EQUITY AND FIXED INCOME

CFA® PROGRAM CURRICULUM
2013 • Level I • Volume 5

CFA Institute

WILEY

John Wiley & Sons, Inc.

ISBN 978-1-937537-04-3 (paper)
ISBN 978-1-937537-25-8 (ebk)

10   9   8   7   6   5   4   3   2

Please visit our website at
www.WileyGlobalFinance.com.

Contents

indicates an optional segment

Contents

◘ indicates an optional segment

How to Use the CFA Program Curriculum

Congratulations on your decision to enter the Chartered Financial Analyst (CFA®) Program. This exciting and rewarding program of study reflects your desire to become a serious investment professional. You are embarking on a program noted for its high ethical standards and the breadth of knowledge, skills, and abilities it develops. Your commitment to the CFA Program should be educationally and professionally rewarding.

The credential you seek is respected around the world as a mark of accomplishment and dedication. Each level of the program represents a distinct achievement in professional development. Successful completion of the program is rewarded with membership in a prestigious global community of investment professionals. CFA charterholders are dedicated to life-long learning and maintaining currency with the ever-changing dynamics of a challenging profession. The CFA Program represents the first step towards a career-long commitment to professional education.

The CFA examination measures your mastery of the core skills required to succeed as an investment professional. These core skills are the basis for the Candidate Body of Knowledge (CBOK™). The CBOK consists of four components:

- A broad topic outline that lists the major top-level topic areas (CBOK Topic Outline)
- Topic area weights that indicate the relative exam weightings of the top-level topic areas
- Learning outcome statements (LOS) that advise candidates about the specific knowledge, skills, and abilities they should acquire from readings covering a topic area (LOS are provided in candidate study sessions and at the beginning of each reading)
- The CFA Program curriculum, readings, and end-of-reading questions, which candidates receive upon exam registration

Therefore, the keys to your success on the CFA exam is studying and understanding the CBOK™. The following sections provide background on the CBOK, the organization of the curriculum, and tips for developing an effective study program.

CURRICULUM DEVELOPMENT PROCESS

The CFA Program is grounded in the practice of the investment profession. Using the Global Body of Investment Knowledge (GBIK) collaborative website, CFA Institute performs a continuous practice analysis with investment professionals around the world to determine the knowledge, skills, and abilities (competencies) that are relevant to the profession. Regional expert panels and targeted surveys are conducted annually to verify and reinforce the continuous feedback from the GBIK collaborative website. The practice analysis process ultimately defines the CBOK. The CBOK contains the competencies that are generally accepted and applied by investment professionals.

These competencies are used in practice in a generalist context and are expected to be demonstrated by a recently qualified CFA charterholder.

A committee consisting of practicing charterholders, in conjunction with CFA Institute staff, designs the CFA Program curriculum in order to deliver the CBOK to candidates. The examinations, also written by practicing charterholders, are designed to allow you to demonstrate your mastery of the CBOK as set forth in the CFA Program curriculum. As you structure your personal study program, you should emphasize mastery of the CBOK and the practical application of that knowledge. For more information on the practice analysis, CBOK, and development of the CFA Program curriculum, please visit www.cfainstitute.org.

ORGANIZATION OF THE CURRICULUM

The Level I CFA Program curriculum is organized into 10 topic areas. Each topic area begins with a brief statement of the material and the depth of knowledge expected.

Each topic area is then divided into one or more study sessions. These study sessions—18 sessions in the Level I curriculum—should form the basic structure of your reading and preparation.

Each study session includes a statement of its structure and objective, and is further divided into specific reading assignments. An outline illustrating the organization of these 18 study sessions can be found at the front of each volume.

The reading assignments are the basis for all examination questions, and are selected or developed specifically to teach the knowledge, skills, and abilities reflected in the CBOK. These readings are drawn from CFA Institute-commissioned content, textbook chapters, professional journal articles, research analyst reports, and cases. All readings include problems and solutions to help you understand and master the topic areas.

Reading-specific Learning Outcome Statements (LOS) are listed at the beginning of each reading. These LOS indicate what you should be able to accomplish after studying the reading. The LOS, the reading, and the end-of-reading questions are dependent on each other, with the reading and questions providing context for understanding the scope of the LOS.

You should use the LOS to guide and focus your study, as each examination question is based on an assigned reading and one or more LOS. The readings provide context for the LOS and enable you to apply a principle or concept in a variety of scenarios. The candidate is responsible for the entirety of all of the required material in a study session, the assigned readings as well as the end-of-reading questions and problems.

We encourage you to review the material on LOS (http://www.cfainstitute.org/cfaprogram/courseofstudy/Pages/cfa_los.aspx), including the descriptions of LOS "command words," (www.cfainstitute.org/Documents/cfa_and_cipm_los_command_words.pdf).

FEATURES OF THE CURRICULUM

OPTIONAL
SEGMENT

- **Required vs. Optional Segments** - You should read all of an assigned reading. In some cases, however, we have reprinted an entire chapter or article and marked certain parts of the reading as "optional." The CFA examination is based only on the required segments, and the optional segments are included only when they might help you to better understand the required segments (by seeing the required material in its full context). When an optional segment begins, you will see text and a dashed vertical bar in the outside margin that will continue until the optional segment ends, accompanied by another icon. *Unless the material is specifically marked as optional, you should assume it is required.* You should rely on the required segments and the reading-specific LOS in preparing for the examination.

**END OPTIONAL
SEGMENT**

- **Problems/Solutions** - *All questions and problems in the readings as well as their solutions (which are provided directly following the problems) are part of the curriculum and are required material for the exam.* When appropriate, we have included problems within and after the readings to demonstrate practical application and reinforce your understanding of the concepts presented. The questions and problems are designed to help you learn these concepts and may serve as a basis for exam questions. Many of these questions are adapted from past CFA examinations.

- **Margins** - The wide margins in each volume provide space for your note-taking.

- **Six-Volume Structure** - For portability of the curriculum, the material is spread over six volumes.

- **Glossary and Index** - For your convenience, we have printed a comprehensive glossary and index in each volume. Throughout the curriculum, a **bolded blue** word in a reading denotes a term defined in the glossary.

- **Source Material** - The authorship, publisher, and copyright owners are given for each reading for your reference. We recommend that you use this CFA Institute curriculum rather than the original source materials because the curriculum may include only selected pages from outside readings, updated sections within the readings, and contains problems and solutions tailored to the CFA Program.

- **LOS Self-Check** - We have inserted checkboxes next to each LOS that you can use to track your progress in mastering the concepts in each reading.

DESIGNING YOUR PERSONAL STUDY PROGRAM

Create a Schedule - An orderly, systematic approach to examination preparation is critical. You should dedicate a consistent block of time every week to reading and studying. Complete all reading assignments and the associated problems and solutions in each study session. Review the LOS both before and after you study each reading to ensure that you have mastered the applicable content and can demonstrate the knowledge, skill, or ability described by the LOS and the assigned reading. Use the LOS self-check to track your progress and highlight areas of weakness for later review.

As you prepare for your exam, we will e-mail you important exam updates, testing policies, and study tips. Be sure to read these carefully. Curriculum errata are periodically updated and posted on the study session page at www.cfainstitute.org. You may also sign up for an RSS feed to alert you to the latest errata update.

Successful candidates report an average of over 300 hours preparing for each exam. Your preparation time will vary based on your prior education and experience. For each level of the curriculum, there are 18 study sessions, so a good plan is to devote 15–20 hours per week, for 18 weeks, to studying the material. Use the final four to six weeks before the exam to review what you've learned and practice with sample and mock exams. This recommendation, however, may underestimate the hours needed for appropriate examination preparation depending on your individual circumstances, relevant experience, and academic background. You will undoubtedly adjust your study time to conform to your own strengths and weaknesses, and your educational and professional background.

You will probably spend more time on some study sessions than on others, but on average you should plan on devoting 15-20 hours per study session. You should allow ample time for both in-depth study of all topic areas and additional concentration on those topic areas for which you feel least prepared.

Online Sample Examinations - CFA Institute online sample examinations are intended to assess your exam preparation as you progress toward the end of your study. After each question, you will receive immediate feedback noting the correct response and indicating the relevant assigned reading, so you will be able to identify areas of weakness for further study. The 120-minute sample examinations reflect the question formats, topics, and level of difficulty of the actual CFA examinations. Aggregate data indicate that the CFA examination pass rate was higher among candidates who took one or more online sample examinations than among candidates who did not take the online sample examinations. For more information on the online sample examinations, please visit www.cfainstitute.org.

Online Mock Examinations - In response to candidate requests, CFA Institute has developed mock examinations that mimic the actual CFA examinations not only in question format and level of difficulty, but also in length and topic weight. The three-hour online mock exams simulate the morning and afternoon sessions of the actual CFA exam, and are intended to be taken after you complete your study of the full curriculum, so you can test your understanding of the CBOK and your readiness for the exam. The mock exams are available in a printable PDF format with feedback provided at the end of the exam, rather than after each question as with the sample exams. CFA Institute recommends that you take these mock exams at the final stage of your preparation toward the actual CFA examination. For more information on the online mock examinations, please visit www.cfainstitute.org.

Preparatory Providers - After you enroll in the CFA Program, you may receive numerous solicitations for preparatory courses and review materials. When considering a prep course make sure the provider is in compliance with the CFA Institute Prep Provider Guidelines Program (www.cfainstitute.org/partners/examprep/Pages/cfa_prep_provider_guidelines.aspx). Just remember, there are no shortcuts to success on the CFA examinations; reading and studying the CFA curriculum is the key to success on the examination. The CFA examinations reference only the CFA Institute assigned curriculum—no preparatory course or review course materials are consulted or referenced.

SUMMARY

Every question on the CFA examination is based on the content contained in the required readings and on one or more LOS. Frequently, an examination question is based on a specific example highlighted within a reading or on a specific end-of-reading question and/or problem and its solution. To make effective use of the CFA Program curriculum, please remember these key points:

1. All pages printed in the curriculum are required reading for the examination except for occasional sections marked as optional. You may read optional pages as background, but you will not be tested on them.

2. All questions, problems, and their solutions - printed at the end of readings - are part of the curriculum and are required study material for the examination.

3. You should make appropriate use of the online sample/mock examinations and other resources available at www.cfainstitute.org.

4. You should schedule and commit sufficient study time to cover the 18 study sessions, review the materials, and take sample/mock examinations.

5. **Note:** Some of the concepts in the study sessions may be superseded by updated rulings and/or pronouncements issued after a reading was published. Candidates are expected to be familiar with the overall analytical framework contained in the assigned readings. Candidates are not responsible for changes that occur after the material was written.

FEEDBACK

At CFA Institute, we are committed to delivering a comprehensive and rigorous curriculum for the development of competent, ethically grounded investment professionals. We rely on candidate and member feedback as we work to incorporate content, design, and packaging improvements. You can be assured that we will continue to listen to your suggestions. Please send any comments or feedback to curriculum@ cfainstitute.org. Ongoing improvements in the curriculum will help you prepare for success on the upcoming examinations, and for a lifetime of learning as a serious investment professional.

Equity

TOPIC LEVEL LEARNING OUTCOME

The candidate should be able to describe characteristics of equity investments, security markets, and indices. The candidate should also be able to analyze industries, companies, and equity securities and to describe and demonstrate the use of basic equity valuation models.

13

Equity:

Market Organization, Market Indices, and Market Efficiency

This study session explains important characteristics of the markets in which equities, fixed-income instruments, derivatives, and alternative investments trade. The reading on market organization and structure describes market classifications, types of assets and market participants, and how assets are traded. The reading on security market indices explains how indices are constructed, managed, and used in investments. The reading on market efficiency discusses the degree to which market prices reflect information and explains the implications of different degrees of market efficiency for security analysis and portfolio management.

READING ASSIGNMENTS

Reading 46 *Market Organization and Structure*
by Larry Harris

Reading 47 *Security Market Indices*
by Paul D. Kaplan, CFA, and Dorothy C. Kelly, CFA

Reading 48 *Market Efficiency*
by W. Sean Cleary, CFA, Howard J. Atkinson, CFA, and Pamela Peterson Drake, CFA

Market Organization and Structure

by Larry Harris

LEARNING OUTCOMES

Mastery	The candidate should be able to:
☐	a explain the main functions of the financial system;
☐	b describe classifications of assets and markets;
☐	c describe the major types of securities, currencies, contracts, commodities, and real assets that trade in organized markets, including their distinguishing characteristics and major subtypes;
☐	d describe types of financial intermediaries and services that they provide;
☐	e compare positions an investor can take in an asset;
☐	f calculate and interpret the leverage ratio, the rate of return on a margin transaction, and the security price at which the investor would receive a margin call;
☐	g compare execution, validity, and clearing instructions;
☐	h compare market orders with limit orders;
☐	i define primary and secondary markets and explain how secondary markets support primary markets;
☐	j describe how securities, contracts, and currencies are traded in quote-driven, order-driven, and brokered markets;
☐	k describe characteristics of a well-functioning financial system;
☐	l describe objectives of market regulation.

1   INTRODUCTION

Financial analysts gather and process information to make investment decisions, including those related to buying and selling assets. Generally, the decisions involve trading securities, currencies, contracts, commodities, and real assets such as real estate. Consider several examples:

- Fixed income analysts evaluate issuer credit-worthiness and macroeconomic prospects to determine which bonds and notes to buy or sell to preserve capital while obtaining a fair rate of return.

- Stock analysts study corporate values to determine which stocks to buy or sell to maximize the value of their stock portfolios.

- Corporate treasurers analyze exchange rates, interest rates, and credit conditions to determine which currencies to trade and which notes to buy or sell to have funds available in a needed currency.

- Risk managers work for producers or users of commodities to calculate how many commodity futures contracts to buy or sell to manage inventory risks.

Financial analysts must understand the characteristics of the markets in which their decisions will be executed. This reading, by examining those markets from the analyst's perspective, provides that understanding.

This reading is organized as follows. Section 2 examines the functions of the financial system. Section 3 introduces assets that investors, information-motivated traders, and risk managers use to advance their financial objectives and presents ways practitioners classify these assets into markets. These assets include such financial instruments as securities, currencies, and some contracts; certain commodities; and real assets. Financial analysts must know the distinctive characteristics of these trading assets.

Section 4 is an overview of financial intermediaries (entities that facilitate the functioning of the financial system). Section 5 discusses the positions that can be obtained while trading assets. You will learn about the benefits and risks of long and short positions, how these positions can be financed, and how the financing affects their risks. Section 6 discusses how market participants order trades and how markets process those orders. These processes must be understood to achieve trading objectives while controlling transaction costs.

Section 7 focuses on describing primary markets. Section 8 describes the structures of secondary markets in securities. Sections 9 and 10 close the reading with discussions of the characteristics of a well-functioning financial system and of how regulation helps make financial markets function better. A summary reviews the reading's major ideas and points, and practice problems conclude.

2   THE FUNCTIONS OF THE FINANCIAL SYSTEM

The financial system includes markets and various financial intermediaries that help transfer financial assets, real assets, and financial risks in various forms from one entity to another, from one place to another, and from one point in time to another. These transfers take place whenever someone exchanges one asset or financial contract for another. The assets and contracts that people (people act on behalf of themselves, companies, charities, governments, etc., so the term "people" has a broad definition in this reading) trade include notes, bonds, stocks, exchange-traded funds, currencies, forward contracts, futures contracts, option contracts, swap contracts, and certain commodities. When the buyer and seller voluntarily arrange their trades, as is usually the case, the buyer and the seller both expect to be better off.

People use the financial system for six main purposes:

1. to save money for the future;
2. to borrow money for current use;
3. to raise equity capital;
4. to manage risks;
5. to exchange assets for immediate and future deliveries; and
6. to trade on information.

The main functions of the financial system are to facilitate:

1. the achievement of the purposes for which people use the financial system;
2. the discovery of the rates of return that equate aggregate savings with aggregate borrowings; and
3. the allocation of capital to the best uses.

These functions are extremely important to economic welfare. In a well-functioning financial system, transaction costs are low, analysts can value savings and investments, and scarce capital resources are used well.

Sections 2.1 through 2.3 expand on these three functions. The six subsections of Section 2.1 cover the six main purposes for which people use the financial system and how the financial system facilitates the achievement of those purposes. Sections 2.2 and 2.3 discuss determining rates of return and capital allocation efficiency, respectively.

2.1 Helping People Achieve Their Purposes in Using the Financial System

People often arrange transactions to achieve more than one purpose when using the financial system. For example, an investor who buys the stock of an oil producer may do so to move her wealth from the present to the future, to hedge the risk that she will have to pay more for energy in the future, and to exploit insightful research that she conducted that suggests the company's stock is undervalued in the marketplace. If the investment proves to be successful, she will have saved money for the future, managed her energy risk exposure, and obtained a return on her research.

The separate discussions of each of the six main uses of the financial system by people will help you better identify the reasons why people trade. Your ability to identify the various uses of the financial system will help you avoid confusion that often leads to poor financial decisions. The financial intermediaries that are mentioned in these discussions are explained further in Section 4.

2.1.1 *Saving*

People often have money that they choose not to spend now and that they want available in the future. For example, workers who save for their retirements need to move some of their current earnings into the future. When they retire, they will use their savings to replace the wages that they will no longer be earning. Similarly, companies save money from their sales revenue so that they can pay vendors when their bills come due, repay debt, or acquire assets (for example, other companies or machinery) in the future.

To move money from the present to the future, savers buy notes, certificates of deposit, bonds, stocks, mutual funds, or real assets such as real estate. These alternatives generally provide a better expected rate of return than simply storing money. Savers function sell these assets in the future to fund their future expenditures. When savers commit money to earn a financial return, they commonly are called investors. They invest when they purchase assets, and they divest when they sell them.

Investors require a fair rate of return while their money is invested. The required fair rate of return compensates them for the use of their money and for the risk that they may lose money if the investment fails or if inflation reduces the real value of their investments.

The financial system facilitates savings when institutions create investment vehicles, such as bank deposits, notes, stocks, and mutual funds, that investors can acquire and sell without paying substantial transaction costs. When these instruments are fairly priced and easy to trade, investors will use them to save more.

2.1.2 *Borrowing*

People, companies, and governments often want to spend money now that they do not have. They can obtain money to fund projects that they wish to undertake now by borrowing it. Companies can also obtain funds by selling ownership or equity interests (covered in Section 2.1.3). Banks and other investors provide those requiring funds with money because they expect to be repaid with interest or because they expect to be compensated with future disbursements, such as dividends and capital gains, as the ownership interest appreciates in value.

People may borrow to pay for such items as vacations, homes, cars, or education. They generally borrow through mortgages and personal loans, or by using credit cards. People typically repay these loans with money they earn later.

Companies often require money to fund current operations or to engage in new capital projects. They may borrow the needed funds in a variety of ways, such as arranging a loan or a line of credit with a bank, or selling fixed income securities to investors. Companies typically repay their borrowing with income generated in the future. In addition to borrowing, companies may raise funds by selling ownership interests.

Governments may borrow money to pay salaries and other expenses, to fund projects, to provide welfare benefits to their citizens and residents, and to subsidize various activities. Governments borrow by selling bills, notes, or bonds. Governments repay their debt using future revenues from taxes and in some instances from the projects funded by these debts.

Borrowers can borrow from lenders only if the lenders believe that they will be repaid. If the lenders believe, however, that repayment in full with interest may not occur, they will demand higher rates of interest to cover their expected losses and to compensate them for the discomfit they experience wondering whether they will lose their money. To lower the costs of borrowing, borrowers often pledge assets as collateral for their loans. The assets pledged as collateral often include those that will be purchased by the proceeds of the loan. If the borrowers do not repay their loans, the lenders can sell the collateral and use the proceeds to settle the loans.

Lenders often will not loan to borrowers who intend to invest in risky projects, especially if the borrowers cannot pledge other collateral. Investors may still be willing to supply capital for these risky projects if they believe that the projects will likely produce valuable future cash flows. Rather than lending money, however, they will contribute capital in exchange for equity in the projects.

The financial system facilitates borrowing. Lenders aggregate from savers the funds that borrowers require. Borrowers must convince lenders that they can repay their loans, and that, in the event they cannot, lenders can recover most of the funds lent. Credit bureaus, credit rating agencies, and governments promote borrowing; credit bureaus and credit rating agencies do so by collecting and disseminating information that lenders need to analyze credit prospects and governments do so by establishing bankruptcy codes and courts that define and enforce the rights of borrowers and lenders. When the transaction costs of loans (i.e., the costs of arranging, monitoring, and collecting them) are low, borrowers can borrow more to fund current expenditures with credible promises to return the money in the future.

2.1.3 *Raising Equity Capital*

Companies often raise money for projects by selling (issuing) ownership interests (e.g., corporate common stock or partnership interests). Although these equity instruments legally represent ownership in companies rather than loans to the companies, selling equity to raise capital is simply another mechanism for moving money from the future to the present. When shareholders or partners contribute capital to a company, the company obtains money in the present in exchange for equity instruments that will be entitled to distributions in the future. Although the repayment of the money is not scheduled as it would be for loans, equity instruments also represent potential claims on money in the future.

The financial system facilitates raising equity capital. Investment banks help companies issue equities, analysts value the securities that companies sell, and regulatory reporting requirements and accounting standards attempt to ensure the production of meaningful financial disclosures. The financial system helps promote capital formation by producing the financial information needed to determine fair prices for equity. Liquid markets help companies raise capital. In these markets, shareholders can easily divest their equities as desired. When investors can easily value and trade equities, they are more willing to fund reasonable projects that companies wish to undertake.

Example 1

Financing Capital Projects

As a chief financial officer (CFO) of a large industrial firm, you need to raise cash within a few months to pay for a project to expand existing and acquire new manufacturing facilities. What are the primary options available to you?

Solution:

Your primary options are to borrow the funds or to raise the funds by selling ownership interests. If the company borrows the funds, you may have the company pledge some or all of the project as collateral to reduce the cost of borrowing.

2.1.4 *Managing Risks*

Many people, companies, and governments face financial risks that concern them. These risks include default risk and the risk of changes in interest rates, exchange rates, raw material prices, and sale prices, among many other risks. These risks are often managed by trading contracts that serve as hedges for the risks.

For example, a farmer and a food processor both face risks related to the price of grain. The farmer fears that prices will be lower than expected when his grain is ready for sale whereas the food processor fears that prices will be higher than expected when she has to buy grain in the future. They both can eliminate their exposures to these risks if they enter into a binding forward contract for the farmer to sell a specified quantity of grain to the food processor at a future date at a mutually agreed upon price. By entering into a forward contract that sets the future trade price, they both eliminate their exposure to changing grain prices.

In general, hedgers trade to offset or insure against risks that concern them. In addition to forward contracts, they may use futures contracts, option contracts, or insurance contracts to transfer risk to other entities more willing to bear the risks (these contracts will be covered in Section 3.4). Often the hedger and the other entity face exactly the opposite risks, so the transfer makes both more secure, as in the grain example.

The financial system facilitates risk management when liquid markets exist in which risk managers can trade instruments that are correlated (or inversely correlated) with the risks that concern them without incurring substantial transaction costs. Investment banks, exchanges, and insurance companies devote substantial resources to designing such contracts and to ensuring that they will trade in liquid markets. When such markets exist, people are better able to manage the risks that they face and often are more willing to undertake risky activities that they expect will be profitable.

2.1.5 Exchanging Assets for Immediate Delivery (Spot Market Trading)

People and companies often trade one asset for another that they rate more highly or, equivalently, that is more useful to them. They may trade one currency for another currency, or money for a needed commodity or right. Following are some examples that illustrate these trades:

- Volkswagen pays its German workers in euros, but the company receives dollars when it sells cars in the United States. To convert money from dollars to euros, Volkswagen trades in the foreign exchange markets.

- A Mexican investor who is worried about the prospects for peso inflation or a potential devaluation of the peso may buy gold in the spot gold market. (This transaction may hedge against the risk of devaluation of the peso because the value of gold may increase with inflation.)

- A plastic producer must buy carbon credits to emit carbon dioxide when burning fuel to comply with environmental regulations. The carbon credit is a legal right that the producer must have to engage in activities that emit carbon dioxide.

In each of these cases, the trades are considered spot market trades because the instruments trade for immediate delivery. The financial system facilitates these exchanges when liquid spot markets exist in which people can arrange and settle trades without substantial transaction costs.

2.1.6 Information-Motivated Trading

Information-motivated traders trade to profit from information that they believe allows them to predict future prices. Like all other traders, they hope to buy at low prices and sell at higher prices. Unlike pure investors, however, they expect to earn a return on their information in addition to the normal return expected for bearing risk through time.

Active investment managers are information-motivated traders who collect and analyze information to identify securities, contracts, and other assets that their analyses indicate are under- or overvalued. They then buy those that they consider undervalued and sell those that they consider overvalued. If successful, they obtain a greater return than the unconditional return that would be expected for bearing the risk in their positions. The return that they expect to obtain is a conditional return earned on the basis of the information in their analyses. Practitioners often call this process active portfolio management.

Note that the distinction between pure investors and information-motivated traders depends on their motives for trading and not on the risks that they take or their expected holding periods. Investors trade to move wealth from the present to the future whereas information-motivated traders trade to profit from superior information about future values. When trading to move wealth forward, the time period may be short or long. For example, a bank treasurer may only need to move money overnight and might use money market instruments trading in an interbank funds market to accomplish that. A pension fund, however, may need to move money

30 years forward and might do that by using shares trading in a stock market. Both are investors although their expected holding periods and the risks in the instruments that they trade are vastly different.

In contrast, information-motivated traders trade because their information-based analyses suggest to them that prices of various instruments will increase or decrease in the future at a rate faster than others without their information or analytical models would expect. After establishing their positions, they hope that prices will change quickly in their favor so that they can close their positions, realize their profits, and redeploy their capital. These price changes may occur almost instantaneously, or they may take years to occur if information about the mispricing is difficult to obtain or understand.

The two categories of traders are not mutually exclusive. Investors also are often information-motivated traders. Many investors who want to move wealth forward through time collect and analyze information to select securities that will allow them to obtain conditional returns that are greater than the unconditional returns expected for securities in their assets classes. If they have rational reasons to expect that their efforts will indeed produce superior returns, they are information-motivated traders. If they consistently fail to produce such returns, their efforts will be futile, and they would have been better off simply buying and holding well-diversified portfolios.

Example 2

Investing versus Information-Motivated Trading

The head of a large labor union with a pension fund asks you, a pension consultant, to distinguish between investing and information-motivated trading. You are expected to provide an explanation that addresses the financial problems that she faces. How would you respond?

Solution:

The object of investing for the pension fund is to move the union's pension assets from the present to the future when they will be needed to pay the union's retired pensioners. The pension fund managers will typically do this by buying stocks, bonds, and perhaps other assets. The pension fund managers expect to receive a fair rate of return on the pension fund's assets without paying excessive transaction costs and management fees. The return should compensate the fund for the risks that it bears and for the time that other people are using the fund's money.

The object of information-motivated trading is to earn a return in excess of the fair rate of return. Information-motivated traders analyze information that they collect with the hope that their analyses will allow them to predict better than others where prices will be in the future. They then buy assets that they think will produce excess returns and sell those that they think will underperform. Active investment managers are information-motivated traders.

The characteristic that most distinguishes investors from information-motivated traders is the return that they expect. Although both types of traders hope to obtain extraordinary returns, investors rationally expect to receive only fair returns during the periods of their investments. In contrast, information-motivated traders expect to make returns in excess of required fair rates of return. Of course, not all investing or information-motivated trading is successful (in other words, the actual returns may not equal or exceed the expected returns).

The financial system facilitates information-motivated trading when liquid markets allow active managers to trade without significant transaction costs. Accounting standards and reporting requirements that produce meaningful financial disclosures reduce the costs of being well informed, but do not necessarily help informed traders profit because they often compete with each other. The most profitable well-informed traders are often those that have the most unique insights into future values.

2.1.7 *Summary*

People use the financial system for many purposes, the most important of which are saving, borrowing, raising equity capital, managing risk, exchanging assets in spot markets, and information-motivated trading. The financial system best facilitates these uses when people can trade instruments that interest them in liquid markets, when institutions provide financial services at low cost, when information about assets and about credit risks is readily available, and when regulation helps ensure that everyone faithfully honors their contracts.

2.2 Determining Rates of Return

Saving, borrowing, and selling equity are all means of moving money through time. Savers move money from the present to the future whereas borrowers and equity issuers move money from the future to the present.

Because time machines do not exist, money can travel forward in time only if an equal amount of money is travelling in the other direction. This equality always occurs because borrowers and equity sellers create the securities in which savers invest. For example, the bond sold by a company that needs to move money from the future to the present is the same bond bought by a saver who needs to move money from the present to the future.

The aggregate amount of money that savers will move from the present to the future is related to the expected rate of return on their investments. If the expected return is high, they will forgo current consumption and move more money to the future. Similarly, the aggregate amount of money that borrowers and equity sellers will move from the future to the present depends on the costs of borrowing funds or of giving up ownership. These costs can be expressed as the rate of return that borrowers and equity sellers are expected to deliver in exchange for obtaining current funds. It is the same rate that savers expect to receive when delivering current funds. If this rate is low, borrowers and equity sellers will want to move more money to the present from the future. In other words, they will want to raise more funds.

Because the total money saved must equal the total money borrowed and received in exchange for equity, the expected rate of return depends on the aggregate supply of funds through savings and the aggregate demand for funds. If the rate is too high, savers will want to move more money to the future than borrowers and equity issuers will want to move to the present. The expected rate will have to be lower to discourage the savers and to encourage the borrowers and equity issuers. Conversely, if the rate is too low, savers will want to move less money forward than borrowers and equity issuers will want to move to the present. The expected rate will have to be higher to encourage the savers and to discourage the borrowers and equity issuers. Between rates too high and too low, an expected rate of return exists, in theory, in which the aggregate supply of funds for investing (supply of funds saved) and the aggregate demand for funds through borrowing and equity issuing are equal.

Economists call this rate the equilibrium interest rate. It is the price for moving money through time. Determining this rate is one of the most important functions of the financial system. The equilibrium interest rate is the only interest rate that would exist if all securities were equally risky, had equal terms, and were equally liquid. In fact, the required rates of return for securities vary by their risk characteristics, terms, and liquidity. For a given issuer, investors generally require higher rates of return for equity than for debt, for long-term securities than for short-term securities, and for illiquid securities than for liquid ones. Financial analysts recognize that all required rates of return depend on a common equilibrium interest rate plus adjustments for risk.

Example 3

Interest Rates

For a presentation to private wealth clients by your firm's chief economist, you are asked to prepare the audience by explaining the most fundamental facts concerning the role of interest rates in the economy. You agree. What main points should you try to convey?

Solution:

Savers have money now that they will want to use in the future. Borrowers want to use money now that they do not have, but they expect that they will have money in the future. Borrowers are loaned money by savers and promise to repay it in the future.

The interest rate is the return that lenders, the savers, expect to receive from borrowers for allowing borrowers to use the savers' money. The interest rate is the price of using money.

Interest rates depend on the total amount of money that people want to borrow and the total amount of money that people are willing to lend. Interest rates are high when, in aggregate, people value having money now substantially more than they value having money in the future. In contrast, if many people with money want to use it in the future and few people presently need more money than they have, interest rates will be low.

2.3 Capital Allocation Efficiency

Primary capital markets (primary markets) are the markets in which companies and governments raise capital (funds). Companies may raise funds by borrowing money or by issuing equity. Governments may raise funds by borrowing money.

Economies are said to be allocationally efficient when their financial systems allocate capital (funds) to those uses that are most productive. Although companies may be interested in getting funding for many potential projects, not all projects are worth funding. One of the most important functions of the financial system is to ensure that only the best projects obtain scarce capital funds; the funds available from savers should be allocated to the most productive uses.

In market-based economies, savers determine, directly or indirectly, which projects obtain capital. Savers determine capital allocations directly by choosing which securities they will invest in. Savers determine capital allocations indirectly by giving funds to financial intermediaries that then invest the funds. Because investors fear the loss of their money, they will lend at lower interest rates to borrowers with the best credit prospects or the best collateral, and they will lend at higher rates to other borrowers with less secure prospects. Similarly, they will buy only those equities that they believe have the best prospects relative to their prices and risks.

To avoid losses, investors carefully study the prospects of the various investment opportunities available to them. The decisions that they make tend to be well informed, which helps ensure that capital is allocated efficiently. The fear of losses by investors and by those raising funds to invest in projects ensures that only the best projects tend to be funded. The process works best when investors are well informed about the prospects of the various projects.

In general, investors will fund an equity project if they expect that the value of the project is greater than its cost, and they will not fund projects otherwise. If the investor expectations are accurate, only projects that should be undertaken will be funded and all such projects will be funded. Accurate market information thus leads to efficient capital allocation.

Example 4

Primary Market Capital Allocation

How can poor information about the value of a project result in poor capital allocation decisions?

Solution:

Projects should be undertaken only if their value is greater than their cost. If investors have poor information and overestimate the value of a project in which its true value is less than its cost, a wealth-diminishing project may be undertaken. Alternatively, if investors have poor information and underestimate the value of a project in which its true value is greater than its cost, a wealth-enhancing project may not be undertaken.

---

3   ASSETS AND CONTRACTS

People, companies, and governments use many different assets and contracts to further their financial goals and to manage their risks. The most common assets include financial assets (such as bank deposits, certificates of deposit, loans, mortgages, corporate and government bonds and notes, common and preferred stocks, real estate investment trusts, master limited partnership interests, pooled investment products, and exchange-traded funds), currencies, certain commodities (such as gold and oil), and real assets (such as real estate). The most common contracts are option, futures, forward, swap, and insurance contracts. People, companies, and governments use these assets and contracts to raise funds, to invest, to profit from information-motivated trading, to hedge risks, and/or to transfer money from one form to another.

3.1 Classifications of Assets and Markets

Practitioners often classify assets and the markets in which they trade by various common characteristics to facilitate communications with their clients, with each other, and with regulators.

The most actively traded assets are securities, currencies, contracts, and commodities. In addition, real assets are traded. Securities generally include debt instruments, equities, and shares in pooled investment vehicles. **Currencies** are monies issued by national monetary authorities. Contracts are agreements to exchange securities, currencies, commodities or other contracts in the future. Commodities include precious metals, energy products, industrial metals, and agricultural products. Real assets are tangible properties such as real estate, airplanes, or machinery. Securities, currencies, and contracts are classified as financial assets whereas commodities and real assets are classified as physical assets.

Securities are further classified as debt or equity. Debt instruments (also called fixed-income instruments) are promises to repay borrowed money. Equities represent ownership in companies. Pooled investment vehicle shares represent ownership of an undivided interest in an investment portfolio. The portfolio may include securities, currencies, contracts, commodities, or real assets. Pooled investment vehicles, such as exchange-traded funds, which exclusively own shares in other companies, generally are also considered equities.

Securities are also classified by whether they are public or private securities. Public securities are those registered to trade in public markets, such as on exchanges or through dealers. In most jurisdictions, issuers must meet stringent minimum regulatory standards, including reporting and corporate governance standards, to issue publicly traded securities.

Private securities are all other securities. Often, only specially qualified investors can purchase private equities and private debt instruments. Investors may purchase them directly from the issuer or indirectly through an investment vehicle specifically formed to hold such securities. Issuers often issue private securities when they find public reporting standards too burdensome or when they do not want to conform to the regulatory standards associated with public equity. Venture capital is private equity that investors supply to companies when or shortly after they are founded. Private securities generally are illiquid. In contrast, many public securities trade in liquid markets in which sellers can easily find buyers for their securities.

Contracts are derivative contracts if their values depend on the prices of other underlying assets. Derivative contracts may be classified as physical or financial depending on whether the underlying instruments are physical products or financial securities. Equity derivatives are contracts whose values depend on equities or indices of equities. Fixed-income derivatives are contracts whose values depend on debt securities or indices of debt securities.

Practitioners classify markets by whether the markets trade instruments for immediate delivery or for future delivery. Markets that trade contracts that call for delivery in the future are forward or futures markets. Those that trade for immediate delivery are called **spot markets** to distinguish them from forward markets that trade contracts on the same underlying instruments. Options markets trade contracts that deliver in the future, but delivery takes place only if the holders of the options choose to exercise them.

When issuers sell securities to investors, practitioners say that they trade in the **primary market**. When investors sell those securities to others, they trade in the **secondary market**. In the primary market, funds flow to the issuer of the security from the purchaser. In the secondary market, funds flow between traders.

Practitioners classify financial markets as money markets or capital markets. **Money markets** trade debt instruments maturing in one year or less. The most common such instruments are repurchase agreements (defined in Section 3.2.1), negotiable certificates of deposit, government bills, and commercial paper. In contrast, **capital markets** trade instruments of longer duration, such as bonds and equities, whose values depend on the credit-worthiness of the issuers and on payments of interest or dividends that will be made in the future and may be uncertain. Corporations generally finance their operations in the capital markets, but some also finance a portion of their operations by issuing short-term securities, such as commercial paper.

Finally, practitioners distinguish between **traditional investment markets** and **alternative investment markets**. Traditional investments include all publicly traded debts and equities and shares in pooled investment vehicles that hold publicly traded debts and/or equities. Alternative investments include hedge funds, private equities (including venture capital), commodities, real estate securities and real estate properties, securitized debts, operating leases, machinery, collectibles, and precious gems. Because these investments are often hard to trade and hard to value, they may sometimes trade at substantial deviations from their intrinsic values. The discounts compensate investors for the research that they must do to value these assets and for their inability to easily sell the assets if they need to liquidate a portion of their portfolios.

The remainder of this section describes the most common assets and contracts that people, companies, and governments trade.

Example 5

Asset and Market Classification

The investment policy of a mutual fund only permits the fund to invest in public equities traded in secondary markets. Would the fund be able to purchase:

1. Common stock of a company that trades on a large stock exchange?
2. Common stock of a public company that trades only through dealers?
3. A government bond?
4. A single stock futures contract?
5. Common stock sold for the first time by a properly registered public company?
6. Shares in a privately held bank with €10 billion of capital?

Solution to 1:

Yes. Common stock is equity. Those common stocks that trade on large exchanges invariably are public equities that trade in secondary markets.

Solution to 2:

Yes. Dealer markets are secondary markets and the security is a public equity.

Solution to 3:

No. Although government bonds are public securities, they are not equities. They are debt securities.

Solution to 4:

No. Although the underlying instruments for single stock futures are invariably public equities, single stock futures are derivative contracts, not equities.

Solution to 5:

No. The fund would not be able to buy these shares because a purchase from the issuer would be in the primary market. The fund would have to wait until it could buy the shares from someone other than the issuer.

Solution to 6:

No. These shares are private equities, not public equities. The public prominence of the company does not make its securities public securities unless they have been properly registered as public securities.

3.2 Securities

People, companies, and governments sell securities to raise money. Securities include bonds, notes, commercial paper, mortgages, common stocks, preferred stocks, warrants, mutual fund shares, unit trusts, and depository receipts. These can be classified broadly as fixed-income instruments, equities, and shares in pooled investment vehicles. Note that the legal definition of a security varies by country and may or may not coincide with the usage here. Securities that are sold to the public or that can be resold to the public are called issues. Companies and governments are the most common issuers.

3.2.1 *Fixed Income*

Fixed-income instruments contractually include predetermined payment schedules that usually include interest and principal payments. Fixed-income instruments generally are promises to repay borrowed money but may include other instruments with payment schedules, such as settlements of legal cases or prizes from lotteries. The payment amounts may be pre-specified or they may vary according to a fixed formula that depends on the future values of an interest rate or a commodity price. Bonds, notes, bills, certificates of deposit, commercial paper, repurchase agreements, loan agreements, and mortgages are examples of promises to repay money in the future. People, companies, and governments create fixed-income instruments when they borrow money.

Corporations and governments issue bonds and notes. Fixed-income securities with shorter maturities are called "notes," those with longer maturities are called "bonds." The cutoff is usually at 10 years. In practice, however, the terms are generally used interchangeably. Both become short-term instruments when the remaining time until maturity is short, usually taken to be one year or less.

Some corporations issue convertible bonds, which are typically convertible into stock, usually at the option of the holder after some period. If stock prices are high so that conversion is likely, convertibles are valued like stock. Conversely, if stock prices are low so that conversion is unlikely, convertibles are valued like bonds.

Bills, certificates of deposit, and commercial paper are respectively issued by governments, banks, and corporations. They usually mature within a year of being issued; certificates of deposit sometimes have longer initial maturities.

Repurchase agreements (repos) are short-term lending instruments. The term can be as short as overnight. A borrower seeking funds will sell an instrument—typically a high quality bond—to a lender with an agreement to repurchase it later at a slightly higher price based on an agreed upon interest rate.

Practitioners distinguish between short-term, intermediate-term, and long-term fixed-income securities. No general consensus exists about the definition of short-term, intermediate-term, and long-term. Instruments that mature in less than one to two years are considered short-term instruments whereas those that mature in more than five to ten years are considered long-term instruments. In the middle are intermediate-term instruments.

Instruments trading in money markets are called money market instruments. Such instruments are traded debt instruments maturing in one year or less. Money market funds and corporations seeking a return on their short-term cash balances typically hold money market instruments.

3.2.2 *Equities*

Equities represent ownership rights in companies. These include common and preferred shares. Common shareholders own residual rights to the assets of the company. They have the right to receive any dividends declared by the boards of directors, and in the event of liquidation, any assets remaining after all other claims are paid. Acting through the boards of directors that they elect, common shareholders usually can select the managers who run the corporations.

Preferred shares are equities that have preferred rights (relative to common shares) to the cash flows and assets of the company. Preferred shareholders generally have the right to receive a specific dividend on a regular basis. If the preferred share is a cumulative preferred equity, the company must pay the preferred shareholders any previously omitted dividends before it can pay dividends to the common shareholders. Preferred shareholders also have higher claims to assets relative to common shareholders in the event of corporate liquidation. For valuation purposes, financial analysts generally treat preferred stocks as fixed-income securities when the issuers will clearly be able to pay their promised dividends in the foreseeable future.

Warrants are securities issued by a corporation that allow the warrant holders to buy a security issued by that corporation, if they so desire, usually at any time before the warrants expire or, if not, upon expiration. The security that warrant holders can buy usually is the issuer's common stock, in which case the warrants are considered equities because the warrant holders can obtain equity in the company by exercising their warrants. The warrant **exercise price** is the price that the warrant holder must pay to buy the security.

Example 6

Securities

What factors distinguish fixed-income securities from equities?

Solution:

Fixed-income securities generate income on a regular schedule. They derive their value from the promise to pay a scheduled cash flow. The most common fixed-income securities are promises made by people, companies, and governments to repay loans.

Equities represent residual ownership in companies after all other claims—including any fixed-income liabilities of the company—have been satisfied. For corporations, the claims of preferred equities typically have priority over the claims of common equities. Common equities have the residual ownership in corporations.

3.2.3 *Pooled Investments*

Pooled investment vehicles are mutual funds, trusts, depositories, and hedge funds, that issue securities that represent shared ownership in the assets that these entities hold. The securities created by mutual funds, trusts, depositories, and hedge fund are respectively called *shares*, *units*, *depository receipts*, and *limited partnership interests* but practitioners often use these terms interchangeably. People invest in pooled investment vehicles to benefit from the investment management services of their managers and from diversification opportunities that are not readily available to them on an individual basis.

Mutual funds are investment vehicles that pool money from many investors for investment in a portfolio of securities. They are often legally organized as investment trusts or as corporate investment companies. Pooled investment vehicles may be open-ended or closed-ended. Open-ended funds issue new shares and redeem existing shares on demand, usually on a daily basis. The price at which a fund redeems and sells the fund's shares is based on the net asset value of the fund's portfolio, which is the difference between the fund's assets and liabilities, expressed on a per share basis. Investors generally buy and sell open-ended mutual funds by trading with the mutual fund.

In contrast, closed-end funds issue shares in primary market offerings that the fund or its investment bankers arrange. Once issued, investors cannot sell their shares of the fund back to the fund by demanding redemption. Instead, investors in closed-end funds must sell their shares to other investors in the secondary market. The secondary market prices of closed-end funds may differ—sometimes quite significantly—from their net asset values. Closed-end funds generally trade at a discount to their net asset values. The discount reflects the expenses of running the fund and sometimes investor concerns about the quality of the management. Closed-end funds may also trade at a discount or a premium to net asset value when investors believe that the portfolio securities are overvalued or undervalued. Many financial analysts thus believe that discounts and premiums on closed-end funds measure market sentiment.

Exchange-traded funds (ETFs) and exchange-traded notes (ETNs) are open-ended funds that investors can trade among themselves in secondary markets. The prices at which ETFs trade rarely differ much from net asset values because a class of investors, known as authorized participants (APs), has the option of trading directly with the ETF. If the market price of an equity ETF is sufficiently below its net asset value, APs will buy shares in the secondary market at market price and redeem shares at net asset value with the fund. Conversely, if the price of an ETF is sufficiently above its net asset value, APs will buy shares from the fund at net asset value and sell shares in the secondary market at market price. As a result, the market price and net asset values of ETFs tend to converge.

Many ETFs permit only in-kind deposits and redemptions. Buyers who buy directly from such a fund pay for their shares with a portfolio of securities rather than with cash. Similarly, sellers receive a portfolio of securities. The transaction portfolio generally is very similar—often essentially identical—to the portfolio held by the fund. Practitioners sometimes call such funds "depositories" because they issue depository receipts for the portfolios that traders deposit with them. The traders then trade the receipts in the secondary market. Some warehouses holding industrial materials and precious metals also issue tradable warehouse receipts.

Asset-backed securities are securities whose values and income payments are derived from a pool of assets, such as mortgage bonds, credit card debt, or car loans. These securities typically pass interest and principal payments received from the pool of assets through to their holders on a monthly basis. These payments may depend on formulas that give some classes of securities—called tranches—backed by the pool more value than other classes.

Hedge funds are investment funds that generally organize as limited partnerships. The hedge fund managers are the general partners. The limited partners are qualified investors who are wealthy enough and well informed enough to tolerate and accept substantial losses, should they occur. The regulatory requirements to participate in a hedge fund and the regulatory restrictions on hedge funds vary by jurisdiction. Most hedge funds follow only one investment strategy, but no single investment strategy characterizes hedge funds as a group. Hedge funds exist that follow almost every imaginable strategy ranging from long–short arbitrage in the stock markets to direct investments in exotic alternative assets.

The primary distinguishing characteristic of hedge funds is their management compensation scheme. Almost all funds pay their managers with an annual fee that is proportional to their assets and with an additional performance fee that depends on the wealth that the funds generate for their shareholders. A secondary distinguishing characteristic of many hedge funds is the use of leverage to increase risk exposure and to hopefully increase returns.

3.3 Currencies

Currencies are monies issued by national monetary authorities. Approximately 175 currencies are currently in use throughout the world. Some of these currencies are regarded as reserve currencies. Reserve currencies are currencies that national central banks and other monetary authorities hold in significant quantities. The primary reserve currencies are the U.S. dollar and the euro. Secondary reserve currencies include the British pound, the Japanese yen, and the Swiss franc.

Currencies trade in foreign exchange markets. In spot currency transactions, one currency is immediately or almost immediately exchanged for another. The rate of exchange is called the spot exchange rate. Traders typically negotiate institutional trades in multiples of large quantities, such as US$1 million or ¥100 million. Institutional trades generally settle in two business days.

Retail currency trades most commonly take place through commercial banks when their customers exchange currencies at a location of the bank, use ATM machines when travelling to withdraw a different currency than the currency in which their bank accounts are denominated, or use credit cards to buy items priced in different currencies. Retail currency trades also take place at airport kiosks, at store front currency exchanges, or on the street.

3.4 Contracts

A contract is an agreement among traders to do something in the future. Contracts include forward, futures, swap, option, and insurance contracts. The values of most contracts depend on the value of an **underlying asset**. The underlying asset may be a commodity, a security, an index representing the values of other instruments, a currency pair or basket, or other contracts.

Contracts provide for some physical or cash settlement in the future. In a physically settled contract, settlement occurs when the parties to the contract physically exchange some item, such as tomatoes, pork bellies, or gold bars. Physical settlement also includes the delivery of such financial instruments as bonds, equities, or futures contracts even though the delivery is electronic. In contrast, cash settled contracts settle through cash payments. The amount of the payment depends on formulas specified in the contracts.

Financial analysts classify contracts by whether they are physical or financial based on the nature of the underlying asset. If the underlying asset is a physical product, the contract is a physical; otherwise, the contract is a financial. Examples of assets classified as physical include contracts for the delivery of petroleum, lumber, and gold. Examples of assets classified as financial include option contracts, and contracts on interest rates, stock indices, currencies, and credit default swaps.

Contracts that call for immediate delivery are called spot contracts, and they trade in spot markets. Immediate delivery generally is three days or less, but depends on each market. All other contracts involve what practitioners call futurity. They derive their values from events that will take place in the future.

Example 7

Contracts for Difference

Contracts for difference (CFD) allow people to speculate on price changes for an underlying asset, such as a common stock or an index. Dealers generally sell CFDs to their clients. When the clients sell the CFDs back to their dealer, they receive any appreciation in the underlying asset's price between the time of purchase and sale (open and close) of the contract. If the underlying asset's price drops over this interval, the client pays the dealer the difference.

1. Are contracts for difference derivative contracts?
2. Are contracts for difference based on copper prices cash settled or physically settled?

> **Solution to 1:**
>
> Contracts for difference are derivative contracts because their values are derived from changes in the prices of the underlying asset on which they are based.
>
> **Solution to 2:**
>
> All contracts for difference are cash settled contracts regardless of the underlying asset on which they are based because they settle in cash and not in the underlying asset.

3.4.1 *Forward Contracts*

A **forward contract** is an agreement to trade the underlying asset in the future at a price agreed upon today. For example, a contract for the sale of wheat after the harvest is a forward contract. People often use forward contracts to reduce risk. Before planting wheat, farmers like to know the price at which they will sell their crop. Similarly, before committing to sell flour to bakers in the future, millers like to know the prices that they will pay for wheat. The farmer and the miller both reduce their operating risks by agreeing to trade wheat forward.

Practitioners call such traders hedgers because they use their contractual commitments to hedge their risks. If the price of wheat falls, the wheat farmer's crop will drop in value on the spot market but he has a contract to sell wheat in the future at a higher fixed price. The forward contract has become more valuable to the farmer. Conversely, if the price of wheat rises, the miller's future obligation to sell flour will become more burdensome because of the high price he would have to pay for wheat on the spot market, but the miller has a contract to buy wheat at a lower fixed price. The forward contract has become more valuable to the miller. In both cases, fluctuations in the spot price are hedged by the forward contract. The forward contract offsets the operating risks that the hedgers face.

Consider a simple example of hedging. A tomato farmer in southern Ontario, Canada, grows tomatoes for processing into tomato sauce. The farmer expects to harvest 250,000 bushels and that the price at harvest will be $1.03. That price, however, could fluctuate significantly before the harvest. If the price of tomatoes drops to $0.75, the farmer would lose $0.28 per bushel ($1.03 – $0.75) relative to his expectations, or a total of $70,000. Now, suppose that the farmer can sell tomatoes forward to Heinz at $1.01 for delivery at the harvest. If the farmer sells 250,000 bushels forward, and the price of tomatoes drops to $0.75, the farmer would still be able to sell his tomatoes for $1.01, and thus would not suffer from the drop in price of tomatoes.

Example 8

Hedging Gold Production

An Indonesian gold producer invests in a mine expansion project on the expectation that gold prices will remain at or above 35,000 rupiah per gram when the new project starts producing ore.

1. What risks does the gold producer face with respect to the price of gold?
2. How might the gold producer hedge its gold price risk?

> **Solution to 1:**
>
> The gold producer faces the risk that the price of gold could fall below 35,000 rupiah before it can sell its new production. If so, the investment in the expansion project will be less profitable than expected, and may even generate losses for the mine.
>
> **Solution to 2:**
>
> The gold producer could hedge the gold price risk by selling gold forward, hopefully at a price near 35,000 rupiah. Even if the price of gold falls, the gold producer would get paid the contract price.

Forward contracts are very common, but two problems limit their usefulness for many market participants. The first problem is counterparty risk. **Counterparty risk** is the risk that the other party to a contract will fail to honor the terms of the contract. Concerns about counterparty risk ensure that generally only parties who have long-standing relationships with each other execute forward contracts. Trustworthiness is critical when prices are volatile because, after a large price change, one side or the other may prefer not to settle the contract.

The second problem is liquidity. Trading out of a forward contract is very difficult because it can only be done with the consent of the other party. The liquidity problem ensures that forward contracts tend to be executed only among participants for whom delivery is economically efficient and quite certain at the time of contracting so that both parties will want to arrange for delivery.

The counterparty risk problem and the liquidity problem often make it difficult for market participants to obtain the hedging benefits associated with forward contracting. Fortunately, futures contracts have been developed to mitigate these problems.

3.4.2 *Futures Contracts*

A **futures contract** is a standardized forward contract for which a clearinghouse guarantees the performance of all traders. The buyer of a futures contract is the side that will take physical delivery or its cash equivalent. The seller of a futures contract is the side that is liable for the delivery or its cash equivalent. A **clearinghouse** is an organization that ensures that no trader is harmed if another trader fails to honor the contract. In effect, the clearinghouse acts as the buyer for every seller and as the seller for every buyer. Buyers and sellers, therefore, can trade futures without worrying whether their counterparties are creditworthy. Because futures contracts are standardized, a buyer can eliminate his obligation to buy by selling his contract to anyone. A seller similarly can eliminate her obligation to deliver by buying a contact from anyone. In either case, the clearinghouse will release the trader from all future obligations if his or her long and short positions exactly offset each other.

To protect against defaults, futures clearinghouses require that all participants post with the clearinghouse an amount of money known as **initial margin** when they enter a contract. The clearinghouse then settles the margin accounts on a daily basis. All participants who have lost on their contracts that day will have the amount of their losses deducted from their margin by the clearinghouse. The clearinghouse similarly increases margins for all participants who gained on that day. Participants whose margins drop below the required **maintenance margin** must replenish their accounts. If a participant does not provide sufficient additional margin when required, the participant's broker will immediately trade to offset the participant's position. These **variation margin payments** ensure that the liabilities associated with futures contracts do not grow large.

Example 9

Futures Margin

NYMEX's Light Sweet Crude Oil futures contract specifies the delivery of 1,000 barrels of West Texas Intermediate (WTI) Crude Oil when the contract finally settles. A broker requires that its clients post an initial overnight margin of $7,763 per contract and an overnight maintenance margin of $5,750 per contract. A client buys ten contracts at $75 per barrel through this broker. On the next day, the contract settles for $72 per barrel. How much additional margin will the client have to provide to his broker?

Solution:

The client lost three dollars per barrel (he is the side committed to take delivery or its cash equivalent at $75 per barrel).This results in a $3,000 loss on each of his 10 contracts, and a total loss of $30,000. His initial margin of $77,630 is reduced by $30,000 leaving $47,630 in his margin account. Because his account has dropped below the maintenance margin requirement of $57,500, the client will get a margin call. The client must provide an additional $30,000 = $77,630 − $47,630 to replenish his margin account; the account is replenished to the amount of the initial margin. The client will only receive another margin call if his account drops to below $57,500 again.

Futures contracts have vastly improved the efficiency of forward contracting markets. Traders can trade standardized futures contracts with anyone without worrying about counterparty risk, and they can close their positions by arranging offsetting trades. Hedgers for whom the terms of the standard contract are not ideal generally still use the futures markets because the contracts embody most of the price risk that concerns them. They simply offset (close out) their futures positions, at the same time they enter spot contracts on which they make or take ultimate delivery.

Example 10

Forward and Futures Contracts

What feature most distinguishes futures contracts from forward contracts?

Solution:

A futures contract is a standardized forward contract for which a clearinghouse guarantees the performance of all buyers and sellers. The clearinghouse reduces the counterparty risk problem. The clearinghouse allows a buyer who has bought a contract from one person and sold the same contract to another person to net out the two obligations so that she is no longer liable for either side of the contract; the positions are closed. The ability to trade futures contracts provides liquidity in futures contracts compared with forward contracts.

3.4.3 *Swap Contracts*

A **swap contract** is an agreement to exchange payments of periodic cash flows that depend on future asset prices or interest rates. For example, in a typical **interest rate swap**, at periodic intervals, one party makes fixed cash payments to the counterparty in exchange for variable cash payments from the counterparty. The variable payments are based on a pre-specified variable interest rate such as the London Interbank Offered

Rate (LIBOR). This swap effectively exchanges fixed interest payments for variable interest payments. Because the variable rate is set in the future, the cash flows for this contract are uncertain when the parties enter the contract.

Investment managers often enter interest rate swaps when they own a fixed long-term income stream that they want to convert to a cash flow that varies with current short-term interest rates, or vice versa. The conversion may allow them to substantially reduce the total interest rate risk to which they are exposed. Hedgers often use swap contracts to manage risks.

In a **commodity swap**, one party typically makes fixed payments in exchange for payments that depend on future prices of a commodity such as oil. In a **currency swap**, the parties exchange payments denominated in different currencies. The payments may be fixed, or they may vary depending on future interest rates in the two countries. In an **equity swap**, the parties exchange fixed cash payments for payments that depend on the returns to a stock or a stock index.

Example 11

Swap and Forward Contracts

What feature most distinguishes a swap contract from a cash-settled forward contract?

Solution:

Both contracts provide for the exchange of cash payments in the future. A forward contract only has a single cash payment at the end that depends on an underlying price or index at the end. In contrast, a swap contract has several scheduled periodic payments, each of which depends on an underlying price or index at the time of the payment.

3.4.4 Option Contracts

An **option contract** allows the holder (the purchaser) of the option to buy or sell, depending on the type of option, an underlying instrument at a specified price at or before a specified date in the future. Those that do buy or sell are said to **exercise** their contracts. An option to buy is a **call option**, and an option to sell is a **put option**. The specified price is called the strike price (exercise price). If the holders can exercise their contracts only when they mature, they are **European-style contracts**. If they can exercise the contracts earlier, they are **American-style contracts**. Many exchanges list standardized option contracts on individual stocks, stock indices, futures contracts, currencies, swaps, and precious metals. Institutions also trade many customized option contracts with dealers in the over-the-counter derivative market.

Option holders generally will exercise call options if the strike price is below the market price of the underlying instrument, in which case, they will be able to buy at a lower price than the market price. Similarly, they will exercise put options if the strike price is above the underlying instrument price so that they sell at a higher price than the market price. Otherwise, option holders allow their options to expire as worthless.

The price that traders pay for an option is the option premium. Options can be quite expensive because, unlike forward and futures contracts, they do not impose any liability on the holder. The premium compensates the sellers of options—called option writers—for giving the call option holders the right to potentially buy below market prices and put option holders the right to potentially sell above market prices. Because the writers must trade if the holders exercise their options, option contracts may impose substantial liabilities on the writers.

Example 12

Option and Forward Contracts

What feature most distinguishes option contracts from forward contracts?

Solution:

The holder of an option contract has the right, but not the obligation, to buy (for a call option) or sell (for a put option) the underlying instrument at some time in the future. The writer of an option contract must trade the underlying instrument if the holder exercises the option.

In contrast, the two parties to a forward contract must trade the underlying instrument (or its equivalent value for a cash-settled contract) at some time in the future if either party wants to settle the contract.

3.4.5 *Other Contracts*

Insurance contracts pay their beneficiaries a cash benefit if some event occurs. Life, liability, and automobile insurance are examples of insurance contracts sold to retail clients. People generally use insurance contracts to compensate for losses that they will experience if bad things happen unexpectedly. Insurance contracts allow them to hedge risks that they face.

Credit default swaps (CDS) are insurance contracts that promise payment of principal in the event that a company defaults on its bonds. Bondholders use credit default swaps to convert risky bonds into more secure investments. Other creditors of the company may also buy them to hedge against the risk they will not be paid if the company goes bankrupt.

Well-informed traders who believe that a corporation will default on its bonds may buy credit default swaps written on the corporation's bonds if the swap prices are sufficiently low. If they are correct, the traders will profit if the payoff to the swap is more than the cost of buying and maintaining the swap position.

People sometimes also buy insurance contracts as investments, especially in jurisdictions where payouts from insurance contracts are not subject to as much taxation as are payouts to other investment vehicles. They may buy these contracts directly from insurance companies, or they may buy already issued contracts from their owners. For example, the life settlements market trades life insurance contracts that people sell to investors when they need cash.

3.5 Commodities

Commodities include precious metals, energy products, industrial metals, agricultural products, and carbon credits. Spot commodity markets trade commodities for immediate delivery whereas the forward and futures markets trade commodities for future delivery. Managers seeking positions in commodities can acquire them directly by trading in the spot markets or indirectly by trading forward and futures contracts.

The producers and processors of industrial metals and agricultural products are the primary users of the spot commodity markets because they generally are best able to take and make delivery and to store physical products. They undertake these activities in the normal course of operating their businesses. Their ability to handle physical products and the information that they gather operating businesses also gives them substantial advantages as information-motivated traders in these markets. Many producers employ financial analysts to help them analyze commodity market conditions so that they can best manage their inventories to hedge their operational risks and to speculate on future price changes.

Commodities also interest information-motivated traders and investment managers because they can use them as hedges against risks that they hold in their portfolios or as vehicles to speculate on future price changes. Most such traders take positions in the futures markets because they usually do not have facilities to handle most physical products nor can they easily obtain them. They also cannot easily cope with the normal variation in qualities that characterizes many commodities. Information-motivated traders and investment managers also prefer to trade in futures markets because most futures markets are more liquid than their associated spot markets and forward markets. The liquidity allows them to easily close their positions before delivery so that they can avoid handling physical products.

Some information-motivated traders and investment managers, however, trade in the spot commodity markets, especially when they can easily contract for low-cost storage. Commodities for which delivery and storage costs are lowest are nonperishable products for which the ratio of value to weight is high and variation in quality is low. These generally include precious metals, industrial diamonds, such high-value industrial metals as copper, aluminum, and mercury, and carbon credits.

3.6 Real Assets

Real assets include such tangible properties as real estate, airplanes, machinery, or lumber stands. These assets normally are held by operating companies, such as real estate developers, airplane leasing companies, manufacturers, or loggers. Many institutional investment managers, however, have been adding real assets to their portfolios as direct investments (involving direct ownership of the real assets) and indirect investments (involving indirect ownership, for example, purchase of securities of companies that invest in real assets or real estate investment trusts). Investments in real assets are attractive to them because of the income and tax benefits that they often generate, and because changes in their values may have a low correlation with other investments that the managers hold.

Direct investments in real assets generally require substantial management to ensure that the assets are maintained and used efficiently. Investment managers investing in such assets must either hire personnel to manage them or hire outside management companies. Either way, management of real assets is quite costly.

Real assets are unique properties in the sense that no two assets are alike. An example of a unique property is a real estate parcel. No two parcels are the same because, if nothing else, they are located in different places. Real assets generally differ in their conditions, remaining useful lives, locations, and suitability for various purposes. These differences are very important to the people who use them, so the market for a given real asset may be very limited. Thus, real assets tend to trade in very illiquid markets.

The heterogeneity of real assets, their illiquidity, and the substantial costs of managing them are all factors that complicate the valuation of real assets and generally make them unsuitable for most investment portfolios. These same problems, however, often cause real assets to be misvalued in the market, so astute information-motivated traders may occasionally identify significantly undervalued assets. The benefits from purchasing such assets, however, are often offset by the substantial costs of searching for them and by the substantial costs of managing them.

Many financial intermediaries create entities, such as real estate investment trusts (REITs) and master limited partnerships (MLPs), to securitize real assets and to facilitate indirect investment in real assets. The financial intermediaries manage the assets and pass through the net benefits after management costs to the investors who hold these securities. Because these securities are much more homogenous and divisible than the real assets that they represent, they tend to trade in much more liquid markets. Thus, they are much more suitable as investments than the real assets themselves.

Of course, investors seeking exposure to real assets can also buy shares in corporations that hold and operate real assets. Although almost all corporations hold and operate real assets, many specialize in assets that particularly interest investors seeking exposure to specific real asset classes. For example, investors interested in owning aircraft can buy an aircraft leasing company such as Waha Capital (Abu Dhabi Securities Exchange) and Aircastle Limited (NYSE).

Example 13

Assets and Contracts

Consider the following assets and contracts:

Bank deposits	Hedge funds
Certificates of deposit	Master limited partnership interests
Common stocks	Mortgages
Corporate bonds	Mutual funds
Currencies	Stock option contracts
Exchange-traded funds	Preferred stocks
Lumber forward contracts	Real estate parcels
Crude oil futures contracts	Interest rate swaps
Gold	Treasury notes

1. Which of these represent ownership in corporations?
2. Which of these are debt instruments?
3. Which of these are created by traders rather than by issuers?
4. Which of these are pooled investment vehicles?
5. Which of these are real assets?
6. Which of these would a home builder most likely use to hedge construction costs?
7. Which of these would a corporation trade when moving cash balances among various countries?

Solution to 1:

Common and preferred stocks represent ownership in corporations.

Solution to 2:

Bank deposits, certificates of deposit, corporate bonds, mortgages, and Treasury notes are all debt instruments. They respectively represent loans made to banks, corporations, mortgagees (typically real estate owners), and the Treasury.

Solution to 3:

Lumber forward contracts, crude oil futures contracts, stock option contracts, and interest rate swaps are created when the seller sells them to a buyer.

Solution to 4:

Exchange-traded funds, hedge funds, and mutual funds are pooled investment vehicles. They represent shared ownership in a portfolio of other assets.

Solution to 5:

Real estate parcels are real assets.

> **Solution to 6:**
>
> A builder would buy lumber forward contracts to lock in the price of lumber needed to build homes.
>
> **Solution to 7:**
>
> Corporations often trade currencies when moving cash from one country to another.

4 FINANCIAL INTERMEDIARIES

Financial intermediaries help entities achieve their financial goals. These intermediaries include commercial, mortgage, and investment banks; credit unions, credit card companies, and various other finance corporations; brokers and exchanges; dealers and arbitrageurs; clearinghouses and depositories; mutual funds and hedge funds; and insurance companies. The services and products that financial intermediaries provide allow their clients to solve the financial problems that they face more efficiently than they could do so by themselves. Financial intermediaries are essential to well-functioning financial systems.

Financial intermediaries are called intermediaries because the services and products that they provide help connect buyers to sellers in various ways. Whether the connections are easy to identify or involve complex financial structures, financial intermediaries stand between one or more buyers and one or more sellers and help them transfer capital and risk between them. Financial intermediaries' activities allow buyers and sellers to benefit from trading, often without any knowledge of the other.

This section introduces the main financial intermediaries that provide services and products in well-developed financial markets. The discussion starts with those intermediaries whose services most obviously connect buyers to sellers and then proceeds to those intermediaries whose services create more subtle connections. Because many financial intermediaries provide many different types of services, some are mentioned more than once. The section concludes with a general characterization of the various ways in which financial intermediaries add value to the financial system.

4.1 Brokers, Exchanges, and Alternative Trading Systems

Brokers are agents who fill orders for their clients. They do not trade with their clients. Instead, they search for traders who are willing to take the other side of their clients' orders. Individual brokers may work for large brokerage firms, the brokerage arm of banks, or at exchanges. Some brokers match clients to clients personally. Others use specialized computer systems to identify potential trades and help their clients fill their orders. Brokers help their clients trade by reducing the costs of finding counterparties for their trades.

Block brokers provide brokerage service to large traders. Large orders are hard to fill because finding a counterparty willing to do a large trade is often quite difficult. A large buy order generally will trade at a premium to the current market price, and a large sell order generally will trade at a discount to the current market price. These price concessions encourage other traders to trade with the large traders. They also make large traders reluctant, however, to expose their orders to the public before their trades are arranged because they do not want to move the market. Block brokers, therefore, carefully manage the exposure of the orders entrusted to them, which makes filling them difficult.

Investment banks provide advice to their mostly corporate clients and help them arrange transactions such as initial and seasoned securities offerings. Their corporate finance divisions help corporations finance their business by issuing securities, such as common and preferred shares, notes, and bonds. Another function of corporate finance divisions is to help companies identify and acquire other companies (i.e., in mergers and acquisitions).

Exchanges provide places where traders can meet to arrange their trades. Historically, brokers and dealers met on an exchange floor to negotiate trades. Increasingly, exchanges arrange trades for traders based on orders that brokers and dealers submit to them. Such exchanges essentially act as brokers. The distinction between exchanges and brokers has become quite blurred. Exchanges and brokers that use electronic order matching systems to arrange trades among their clients are functionally indistinguishable in this respect. Examples of exchanges include the NYSE-Euronext, Eurex, Deutsche Börse, the Chicago Mercantile Exchange, the Tokyo Stock Exchange, and the Singapore Exchange.

Exchanges are easily distinguished from brokers by their regulatory operations. Most exchanges regulate their members' behavior when trading on the exchange, and sometimes away from the exchange.

Many securities exchanges regulate the issuers that list their securities on the exchange. These regulations generally require timely financial disclosure. Financial analysts use this information to value the securities traded at the exchange. Without such disclosure, valuing securities could be very difficult and market prices might not reflect the fundamental values of the securities. In such situations, well-informed participants may profit from less-informed participants. To avoid such losses, the less-informed participants may withdraw from the market, which can greatly increase corporate costs of capital.

Some exchanges also prohibit issuers from creating capital structures that would concentrate voting rights in the hands of a few owners who do not own a commensurate share of the equity. These regulations attempt to ensure that corporations are run for the benefit of all shareholders and not to promote the interests of controlling shareholders who do not have significant economic stakes in the company.

Exchanges derive their regulatory authority from their national or regional governments, or through the voluntary agreements of their members and issuers to subject themselves to the exchange regulations. In most countries, government regulators oversee the exchange rules and the regulatory operations. Most countries also impose financial disclosure standards on public issuers. Examples of government regulatory bodies include the Japanese Financial Services Agency, the Hong Kong Securities and Futures Commission, the British Financial Services Authority, the German Bundesanstalt für Finanzdienstleistungsaufsicht, the U.S. Securities and Exchange Commission, the Ontario Securities Commission, and the Mexican Comisión Nacional Bancaria y de Valores.

Alternative trading systems (ATSs), also known as **electronic communications networks** (ECNs) or **multilateral trading facilities** (MTFs) are trading venues that function like exchanges but that do not exercise regulatory authority over their subscribers except with respect to the conduct of their trading in their trading systems. Some ATSs operate electronic trading systems that are otherwise indistinguishable from the trading systems operated by exchanges. Others operate innovative trading systems that suggest trades to their customers based on information that their customers share with them or that they obtain through research into their customers' preferences. Many ATSs are known as **dark pools** because they do not display the orders that their clients send to them. Large investment managers especially like these systems because market prices often move to their disadvantage when other traders know about their large orders. ATSs may be owned and operated by broker–dealers, exchanges, banks, or by companies organized solely for this purpose, many of which may be owned by a consortia of brokers–dealers and banks. Examples of ATSs include PureTrading (Canada), the Order Machine (Netherlands), Chi-X Europe, BATS (U.S.), POSIT (U.S.), Liquidnet (U.S.), Baxter-FX (Ireland), and Turquoise (Europe). Many of these ATSs provide services in many markets besides the ones in which they are domiciled.

4.2 Dealers

Dealers fill their clients' orders by trading with them. When their clients want to sell securities or contracts, dealers buy the instruments for their own accounts. If their clients want to buy securities, dealers sell securities that they own or have borrowed. After completing a transaction, dealers hope to reverse the transaction by trading with another client on the other side of the market. When they are successful, they effectively connect a buyer who arrived at one point in time with a seller who arrived at another point in time.

The service that dealers provide is liquidity. **Liquidity** is the ability to buy or sell with low transactions costs when you want to trade. By allowing their clients to trade when they want to trade, dealers provide liquidity to them. In over-the-counter markets, dealers offer liquidity when their clients ask them to trade with them. In exchange markets, dealers offer liquidity to anyone who is willing to trade at the prices that the dealers offer at the exchange. Dealers profit when they can buy at prices that on average are lower than the prices at which they sell.

Dealers may organize their operations within proprietary trading houses, investment banks, and hedge funds, or as sole proprietorships. Some dealers are traditional dealers in the sense that individuals make trading decisions. Others use computerized trading to make all trading decisions. Examples of companies with large dealing operations include Deutsche Securities (Germany), RBC Capital Markets (Canada), Nomura (Japan), Timber Hill (U.S.), Knight Securities (U.S.), Goldman Sachs (U.S.), and IG Group plc (U.K.). Almost all investment banks have large dealing operations.

Most dealers also broker orders, and many brokers deal to their customers. Accordingly, practitioners often use the term **broker–dealer** to refer to dealers and brokers. Broker–dealers have a conflict of interest with respect to how they fill their customers' orders. When acting as a broker, they must seek the best price for their customers' orders. When acting as dealers, however, they profit most when they sell to their customers at high prices or buy from their customers at low prices. The problem is most serious when the customer allows the broker–dealer to decide whether to trade the order with another trader or to fill it as a dealer. Consequently, when trading with a broker–dealer, some customers specify how they want their orders filled. They may also trade only with pure agency brokers who do not also deal.

Primary dealers are dealers with whom central banks trade when conducting monetary policy. They buy bills, notes, and bonds when the central banks sell them to decrease the money supply. The dealers then sell these instruments to their clients. Similarly, when the central banks want to increase the money supply, the primary dealers buy these instruments from their clients and sell them to the central banks.

Example 14

Brokers and Dealers

What characteristic *most likely* distinguishes brokers from dealers?

Solution:

Brokers are agents that arrange trades on behalf of their clients. They do not trade with their clients. In contrast, dealers are proprietary traders who trade with their clients.

4.3 Securitizers

Banks and investment companies create new financial products when they buy and repackage securities or other assets. For example, mortgage banks commonly originate hundreds or thousands of residential mortgages by lending money to homeowners. They then place the mortgages in a pool and sell shares of the pool to investors as mortgage pass-through securities, which are also known as mortgage-backed securities. All payments of principal and interest are passed through to the investors each month, after deducting the costs of servicing the mortgages. Investors who purchase these pass-through securities obtain securities that in aggregate have the same net cash flows and associated risks as the pool of mortgages.

The process of buying assets, placing them in a pool, and then selling securities that represent ownership of the pool is called securitization.

Mortgage-backed securities have the advantage that default losses and early repayments are much more predictable for a diversified portfolio of mortgages than they are for individual mortgages. They are also attractive to investors who cannot efficiently service mortgages but wish to invest in mortgages. By securitizing mortgage pools, the mortgage banks allow investors who are not large enough to buy hundreds of mortgages to obtain the benefits of diversification and economies of scale in loan servicing.

Securitization greatly improves liquidity in the mortgage markets because it allows investors in the pass-through securities to buy mortgages indirectly that they otherwise would not buy. Because the financial risks associated with mortgage-backed securities (debt securities with specified claims on the cash flows of a portfolio of mortgages) are much more predictable than those of individual mortgages, mortgage-backed securities are easier to price and thus easier to sell when investors need to raise cash. These characteristics make the market for mortgage-backed securities much more liquid than the market for individual mortgages. Because investors value liquidity—the ability to sell when they want to—they will pay more for securitized mortgages than for individual mortgages. The homeowners benefit because higher mortgage prices imply lower interest rates.

The mortgage bank is a financial intermediary because it connects investors who want to buy mortgages to homeowners who want to borrow money. The homeowners sell mortgages to the bank when the bank lends them money.

Some mortgage banks form mortgage pools from mortgages that they buy from other banks that originate the loans. These mortgage banks are also financial intermediaries because they connect sellers of mortgages to buyers of mortgage-backed securities. Although the sellers of the mortgages are the originating lenders and not the borrowers, the benefits of creating liquid mortgage-backed securities ultimately flow back to the borrowers.

The creation of the pass-through securities generally takes place on the accounts of the mortgage bank. The bank buys mortgages and sells pass-through securities whose values depend on the mortgage pool. The mortgages appear on the bank's accounts as assets and the mortgage-backed securities appear as liabilities.

In many securitizations, the financial intermediary avoids placing the assets and liabilities on its balance sheet by setting up a special corporation or trust that buys the assets and issues the securities. Those corporations and trusts are called **special purpose vehicles** (SPVs) or alternatively **special purpose entities** (SPEs). Conducting a securitization through a special purpose vehicle is advantageous to investors because their interests in the asset pool are better protected in an SPV than they would be on the balance sheet of the financial intermediary if the financial intermediary were to go bankrupt.

Financial intermediaries securitize many assets. Besides mortgages, banks securitize car loans, credit card receivables, bank loans, and airplane leases, to name just a few assets. As a class, these securities are called asset-backed securities.

When financial intermediaries securitize assets, they often create several classes of securities, called tranches, that have different rights to the cash flows from the asset pool. The tranches are structured so that some produce more predictable cash flows than do others. The senior tranches have first rights to the cash flow from the asset pool. Because the overall risk of a given asset pool cannot be changed, the more junior tranches bear a disproportionate share of the risk of the pool. Practitioners often call the most junior tranche toxic waste because it is so risky. The complexity associated with slicing asset pools into tranches can make the resulting securities difficult to value. Mistakes in valuing these securities contributed to the financial crisis that started in 2007.

Investment companies also create pass-through securities based on investment pools. For example, an exchange-traded fund is an asset-backed security that represents ownership in the securities and contracts held by the fund. The shareholders benefit from the securitization because they can buy or sell an entire portfolio in a single transaction. Because the transaction cost savings are quite substantial, exchange-traded funds often trade in very liquid markets. The investment companies (and sometimes the arbitrageurs) that create exchange-traded funds are financial intermediaries because they connect the buyers of the funds to the sellers of the assets that make up the fund portfolios.

More generally, the creators of all pooled investment vehicles are financial intermediaries that transform portfolios of securities and contracts into securities that represent undivided ownership of the portfolios. The investors in these funds thus indirectly invest in the securities held by the fund. They benefit from the expertise of the investment manager and from obtaining a portfolio that may be more diversified than one they might otherwise be able to hold.

4.4 Depository Institutions and Other Financial Corporations

Depository institutions include commercial banks, savings and loan banks, credit unions, and similar institutions that raise funds from depositors and other investors and lend it to borrowers. The banks give their depositors interest and transaction services, such as check writing and check cashing, in exchange for using their money. They may also raise funds by selling bonds or equity in the bank.

These banks are financial intermediaries because they transfer funds from their depositors and investors to their borrowers. The depositors and investors benefit because they obtain a return (in interest, transaction services, dividends, or capital appreciation) on their funds without having to contract with the borrowers and manage their loans. The borrowers benefit because they obtain the funds that they need without having to search for investors who will trust them to repay their loans.

Many other financial corporations provide credit services. For example, acceptance corporations, discount corporations, payday advance corporations, and factors provide credit to borrowers by lending them money secured by such assets as consumer loans, machinery, future paychecks, or accounts receivables. They finance these loans by selling commercial paper, bonds, and shares to investors. These corporations are intermediaries because they connect investors to borrowers. The investors obtain investments secured by a diversified portfolio of loans while the borrowers obtain funds without having to search for investors.

Brokers also act as financial intermediaries when they lend funds to clients who want to buy securities on margin. They generally obtain the funds from other clients who deposit them in their accounts. Brokers who provide these services to hedge funds and other similar institutions are called prime brokers.

Banks, financial corporations, and brokers can only raise money from depositors and other lenders because their equity owners retain residual interests in the performance of the loans that they make. If the borrowers default, the depositors and other lenders have priority claims over the equity owners. If insufficient money is collected from the borrowers, shareholders' equity is used to pay their depositors and other lenders. The risk of losing capital focuses the equity owners' and management's attention so that credit is not offered foolishly.

Because the ability of these companies to cover their credit losses is limited by the capital that their owners invest in them, the depositors and other investors who lend them money pay close attention to how much money the owners have at risk. For example, if a finance corporation is poorly capitalized, its shareholders will lose little if its clients default on the loans that the finance corporation makes to them. In that case, the finance corporation will have little incentive to lend only to creditworthy borrowers and to effectively manage collection on those loans once they have been made. Worse, it may even choose to lend to borrowers with poor credit because the interest rates that they can charge such borrowers are higher. Until those loans default, the higher income will make the corporation appear to be more profitable than it actually is. Depositors and other investors are aware of these problems and generally pay close attention to them. Accordingly, poorly capitalized financial institutions cannot easily borrow money to finance their operations at favorable rates.

Depository banks and financial corporations are similar to securitized asset pools that issue pass-through securities. Their depositors and investors own securities that ultimately are backed by an asset pool consisting of their loan portfolios. The depositors generally hold the most senior tranche, followed by the other creditors. The shareholders hold the most junior tranche. In the event of bankruptcy, they are paid only if everyone else is paid.

Example 15

Commercial Banks

What services do commercial banks provide that make them financial intermediaries?

Solution:

Commercial banks collect deposits from investors and lend them to borrowers. They are intermediaries because they connect lenders to borrowers. Commercial banks also provide transaction services that make it easier for the banks' depository customers to pay bills and collect funds from their own customers.

4.5 Insurance Companies

Insurance companies help people and companies offset risks that concern them. They do this by creating insurance contracts (policies) that provide a payment in the event that some loss occurs. The insured buy these contracts to hedge against potential losses. Common examples of insurance contracts include auto, fire, life, liability, medical, theft, and disaster insurance contracts.

Credit default swaps are also insurance contracts, but historically they have not been subject to the same reserve requirements that most governments apply to more traditional insurance contracts. They may be sold by insurance companies or by other financial entities, such as investment banks or hedge funds.

Insurance contracts transfer risk from those who buy the contracts to those who sell them. Although insurance companies occasionally broker trades between the insured and the insurer, they more commonly provide the insurance themselves. In that case, the insurance company's owners and creditors become the indirect insurers of the risks that the insurance company assumes. Insurance companies also often transfer risks that they do not wish to bear by buying reinsurance policies from reinsurers.

Insurers are financial intermediaries because they connect the buyers of their insurance contracts with investors, creditors, and reinsurers who are willing to bear the insured risks. The buyers benefit because they can easily obtain the risk transfers that they seek without searching for entities that would be willing to assume those risks.

The owners, creditors, and reinsurers of the insurance company benefit because the company allows them to sell their tolerance for risk easily without having to manage the insurance contracts. Instead, the company manages the relationships with the insured—primarily collections and claims—and hopefully controls the various problems—fraud, moral hazard, and adverse selection—that often plague insurance markets. Fraud occurs when people deliberately cause or falsely report losses to collect on insurance. Moral hazard occurs when people are less careful about avoiding insured losses than they would be if they were not insured so that losses occur more often than they would otherwise. Adverse selection occurs when only those who are most at risk buy insurance so that insured losses tend to be greater than average.

Everyone benefits because insurance companies hold large diversified portfolios of policies. Loss rates for well-diversified portfolios of insurance contracts are much more predictable than for single contracts. For such contracts as auto insurance in which losses are almost uncorrelated across policies, diversification ensures that the financial performance of a large portfolio of contracts will be quite predictable and so holding the portfolio will not be very risky. The insured benefit because they do not have to pay the insurers much to compensate them for bearing risk (the expected loss is quite predictable so the risk is relatively low). Instead, their insurance premiums primarily reflect the expected loss rate in the portfolio plus the costs of running and financing the company.

4.6 Arbitrageurs

Arbitrageurs trade when they can identify opportunities to buy and sell identical or essentially similar instruments at different prices in different markets. They profit when they can buy in one market for less than they sell in another market. Arbitrageurs are financial intermediaries because they connect buyers in one market to sellers in another market.

The purest form of arbitrage involves buying and selling the same instrument in two different markets. Arbitrageurs who do such trades sell to buyers in one market and buy from sellers in the other market. They provide liquidity to the markets because they make it easier for buyers and sellers to trade when and where they want to trade.

Because dealers and arbitrageurs both provide liquidity to other traders, they compete with each other. The dealers connect buyers and sellers who arrive in the same market at different times whereas the arbitrageurs connect buyers and sellers who arrive at the same time in different markets. In practice, traders who profit from offering liquidity rarely are purely dealers or purely arbitrageurs. Instead, most traders attempt to identify and exploit every opportunity they can to manage their inventories profitably.

If information about prices is readily available to market participants, pure arbitrages involving the same instrument will be quite rare. Traders who are well informed about market conditions usually route their orders to the market offering the best price so that arbitrageurs will have few opportunities to match traders across markets when they want to trade the exact same instrument.

Arbitrageurs often trade securities or contracts whose values depend on the same underlying factors. For example, dealers in equity option contracts often sell call options in the contract market and buy the underlying shares in the stock market. Because the values of the call options and of the underlying shares are closely correlated (the value of the call increases with the value of the shares), the long stock position hedges the risk in the short call position so that the dealer's net position is not too risky.

Similar to the pure arbitrage that involves the same instrument in different markets, these arbitrage trades connect buyers in one market to sellers in another market. In this case, however, the buyers and sellers are interested in different instruments whose values are closely related. In the example, the buyer is interested in buying a call options contract, the value of which is a nonlinear function of the value of the underlying stock; the seller is interested in selling the underlying stock.

Options dealers buy stock and sell calls when calls are overpriced relative to the underlying stocks. They use complicated financial models to value options in relation to underlying stock values, and they use financial engineering techniques to control the risk of their portfolios. Successful arbitrageurs must know valuation relations well and they must manage the risk in their portfolios well to trade profitably. They profit by buying the relatively undervalued instrument and selling the relatively overvalued instrument.

Buying a risk in one form and selling it another form involves a process called replication. Arbitrageurs use various trading strategies to replicate the returns to securities and contracts. If they can substantially replicate those returns, they can use the replication trading strategy to offset the risk of buying or selling the actual securities and contracts. The combined effect of their trading is to transform risk from one form to another. This process allows them to create or eliminate contracts in response to the excess demand for, and supply of, contracts.

For example, when traders want to buy more call contracts than are presently available, they push the call contract prices up so that calls become overvalued relative to the underlying stock. The arbitrageurs replicate calls by using a particular financial engineering strategy to buy the underlying stock, and then create the desired call option contracts by selling them short. In contrast, if more calls have been created than traders want to hold, call prices will fall so that calls become undervalued relative to the underlying stock. The arbitrageurs will trade stocks and contracts to absorb the excess contracts. Arbitrageurs who use these strategies are financial intermediaries because they connect buyers and sellers who want to trade the same underlying risks but in different forms.

Example 16

Dealers and Arbitrageurs

With respect to providing liquidity to market participants, what characteristics most clearly distinguish dealers from arbitrageurs?

Solution:

Dealers provide liquidity to buyers and sellers who arrive at the same market at different times. They move liquidity through time. Arbitrageurs provide liquidity to buyers and sellers who arrive at different markets at the same time. They move liquidity across markets.

4.7 Settlement and Custodial Services

In addition to connecting buyers to sellers through a variety of direct and indirect means, financial intermediaries also help their customers settle their trades and ensure that the resulting positions are not stolen or pledged more than once as collateral.

Clearinghouses arrange for final settlement of trades. In futures markets, they guarantee contract performance. In other markets, they may act only as escrow agents, transferring money from the buyer to the seller while transferring securities from the seller to the buyer.

The members of a clearinghouse are the only traders for whom the clearinghouse will settle trades. To ensure that their members settle the trades that they present to the clearinghouse, clearinghouses require that their members have adequate capital and post-performance bonds (margins). Clearinghouses also limit the aggregate net (buy minus sell) quantities that their members can settle.

Brokers and dealers who are not members of the clearinghouse must arrange to have a clearinghouse member settle their trades. To ensure that the non-member brokers and dealers can settle their trades, clearinghouse members require that their customers (the non-member brokers and dealers) have adequate capital and post-margins. They also limit the aggregate net quantities that their customers can settle and they monitor their customers' trading to ensure that they do not arrange trades that they cannot settle.

Brokers and dealers similarly monitor the trades made by their retail and institutional customers, and regulate their customers to ensure that they do not arrange trades that they cannot settle.

This hierarchical system of responsibility generally ensures that traders settle their trades. The brokers and dealers guarantee settlement of the trades they arrange for their retail and institutional customers. The clearinghouse members guarantee settlement of the trades that their customers present to them, and clearinghouses guarantee settlement of all trades presented to them by their members. If a clearinghouse member fails to settle a trade, the clearinghouse settles the trade using its own capital or capital drafted from the other members.

Reliable settlement of all trades is extremely important to a well-functioning financial system because it allows strangers to confidently contract with each other without worrying too much about **counterparty risk**, the risk that their counterparties will not settle their trades. A secure clearinghouse system thus greatly increases liquidity because it greatly increases the number of counterparties with whom a trader can safely arrange a trade.

In many national markets, clearinghouses clear all securities trades so that traders can trade securities through any exchange, broker, alternative trading system, or dealer. These clearinghouse systems promote competition among these exchange service providers.

In contrast, most futures exchanges have their own clearinghouses. These clearinghouses usually will not accept trades arranged away from their exchanges so that a competing exchange cannot trade another exchange's contracts. Competing exchanges may create similar contracts, but moving traders from one established market to a new market is extraordinarily difficult because traders prefer to trade where other traders trade.

Depositories or custodians hold securities on behalf of their clients. These services, which are often offered by banks, help prevent the loss of securities through fraud, oversight, or natural disaster. Broker–dealers also often hold securities on behalf of their customers so that the customers do not have to hold the securities in certificate form. To avoid problems with lost certificates, securities increasingly are issued only in electronic form.

Example 17

Financial Intermediaries

As a relatively new member of the business community, you decide it would be advantageous to join the local lunch club to network with businessmen. Upon learning that you are a financial analyst, club members soon enlist you to give a lunch speech. During the question and answer session afterwards, a member of the audience asks, "I keep reading in the newspaper about the need to regulate 'financial intermediaries', but really don't understand exactly what they are. Can you tell me?" How do you answer?

Solution:

Financial intermediaries are companies that help their clients achieve their financial goals. They are called intermediaries because, in some way or another, they stand between two or more people who would like to trade with each other, but for various reasons find it difficult to do so directly. The intermediary arranges the trade for them, or more often, trades with both sides.

For example, a commercial bank is an intermediary that connects investors with money to borrowers who need money. The investors buy certificates of deposit from the bank, buy bonds or stock issued by the bank, or simply are depositors in the bank. The borrowers borrow this money from the bank when they arrange loans. Without the bank's intermediation, the investors would have to find trustworthy borrowers themselves, which would be difficult, and the borrowers would have to find trusting lenders, which would also be difficult.

Similarly, an insurance company is an intermediary because it connects customers who want to insure risks with investors who are willing to bear those risks. The investors own shares or bonds issued by the insurance company, or they have sold reinsurance contracts to the insurance company. The insured benefit because they can more easily buy a policy from an insurance company than they can find counterparties who would be willing to bear their risks. The investors benefit because the insurance company creates a diversified portfolio of risks by selling insurance to thousands or millions of customers. Diversification ensures that the net risk borne by the insurance company and its investors will be predictable and thus financially manageable.

In both cases, the financial intermediary also manages the relationships with its customers and investors so that neither side has to worry about the credit-worthiness or trust-worthiness of its counterparties. For example, the bank manages credit quality and collections on its loans and the insurance company manages risk exposure and collections on its policies. These services benefit both sides by reducing the costs of connecting investors to borrowers or of insured to insurers.

These are only two examples of financial intermediation. Many others involve firms engaged in brokerage, dealing, arbitrage, securitization, investment management, and the clearing and settlement of trades. In all cases, the financial intermediary stands between a buyer and a seller, offering them services that allow them to better achieve their financial goals in a cost effective and efficient manner.

4.8 Summary

By facilitating transactions among buyers and sellers, financial intermediaries provide services essential to a well-functioning financial system. They facilitate transactions the following ways:

1. Brokers, exchanges, and various alternative trading systems match buyers and sellers interested in trading the same instrument at the same place and time. These financial intermediaries specialize in discovering and organizing information about who wants to trade.

2. Dealers and arbitrageurs connect buyers to sellers interested in trading the same instrument but who are not present at the same place and time. Dealers connect buyers to sellers who are present at the same place but at different times whereas arbitrageurs connect buyers to sellers who are present at the same time but in different places. These financial intermediaries trade for their own accounts when providing these services. Dealers buy or sell with one client and hope to do the offsetting transaction later with another client. Arbitrageurs buy from a seller in one market while simultaneously selling to a buyer in another market.

3. Many financial intermediaries create new instruments that depend on the cash flows and associated financial risks of other instruments. The intermediaries provide these services when they securitize assets, manage investment funds, operate banks and other finance corporations that offer investments to investors and loans to borrowers, and operate insurance companies that pool risks. The instruments that they create generally are more attractive to their clients than the instruments on which they are based. The new instruments also may be differentiated to appeal to diverse clienteles. Their efforts connect buyers of one or more instruments to sellers of other instruments, all of which in aggregate provide the same cash flows and risk exposures. Financial intermediaries thus effectively arrange trades among traders who otherwise would not trade with each other.

4. Arbitrageurs who conduct arbitrage among securities and contracts whose values depend on common factors convert risk from one form to another. Their trading connects buyers and sellers who want to trade similar risks expressed in different forms.

5. Banks, clearinghouses, and depositories provide services that ensure traders settle their trades and that the resulting positions are not stolen or pledged more than once as collateral.

5   POSITIONS

People generally solve their financial and risk management problems by taking positions in various assets or contracts. A **position** in an asset is the quantity of the instrument that an entity owns or owes. A **portfolio** consists of a set of positions.

People have **long positions** when they own assets or contracts. Examples of long positions include ownership of stocks, bonds, currencies, contracts, commodities, or real assets. Long positions benefit from an appreciation in the prices of the assets or contracts owned.

People have **short positions** when they have sold assets that they do not own, or when they write and sell contracts. Short positions benefit from a decrease in the prices of the assets or contracts sold. Short sellers profit by selling at high prices and repurchasing at lower prices. Information-motivated traders sell assets and contracts short positions when they believe that prices will fall.

Hedgers also often sell instruments short. They short securities and contracts when the financial risks inherent in the instruments are positively correlated with the risks to which they are exposed. For example, to hedge the risk associated with holding copper inventories, a wire manufacturer would sell short copper futures. If the price of copper falls, the manufacturer will lose on his copper inventories but gain on his short futures position. (If the risk in an instrument is inversely correlated with a risk to which hedgers are exposed, the hedgers will hedge with long positions.)

Contracts have long sides and short sides. The long side of a forward or futures contract is the side that will take physical delivery or its cash equivalent. The short side of such contracts is the side that is liable for the delivery. The long side of a futures contract increases in value when the value of the underlying asset increases in value.

The identification of the two sides can be confusing for option contracts. The long side of an option contract is the side that holds the right to exercise the option. The short side is the side that must satisfy the obligation. Practitioners say that that the long side *holds* the option and the short side *writes* the option, so the long side is the holder and the short side is the writer. The put contracts are the source of the potential confusion. The put contract holder has the right to sell the underlying to the writer. The holder will benefit if the price of the underlying falls, in which case the price of the put contract will rise. The holder is long the put contract and has an indirect short position in the underlying instrument. Analysts call the indirect short position short exposure to the underlying. The put contract holders have long exposure to their option contract and short exposure to the underlying instrument.

Exhibit 1	Option Positions and Their Associated Underlying Risk Exposures	
Type of Option	**Option Position**	**Exposure to Underlying Risk**
Call	Long	Long
Call	Short	Short
Put	Long	Short
Put	Short	Long

The identification of the long side in a swap contract is often arbitrary because swap contracts call for the exchange of contractually determined cash flows rather than for the purchase (or the cash equivalent) of some underlying instrument. In general, the side that benefits from an increase in the quoted price is the long side.

The identification of the long side in currency contracts also may be confusing. In this case, the confusion stems from symmetry in the contracts. The buyer of one currency is the seller of the other currency, and vice versa for the seller. Thus, a long forward position in one currency is a short forward position in the other currency. When practitioners describe a position, they generally will say, "I'm long the dollar against the yen," which means they have bought dollars and sold yen.

5.1 Short Positions

Short sellers create short positions in contracts by selling contracts that they do not own. In a sense, they become the issuers of the contract when they create the liabilities associated with their contracts. This analogy will also help you better understand risk when you study corporate finance: Corporations create short positions in their bonds when they issue bonds in exchange for cash. Although bonds are generally considered to be securities, they are also contracts between the issuer and the bondholder.

Short sellers create short positions in securities by borrowing securities from security lenders who are long holders. The short sellers then sell the borrowed securities to other traders. Short sellers close their positions by repurchasing the securities and returning them to the security lenders. If the securities drop in value, the short sellers profit because they repurchase the securities at lower prices than the prices at which they sold the securities. If the securities rise in value, they will lose. Short sellers who buy to close their positions are said to cover their positions.

The potential gains in a long position generally are unbounded. For example, the stock prices of such highly successful companies as Yahoo! have increased more than 50-fold since they were first publicly traded. The potential losses on long positions, however, are limited to no more than 100 percent—a complete loss—for long positions without any associated liabilities.

In contrast, the potential gains on a short position are limited to no more than 100 percent whereas the potential losses are unbounded. The unbounded potential losses on short positions make short positions very risky in volatile instruments. For example, if you shorted 100 shares of Yahoo! in July 1996 at $20 and you kept your position open for four years, you would have lost $148,000 on your $2,000 initial short position. During this period, Yahoo! rose 75-fold to $1,500 on a split-adjusted equivalent basis.

Although security lenders generally believe that they are long the securities that they lend, in fact, they do not actually own the securities during the periods of their loans. Instead, they own promises made by the short sellers to return the securities. These promises are memorialized in security lending agreements. These agreements specify that the short sellers will pay the long sellers all dividends or interest that they otherwise would have received had they not lent their securities. These payments are called payments-in-lieu of dividends (or of interest), and they may have different tax treatments than actual dividends and interest. The security lending agreements also protect the lenders in the event of a stock split.

To secure the security loans, lenders require that the short seller leave the proceeds of the short sale on deposit with them as collateral for the stock loan. They invest the collateral in short-term securities, and they rebate the interest to the short sellers at rates called short rebate rates. The short rebate rates are determined in the market and generally are available only to institutional short-sellers and some large retail traders. If a security is hard to borrow, the rebate rate may be very small or even negative. Such securities are said to be on special. Otherwise, the rebate rate is usually 10 basis points less than the overnight rate in the interbank funds market. Most security lending agreements require various margin payments to keep the credit risk among the parties from growing when prices change.

Securities lenders lend their securities because the short rebate rates they pay on the collateral are lower than the interest rates they receive from investing the collateral. The difference is because of the implicit loan fees that they receive from the borrowers for borrowing the stock. The difference also compensates lenders for risks that the lenders take when investing the collateral and for the risk that the borrowers will default if prices rise significantly.

Example 18

Short Positions in Securities and Contracts

How is the process of short selling shares of Siemens different from that of short selling a Siemens equity call option contract?

Solution:

To short sell shares of Siemens, the seller (or his broker) must borrow the shares from a long holder so that he can deliver them to the buyer. To short sell a Siemens equity call option contract, the seller simply creates the contract when he sells it to the buyer.

5.2 Leveraged Positions

In many markets, traders can buy securities by borrowing some of the purchase price. They usually borrow the money from their brokers. The borrowed money is called the **margin loan**, and they are said to buy on margin. The interest rate that the buyers pay for their margin loan is called the **call money rate**. The call money rate is above the government bill rate and is negotiable. Large buyers generally obtain more favorable rates than do retail buyers. For institutional-size buyers, the call money rate is quite low because the loans are generally well secured by securities held as collateral by the lender.

Trader's equity is that portion of the security price that the buyer must supply. Traders who buy securities on margin are subject to minimum margin requirements. The **initial margin requirement** is the minimum fraction of the purchase price that must be trader's equity. This requirement may be set by the government, the exchange, or the exchange clearinghouse. For example, in the United States, the Federal Reserve Board sets the initial margin requirement through Regulation T. In Hong Kong, the Securities and Futures Commission sets the margin requirements. In all markets, brokers often require more equity than the government-required minimum from their clients when lending to them.

Many markets allow brokers to lend their clients more money if the brokers use risk models to measure and control the overall risk of their clients' portfolios. This system is called portfolio margining.

Buying securities on margin can greatly increase the potential gains or losses for a given amount of equity in a position because the trader can buy more securities on margin than he could otherwise. The buyer thus earns greater profits when prices rise and suffers greater losses when prices fall. The relation between risk and borrowing is called **financial leverage** (often simply called leverage). Traders leverage their positions when they borrow to buy more securities. A highly leveraged position is large relative to the equity that supports it.

The leverage ratio is the ratio of the value of the position to the value of the equity investment in it. The leverage ratio indicates how many times larger a position is than the equity that supports it. The maximum leverage ratio associated with a position financed by the minimum margin requirement is one divided by the minimum margin requirement. If the requirement is 40 percent, then the maximum leverage ratio is 2.5 = 100% position ÷ 40% equity.

The leverage ratio indicates how much more risky a leveraged position is relative to an unleveraged position. For example, if a stock bought on 40 percent margin rises 10 percent, the buyer will experience a 25 percent (2.5 × 10%) return on the equity investment in her leveraged position. But if the stock falls by 10 percent, the return on the equity investment will be −25 percent (before the interest on the margin loan and before payment of commissions).

Financial analysts must be able to compute the total return to the equity investment in a leveraged position. The total return depends on the price change of the purchased security, the dividends or interest paid by the security, the interest paid on the margin loan, and the commissions paid to buy and sell the security. The following example illustrates the computation of the total return to a leveraged purchase of stock that pays a dividend.

Example 19

Computing Total Return to a Leveraged Stock Purchase

A buyer buys stock on margin and holds the position for exactly one year, during which time the stock pays a dividend. For simplicity, assume that the interest on the loan and the dividend are both paid at the end of the year.

Purchase price	$20/share
Sale price	$15/share
Shares purchased	1,000
Leverage ratio	2.5
Call money rate	5%
Dividend	$0.10/share
Commission	$0.01/share

1. What is the total return on this investment?
2. Why is the loss greater than the 25 percent decrease in the market price?

Solution to 1:

To find the return on this investment, first determine the initial equity and then determine the equity remaining after the sale. The total purchase price is $20,000. The leverage ratio of 2.5 indicates that the buyer's equity financed 40 percent = (1 ÷ 2.5) of the purchase price. Thus, the equity investment is $8,000 = 40% of $20,000. The $12,000 remainder is borrowed. The actual investment is slightly higher because the buyer must pay a commission of $10 = $0.01/share × 1,000 shares to buy the stock. The total initial investment is $8,010.

At the end of the year, the stock price has declined by $5/share. The buyer lost $5,000 = $5/share × 1,000 shares as a result of the price change. In addition, the buyer has to pay interest at 5 percent on the $12,000 loan, or $600. The buyer also receives a dividend of $0.10/share, or $100. The trader's equity remaining after the sale is computed from the initial equity investment as follows:

Initial investment	$8,010
Purchase commission	−10
Trading gains/losses	−5,000
Margin interest paid	−600
Dividends received	100
Sales commission paid	−10
Remaining equity	$2,490

or

Proceeds on sale	$15,000
Payoff loan	−12,000
Margin interest paid	−600
Dividends received	100
Sales commission paid	−10
Remaining equity	$2,490

so that the return on the initial investment of $8,010 is $(2,490 − 8,010)/8,010 = −68.9\%$.

Solution to 2:

The realized loss is substantially greater than the stock price return of $($15 − $20)/$20 = −25\%$. Most of the difference is because of the leverage with the remainder primarily the result of the interest paid on the loan. Based on the leverage alone and ignoring the other cash flows, we would expect that the return on the equity would be −62.5% = 2.5 leverage times the −25% stock price return.

In the above example, if the stock dropped more than the buyer's original 40 percent margin (ignoring commissions, interest, and dividends), the trader's equity would have become negative. In that case, the investor would owe his broker more than the stock is worth. Brokers often lose money in such situations if the buyer does not repay the loan out of other funds.

To prevent such losses, brokers require that margin buyers always have a minimum amount of equity in their positions. This minimum is called the **maintenance margin requirement**. It is usually 25 percent of the current value of the position, but it may be higher or lower depending on the volatility of the instrument and the policies of the broker.

If the value of the equity falls below the maintenance margin requirement, the buyer will receive a **margin call**, or request for additional equity. If the buyer does not deposit additional equity with the broker in a timely manner, the broker will close the position to prevent further losses and thereby secure repayment of the margin loan.

When you buy securities on margin, you must know the price at which you will receive a margin call if prices drop. The answer to this question depends on your initial equity and on the maintenance margin requirement.

Example 20

Margin Call Price

A trader buys stock on margin posting 40 percent of the initial stock price of $20 as equity. The maintenance margin requirement for the position is 25 percent. Below what price will a margin call occur?

Solution:

The trader's initial equity is 40 percent of the initial stock price of $20, or $8 per share. Subsequent changes in equity per share are equal to the share price change so that equity per share is equal to $8 + (P − 20) where P is the current share price. The margin call takes place when equity drops below the 25 percent maintenance margin requirement. The price below which a margin call will take place is the solution to the following equation:

$$\frac{\text{Equity/share}}{\text{Price/share}} = \frac{\$8 + P - 20}{P} = 25\%$$

which occurs at P = 16. When the price drops below $16, the equity will be under $4/share, which is less than 25 percent of the price.

Traders who sell securities short are also subject to margin requirements because they have borrowed securities. Initially, the trader's equity supporting the short position must be at least equal to the margin requirement times the initial value of the short position. If prices rise, equity will be lost. At some point, the short seller will have to contribute additional equity to meet the maintenance margin requirement. Otherwise, the broker will buy the security back to cover the short position to prevent further losses and thereby secure repayment of the stock loan.

ORDERS

6

Buyers and sellers communicate with the brokers, exchanges, and dealers that arrange their trades by issuing **orders**. All orders specify what instrument to trade, how much to trade, and whether to buy or sell. Most orders also have other instructions attached to them. These additional instructions may include execution instructions, validity instructions, and clearing instructions. **Execution instructions** indicate how to fill the order, **validity instructions** indicate when the order may be filled, and **clearing instructions** indicate how to arrange the final settlement of the trade.

In this section, we introduce various order instructions and explain how traders use them to achieve their objectives. We discuss execution mechanisms—how exchanges, brokers and dealers fill orders—in the next section. To understand the concepts in this section, however, you need to know a little about order execution mechanisms.

In most markets, dealers and various other proprietary traders often are willing to buy from, or sell to, other traders seeking to sell or buy. The prices at which they are willing to buy are called **bid** prices and those at which they are willing to sell are called **ask** prices, or sometimes **offer** prices. The ask prices are invariably higher than the bid prices.

The traders who are willing to trade at various prices may also indicate the quantities that they will trade at those prices. These quantities are called **bid sizes** and **ask sizes** depending on whether they are attached to bids or offers.

Practitioners say that the traders who offer to trade make a market. Those who trade with them take the market.

The highest bid in the market is the **best bid**, and the lowest ask in the market is the **best offer**. The difference between the best bid and the best offer is the **market bid–ask spread**. When traders ask, "What's the market?" they want to know the best bid and ask prices and their associated sizes. Bid–ask spreads are an implicit cost of trading. Markets with small bid–ask spreads are markets in which the costs of trading are small, at least for the sizes quoted. Dealers often quote both bid and ask prices, and in that case, practitioners say that they quote a two-sided market. The market spread is never more than any dealer spread.

6.1 Execution Instructions

Market and limit orders convey the most common execution instructions. A **market order** instructs the broker or exchange to obtain the best price immediately available when filling the order. A **limit order** conveys almost the same instruction: Obtain the best price immediately available, but in no event accept a price higher than a specified limit price when buying or accept a price lower than a specified limit price when selling.

Many people mistakenly believe that limit orders specify the prices at which the orders will trade. Although limit orders do often trade at their limit prices, remember that the first instruction is to obtain the best price available. If better prices are available than the limit price, brokers and exchanges should obtain those prices for their clients.

Market orders generally execute immediately if other traders are willing to take the other side of the trade. The main drawback with market orders is that they can be expensive to execute, especially when the order is placed in a market for a thinly traded security, or more generally, when the order is large relative to the normal trading activity in the market. In that case, a market buy order may fill at a high price, or a market sell order may fill at a low price if no traders are willing to trade at better prices. High purchase prices and low sale prices represent price concessions given to other traders to encourage them to take the other side of the trade. Because the sizes of price concessions can be difficult to predict, and because prices often change between when a trader submits an order and when the order finally fills, the execution prices for market orders are often uncertain.

Buyers and sellers who are concerned about the possibility of trading at unacceptable prices add limit price instructions to their orders. The main problem with limit orders is that they may not execute. Limit orders do not execute if the limit price on a buy order is too low, or if the limit price on a sell order is too high. For example, if an investment manager submits a limit order to buy at the limit price of 20 (buy limit 20) and nobody is willing to sell at or below 20, the order will not trade. If prices never drop to 20, the manager will never buy. If the price subsequently rises, the manager will have lost the opportunity to profit from the price rise.

Whether traders use market orders or limit orders when trying to arrange trades depends on their concerns about price, trading quickly, and failing to trade. On average, limit orders trade at better prices than do market orders, but they often do not trade. Traders generally regret when their limit orders fail to trade because they usually would have profited if they had traded. Limit buy orders do not fill when prices are rising, and limit sell orders do not fill when prices are falling. In both cases, traders would be better off if their orders had filled.

The probability that a limit order will execute depends on where the order is placed relative to market prices. An aggressively priced order is more likely to trade than is a less aggressively priced order. A limit buy order is aggressively priced when the limit price is high relative to the market bid and ask prices. If the limit price is placed above the best offer, the buy order generally will partially or completely fill at the best offer price, depending on the size available at the best offer. Such limit orders are called **marketable limit orders** because at least part of the order can trade immediately. A limit buy order with a very high price relative to the market is essentially a market order.

If the buy order is placed above the best bid but below the best offer, traders say the order makes a new market because it becomes the new best bid. Such orders generally will not immediately trade, but they may attract sellers who are interested in trading. A buy order placed at the best bid is said to make market. It may have to wait until all other buy orders at that price trade first. Finally, a buy order placed below the best bid is **behind the market**. It will not execute unless market prices drop. Traders call limit orders that are waiting to trade **standing limit orders**.

Sell limit orders are aggressively priced if the limit price is low relative to market prices. The limit price of a marketable sell limit order is below the best bid. A limit sell order placed between the best bid and the best offer makes a new market on the sell side, one placed at the best offer makes market, and one placed above the best offer is behind the market.

Exhibit 2 presents a simplified **limit order book** in which orders are presented ranked by their limit prices for a hypothetical market. The market is "26 bid, offered at 28" because the best bid is 26 and the best offer (ask) is 28.

Exhibit 2	Terms Traders Use to Describe Standing Limit Orders

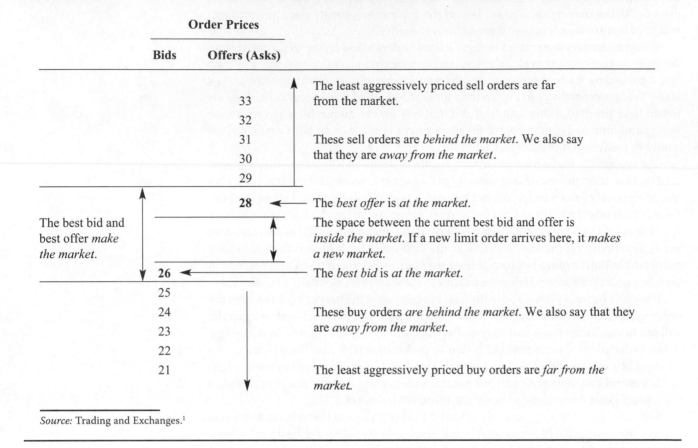

Order Prices

Bids	Offers (Asks)	
	33	The least aggressively priced sell orders are far from the market.
	32	
	31	These sell orders are *behind the market*. We also say that they are *away from the market*.
	30	
	29	
	28	The *best offer* is *at the market*.
		The space between the current best bid and offer is *inside the market*. If a new limit order arrives here, it *makes a new market*.
The best bid and best offer *make the market*.	**26**	The *best bid* is *at the market*.
	25	
	24	These buy orders *are behind the market*. We also say that they are *away from the market*.
	23	
	22	
	21	The least aggressively priced buy orders are *far from the market*.

Source: Trading and Exchanges.[1]

Example 21

Making and Taking

1. What is the difference between making a market and taking a market?
2. What order types are most likely associated with making a market and taking a market?

Solution to 1:

A trader makes a market when the trader offers to trade. A trader takes a market when the trader accepts an offer to trade.

Solution to 2:

Traders place standing limit orders to give other traders opportunities to trade. Standing limit orders thus make markets. In contrast, traders use market orders or marketable limit orders to take offers to trade. These marketable orders take the market.

A trade-off exists between how aggressively priced an order is and the ultimate trade price. Although aggressively priced orders fill faster and with more certainty then do less aggressively priced limit orders, the prices at which they execute are inferior.

1 Harris, Larry. 2003. *Trading and Exchanges: Market Microstructure for Practitioners*. New York: Oxford University Press.

Buyers seeking to trade quickly must pay higher prices to increase the probability of trading quickly. Similarly, sellers seeking to trade quickly must accept lower prices to increase the probability of trading quickly.

Some order execution instructions specify conditions on size. For example, **all-or-nothing orders (AON)** can only trade if their entire sizes can be traded. Traders can similarly specify minimum fill sizes. This specification is common when settlement costs depend on the number of trades made to fill an order and not on the aggregate size of the order.

Exposure instructions indicate whether, how, and perhaps to whom orders should be exposed. **Hidden orders** are exposed only to the brokers or exchanges that receive them. These agencies cannot disclose hidden orders to other traders until they can fill them. Traders use hidden orders when they are afraid that other traders might behave strategically if they knew that a large order was in the market. Traders can discover hidden size only by submitting orders that will trade with that size. Thus, traders can only learn about hidden size after they have committed to trading with it.

Traders also often indicate a specific **display size** for their orders. Brokers and exchanges then expose only the display size for these orders. Any additional size is hidden from the public but can be filled if a suitably large order arrives. Traders sometimes call such orders **iceberg orders** because most of the order is hidden. Traders specify display sizes when they do not want to display their full sizes, but still want other traders to know that someone is willing to trade at the displayed price. Traders on the opposite side who wish to trade additional size at that price can discover the hidden size only if they trade the displayed size, at which point the broker or exchange will display any remaining size up to the display size. They also can discover the hidden size by submitting large orders that will trade with that size.

Example 22

Market versus Limit and Hidden versus Displayed Orders

You are the buy-side trader for a very clever investment manager. The manager has hired a commercial satellite firm to take regular pictures of the parking lots in which new car dealers store their inventories. It has also hired some part-time workers to count the cars on the lots. With this information and some econometric analyses, the manager can predict weekly new car sale announcements more accurately than can most analysts. The manager typically makes a quarter percent each week on this strategy. Once a week, a day before the announcements are made, the manager gives you large orders to buy or sell car manufacturers based on his insights into their dealers' sales. What primary issues should you consider when deciding whether to:

1. use market or limit orders to fill his orders?

2. display the orders or hide them?

Solution to 1:

The manager's information is quite perishable. If his orders are not filled before the weekly sales are reported to the public, the manager will lose the opportunity to profit from the information as prices immediately adjust to the news. The manager, therefore, needs to get the orders filled quickly. This consideration suggests that the orders should be submitted as market orders. If submitted as limit orders, the orders might not execute and the firm would lose the opportunity to profit.

Large market orders, however, can be very expensive to execute, especially if few people are willing to trade significant size on the other side of the market. Because transaction costs can easily exceed the expected quarter percent return, you should submit limit orders to limit the execution prices that you are willing to accept. It is better to fail to trade than to trade at losing prices.

Solution to 2:

Your large orders could easily move the market if many people were aware of them, and even more so if others were aware that you are trading on behalf of a successful information-motivated trader. You thus should consider submitting hidden orders. The disadvantage of hidden orders is that they do not let people know that they can trade the other side if they want to.

6.2 Validity Instructions

Validity instructions indicate when an order may be filled. The most common validity instruction is the **day order**. A day order is good for the day on which it is submitted. If it has not been filled by the close of business, the order expires unfilled.

Good-till-cancelled orders (GTC) are just that. In practice, most brokers limit how long they will manage an order to ensure that they do not fill orders that their clients have forgotten. Such brokers may limit their GTC orders to a few months.

Immediate or cancel orders (IOC) are good only upon receipt by the broker or exchange. If they cannot be filled in part or in whole, they cancel immediately. In some markets these orders are also known as **fill or kill** orders. When searching for hidden liquidity, electronic algorithmic trading systems often submit thousands of these IOC orders for every order that they fill.

Good-on-close orders can only be filled at the close of trading. These orders often are market orders, so traders call them **market-on-close** orders. Traders often use on-close orders when they want to trade at the same prices that will be published as the closing prices of the day. Mutual funds often like to trade at such prices because they value their portfolios at closing prices. Many traders also use **good-on-open** orders.

6.2.1 Stop Orders

A **stop order** is an order in which a trader has specified a stop price condition. The stop order may not be filled until the stop price condition has been satisfied. For a sell order, the stop price condition suspends execution of the order until a trade occurs at or below the stop price. After that trade, the stop condition is satisfied and the order becomes valid for execution, subject to all other execution instructions attached to it. If the market price subsequently rises above the sell order's stop price before the order trades, the order remains valid. Similarly, a buy order with a stop condition becomes valid only after a price rises above the specified stop price.

Traders often call stop orders **stop-loss orders** because many traders use them with the hope of stopping losses on positions that they have established. For example, a trader who has bought stock at 40 may want to sell the stock if the price falls below 30. In that case, the trader might submit a "GTC, stop 30, market sell" order. If the price falls to or below 30, the market order becomes valid and it should immediately execute at the best price then available in the market. That price may be substantially lower than 30 if the market is falling quickly. The stop-loss order thus does not guarantee a stop to losses at the stop price. If potential sellers are worried about trading at too low of a price, they can attach stop instructions to limit orders instead of market orders. In this example, if the trader is unwilling to sell below 25, the trader would submit a "GTC, stop 30, limit 25 sell" order.

If a trader wants to guarantee that he can sell at 30, the trader would buy a put option contract struck at 30. The purchase price of the option would include a premium for the insurance that the trader is buying. Option contracts can be viewed as limit orders for which execution is guaranteed at the strike price. A trader similarly might use a stop-buy order or a call option to limit losses on a short position.

A portfolio manager might use a stop-buy order when the manager believes that a security is undervalued but is unwilling to trade without market confirmation. For example, suppose that a stock currently trades for 50 RMB and a manager believes that it should be worth 100 RMB. Further, the manager believes that the stock will much more likely be worth 100 RMB if other traders are willing to buy it above 65 RMB. To best take advantage of this information, the manager would consider issuing a "GTC, stop 65 RMB, limit 100 RMB buy" order. Note that if the manager relies too much on the market when making this trading decision, however, he may violate CFA Standard of Professional Conduct V.A.2, which requires that all investment actions have a reasonable and adequate basis supported by appropriate research and investigation.

Because stop-sell orders become valid when prices are falling and stop-buy orders become valid when prices are rising, traders using stop orders contribute to market momentum as their sell orders push prices down further and their buy orders push prices up. Execution prices for stop orders thus are often quite poor.

Example 23

Limit and Stop Instructions

In what ways do limit and stop instructions differ?

Solution:

Although both limit and stop instructions specify prices, the role that these prices play in the arrangement of a trade are completely different. A limit price places a limit on what trade prices will be acceptable to the trader. A buyer will accept prices only at or lower than the limit price whereas a seller will accept prices only at or above the limit price.

In contrast, a stop price indicates when an order can be filled. A buy order can only be filled once the market has traded at a price at or above the stop price. A sell order can only be filled once the market has traded at a price at or below the stop price.

Both order instructions may delay or prevent the execution of an order. A buy limit order will not execute until someone is willing to sell at or below the limit price. Similarly, a sell limit order will not execute until someone is willing to buy at or above the limit sell price. In contrast, a stop-buy order will not execute if the market price never rises to the stop price. Similarly, a stop-sell order will not execute if the market price never falls to the stop price.

6.3 Clearing Instructions

Clearing instructions tell brokers and exchanges how to arrange final settlement of trades. Traders generally do not attach these instructions to each order—instead they provide them as standing instructions. These instructions indicate what entity is responsible for clearing and settling the trade. For retail trades, that entity is the customer's broker. For institutional trades, that entity may be a custodian or another broker. When a client uses one broker to arrange trades and another broker to settle trades, traders say that the first broker gives up the trade to the other broker, who is often known as the prime broker. Institutional traders provide these instructions so they can obtain specialized execution services from different brokers while maintaining a single account for custodial services and other prime brokerage services, such as margin loans.

An important clearing instruction that must appear on security sale orders is an indication of whether the sale is a long sale or a short sale. In either case, the broker representing the sell order must ensure that the trader can deliver securities for settlement. For a long sale, the broker must confirm that the securities held are available for delivery. For a short sale, the broker must either borrow the security on behalf of the client or confirm that the client can borrow the security.

7 PRIMARY SECURITY MARKETS

When issuers first sell their securities to investors, practitioners say that the trades take place in the **primary markets**. An issuer makes an **initial public offering** (IPO)— sometimes called a placing—of a security issue when it sells the security to the public for the first time. A **seasoned security** is a security that an issuer has already issued. If the issuer wants to sell additional units of a previously issued security, it makes a **seasoned offering** (sometimes called a secondary offering). Both types of offerings occur in the **primary market** where issuers sell their securities to investors. Later, if investors trade these securities among themselves, they trade in **secondary markets**. This section discusses primary markets and the procedures that issuers use to offer their securities to the public.

7.1 Public Offerings

Corporations generally contract with an investment bank to help them sell their securities to the public. The investment bank then lines up subscribers who will buy the security. Investment bankers call this process **book building**. In London, the book builder is called the book runner. The bank tries to build a book of orders to which they can sell the offering. Investment banks often support their book building by providing investment information and opinion about the issuer to their clients and to the public. Before the offering, the issuer generally makes a very detailed disclosure of its business, of the risks inherent in it, and of the uses to which the new funds will be placed.

When time is of the essence, issuers in Europe may issue securities through an **accelerated book build**, in which the investment bank arranges the offering in only one or two days. Such sales often occur at discounted prices.

The first public offering of common stock in a company consists of newly issued shares to be sold by the company. It may also include shares that the founders and other early investors in the company seek to sell. The initial public offering provides these investors with a means of liquidating their investments.

In an **underwritten offering**—the most common type of offering—the investment bank guarantees the sale of the issue at an offering price that it negotiates with the issuer. If the issue is undersubscribed, the bank will buy whatever securities it cannot sell at the offering price. In the case of an IPO, the underwriter usually also promises to make a market in the security for about a month to ensure that the secondary market will be liquid and to provide price support, if necessary. For large issues, a syndicate of investment banks and broker–dealers helps the **lead underwriter** build the book. The issuer usually pays an underwriting fee of about 7 percent for these various services. The underwriting fee is a placement cost of the offering.

In a **best efforts offering**, the investment bank acts only as broker. If the offering is undersubscribed, the issuer will not sell as much as it hoped to sell.

For both types of offerings, the issuer and the bank usually jointly set the offering price following a negotiation. If they set a price that buyers consider too high, the offering will be undersubscribed, and they will fail to sell the entire issue. If they set the price too low, the offering will be oversubscribed, in which case the securities are often allocated to preferred clients or on a pro-rata basis.

(Note that CFA Standard of Professional Conduct III.B—fair dealing—requires that the allocation be based on a written policy disclosed to clients and suggests that the securities be offered on a pro-rata basis among all clients who have comparable relationships with their broker–dealers.)

Investment banks have a conflict of interest with respect to the offering price in underwritten offerings. As agents for the issuers, they generally are supposed to select the offering price that will raise the most money. But as underwriters, they have strong incentives to choose a low price. If the price is low, the banks can allocate valuable shares to benefit their clients and thereby indirectly benefit the banks. If the price is too high, the underwriters will have to buy overvalued shares in the offering and perhaps also during the following month if they must support the price in the secondary market, which directly costs the banks. These considerations tend to lower initial offering prices so that prices in the secondary market often rise immediately following an IPO. They are less important in a seasoned offering because trading in the secondary market helps identify the proper price for the offering.

First time issuers generally accept lower offering prices because they and many others believe that an undersubscribed IPO conveys very unfavorable information to the market about the company's prospects at a time when it is most vulnerable to public opinion about its prospects. They fear that an undersubscribed initial public offering will make it substantially harder to raise additional capital in subsequent seasoned offerings.

Example 24

The Playtech Initial Public Offering

Playtech is a designer, developer, and licensor of software for the gambling industry. On 28 March 2006, Playtech raised approximately £265 million gross through an initial public offering of 103,142,466 ordinary shares at £2.57 per ordinary share. After the initial public offering, Playtech had 213,333,333 ordinary shares issued and outstanding.

Playtech received gross proceeds of approximately £34.3 million and net proceeds of £31.8 million. The ordinary shares that were sold to the public represented approximately 48 percent of Playtech's total issued ordinary shares.

The shares commenced trading at 8:00 AM on the AIM market of the London Stock Exchange where Playtech opened at £2.74, traded 37 million shares between £2.68 and £2.74, and closed at £2.73.

1. Approximately how many new shares were issued by the company and how many shares were sold by the company's founders? What fraction of their holdings in the company did the founders sell?

2. Approximately what return did the subscribers who participated in the IPO make on the first day it traded?

3. Approximately how much did Playtech pay in placement costs as a percentage of the new funds raised?

Solution to 1:

Playtech received gross proceeds of £34.3 million at £2.57 per share so the company issued and sold 13,346,304 shares (= £34.3 million/£2.57 per share).

The total placement was for 103,142,466 shares, so the founders sold 89,796,162 shares (= 103,142,466 shares − 13,346,304 shares). Because approximately 200 million = 213.3 million − 13.3 million shares were outstanding before the placement, the founders sold approximately 45 percent (= 90 million/200 million) of the company.

Solution to 2:

The subscribers bought the stock for £2.57 per share and it closed at £2.73. The first day return thus was $6.2\% = \dfrac{2.73 - 2.57}{2.57} \times 100$.

Solution to 3:

Playtech obtained gross proceeds of £34.3 million, but only raised net proceeds of £31.8 million. The £2.5 million difference was the total cost of the placement to the firm, which is 7.9 percent of £31.8 million net proceeds.

7.2 Private Placements and Other Primary Market Transactions

Corporations sometimes issue their securities in private placements. In a **private placement**, corporations sell securities directly to a small group of qualified investors, usually with the assistance of an investment bank. Qualified investors have sufficient knowledge and experience to recognize the risks that they assume, and sufficient wealth to assume those risks responsibly. Most countries allow corporations to do private placements without nearly as much public disclosure as is required for public offerings. Private placements, therefore, may be cheaper than public offerings, but the buyers generally require higher returns (lower purchase prices) because they cannot subsequently trade the securities in an organized secondary market.

Corporations sometimes sell new issues of seasoned securities directly to the public on a piecemeal basis via a shelf registration. In a **shelf registration**, the corporation makes all public disclosures that it would for a regular offering, but it does not sell the shares in a single transaction. Instead, it sells the shares directly into the secondary market over time, generally when it needs additional capital. Shelf registrations provide corporations with flexibility in the timing of their capital transactions, and they can alleviate the downward price pressures often associated with large secondary offerings.

Many corporations may also issue shares via dividend reinvestment plans (DRPs or DRIPs, for short) that allow their shareholders to reinvest their dividends in newly issued shares of the corporation (in particular, DRPs specify that the corporation issue new shares for the plan rather than purchase them on the open market). These plans sometimes also allow existing shareholders and other investors to buy additional stock at a slight discount to current prices.

Finally, corporations can issue new stock via a rights offering. In a rights offering, the corporation distributes rights to buy stock at a fixed price to existing shareholders in proportion to their holdings. Because the rights need not be exercised, they are options. The exercise price, however, is set below the current market price of the stock so that buying stock with the rights is immediately profitable. Consequently, shareholders will experience dilution in the value of their existing shares. They can offset the dilution loss by exercising their rights or by selling the rights to others who will exercise them. Shareholders generally do not like rights offerings because they must provide additional capital (or sell their rights) to avoid losses through dilution. Financial analysts recognize that these securities, although called rights, are actually short-term stock warrants and value them accordingly.

The national governments of financially strong countries generally issue their bonds, notes, and bills in public auctions organized by a government agency (usually associated with the finance ministry). They may also sell them directly to dealers.

Smaller and less financially secure national governments and most regional governments often contract with investment banks to help them sell and distribute their securities. The laws of many governments, however, require that they auction their securities.

Example 25

Private and Public Placements

In what ways do private placements differ from public placements?

Solution:

Issuers make private placements to a limited number of investors that generally are financially sophisticated and well informed about risk. The investors generally have some relationship to the issuer. Issuers make public placements when they sell securities to the general public. Public placements generally require substantially more financial disclosure than do private placements.

7.3 Importance of Secondary Markets to Primary Markets

Corporations and governments can raise money in the primary markets at lower cost when their securities will trade in liquid secondary markets. In a **liquid market**, traders can buy or sell with low transaction costs and small price concessions when they want to trade. Buyers value liquidity because they may need to sell their securities to meet liquidity needs. Investors thus will pay more for securities that they can easily sell than for those that they cannot easily sell. Higher prices translate into lower costs of capital for the issuers.

SECONDARY SECURITY MARKET AND CONTRACT MARKET STRUCTURES

8

Trading is the successful outcome to a bilateral search in which buyers look for sellers and sellers look for buyers. Many market structures have developed to reduce the costs of this search. Markets are liquid when the costs of finding a suitable counterparty to a trade are low.

Trading in securities and contracts takes place in a variety of market structures. The structures differ by when trades can be arranged, who arranges the trades, how they do so, and how traders learn about possible trading opportunities and executed trades. This section introduces the various market structures used to trade securities and contracts. We first consider trading sessions, then execution mechanisms, and finally market information systems.

8.1 Trading Sessions

Markets are organized as call markets or as continuous trading markets. In a **call market**, trades can be arranged only when the market is called at a particular time and place. In contrast in a **continuous trading market**, trades can be arranged and executed anytime the market is open.

Buyers can easily find sellers and vice versa in call markets because all traders interested in trading (or orders representing their interests) are present at the same time and place. Call markets thus have the potential to be very liquid when they are called. But they are completely illiquid between trading sessions. In contrast, traders can arrange and execute their trades at anytime in continuous trading markets, but doing so can be difficult if the buyers and sellers (or their orders) are not both present at the same time.

Most call markets use single price auctions to match buyers to sellers. In these auctions, the market constructs order books representing all buy orders and all seller orders. The market then chooses a single trade price that will maximize the total volume of trade. The order books are supply and demand schedules, and the point at which they cross determines the trade price.

Call markets usually are organized just once a day, but some markets organize calls at more frequent intervals.

Many continuous trading markets start their trading with a call market auction. During a pre-opening period, traders submit their orders for the market call. At the opening, any possible trades are arranged and then trading continues in the continuous trading session. Some continuous trading markets also close their trading with a call. In these markets, traders who are only interested in trading in the closing call submit market- or limit-on-close orders.

Example 26

Call Markets and Continuous Trading Markets

1. What is the main advantage of a call market compared with a continuous trading market?

2. What is the main advantage of a continuous trading market compared with a call market?

Solution to 1:

By gathering all traders to the same place at the same time, a call market makes it easier for buyers to find sellers and vice versa. In contrast, if buyers and sellers (or their orders) are not present at the same time in a continuous market, they cannot trade.

Solution to 2:

In a continuous trading market, a willing buyer and seller can trade at anytime the market is open. In contrast, in a call market trading can take place only when the market is called.

8.2 Execution Mechanisms

The three main types of market structures are quote-driven markets (sometimes called price-driven or dealer markets), order-driven markets, and brokered markets. In **quote-driven markets**, customers trade with dealers. In **order-driven markets**, an order matching system run by an exchange, a broker, or an alternative trading system uses rules to arrange trades based on the orders that traders submit. Most exchanges and ECNs organize order-driven markets. In **brokered markets**, brokers arrange trades between their customers. Brokered markets are common for transactions of unique instruments, such as real estate properties, intellectual properties, or large blocks of securities. Many trading systems use more than one type of market structure.

8.2.1 *Quote-Driven Markets*

Worldwide, most trading, other than in stocks, takes place in quote-driven markets. Almost all bonds and currencies and most spot commodities trade in quote-driven markets. Traders call them quote-driven (or price-driven or dealer) because customers trade at the prices quoted by dealers. Depending on the instrument traded, the dealers work for commercial banks, for investment banks, for broker–dealers, or for proprietary trading houses.

Quote-driven markets also often are called over-the-counter (OTC) markets because securities used to be literally traded over the dealer's counter in the dealer's office. Now, most trades in OTC markets are conducted over proprietary computer communications networks, by telephone, or sometimes over instant messaging systems.

8.2.2 *Order-Driven Markets*

Order-driven markets arrange trades using rules to match buy orders to sell orders. The orders may be submitted by customers or by dealers. Almost all exchanges use order-driven trading systems, and every automated trading system is an order-driven system.

Because rules match buyers to sellers, traders often trade with complete strangers. Order-driven markets thus must have procedures to ensure that buyers and sellers perform on their trade contracts. Otherwise, dishonest traders would enter contracts that they would not settle if a change in market conditions made settlement unprofitable.

Two sets of rules characterize order-driven market mechanisms: Order matching rules and trade pricing rules. The order matching rules match buy orders to sell orders. The trade pricing rules determine the prices at which the matched trades take place.

8.2.2.1 Order Matching Rules   Order-driven trading systems match buyers to sellers using rules that rank the buy orders and the sell orders based on price, and often along with other secondary criteria. The systems then match the highest ranking buy order with the highest ranking sell order. If the buyer is willing to pay at least as much as the seller is willing to receive, the system will arrange a trade for the minimum of the buy and sell quantities. The remaining size, if any, is then matched with the next order on the other side and the process continues until no further trades can be arranged.

The **order precedence hierarchy** determines which orders go first. The first rule is **price priority**: The highest priced buy orders and the lowest priced sell orders go first. They are the most aggressively priced orders. **Secondary precedence rules** determine how to rank orders at the same price. Most trading systems use time precedence to rank orders at the same price. The first order to arrive has precedence over other orders. In trading systems that permit hidden and partially hidden orders, displayed quantities at a given price generally have precedence over the undisplayed quantities. So the complete precedence hierarchy is given by price priority, display precedence at a given price, and finally time precedence among all orders with the same display status at a given price. These rules give traders incentives to improve price, display their orders, and arrive early if they want to trade quickly. These incentives increase market liquidity.

8.2.2.2 Trade Pricing Rules   After the orders are matched, the trading system then uses its trade pricing rule to determine the trade price. The three rules that various order-driven markets use to price their trades are the uniform pricing rule, the discriminatory pricing rule, and the derivative pricing rule.

Call markets commonly use the uniform pricing rule. Under this rule, all trades execute at the same price. The market chooses the price that maximizes the total quantity traded.

Continuous trading markets use the **discriminatory pricing rule**. Under this rule, the limit price of the order or quote that first arrived—the standing order—determines the trade price. This rule allows a large arriving trader to discriminate among standing limit orders by filling the most aggressively priced orders first at their limit prices and then filling less aggressively priced orders at their less favorable (from the point of view of the arriving trader) limit prices. If trading systems did not use this pricing rule, large traders would break their orders into pieces to price discriminate on their own.

Example 27

Filling a Large Order in a Continuous Trading Market

Before the arrival of a large order, a market has the following limit orders standing on its book:

Buyer	Bid Size	Limit Price(¥)	Offer Size	Seller
Takumi	15	100.1		
Hiroto	8	100.2		
Shou	10	100.3		
		100.4	4	Hina
		100.5	6	Sakur
		100.6	12	Miku

Buyer Tsubasa submits a day order to buy 15 contracts, limit ¥100.5. With whom does he trade, what is his average trade price, and what does the limit order book look like afterward?

Solution:

Tsubasa's buy order first fills with the most aggressively priced sell order, which is Hina's order for four contracts. A trade takes place at ¥100.4 for four contracts, Hina's order fills completely, and Tsubasa still has 11 more contracts remaining.

The next most aggressively priced sell order is Sakur's order for six contracts. A second trade takes place at ¥100.5 for six contracts, Sakur's order fills completely, and Tsubasa still has five more contracts remaining.

The next most aggressively priced sell order is Miku's order at ¥100.6. No further trade is possible, however, because her limit sell price is above Tsubasa's limit buy price. Tsubasa's average trade price is $¥100.46 = \dfrac{4 \times ¥100.4 + 6 \times ¥100.5}{4 + 6}$.

Because Tsubasa issued a day order, the remainder of his order is placed on the book on the buy side at ¥100.5. The following orders are then on the book:

Buyer	Bid Size	Limit Price (¥)	Offer Size	Seller
Takumi	15	100.1		
Hiroto	8	100.2		
Shou	10	100.3		
		100.4		
Tsubasa	5	100.5		
		100.6	12	Miku

If Tsubasa had issued an immediate-or-cancel order, the remaining five contracts would have been cancelled.

Crossing networks use the derivative pricing rule. **Crossing networks** are trading systems that match buyers and sellers who are willing to trade at prices obtained from other markets. Most systems cross their trades at the midpoint of the best bid and ask quotes published by the exchange at which the security primarily trades. This pricing rule is called a **derivative pricing rule** because the price is derived from another market. In particular, the price does not depend on the orders submitted to the crossing network. Some crossing networks are organized as call markets and others as continuously trading markets. The most important crossing market is the equity trading system POSIT.

8.2.3 Brokered Markets

The third execution mechanism is the **brokered market**, in which brokers arrange trades among their clients. Brokers organize markets for instruments for which finding a buyer or a seller willing to trade is difficult because the instruments are unique and thus of interest only to a limited number of people or institutions. These instruments generally are also infrequently traded and expensive to carry in inventory. Examples of such instruments include very large blocks of stock, real estate properties, fine art masterpieces, intellectual properties, operating companies, liquor licenses, and taxi medallions. Because dealers generally are unable or unwilling to hold these assets in their inventories, they will not make markets in them. Organizing order-driven markets for these instruments is not sensible because too few traders would submit orders to them.

Successful brokers in these markets try to know everyone who might now or in the future be willing to trade. They spend most of their time on the telephone and in meetings building their networks.

Example 28

Quote-Driven, Order-Driven, and Brokered Markets

What are the primary advantages of quote-driven, order-driven, and brokered markets?

Solution:

In a quote-driven market, dealers generally are available to supply liquidity. In an order-driven market, traders can supply liquidity to each other. In a brokered market, brokers help find traders who are willing to trade when dealers would not be willing to make markets and when traders would not be willing to post orders.

8.3 Market Information Systems

Markets vary in the type and quantity of data that they disseminate to the public. Traders say that a market is pre-trade transparent if the market publishes real-time data about quotes and orders. Markets are post-trade transparent if the market publishes trade prices and sizes soon after trades occur.

Buy-side traders value transparency because it allows them to better manage their trading, understand market values, and estimate their prospective and actual transaction costs. In contrast, dealers prefer to trade in opaque markets because, as frequent traders, they have an information advantage over those who know less than they do. Bid–ask spreads tend to be wider and transaction costs tend to be higher in opaque markets because finding the best available price is harder for traders in such markets.

9   WELL-FUNCTIONING FINANCIAL SYSTEMS

The financial system allows traders to solve financing and risk management problems. In a well-functioning financial system:

- investors can easily move money from the present to the future while obtaining a fair rate of return for the risks that they bear;
- borrowers can easily obtain funds that they need to undertake current projects if they can credibly promise to repay the funds in the future;
- hedgers can easily trade away or offset the risks that concern them; and
- traders can easily trade currencies for other currencies or commodities that they need.

If the assets or contracts needed to solve these problems are available to trade, the financial system has **complete markets**. If the costs of arranging these trades are low, the financial system is **operationally efficient**. If the prices of the assets and contracts reflect all available information related to fundamental values, the financial system is **informationally efficient**.

Well-functioning financial systems are characterized by:

- the existence of well-developed markets that trade instruments that help people solve their financial problems (complete markets);
- liquid markets in which the costs of trading—commissions, bid–ask spreads, and order price impacts—are low (operationally efficient markets);
- timely financial disclosures by corporations and governments that allow market participants to estimate the fundamental values of securities (support informationally efficient markets); and
- prices that reflect fundamental values so that prices vary primarily in response to changes in fundamental values and not to demands for liquidity made by uninformed traders (informationally efficient markets).

Such complete and operationally efficient markets are produced by financial intermediaries who:

- organize exchanges, brokerages, and alternative trading systems that match buyers to sellers;
- provide liquidity on demand to traders;
- securitize assets to produce investment instruments that are attractive to investors and thereby lower the costs of funds for borrowers;
- run banks that match investors to borrowers by taking deposits and making loans;
- run insurance companies that pool uncorrelated risks;
- provide investment advisory services that help investors manage and grow their assets at low cost;
- organize clearinghouses that ensure everyone settles their trades and contracts; and
- organize depositories that ensure nobody loses their assets.

The benefits of a well-functioning financial system are huge. In such systems, investors who need to move money to the future can easily connect with entrepreneurs who need money now to develop new products and services. Similarly, producers who would otherwise avoid valuable projects because they are too risky can easily transfer those risks to others who can better bear them. Most importantly, these transactions generally can take place among strangers so that the benefits from trading can be derived from an enormous number of potential matches.

In contrast, economies that have poorly functioning financial systems have great difficulties allocating capital among the many companies who could use it. Financial transactions tend to be limited to arrangements within families when people cannot easily find trustworthy counterparties who will honor their contracts. In such economies, capital is allocated inefficiently, risks are not easily shared, and production is inefficient.

An extraordinarily important byproduct of an operationally efficient financial system is the production of informationally efficient prices. Prices are informationally efficient when they reflect all available information about fundamental values. Informative prices are crucially important to the welfare of an economy because they help ensure that resources go where they are most valuable. Economies that use resources where they are most valuable are **allocationally efficient**. Economies that do not use resources where they are most valuable waste their resources and consequently often are quite poor.

Well-informed traders make prices informationally efficient. When they buy assets and contracts that they think are undervalued, they tend to push the assets' prices up. Similarly, when they sell assets and contracts that they think are overvalued, they tend to push the assets' prices down. The effect of their trading thus causes prices to reflect their information about values.

How accurately prices reflect fundamental information depends on the costs of obtaining fundamental information and on the liquidity available to well-informed traders. Accounting standards and reporting requirements that produce meaningful and timely financial disclosures reduce the costs of obtaining fundamental information and thereby allow analysts to form more accurate estimates of fundamental values. Liquid markets allow well-informed traders to fill their orders at low cost. If filling orders is very costly, informed trading may not be profitable. In that case, information-motivated traders will not commit resources to collect and analyze data and they will not trade. Without their research and their associated trading, prices would be less informative.

Example 29

Well-Functioning Financial Systems

As a financial analyst specializing in emerging market equities, you understand that a well-functioning financial system contributes to the economic prosperity of a country. You are asked to start covering a new small market country. What factors will you consider when characterizing the quality of its financial markets?

Solution:

In general, you will consider whether:

■ the country has markets that allow its companies and residents to finance projects, save for the future, and exchange risk;

■ the costs of trading in those markets is low; and

■ prices reflect fundamental values.

You may specifically check to see whether:

■ fixed income and stock markets allow borrowers to easily obtain capital from investors;

- corporations disclose financial and operating data on a timely basis in conformity to widely respected reporting standards, such as IFRS;

- forward, futures, and options markets trade instruments that companies need to hedge their risks;

- dealers and arbitrageurs allow traders to trade when they want to;

- bid–ask spreads are small;

- trades and contracts invariably settle as expected;

- investment managers provide high-quality management services for reasonable fees;

- banks and other financing companies are well capitalized and thus able to help investors provide capital to borrowers;

- securitized assets are available and represent reasonable credit risks;

- insurance companies are well capitalized and thus able to help those exposed to risks insure against them; and

- price volatility appears consistent with changes in fundamental values.

10   MARKET REGULATION

Government agencies and practitioner organizations regulate many markets and the financial intermediaries that participate in them. The regulators generally seek to promote fair and orderly markets in which traders can trade at prices that accurately reflect fundamental values without incurring excessive transaction costs. This section identifies the problems that financial regulators hope to solve and the objectives of their regulations.

Regrettably, some people will steal from each other if given a chance, especially if the probability of detection is low or if the penalty for being caught is low. The number of ways that people can steal or misappropriate wealth generally increases with the complexity of their relationships and with asymmetries in their knowledge. Because financial markets tend to be complex, and because customers are often much less sophisticated than the professionals that serve them, the potential for losses through various frauds can be unacceptably high in unregulated markets.

Regulators thus ensure that systems are in place to protect customers from fraud. In principle, the customers themselves would demand such systems as a condition of doing business. When customers are unsophisticated or poorly informed, however, they may not know how to protect themselves. When the costs of learning are large—as they often are in complex financial markets—having regulators look out for the public interest can be economically efficient.

More customer money is probably lost in financial markets through negligence than through outright fraud. Most customers in financial markets use various agents to help them solve problems that they do not understand well. These agents include securities brokers, financial advisers, investment managers, and insurance agents. Because customers generally do not have much information about market conditions, they find it extremely difficult to measure the added value they obtain from their agents. This problem is especially challenging when performance has a strong random component. In that case, determining whether agents are skilled or lucky is very difficult. Moreover, if the agent is a good salesman, the customer may not critically evaluate their agent's performance. These conditions, which characterize most financial markets, ensure that customers cannot easily determine whether their agents are working faithfully for them. They tend to lose if their agents are unqualified or lazy, or if they unconsciously favor themselves and their friends over their clients, as is natural for even the most honest people.

Regulators help solve these agency problems by setting minimum standards of competence for agents and by defining and enforcing minimum standards of practice. CFA Institute provides significant standard setting leadership in the areas of investment management and investment performance reporting through its Chartered Financial Analyst Program, in which you are studying, and its Global Investment Performance Standards. In principle, regulation would not be necessary if customers could identify competent agents and effectively measure their performance. In the financial markets, doing so is very difficult.

Regulators often act to level the playing field for market participants. For example, in many jurisdictions, insider trading in securities is illegal. The rule prevents corporate insiders and others with access to corporate information from trading on material information that has not been released to the public. The purpose of the rule is to reduce the profits that insiders could extract from the markets. These profits would come from other traders who would lose when they trade with well-informed insiders. Because traders tend to withdraw from markets when they lose, rules against insider trading help keep markets liquid. They also keep corporate insiders from hoarding information.

Many situations arise in financial markets in which common standards benefit everyone involved. For example, having all companies report financial results on a common basis allows financial analysts to easily compare companies. Accordingly, the International Accounting Standards Board (IASB) and the U.S.-based Financial Accounting Standards Board, among many others, promulgate common financial standards to which all companies must report. The benefits of having common reporting standards has led to a very successful and continuing effort to converge all accounting standards to a single worldwide standard. Without such regulations, investors might eventually refuse to invest in companies that do not report to a common standard, but such market-based discipline is a very slow regulator of behavior, and it would have little effect on companies that do not need to raise new capital.

Regulators generally require that financial firms maintain minimum levels of capital. These capital requirements serve two purposes. First, they ensure that the companies will be able to honor their contractual commitments when unexpected market movements or poor decisions cause them to lose money. Second, they ensure that the owners of financial firms have substantial interest in the decisions that they make. Without a substantial financial interest in the decisions that they make, companies often take too many risks and exercise poor judgment about extending credit to others. When such companies fail, they impose significant costs on others. Minimum capital requirements reduce the probability that financial firms will fail and they reduce the disruptions associated with those failures that do occur. In principle, a firm's customers and counterparties could require minimum capital levels as a condition of doing business with the firm, but they have more difficulty enforcing their contracts than do governments who can imprison people.

Regulators similarly regulate insurance companies and pension funds that make long-term promises to their clients. Such entities need to maintain adequate reserves to ensure that they can fund their liabilities. Unfortunately, their managers have a tendency to underestimate these reserves if they will not be around when the liabilities come due. Again, in principle, policyholders and employees could regulate the behavior of their insurance funds and their employers by refusing to contract with them if they do not promise to adequately fund their liabilities. In practice, however, the sophistication, information, and time necessary to write and enforce contracts that control these problems are beyond the reach of most people. The government thus is a sensible regulator of such problems.

Many regulators are self-regulating organizations (SROs) that regulate their members. Exchanges, clearinghouses, and dealer trade organizations are examples of self-regulating organizations. In some cases, the members of these organizations voluntarily subject themselves to the SRO's regulations to promote the common good. In other cases, governments delegate regulatory and enforcement authorities to SROs, usually subject to the supervision of a government agency, such as a national securities and exchange authority. Exchanges, dealer associations, and clearing agencies often regulate their members with these delegated powers.

By setting high standards of behavior, SROs help their members obtain the confidence of their customers. They also reduce the chance that members of the SRO will incur losses when dealing with other members of the SRO.

When regulators fail to solve the problems discussed here, the financial system does not function well. People who lose money stop saving and borrowers with good ideas cannot fund their projects. Similarly, hedgers withdraw from markets when the costs of hedging are high. Without the ability to hedge, producers become reluctant to specialize because specialization generally increases risk. Because specialization also decreases costs, however, production becomes less efficient as producers chose safer technologies. Economies that cannot solve the regulatory problems described in this section tend to operate less efficiently than do better regulated economies, and they tend to be less wealthy.

To summarize, the objectives of market regulation are to:

1. control fraud;

2. control agency problems;

3. promote fairness;

4. set mutually beneficial standards;

5. prevent undercapitalized financial firms from exploiting their investors by making excessively risky investments; and

6. ensure that long-term liabilities are funded.

Regulation is necessary because regulating certain behaviors through market-based mechanisms is too costly for people who are unsophisticated and uninformed. Effectively regulated markets allow people to better achieve their financial goals.

Example 30

Bankrupt Traders

You are the chief executive officer of a brokerage that is a member of a clearinghouse. A trader who clears through your firm is bankrupt at midday, but you do not yet know it even though your clearing agreement with him explicitly requires that he immediately report significant losses. The trader knows that if he takes a large position, prices might move in his favor so that he will no longer be bankrupt. The trader attempts to do so and succeeds. You find out about this later in the evening.

1. Why does the clearinghouse regulate its members?

2. What should you do about the trader?

3. Why would the clearinghouse allow you to keep his trading profits?

Solution to 1:

The clearinghouse regulates its members to ensure that no member imposes costs on another member by failing to settle a trade.

> **Solution to 2:**
>
> You should immediately end your clearing relationship with the trader and confiscate his trading profits. The trader was trading with your firm's capital after he became bankrupt. Had he lost, your firm would have borne the loss.
>
> **Solution to 3:**
>
> If the clearinghouse did not permit you to keep his trading profits, other traders similarly situated might attempt the same strategy.

SUMMARY

This reading introduces how the financial system operates and explains how well-functioning financial systems lead to wealthy economies. Financial analysts need to understand how the financial system works because their analyses often lead to trading decisions.

The financial system consists of markets and the financial intermediaries that operate in them. These institutions allow buyers to connect with sellers. They may trade directly with each other when they trade the same instrument or they only may trade indirectly when a financial intermediary connects the buyer to the seller through transactions with each that appear on the intermediary's balance sheet. The buyer and seller may exchange instruments, cash flows, or risks.

The following points, among others, were made in this reading:

- The financial system consists of mechanisms that allow strangers to contract with each other to move money through time, to hedge risks, and to exchange assets that they value less for those that they value more.

- Investors move money from the present to the future when they save. They expect a normal rate of return for bearing risk through time. Borrowers move money from the future to the present to fund current projects and expenditures. Hedgers trade to reduce their exposure to risks they prefer not to take. Information-motivated traders are active investment managers who try to indentify under- and overvalued instruments.

- Securities are first sold in primary markets by their issuers. They then trade in secondary markets.

- People invest in pooled investment vehicles to benefit from the investment management services of their managers.

- Forward contracts allow buyers and sellers to arrange for future sales at predetermined prices. Futures contracts are forward contracts guaranteed by clearinghouses. The guarantee ensures that strangers are willing to trade with each other and that traders can offset their positions by trading with anybody. These features of futures contract markets make them highly attractive to hedgers and information-motivated traders.

- Many financial intermediaries connect buyers to sellers in a given instrument, acting directly as brokers and exchanges or indirectly as dealers and arbitrageurs.

- Financial intermediaries create instruments when they conduct arbitrage, securitize assets, borrow to lend, manage investment funds, or pool insurance contracts. These activities all transform cash flows and risks from one form to another. Their services allow buyers and sellers to connect with each other through instruments that meet their specific needs.

■ Financial markets work best when strangers can contract with each other without worrying about whether their counterparts are able and willing to honor their contract. Clearinghouses, variation margins, maintenance margins, and settlement guarantees made by creditworthy brokers on behalf of their clients help manage credit risk and ultimately allow strangers to contract with each other.

■ Information-motivated traders short sell when they expect that prices will fall. Hedgers short sell to reduce the risks of a long position in a related contract or commodity.

■ Margin loans allow people to buy more securities than their equity would otherwise permit them to buy. The larger positions expose them to more risk so that gains and losses for a given amount of equity will be larger. The leverage ratio is the value of a position divided by the value of the equity supporting it. The returns to the equity in a position are equal to the leverage ratio times the returns to the unleveraged position.

■ To protect against credit losses, brokers demand maintenance margin payments from their customers who have borrowed cash or securities when adverse price changes cause their customer's equity to drop below the maintenance margin ratio. Brokers close positions for customers who do not satisfy these margin calls.

■ Orders are instructions to trade. They always specify instrument, side (buy or sell), and quantity. They usually also provide several other instructions.

■ Market orders tend to fill quickly but often at inferior prices. Limit orders generally fill at better prices if they fill, but they may not fill. Traders choose order submission strategies on the basis of how quickly they want to trade, the prices they are willing to accept, and the consequences of failing to trade.

■ Stop instructions are attached to other orders to delay efforts to fill them until the stop condition is satisfied. Although stop orders are often used to stop losses, they are not always effective.

■ Issuers sell their securities using underwritten public offerings, best efforts public offerings, private placements, shelf registrations, dividend reinvestment programs, and rights offerings. Investment banks have a conflict of interests when setting the initial offering price in an IPO.

■ Well-functioning secondary markets are essential to raising capital in the primary markets because investors value the ability to sell their securities if they no longer want to hold them or if they need to disinvest to raise cash. If they cannot trade their securities in a liquid market, they will not pay as much for them.

■ Matching buyers and sellers in call markets is easy because the traders (or their orders) come together at the same time and place.

■ Dealers provide liquidity in quote-driven markets. Public traders as well as dealers provide liquidity in order-driven markets.

■ Order-driven markets arrange trades by ranking orders using precedence rules. The rules generally ensure that traders who provide the best prices, display the most size, and arrive early trade first. Continuous order-driven markets price orders using the discriminatory pricing rule. Under this rule, standing limit orders determine trade prices.

- Brokers help people trade unique instruments or positions for which finding a buyer or a seller is difficult.

- Transaction costs are lower in transparent markets than in opaque markets because traders can more easily determine market value and more easily manage their trading in transparent markets.

- A well-functioning financial system allows people to trade instruments that best solve their wealth and risk management problems with low transaction costs. Complete and liquid markets characterize a well-functioning financial system. Complete markets are markets in which the instruments needed to solve investment and risk management problems are available to trade. Liquid markets are markets in which traders can trade when they want to trade at low cost.

- The financial system is operationally efficient when its markets are liquid. Liquid markets lower the costs of raising capital.

- A well-functioning financial system promotes wealth by ensuring that capital allocation decisions are well made. A well-functioning financial system also promotes wealth by allowing people to share the risks associated with valuable products that would otherwise not be undertaken.

- Prices are informationally efficient when they reflect all available information about fundamental values. Information-motivated traders make prices informationally efficient. Prices will be most informative in liquid markets because information-motivated traders will not invest in information and research if establishing positions based on their analyses is too costly.

- Regulators generally seek to promote fair and orderly markets in which traders can trade at prices that accurately reflect fundamental values without incurring excessive transaction costs. Governmental agencies and self-regulating organizations of practitioners provide regulatory services that attempt to make markets safer and more efficient.

- Mandated financial disclosure programs for the issuers of publicly traded securities ensure that information necessary to estimate security values is available to financial analysts on a consistent basis.

PRACTICE PROBLEMS FOR READING 46

1. Akihiko Takabe has designed a sophisticated forecasting model, which predicts the movements in the overall stock market, in the hope of earning a return in excess of a fair return for the risk involved. He uses the predictions of the model to decide whether to buy, hold, or sell the shares of an index fund that aims to replicate the movements of the stock market. Takabe would *best* be characterized as a(n):

    A. hedger.

    B. investor.

    C. information-motivated trader.

2. James Beach is young and has substantial wealth. A significant proportion of his stock portfolio consists of emerging market stocks that offer relatively high expected returns at the cost of relatively high risk. Beach believes that investment in emerging market stocks is appropriate for him given his ability and willingness to take risk. Which of the following labels *most appropriately* describes Beach?

    A. Hedger.

    B. Investor.

    C. Information-motivated trader.

3. Lisa Smith owns a manufacturing company in the United States. Her company has sold goods to a customer in Brazil and will be paid in Brazilian real (BRL) in three months. Smith is concerned about the possibility of the BRL depreciating more than expected against the U.S. dollar (USD). Therefore, she is planning to sell three-month futures contracts on the BRL. The seller of such contracts generally gains when the BRL depreciates against the USD. If Smith were to sell these future contracts, she would *most appropriately* be described as a(n):

    A. hedger.

    B. investor.

    C. information-motivated trader.

4. Which of the following is *not* a function of the financial system?

    A. To regulate arbitrageurs' profits (excess returns).

    B. To help the economy achieve allocational efficiency.

    C. To facilitate borrowing by businesses to fund current operations.

5. An investor primarily invests in stocks of publicly traded companies. The investor wants to increase the diversification of his portfolio. A friend has recommended investing in real estate properties. The purchase of real estate would *best* be characterized as a transaction in the:

    A. derivative investment market.

    B. traditional investment market.

    C. alternative investment market.

6. A hedge fund holds its excess cash in 90-day commercial paper and negotiable certificates of deposit. The cash management policy of the hedge fund is *best described* as using:

    A. capital market instruments.

    B. money market instruments.

    C. intermediate-term debt instruments.

7. An oil and gas exploration and production company announces that it is offering 30 million shares to the public at $45.50 each. This transaction is *most likely* a sale in the:

   A. futures market.

   B. primary market.

   C. secondary market.

8. Consider a mutual fund that invests primarily in fixed-income securities that have been determined to be appropriate given the fund's investment goal. Which of the following is *least likely* to be a part of this fund?

   A. Warrants.

   B. Commercial paper.

   C. Repurchase agreements.

9. A friend has asked you to explain the differences between open-end and closed-end funds. Which of the following will you *most likely* include in your explanation?

   A. Closed-end funds are unavailable to new investors.

   B. When investors sell the shares of an open-end fund, they can receive a discount or a premium to the fund's net asset value.

   C. When selling shares, investors in an open-end fund sell the shares back to the fund whereas investors in a closed-end fund sell the shares to others in the secondary market.

10. The usefulness of a forward contract is limited by some problems. Which of the following is *most likely* one of those problems?

    A. Once you have entered into a forward contract, it is difficult to exit from the contract.

    B. Entering into a forward contract requires the long party to deposit an initial amount with the short party.

    C. If the price of the underlying asset moves adversely from the perspective of the long party, periodic payments must be made to the short party.

11. Tony Harris is planning to start trading in commodities. He has heard about the use of futures contracts on commodities and is learning more about them. Which of the following is Harris *least likely* to find associated with a futures contract?

    A. Existence of counterparty risk.

    B. Standardized contractual terms.

    C. Payment of an initial margin to enter into a contract.

12. A German company that exports machinery is expecting to receive $10 million in three months. The firm converts all its foreign currency receipts into euros. The chief financial officer of the company wishes to lock in a minimum fixed rate for converting the $10 million to euro but also wants to keep the flexibility to use the future spot rate if it is favorable. What hedging transaction is *most likely* to achieve this objective?

    A. Selling dollars forward.

    B. Buying put options on the dollar.

    C. Selling futures contracts on dollars.

13. A book publisher requires substantial quantities of paper. The publisher and a paper producer have entered into an agreement for the publisher to buy and

the producer to supply a given quantity of paper four months later at a price agreed upon today. This agreement is a:

   A. futures contract.

   B. forward contract.

   C. commodity swap.

14. The Standard & Poor's Depositary Receipts (SPDRs) is an investment that tracks the S&P 500 stock market index. Purchases and sales of SPDRs during an average trading day are *best* described as:

   A. primary market transactions in a pooled investment.

   B. secondary market transactions in a pooled investment.

   C. secondary market transactions in an actively managed investment.

15. The Standard & Poor's Depositary Receipts (SPDRs) is an exchange-traded fund in the United States that is designed to track the S&P 500 stock market index. The current price of a share of SPDRs is $113. A trader has just bought call options on shares of SPDRs for a premium of $3 per share. The call options expire in five months and have an exercise price of $120 per share. On the expiration date, the trader will exercise the call options (ignore any transaction costs) if and only if the shares of SPDRs are trading:

   A. below $120 per share.

   B. above $120 per share.

   C. above $123 per share.

16. Which of the following statements about exchange-traded funds is *most correct*?

   A. Exchange-traded funds are not backed by any assets.

   B. The investment companies that create exchange-traded funds are financial intermediaries.

   C. The transaction costs of trading shares of exchange-traded funds are substantially greater than the combined costs of trading the underlying assets of the fund.

17. Jason Schmidt works for a hedge fund and he specializes in finding profit opportunities that are the result of inefficiencies in the market for convertible bonds—bonds that can be converted into a predetermined amount of a company's common stock. Schmidt tries to find convertibles that are priced inefficiently relative to the underlying stock. The trading strategy involves the simultaneous purchase of the convertible bond and the short sale of the underlying common stock. The above process could best be described as:

   A. hedging.

   B. arbitrage.

   C. securitization.

18. Pierre-Louis Robert just purchased a call option on shares of the Michelin Group. A few days ago he wrote a put option on Michelin shares. The call and put options have the same exercise price, expiration date, and number of shares underlying. Considering both positions, Robert's exposure to the risk of the stock of the Michelin Group is:

   A. long.

   B. short.

   C. neutral.

19. An online brokerage firm has set the minimum margin requirement at 55 percent. What is the maximum leverage ratio associated with a position financed by this minimum margin requirement?

　A. 1.55.

　B. 1.82.

　C. 2.22.

20. A trader has purchased 200 shares of a non-dividend-paying firm on margin at a price of $50 per share. The leverage ratio is 2.5. Six months later, the trader sells these shares at $60 per share. Ignoring the interest paid on the borrowed amount and the transaction costs, what was the return to the trader during the six-month period?

　A. 20 percent.

　B. 33.33 percent.

　C. 50 percent.

21. Jason Williams purchased 500 shares of a company at $32 per share. The stock was bought on 75 percent margin. One month later, Williams had to pay interest on the amount borrowed at a rate of 2 percent per month. At that time, Williams received a dividend of $0.50 per share. Immediately after that he sold the shares at $28 per share. He paid commissions of $10 on the purchase and $10 on the sale of the stock. What was the rate of return on this investment for the one-month period?

　A. −12.5 percent.

　B. −15.4 percent.

　C. −50.1 percent.

22. Caroline Rogers believes the price of Gamma Corp. stock will go down in the near future. She has decided to sell short 200 shares of Gamma Corp. at the current market price of €47. The initial margin requirement is 40 percent. Which of the following is an appropriate statement regarding the margin requirement that Rogers is subject to on this short sale?

　A. She will need to contribute €3,760 as margin.

　B. She will need to contribute €5,640 as margin.

　C. She will only need to leave the proceeds from the short sale as deposit and does not need to contribute any additional funds.

23. The current price of a stock is $25 per share. You have $10,000 to invest. You borrow an additional $10,000 from your broker and invest $20,000 in the stock. If the maintenance margin is 30 percent, at what price will a margin call first occur?

　A. $9.62.

　B. $17.86.

　C. $19.71.

24. You have placed a sell market-on-open order—a market order that would automatically be submitted at the market's open tomorrow and would fill at the market price. Your instruction, to sell the shares at the market open, is a(n):

　A. execution instruction.

　B. validity instruction.

　C. clearing instruction.

25. A market has the following limit orders standing on its book for a particular stock. The bid and ask sizes are number of shares in hundreds.

Bid Size	Limit Price (€)	Offer Size
5	9.73	
12	9.81	
4	9.84	
6	9.95	
	10.02	5
	10.10	12
	10.14	8

What is the market?

A. 9.73 bid, offered at 10.14.

B. 9.81 bid, offered at 10.10.

C. 9.95 bid, offered at 10.02.

26. Consider the following limit order book for a stock. The bid and ask sizes are number of shares in hundreds.

Bid Size	Limit Price (¥)	Offer Size
3	122.80	
8	123.00	
4	123.35	
	123.80	7
	124.10	6
	124.50	7

A new buy limit order is placed for 300 shares at ¥123.40. This limit order is said to:

A. take the market.

B. make the market.

C. make a new market.

27. Currently, the market in a stock is "$54.62 bid, offered at $54.71." A new sell limit order is placed at $54.62. This limit order is said to:

A. take the market.

B. make the market.

C. make a new market.

28. Jim White has sold short 100 shares of Super Stores at a price of $42 per share. He has also simultaneously placed a "good-till-cancelled, stop 50, limit 55 buy" order. Assume that if the stop condition specified by White is satisfied and the order becomes valid, it will get executed. Excluding transaction costs, what is the maximum possible loss that White can have?

A. $800.

B. $1,300.

C. Unlimited.

29. You own shares of a company that are currently trading at $30 a share. Your technical analysis of the shares indicates a support level of $27.50. That is, if

the price of the shares is going down, it is more likely to stay above this level rather than fall below it. If the price does fall below this level, however, you believe that the price may continue to decline. You have no immediate intent to sell the shares but are concerned about the possibility of a huge loss if the share price declines below the support level. Which of the following types of orders could you place to most appropriately address your concern?

A. Short sell order.

B. Good-till-cancelled stop sell order.

C. Good-till-cancelled stop buy order.

30. In an underwritten offering, the risk that the entire issue may not be sold to the public at the stipulated offering price is borne by the:

A. issuer.

B. investment bank.

C. buyers of the part of the issue that is sold.

31. A British company listed on the Alternative Investment Market of the London Stock Exchange, announced the sale of 6,686,665 shares to a small group of qualified investors at £0.025 per share. Which of the following *best describes* this sale?

A. Shelf registration.

B. Private placement.

C. Initial public offering.

32. A German publicly traded company, to raise new capital, gave its existing shareholders the opportunity to subscribe for new shares. The existing shareholders could purchase two new shares at a subscription price of €4.58 per share for every 15 shares held. This is an example of a(n):

A. rights offering.

B. private placement.

C. initial public offering.

33. Consider an order-driven system that allows hidden orders. The following four sell orders on a particular stock are currently in the system's limit order book. Based on the commonly used order precedence hierarchy, which of these orders will have precedence over others?

Order	Time of Arrival (HH:MM:SS)	Limit Price (€)	Special Instruction (If any)
I	9:52:01	20.33	
II	9:52:08	20.29	Hidden order
III	9:53:04	20.29	
IV	9:53:49	20.29	

A. Order I (time of arrival of 9:52:01).

B. Order II (time of arrival of 9:52:08).

C. Order III (time of arrival of 9:53:04).

34. Zhenhu Li has submitted an immediate-or-cancel buy order for 500 shares of a company at a limit price of CNY 74.25. There are two sell limit orders standing in that stock's order book at that time. One is for 300 shares at a limit price of CNY 74.30 and the other is for 400 shares at a limit price of CNY 74.35. How many shares in Li's order would get cancelled?

A. None (the order would remain open but unfilled).

B. 200 (300 shares would get filled).

C. 500 (there would be no fill).

35. A market has the following limit orders standing on its book for a particular stock:

Buyer	Bid Size (Number of Shares)	Limit Price (£)	Offer Size (Number of Shares)	Seller
Keith	1,000	19.70		
Paul	200	19.84		
Ann	400	19.89		
Mary	300	20.02		
		20.03	800	Jack
		20.11	1,100	Margaret
		20.16	400	Jeff

Ian submits a day order to sell 1,000 shares, limit £19.83. Assuming that no more buy orders are submitted on that day after Ian submits his order, what would be Ian's average trade price?

A. £19.70.

B. £19.92.

C. £20.05.

36. A financial analyst is examining whether a country's financial market is well functioning. She finds that the transaction costs in this market are low and trading volumes are high. She concludes that the market is quite liquid. In such a market:

A. traders will find it hard to make use of their information.

B. traders will find it easy to trade and their trading will make the market less informationally efficient.

C. traders will find it easy to trade and their trading will make the market more informationally efficient.

37. The government of a country whose financial markets are in an early stage of development has hired you as a consultant on financial market regulation. Your first task is to prepare a list of the objectives of market regulation. Which of the following is *least likely* to be included in this list of objectives?

A. Minimize agency problems in the financial markets.

B. Ensure that financial markets are fair and orderly.

C. Ensure that investors in the stock market achieve a rate of return that is at least equal to the risk-free rate of return.

SOLUTIONS FOR READING 46

1. C is correct. Takabe is best characterized as an information-motivated trader. Takabe believes that his model provides him superior information about the movements in the stock market and his motive for trading is to profit from this information.

2. B is correct. Beach is an investor. He is simply investing in risky assets consistent with his level of risk aversion. Beach is not hedging any existing risk or using information to identify and trade mispriced securities. Therefore, he is not a hedger or an information-motivated trader.

3. A is correct. Smith is a hedger. The short position on the BRL futures contract offsets the BRL long position in three months. She is hedging the risk of the BRL depreciating against the USD. If the BRL depreciates, the value of the cash inflow goes down in USD terms but there is a gain on the futures contracts.

4. A is correct. Regulation of arbitrageurs' profits is not a function of the financial system. The financial system facilitates the allocation of capital to the best uses and the purposes for which people use the financial system, including borrowing money.

5. C is correct. The purchase of real estate properties is a transaction in the alternative investment market.

6. B is correct. The 90-day commercial paper and negotiable certificates of deposit are money market instruments.

7. B is correct. This transaction is a sale in the primary market. It is a sale of shares from the issuer to the investor and funds flow to the issuer of the security from the purchaser.

8. A is correct. Warrants are least likely to be part of the fund. Warrant holders have the right to buy the issuer's common stock. Thus, warrants are typically classified as equity and are least likely to be a part of a fixed-income mutual fund. Commercial paper and repurchase agreements are short-term fixed-income securities.

9. C is correct. When investors want to sell their shares, investors of an open-end fund sell the shares back to the fund whereas investors of a closed-end fund sell the shares to others in the secondary market. Closed-end funds are available to new investors but they must purchase shares in the fund in the secondary market. The shares of a closed-end fund trade at a premium or discount to net asset value.

10. A is correct. Once you have entered into a forward contract, it is difficult to exit from the contract. As opposed to a futures contract, trading out of a forward contract is quite difficult. There is no exchange of cash at the origination of a forward contract. There is no exchange on a forward contract until the maturity of the contract.

11. A is correct. Harris is least likely to find counterparty risk associated with a futures contract. There is limited counterparty risk in a futures contract because the clearinghouse is on the other side of every contract.

12. B is correct. Buying a put option on the dollar will ensure a minimum exchange rate but does not have to be exercised if the exchange rate moves in a favorable direction. Forward and futures contracts would lock in a fixed rate but would not allow for the possibility to profit in case the value of the dollar three months later in the spot market turns out to be greater than the value in the forward or futures contract.

13. B is correct. The agreement between the publisher and the paper supplier to respectively buy and supply paper in the future at a price agreed upon today is a forward contract.

14. B is correct. SPDRs trade in the secondary market and are a pooled investment vehicle.

15. B is correct. The holder of the call option will exercise the call options if the price is above the exercise price of $120 per share. Note that if the stock price is above $120 but less than $123, the option would be exercised even though the net result for the option buyer after considering the premium is a loss. For example, if the stock price is $122, the option buyer would exercise the option to make $2 = $122 − $120 per share, resulting in a loss of $1 = $3 − $2 after considering the premium. It is better to exercise and have a loss of only $1, however, rather than not exercise and lose the entire $3 premium.

16. B is correct. The investment companies that create exchange-traded funds (ETFs) are financial intermediaries. ETFs are securities that represent ownership in the assets held by the fund. The transaction costs of trading shares of ETFs are substantially lower than the combined costs of trading the underlying assets of the ETF.

17. B is correct. The process can best be described as arbitrage because it involves buying and selling instruments, whose values are closely related, at different prices in different markets.

18. A is correct. Robert's exposure to the risk of the stock of the Michelin Group is long. The exposure as a result of the long call position is long. The exposure as a result of the short put position is also long. Therefore, the combined exposure is long.

19. B is correct. The maximum leverage ratio is 1.82 = 100% position ÷ 55% equity. The maximum leverage ratio associated with a position financed by the minimum margin requirement is one divided by the minimum margin requirement.

20. C is correct. The return is 50 percent. If the position had been unleveraged, the return would be 20% = (60 − 50)/50. Because of leverage, the return is 50% = 2.5 × 20%.

    Another way to look at this problem is that the equity contributed by the trader (the minimum margin requirement) is 40% = 100% ÷ 2.5. The trader contributed $20 = 40% of $50 per share. The gain is $10 per share, resulting in a return of 50% = 10/20.

21. B is correct. The return is −15.4 percent.

    Total cost of the purchase = $16,000 = 500 × $32

    Equity invested = $12,000 = 0.75 × $16,000

    Amount borrowed = $4,000 = 16,000 − 12,000

    Interest paid at month end = $80 = 0.02 × $4,000

    Dividend received at month end = $250 = 500 × $0.50

    Proceeds on stock sale = $14,000 = 500 × $28

    Total commissions paid = $20 = $10 + $10

    Net gain/loss = −$1,850 = −16,000 − 80 + 250 + 14,000 − 20

    Initial investment including commission on purchase = $12,010

    Return = −15.4% = −$1,850/$12,010

22. A is correct. She will need to contribute €3,760 as margin. In view of the possibility of a loss, if the stock price goes up, she will need to contribute

€3,760 = 40% of €9,400 as the initial margin. Rogers will need to leave the proceeds from the short sale (€9,400 = 200 × €47) on deposit.

23. B is correct. A margin call will first occur at a price of $17.86. Because you have contributed half and borrowed the remaining half, your initial equity is 50 percent of the initial stock price, or $12.50 = 0.50 × $25. If P is the subsequent price, your equity would change by an amount equal to the change in price. So, your equity at price P would be 12.50 + (P – 25). A margin call will occur when the percentage margin drops to 30 percent. So, the price at which a margin call will occur is the solution to the following equation.

$$\frac{Equity\ /\ Share}{Price\ /\ Share} = \frac{12.50 + P - 25}{P} = 30\%$$

The solution is P = $17.86.

24. B is correct. An instruction regarding when to fill an order is considered a validity instruction.

25. C is correct. The market is 9.95 bid, offered at 10.02. The best bid is at €9.95 and the best offer is €10.02.

26. C is correct. This order is said to make a new market. The new buy order is at ¥123.40, which is better than the current best bid of ¥123.35. Therefore, the buy order is making a new market. Had the new order been at ¥123.35, it would be said to make the market. Because the new buy limit order is at a price less than the best offer of ¥123.80, it will not immediately execute and is not taking the market.

27. A is correct. This order is said to take the market. The new sell order is at $54.62, which is at the current best bid. Therefore, the new sell order will immediately trade with the current best bid and is taking the market.

28. B is correct. The maximum possible loss is $1,300. If the stock price crosses $50, the stop buy order will become valid and will get executed at a maximum limit price of $55. The maximum loss per share is $13 = $55 – $42, or $1,300 for 100 shares.

29. B is correct. The most appropriate order is a good-till-cancelled stop sell order. This order will be acted on if the stock price declines below a specified price (in this case, $27.50). This order is sometimes referred to as a good-till-cancelled stop loss sell order. You are generally bullish about the stock, as indicated by no immediate intent to sell, and would expect a loss on short selling the stock. A stop buy order is placed to buy a stock when the stock is going up.

30. B is correct. The investment bank bears the risk that the issue may be undersubscribed at the offering price. If the entire issue is not sold, the investment bank underwriting the issue will buy the unsold securities at the offering price.

31. B is correct. This sale is a private placement. As the company is already publicly traded, the share sale is clearly not an initial public offering. The sale also does not involve a shelf registration because the company is not selling shares to the public on a piecemeal basis.

32. A is correct. This offering is a rights offering. The company is distributing rights to buy stock at a fixed price to existing shareholders in proportion to their holdings.

33. C is correct. Order III (time of arrival of 9:53:04) has precedence. In the order precedence hierarchy, the first rule is price priority. Based on this rule, sell

orders II, III, and IV get precedence over order I. The next rule is display precedence at a given price. Because order II is a hidden order, orders III and IV get precedence. Finally, order III gets precedence over order IV based on time priority at same price and same display status.

34. C is correct. The order for 500 shares would get cancelled; there would be no fill. Li is willing to buy at CNY 74.25 or less but the minimum offer price in the book is CNY 74.30; therefore, no part of the order would be filled. Because Li's order is immediate-or-cancel, it would be cancelled.

35. B is correct. Ian's average trade price is:

$$£19.92 = \frac{300 \times £20.02 + 400 \times £19.89 + 200 \times £19.84}{300 + 400 + 200}$$

Ian's sell order first fills with the most aggressively priced buy order, which is Mary's order for 300 shares at £20.02. Ian still has 700 shares for sale. The next most aggressively priced buy order is Ann's order for 400 shares at £19.89. This order is filled. Ian still has 300 shares for sale. The next most aggressively priced buy order is Paul's order for 200 shares at £19.84. A third trade takes place. Ian still has 100 shares for sale.

The next buy order is Keith's order for 1,000 shares at £19.70. However, this price is below Ian's limit price of £19.83. Therefore, no more trade is possible.

36. C is correct. In such a market, well-informed traders will find it easy to trade and their trading will make the market more informationally efficient. In a liquid market, it is easier for informed traders to fill their orders. Their trading will cause prices to incorporate their information and the prices will be more in line with the fundamental values.

37. C is correct. Ensure that investors in the stock market achieve a rate of return that is at least equal to the risk-free rate of return is least likely to be included as an objective of market regulation. Stocks are risky investments and there would be occasions when a stock market investment would not only have a return less than the risk-free rate but also a negative return. Minimizing agency costs and ensuring that financial markets are fair and orderly are objectives of market regulation.

Security Market Indices

by Paul D. Kaplan, CFA, and Dorothy C. Kelly, CFA

LEARNING OUTCOMES

Mastery	The candidate should be able to:
☐	**a** describe a security market index;
☐	**b** calculate and interpret the value, price return, and total return of an index;
☐	**c** describe the choices and issues in index construction and management;
☐	**d** compare the different weighting methods used in index construction;
☐	**e** calculate and analyze the value and return of an index on the basis of its weighting method;
☐	**f** describe rebalancing and reconstitution of an index;
☐	**g** describe uses of security market indices;
☐	**h** describe types of equity indices;
☐	**i** describe types of fixed-income indices;
☐	**j** describe indices representing alternative investments;
☐	**k** compare types of security market indices.

INTRODUCTION

1

Investors gather and analyze vast amounts of information about security markets on a continual basis. Because this work can be both time consuming and data intensive, investors often use a single measure that consolidates this information and reflects the performance of an entire security market.

Security market indices were first introduced as a simple measure to reflect the performance of the U.S. stock market. Since then, security market indices have evolved into important multi-purpose tools that help investors track the performance of various security markets, estimate risk, and evaluate the performance of investment managers. They also form the basis for new investment products.

in·dex, *noun* (*pl.***in·dex·es** *or* **in·di·ces**) Latin *indic-*, *index*, from *indicare* to indicate: an indicator, sign, or measure of something.

ORIGIN OF MARKET INDICES

Investors had access to regularly published data on individual security prices in London as early as 1698, but nearly 200 years passed before they had access to a simple indicator to reflect security market information.[1] To give readers a sense of how the U.S. stock market in general performed on a given day, publishers Charles H. Dow and Edward D. Jones introduced the Dow Jones Average, the world's first security market index, in 1884.[2] The index, which appeared in *The Customers' Afternoon Letter*, consisted of the stocks of nine railroads and two industrial companies. It eventually became the Dow Jones Transportation Average.[3] Convinced that industrial companies, rather than railroads, would be "the great speculative market" of the future, Dow and Jones introduced a second index in May 1896—the Dow Jones Industrial Average (DJIA). It had an initial value of 40.94 and consisted of 12 stocks from major U.S. industries.[4,5] Today, investors can choose from among thousands of indices to measure and monitor different security markets and asset classes.

This reading is organized as follows. Section 2 defines a security market index and explains how to calculate the price return and total return of an index for a single period and over multiple periods. Section 3 describes how indices are constructed and managed. Section 4 discusses the use of market indices. Sections 5, 6, and 7 discuss various types of indices, and the final section summarizes the reading. Practice problems follow the conclusions and summary.

2   INDEX DEFINITION AND CALCULATIONS OF VALUE AND RETURNS

A **security market index** represents a given security market, market segment, or asset class. Most indices are constructed as portfolios of marketable securities.

The value of an index is calculated on a regular basis using either the actual or estimated market prices of the individual securities, known as **constituent securities**, within the index. For each security market index, investors may encounter two versions of the same index (i.e., an index with identical constituent securities and weights): one version based on price return and one version based on total return. As the name suggests, a **price return index**, also known as a **price index**, reflects *only* the prices of the constituent securities within the index. A **total return index**, in contrast, reflects not only the prices of the constituent securities but also the reinvestment of all income received since inception.

---

1 London Stock Exchange, "Our History" (2009): www.londonstockexchange.com.
2 Dow Jones & Company, "Dow Jones Industrial Average Historical Components," (2008): 2.
3 Dow Jones & Company, "Dow Jones History" (2009): www.dowjones.com/TheCompany/History/History.htm.
4 Dow Jones & Company, *The Market's Measure*, edited by John A. Presbo (1999): 11.
5 Dow Jones & Company, "Dow Jones Industrial Average Historical Components" (2008): 2.

At inception, the values of the price and total return versions of an index are equal. As time passes, however, the value of the total return index, which includes the reinvestment of all dividends and/or interest received, will exceed the value of the price return index by an increasing amount. A look at how the values of each version are calculated over multiple periods illustrates why.

The value of a price return index is calculated as:

$$V_{PRI} = \frac{\sum_{i=1}^{N} n_i P_i}{D}$$

(1)

where

V_{PRI} = the value of the price return index
n_i = the number of units of constituent security i held in the index portfolio
N = the number of constituent securities in the index
P_i = the unit price of constituent security i
D = the value of the divisor

The **divisor** is a number initially chosen at inception. It is frequently chosen so that the price index has a convenient initial value, such as 1,000. The index provider then adjusts the value of the divisor as necessary to avoid changes in the index value that are unrelated to changes in the prices of its constituent securities. For example, when changing index constituents, the index provider may adjust the divisor so that the value of the index with the new constituents equals the value of the index prior to the changes.

Index return calculations, like calculations of investment portfolio returns, may measure price return or total return. **Price return** measures only price appreciation or percentage change in price. **Total return** measures price appreciation plus interest, dividends, and other distributions.

2.1 Calculation of Single-Period Returns

For a security market index, price return can be calculated in two ways: either the percentage change in value of the price return index, or the weighted average of price returns of the constituent securities. The price return of an index can be expressed as:

$$PR_I = \frac{V_{PRI1} - V_{PRI0}}{V_{PRI0}}$$

(2)

where

PR_I = the price return of the index portfolio (as a decimal number, i.e., 12 percent is 0.12)
V_{PRI1} = the value of the price return index at the end of the period
V_{PRI0} = the value of the price return index at the beginning of the period

Similarly, the price return of each constituent security can be expressed as:

$$PR_i = \frac{P_{i1} - P_{i0}}{P_{i0}}$$

(3)

where

PR_i = the price return of constituent security i (as a decimal number)
P_{i1} = the price of constituent security i at the end of the period
P_{i0} = the price of constituent security i at the beginning of the period

Because the price return of the index equals the weighted average of price returns of the individual securities, we can write:

$$PR_I = \sum_{i=1}^{N} w_i PR_i = \sum_{i=1}^{N} w_i \left(\frac{P_{i1} - P_{i0}}{P_{i0}} \right) = 1 \qquad \text{(4)}$$

where:

PR_I = the price return of index portfolio (as a decimal number)

PR_i = the price return of constituent security i (as a decimal number)

N = the number of individual securities in the index

w_i = the weight of security i (the fraction of the index portfolio allocated to security i)

P_{i1} = the price of constituent security i at the end of the period

P_{i0} = the price of constituent security i at the beginning of the period

Equation 4 can be rewritten simply as:

$$PR_I = w_1 PR_1 + w_2 PR_2 + ... + w_N PR_N \qquad \text{(5)}$$

where

PR_I = the price return of index portfolio (as a decimal number)

PR_i = the price return of constituent security i (as a decimal number)

w_i = the weight of security i (the fraction of the index portfolio allocated to security i)

N = the number of securities in the index

Total return measures price appreciation plus interest, dividends, and other distributions. Thus, the **total return of an index** is the price appreciation, or change in the value of the price return index, plus income (dividends and/or interest) over the period, expressed as a percentage of the beginning value of the price return index. The total return of an index can be expressed as:

$$TR_I = \frac{V_{PRI1} - V_{PRI0} + Inc_I}{V_{PRI0}} \qquad \text{(6)}$$

where

TR_I = the total return of the index portfolio (as a decimal number)

V_{PRI1} = the value of the price return index at the end of the period

V_{PRI0} = the value of the price return index at the beginning of the period

Inc_I = the total income (dividends and/or interest) from all securities in the index held over the period

The total return of an index can also be calculated as the weighted average of total returns of the constituent securities. The total return of each constituent security in the index is calculated as:

$$TR_i = \frac{P_{1i} - P_{0i} + Inc_i}{P_{0i}} \qquad \text{(7)}$$

where

TR_i = the total return of constituent security i (as a decimal number)

P_{1i} = the price of constituent security i at the end of the period

P_{0i} = the price of constituent security i at the beginning of the period

Inc_i = the total income (dividends and/or interest) from security i over the period

Because the total return of an index can be calculated as the weighted average of total returns of the constituent securities, we can express total return as:

$$TR_I = \sum_{i=1}^{N} w_i TR_i = \sum_{i=1}^{N} w_i \left(\frac{P_{1i} - P_{0i} + Inc_i}{P_{0i}} \right) \tag{8}$$

Equation 8 can be rewritten simply as

$$TR_I = w_1 TR_1 + w_2 TR_2 + \ldots + w_N TR_N \tag{9}$$

where

> TR_I = the total return of the index portfolio (as a decimal number)
> TR_i = the total return of constituent security i (as a decimal number)
> w_i = the weight of security i (the fraction of the index portfolio allocated to security i)
> N = the number of securities in the index

2.2 Calculation of Index Values over Multiple Time Periods

The calculation of index values over multiple time periods requires geometrically linking the series of index returns. With a series of price returns for an index, we can calculate the value of the price return index with the following equation:

$$V_{PRIT} = V_{PRI0} (1+PR_{I1})(1+PR_{I2})\ldots(1+PR_{IT}) \tag{10}$$

where

> V_{PRI0} = the value of the price return index at inception
> V_{PRIT} = the value of the price return index at time t
> PR_{IT} = the price return (as a decimal number) on the index over period t, $t = 1$, 2, ..., T

For an index with an inception value set to 1,000 and price returns of 5 percent and 3 percent for Periods 1 and 2 respectively, the values of the price return index would be calculated as follows:

Period	Return (%)	Calculation	Ending Value
0		1,000(1.00)	1,000.00
1	5.00	1,000(1.05)	1,050.00
2	3.00	1,000(1.05)(1.03)	1,081.50

Similarly, the series of total returns for an index is used to calculate the value of the total return index with the following equation:

$$V_{TRIT} = V_{TRI0} (1+TR_{I1})(1+TR_{I2})\ldots(1+TR_{IT}) \tag{11}$$

where

> V_{TRI0} = the value of the index at inception
> V_{TRIT} = the value of the total return index at time t
> TR_{IT} = the total return (as a decimal number) on the index over period t, $t = 1$, 2, ..., T

Suppose that the same index yields an additional 1.5 percent return from income in Period 1 and an additional 2.0 percent return from income in Period 2, bringing the total returns for Periods 1 and 2, respectively, to 6.5 percent and 5 percent. The values of the total return index would be calculated as follows:

Period	Return (%)	Calculation	Ending Value
0		1,000(1.00)	1,000.00
1	6.50	1,000(1.065)	1,065.00
2	5.00	1,000(1.065)(1.05)	1,118.25

As illustrated above, as time passes, the value of the total return index, which includes the reinvestment of all dividends and/or interest received, exceeds the value of the price return index by an increasing amount.

3 INDEX CONSTRUCTION AND MANAGEMENT

Constructing and managing a security market index is similar to constructing and managing a portfolio of securities. Index providers must decide the following:

1. Which target market should the index represent?
2. Which securities should be selected from that target market?
3. How much weight should be allocated to each security in the index?
4. When should the index be rebalanced?
5. When should the security selection and weighting decision be re-examined?

3.1 Target Market and Security Selection

The first decision in index construction is identifying the target market, market segment, or asset class that the index is intended to represent. The target market may be defined very broadly or narrowly. It may be based on asset class (e.g., equities, fixed income, real estate, commodities, hedge funds); geographic region (e.g., Japan, South Africa, Latin America, Europe); the exchange on which the securities are traded (e.g., Shanghai, Toronto, Tokyo), and/or other characteristics (e.g., economic sector, company size, investment style, duration, or credit quality).

The target market determines the investment universe and the securities available for inclusion in the index. Once the investment universe is identified, the number of securities and the specific securities to include in the index must be determined. The constituent securities could be nearly all those in the target market or a representative sample of the target market. Some equity indices, such as the S&P 500 Index and the FTSE 100, fix the number of securities included in the index and indicate this number in the name of the index. Other indices allow the number of securities to vary to reflect changes in the target market or to maintain a certain percentage of the target market. For example, the Tokyo Stock Price Index (TOPIX) represents and includes all of the largest stocks, known as the First Section, listed on the Tokyo Stock Exchange. To be included in the First Section—and thus the TOPIX—stocks must meet certain criteria, such as the number of shares outstanding, the number of shareholders, and market capitalization. Stocks that no longer meet the criteria are removed from the First Section and also the TOPIX. Objective or mechanical rules determine the constituent securities of most, but not all, indices. The Sensex of Bombay and the S&P 500, for example, use a selection committee and more subjective decision-making rules to determine constituent securities.

3.2 Index Weighting

The weighting decision determines how much of each security to include in the index and has a substantial impact on an index's value. Index providers use a number of methods to weight the constituent securities in an index. Indices can be price weighted, equal weighted, market-capitalization weighted, or fundamentally weighted. Each weighting method has its advantages and disadvantages.

3.2.1 *Price Weighting*

The simplest method to weight an index and the one used by Charles Dow to construct the Dow Jones Industrial Average is **price weighting**. In price weighting, the weight on each constituent security is determined by dividing its price by the sum of all the prices of the constituent securities. The weight is calculated using the following formula:

$$w_i^P = \frac{P_i}{\sum\limits_{i=1}^{N} P_i} \tag{12}$$

Exhibit 1 illustrates the values, weights, and single-period returns following inception of a price-weighted equity index with five constituent securities. The value of the price-weighted index is determined by dividing the sum of the security values (101.50) by the divisor, which is typically set at inception to equal the initial number of securities in the index. Thus, in our example, the divisor is 5 and the initial value of the index is calculated as 101.50 ÷ 5 = 20.30.

As illustrated in this exhibit, Security A, which has the highest price, also has the highest weighting and thus will have the greatest impact on the return of the index. Note how both the price return and the total return of the index are calculated on the basis of the corresponding returns on the constituent securities.

A property unique to price-weighted indices is that a stock split on one constituent security changes the weights on all the securities in the index.[6] To prevent the stock split and the resulting new weights from changing the value of the index, the index provider must adjust the value of the divisor as illustrated in Exhibit 2. Given a 2-for-1 split in Security A, the divisor is adjusted by dividing the sum of the constituent prices *after* the split (77.50) by the value of the index *before* the split (21.00). This adjustment results in changing the divisor from 5 to 3.69 so that the index value is maintained at 21.00.

---

6 A stock split is an increase in the number of shares outstanding and a proportionate decrease in the price per share such that the total market value of equity, as well as investors' proportionate ownership in the company, does not change.

Exhibit 1 Example of a Price-Weighted Equity Index

Security	Shares in Index	BOP Price	Value (Shares × BOP Price)	BOP Weight (%)	EOP Price	Dividends per Share	Total Dividends	Value (Shares × EOP Price)	Price Return (%)	Total Return (%)	BOP Weight × Price Return (%)	BOP Weight × Total Return (%)	EOP Weight (%)
A	1	50.00	50.00	49.26	55.00	0.75	0.75	55.00	10.00	11.50	4.93	5.66	52.38
B	1	25.00	25.00	24.63	22.00	0.10	0.10	22.00	−12.00	−11.60	−2.96	−2.86	20.95
C	1	12.50	12.50	12.32	8.00	0.00	0.00	8.00	−36.00	−36.00	−4.43	−4.43	7.62
D	1	10.00	10.00	9.85	14.00	0.05	0.05	14.00	40.00	40.50	3.94	3.99	13.33
E	1	4.00	4.00	3.94	6.00	0.00	0.00	6.00	50.00	50.00	1.97	1.97	5.72
Total			101.50	100.00			0.90	105.00	3.45		3.45	4.33	100.00
Index Value			20.30				0.18	21.00					

Divisor = 5
BOP = Beginning of period
EOP = End of period

Type of Index	BOP Value	Return (%)	EOP Value
Price Return	20.30	3.45	21.00
Total Return	20.30	4.33	21.18

	Exhibit 2	Impact of 2-for-1 Split in Security A		
Security	**Price before Split**	**Weight before Split (%)**	**Price after Split**	**Weight after Split (%)**
A	55.00	52.38	27.50	35.48
B	22.00	20.95	22.00	28.39
C	8.00	7.62	8.00	10.32
D	14.00	13.33	14.00	18.07
E	6.00	5.72	6.00	7.74
Total	105.00	100.00	77.50	100.00
Divisor	5.00		3.69	
Index Value	21.00		21.00	

The primary advantage of price weighting is its simplicity. The main disadvantage of price weighting is that it results in arbitrary weights for each security. In particular, a stock split in any one security causes arbitrary changes in the weights of all the constituents' securities.

3.2.2 Equal Weighting

Another simple index weighting method is **equal weighting**. This method assigns an equal weight to each constituent security at inception. The weights are calculated as:

$$w_i^E = \frac{1}{N} \tag{13}$$

where

w_i = fraction of the portfolio that is allocated to security i or weight of security i
N = number of securities in the index

To construct an equal-weighted index from the five securities in Exhibit 1, the index provider allocates one-fifth (20 percent) of the value of the index (at the beginning of the period) to each security. Dividing the value allocated to each security by each security's individual share price determines the number of shares of each security to include in the index. Unlike a price-weighted index, where the weights are arbitrarily determined by the market prices, the weights in an equal-weighted index are arbitrarily assigned by the index provider.

Exhibit 3 illustrates the values, weights, and single-period returns following inception of an equal-weighted index with the same constituent securities as those in Exhibit 1. This example assumes a beginning index portfolio value of 10,000 (i.e., an investment of 2,000 in each security). To set the initial value of the index to 1,000, the divisor is set to 10 (10,000 ÷ 10 = 1,000).

Exhibits 1 and 3 demonstrate how different weighting methods result in different returns. The 10.4 percent price return of the equal-weighted index shown in Exhibit 3 differs significantly from the 3.45 percent price return of the price-weighted index in Exhibit 1.

Like price weighting, the primary advantage of equal weighting is its simplicity. Equal weighting, however, has a number of disadvantages. First, securities that constitute the largest fraction of the target market value are underrepresented, and securities that constitute a small fraction of the target market value are overrepresented. Second, after the index is constructed and the prices of constituent securities change, the index is no longer equally weighted. Therefore, maintaining equal weights requires frequent adjustments (rebalancing) to the index.

Exhibit 3   Example of an Equal-Weighted Equity Index

Security	Shares in Index	BOP Price	Value (Shares × BOP Price)	Weight (%)	EOP Price	Dividends per Share	Value (Shares × EOP Price)	Total Dividends	Price Return (%)	Total Return (%)	Weight × Price Return (%)	Weight × Total Return (%)	EOP Weight (%)
A	40	50.00	2,000	20.00	55.00	0.75	2,200	30	10.00	11.50	2.00	2.30	19.93
B	80	25.00	2,000	20.00	22.00	0.10	1,760	8	-12.00	-11.60	-2.40	-2.32	15.94
C	160	12.50	2,000	20.00	8.00	0.00	1,280	0	-36.00	-36.00	-7.20	-7.20	11.60
D	200	10.00	2,000	20.00	14.00	0.05	2,800	10	40.00	40.50	8.00	8.10	25.36
E	500	4.00	2,000	20.00	6.00	0.00	3,000	0	50.00	50.00	10.00	10.00	27.17
Total			10,000	100.00			11,040	48			10.40	10.88	100.00
Index Value			1,000				1,104	4.80	10.40	10.88			

Divisor = 10
BOP = Beginning of period
EOP = End of period

Type of Index	BOP Value	Return (%)	EOP Value
Price Return	1,000.00	10.40	1,104.00
Total Return	1,000.00	10.88	1,108.80

3.2.3 *Market-Capitalization Weighting*

In **market-capitalization weighting**, or value weighting, the weight on each constituent security is determined by dividing its market capitalization by the total market capitalization (the sum of the market capitalization) of all the securities in the index. Market capitalization or value is calculated by multiplying the number of shares outstanding by the market price per share.

The market-capitalization weight of security i is:

$$w_i^M = \frac{Q_i P_i}{\sum_{j=1}^{N} Q_j P_j} \tag{14}$$

where

w_i = fraction of the portfolio that is allocated to security i or weight of security i
Q_i = number of shares outstanding of security i
P_i = share price of security i
N = number of securities in the index

Exhibit 4 illustrates the values, weights, and single-period returns following inception of a market-capitalization-weighted index for the same five-security market. Security A, with 3,000 shares outstanding and a price of 50 per share, has a market capitalization of 150,000 or 26.29 percent (150,000/570,500) of the entire index portfolio. The resulting index weights in the exhibit reflect the relative value of each security as measured by its market capitalization.

As shown in Exhibits 1, 3, and 4, the weighting method affects the index's returns. The price and total returns of the market-capitalization index in Exhibit 4 (1.49 percent and 2.13 percent, respectively) differ significantly from those of the price-weighted (3.45 percent and 4.33 percent, respectively) and equal-weighted (10.40 percent and 10.88 percent respectively) indices. To understand the source and magnitude of the difference, compare the weights and returns of each security under each of the weighting methods. The weight of Security A, for example, ranges from 49.26 percent in the price-weighted index to 20 percent in the equal-weighted index. With a price return of 10 percent, Security A contributes 4.93 percent to the price return of the price-weighted index, 2.00 percent to the price return of the equal-weighted index, and 2.63 percent to the price return of the market-capitalization-weighted index. With a total return of 11.50 percent, Security A contributes 5.66 percent to the total return of the price-weighted index, 2.30 percent to the total return of the equal-weighted index, and 3.02 percent to the total return of the market-capitalization-weighted index.

3.2.3.1 Float-Adjusted Market-Capitalization Weighting   In **float-adjusted market-capitalization weighting**, the weight on each constituent security is determined by adjusting its market capitalization for its **market float**. Typically, market float is the number of shares of the constituent security that are available to the investing public. For companies that are closely held, only a portion of the shares outstanding are available to the investing public (the rest are held by a small group of controlling investors). In addition to excluding shares held by controlling shareholders, most float-adjusted market-capitalization-weighted indices also exclude shares held by other corporations and governments. Some providers of indices that are designed to represent the investment opportunities of global investors further reduce the number of shares included in the index by excluding shares that are not available to foreigner investors. The index providers may refer to these indices as "free-float-adjusted market-capitalization-weighted indices."

Float-adjusted market-capitalization-weighted indices reflect the shares available for public trading by multiplying the market price per share by the number of shares

Exhibit 4   Example of a Market-Capitalization-Weighted Equity Index

Stock	Shares Out-standing	BOP Price	BOP Market Cap	BOP Weight (%)	EOP Price	Dividends per Share	EOP Market Cap	Total Dividends	Price Return (%)	Total Return (%)	BOP Weight × Price Return (%)	BOP Weight × Total Return (%)	EOP Weight (%)
A	3,000	50.00	150,000	26.29	55.00	0.75	165,000	2,250	10.00	11.50	2.63	3.02	28.50
B	10,000	25.00	250,000	43.82	22.00	0.10	220,000	1,000	−12.00	−11.60	−5.26	−5.08	38.00
C	5,000	12.50	62,500	10.96	8.00	0.00	40,000	0	−36.00	−36.00	−3.95	−3.95	6.91
D	8,000	10.00	80,000	14.02	14.00	0.05	112,000	400	40.00	40.50	5.61	5.68	19.34
E	7,000	4.00	28,000	4.91	6.00	0.00	42,000	0	50.00	50.00	2.46	2.46	7.25
Total			570,500	100.00			579,000	3,650			1.49	2.13	100.00
Index Value			1,000				1,014.90		1.49	2.13			

Divisor = 570.50
BOP = Beginning of period
EOP = End of period

Type of Index	BOP Value	Return (%)	EOP Value
Price Return	1,000.00	1.49	1,014.90
Total Return	1,000.00	2.13	1,021.30

available to the investing public (i.e., the float-adjusted market capitalization) rather than the total number of shares outstanding (total market capitalization). Currently, most market-capitalization-weighted indices are float adjusted. Therefore, unless otherwise indicated, for the remainder of this reading, "market-capitalization" weighting refers to float-adjusted market-capitalization weighting.

The float-adjusted market-capitalization weight of security i is calculated as:

$$w_i^M = \frac{f_i Q_i P_i}{\sum_{j=1}^{N} f_j Q_j P_j} \tag{15}$$

where

f_i = fraction of shares outstanding in the market float
w_i = fraction of the portfolio that is allocated to security i or weight of security i
Q_i = number of shares outstanding of security i
P_i = share price of security i
N = number of securities in the index

Exhibit 5 illustrates the values, weights, and single-period returns following inception of a float-adjusted market-capitalization-weighted equity index using the same five securities as before. The low percentage of shares of Security D in the market float compared with the number of shares outstanding indicates that the security is closely held.

The primary advantage of market-capitalization weighting (including float adjusted) is that constituent securities are held in proportion to their value in the target market. The primary disadvantage is that constituent securities whose prices have risen the most (or fallen the most) have a greater (or lower) weight in the index (i.e., as a security's price rises relative to other securities in the index, its weight increases; and as its price decreases in value relative to other securities in the index, its weight decreases). This weighting method leads to overweighting stocks that have risen in price (and may be overvalued) and underweighting stocks that have declined in price (and may be undervalued). The effect of this weighting method is similar to a momentum investment strategy in that over time, the securities that have risen in price the most will have the largest weights in the index.

3.2.4 Fundamental Weighting

Fundamental weighting attempts to address the disadvantages of market-capitalization weighting by using measures of a company's size that are independent of its security price to determine the weight on each constituent security. These measures include book value, cash flow, revenues, earnings, dividends, and number of employees.

Some fundamental indices use a single measure, such as total dividends, to weight the constituent securities, whereas others combine the weights from several measures to form a composite value that is used for weighting.

Letting F_i denote a given fundamental size measure of company i, the fundamental weight on security i is:

$$w_i^F = \frac{F_i}{\sum_{j=1}^{N} F_j} \tag{16}$$

Relative to a market-capitalization-weighted index, a fundamental index with weights based on such an item as earnings will result in greater weights on constituent securities with earnings yields (earnings divided by price) that are higher than the earnings yield of the overall market-weighted portfolio. Similarly, stocks with earnings

Exhibit 5   Example of Float-Adjusted Market-Capitalization-Weighted Equity Index

Stock	Shares Out-standing	% Shares in Market Float	Shares in Index	BOP Price	BOP Float-Adjusted Market Cap	BOP Weight (%)	EOP Price	Dividends per Share	Total Dividends	Ending Float-Adjusted Market Cap	Price Return (%)	Total Return (%)	BOP Weight × Price Return (%)	BOP Weight × Total Return (%)	EOP Weight (%)
A	3,000	100	3,000	50.00	150,000	35.40	55.00	0.75	2,250	165,000	10.00	11.50	3.54	4.07	39.61
B	10,000	70	7,000	25.00	175,000	41.31	22.00	0.10	700	154,000	-12.00	-11.60	-4.96	-4.79	36.97
C	5,000	90	4,500	12.50	56,250	13.28	8.00	0.00	0	36,000	-36.00	-36.00	-4.78	-4.78	8.64
D	8,000	25	2,000	10.00	20,000	4.72	14.00	0.05	100	28,000	40.00	40.50	1.89	1.91	6.72
E	7,000	80	5,600	4.00	22,400	5.29	6.00	0.00	0	33,600	50.00	50.00	2.65	2.65	8.06
Total					423,650	100.00			3,050	416,600			-1.66	-0.94	100.00
Index Value					1,000				7.20	983.36	-1.66	-0.94			

Divisor = 423.65
BOP = Beginning of period
EOP = End of period

Type of Index	Initial Value	Return (%)	Ending Value
Price Return	1,000.00	-1.66	983.36
Total Return	1,000.00	-0.94	990.56

yields less than the yield on the overall market-weighted portfolio will have lower weights. For example, suppose there are two stocks in an index. Stock A has a market capitalization of €200 million, Stock B has a market capitalization of €800 million, and their aggregate market capitalization is €1 billion (€1,000 million). Both companies have earnings of €20 million and aggregate earnings of €40 million. Thus, Stock A has an earnings yield of 10 percent (20/200) and Stock B has an earnings yield of 2.5 percent (20/800). The earnings weight of Stock A is 50 percent (20/40), which is higher than its market-capitalization weight of 20 percent (200/1,000). The earnings weight of Stock B is 50 percent (20/40), which is less than its market-capitalization weight of 80 percent (800/1,000). Relative to the market-cap-weighted index, the earnings-weighted index over-weights the high-yield Stock A and under-weights the low-yield Stock B.

The most important property of fundamental weighting is that it leads to indices that have a "value" tilt. That is, a fundamentally weighted index has ratios of book value, earnings, dividends, etc. to market value that are higher than its market-capitalization-weighted counterpart. Also, in contrast to the momentum "effect" of market-capitalization-weighted indices, fundamentally weighted indices generally will have a contrarian "effect" in that the portfolio weights will shift away from securities that have increased in relative value and toward securities that have fallen in relative value whenever the portfolio is rebalanced.

3.3 Index Management: Rebalancing and Reconstitution

So far, we have discussed index construction. Index management entails the two remaining questions:

- When should the index be rebalanced?
- When should the security selection and weighting decisions be re-examined?

3.3.1 *Rebalancing*

Rebalancing refers to adjusting the weights of the constituent securities in the index. To maintain the weight of each security consistent with the index's weighting method, the index provider rebalances the index by adjusting the weights of the constituent securities on a regularly scheduled basis (rebalancing dates)—usually quarterly. Rebalancing is necessary because the weights of the constituent securities change as their market prices change. Note, for example, that the weights of the securities in the equal-weighted index (Exhibit 3) at the end of the period are no longer equal (i.e., 20 percent):

Security A	19.93%
Security B	15.94
Security C	11.60
Security D	25.36
Security E	27.17

In rebalancing the index, the weights of Securities D and E (which had the highest returns) would be decreased and the weights of Securities A, B, and C (which had the lowest returns) would be increased. Thus, rebalancing creates turnover within an index.

Price-weighted indices are not rebalanced because the weight of each constituent security is determined by its price. For market-capitalization-weighted indices, rebalancing is less of a concern because the indices largely rebalance themselves. In our market-capitalization index, for example, the weight of Security C automatically declined from 10.96 percent to 6.91 percent, reflecting the 36 percent decline in its market price. Market-capitalization weights are only adjusted to reflect mergers, acquisitions, liquidations, and other corporate actions between rebalancing dates.

3.3.2 *Reconstitution*

Reconstitution is the process of changing the constituent securities in an index. It is similar to a portfolio manager deciding to change the securities in his or her portfolio. Reconstitution is part of the rebalancing cycle. The reconstitution date is the date on which index providers review the constituent securities, re-apply the initial criteria for inclusion in the index, and select which securities to retain, remove, or add. Constituent securities that no longer meet the criteria are replaced with securities that do meet the criteria. Once the revised list of constituent securities is determined, the weighting method is re-applied. Indices are reconstituted to reflect changes in the target market (bankruptcies, de-listings, mergers, acquisitions, etc.) and/or to reflect the judgment of the selection committee.

Reconstitution creates turnover in a number of different ways, particularly for market-capitalization-weighted indices. When one security is removed and another is added, the index provider has to change the weights of the other securities in order to maintain the market-capitalization weighting of the index.

The frequency of reconstitution is a major issue for widely used indices and their constituent securities. The Russell 2000 Index, for example, reconstitutes annually. It is used as a benchmark by numerous investment funds, and each year, prior to the index's reconstitution, the managers of these funds buy stocks they think will be added to the index—driving those stocks' prices up—and sell stocks they think will be deleted from the index—driving those stocks' prices down. Exhibit 6 illustrates the potential impact of these decisions. Beginning in late April 2009, some managers began acquiring and bidding up the price of Uranium Energy Corporation (UEC) because they believed that it would be included in the reconstituted Russell 2000 Index. On 12 June, Russell listed UEC as a preliminary addition to the Russell 2000 Index and the Russell 3000 Index.[7] By that time, the stock value had increased by more than 300 percent. Investors continued to bid up the stock price in the weeks following the announcement, and the stock closed on the reconstitution date of 30 June at USD2.90, up nearly 400 percent for the quarter.

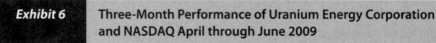

| Exhibit 6 | Three-Month Performance of Uranium Energy Corporation and NASDAQ April through June 2009 |

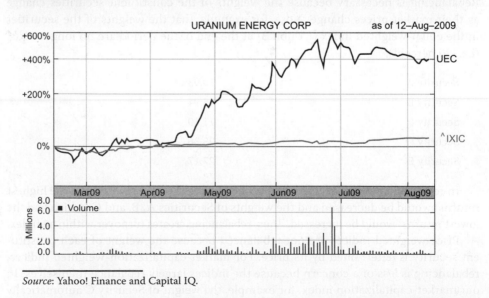

Source: Yahoo! Finance and Capital IQ.

---

7 According to the press release, final membership in the index would be published after market close on Friday, 26 June.

USES OF MARKET INDICES

Indices were initially created to give a sense of how a particular security market performed on a given day. With the development of modern financial theory, their uses in investment management have expanded significantly. Some of the major uses of indices include:

- gauges of market sentiment;
- proxies for measuring and modeling returns, systematic risk, and risk-adjusted performance;
- proxies for asset classes in asset allocation models;
- benchmarks for actively managed portfolios; and
- model portfolios for such investment products as index funds and exchange-traded funds (ETFs).

Investors using security market indices must be familiar with how various indices are constructed in order to select the index or indices most appropriate for their needs.

4.1 Gauges of Market Sentiment

The original purpose of stock market indices was to provide a gauge of investor confidence or market sentiment. As indicators of the collective opinion of market participants, indices reflect investor attitudes and behavior. The Dow Jones Industrial Average has a long history, is frequently quoted in the media, and remains a popular gauge of market sentiment. It may not accurately reflect the overall attitude of investors or the "market," however, because the index consists of only 30 of the thousands of U.S. stocks traded each day.

4.2 Proxies for Measuring and Modeling Returns, Systematic Risk, and Risk-Adjusted Performance

The capital asset pricing model (CAPM) defines beta as the systematic risk of a security with respect to the entire market. The market portfolio in the CAPM consists of all risky securities. To represent the performance of the market portfolio, investors use a broad index. For example, the Tokyo Price Index (TOPIX) and the S&P 500 often serve as proxies for the market portfolio in Japan and the United States, respectively, and are used for measuring and modeling systematic risk and market returns.

Security market indices also serve as market proxies when measuring risk-adjusted performance. The beta of an actively managed portfolio allows investors to form a passive alternative with the same level of systematic risk. For example, if the beta of an actively managed portfolio of global stocks is 0.95 with respect to the MSCI World Index, investors can create a passive portfolio with the same systematic risk by investing 95 percent of their portfolio in a MSCI World Index fund and holding the remaining 5 percent in cash. Alpha, the difference between the return of the actively managed portfolio and the return of the passive portfolio, is a measure of risk-adjusted return or investment performance. Alpha can be the result of manager skill (or lack thereof), transaction costs, and fees.

4.3 Proxies for Asset Classes in Asset Allocation Models

Because indices exhibit the risk and return profiles of select groups of securities, they play a critical role as proxies for asset classes in asset allocation models. They provide the historical data used to model the risks and returns of different asset classes.

4.4 Benchmarks for Actively Managed Portfolios

Investors often use indices as benchmarks to evaluate the performance of active portfolio managers. The index selected as the benchmark should reflect the investment strategy used by the manager. For example, an active manager investing in global small-capitalization stocks should be evaluated using a benchmark index, such as the FTSE Global Small Cap Index, which includes 4,600 small-capitalization stocks across 48 countries.

The choice of an index to use as a benchmark is important because an inappropriate index could lead to incorrect conclusions regarding an active manager's investment performance. Suppose that the small-cap manager underperformed the small-cap index but outperformed a broad equity market index. If investors use the broad market index as a benchmark, they might conclude that the small-cap manager is earning his or her fees and should be retained or given additional assets to invest. Using the small-cap index as a benchmark might lead to a very different conclusion.

4.5 Model Portfolios for Investment Products

Indices also serve as the basis for the development of new investment products. Using indices as benchmarks for actively managed portfolios has led some investors to conclude that they should invest in the benchmarks instead. Based on the CAPM's conclusion that investors should hold the market portfolio, broad market index funds have been developed to function as proxies for the market portfolio.

Investment management firms initially developed and managed index portfolios for institutional investors. Eventually, mutual fund companies introduced index funds for individual investors. Subsequently, investment management firms introduced exchange-traded funds, which are managed the same way as index mutual funds but trade like stocks.

The first ETFs were based on existing indices. As the popularity of ETFs increased, index providers created new indices for the specific purpose of forming ETFs, leading to the creation of numerous narrowly defined indices with corresponding ETFs. The Market Vectors Vietnam ETF, for example, allows investors to invest in the equity market of Vietnam.

The choice of indices to meet the needs of investors is extensive. Index providers are constantly looking for opportunities to develop indices to meet the needs of investors.

5   EQUITY INDICES

A wide variety of equity indices exist, including broad market, multi-market, sector, and style indices.

5.1 Broad Market Indices

A broad equity market index, as its name suggests, represents an entire given equity market and typically includes securities representing more than 90 percent of the selected market. For example, the Shanghai Stock Exchange Composite Index (SSE) is a market-capitalization-weighted index of all shares that trade on the Shanghai Stock Exchange. In the United States, the Wilshire 5000 Total Market Index is a market-capitalization-weighted index that includes more than 6,000 equity securities and is designed to represent the entire U.S. equity market.[8] The Russell 3000, consisting of

---

8 Despite its name, the Wilshire 5000 has no constraint on the number of securities that can be included. It included approximately 5,000 securities at inception.

the largest 3,000 stocks by market capitalization, represents 99 percent of the U.S. equity market.

5.2 Multi-Market Indices

Multi-market indices usually comprise indices from different countries and are designed to represent multiple security markets. Multi-market indices may represent multiple national markets, geographic regions, economic development groups, and, in some cases, the entire world. World indices are of importance to investors who take a global approach to equity investing without any particular bias toward a particular country or region. A number of index providers publish families of multi-market equity indices.

MSCI Barra offers a number of multi-market indices. As shown in Exhibit 7, MSCI Barra classifies countries along two dimensions: level of economic development and geographic region. Developmental groups, which MSCI Barra refers to as market classifications, include developed markets, emerging markets, and frontier markets. The geographic regions are largely divided by longitudinal lines of the globe: the Americas, Europe with Africa, and Asia with the Pacific. MSCI Barra provides country-specific indices for each of the developed and emerging market countries within its multi-market indices. MSCI Barra periodically reviews the market classifications of countries in its indices for movement from frontier markets to emerging markets and from emerging markets to developed markets and reconstitutes the indices accordingly.

Exhibit 7	MSCI International Equity Indices—Country and Market Coverage (as of June 2009)

Developed Markets

Americas	Europe	Pacific
Canada, United States	Austria, Belgium, Denmark, Finland, France, Germany, Greece, Ireland, Italy, Netherlands, Norway, Portugal, Spain, Sweden, Switzerland, United Kingdom	Australia, Hong Kong, Japan, New Zealand, Singapore

Emerging Markets

Americas	Europe, Middle East, Africa	Asia
Argentina[1], Brazil, Chile, Colombia, Mexico, Peru	Czech Republic, Egypt, Hungary, Israel, Jordan, Morocco, Poland, Russia, South Africa, Turkey	China, India, Indonesia, South Korea, Malaysia, Pakistan[2], Philippines, Taiwan, Thailand

Frontier Markets

Americas	Central & Eastern Europe & CIS	Africa	Middle East	Asia
Jamaica[3], Trinidad & Tobago[3]	Bulgaria, Croatia, Estonia, Lithuania, Kazakhstan, Romania, Serbia, Slovenia, Ukraine	Botswana[4], Ghana[4], Kenya, Mauritius, Nigeria, Tunisia	Lebanon, Bahrain, Kuwait, Oman, Qatar, United Arab Emirates, Saudi Arabia[5]	Sri Lanka, Vietnam

[1]The MSCI Argentina Index was reclassified from the MSCI Emerging Markets Index to the MSCI Frontier Markets Index at the end of May 2009 to coincide with the May 2009 Semi-Annual Index Review.

(continued)

Exhibit 7	Continued

5.2.1 *Fundamental Weighting in Multi-Market Indices*

Some index providers weight the securities within each country by market capitalization and then weight each country in the overall index in proportion to its relative GDP, effectively creating fundamental weighting in multi-market indices. GDP-weighted indices were some of the first fundamentally weighted indices created. Introduced in 1987 by MSCI to address the 60 percent weight of Japanese equities in the market-capitalization-weighted MSCI EAFE Index at the time, GDP-weighted indices reduced the allocation to Japanese equities by half.[9]

5.3 Sector Indices

Sector indices represent and track different economic sectors—such as consumer goods, energy, finance, health care, and technology—on either a national, regional, or global basis. Because different sectors of the economy behave differently over the course of the business cycle, some investors may seek to overweight or underweight their exposure to particular sectors.

Sector indices are organized as families; each index within the family represents an economic sector. Typically, the aggregation of a sector index family is equivalent to a broad market index. Economic sector classification can be applied on a global, regional, or country-specific basis, but no universally agreed upon sector classification method exists.

Sector indices play an important role in performance analysis because they provide a means to determine whether a portfolio manager is more successful at stock selection or sector allocation. Sector indices also serve as model portfolios for sector-specific ETFs and other investment products.

5.4 Style Indices

Style indices represent groups of securities classified according to market capitalization, value, growth, or a combination of these characteristics. They are intended to reflect the investing styles of certain investors, such as the growth investor, value investor, and small-cap investor.

5.4.1 *Market Capitalization*

Market-capitalization indices represent securities categorized according to the major capitalization categories: large cap, midcap, and small cap. With no universal definition of these categories, the indices differ on the distinctions between large cap and midcap and between midcap and small cap, as well as the minimum market-capitalization size required to be included in a small-cap index. Classification into categories can be

---

9 Steven A. Schoenfeld, *Active Index Investing* (Hoboken, NJ: John Wiley & Sons, 2004): 220.

based on absolute market capitalization (e.g., below €100 million) or relative market capitalization (e.g., the smallest 2,500 stocks).

5.4.2 *Value/Growth Classification*

Some indices represent categories of stocks based on their classifications as either value or growth stocks. Different index providers use different factors and valuation ratios (low price-to-book ratios, low price-to-earnings ratios, high dividend yields, etc.) to distinguish between value and growth equities.

5.4.3 *Market Capitalization and Value/Growth Classification*

Combining the three market-capitalization groups with value and growth classifications results in six basic style index categories:

- Large-Cap Value
- Mid-Cap Value
- Small-Cap Value
- Large-Cap Growth
- Mid-Cap Growth
- Small-Cap Growth

Because indices use different size and valuation classifications, the constituents of indices designed to represent a given style, such as small-cap value, may differ—sometimes substantially.

Because valuation ratios and market capitalizations change over time, stocks frequently migrate from one style index category to another on reconstitution dates. As a result, style indices generally have much higher turnover than do broad market indices.

FIXED-INCOME INDICES

6

A wide variety of fixed-income indices exists, but the nature of the fixed-income markets and fixed-income securities leads to some very important challenges to fixed-income index construction and replication. These challenges are the number of securities in the fixed-income universe, the availability of pricing data, and the liquidity of the securities.

6.1 Construction

The fixed-income universe includes securities issued by governments, government agencies, and corporations. Each of these entities may issue a variety of fixed-income securities with different characteristics. As a result, the number of fixed-income securities is many times larger than the number of equity securities. To represent a specific fixed-income market or segment, indices may include thousands of different securities. Over time, these fixed-income securities mature, and issuers offer new securities to meet their financing needs, leading to turnover in fixed-income indices.

Another challenge in index construction is that fixed-income markets are predominantly dealer markets. This means that firms (dealers) are assigned to specific securities and are responsible for creating liquid markets for those securities by purchasing and selling them from their inventory. In addition, many securities do not trade frequently and, as a result, are relatively illiquid. As a result, index providers must contact dealers to obtain current prices on constituent securities to update the index or they must estimate the prices of constituent securities using the prices of traded fixed-income securities with similar characteristics.

These challenges can result in indices with dissimilar numbers of bonds representing the same markets. As seen in Exhibit 8, the differences can be large. The large number of fixed-income securities—combined with the lack of liquidity of some securities—has made it more costly and difficult, compared with equity indices, for investors to replicate fixed-income indices and duplicate their performance.

Exhibit 8	Comparison of Minimum Issue Size and Bond Holdings by Index					
	Barclays Capital		**Markit iBoxx**		**Morningstar**	
Index	Min. (Thousands)	No. of Bonds	Min. (Thousands)	No. of Bonds	Min. (Thousands)	No. of Bonds
U.S. agency	250,000	988	500,000	435	1,000,000	193
U.S. corporate	250,000	3,134	500,000	1,694	500,000	1,862
U.K. corporate	250,000	916	100,000	713	225,000	303
Euro corporate	300,000	1,285	500,000	1,167	325,000	829

Source: Morningstar.

6.2 Types of Fixed-Income Indices

The wide variety of fixed-income securities, ranging from zero-coupon bonds to bonds with embedded options (i.e., callable or putable bonds), results in a number of different types of fixed-income indices. Similar to equities, fixed-income securities can be categorized according to the issuer's economic sector, the issuer's geographic region, or the economic development of the issuer's geographic region. Fixed-income securities can also be classified along the following dimensions:

■ type of issuer (government, government agency, corporation);

■ type of financing (general obligation, collateralized);

■ currency of payments;

■ maturity;

■ credit quality (investment grade, high yield, credit agency ratings); and

■ absence or presence of inflation protection.

Fixed-income indices are based on these various dimensions and can be categorized as follows:

■ aggregate or broad market indices;

■ market sector indices;

■ style indices;

■ economic sector indices; and

■ specialized indices such as high-yield, inflation-linked, and emerging market indices.

The first fixed-income index created, the Barclays Capital U.S. Aggregate Bond Index (formerly the Lehman Brothers Aggregate Bond Index), is an example of a single-country aggregate index. Designed to represent the broad market of U.S. fixed-income securities, it comprises more than 9,200 securities, including U.S. Treasury, government-related, corporate, mortgage-backed, asset-backed, and commercial mortgage-backed securities.

Aggregate indices can be subdivided by market sector (government, government agency, collateralized, corporate); style (maturity, credit quality); economic sector, or some other characteristic to create more narrowly defined indices. A common distinction reflected in indices is between investment grade (e.g., those with a Standard & Poor's credit rating of BBB– or better) and high-yield securities. Investment-grade indices are typically further subdivided by maturity (i.e., short, intermediate, or long) and by credit rating (e.g., AAA, BBB, etc.).[10] The wide variety of fixed-income indices reflects the partitioning of fixed-income securities on the basis of a variety of dimensions.

Exhibit 9 illustrates how the major types of fixed-income indices can be organized on the basis of various dimensions.

Exhibit 9	Dimensions of Fixed-Income Indices			
Market	Global			
	Regional			
	Country or Currency Zone			
Type	Corporate	Collateralized *Securitized* *Mortgage-backed*	Government agency	Government
Maturity	For example, 1–3, 3–5, 5–7, 7–10, 10+ years; short-term, medium-term, or long-term			
Credit quality	For example, AAA, AA, A, BBB, etc.; Aaa, Aa, A, Baa, etc.; investment grade, high yield			

All aggregate indices include a variety of market sectors and credit ratings. The breakdown of the Barclays Capital Global Aggregate Bond Index by market sectors and by credit rating is shown in Exhibit 10 and Exhibit 11, respectively.

Exhibit 10	Market Sector Breakdown of the Barclays Capital Global Aggregate Bond Index

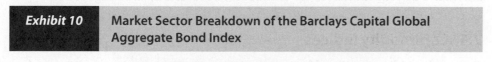

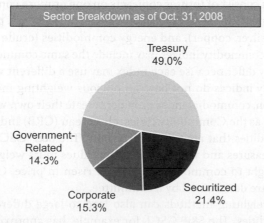

Sector Breakdown as of Oct. 31, 2008

- Treasury 49.0%
- Securitized 21.4%
- Corporate 15.3%
- Government-Related 14.3%

Source: Barclays Capital, "The Benchmark in Fixed Income: Barclays Capital Indices" (December 2008).

---

10 The credit rating categories vary based on the credit rating agency used by the index provider.

Exhibit 11	Credit Breakdown of the Barclays Capital Global Aggregate Bond Index

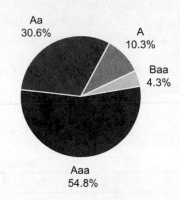

Quality Breakdown as of Oct. 31, 2008

Aa 30.6%

A 10.3%

Baa 4.3%

Aaa 54.8%

Source: Barclays Capital, "The Benchmark in Fixed Income: Barclays Capital Indices" (December 2008).

7   INDICES FOR ALTERNATIVE INVESTMENTS

Many investors seek to lower the risk or enhance the performance of their portfolios by investing in assets classes other than equities and fixed income. Interest in alternative assets and investment strategies has led to the creation of indices designed to represent broad classes of alternative investments. Three of the most widely followed alternative investment classes are commodities, real estate, and hedge funds.

7.1 Commodity Indices

Commodity indices consist of futures contracts on one or more commodities, such as agricultural products (rice, wheat, sugar), livestock (cattle, hogs), precious and common metals (gold, silver, copper), and energy commodities (crude oil, natural gas).

Although some commodity indices may include the same commodities, the returns of these indices may differ because each index may use a different weighting method. Because commodity indices do not have an obvious weighting mechanism, such as market capitalization, commodity index providers create their own weighting methods. Some indices, such as the Commodity Research Bureau (CRB) Index, contain a fixed number of commodities that are weighted equally. The S&P GSCI uses a combination of liquidity measures and world production values in its weighting scheme and allocates more weight to commodities that have risen in price. Other indices have fixed weights that are determined by a committee.

The different weighting methods can also lead to large differences in exposure to specific commodities. The S&P GSCI, for example, has approximately double the energy-sector weighting and one-third the agriculture sector weighting of the CRB Index. These differences result in indices with very different risk and return profiles. Unlike commodity indices, broad equity and fixed-income indices that target the same markets share similar risk and return profiles.

The performance of commodity indices can also be quite different from their underlying commodities because the indices consist of futures contracts on the commodities rather than the actual commodities. Index returns are affected by factors other than changes in the prices of the underlying commodities because futures contracts must be continually "rolled over" (i.e., replacing a contract nearing expiration with a new contract). Commodity index returns reflect the risk-free interest rate, the changes in future prices, and the roll yield. Therefore, a commodity index return can be quite different from the return based on changes in the prices of the underlying commodities.

7.2 Real Estate Investment Trust Indices

Real estate indices represent not only the market for real estate securities but also the market for real estate—a highly illiquid market and asset class with infrequent transactions and pricing information. Real estate indices can be categorized as appraisal indices, repeat sales indices, and real estate investment trust (REIT) indices.

REIT indices consist of shares of publicly traded REITs. REITS are public or private corporations organized specifically to invest in real estate, either through ownership of properties or investment in mortgages. Shares of public REITs are traded on the world's various stock exchanges and are a popular choice for investing in commercial real estate properties. Because REIT indices are based on publicly traded REITs with continuous market pricing, the value of REIT indices is calculated continuously.

The FTSE EPRA/NAREIT global family of REIT indices shown in Exhibit 12 seeks to represent trends in real estate stocks worldwide and includes representation from the European Real Estate Association (EPRA) and the National Association of Real Estate Investment Trusts (NAREIT).

| Exhibit 12 | The FTSE EPRA/NAREIT Global REIT Index Family |

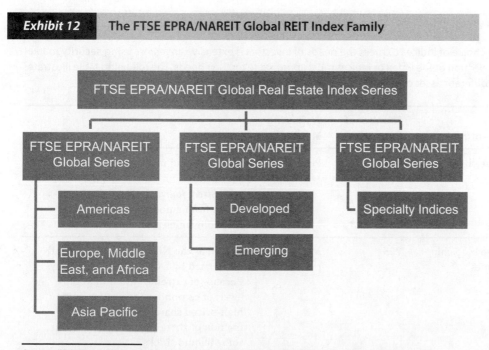

Source: FTSE International, "FTSE EPRA/NAREIT Global & Global Ex US Indices" Factsheet 2009). "FTSE®" is a trade mark of the London Stock Exchange Plc, "NAREIT®" is the a trade mark of the National Association of Real Estate Investment Trusts ("NAREIT") and "EPRA®" is a trade mark of the European Public Real Estate Association ("EPRA") and all are used by FTSE International Limited ("FTSE") under license.

7.3 Hedge Fund Indices

Hedge fund indices reflect the returns on hedge funds. **Hedge funds** are private investment vehicles that typically use leverage and long and short investment strategies.

A number of research organizations maintain databases of hedge fund returns and summarize these returns into indices. These database indices are designed to represent the performance of the hedge funds on a very broad global level (hedge funds in general) or the strategy level. Most of these indices are equal weighted and represent the performance of the hedge funds within a particular database.

Most research organizations rely on the voluntary cooperation of hedge funds to compile performance data. As unregulated entities, however, hedge funds are not required to report their performance to any party other than their investors. Therefore, each hedge fund decides to which database(s) it will report its performance. As a result, rather than index providers determining the constituents, the constituents determine the index.

Frequently, a hedge fund reports its performance to only one database. The result is little overlap of funds covered by the different indices. With little overlap between their constituents, different global hedge fund indices may reflect very different performance for the hedge fund industry over the same period of time.

Another consequence of the voluntary performance reporting is the potential for survivorship bias and, therefore, inaccurate performance representation. This means that hedge funds with poor performance may be less likely to report their performance to the database or may stop reporting to the database, so their returns may be excluded when measuring the return of the index. As a result, the index may not accurately reflect actual hedge fund performance so much as the performance of hedge funds that are performing well.

REPRESENTATIVE INDICES WORLDWIDE

As indicated in this reading, the choice of indices to meet the needs of investors is extensive. Investors using security market indices must be careful in their selection of the index or indices most appropriate for their needs. The following table illustrates the variety of indices reflecting different asset classes, markets, and weighting methods.

Index	Representing	Number of Securities	Weighting Method	Comments
Dow Jones Industrial Average	U.S. blue chip companies	30	Price	The oldest and most widely known U.S. equity index. *Wall Street Journal* editors choose 30 stocks from among large, mature blue-chip companies.
Nikkei Stock Average	Japanese blue chip companies	225	Modified price	Known as the Nikkei 225 and originally formulated by Dow Jones & Company. Because of extreme variation in price levels of component securities, some high-priced shares are weighted as a fraction of share price. Index contains some illiquid stocks.
TOPIX	All companies listed on the Tokyo Stock Exchange First Section	Varies	Float-adjusted market cap	Represents about 93 percent of the market value of all Japanese equities. Contains a large number of very small, illiquid stocks, making exact replication difficult.

Index	Representing	Number of Securities	Weighting Method	Comments
MSCI All Country World Index	Stocks of 23 developed and 22 emerging markets	Varies	Free-float-adjusted market cap	Composed of companies representative of the market structure of developed and emerging market countries in the Americas, Europe/Middle East, and Asia/Pacific regions. Price return and total return versions available in both USD and local currencies.
S&P Developed Ex-U.S. BMI Energy Sector Index	Energy sector of developed global markets outside the United States	Varies	Float-adjusted market cap	Serves as a model portfolio for the SPDR® S&P Energy Sector Exchange-Traded Fund (ETF).
Barclays Capital Global Aggregate Bond Index	Investment-grade bonds in the North American, European, and Asian markets	Varies	Market cap	Formerly known as Lehman Brothers Global Aggregate Bond Index.
Markit iBoxx Euro High-Yield Bond Indices	Sub-investment-grade euro-denominated corporate bonds	Varies	Market cap and variations	Rebalanced monthly. Represents tradable part of market. Price and total return versions available with such analytical values as yield, duration, modified duration, and convexity. Provides platform for research and structured products.
FTSE EPRA/NAREIT Global Real Estate Index	Real estate securities in the North American, European, and Asian markets	335	Float-adjusted market cap	The stocks of REITs that constitute the index trade on public stock exchanges and may be constituents of equity market indices.
HFRX Global Hedge Fund Index	Overall composition of the HFR database	Varies	Asset weighted	Comprises all eligible hedge fund strategies. Examples include convertible arbitrage, distressed securities, market neutral, event driven, macro, and relative value arbitrage. Constituent strategies are asset weighted on the basis of asset distribution within the hedge fund industry.
HFRX Equal Weighted Strategies EUR Index	Overall composition of the HFR database	Varies	Equal weighted	Denominated in euros and is constructed from the same strategies as the HFRX Global Hedge Fund Index.
Morningstar Style Indices	U.S. stocks classified by market cap and value/growth orientation	Varies	Float-adjusted market cap	The nine indices defined by combinations of market cap (large, mid, and small) and value/growth orientation (value, core, growth) have mutually exclusive constituents and are exhaustive with respect to the Morningstar U.S. Market Index. Each is a model portfolio for one of the iShares Morningstar ETFs.

SUMMARY

This reading explains and illustrates the construction, management, and uses of security market indices. It also discusses various types of indices. Security market indices are invaluable tools for investors, who can select from among thousands of indices representing a variety of security markets, market segments, and asset classes. These indices range from those representing the global market for major asset classes to those representing alternative investments in specific geographic markets. To benefit from the use of security market indices, investors must understand their construction and determine whether the selected index is appropriate for their purposes. Frequently, an index that is well suited for one purpose may not be well suited for other purposes. Users of indices must be familiar with how various indices are constructed in order to select the index or indices most appropriate for their needs.

Among the key points made in this reading are the following:

- Security market indices are intended to measure the values of different target markets (security markets, market segments, or asset classes).

- The constituent securities selected for inclusion in the security market index are intended to represent the target market.

- A price return index reflects only the prices of the constituent securities.

- A total return index reflects not only the prices of the constituent securities but also the reinvestment of all income received since the inception of the index.

- Methods used to weight the constituents of an index range from the very simple, such as price and equal weightings, to the more complex, such as market-capitalization and fundamental weightings.

- Choices in index construction—in particular, the choice of weighting method—affect index valuation and returns.

- Index management includes 1) periodic rebalancing to ensure that the index maintains appropriate weightings and 2) reconstitution to ensure the index represents the desired target market.

- Rebalancing and reconstitution create turnover in an index. Reconstitution can dramatically affect prices of current and prospective constituents.

- Indices serve a variety of purposes. They gauge market sentiment and serve as benchmarks for actively managed portfolios. They act as proxies for measuring systematic risk and risk-adjusted performance. They also serve as proxies for asset classes in asset allocation models and as model portfolios for investment products.

- Investors can choose from security market indices representing various asset classes, including equity, fixed-income, commodity, real estate, and hedge fund indices.

- Within most asset classes, index providers offer a wide variety of indices, ranging from broad market indices to highly specialized indices based on the issuer's geographic region, economic development group, or economic sector or other factors.

- Proper use of security market indices depends on understanding their construction and management.

PRACTICE PROBLEMS FOR READING 47

1. A security market index represents the:

    A. risk of a security market.

    B. security market as a whole.

    C. security market, market segment, or asset class.

2. Security market indices are:

    A. constructed and managed like a portfolio of securities.

    B. simple interchangeable tools for measuring the returns of different asset classes.

    C. valued on a regular basis using the actual market prices of the constituent securities.

3. When creating a security market index, an index provider must first determine the:

    A. target market.

    B. appropriate weighting method.

    C. number of constituent securities.

4. One month after inception, the price return version and total return version of a single index (consisting of identical securities and weights) will be equal if:

    A. market prices have not changed.

    B. capital gains are offset by capital losses.

    C. the securities do not pay dividends or interest.

5. The values of a price return index and a total return index consisting of identical equal-weighted dividend-paying equities will be equal:

    A. only at inception.

    B. at inception and on rebalancing dates.

    C. at inception and on reconstitution dates.

6. An analyst gathers the following information for an equal-weighted index comprised of assets Able, Baker, and Charlie:

Security	Beginning of Period Price (€)	End of Period Price (€)	Total Dividends (€)
Able	10.00	12.00	0.75
Baker	20.00	19.00	1.00
Charlie	30.00	30.00	2.00

    The price return of the index is:

    A. 1.7%.

    B. 5.0%.

    C. 11.4%.

7. An analyst gathers the following information for an equal-weighted index comprised of assets Able, Baker, and Charlie:

Security	Beginning of Period Price (€)	End of Period Price (€)	Total Dividends (€)
Able	10.00	12.00	0.75
Baker	20.00	19.00	1.00
Charlie	30.00	30.00	2.00

The total return of the index is:

A. 5.0%.

B. 7.9%.

C. 11.4%.

8. An analyst gathers the following information for a price-weighted index comprised of securities ABC, DEF, and GHI:

Security	Beginning of Period Price (£)	End of Period Price (£)	Total Dividends (£)
ABC	25.00	27.00	1.00
DEF	35.00	25.00	1.50
GHI	15.00	16.00	1.00

The price return of the index is:

A. −4.6%.

B. −9.3%.

C. −13.9%.

9. An analyst gathers the following information for a market-capitalization-weighted index comprised of securities MNO, QRS, and XYZ:

Security	Beginning of Period Price (¥)	End of Period Price (¥)	Dividends per Share (¥)	Shares Outstanding
MNO	2,500	2,700	100	5,000
QRS	3,500	2,500	150	7,500
XYZ	1,500	1,600	100	10,000

The price return of the index is:

A. −9.33%.

B. −10.23%.

C. −13.90%.

10. An analyst gathers the following information for a market-capitalization-weighted index comprised of securities MNO, QRS, and XYZ:

Security	Beginning of Period Price (¥)	End of Period Price (¥)	Dividends per Share (¥)	Shares Outstanding
MNO	2,500	2,700	100	5,000
QRS	3,500	2,500	150	7,500
XYZ	1,500	1,600	100	10,000

The total return of the index is:

A. 1.04%.

B. −5.35%.

C. −10.23%.

11. When creating a security market index, the target market:

A. determines the investment universe.

B. is usually a broadly defined asset class.

C. determines the number of securities to be included in the index.

12. An analyst gathers the following data for a price-weighted index:

	Beginning of Period		End of Period	
Security	Price (€)	Shares	Price (€)	Shares
A	20.00	300	22.00	300
B	50.00	300	48.00	300
C	26.00	2,000	30.00	2,000

The price return of the index over the period is:

A. 4.2%.

B. 7.1%.

C. 21.4%.

13. An analyst gathers the following data for a value-weighted index:

	Beginning of Period		End of Period	
Security	Price (£)	Shares	Price (£)	Shares
A	20.00	300	22.00	300
B	50.00	300	48.00	300
C	26.00	2,000	30.00	2,000

The return on the value-weighted index over the period is:

A. 7.1%.

B. 11.0%.

C. 21.4%.

14. An analyst gathers the following data for an equally weighted index:

	Beginning of Period		End of Period	
Security	Price (¥)	Shares	Price (¥)	Shares
A	20.00	300	22.00	300
B	50.00	300	48.00	300
C	26.00	2,000	30.00	2,000

The return on the index over the period is:

A. 4.2%.

B. 6.8%.

C. 7.1%.

15. Which of the following index weighting methods requires an adjustment to the divisor after a stock split?
    - **A.** Price weighting.
    - **B.** Fundamental weighting.
    - **C.** Market-capitalization weighting.

16. If the price return of an equal-weighted index exceeds that of a market-capitalization-weighted index comprised of the same securities, the *most likely* explanation is:
    - **A.** stock splits.
    - **B.** dividend distributions.
    - **C.** outperformance of small-market-capitalization stocks.

17. A float-adjusted market-capitalization-weighted index weights each of its constituent securities by its price and:
    - **A.** its trading volume.
    - **B.** the number of its shares outstanding.
    - **C.** the number of its shares available to the investing public.

18. Which of the following index weighting methods is most likely subject to a value tilt?
    - **A.** Equal weighting.
    - **B.** Fundamental weighting.
    - **C.** Market-capitalization weighting.

19. Rebalancing an index is the process of periodically adjusting the constituent:
    - **A.** securities' weights to optimize investment performance.
    - **B.** securities to maintain consistency with the target market.
    - **C.** securities' weights to maintain consistency with the index's weighting method.

20. Which of the following index weighting methods requires the most frequent rebalancing?
    - **A.** Price weighting.
    - **B.** Equal weighting.
    - **C.** Market-capitalization weighting.

21. Reconstitution of a security market index reduces:
    - **A.** portfolio turnover.
    - **B.** the need for rebalancing.
    - **C.** the likelihood that the index includes securities that are not representative of the target market.

22. Security market indices are used as:
    - **A.** measures of investment returns.
    - **B.** proxies to measure unsystematic risk.
    - **C.** proxies for specific asset classes in asset allocation models.

23. Uses of market indices do not include serving as a:
    - **A.** measure of systematic risk.
    - **B.** basis for new investment products.
    - **C.** benchmark for evaluating portfolio performance.

24. Which of the following statements regarding sector indices is *most* accurate? Sector indices:

    A. track different economic sectors and cannot be aggregated to represent the equivalent of a broad market index.

    B. provide a means to determine whether an active investment manager is more successful at stock selection or sector allocation.

    C. apply a universally agreed upon sector classification system to identify the constituent securities of specific economic sectors, such as consumer goods, energy, finance, health care.

25. Which of the following is an example of a style index? An index based on:

    A. geography.

    B. economic sector.

    C. market capitalization.

26. Which of the following statements regarding fixed-income indices is *most* accurate?

    A. Liquidity issues make it difficult for investors to easily replicate fixed-income indices.

    B. Rebalancing and reconstitution are the only sources of turnover in fixed-income indices.

    C. Fixed-income indices representing the same target market hold similar numbers of bonds.

27. An aggregate fixed-income index:

    A. comprises corporate and asset-backed securities.

    B. represents the market of government-issued securities.

    C. can be subdivided by market or economic sector to create more narrowly defined indices.

28. Fixed-income indices are *least likely* constructed on the basis of:

    A. maturity.

    B. type of issuer.

    C. coupon frequency.

29. Commodity index values are based on:

    A. futures contract prices.

    B. the market price of the specific commodity.

    C. the average market price of a basket of similar commodities.

30. Which of the following statements is *most* accurate?

    A. Commodity indices all share similar weighting methods.

    B. Commodity indices containing the same underlying commodities offer similar returns.

    C. The performance of commodity indices can be quite different from that of the underlying commodities.

31. Which of the following is *not* a real estate index category?

    A. Appraisal index.

    B. Initial sales index.

    C. Repeat sales index.

32. A unique feature of hedge fund indices is that they:

   A. are frequently equal weighted.

   B. are determined by the constituents of the index.

   C. reflect the value of private rather than public investments.

33. The returns of hedge fund indices are *most likely*:

   A. biased upward.

   B. biased downward.

   C. similar across different index providers.

34. In comparison to equity indices, the constituent securities of fixed-income indices are:

   A. more liquid.

   B. easier to price.

   C. drawn from a larger investment universe.

SOLUTIONS FOR READING 47

1. C is correct. A security market index represents the value of a given security market, market segment, or asset class.

2. A is correct. Security market indices are constructed and managed like a portfolio of securities.

3. A is correct. The first decision is identifying the target market that the index is intended to represent because the target market determines the investment universe and the securities available for inclusion in the index.

4. C is correct. The difference between a price return index and a total return index consisting of identical securities and weights is the income generated over time by the underlying securities. If the securities in the index do not generate income, both indices will be identical in value.

5. A is correct. At inception, the values of the price return and total return versions of an index are equal.

6. B is correct. The price return is the sum of the weighted returns of each security. The return of Able is 20 percent $[(12 - 10)/10]$; of Baker is -5 percent $[(19 - 20)/20]$; and of Charlie is 0 percent $[(30 - 30)/30]$. The price return index assigns a weight of 1/3 to each asset; therefore, the price return is $1/3 \times [20\% + (-5\%) + 0\%] = 5\%$.

7. C is correct. The total return of an index is calculated on the basis of the change in price of the underlying securities plus the sum of income received or the sum of the weighted total returns of each security. The total return of Able is 27.5 percent; of Baker is 0 percent; and of Charlie is 6.7 percent:

    Able: $(12 - 10 + 0.75)/10 = 27.5\%$

    Baker: $(19 - 20 + 1)/20 = 0\%$

    Charlie: $(30 - 30 + 2)/30 = 6.7\%$

    An equal-weighted index applies the same weight (1/3) to each security's return; therefore, the total return $= 1/3 \times (27.5\% + 0\% + 6.7\%) = 11.4\%$.

8. B is correct. The price return of the price-weighted index is the percentage change in price of the index: $(68 - 75)/75 = -9.33\%$.

Security	Beginning of Period Price (£)	End of Period Price (£)
ABC	25.00	27.00
DEF	35.00	25.00
GHI	15.00	16.00
TOTAL	75.00	68.00

9. B is correct. The price return of the index is (48,250,000 − 53,750,000)/53,750,000 = −10.23%.

Security	Beginning of Period Price (¥)	Shares Outstanding	Beginning of Period Value (¥)	End of Period Price (¥)	End of Period Value (¥)
MNO	2,500	5,000	12,500,000	2,700	13,500,000
QRS	3,500	7,500	26,250,000	2,500	18,750,000
XYZ	1,500	10,000	15,000,000	1,600	16,000,000
Total			53,750,000		48,250,000

10. B is correct. The total return of the market-capitalization-weighted index is calculated below:

Security	Beginning of Period Value (¥)	End of Period Value (¥)	Total Dividends (¥)	Total Return (%)
MNO	12,500,000	13,500,000	500,000	12.00
QRS	26,250,000	18,750,000	1,125,000	−24.29
XYZ	15,000,000	16,000,000	1,000,000	13.33
Total	53,750,000	48,250,000	2,625,000	−5.35

11. A is correct. The target market determines the investment universe and the securities available for inclusion in the index.

12. A is correct. The sum of prices at the beginning of the period is 96; the sum at the end of the period is 100. Regardless of the divisor, the price return is 100/96 − 1 = 0.042 or 4.2 percent.

13. B is correct. It is the percentage change in the market value over the period:

    Market value at beginning of period: (20 × 300) + (50 × 300) + (26 × 2,000) = 73,000

    Market value at end of period: (22 × 300) + (48 × 300) + (30 × 2,000) = 81,000

    Percentage change is 81,000/73,000 − 1 = 0.1096 or 11.0 percent with rounding.

14. C is correct. With an equal-weighted index, the same amount is invested in each security. Assuming $1,000 is invested in each of the three stocks, the index value is $3,000 at the beginning of the period and the following number of shares is purchased for each stock:

    Security A: 50 shares

    Security B: 20 shares

    Security C: 38.46 shares.

    Using the prices at the beginning of the period for each security, the index value at the end of the period is $3,213.8: ($22 × 50) + ($48 × 20) + ($30 × 38.46). The price return is $3,213.8/$3,000 − 1 = 7.1%.

15. A is correct. In the price weighting method, the divisor must be adjusted so the index value immediately after the split is the same as the index value immediately prior to the split.

16. C is correct. The main source of return differences arises from outperformance of small-cap securities or underperformance of large-cap securities. In an

equal-weighted index, securities that constitute the largest fraction of the market are underrepresented and securities that constitute only a small fraction of the market are overrepresented. Thus, higher equal-weighted index returns will occur if the smaller-cap equities outperform the larger-cap equities.

17. C is correct. "Float" is the number of shares available for public trading.

18. B is correct. Fundamental weighting leads to indices that have a value tilt.

19. C is correct. Rebalancing refers to adjusting the weights of constituent securities in an index to maintain consistency with the index's weighting method.

20. B is correct. Changing market prices will cause weights that were initially equal to become unequal, thus requiring rebalancing.

21. C is correct. Reconstitution is the process by which index providers review the constituent securities, re-apply the initial criteria for inclusion in the index, and select which securities to retain, remove, or add. Constituent securities that no longer meet the criteria are replaced with securities that do. Thus, reconstitution reduces the likelihood that the index includes securities that are not representative of the target market.

22. C is correct. Security market indices play a critical role as proxies for asset classes in asset allocation models.

23. A is correct. Security market indices are used as proxies for measuring market or systematic risk, not as measures of systematic risk.

24. B is correct. Sector indices provide a means to determine whether a portfolio manager is more successful at stock selection or sector allocation.

25. C is correct. Style indices represent groups of securities classified according to market capitalization, value, growth, or a combination of these characteristics.

26. A is correct. The large number of fixed-income securities—combined with the lack of liquidity of some securities—makes it costly and difficult for investors to replicate fixed-income indices.

27. C is correct. An aggregate fixed-income index can be subdivided by market sector (government, government agency, collateralized, corporate), style (maturity, credit quality), economic sector, or some other characteristic to create more narrowly defined indices.

28. C is correct. Coupon frequency is not a dimension on which fixed-income indices are based.

29. A is correct. Commodity indices consist of futures contracts on one or more commodities.

30. C is correct. The performance of commodity indices can be quite different from that of the underlying commodities because the indices consist of futures contracts on the commodities rather than the actual commodities.

31. B is correct. It is not a real estate index category.

32. B is correct. Hedge funds are not required to report their performance to any party other than their investors. Therefore, each hedge fund decides to which database(s) it will report its performance. Thus, for a hedge fund index, constituents determine the index rather than index providers determining the constituents.

33. A is correct. Voluntary performance reporting may lead to survivorship bias, and poorer performing hedge funds will be less likely to report their performance.

34. C is correct. The fixed-income market has more issuers and securities than the equity market.

48

Market Efficiency

by W. Sean Cleary, CFA, Howard J. Atkinson, CFA, and Pamela Peterson Drake, CFA

LEARNING OUTCOMES

Mastery	The candidate should be able to:
☐	**a** describe market efficiency and related concepts, including their importance to investment practitioners;
☐	**b** distinguish between market value and intrinsic value;
☐	**c** explain factors that affect a market's efficiency;
☐	**d** contrast weak-form, semi-strong-form, and strong-form market efficiency;
☐	**e** explain the implications of each form of market efficiency for fundamental analysis, technical analysis, and the choice between active and passive portfolio management;
☐	**f** describe selected market anomalies;
☐	**g** contrast the behavioral finance view of investor behavior to that of traditional finance.

INTRODUCTION

1

Market efficiency concerns the extent to which market prices incorporate available information. If market prices do not fully incorporate information, then opportunities may exist to make a profit from the gathering and processing of information. The subject of market efficiency is, therefore, of great interest to investment managers, as illustrated in Example 1.

Example 1

Market Efficiency and Active Manager Selection

The chief investment officer (CIO) of a major university endowment fund has listed eight steps in the active manager selection process that can be applied both to traditional investments (e.g., common equity and fixed-income securities) and to alternative investments (e.g., private equity, hedge funds, and real assets). The first step specified is the evaluation of market opportunity:

What is the opportunity and why is it there? To answer this question we start by studying capital markets and the types of managers operating within those markets. We identify market inefficiencies and try to understand their causes, such as regulatory structures or behavioral biases. We can rule out many broad groups of managers and strategies by simply determining that the degree of market inefficiency necessary to support a strategy is implausible. Importantly, we consider the past history of active returns meaningless unless we understand why markets will allow those active returns to continue into the future.[1]

The CIO's description underscores the importance of not assuming that past active returns that might be found in a historical dataset will repeat themselves in the future. **Active returns** refer to returns earned by strategies that do *not* assume that all information is fully reflected in market prices.

Governments and market regulators also care about the extent to which market prices incorporate information. Efficient markets imply informative prices—prices that accurately reflect available information about fundamental values. In market-based economies, market prices help determine which companies (and which projects) obtain capital. If these prices do not efficiently incorporate information about a company's prospects, then it is possible that funds will be misdirected. By contrast, prices that are informative help direct scarce resources and funds available for investment to their highest-valued uses.[2] Informative prices thus promote economic growth. The efficiency of a country's capital markets (in which businesses raise financing) is an important characteristic of a well-functioning financial system.

The remainder of this reading is organized as follows. Section 2 provides specifics on how the efficiency of an asset market is described and discusses the factors affecting (i.e., contributing to and impeding) market efficiency. Section 3 presents an influential three-way classification of the efficiency of security markets and discusses its implications for fundamental analysis, technical analysis, and portfolio management. Section 4 presents several market anomalies (apparent market inefficiencies that have received enough attention to be individually identified and named) and describes how these anomalies relate to investment strategies. Section 5 introduces behavioral finance and how that field of study relates to market efficiency. A summary concludes the reading.

2

THE CONCEPT OF MARKET EFFICIENCY

2.1 The Description of Efficient Markets

An **informationally efficient market** (an **efficient market**) is a market in which asset prices reflect new information quickly and rationally. An efficient market is thus a market in which asset prices reflect all past and present information.[3]

---

1 The CIO is Christopher J. Brightman, CFA, of the University of Virginia Investment Management Company, as reported in Yau, Schneeweis, Robinson, and Weiss (2007, pp. 481–482).
2 This concept is known as allocative efficiency.
3 This definition is convenient for making several instructional points. The definition that most simply explains the sense of the word *efficient* in this context can be found in Fama (1976): "An efficient capital market is a market that is efficient in processing information" (p. 134).

In this section we expand on this definition by clarifying the time frame required for an asset's price to incorporate information as well as describing the elements of information releases assumed under market efficiency. We discuss the difference between market value and intrinsic value and illustrate how inefficiencies or discrepancies between these values can provide profitable opportunities for active investment. As financial markets are generally not considered being either completely efficient or inefficient, but rather falling within a range between the two extremes, we describe a number of factors that contribute to and impede the degree of efficiency of a financial market. Finally, we conclude our overview of market efficiency by illustrating how the costs incurred by traders in identifying and exploiting possible market inefficiencies affect how we interpret market efficiency.

Investment managers and analysts, as noted, are interested in market efficiency because the extent to which a market is efficient affects how many profitable trading opportunities (market inefficiencies) exist. Consistent, superior, risk-adjusted returns (net of all expenses) are not achievable in an efficient market.[4] In a highly efficient market, a **passive investment** strategy (i.e., buying and holding a broad market portfolio) that does not seek superior risk-adjusted returns is preferred to an **active investment** strategy because of lower costs (for example, transaction and information-seeking costs). By contrast, in a very inefficient market, opportunities may exist for an active investment strategy to achieve superior risk-adjusted returns (net of all expenses in executing the strategy) as compared with a passive investment strategy. In inefficient markets, an active investment strategy may outperform a passive investment strategy on a risk-adjusted basis. Understanding the characteristics of an efficient market and being able to evaluate the efficiency of a particular market are important topics for investment analysts and portfolio managers.

An efficient market is a market in which asset prices reflect information quickly. But what is the time frame of "quickly"? Trades are the mechanism by which information can be incorporated into asset transaction prices. The time needed to execute trades to exploit an inefficiency may provide a baseline for judging speed of adjustment.[5] The time frame for an asset's price to incorporate information must be at least as long as the shortest time a trader needs to execute a transaction in the asset. In certain markets, such as foreign exchange and developed equity markets, market efficiency relative to certain types of information has been studied using time frames as short as one minute or less. If the time frame of price adjustment allows many traders to earn profits with little risk, then the market is relatively inefficient. These considerations lead to the observation that market efficiency can be viewed as falling on a continuum.

Finally, an important point is that in an efficient market, prices should be expected to react only to the elements of information releases that are not anticipated fully by investors—that is, to the "unexpected" or "surprise" element of such releases. Investors process the unexpected information and revise expectations (for example, about an asset's future cash flows, risk, or required rate of return) accordingly. The revised expectations enter or get incorporated in the asset price through trades in the asset. Market participants who process the news and believe that at the current market price an asset does not offer sufficient compensation for its perceived risk will tend to sell it or even sell it short. Market participants with opposite views should be buyers. In this way the market establishes the price that balances the various opinions after expectations are revised.

---

4 The technical term for *superior* in this context is *positive abnormal* in the sense of higher than expected given the asset's risk (as measured, according to capital market theory, by the asset's contribution to the risk of a well-diversified portfolio).

5 Although the original theory of market efficiency does not quantify this speed, the basic idea is that it is sufficiently swift to make it impossible to consistently earn abnormal profits. Chordia, Roll, and Subrahmanyam (2005) suggest that the adjustment to information on the New York Stock Exchange (NYSE) is between 5 and 60 minutes.

Example 2

Price Reaction to the Default on a Bond Issue

Suppose that a speculative-grade bond issuer announces, just before bond markets open, that it will default on an upcoming interest payment. In the announcement, the issuer confirms various reports made in the financial media in the period leading up to the announcement. Prior to the issuer's announcement, the financial news media reported the following: 1) suppliers of the company were making deliveries only for cash payment, reducing the company's liquidity; 2) the issuer's financial condition had probably deteriorated to the point that it lacked the cash to meet an upcoming interest payment; and 3) although public capital markets were closed to the company, it was negotiating with a bank for a private loan that would permit it to meet its interest payment and continue operations for at least nine months. If the issuer defaults on the bond, the consensus opinion of analysts is that bondholders will recover approximately $0.36 to $0.38 per dollar face value.

1. If the market for the bond is highly efficient, the bond's market price is *most likely* to fully reflect the bond's value after default:

   A. in the period leading up to the announcement.

   B. in the first trade prices after the market opens on the announcement day.

   C. when the issuer actually misses the payment on the interest payment date.

2. If the market for the bond is highly efficient, the piece of information that bond investors *most likely* focused on in the issuer's announcement was that the issuer:

   A. had failed in its negotiations for a bank loan.

   B. lacked the cash to meet the upcoming interest payment.

   C. had been required to make cash payments for supplier deliveries.

Solution to 1:

B is correct. The announcement removed any uncertainty about default. In the period leading up to the announcement, the bond's market price incorporated a probability of default but the price would not have fully reflected the bond's value after default. The possibility that a bank loan might permit the company to avoid default was not eliminated until the announcement.

Solution to 2:

A is correct. The failure of the loan negotiations first becomes known in this announcement. The failure implies default.

2.2 Market Value versus Intrinsic Value

Market value is the price at which an asset can currently be bought or sold. **Intrinsic value** (sometimes called **fundamental value**) is, broadly speaking, the value that would be placed on it by investors if they had a complete understanding of the asset's investment characteristics.[6] For a bond, for example, such information would include its interest (coupon) rate, principal value, the timing of its interest and principal

---

6 Intrinsic value is often defined as the present value of all expected future cash flows of the asset.

payments, the other terms of the bond contract (indenture), a precise understanding of its default risk, the liquidity of its market, and other issue-specific items. In addition, market variables such as the term structure of interest rates and the size of various market premiums applying to the issue (for default risk, etc.) would enter into a discounted cash flow estimate of the bond's intrinsic value (discounted cash flow models are often used for such estimates). The word *estimate* is used because in practice, intrinsic value can be estimated but is not known for certain.

If investors believe a market is highly *efficient*, they will usually accept market prices as accurately reflecting intrinsic values. Discrepancies between market price and intrinsic value are the basis for profitable active investment. Active investors seek to own assets selling below perceived intrinsic value in the marketplace and to sell or sell short assets selling above perceived intrinsic value.

If investors believe an asset market is relatively *inefficient*, they may try to develop an independent estimate of intrinsic value. The challenge for investors and analysts is estimating an asset's intrinsic value. Numerous theories and models, including the dividend discount model, can be used to estimate an asset's intrinsic value, but they all require some form of judgment regarding the size, timing, and riskiness of the future cash flows associated with the asset. The more complex an asset's future cash flows, the more difficult it is to estimate its intrinsic value. These complexities and the estimates of an asset's market value are reflected in the market through the buying and selling of assets. The market value of an asset represents the intersection of supply and demand—the point that is low enough to induce at least one investor to buy while being high enough to induce at least one investor to sell. Because information relevant to valuation flows continually to investors, estimates of intrinsic value change, and hence, market values change.

Example 3

Intrinsic Value

1. An analyst estimates that a security's intrinsic value is lower than its market value. The security appears to be:
   A. undervalued.
   B. fairly valued.
   C. overvalued.

2. A market in which assets' market values are, on average, equal to or nearly equal to intrinsic values is *best described* as a market that is attractive for:
   A. active investment.
   B. passive investment.
   C. both active and passive investment.

3. Suppose that the future cash flows of an asset are accurately estimated. The asset trades in a market that you believe is highly efficient based on most evidence. But your intrinsic value estimate exceeds market value by a moderate amount. The *most likely* conclusion is that you have:
   A. overestimated the asset's risk.
   B. underestimated the asset's risk.
   C. identified a market inefficiency.

Solution to 1:

C is correct. The market is valuing the asset at more than its true worth.

Solution to 2:

B is correct because an active investment is not expected to earn superior risk-adjusted returns. The additional costs of active investment are not justified in such a market.

Solution to 3:

B is correct. If risk is underestimated, the discount rate being applied to find the present value of the expected cash flows (estimated intrinsic value) will be too low and the intrinsic value estimate will be too high.

2.3 Factors Contributing to and Impeding a Market's Efficiency

For markets to be efficient, prices should adjust quickly and rationally to the release of new information. In other words, prices of assets in an efficient market should "fully reflect" all information. Financial markets, however, are generally not classified at the two extremes as either completely inefficient or completely efficient but, rather, as exhibiting various degrees of efficiency. In other words, market efficiency should be viewed as falling on a continuum between extremes of completely efficient, at one end, and completely inefficient, at the other. Asset prices in a highly efficient market, by definition, reflect information more quickly and more accurately than in a less-efficient market. These degrees of efficiency also vary through time, across geographical markets, and by type of market. A number of factors contribute to and impede the degree of efficiency in a financial market.

2.3.1 *Market Participants*

One of the most critical factors contributing to the degree of efficiency in a market is the number of market participants. Consider the following example that illustrates the relationship between the number of market participants and market efficiency.

Example 4

Illustration of Market Efficiency

Assume that the shares of a small market capitalization (cap) company trade on a public stock exchange. Because of its size, it is not considered "blue-chip" and not many professional investors follow the activities of the company.[7] A small-cap fund analyst reports that the most recent annual operating performance of the company has been surprisingly good, considering the recent slump in its industry. The company's share price, however, has been slow to react to the positive financial results because the company is not being recommended by the majority of research analysts. This mispricing implies that the market for this company's shares is less than fully efficient. The small-cap fund analyst recognizes the opportunity and immediately recommends the purchase of the company's shares. The share price gradually increases as more investors purchase the shares once the news of the mispricing spreads through the market. As a result, it takes a few days for the share price to fully reflect the information.

Six months later, the company reports another solid set of interim financial results. But because the previous mispricing and subsequent profit opportunities

---

7 A "blue-chip" share is one from a well-recognized company that is considered to be high quality but low risk. This term generally refers to a company that has a long history of earnings and paying dividends.

have become known in the market, the number of analysts following the company's shares has increased substantially. As a result, as soon as unexpected information about the positive interim results are released to the public, a large number of buy orders quickly drive up the stock price, thereby making the market for these shares more efficient than before.

A large number of investors (individual and institutional) follow the major financial markets closely on a daily basis, and if mispricings exist in these markets, as illustrated by the example, investors will act so that these mispricings disappear quickly. Besides the number of investors, the number of financial analysts who follow or analyze a security or asset should be positively related to market efficiency. The number of market participants and resulting trading activity can vary significantly through time. A lack of trading activity can cause or accentuate other market imperfections that impede market efficiency. In fact, in many of these markets, such as China, trading in many of the listed stocks is restricted for foreigners. By nature, this limitation reduces the number of market participants, restricts the potential for trading activity, and hence reduces market efficiency.

Example 5

Factors Affecting Market Efficiency

The expected effect on market efficiency of opening a securities market to trading by foreigners would be to:

A. decrease market efficiency.

B. leave market efficiency unchanged.

C. increase market efficiency.

Solution:

C is correct. The opening of markets as described should increase market efficiency by increasing the number of market participants.

2.3.2 *Information Availability and Financial Disclosure*

Information availability (e.g., an active financial news media) and financial disclosure should promote market efficiency. Information regarding trading activity and traded companies in such markets as the New York Stock Exchange, the London Stock Exchange, and the Tokyo Stock Exchange is readily available. Many investors and analysts participate in these markets, and analyst coverage of listed companies is typically substantial. As a result, these markets are quite efficient. In contrast, trading activity and material information availability may be lacking in smaller securities markets, such as those operating in some emerging markets.

Similarly, significant differences may exist in the efficiency of different types of markets. For example, many securities trade primarily or exclusively in dealer or over-the-counter (OTC) markets, including bonds, money market instruments, currencies, mortgage-backed securities, swaps, and forward contracts. The information provided by the dealers that serve as market makers for these markets can vary significantly in quality and quantity, both through time and across different product markets.

Treating all market participants fairly is critical for the integrity of the market and explains why regulators place such an emphasis on "fair, orderly, and efficient markets."[8] A key element of this fairness is that all investors have access to the information necessary to value securities that trade in the market. Rules and regulations that promote fairness and efficiency in a market include those pertaining to the disclosure of information and illegal insider trading.

For example, U.S. Securities and Exchange Commission's (SEC's) Regulation FD (Fair Disclosure) requires that if security issuers provide nonpublic information to some market professionals or investors, they must also disclose this information to the public.[9] This requirement helps provide equal and fair opportunities, which is important in encouraging participation in the market. A related issue deals with illegal insider trading. The SEC's rules, along with court cases, define illegal insider trading as trading in securities by market participants who are considered insiders "while in possession of material, nonpublic information about the security."[10,11] Although these rules cannot guarantee that some participants will not have an advantage over others and that insiders will not trade on the basis of inside information, the civil and criminal penalties associated with breaking these rules are intended to discourage illegal insider trading and promote fairness.

2.3.3 Limits to Trading

Arbitrage is a set of transactions that produces riskless profits. Arbitrageurs are traders who engage in such trades to benefit from pricing discrepancies (inefficiencies) in markets. Such trading activity contributes to market efficiency. For example, if an asset is traded in two markets but at different prices, the actions of buying the asset in the market in which it is underpriced and selling the asset in the market in which it is overpriced will eventually bring these two prices together. The presence of these arbitrageurs helps pricing discrepancies disappear quickly. Obviously, market efficiency is impeded by any limitation on arbitrage resulting from operating inefficiencies, such as difficulties in executing trades in a timely manner, prohibitively high trading costs, and a lack of transparency in market prices.

Some market experts argue that restrictions on short selling limit arbitrage trading, which impedes market efficiency. **Short selling** is the transaction whereby an investor sells shares that he or she does not own by borrowing them from a broker and agreeing to replace them at a future date. Short selling allows investors to sell securities they believe to be overvalued, much in the same way they can buy those they believe to be undervalued. In theory, such activities promote more efficient pricing. Regulators and others, however, have argued that short selling may exaggerate downward market movements, leading to crashes in affected securities. In contrast, some researchers report evidence indicating that when investors are unable to borrow securities, that is to short the security, or when costs to borrow shares are high, market prices may deviate from intrinsic values.[12] Furthermore, research suggests that short selling is helpful in price discovery (that is, it facilitates supply and demand in determining prices).[13]

---

8 "The Investor's Advocate: How the SEC Protects Investors, Maintains Market Integrity, and Facilitates Capital Formation," U.S. Securities and Exchange Commission (www.sec.gov/about/whatwedo.shtml).

9 Regulation FD, "Selective Disclosure and Insider Trading," 17 CFR Parts 240, 243, and 249, effective 23 October 2000.

10 Although not the focus of this particular reading, it is important to note that a party is considered an insider not only when the individual is a corporate insider, such as an officer or director, but also when the individual is aware that the information is nonpublic information [Securities and Exchange Commission, Rules 10b5-1 ("Trading on the Basis of Material Nonpublic Information in Insider Trading Cases") and Rule 10b5-2 "Duties of Trust or Confidence in Misappropriation Insider Trading Cases")].

11 In contrast to the situation in the United States, in other developed markets, the insider trading laws are generally promulgated by the courts, although the definition of "insider trading" is generally through statutes. See, for example, the European Community's (EC's) Insider Trading Directive, *Council Directive Coordinating Regulations on Insider Dealing*, Directive 89/592, article 32, 1989 OJ (L 334) 30, 1.

12 A significant amount of research supports this view, including Jones and Lamont (2002) and Duffie, Garleanu, and Pederson (2002).

13 See Bris, Goetzmann, and Zhu (2009).

2.4 Transaction Costs and Information-Acquisition Costs

The costs incurred by traders in identifying and exploiting possible market inefficiencies affect the interpretation of market efficiency. The two types of costs to consider are transaction costs and information-acquisition costs.

■ *Transaction costs*: Practically, transaction costs are incurred in trading to exploit any perceived market inefficiency. Thus, "efficient" should be viewed as efficient within the bounds of transaction costs. For example, consider a violation of the principle that two identical assets should sell for the same price in different markets. Such a violation can be considered to be a rather simple possible exception to market efficiency because prices appear to be inconsistently processing information. To exploit the violation, a trader could arbitrage by simultaneously shorting the asset in the higher-price market and buying the asset in the lower-price market. If the price discrepancy between the two markets is smaller than the transaction costs involved in the arbitrage for the lowest cost traders, the arbitrage will not occur, and both prices are in effect efficient within the bounds of arbitrage. These bounds of arbitrage are relatively narrow in highly liquid markets, such as the market for U.S. Treasury bills, but could be wide in illiquid markets.

■ *Information-acquisition costs:* Practically, expenses are always associated with gathering and analyzing information. New information is incorporated in transaction prices by traders placing trades based on their analysis of information. Active investors who place trades based on information they have gathered and analyzed play a key role in market prices adjusting to reflect new information. The classic view of market efficiency is that active investors incur information acquisition costs but that money is wasted because prices already reflect all relevant information. This view of efficiency is very strict in the sense of viewing a market as inefficient if active investing can recapture any part of the costs, such as research costs and active asset selection. Grossman and Stiglitz (1980) argue that prices must offer a return to information acquisition; in equilibrium, if markets are efficient, returns net of such expenses are just fair returns for the risk incurred. The modern perspective views a market as inefficient if, after deducting such costs, active investing can earn superior returns. Gross of expenses, a return should accrue to information acquisition in an efficient market.

In summary, a modern perspective calls for the investor to consider transaction costs and information-acquisition costs when evaluating the efficiency of a market. A price discrepancy must be sufficiently large to leave the investor with a profit (adjusted for risk) after taking account of the transaction costs and information-acquisition costs to reach the conclusion that the discrepancy may represent a market inefficiency. Prices may somewhat less than fully reflect available information without there being a true market opportunity for active investors.

FORMS OF MARKET EFFICIENCY   3

Eugene Fama developed a framework for describing the degree to which markets are efficient.[14] In his efficient market hypothesis, markets are efficient when prices reflect *all* relevant information at any point in time. This means that the market prices observed for securities, for example, reflect the information available at the time.

---

14 Fama (1970).

In his framework, Fama defines three forms of efficiency: weak, semi-strong, and strong. Each form is defined with respect to the available information that is reflected in prices.

	Market Prices Reflect:		
Forms of Market Efficiency	**Past Market Data**	**Public Information**	**Private Information**
Weak form of market efficiency	✓		
Semi-strong form of market efficiency	✓	✓	
Strong form of market efficiency	✓	✓	✓

A finding that investors can consistently earn **abnormal returns** by trading on the basis of information is evidence contrary to market efficiency. In general, abnormal returns are returns in excess of those expected given a security's risk and the market's return. In other words, abnormal return equals actual return less expected return.

3.1 Weak Form

In the **weak-form efficient market hypothesis**, security prices fully reflect *all past market data*, which refers to all historical price and trading volume information. If markets are weak-form efficient, past trading data are already reflected in current prices and investors cannot predict future price changes by extrapolating prices or patterns of prices from the past.[15]

Tests of whether securities markets are weak-form efficient require looking at patterns of prices. One approach is to see whether there is any serial correlation in security returns, which would imply a predictable pattern.[16] Although there is some weak correlation in daily security returns, there is not enough correlation to make this a profitable trading rule after considering transaction costs.

An alternative approach to test weak-form efficiency is to examine specific trading rules that attempt to exploit historical trading data. If any such trading rule consistently generates abnormal risk-adjusted returns after trading costs, this evidence will contradict weak-form efficiency. This approach is commonly associated with **technical analysis**, which involves the analysis of historical trading information (primarily pricing and volume data) in an attempt to identify recurring patterns in the trading data that can be used to guide investment decisions. Many technical analysts, also referred to as "technicians," argue that many movements in stock prices are based, in large part, on psychology. Many technicians attempt to predict how market participants will behave, based on analyses of past behavior, and then trade on those predictions. Technicians often argue that simple statistical tests of trading rules are not conclusive because they are not applied to the more sophisticated trading strategies that can be used and that the research excludes the technician's subjective judgment. Thus, it is difficult to definitively refute this assertion because there are an unlimited number of possible technical trading rules.

---

15 Market efficiency should not be confused with the random walk hypothesis, in which price changes over time are independent of one another. A random walk model is one of many alternative expected return generating models. Market efficiency does not require that returns follow a random walk.

16 Serial correlation is a statistical measure of the degree to which the returns in one period are related to the returns in another period.

Can technical analysts profit from trading on past trends? Overall, the evidence indicates that investors cannot consistently earn abnormal profits using past prices or other technical analysis strategies in developed markets.[17] Some evidence suggests, however, that there are opportunities to profit on technical analysis in countries with developing markets, including China, Hungary, Bangladesh, and Turkey.[18]

3.2 Semi-Strong Form

In a **semi-strong-form efficient market**, prices reflect all publicly known and available information. Publicly available information includes financial statement data (such as earnings, dividends, corporate investments, changes in management, etc.) and financial market data (such as closing prices, shares traded, etc.). Therefore, the semi-strong form of market efficiency encompasses the weak form. In other words, if a market is semi-strong efficient, then it must also be weak-form efficient. A market that quickly incorporates all publicly available information into its prices is semi-strong efficient.

In a semi-strong market, efforts to analyze publicly available information are futile. That is, analyzing earnings announcements of companies to identify underpriced or overpriced securities is pointless because the prices of these securities already reflect all publicly available information. If markets are semi-strong efficient, no single investor has access to information that is not already available to other market participants, and as a consequence, no single investor can gain an advantage in predicting future security prices. In a semi-strong efficient market, prices adjust quickly and accurately to new information. Suppose a company announces earnings that are higher than expected. In a semi-strong efficient market, investors would not be able to act on this announcement and earn abnormal returns.

A common empirical test of investors' reaction to information releases is the event study. Suppose a researcher wants to test whether investors react to the announcement that the company is paying a special dividend. The researcher identifies a sample period and then those companies that paid a special dividend in the period and the date of the announcement. Then, for each company's stock, the researcher calculates the expected return on the share for the event date. This expected return may be based on many different models, including the capital asset pricing model, a simple market model, or a market index return. The researcher calculates the excess return as the difference between the actual return and the expected return. Once the researcher has calculated the event's excess return for each share, statistical tests are conducted to see whether the abnormal returns are statistically different from zero. The process of an event study is outlined in Exhibit 1.

---

17 Bessembinder and Chan (1998) and Fifield, Power, and Sinclair (2005).
18 Fifield, Power, and Sinclair (2005), Chen and Li (2006), and Mobarek, Mollah, and Bhuyan (2008).

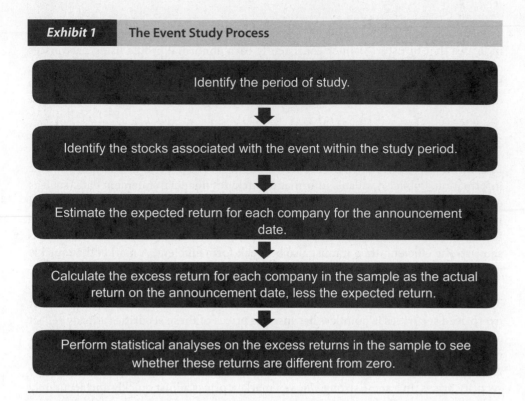

| Exhibit 1 | The Event Study Process |

How do event studies relate to efficient markets? In a semi-strong efficient market, share prices react quickly and accurately to public information. Therefore, if the information is good news, such as better-than-expected earnings, one would expect the company's shares to increase immediately at the time of the announcement; if it is bad news, one would expect a swift, negative reaction. If actual returns exceed what is expected in absence of the announcement and these returns are confined to the announcement period, then they are consistent with the idea that market prices react quickly to new information. In other words, the finding of excess returns at the time of the announcement does not necessarily indicate market inefficiency. In contrast, the finding of consistent excess returns following the announcement would suggest a trading opportunity. Trading on the basis of the announcement—that is, once the announcement is made—would not, on average, yield abnormal returns.

Example 6

Information Arrival and Market Reaction

Consider an example of a news item and its effect on a share's price. In June 2008, the U.S. Federal Trade Commission (FTC) began an investigation of Intel Corporation regarding non-competitiveness, and on 16 December 2009, the FTC announced that it was suing Intel over non-competitive issues. This announcement was made before the market opened for trading on 16 December.

Intel stock closed at $19.78 on 15 December 2009 but opened at $19.50 on 16 December. The stock then traded in the range from $19.45 to $19.68 within the first half hour as the news of the suit and Intel's initial response were spreading among investors. Exhibit 2 illustrates the price of Intel for the first 90 minutes of trading on 16 December.

Exhibit 2	Price of Intel: 16 December 2009

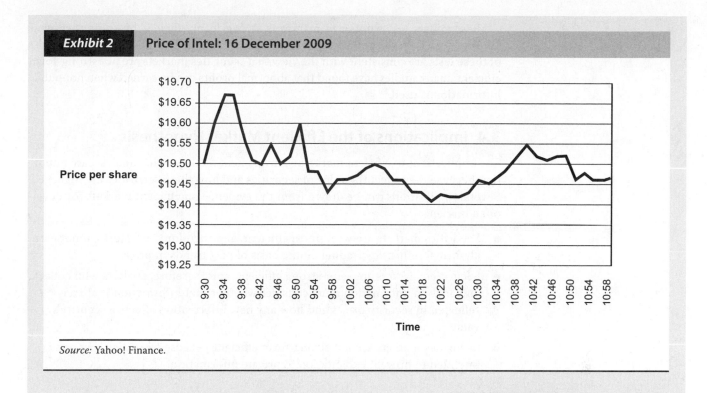

Price per share

Source: Yahoo! Finance.

Is the fact that the price of Intel moves up immediately and then comes down indicative of an inefficiency regarding information? Not necessarily. Does it mean that investors overreacted? Not necessarily. During the morning, both before and after the market opened, news flowed about the lawsuit and the company's reaction to the lawsuit. The price of the shares reflects investors' reactions to this news. Why didn't Intel's shares simply move to a new level and stay there? Because 1) information continued to flow during the day on Intel and investors' estimate of the importance of this news on Intel's stock value continued to change, and 2) other news, related to other events and issues (such as the economy), affected stock prices.

Researchers have examined many different company-specific information events, including stock splits, dividend changes, and merger announcements, as well as economy-wide events, such as regulation changes and tax rate changes. The results of most research are consistent with the view that developed securities markets might be semi-strong efficient. But some evidence suggests that the markets in developing countries may not be semi-strong efficient.[19]

3.3 Strong Form

In a **strong-form efficient market**, security prices fully reflect both public and private information. A market that is strong-form efficient is, by definition, also semi-strong and weak-form efficient. In the case of a strong-form efficient market, insiders would not be able to earn abnormal returns from trading on the basis of private information. A strong-form efficient market also means that prices reflect all private information, which means that prices reflect everything that the management of a company knows about the financial condition of the company that has not been publicly released. However, this is not likely because of the strong prohibitions against insider trading that are found in most countries. If a market is strong-form efficient, those with insider information cannot earn abnormal returns.

---

19 See Gan, Lee, Hwa, and Zhang (2005) and Raja, Sudhahar, and Selvam (2009).

Researchers test whether a market is strong-form efficient by testing whether investors can earn abnormal profits by trading on nonpublic information. The results of these tests are consistent with the view that securities markets are not strong-form efficient; many studies have found that abnormal profits can be earned when nonpublic information is used.[20]

3.4 Implications of the Efficient Market Hypothesis

The implications of efficient markets to investment managers and analysts are important because they affect the value of securities and how these securities are managed. Several implications can be drawn from the evidence on efficient markets for developed markets:

▪ Securities markets are weak-form efficient, and therefore, investors cannot earn abnormal returns by trading on the basis of past trends in price.

▪ Securities markets are semi-strong efficient, and therefore, analysts who collect and analyze information must consider whether that information is already reflected in security prices and how any new information affects a security's value.[21]

▪ Securities markets are not strong-form efficient because securities laws are intended to prevent exploitation of private information.

3.4.1 *Fundamental Analysis*

Fundamental analysis is the examination of publicly available information and the formulation of forecasts to estimate the intrinsic value of assets. Fundamental analysis involves the estimation of an asset's value using company data, such as earnings and sales forecasts, and risk estimates as well as industry and economic data, such as economic growth, inflation, and interest rates. Buy and sell decisions depend on whether the current market price is less than or greater than the estimated intrinsic value.

The semi-strong form of market efficiency says that all available public information is reflected in current prices. So, what good is fundamental analysis? Fundamental analysis is necessary in a well-functioning market because this analysis helps the market participants understand the value implications of information. In other words, fundamental analysis facilitates a semi-strong efficient market by disseminating value-relevant information. And, although fundamental analysis requires costly information, this analysis can be profitable in terms of generating abnormal returns if the analyst creates a comparative advantage with respect to this information.[22]

3.4.2 *Technical Analysis*

Investors using **technical analysis** attempt to profit by looking at patterns of prices and trading volume. Although some price patterns persist, exploiting these patterns may be too costly and, hence, would not produce abnormal returns.

Consider a situation in which a pattern of prices exists. With so many investors examining prices, this pattern will be detected. If profitable, exploiting this pattern will eventually affect prices such that this pattern will no longer exist; it will be arbitraged away. In other words, by detecting and exploiting patterns in prices, technical analysts assist markets in maintaining weak-form efficiency. Does this mean that

---

20 Evidence that finds that markets are not strong-form efficient include Jaffe (1974) and Rozeff and Zaman (1988).
21 In the case of the Intel example, this implication would mean estimating how the actual filing of the lawsuit and the company's reaction to the lawsuit affect the value of Intel, while keeping in mind that the expectation of a lawsuit was already impounded in Intel's stock price.
22 Brealey (1983).

technical analysts cannot earn abnormal profits? Not necessarily, because there may be a possibility of earning abnormal profits from a pricing inefficiency. But would it be possible to earn abnormal returns on a consistent basis from exploiting such a pattern? No, because the actions of market participants will arbitrage this opportunity quickly, and the inefficiency will no longer exist.

3.4.3 Portfolio Management

If securities markets are weak-form and semi-strong-form efficient, the implication is that active trading, whether attempting to exploit price patterns or public information, is not likely to generate abnormal returns. In other words, portfolio managers cannot beat the market on a consistent basis, so therefore, passive portfolio management should outperform active portfolio management. Researchers have observed that mutual funds do not, on average, outperform the market on a risk-adjusted basis.[23] Mutual funds perform, on average, similar to the market before considering fees and expenses and perform worse than the market, on average, once fees and expenses are considered. Even if a mutual fund is not actively managed, there are costs to managing these funds, which reduces net returns.

So, what good are portfolio managers? The role of a portfolio manager is not necessarily to beat the market but, rather, to establish and manage a portfolio consistent with the portfolio's objectives, with appropriate diversification and asset allocation, while taking into consideration the risk preferences and tax situation of the investor.

MARKET PRICING ANOMALIES

4

Although considerable evidence shows that markets are efficient, researchers have also reported a number of potential inefficiencies, or anomalies, that result in the mispricing of securities. These market anomalies, if persistent, are exceptions to the notion of market efficiency. In other words, a **market anomaly** occurs if a change in the price of an asset or security cannot directly be linked to current relevant information known in the market or to the release of new information into the market. Although the list is far from exhaustive, in this section, several well-known anomalies in financial markets are discussed.

The validity of any evidence supporting the existence of such market inefficiencies must be *consistent* over reasonably long periods. Otherwise, a detected market anomaly may largely be an artifact of the sample period chosen. In the widespread search for discovering profitable anomalies, many findings could simply be the product of a process called **data mining**, also known as **data snooping**. In generally accepted research practice, an initial hypothesis is developed which is based on economic rationale, followed by tests conducted on objectively selected data to either confirm or reject the original hypothesis. However, with data mining the process is reversed where data is often examined with the intent to develop a hypothesis, instead of developing a hypothesis first. This is done by analyzing data in various manners, and even utilizing different empirical approaches until you find support for a desired result, in this case a profitable anomaly. Can researchers look back on data and find a trading strategy that would have yielded abnormal returns? Absolutely. Will this trading strategy provide abnormal returns in the future? Perhaps not. It is always possible that enough data snooping can detect a trading strategy that would have worked in the past, and it is always possible that some trading strategy can produce abnormal returns simply by chance. But in an efficient market, such a strategy is unlikely to

---

23 See Malkiel (1995). One of the challenges to evaluating mutual fund performance is that the researcher must control for survivorship bias.

generate abnormal returns on a consistent basis in the future. Although identified anomalies may frequently appear to produce excess returns, it is generally difficult to profitably exploit the anomalies after accounting for risk, trading costs, and so on.

Several anomalies are listed in Exhibit 3. This list is by no means exhaustive, but it provides information on the breadth of the anomalies. A few of these anomalies are discussed in more detail in the following sections. The anomalies are placed into categories based on the research method that identified the anomaly. Time-series anomalies were identified using time series of data. Cross-sectional anomalies were identified based on analyzing a cross section of companies that differ on some key characteristics. Other anomalies were identified by a variety of means, including event studies.

Exhibit 3	Sampling of Observed Pricing Anomalies	
Time Series	**Cross-Sectional**	**Other**
January effect	Size effect	Closed-end fund discount
Day-of-the-week effect	Value effect	Earnings surprise
Weekend effect	Book-to-market ratios	Initial public offerings
Turn-of-the-month effect	P/E ratio effect	Distressed securities effect
Holiday effect	Value Line enigma	Stock splits
Time-of-day effect		Super Bowl
Momentum		
Overreaction		

4.1 Time-Series Anomalies

Two of the major categories of time-series anomalies that have been documented are 1) calendar anomalies and 2) momentum and overreaction anomalies.

4.1.1 *Calendar Anomalies*

In the 1980s, a number of researchers reported that stock market returns in January were significantly higher compared to the rest of the months of the year, with most of the abnormal returns reported during the first five trading days in January. Since its first documentation in the 1980s, this pattern, known as the **January effect**, has been observed in most equity markets around the world. This anomaly is also known as the **turn-of-the-year effect**, or even often referred to as the "small firm in January effect" because it is most frequently observed for the returns of small market capitalization stocks.[24]

The January effect contradicts the efficient market hypothesis because excess returns in January are not attributed to any new and relevant information or news. A number of reasons have been suggested for this anomaly, including tax-loss selling. Researchers have speculated that, in order to reduce their tax liabilities, investors sell their "loser" securities in December for the purpose of creating capital losses, which can then be used to offset any capital gains. A related explanation is that these losers tend to be small-cap stocks with high volatility.[25] This increased supply of equities in December depresses their prices, and then these shares are bought in early January at

---

24 There is also evidence of a January effect in bond returns that is more prevalent in high-yield corporate bonds, similar to the small-company effect for stocks.
25 See Roll (1983).

relatively attractive prices. This demand then drives their prices up again. Overall, the evidence indicates that tax-loss selling may account for a portion of January abnormal returns, but it does not explain all of it.

Another possible explanation for the anomaly is so-called "window dressing", a practice in which portfolio managers sell their riskier securities prior to 31 December. The explanation is as follows: many portfolio managers prepare the annual reports of their portfolio holdings as of 31 December. Selling riskier securities is an attempt to make their portfolios appear less risky. After 31 December, a portfolio manager would then simply purchase riskier securities in an attempt to earn higher returns. However, similar to the tax-loss selling hypothesis, the research evidence in support of the window dressing hypothesis explains some, but not all, of the anomaly.

Recent evidence for both stock and bond returns suggests that the January effect is not persistent and, therefore, is not a pricing anomaly. Once an appropriate adjustment for risk is made, the January "effect" does not produce abnormal returns.[26]

Several other calendar effects, including the day-of-the-week and the weekend effects,[27] have been found. These anomalies are summarized in Exhibit 4.[28] But like the size effect, which will be described later, most of these anomalies have been eliminated over time. One view is that the anomalies have been exploited such that the effect has been arbitraged away. Another view, however, is that increasingly sophisticated statistical methodologies fail to detect pricing inefficiencies.

Exhibit 4	Calendar-Based Anomalies
Anomaly	**Observation**
Turn-of-the-month effect	Returns tend to be higher on the last trading day of the month and the first three trading days of the next month.
Day-of-the-week effect	The average Monday return is negative and lower than the average returns for the other four days, which are all positive.
Weekend effect	Returns on weekends tend to be lower than returns on weekdays.
Holiday effect	Returns on stocks in the day prior to market holidays tend to be higher than other days.

4.1.2 *Momentum and Overreaction Anomalies*

Momentum anomalies relate to short-term share price patterns. One of the earliest studies to identify this type of anomaly was conducted by Werner DeBondt and Richard Thaler, who argued that investors overreact to the release of unexpected public information.[29] Therefore, stock prices will be inflated (depressed) for those companies releasing good (bad) information. This anomaly has become known as the overreaction effect. Using the overreaction effect, they proposed a strategy that involved buying "loser" portfolios and selling "winner" portfolios. They defined stocks as winners or losers based on their total returns over the previous three- to five-year

---

26 See, for example, Kim (2006).
27 For a discussion of several of these anomalous patterns, see Jacobs and Levy (1988).
28 The weekend effect consists of a pattern of returns around the weekend: abnormal positive returns on Fridays followed by abnormally negative returns on Mondays. This is a day-of-the-week effect that specifically links Friday and Monday returns. It is interesting to note that in 2009, the weekend effect in the United States was inverted, with 80 percent of the gains from March 2009 onward coming from the first trading day of the week.
29 DeBondt and Thaler (1985).

period. They found that in a subsequent period, the loser portfolios outperformed the market, while the winner portfolios underperformed the market. Similar patterns have been documented in many, but not all, global stock markets as well as in bond markets. One criticism is that the observed anomaly may be the result of statistical problems in the analysis.

A contradiction to weak-form efficiency occurs when securities that have experienced high returns in the short term tend to continue to generate higher returns in subsequent periods.[30] Empirical support for the existence of momentum in stock returns in most stock markets around the world is well documented. If investors can trade on the basis of momentum and earn abnormal profits, then this anomaly contradicts the weak form of the efficient market hypothesis because it represents a pattern in prices that can be exploited by simply using historical price information.[31]

Researchers have argued that the existence of momentum is rational and not contrary to market efficiency because it is plausible that there are shocks to the expected growth rates of cash flows to shareholders and that these shocks induce a serial correlation that is rational and short lived.[32] In other words, having stocks with some degree of momentum in their security returns may not imply irrationality but, rather, may reflect prices adjusting to a shock in growth rates.

4.2 Cross-Sectional Anomalies

Two of the most researched cross-sectional anomalies in financial markets are the size effect and the value effect.

4.2.1 Size Effect

The size effect results from the observation that equities of small-cap companies tend to outperform equities of large-cap companies on a risk-adjusted basis. Many researchers documented a small-company effect soon after the initial research was published in 1981. This effect, however, was not apparent in subsequent studies.[33] Part of the reason that the size effect was not confirmed by subsequent studies may be because of the fact that if it were truly an anomaly, investors acting on this effect would reduce any potential returns. But some of the explanation may simply be that the effect as originally observed was a chance outcome and, therefore, not actually an inefficiency.

4.2.2 Value Effect

A number of global empirical studies have shown that value stocks, which are generally referred to as stocks that have below-average price-to-earnings (P/E) and market-to-book (M/B) ratios, and above-average dividend yields, have consistently outperformed growth stocks over long periods of time.[34] If the effect persists, the value stock anomaly contradicts semi-strong market efficiency because all the information used to categorize stocks in this manner is publicly available.

---

30 Notice that this pattern lies in sharp contrast to DeBondt and Thaler's reversal pattern that is displayed over longer periods of time. In theory, the two patterns could be related. In other words, it is feasible that prices are bid up extremely high, perhaps too high, in the short term for companies that are doing well. In the longer term (three-to-five years), the prices of these short-term winners correct themselves and they do poorly.

31 Jegadeesh and Titman (2001).

32 Johnson (2002).

33 Although a large number of studies documents a small-company effect, these studies are concentrated in a period similar to that of the original research and, therefore, use a similar data set. The key to whether something is a true anomaly is persistence in out-of-sample tests. Fama and French (2008) document that the size effect is apparent only in microcap stocks but not in small- and large-cap stocks and these microcap stocks may have a significant influence in studies that document a size effect.

34 For example, see Capaul, Rowley, and Sharpe (1993) and Fama and French (1998).

Fama and French developed a three-factor model to predict stock returns.[35] In addition to the use of market returns as specified by the capital asset pricing model (CAPM), the Fama and French model also includes the size of the company as measured by the market value of its equity and the company's book value of equity divided by its market value of equity, which is a value measure. The Fama and French model captures risk dimensions related to stock returns that the CAPM model does not consider. Fama and French find that when they apply the three-factor model instead of the CAPM, the value stock anomaly disappears.

4.3 Other Anomalies

A number of additional anomalies has been documented in the financial markets, including the existence of closed-end investment fund discounts, price reactions to the release of earnings information, returns of initial public offerings, and the predictability of returns based on prior information.

4.3.1 Closed-End Investment Fund Discounts

A closed-end investment fund issues a fixed number of shares at inception and does not sell any additional shares after the initial offering. Therefore, the fund capitalization is fixed unless a secondary public offering is made. The shares of closed-end funds trade on stock markets like any other shares in the equity market (i.e., their prices are determined by supply and demand).

Theoretically, these shares should trade at a price approximately equal to their net asset value (NAV) per share, which is simply the total market value of the fund's security holdings less any liabilities divided by the number of shares outstanding. An abundance of research, however, has documented that, on average, closed-end funds trade at a discount from NAV. Most studies have documented average discounts in the 4–10 percent range, although individual funds have traded at discounts exceeding 50 percent and others have traded at large premiums.[36]

The closed-end fund discount presents a puzzle because conceptually, an investor could purchase all the shares in the fund, liquidate the fund, and end up making a profit. Some researchers have suggested that these discounts are attributed to management fees or expectations of the managers' performance, but these explanations are not supported by the evidence.[37] An alternative explanation for the discount is that tax liabilities are associated with unrealized capital gains and losses that exist prior to when the investor bought the shares, and hence, the investor does not have complete control over the timing of the realization of gains and losses.[38] Although the evidence supports this hypothesis to a certain extent, the tax effect is not large enough to explain the entire discount. Finally, it has often been argued that the discounts exist because of liquidity problems and errors in calculating NAV. The illiquidity explanation is plausible if shares are recorded at the same price as more liquid, publicly traded stocks; some evidence supports this assertion. But as with tax reasons, liquidity issues explain only a portion of the discount effect.

Can these discounts be exploited to earn abnormal returns if transaction costs are taken into account? No. First, the transaction costs involved in exploiting the

---

35 Fama and French (1995).
36 See Dimson and Minio-Kozerski (1999) for a review of this literature.
37 See Lee, Sheifer, and Thaler (1990).
38 The return to owners of closed-end fund shares has three parts: 1) the price appreciation or depreciation of the shares themselves, 2) the dividends earned and distributed to owners by the fund, and 3) the capital gains and losses earned by the fund that are distributed by the fund. The explanation of the anomalous pricing has to do with the timing of the distribution of capital gains.

discount—buying all the shares and liquidating the fund—would eliminate any profit.[39] Second, these discounts tend to revert to zero over time. Hence, a strategy to trade on the basis of these discounts would not likely be profitable.[40]

4.3.2 *Earnings Surprise*

Although most event studies have supported semi-strong market efficiency, some researchers have provided evidence that questions semi-strong market efficiency. One of these studies relates to the extensively examined adjustment of stock prices to earnings announcements.[41] The unexpected part of the earnings announcement, or **earnings surprise**, is the portion of earnings that is unanticipated by investors and, according to the efficient market hypothesis, merits a price adjustment. Positive (negative) surprises should cause appropriate and rapid price increases (decreases). Several studies have been conducted using data from numerous markets around the world. Most of the results indicate that earnings surprises are reflected quickly in stock prices, but the adjustment process is not always efficient. In particular, although a substantial adjustment occurs prior to and at the announcement date, an adjustment also occurs after the announcement.[42]

As a result of these slow price adjustments, companies that display the largest positive earnings surprises subsequently display superior stock return performance, whereas poor subsequent performance is displayed by companies with low or negative earnings surprises.[43] This finding implies that investors could earn abnormal returns using publicly available information by buying stocks of companies that had positive earnings surprises and selling those with negative surprises.

Although there is support for abnormal returns associated with earnings surprises, and some support for such returns beyond the announcement period, there is also evidence indicating that these observed abnormal returns are an artifact of studies that do not sufficiently control for transaction costs and risk.[44]

4.3.3 *Initial Public Offerings (IPOs)*

When a company offers shares of its stock to the public for the first time, it does so through an initial public offering (or IPO). This offering involves working with an investment bank that helps price and market the newly issued shares. After the offering is complete, the new shares trade on a stock market for the first time. Given the risk that investment bankers face in trying to sell a new issue for which the true price is unknown, it is perhaps not surprising to find that, on average, the initial selling price is set too low and that the price increases dramatically on the first trading day. The percentage difference between the issue price and the closing price at the end of the first day of trading is often referred to as the degree of underpricing.

The evidence suggests that, on average, investors who are able to buy the shares of an IPO at their offering price may be able to earn abnormal profits. For example, during the internet bubble of 1995–2000, many IPOs ended their first day of trading up by more than 100 percent. Such performance, however, is not always the case. Sometimes the issues are priced too high, which means that share prices drop on

---

39 See, for example, the study by Pontiff (1996), which shows how the cost of arbitraging these discounts eliminates the profit.

40 See Pontiff (1995).

41 See Jones, Rendleman, and Latané (1984).

42 Not surprisingly, it is often argued that this slow reaction contributes to a momentum pattern.

43 A similar pattern has been documented in the corporate bond market, where bond prices react too slowly to new company earnings announcements as well as to changes in company debt ratings.

44 See Brown (1997) for a summary of evidence supporting the existence of this anomaly. See Zarowin (1989) for evidence regarding the role of size in explaining abnormal returns to surprises; Alexander, Goff, and Peterson (1989) for evidence regarding transaction costs and unexpected earnings strategies; and Kim and Kim (2003) for evidence indicating that the anomalous returns can be explained by risk factors.

their first day of trading. In addition, the evidence also suggests that investors buying after the initial offering are not able to earn abnormal profits because prices adjust quickly to the "true" values, which supports semi-strong market efficiency. In fact, the subsequent long-term performance of IPOs is generally found to be below average. Taken together, the IPO underpricing and the subsequent poor performance suggests that the markets are overly optimistic initially (i.e., investors overreact).

Some researchers have examined closely why IPOs may appear to have anomalous returns. Because of the small size of the IPO companies and the method of equally weighting the samples, what appears to be an anomaly may simply be an artifact of the methodology.[45]

4.3.4 *Predictability of Returns Based on Prior Information*

A number of researchers have documented that equity returns are related to prior information on such factors as interest rates, inflation rates, stock volatility, and dividend yields.[46] But finding that equity returns are affected by changes in economic fundamentals is not evidence of market inefficiency and would not result in abnormal trading returns.[47]

Furthermore, the relationship between stock returns and the prior information is not consistent over time. For example, in one study, the relationship between stock prices and dividend yields changed from positive to negative in different periods.[48] Hence, a trading strategy based on dividend yields would not yield consistent abnormal returns.

4.4 Implications for Investment Strategies

Although it is interesting to consider the anomalies just described, attempting to benefit from them in practice is not easy. In fact, most researchers conclude that observed anomalies are not violations of market efficiency but, rather, are the result of statistical methodologies used to detect the anomalies. As a result, if the methodologies are corrected, most of these anomalies disappear.[49] Another point to consider is that in an efficient market, overreactions may occur, but then so do under-reactions.[50] Therefore, on average, the markets are efficient. In other words, investors face challenges when they attempt to translate statistical anomalies into economic profits. Consider the following quote regarding anomalies from the *Economist* ("Frontiers of Finance Survey," 9 October 1993):

> Many can be explained away. When transactions costs are taken into account, the fact that stock prices tend to over-react to news, falling back the day after good news and bouncing up the day after bad news, proves unexploitable: price reversals are always within the bid-ask spread. Others such as the small-firm effect, work for a few years and then fail for a few years. Others prove to be merely proxies for the reward for risk taking. Many have disappeared since (and because) attention has been drawn to them.

It is difficult to envision entrusting your retirement savings to a manager whose strategy is based on buying securities on Mondays, which tends to have negative returns on average, and selling them on Fridays. For one thing, the negative Monday returns are merely an average, so on any given week, they could be positive. In addition, such

---

45 See Brav and Gompers (1997) and Brav, Geczy, and Gompers (1995).
46 See, for example, Fama and Schwert (1977) and Fama and French (1988).
47 See Fama and French (2008).
48 Schwert (2003, Chapter 15).
49 Fama (1998).
50 This point is made by Fama (1998).

a strategy would generate large trading costs. Even more importantly, investors would likely be uncomfortable investing their funds in a strategy that has no compelling underlying economic rationale.

5 BEHAVIORAL FINANCE

Behavioral finance is a field of financial thought that examines investor behavior and how this behavior affects what is observed in the financial markets. The behavior of individuals, in particular their cognitive biases, has been offered as a possible explanation for a number of pricing anomalies. In a broader sense, behavioral finance attempts to explain why individuals make the decisions that they do, whether these decisions are rational or irrational. The focus of much of the work in this area is on the cognitive biases that affect investment decisions.

Most asset-pricing models assume that markets are rational and that the intrinsic value of a security reflects this rationality. But market efficiency and asset-pricing models do not require that each individual is rational—rather, only that the market is rational. This leaves a lot of room for individual behavior to deviate from rationality. Even if individuals deviate from rationality, however, there may still be no room for profitable arbitrage for any observed mispricing in the financial markets.

5.1 Loss Aversion

In most financial models, the assumption is that investors are risk averse. **Risk aversion** implies that, although investors dislike risk, they are willing to assume risk if adequately compensated in the form of higher expected returns. In the most general models, researchers assume that investors do not like risk, whether the risk is that the returns are higher than expected or lower than expected. Behavioralists, however, allow for the possibility that this dislike for risk is not symmetrical. For example, some argue that behavioral theories of loss aversion can explain observed overreaction in markets, such that investors dislike losses more than they like comparable gains.[51] If loss aversion is more important than risk aversion, researchers should observe that investors overreact.[52] Although this can explain the overreaction anomaly, evidence also suggests that under reaction is just as prevalent as overreaction, which counters these arguments.

5.2 Overconfidence

One of the behavioral biases offered to explain pricing anomalies is overconfidence. If investors are overconfident, they place too much emphasis on their ability to process and interpret information about a security. Overconfident investors do not process information appropriately, and if there is a sufficient number of these investors, stocks will be mispriced.[53] But most researchers argue that this mispricing is temporary, with prices correcting eventually. The issues, however, are how long it takes prices to become correctly priced, whether this mispricing is predictable, and whether investors can consistently earn abnormal profits.

---

51 See DeBondt and Thaler (1985) and Tversky and Kahneman (1981).
52 See Fama (1998).
53 Another aspect to overconfidence is that investors who are overconfident in their ability to select investments and manage a portfolio tend to use less diversification, investing in what is most familiar. Therefore, investor behavior may affect investment results—returns and risk—without implications for the efficiency of markets.

Evidence has suggested that overconfidence results in mispricing for U.S., U.K., German, French, and Japanese markets.[54] This overconfidence, however, is predominantly in higher-growth companies, whose prices react slowly to new information.[55]

5.3 Other Behavioral Biases

Other behavioral theories that have been put forth as explaining investor behavior include the following:

- **representativeness**, with investors assessing probabilities of outcomes depending on how similar they are to the current state;

- **gambler's fallacy**, in which recent outcomes affect investors' estimates of future probabilities;

- **mental accounting**, in which investors keep track of the gains and losses for different investments in separate mental accounts;

- **conservatism**, where investors tend to be slow to react to changes;

- **disposition effect**, in which investors tend to avoid realizing losses but, rather, seek to realize gains; and

- **narrow framing**, in which investors focus on issues in isolation.[56]

The basic idea of these theories is that investors are humans and, therefore, imperfect and that the beliefs they have about a given asset's value may not be homogeneous. These behaviors help explain observed pricing anomalies. But the issue, which is controversial, is whether these insights help exploit any mispricing. In other words, researchers can use investor behavior to explain pricing, but can investors use it to predict how asset prices will be affected?

5.4 Information Cascades

One application of behavioral theories to markets and pricing focuses on the role of personal learning in markets, where personal learning is what investors learn by observing trading outcomes and what they learn from "conversations"—ideas shared among investors about specific assets and the markets.[57] This approach argues that social interaction and the resultant contagion is important in pricing and can explain such phenomena as price changes without accompanying news and mistakes in valuation.

Biases that investors possess, such as framing or mental accounting, can lead to herding behavior or information cascades. Herding and information cascades are related but not identical concepts. **Herding** is clustered trading that may or may not be based on information.[58] An **information cascade**, in contrast, is the transmission of information from those participants who act first and whose decisions influence the decisions of others. Those who are acting on the choices of others may be ignoring their own preferences in favor of imitating the choices of others. In particular, information cascades may occur with respect to the release of accounting information because accounting information is noisy. For example, the release of earnings is noisy because it is uncertain what the current earnings imply about future earnings.

Information cascades may result in serial correlation of stock returns, which is consistent with overreaction anomalies. Do information cascades result in correct pricing? Some argue that if a cascade is leading toward an incorrect value, this cascade

---

54 Scott, Stumpp, and Xu (2003) and Boujelbene Abbes, Boujelbene, and Bouri (2009).
55 Scott, Stumpp, and Xu (2003).
56 For a review of these behavioral issues, see Hirshleifer (2001).
57 Hirshleifer and Teoh (2009).
58 The term used when there is herding without information is "spurious herding."

is "fragile" and will be corrected because investors will ultimately give more weight to public information or the trading of a recognized informed trader.[59] Information cascades, although documented in markets, do not necessarily mean that investors can exploit them as profitable trading opportunities.

Are information cascades rational? If the informed traders act first and uninformed traders imitate the informed traders, this behavior is consistent with rationality. The imitation trading by the uninformed traders helps the market incorporate relevant information and improves market efficiency.[60] The empirical evidence is consistent with the idea that information cascades are greater for a stock when the information quality regarding the company is poor.[61] Hence, information cascades are enhancing the information available to traders.

5.5 Behavioral Finance and Efficient Markets

The use of behavioral theories to explain observed pricing is an important part of the understanding of how markets function and how prices are determined. Whether there is a behavioral explanation for market anomalies remains a debate. Pricing anomalies are continually being uncovered, and then statistical and behavioral explanations are offered to explain these anomalies.

On the one hand, if investors must be rational for efficient markets to exist, then all the foibles of human investors suggest that markets cannot be efficient. On the other hand, if all that is required for markets to be efficient is that investors cannot consistently beat the market on a risk-adjusted basis, then the evidence does support market efficiency.

SUMMARY

This reading has provided an overview of the theory and evidence regarding market efficiency and has discussed the different forms of market efficiency as well as the implications for fundamental analysis, technical analysis, and portfolio management. The general conclusion drawn from the efficient market hypothesis is that it is not possible to beat the market on a consistent basis by generating returns in excess of those expected for the level of risk of the investment.

Additional key points include the following:

■ The efficiency of a market is affected by the number of market participants and depth of analyst coverage, information availability, and limits to trading.

■ There are three forms of efficient markets, each based on what is considered to be the information used in determining asset prices. In the weak form, asset prices fully reflect all market data, which refers to all past price and trading volume information. In the semi-strong form, asset prices reflect all publicly known and available information. In the strong form, asset prices fully reflect all information, which includes both public and private information.

■ Intrinsic value refers to the true value of an asset, whereas market value refers to the price at which an asset can be bought or sold. When markets are

---

59 Avery and Zemsky (1999).

60 Another alternative is that the uninformed traders are the majority of the market participants and the imitators are imitating not because they agree with the actions of the majority but because they are looking to act on the actions of the uninformed traders.

61 Avery and Zemsky (1999) and Bikhchandani, Hirshleifer, and Welch (1992).

efficient, the two should be the same or very close. But when markets are not efficient, the two can diverge significantly.

- Most empirical evidence supports the idea that securities markets in developed countries are semi-strong-form efficient; however, empirical evidence does not support the strong form of the efficient market hypothesis.

- A number of anomalies have been documented that contradict the notion of market efficiency, including the size anomaly, the January anomaly, and the winners–losers anomalies. In most cases, however, contradictory evidence both supports and refutes the anomaly.

- Behavioral finance uses human psychology, such as cognitive biases, in an attempt to explain investment decisions. Whereas behavioral finance is helpful in understanding observed decisions, a market can still be considered efficient even if market participants exhibit seemingly irrational behaviors, such as herding.

REFERENCES

Alexander, John C., Delbert Goff, and Pamela P. Peterson. 1989. "Profitability of a Trading Strategy Based on Unexpected Earnings." *Financial Analysts Journal*, vol. 45, no. 4 : 65–71.

Avery, Christopher, and Peter Zemsky. 1998. "Multi-Dimensional Uncertainty and Herding in Financial Markets." *American Economic Review*, vol. 88, no. 4 : 724–748.

Bessembinder, Hendrik, and Kalok Chan. 1998. "Market Efficiency and the Returns to Technical Analysis." *Financial Management*, vol. 27, no. 2 : 5–17.

Bikhchandani, Sushil, David Hirshleifer, and Ivo Welch. 1992. "A Theory of Fads, Fashion, Custom, and Cultural Change as Informational Cascades." *Journal of Political Economy*, vol. 100, no. 5 : 992–1026.

Bouljelbene Abbes, Mouna, Younes Boujelbene, and Abdelfettah Bouri. 2009. "Overconfidence Bias: Explanation of Market Anomalies French Market Case." *Journal of Applied Economic Sciences*, vol. 4, no. 1 : 12–25.

Brav, Alon, and Paul A. Gompers. 1997. "Myth or Reality? The Long-Run Underperformance of Initial Public Offerings: Evidence from Venture and Nonventure Capital-Backed Companies." *Journal of Finance*, vol. 52, no. 5 : 1791–1821.

Brav, Alon, Christopher Geczy, and Paul A. Gompers. 1995. "The Long-Run Underperformance of Seasoned Equity Offerings Revisited." Working paper, Harvard University.

Brealey, Richard. 1983. "Can Professional Investors Beat the Market?" *An Introduction to Risk and Return from Common Stocks*, 2nd edition. Cambridge, MA: MIT Press.

Bris, Arturo, William N. Goetzmann, and Ning Zhu. 2009. "Efficiency and the Bear: Short Sales and Markets around the World." *Journal of Finance*, vol. 62, no. 3 : 1029–1079.

Brown, Laurence D. 1997. "Earning Surprise Research: Synthesis and Perspectives." *Financial Analysts Journal*, vol. 53, no. 2 : 13–19.

Capaul, Carlo, Ian Rowley, and William Sharpe. 1993. "International Value and Growth Stock Returns." *Financial Analysts Journal*, vol. 49: 27–36.

Chen, Kong-Jun, and Xiao-Ming Li. 2006. "Is Technical Analysis Useful for Stock Traders in China? Evidence from the Szse Component A-Share Index." *Pacific Economic Review*, vol. 11, no. 4 : 477–488.

Chordia, Tarun, Richard Roll, and Avanidhar Subrahmanyam. 2005. "Evidence on the Speed of Convergence to Market Efficiency." *Journal of Financial Economics*, vol. 76, no. 2 : 271–292.

DeBondt, Werner, and Richard Thaler. 1985. "Does the Stock Market Overreact?" *Journal of Finance*, vol. 40, no. 3 : 793–808.

Dimson, Elroy, and Carolina Minio-Kozerski. 1999. "Closed-End Funds: A Survey." *Financial Markets, Institutions & Instruments*, vol. 8, no. 2 : 1–41.

Duffie, Darrell, Nicholae Garleanu, and Lasse Heje Pederson. 2002. "Securities Lending, Shorting and Pricing." *Journal of Financial Economics*, vol. 66, no. 2–3: 307–339.

Fama, Eugene F. 1970. "Efficient Capital Markets: A Review of Theory and Empirical Work." *Journal of Finance*, vol. 25, no. 2 : 383–417.

Fama, Eugene F. 1976. *Foundations of Finance*. New York: Basic Books.

Fama, Eugene F. 1998. "Market Efficiency, Long-Term Returns, and Behavioral Finance." *Journal of Financial Economics*, vol. 50, no. 3 : 283–306.

Fama, Eugene F., and G. William Schwert. 1977. "Asset Returns and Inflation." *Journal of Financial Economics*, vol. 5, no. 2 : 115–146.

Fama, Eugene F., and Kenneth R. French. 1988. "Dividend Yields and Expected Stock Returns." *Journal of Financial Economics*, vol. 22, no. 1 : 3–25.

Fama, Eugene F., and Kenneth R. French. 1995. "Size and Book-to-Market Factors in Earnings and Returns." *Journal of Finance*, vol. 50, no. 1 : 131–155.

Fama, Eugene F., and Kenneth R. French. 1998. "Value versus Growth: The International Evidence." *Journal of Finance*, vol. 53: 1975–1999.

Fama, Eugene F., and Kenneth R. French. 2008. "Dissecting Anomalies." *Journal of Finance*, vol. 63, no. 4 : 1653–1678.

Fifield, Suzanne, David Power, and C. Donald Sinclair. 2005. "An Analysis of Trading Strategies in Eleven European Stock Markets." *European Journal of Finance*, vol. 11, no. 6 : 531–548.

Gan, Christopher, Minsoo Lee, Au Yong Hue Hwa, and Jun Zhang. 2005. "Revisiting Share Market Efficiency: Evidence from the New Zealand, Australia, US and Japan Stock Indices." *American Journal of Applied Sciences*, vol. 2, no. 5 : 996–1002.

Grossman, Sanford J., and Joseph E. Stiglitz. 1980. "On the Impossibility of Informationally Efficient Markets." *American Economic Review*, vol. 70, no. 3 : 393–408.

Hirshleifer, David. 2001. "Investor Psychology and Asset Pricing." *Journal of Finance*, vol. 56, no. 4 : 1533–1597.

Hirshleifer, David, and Siew Hong Teoh. 2009. "Thought and Behavior Contagion in Capital Markets." In *Handbook of Financial Markets: Dynamics and Evolution*. Edited by Klaus Reiner Schenk-Hoppe and Thorstein Hens. Amsterdam: North Holland.

Jacobs, Bruce I., and Kenneth N. Levy. 1988. "Calendar Anomalies: Abnormal Returns at Calendar Turning Points." *Financial Analysts Journal*, vol. 44, no. 6 : 28–39.

Jaffe, Jeffrey. 1974. "Special Information and Insider Trading." *Journal of Business*, vol. 47, no. 3 : 410–428.

Jegadeesh, Narayan, and Sheridan Titman. 2001. "Profitability of Momentum Strategies: An Evaluation of Alternative Explanations." *Journal of Finance*, vol. 56: 699–720.

Johnson, Timothy C. 2002. "Rational Momentum Effects." *Journal of Finance*, vol. 57, no. 2 : 585–608.

Jones, Charles M., and Owen A. Lamont. 2002. "Short-Sale Constraints and Stock Returns." *Journal of Financial Economics*, vol. 66, no. 2–3 : 207–239.

Jones, Charles P., Richard J. Rendleman, and Henry. A. Latané. 1984. "Stock Returns and SUEs during the 1970's." *Journal of Portfolio Management*, vol. 10: 18–22.

Kim, Donchoi, and Myungsun Kim. 2003. "A Multifactor Explanation of Post-Earnings Announcement Drift." *Journal of Financial and Quantitative Analysis*, vol. 38, no. 2 : 383–398.

Kim, Dongcheol. 2006. "On the Information Uncertainty Risk and the January Effect." *Journal of Business*, vol. 79, no. 4 : 2127–2162.

Lee, Charles M.C., Andrei Sheifer, and Richard H. Thaler. 1990. "Anomalies: Closed-End Mutual Funds." *Journal of Economic Perspectives*, vol. 4, no. 4 : 153–164.

Malkiel, Burton G. 1995. "Returns from Investing in Equity Mutual Funds 1971 to 1991." *Journal of Finance*, vol. 50: 549–572.

Mobarek, Asma, A. Sabur Mollah, and Rafiqul Bhuyan. 2008. "Market Efficiency in Emerging Stock Market." *Journal of Emerging Market Finance*, vol. 7, no. 1 : 17–41.

Pontiff, Jeffrey. 1995. "Closed-End Fund Premia and Returns: Implications for Financial Market Equilibrium." *Journal of Financial Economics*, vol. 37: 341–370.

Pontiff, Jeffrey. 1996. "Costly Arbitrage: Evidence from Closed-End Funds." *Quarterly Journal of Economics*, vol. 111, no. 4 : 1135–1151.

Raja, M., J. Clement Sudhahar, and M. Selvam. 2009. "Testing the Semi-Strong Form Efficiency of Indian Stock Market with Respect to Information Content of Stock Split Announcement—A Study of IT Industry." *International Research Journal of Finance and Economics*, vol. 25: 7–20.

Roll, Richard. 1983. "On Computing Mean Returns and the Small Firm Premium." *Journal of Financial Economics*, vol. 12: 371–386.

Rozeff, Michael S., and Mir A. Zaman. 1988. "Market Efficiency and Insider Trading: New Evidence." *Journal of Business*, vol. 61: 25–44.

Schwert, G. William. 2003. "Anomalies and Market Efficiency." *Handbook of the Economics of Finance*. Edited by George M. Constantinides, M. Harris, and Rene Stulz. Amsterdam: Elsevier Science, B. V.

Scott, James, Margaret Stumpp, and Peter Xu. 2003. "Overconfidence Bias in International Stock Prices." *Journal of Portfolio Management*, vol. 29, no. 2 : 80–89.

Tversky, Amos, and Daniel Kahneman. 1981. "The Framing of Decisions and the Psychology of Choice." *Science*, vol. 211, no. 30 : 453–458.

Yau, Jot, Thomas Schneeweis, Thomas Robinson, and Lisa Weiss. 2007. "Alternative Investments Portfolio Management." *Managing Investment Portfolios: A Dynamic Process*. Hoboken, NJ: John Wiley & Sons.

Zarowin, P. 1989. "Does the Stock Market Overreact to Corporate Earnings Information?" *Journal of Finance*, vol. 44: 1385–1399.

PRACTICE PROBLEMS FOR READING 48

1. In an efficient market, the change in a company's share price is *most likely* the result of:

   A. insiders' private information.

   B. the previous day's change in stock price.

   C. new information coming into the market.

2. Regulation that restricts some investors from participating in a market will *most likely*:

   A. impede market efficiency.

   B. not affect market efficiency.

   C. contribute to market efficiency.

3. With respect to efficient market theory, when a market allows short selling, the efficiency of the market is *most likely* to:

   A. increase.

   B. decrease.

   C. remain the same.

4. Which of the following regulations will *most likely* contribute to market efficiency? Regulatory restrictions on:

   A. short selling.

   B. foreign traders.

   C. insiders trading with nonpublic information.

5. Which of the following market regulations will *most likely* impede market efficiency?

   A. Restricting traders' ability to short sell.

   B. Allowing unrestricted foreign investor trading.

   C. Penalizing investors who trade with nonpublic information.

6. If markets are efficient, the difference between the intrinsic value and market value of a company's security is:

   A. negative.

   B. zero.

   C. positive.

7. The intrinsic value of an undervalued asset is:

   A. less than the asset's market value.

   B. greater than the asset's market value.

   C. the value at which the asset can currently be bought or sold.

8. The market value of an undervalued asset is:

   A. greater than the asset's intrinsic value.

   B. the value at which the asset can currently be bought or sold.

   C. equal to the present value of all the asset's expected cash flows.

9. With respect to the efficient market hypothesis, if security prices reflect *only* past prices and trading volume information, then the market is:

   A. weak-form efficient.

   B. strong-form efficient.

   C. semi-strong-form efficient.

10. Which one of the following statements *best* describes the semi-strong form of market efficiency?

    A. Empirical tests examine the historical patterns in security prices.

    B. Security prices reflect all publicly known and available information.

    C. Semi-strong-form efficient markets are not necessarily weak-form efficient.

11. If markets are semi-strong efficient, standard fundamental analysis will yield abnormal trading profits that are:

    A. negative.

    B. equal to zero.

    C. positive.

12. If prices reflect all public and private information, the market is *best* described as:

    A. weak-form efficient.

    B. strong-form efficient.

    C. semi-strong-form efficient.

13. If markets are semi-strong-form efficient, then passive portfolio management strategies are *most likely* to:

    A. earn abnormal returns.

    B. outperform active trading strategies.

    C. underperform active trading strategies.

14. If a market is semi-strong-form efficient, the risk-adjusted returns of a passively managed portfolio relative to an actively managed portfolio are *most likely*:

    A. lower.

    B. higher.

    C. the same.

15. Technical analysts assume that markets are:

    A. weak-form efficient.

    B. weak-form inefficient.

    C. semi-strong-form efficient.

16. Fundamental analysts assume that markets are:

    A. weak-form inefficient.

    B. semi-strong-form efficient.

    C. semi-strong-form inefficient.

17. If a market is weak-form efficient but semi-strong-form inefficient, then which of the following types of portfolio management is *most likely* to produce abnormal returns?

    A. Passive portfolio management.

    B. Active portfolio management based on technical analysis.

    C. Active portfolio management based on fundamental analysis.

18. An increase in the time between when an order to trade a security is placed and when the order is executed *most likely* indicates that market efficiency has:

    A. decreased.

    B. remained the same.

    C. increased.

19. With respect to efficient markets, a company whose share price reacts gradually to the public release of its annual report *most likely* indicates that the market where the company trades is:

    A. semi-strong-form efficient.

    B. subject to behavioral biases.

    C. receiving additional information about the company.

20. Which of the following is *least likely* to explain the January effect anomaly?

    A. Tax-loss selling.

    B. Release of new information in January.

    C. Window dressing of portfolio holdings.

21. If a researcher conducting empirical tests of a trading strategy using time series of returns finds statistically significant abnormal returns, then the researcher has *most likely* found:

    A. a market anomaly.

    B. evidence of market inefficiency.

    C. a strategy to produce future abnormal returns.

22. Which of the following market anomalies is inconsistent with weak-form market efficiency?

    A. Earnings surprise.

    B. Momentum pattern.

    C. Closed-end fund discount.

23. Researchers have found that value stocks have consistently outperformed growth stocks. An investor wishing to exploit the value effect should purchase the stock of companies with above-average:

    A. dividend yields.

    B. market-to-book ratios.

    C. price-to-earnings ratios.

24. With respect to rational and irrational investment decisions, the efficient market hypothesis requires:

    A. only that the market is rational.

    B. that all investors make rational decisions.

    C. that some investors make irrational decisions.

25. Observed overreactions in markets can be explained by an investor's degree of:

    A. risk aversion.

    B. loss aversion.

    C. confidence in the market.

26. Like traditional finance models, the behavioral theory of loss aversion assumes that investors dislike risk; however, the dislike of risk in behavioral theory is assumed to be:

    A. leptokurtic.

    B. symmetrical.

    C. asymmetrical.

SOLUTIONS FOR READING 48

1. C is correct. Today's price change is independent of the one from yesterday, and in an efficient market, investors will react to new, independent information as it is made public.

2. A is correct. Reducing the number of market participants can accentuate market imperfections and impede market efficiency (e.g., restrictions on foreign investor trading).

3. A is correct. According to theory, reducing the restrictions on trading will allow for more arbitrage trading, thereby promoting more efficient pricing. Although regulators argue that short selling exaggerates downward price movements, empirical research indicates that short selling is helpful in price discovery.

4. C is correct. Regulation to restrict unfair use of nonpublic information encourages greater participation in the market, which increases market efficiency. Regulators (e.g., U.S. SEC) discourage illegal insider trading by issuing penalties to violators of their insider trading rules.

5. A is correct. Restricting short selling will reduce arbitrage trading, which promotes market efficiency. Permitting foreign investor trading increases market participation, which makes markets more efficient. Penalizing insider trading encourages greater market participation, which increases market efficiency.

6. B is correct. A security's intrinsic value and market value should be equal when markets are efficient.

7. B is correct. The intrinsic value of an undervalued asset is greater than the market value of the asset, where the market value is the transaction price at which an asset can be currently bought or sold.

8. B is correct. The market value is the transaction price at which an asset can be currently bought or sold.

9. A is correct. The weak-form efficient market hypothesis is defined as a market where security prices fully reflect all market data, which refers to all past price and trading volume information.

10. B is correct. In semi-strong-form efficient markets, security prices reflect all publicly available information.

11. B is correct. If all public information should already be reflected in the market price, then the abnormal trading profit will be equal to zero when fundamental analysis is used.

12. B is correct. The strong-form efficient market hypothesis assumes all information, public or private, has already been reflected in the prices.

13. B is correct. Costs associated with active trading strategies would be difficult to recover; thus, such active trading strategies would have difficulty outperforming passive strategies on a consistent after-cost basis.

14. B is correct. In a semi-strong-form efficient market, passive portfolio strategies should outperform active portfolio strategies on a risk-adjusted basis.

15. B is correct. Technical analysts use past prices and volume to predict future prices, which is inconsistent with the weakest form of market efficiency (i.e., weak-form market efficiency). Weak-form market efficiency states that investors cannot earn abnormal returns by trading on the basis of past trends in price and volume.

16. C is correct. Fundamental analysts use publicly available information to estimate a security's intrinsic value to determine if the security is mispriced, which is inconsistent with the semi-strong form of market efficiency. Semi-strong-form market efficiency states that investors cannot earn abnormal returns by trading based on publicly available information.

17. C is correct. If markets are not semi-strong-form efficient, then fundamental analysts are able to use publicly available information to estimate a security's intrinsic value and identify misvalued securities. Technical analysis is not able to earn abnormal returns if markets are weak-form efficient. Passive portfolio managers outperform fundamental analysis if markets are semi-strong-form efficient.

18. A is correct. Operating inefficiencies reduce market efficiency.

19. C is correct. If markets are efficient, the information from the annual report is reflected in the stock prices; therefore, the gradual changes must be from the release of additional information.

20. B is correct. The excess returns in January are not attributed to any new information or news; however, research has found that part of the seasonal pattern can be explained by tax-loss selling and portfolio window dressing.

21. A is correct. Finding significant abnormal returns does not necessarily indicate that markets are inefficient or that abnormal returns can be realized by applying the strategy to future time periods. Abnormal returns are considered market anomalies because they may be the result of the model used to estimate the expected returns or may be the result of underestimating transaction costs or other expenses associated with implementing the strategy, rather than because of market inefficiency.

22. B is correct. Trading based on historical momentum indicates that price patterns exist and can be exploited by using historical price information. A momentum trading strategy that produces abnormal returns contradicts the weak form of the efficient market hypothesis, which states that investors cannot earn abnormal returns on the basis of past trends in prices.

23. A is correct. Higher than average dividend yield is a characteristic of a value stock, along with low price-to-earnings and low market-to-book ratios. Growth stocks are characterized by low dividend yields and high price-to-earnings and high market-to-book ratios.

24. A is correct. The efficient market hypothesis and asset-pricing models only require that the market is rational. Behavioral finance is used to explain *some* of the market anomalies as irrational decisions.

25. B is correct. Behavioral theories of loss aversion can explain observed overreaction in markets, such that investors dislike losses more than comparable gains (i.e., risk is not symmetrical).

26. C is correct. Behavioral theories of loss aversion allow for the possibility that the dislike for risk is not symmetrical, which allows for loss aversion to explain observed overreaction in markets such that investors dislike losses more than they like comparable gains.

14

Equity Analysis and Valuation

This study session focuses on the characteristics, analysis, and valuation of equity securities. The first reading discusses various types and features of equity securities and their roles in investment management. The second reading explains how to conduct industry and company analyses; the reading's major focus is on understating a company's competitive position. The first two readings constitute necessary background knowledge for the third reading, which introduces the subject of equity valuation.

READING ASSIGNMENTS

Reading 49 *Overview of Equity Securities*
        by Ryan C. Fuhrmann, CFA, and Asjeet S. Lamba, CFA

Reading 50 *Introduction to Industry and Company Analysis*
        by Patrick W. Dorsey, CFA, Anthony M. Fiore, CFA, and Ian Rossa
        O'Reilly, CFA

Reading 51 *Equity Valuation: Concepts and Basic Tools*
        by John J. Nagorniak, CFA, and Stephen E. Wilcox, CFA

READING

49

Overview of Equity Securities

by Ryan C. Fuhrmann, CFA, and Asjeet S. Lamba, CFA

LEARNING OUTCOMES

Mastery	The candidate should be able to:
☐	**a** describe characteristics of types of equity securities;
☐	**b** describe differences in voting rights and other ownership characteristics among different equity classes;
☐	**c** distinguish between public and private equity securities;
☐	**d** describe methods for investing in non-domestic equity securities;
☐	**e** compare the risk and return characteristics of types of equity securities;
☐	**f** explain the role of equity securities in the financing of a company's assets;
☐	**g** distinguish between the market value and book value of equity securities;
☐	**h** compare a company's cost of equity, its (accounting) return on equity, and investors' required rates of return.

INTRODUCTION

1

Equity securities represent ownership claims on a company's net assets. As an asset class, equity plays a fundamental role in investment analysis and portfolio management because it represents a significant portion of many individual and institutional investment portfolios.

The study of equity securities is important for many reasons. First, the decision on how much of a client's portfolio to allocate to equities affects the risk and return characteristics of the entire portfolio. Second, different types of equity securities have different ownership claims on a company's net assets, which affect their risk and return characteristics in different ways. Finally, variations in the features of equity securities are reflected in their market prices, so it is important to understand the valuation implications of these features.

This reading provides an overview of equity securities and their different features and establishes the background required to analyze and value equity securities in a global context. It addresses the following questions:

- What distinguishes common shares from preference shares, and what purposes do these securities serve in financing a company's operations?

- What are convertible preference shares, and why are they often used to raise equity for unseasoned or highly risky companies?

- What are private equity securities, and how do they differ from public equity securities?

- What are depository receipts and their various types, and what is the rationale for investing in them?

- What are the risk factors involved in investing in equity securities?

- How do equity securities create company value?

- What is the relationship between a company's cost of equity, its return on equity, and investors' required rate of return?

The remainder of this reading is organized as follows. Section 2 provides an overview of global equity markets and their historical performance. Section 3 examines the different types and characteristics of equity securities, and Section 4 outlines the differences between public and private equity securities. Section 5 provides an overview of the various types of equity securities listed and traded in global markets. Section 6 discusses the risk and return characteristics of equity securities. Section 7 examines the role of equity securities in creating company value and the relationship between a company's cost of equity, its return on equity, and investors' required rate of return. The final section summarizes the reading.

2 EQUITY SECURITIES IN GLOBAL FINANCIAL MARKETS

This section highlights the relative importance and performance of equity securities as an asset class. We examine the total market capitalization and trading volume of global equity markets and the prevalence of equity ownership across various geographic regions. We also examine historical returns on equities and compare them to the returns on government bonds and bills.

Exhibit 1 summarizes the contributions of selected countries and geographic regions to global gross domestic product (GDP) and global equity market capitalization. Analysts can examine the relationship between equity market capitalization and GDP as an indicator of whether the global equity market (or a specific country's or region's equity market) is under, over, or fairly valued. Global equity markets expanded at twice the rate of global GDP between 1993 and 2004. At the beginning of 2008, global GDP and equity market capitalization were nearly equal at approximately US$55 trillion.[1] This implies an equity market capitalization to GDP ratio of 100 percent, which was almost twice the long-run average of 50 percent and indicates that global equity markets were overvalued at that time.

Exhibit 1 illustrates the significant value that investors attach to publicly traded equities relative to the sum of goods and services produced globally every year. It shows the continued significance, and the potential over-representation, of U.S. equity markets relative to their contribution to global GDP. That is, while U.S. equity markets

---

1 EconomyWatch.com, http://www.economywatch.com/gdp/world-gdp/.

contribute around 43 percent to the total capitalization of global equity markets, their contribution to the global GDP is only around 21 percent. Following the stock market turmoil in 2008, however, the market capitalization to GDP ratio of the United States fell to 59 percent, which is significantly lower than its long-run average of 79 percent.[2]

As equity markets outside the United States develop and become increasingly global, their total capitalization levels are expected to grow closer to their respective world GDP contributions. Therefore, it is important to understand and analyze equity securities from a global perspective.

| **Exhibit 1** | Country and Regional Contributions to Global GDP and Equity Market Capitalization (2007) |

Contribution to World GDP

Other Asia 3.7%
Canada 2.0%
Other Europe 3.3%
Japan 6.6%
United Kingdom 3.3%
Emerging Markets 43.7%
EU 16.1%
United States 21.3%

Contribution to Global Stock Market Capitalization

Other Europe 5.2%
Other Asia 4.3%
Emerging Markets 10.9%
Canada 3.8%
Japan 10.8%
United Kingdom 8.3%
United States 43.4%
EU 13.3%

Source: MacroMavens, *IMF World Economic Outlook 2008*, Standard & Poor's BMI Global Index weights.

Exhibit 2 lists the top 10 equity markets at the end of 2008 based on total market capitalization (in billions of U.S. dollars), trading volume, and the number of listed companies.[3] Note that the rankings differ based on the criteria used. For example, the top three markets based on total market capitalization are the NYSE Euronext (U.S.), Tokyo Stock Exchange Group, and NASDAQ OMX; however, the top three markets based on total U.S. dollar trading volume are the Nasdaq OMX, NYSE Euronext (U.S.), and London Stock Exchange, respectively.[4] A relatively new entrant to this top 10 list is China's Shanghai Stock Exchange, which is the only emerging equity market represented on this list.

2 For further details, see Bary (2008).
3 The market capitalization of an individual stock is computed as the share price multiplied by the number of shares outstanding. The total market capitalization of an equity market is the sum of the market capitalizations of each individual stock listed on that market. Similarly, the total trading volume of an equity market is computed by value weighting the total trading volume of each individual stock listed on that market. Total dollar trading volume is computed as the average share price multiplied by the number of shares traded.
4 NASDAQ is the acronym for the National Association of Securities Dealers Automated Quotations.

Exhibit 2	Equity Markets Ranked by Total Market Capitalization at the End of 2008 (Billions of U.S. Dollars)			
Rank	Name of Market	Total U.S. Dollar Market Capitalization	Total U.S. Dollar Trading Volume	Number of Listed Companies
1	NYSE Euronext (U.S.)	$9,208.9	$33,638.9	3,011
2	Tokyo Stock Exchange Group	$3,115.8	$5,607.3	2,390
3	NASDAQ OMX	$2,396.3	$36,446.5	2,952
4	NYSE Euronext (Europe)	$2,101.7	$4,411.2	1,002
5	London Stock Exchange	$1,868.2	$6,271.5	3,096
6	Shanghai Stock Exchange	$1,425.4	$2,600.2	864
7	Hong Kong Exchanges	$1,328.8	$1,629.8	1,261
8	Deutsche Börse	$1,110.6	$4,678.8	832
9	TSX Group	$1,033.4	$1,716.2	3,841
10	BME Spanish Exchanges	$948.4	$2,410.7	3,576

Source: Adapted from the *World Federation of Exchanges 2008 Report* (see http://www. world-exchanges.org). Note that market capitalization by company is calculated by multiplying its stock price by the number of shares outstanding. The market's overall capitalization is the aggregate of the market capitalizations of all companies traded on that market. The number of listed companies includes both domestic and foreign companies whose shares trade on these markets.

Exhibit 3 compares the *real* (or inflation-adjusted) compounded returns on government bonds, government bills, and equity securities in 17 countries during 1900–2008.[5] In real terms, government bonds and bills have essentially kept pace with the inflation rate, earning annualized real returns of 1 percent to 2 percent in most countries.[6] By comparison, real returns in equity markets have generally been above 4 percent per year in most markets—with a world average return just over 5 percent and a world average return excluding the United States just under 5 percent. During this period, Australia and Sweden were the best performing markets followed by South Africa, the United States, and Canada.

---

5 The real return for a country is computed by taking the nominal return and subtracting the observed inflation rate in that country.
6 The exceptions are Belgium, Italy, Germany, France, and Japan—where the average real returns on government bonds have been negative. This is due to the very high inflation rates in these countries during the World War years.

Exhibit 3	Real Returns on Global Equity Securities, Bonds, and Bills during 1900–2008

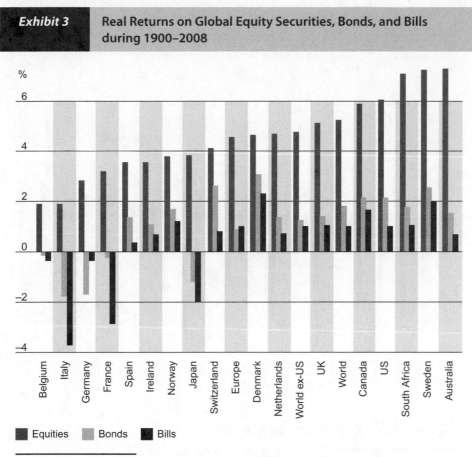

Source: E. Dimson, P. Marsh, and M. Staunton, *Credit Suisse Global Investment Returns Yearbook 2009*, Credit Suisse Research Institute (February 2009).

Exhibit 4 focuses on the real compounded rates of return on equity securities in the same 17 countries during 1900–2008 as well as during the more recent time periods of 1990–1999 and 2000–2008. During 2000–2008, with the exception of Australia, Norway, and South Africa, real returns were negative or close to zero in all markets including the world average. This is in sharp contrast to the performance of these markets during 1990–1999, when inflation rates and interest rates were at record lows in most countries and growth in corporate profits was at record highs.[7]

---

7 The only exception to this was the Japanese equity market, which experienced negative real returns in the 1990s as well. Even in the case of Japan, however, the average real compounded return over the much longer 1900–2008 period has been around 4 percent per year.

Exhibit 4	Real Returns on Global Equity Securities during 1900–2008, 1990–1999, and 2000–2008

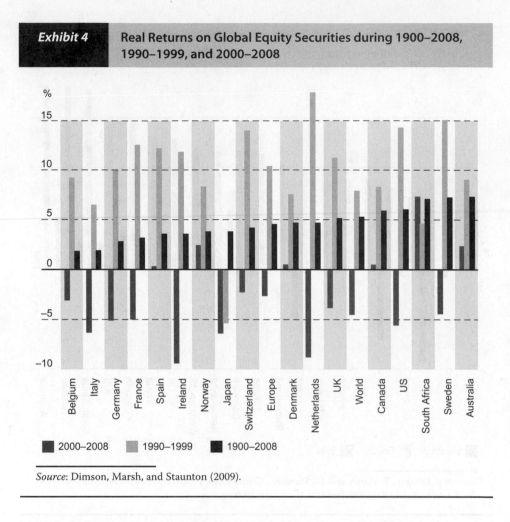

2000–2008   1990–1999   1900–2008

Source: Dimson, Marsh, and Staunton (2009).

The volatility in equity market returns is further highlighted in Exhibit 5, which shows the average performance of world equity markets and the worst performing equity market during World War I, World War II, the technology crash, the oil crisis, the Wall Street crash, and the more recent banking/credit crash. Note that in each period the losses suffered by the worst affected equity market were much larger than the average global losses. The data for the credit crash is as of the end of 2008 and thus does not fully capture the extent of its effects on world equity markets. It is more than likely that in the future, the credit crash of 2007–2008 will be viewed as being the worst of all the extreme market losses.

These observations and historical data are consistent with the concept that the return on securities is directly related to risk level. That is, equity securities have higher risk levels when compared with government bonds and bills, they earn higher rates of return to compensate investors for these higher risk levels, and they also tend to be more volatile over time.

| Exhibit 5 | Extreme Losses in Global Equity Markets during 1900–2008 |

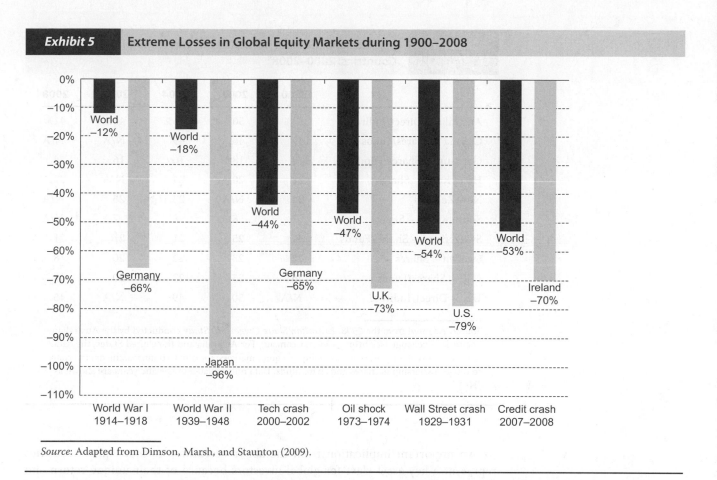

Source: Adapted from Dimson, Marsh, and Staunton (2009).

Given the high risk levels associated with equity securities, it is reasonable to expect that investors' tolerance for risk will tend to differ across equity markets. This is illustrated in Exhibit 6, which shows the results of a series of studies conducted by the Australian Securities Exchange on international differences in equity ownership. During the 2000–2008 period, equity ownership as a percentage of the population was lowest in South Korea (averaging 7.5 percent), followed by Germany (16.6 percent) and Sweden (21 percent). In contrast, Australia, Canada, and the United States had the highest equity ownership as a percentage of the population (averaging almost 50 percent). In addition, there has been a relative decline in share ownership in several countries over recent years, which is not surprising given the recent overall uncertainty in global economies and the volatility in equity markets that this uncertainty has created.

Exhibit 6	International Comparisons of Stock Ownership in Selected Countries: 2000–2008[8]				
	2000	**2002**	**2004**	**2006**	**2008**
Australia – Direct/Indirect	52%	50%	55%	46%	41%
Canada – Shares/Funds	49	46	49	N/A	N/A
Germany – Shares/Funds	19	18	16	16	14
Hong Kong – Shares	22	20	24	N/A	22
New Zealand	24	N/A	23	26	N/A
South Korea – Shares	7	8	8	7	N/A
Switzerland – Shares/Funds	34	25	21	21	21
Sweden – Shares	22	23	22	20	18
U.K. – Shares/Funds	26	25	22	20	18
U.S. – Direct/Indirect	N/A	50	49	N/A	45

Source: Adapted from the *2008 Australian Share Ownership Study* conducted by the Australian Securities Exchange (see http://www.asx.com.au). For Australia and the United States, the data pertain to direct and indirect ownership in equity markets; for other countries, the data pertain to direct ownership in shares and share funds. Data not available in specific years are shown as "N/A."

An important implication from the above discussion is that equity securities represent a key asset class for global investors because of their unique return and risk characteristics. We next examine the various types of equity securities traded on global markets and their salient characteristics.

3 TYPES AND CHARACTERISTICS OF EQUITY SECURITIES

Companies finance their operations by issuing either debt or equity securities. A key difference between these securities is that debt is a liability of the issuing company, whereas equity is not. This means that when a company issues debt, it is contractually obligated to repay the amount it borrows (i.e., the principal or face value of the debt) at a specified future date. The cost of using these funds is called interest, which the company is contractually obligated to pay until the debt matures or is retired.

When the company issues equity securities, it is not contractually obligated to repay the amount it receives from shareholders, nor is it contractually obligated to make periodic payments to shareholders for the use of their funds. Instead, shareholders have a claim on the company's assets after all liabilities have been paid. Because of this residual claim, equity shareholders are considered to be owners of the company. Investors who purchase equity securities are seeking total return (i.e., capital or price

---

8 The percentages reported in the exhibit are based on samples of the adult population in each country who own equity securities either directly or indirectly through investment or retirement funds. For example, 41 percent of the adult population of Australia in 2008 (approximately 6.7 million people) owned equity securities either directly or indirectly. As noted in the study, it is not appropriate to make absolute comparisons across countries given the differences in methodology, sampling, timing, and definitions that have been used in different countries. However, trends across different countries can be identified.

appreciation and dividend income), whereas investors who purchase debt securities (and hold until maturity) are seeking interest income. As a result, equity investors expect the company's management to act in their best interest by making operating decisions that will maximize the market price of their shares (i.e., shareholder wealth).

In addition to common shares (also known as ordinary shares or common stock), companies may also issue preference shares (also known as preferred stock), the other type of equity security. The following sections discuss the different types and characteristics of common and preference securities.

3.1 Common Shares

Common shares represent an ownership interest in a company and are the predominant type of equity security. As a result, investors share in the operating performance of the company, participate in the governance process through voting rights, and have a claim on the company's net assets in the case of liquidation. Companies may choose to pay out some, or all, of their net income in the form of cash dividends to common shareholders, but they are not contractually obligated to do so.[9]

Voting rights provide shareholders with the opportunity to participate in major corporate governance decisions, including the election of its board of directors, the decision to merge with or take over another company, and the selection of outside auditors. Shareholder voting generally takes place during a company's annual meeting. As a result of geographic limitations and the large number of shareholders, it is often not feasible for shareholders to attend the annual meeting in person. For this reason, shareholders may **vote by proxy**, which allows a designated party—such as another shareholder, a shareholder representative, or management—to vote on the shareholders' behalf.

Regular shareholder voting, where each share represents one vote, is referred to as **statutory voting**. Although it is the common method of voting, it is not always the most appropriate one to use to elect a board of directors. To better serve shareholders who own a small number of shares, **cumulative voting** is often used. Cumulative voting allows shareholders to direct their total voting rights to specific candidates, as opposed to having to allocate their voting rights evenly among all candidates. Total voting rights are based on the number of shares owned multiplied by the number of board directors being elected. For example, under cumulative voting, if four board directors are to be elected, a shareholder who owns 100 shares is entitled to 400 votes and can either cast all 400 votes in favor of a single candidate or spread them across the candidates in any proportion. In contrast, under statutory voting, a shareholder would be able to cast only a maximum of 100 votes for each candidate.

The key benefit to cumulative voting is that it allows shareholders with a small number of shares to apply all of their votes to one candidate, thus providing the opportunity for a higher level of representation on the board than would be allowed under statutory voting.

Exhibit 7 describes the rights of Viacom Corporation's shareholders. In this case, a dual-share arrangement allows the founding chairman and his family to control more than 70 percent of the voting rights through the ownership of Class A shares. This arrangement gives them the ability to exert control over the board of director election process, corporate decision making, and other important aspects of managing the company. A cumulative voting arrangement for any minority shareholders of Class A shares would improve their board representation.

---

[9] It is also possible for companies to pay more than the current period's net income as dividends. Such payout policies are, however, generally not sustainable in the long run.

Exhibit 7	Share Class Arrangements at Viacom Corporation[10]

Viacom has two classes of common stock: Class A, which is the voting stock, and Class B, which is the non-voting stock. There is no difference between the two classes except for voting rights; they generally trade within a close price range of each other. There are, however, far more shares of Class B outstanding, so most of the trading occurs in that class.

Voting Rights—Holders of Class A common stock are entitled to one vote per share. Holders of Class B common stock do not have any voting rights, except as required by Delaware law. Generally, all matters to be voted on by Viacom stockholders must be approved by a majority of the aggregate voting power of the shares of Class A common stock present in person or represented by proxy, except as required by Delaware law.

Dividends—Stockholders of Class A common stock and Class B common stock will share ratably in any cash dividend declared by the Board of Directors, subject to any preferential rights of any outstanding preferred stock. Viacom does not currently pay a cash dividend, and any decision to pay a cash dividend in the future will be at the discretion of the Board of Directors and will depend on many factors.

Conversion—So long as there are 5,000 shares of Class A common stock outstanding, each share of Class A common stock will be convertible at the option of the holder of such share into one share of Class B common stock.

Liquidation Rights—In the event of liquidation, dissolution or winding-up of Viacom, all stockholders of common stock, regardless of class, will be entitled to share ratably in any assets available for distributions to stockholders of shares of Viacom common stock subject to the preferential rights of any outstanding preferred stock.

Split, Subdivisions or Combination—In the event of a split, subdivision or combination of the outstanding shares of Class A common stock or Class B common stock, the outstanding shares of the other class of common stock will be divided proportionally.

Preemptive Rights—Shares of Class A common stock and Class B common stock do not entitle a stockholder to any preemptive rights enabling a stockholder to subscribe for or receive shares of stock of any class or any other securities convertible into shares of stock of any class of Viacom.

As seen in Exhibit 7, companies can issue different classes of common shares (Class A and Class B shares), with each class offering different ownership rights.[11] For example, as shown in Exhibit 8, the Ford Motor Company has Class A shares ("Common Stock"), which are owned by the investing public. It also has Class B shares, which are owned only by the Ford family. The exhibit contains an excerpt from Ford's *2008 Annual Report* (p. 115). Class A shareholders have 60 percent voting rights, whereas Class B shareholders have 40 percent. In the case of liquidation, however, Class B shareholders will not only receive the first US$0.50 per share that is available for distribution (as will Class A shareholders), but they will also receive the

---

10 This information has been adapted from Viacom's investor relations website and its 10-K filing with the U.S. Securities and Exchange Commission; see www.viacom.com.
11 In some countries, including the United States, companies can issue different classes of shares, with Class A shares being the most common. The role and function of different classes of shares is described in more detail in Exhibit 8.

next US$1.00 per share that is available for distribution before Class A shareholders receive anything else. Thus, Class B shareholders have an opportunity to receive a larger proportion of distributions upon liquidation than do Class A shareholders.[12]

Exhibit 8	Share Class Arrangements at Ford Motor Company[13]

NOTE 21. CAPITAL STOCK AND AMOUNTS PER SHARE

All general voting power is vested in the holders of Common Stock and Class B Stock. Holders of our Common Stock have 60% of the general voting power and holders of our Class B Stock are entitled to such number of votes per share as will give them the remaining 40%. Shares of Common Stock and Class B Stock share equally in dividends when and as paid, with stock dividends payable in shares of stock of the class held. As discussed in Note 16, we are prohibited from paying dividends (other than dividends payable in stock) under the terms of the Credit Agreement.

If liquidated, each share of Common Stock will be entitled to the first $0.50 available for distribution to holders of Common Stock and Class B Stock, each share of Class B Stock will be entitled to the next $1.00 so available, each share of Common Stock will be entitled to the next $0.50 so available and each share of Common and Class B Stock will be entitled to an equal amount thereafter.

Common shares may also be callable or putable. **Callable common shares** (also known as redeemable common shares) give the issuing company the option (or right), but not the obligation, to buy back shares from investors at a call price that is specified when the shares are originally issued. It is most common for companies to call (or redeem) their common shares when the market price is above the pre-specified call price. The company benefits because it can buy back its shares below the current market price and later resell them at a higher market price, and it can also reduce dividend payments to preserve capital, if required. Investors benefit because they receive a guaranteed return when their shares are called. Exhibit 9 provides an example of callable common shares issued by Genomic Solutions in the U.S. market. The exhibit provides details on the creation of callable common shares used to consummate a strategic alliance between PerkinElmer and Genomic Solutions. The arrangement contains provisions more favorable to PerkinElmer because at the time it was a more established and better capitalized company than Genomic Solutions.

---

12 For example, if US$2.00 per share is available for distribution, the Common Stock (Class A) shareholders will receive US$0.50 per share, while the Class B shareholders will receive US$1.50 per share. However, if there is US$3.50 per share available for distribution, the Common Stock shareholders will receive a total of US$1.50 per share and the Class B shareholders will receive a total of US$2.00 per share.
13 Extracted from Ford Motor Company's *2008 Annual Report* (virtual.stivesonline.com/publication/?i=14030).

Exhibit 9	Callable Stock Arrangement from Genomic Solutions[14]

The following information assumes that the underwriters do not exercise the over-allotment option granted by us to purchase additional shares in the offering:

Callable common stock offered by us:	7,000,000 shares
Callable common stock to be outstanding after the offering:	22,718,888 shares
Common stock to be outstanding after the offering:	1,269,841 shares
Proposed NASDAQ National Market symbol:	GNSL
Use of proceeds:	General corporate purposes and possible future acquisitions

For two years from the completion of this offering, we may require all holders of our callable common stock to sell their shares back to us. We must exercise this right at PerkinElmer's direction. The price for repurchase of our callable common stock generally will be 20% over the market price. PerkinElmer also has a right to match any third party offer for our callable common stock or our business that our board of directors is prepared to accept.

Putable common shares give investors the option or right to sell their shares (i.e., "put" them) back to the issuing company at a price that is specified when the shares are originally issued. Investors will generally sell their shares back to the issuing company when the market price is below the pre-specified put price. Thus, the put option feature limits the potential loss for investors. From the issuing company's perspective, the put option facilitates raising capital because the shares are more appealing to investors.

Exhibit 10 provides an example of putable common shares issued by Dreyer's, now a subsidiary of Switzerland-based Nestlé. In this case, shareholders had the right to sell their shares to Dreyer's for US$83.10, the pre-specified put price.

Exhibit 10	Putable Stock Arrangement for Dreyer's Grand Ice Cream[15]

Dreyer's Grand Ice Cream Holdings, Inc. ("Dreyer's") (NNM: DRYR) announced today that the period during which holders of shares of Dreyer's Class A Callable Putable Common Stock (the "Class A Shares") could require Dreyer's to purchase their Class A Shares (the "Put Right") for a cash payment of $83.10 per Class A Share (the "Purchase Price") expired at 5:00 p.m. New York City time on January 13, 2006 (the "Expiration Time"). According to the report of the depositary agent for the Put Right, holders of an aggregate of 30,518,885 Class A Shares (including 1,792,193 shares subject to guaranteed delivery procedures) properly exercised the Put Right.

3.2 Preference Shares

Preference shares (or preferred stock) rank above common shares with respect to the payment of dividends and the distribution of the company's net assets upon liquidation.[16] However, preference shareholders do not share in the operating performance of

---

14 Genomic Solutions Form S-1 as filed with the U.S. SEC (14 May 2000); see www.edgar-online.com.
15 "Dreyer's Announces Expiration of Put Period and Anticipated Merger with Nestle," *Business Wire* (14 January 2006): www.findarticles.com/p/articles/mi_m0EIN/is_2006_Jan_14/ai_n16001349.
16 Preference shares have a lower priority than debt in the case of liquidation. That is, debt holders have a higher claim on a firm's assets in the event of liquidation and will receive what is owed to them first, followed by preference shareholders and then common shareholders.

the company and generally do not have any voting rights, unless explicitly allowed for at issuance. Preference shares have characteristics of both debt securities and common shares. Similar to the interest payments on debt securities, the dividends on preference shares are fixed and are generally higher than the dividends on common shares. However, unlike interest payments, preference dividends are not contractual obligations of the company. Similar to common shares, preference shares can be perpetual (i.e., no fixed maturity date), can pay dividends indefinitely, and can be callable or putable.

Exhibit 11 provides an example of callable preference shares issued by Goldman Sachs to raise capital during the credit crisis of 2008. In this case, Berkshire Hathaway, the purchaser of the shares, will receive an ongoing dividend from Goldman Sachs. If Goldman Sachs chooses to buy back the shares, it must do so at a 10 percent premium above their par value.

Exhibit 11	Callable Stock Arrangement between Goldman Sachs and Berkshire Hathaway[17]

New York, NY—September 23, 2008—The Goldman Sachs Group, Inc. (NYSE: GS) announced today that it has reached an agreement to sell $5 billion of perpetual preferred stock to Berkshire Hathaway, Inc. in a private offering. The preferred stock has a dividend of 10 percent and is callable at any time at a 10 percent premium. In conjunction with this offering, Berkshire Hathaway will also receive warrants to purchase $5 billion of common stock with a strike price of $115 per share, which are exercisable at any time for a five year term. In addition, Goldman Sachs is raising at least $2.5 billion in common equity in a public offering.

Dividends on preference shares can be cumulative, non-cumulative, participating, non-participating, or some combination thereof (i.e., cumulative participating, cumulative non-participating, non-cumulative participating, non-cumulative non-participating).

Dividends on **cumulative preference shares** accrue so that if the company decides not to pay a dividend in one or more periods, the unpaid dividends accrue and must be paid in full before dividends on common shares can be paid. In contrast, **non-cumulative preference shares** have no such provision. This means that any dividends that are not paid in the current or subsequent periods are forfeited permanently and are not accrued over time to be paid at a later date. However, the company is still not permitted to pay any dividends to common shareholders in the current period unless preferred dividends have been paid first.

Participating preference shares entitle the shareholders to receive the standard preferred dividend plus the opportunity to receive an additional dividend if the company's profits exceed a pre-specified level. In addition, participating preference shares can also contain provisions that entitle shareholders to an additional distribution of the company's assets upon liquidation, above the par (or face) value of the preference shares. **Non-participating preference shares** do not allow shareholders to share in the profits of the company. Instead, shareholders are entitled to receive only a fixed dividend payment and the par value of the shares in the event of liquidation. The use of participating preference shares is much more common for smaller, riskier companies where the possibility of future liquidation is more of a concern to investors.

---

17 Goldman Sachs, "Berkshire Hathaway to Invest $5 Billion in Goldman Sachs," (23 September 2008): www.goldmansachs.com/our-firm/press/press-releases/archived/2008/berkshire-hathaway-invest.html.

Preference shares can also be convertible. **Convertible preference shares** entitle shareholders to convert their shares into a specified number of common shares. This conversion ratio is determined at issuance. Convertible preference shares have the following advantages:

- They allow investors to earn a higher dividend than if they invested in the company's common shares.
- They allow investors the opportunity to share in the profits of the company.
- They allow investors to benefit from a rise in the price of the common shares through the conversion option.
- Their price is less volatile than the underlying common shares because the dividend payments are known and more stable.

As a result, the use of convertible preference shares is a popular financing option in venture capital and private equity transactions in which the issuing companies are considered to be of higher risk and when it may be years before the issuing company "goes public" (i.e., issues common shares to the public).

Exhibit 12 provides examples of the types and characteristics of preference shares as issued by DBS Bank of Singapore.

Exhibit 12	Examples of Preference Shares Issued by DBS Bank[18]

SINGAPORE, MAY 12—DBS Bank said today it plans to offer S$700 million in preference shares and make it available to both retail and institutional investors in Singapore. Called the DBS Preferred Investment Issue, it will yield investors a fixed non-cumulative gross dividend rate of 6% for the first ten years and a floating rate thereafter. The DBS Preferred Investment Issue will be offered in two tranches, consisting of a S$100 million tranche to retail investors via ATMs and a S$600 million placement tranche available to both retail and institutional investors. Depending on investor demand, DBS could increase the offering amount.

Jackson Tai, President and Chief Operating Officer of DBS Group Holdings, said that following the success of the hybrid Tier 1 issue in March, DBS decided to make this new issue available to the local retail investors. "We consider these issues as an important capital management tool. We were pleased with the success of our hybrid Tier 1 issue for institutional investors and wanted to introduce a capital instrument that would be available to retail investors as well."

DBS Preferred Investment Issues are perpetual securities, redeemable after ten years at the option of DBS Bank and at every dividend date thereafter subject to certain redemption conditions. They are issued by DBS Bank and are considered to be core Tier 1 capital under the Monetary Authority of Singapore and Bank of International Settlement's guidelines. They will be listed on the Singapore Exchange Securities Trading Limited and can be traded on the secondary market through a broker. Holders of the DBS Preferred Investment Issue will receive the dividend net of the 24.5% income tax. Investors may claim the tax credit in their tax returns.

---

18 DBS Bank, "DBS Follows US$850 Million Offering of Subordinated Notes to International Markets with Singapore Dollar Market Financing" (12 May 2001): www.dbs.com/newsroom/2001/Pages/press010512.aspx.

PRIVATE VERSUS PUBLIC EQUITY SECURITIES

4

Our discussion so far has focused on equity securities that are issued and traded in public markets and on exchanges. Equity securities can also be issued and traded in private equity markets. **Private equity securities** are issued primarily to institutional investors via non-public offerings, such as private placements. Because they are not listed on public exchanges, there is no active secondary market for these securities. As a result, private equity securities do not have "market determined" quoted prices, are highly illiquid, and require negotiations between investors in order to be traded. In addition, financial statements and other important information needed to determine the fair value of private equity securities may be difficult to obtain because the issuing companies are typically not required by regulatory authorities to publish this information.

There are three primary types of private equity investments: venture capital, leveraged buyouts, and private investment in public equity. **Venture capital** investments provide "seed" or start-up capital, early-stage financing, or mezzanine financing to companies that are in the early stages of development and require additional capital for expansion. These funds are then used to finance the company's product development and growth. Venture capitalists range from family and friends to wealthy individuals and private equity funds. Because the equity securities issued to venture capitalists are not publicly traded, they generally require a commitment of funds for a relatively long period of time; the opportunity to "exit" the investment is typically within 3 to 10 years from the initial start-up. The exit return earned by these private equity investors is based on the price that the securities can be sold for if and when the start-up company first goes public, either via an **initial public offering (IPO)** on the stock market or by being sold to other investors.

A **leveraged buyout (LBO)** occurs when a group of investors (such as the company's management or a private equity partnership) uses a large amount of debt to purchase all of the outstanding common shares of a publicly traded company. In cases where the group of investors acquiring the company is primarily comprised of the company's existing management, the transaction is referred to as a **management buyout (MBO)**. After the shares are purchased, they cease to trade on an exchange and the investor group takes full control of the company. In other words, the company is taken "private" or has been privatized. Companies that are candidates for these types of transactions generally have large amounts of undervalued assets (which can be sold to reduce debt) and generate high levels of cash flows (which are used to make interest and principal payments on the debt). The ultimate objective of a buyout (LBO or MBO) is to restructure the acquired company and later take it "public" again by issuing new shares to the public in the primary market.

The third type of private investment is a **private investment in public equity**, or PIPE.[19] This type of investment is generally sought by a public company that is in need of additional capital quickly and is willing to sell a sizeable ownership position to a private investor or investor group. For example, a company may require a large investment of new equity funds in a short period of time because it has significant expansion opportunities, is facing high levels of indebtedness, or is experiencing a rapid deterioration in its operations. Depending on how urgent the need is and the size of the capital requirement, the private investor may be able to purchase shares in the company at a significant discount to the publicly-quoted market price. Exhibit 13 contains a recent PIPE transaction for the electronics retailer hhgregg, which also included the issuance of additional common shares to the public.

---

19 The term PIPE is widely used in the United States and is also used internationally, including in emerging markets.

Exhibit 13 **Example of a PIPE Transaction**[20]

On July 20, 2009, hhgregg completed a public stock offering of 4,025,000 shares of its common stock at $16.50 per share. Concurrently with the public offering, investment funds affiliated with Freeman Spogli & Co. purchased an additional 1,000,000 shares of common stock, in a private placement transaction, at the price per share paid by the public in the offering. Proceeds, net of underwriting fees, from the public stock offering and private placement, totaled approximately $78.6 million. These proceeds will be used for general corporate purposes, including funding the Company's accelerated new store growth plans.

While the global private equity market is relatively small in comparison to the global public equity market, it has experienced considerable growth over the past three decades. According to a study of the private equity market sponsored by the *World Economic Forum* and spanning the period 1970–2007, approximately US$3.6 trillion in debt and equity were acquired in leveraged buyouts. Of this amount, approximately 75 percent or US$2.7 trillion worth of transactions occurred during 2001–2007.[21] While the U.S. and the U.K. markets were the focus of most private equity investments during the 1980s and 1990s, private equity investments outside of these markets have grown substantially in recent years. In addition, the number of companies operating under private equity ownership has also grown. For example, during the mid-1990s, fewer than 2,000 companies were under LBO ownership compared to close to 14,000 companies that were under LBO ownership globally at the beginning of 2007. The holding period for private equity investments has also increased during this time period from 3 to 5 years (1980s and 1990s) to approximately 10 years.[22]

The move to longer holding periods has given private equity investors the opportunity to more effectively and patiently address any underlying operational issues facing the company and to better manage it for long-term value creation. Because of the longer holding periods, more private equity firms are issuing convertible preference shares because they provide investors with greater total return potential through their dividend payments and the ability to convert their shares into common shares during an IPO.

In operating a publicly traded company, management often feels pressured to focus on short-term results[23] (e.g., meeting quarterly sales and earnings targets from analysts biased toward near-term price performance) instead of operating the company to obtain long-term sustainable revenue and earnings growth. By "going private," management can adopt a more long-term focus and can eliminate certain costs that are necessary to operate a publicly traded company—such as the cost of meeting regulatory and stock exchange filing requirements, the cost of maintaining investor relations departments to communicate with shareholders and the media, and the cost of holding quarterly analyst conference calls.

As described above, public equity markets are much larger than private equity networks and allow companies more opportunities to raise capital that is subsequently actively traded in secondary markets. By operating under public scrutiny, companies are incentivized to be more open in terms of corporate governance and executive

---

20 This information was obtained from hhgregg's first quarter fiscal 2009 earnings report (http://ir.hhgregg.com/releasedetail.cfm?ReleaseID=401980).

21 Stromberg (2008).

22 See, for example, Bailey, Wirth, and Zapol (2005).

23 For further information, see "Overcoming Short-Termism: A Call for a More Responsible Approach to Investment and Business Management" (www.aspeninstitute.org/bsp/cvsg/policy2009).

compensation to ensure that they are acting for the benefit of shareholders. In fact, some studies have shown that private equity firms score lower in terms of corporate governance effectiveness, which may be attributed to the fact that shareholders, analysts, and other stakeholders are able to influence management when corporate governance and other policies are public.

INVESTING IN NON-DOMESTIC EQUITY SECURITIES

5

Technological innovations and the growth of electronic information exchanges (electronic trading networks, the internet, etc.) have accelerated the integration and growth of global financial markets. As detailed previously, global capital markets have expanded at a much more rapid rate than global GDP in recent years; both primary and secondary international markets have benefited from the enhanced ability to rapidly and openly exchange information. Increased integration of equity markets has made it easier and less expensive for companies to raise capital and to expand their shareholder base beyond their local market. Integration has also made it easier for investors to invest in companies that are located outside of their domestic markets. This has enabled investors to further diversify and improve the risk and return characteristics of their portfolios by adding a class of assets with lower correlations to local country assets.

One barrier to investing globally is that many countries still impose "foreign restrictions" on individuals and companies from other countries that want to invest in their domestic companies. There are three primary reasons for these restrictions. The first is to limit the amount of control that foreign investors can exert on domestic companies. For example, some countries prevent foreign investors from acquiring a majority interest in domestic companies. The second is to give domestic investors the opportunity to own shares in the foreign companies that are conducting business in their country. For example, the Swedish home furnishings retailer IKEA abandoned efforts to invest in parts of the Asia/Pacific region because local governments did not want IKEA to maintain complete ownership of its stores. The third reason is to reduce the volatility of capital flows into and out of domestic equity markets. For example, one of the main consequences of the Asian Financial Crisis in 1997–98 was the large outflow of capital from such emerging market countries as Thailand, Indonesia, and South Korea. These outflows led to dramatic declines in the equity markets of these countries and significant currency devaluations and resulted in many governments placing restrictions on capital flows. Today, many of these same markets have built up currency reserves to better withstand capital outflows inherent in economic contractions and periods of financial market turmoil.

Studies have shown that reducing restrictions on foreign ownership has led to improved equity market performance over the long term.[24] Although restrictions vary widely, more countries are allowing increasing levels of foreign ownership. For example, Australia has sought tax reforms as a means to encourage international demand for its managed funds in order to increase its role as an international financial center. China recently announced plans to allow designated foreign institutional investors to invest up to US$1 billion in its domestic yuan-denominated A shares (up from a previous US$800 million) as it seeks to slowly liberalize its stock markets.

Over the past two decades, three trends have emerged: a) an increasing number of companies have issued shares in markets outside of their home country; b) the number of companies whose shares are traded in markets outside of their home has

---

[24] See, for example, Henry and Chari (2007).

increased; and c) an increasing number of companies are dual listed, which means that their shares are simultaneously issued and traded in two or more markets. Companies located in emerging markets have particularly benefited from these trends because they no longer have to be concerned with capital constraints or lack of liquidity in their domestic markets. These companies have found it easier to raise capital in the markets of developed countries because these markets generally have higher levels of liquidity and more stringent financial reporting requirements and accounting standards. Being listed on an international exchange has a number of benefits. It can increase investor awareness about the company's products and services, enhance the liquidity of the company's shares, and increase corporate transparency because of the additional market exposure and the need to meet a greater number of filing requirements.

Technological advancements have made it easier for investors to trade shares in foreign markets. The German insurance company Allianz SE recently delisted its shares from the NYSE and certain European markets because international investors increasingly traded its shares on the Frankfurt Stock Exchange. Exhibit 14 illustrates the extent to which the institutional shareholder base at BASF, a large German chemical corporation, has become increasingly global in nature.

Exhibit 14	Example of Increased Globalization of Share Ownership[25]

BASF is one of the largest publicly owned companies with around 460,000 shareholders and a high free float. An analysis of the shareholder structure carried out in September 2008 showed that, at 22% of share capital, the United States and Canada made up the largest regional group of institutional investors. Institutional investors from Germany made up 13%. Shareholders from Great Britain and Ireland held 14% of BASF shares, while a further 14% are held by institutional investors from the rest of Europe. Around 28% of the company's share capital is held by private investors, most of whom are resident in Germany.

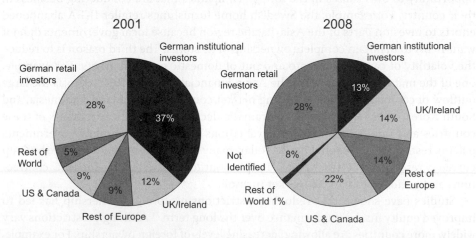

5.1 Direct Investing

Investors can use a variety of methods to invest in the equity of companies outside of their local market. The most obvious is to buy and sell securities directly in foreign markets. However, this means that all transactions—including the purchase and sale of shares, dividend payments, and capital gains—are in the company's, not the investor's,

---

25 Adapted from BASF's investor relations website (www.basf.com). **Free float** refers to the extent that shares are readily and freely tradable in the secondary market.

domestic currency. In addition, investors must be familiar with the trading, clearing, and settlement regulations and procedures of that market. Investing directly often results in less transparency and more volatility because audited financial information may not be provided on a regular basis and the market may be less liquid. Alternatively, investors can use such securities as depository receipts and global registered shares, which represent the equity of international companies and are traded on local exchanges and in the local currencies. With these securities, investors have to worry less about currency conversions (price quotations and dividend payments are in the investor's local currency), unfamiliar market practices, and differences in accounting standards. The sections that follow discuss various securities that investors can invest in outside of their home market.

5.2 Depository Receipts

A **depository receipt**[26] (DR) is a security that trades like an ordinary share on a local exchange and represents an economic interest in a foreign company. It allows the publicly listed shares of a foreign company to be traded on an exchange outside its domestic market. A depository receipt is created when the equity shares of a foreign company are deposited in a bank (i.e., the depository) in the country on whose exchange the shares will trade. The depository then issues receipts that represent the shares that were deposited. The number of receipts issued and the price of each DR is based on a ratio, which specifies the number of depository receipts to the underlying shares. Consequently, a DR may represent one share of the underlying stock, many shares of the underlying stock, or a fractional share of the underlying stock. The price of each DR will be affected by factors that affect the price of the underlying shares, such as company fundamentals, market conditions, analysts' recommendations, and exchange rate movements. In addition, any short-term valuation discrepancies between shares traded on multiple exchanges represent a quick arbitrage profit opportunity for astute traders to exploit. The responsibilities of the **depository bank** that issues the receipts include acting as custodian and as a registrar. This entails handling dividend payments, other taxable events, stock splits, and serving as the transfer agent for the foreign company whose securities the DR represents. The Bank of New York Mellon is the largest depository bank; however, Deutsche Bank, JPMorgan, and Citibank also offer depository services.[27]

A DR can be **sponsored** or **unsponsored**. A sponsored DR is when the foreign company whose shares are held by the depository has a direct involvement in the issuance of the receipts. Investors in sponsored DRs have the same rights as the direct owners of the common shares (e.g., the right to vote and the right to receive dividends). In contrast, with an unsponsored DR, the underlying foreign company has no involvement with the issuance of the receipts. Instead, the depository purchases the foreign company's shares in its domestic market and then issues the receipts through brokerage firms in the depository's local market. In this case, the depository bank, not the investors in the DR, retains the voting rights. Sponsored DRs are generally subject to greater reporting requirements than unsponsored DRs. In the United States, for example, sponsored DRs must be registered (meet the reporting requirements) with the U.S. Securities and Exchange Commission (SEC). Exhibit 15 contains an example of a sponsored DR issued by Japan Airlines.

---

26 Note that the spellings *depositary* and *depository* are used interchangeably in financial markets. In this reading, we use the spelling *depository* throughout.
27 Boubakri, Cosset, and Samet (2008).

| Exhibit 15 | Sponsored versus Unsponsored Depository Receipts[28] |

The Japan Airlines (JAL) Group, Asia's biggest airline grouping, has picked the Bank of New York as the depository bank to make its previously unsponsored American depository receipts (ADRs) sponsored. By taking this action and by boosting investor relations activities in the U.S., the JAL group aims to increase the number of overseas shareholders. The JAL Group's sponsored ADRs became effective on August 19th, 2004 and dealing will start on August 25th. The JAL Group's American depository receipts had been previously issued in the U.S. as unsponsored ADRs by several U.S. depository banks since the 1970s. However, as unsponsored ADRs are issued without the involvement of the company itself, the company has difficulty in identifying ADR holders and controlling ADRs. From now, the JAL Group will be able to better serve its ADR holders and, at the same time, the JAL Group intends to increase its overseas investors.

There are two types of depository receipts: Global depository receipts (GDRs) and American depository receipts (ADRs), which are described below.

5.2.1 Global Depository Receipts

A **global depository receipt** (GDR) is issued outside of the company's home country and outside of the United States. The depository bank that issues GDRs is generally located (or has branches) in the countries on whose exchanges the shares are traded. A key advantage of GDRs is that they are not subject to the foreign ownership and capital flow restrictions that may be imposed by the issuing company's home country because they are sold outside of that country. The issuing company selects the exchange where the GDR is to be traded based on such factors as investors' familiarity with the company or the existence of a large international investor base. The London and Luxembourg exchanges were the first ones to trade GDRs. Other stock exchanges trading GDRs are the Dubai International Financial Exchange, the Singapore Stock Exchange, and the Hong Kong Stock Exchange. Currently, the London and Luxembourg exchanges are where most GDRs are traded because they can be issued in a more timely manner and at a lower cost. Regardless of the exchange they are traded on, the majority of GDRs are denominated in U.S. dollars, although the number of GDRs denominated in pound sterling and euros is increasing. Note that although GDRs cannot be listed on U.S. exchanges, they can be privately placed with institutional investors based in the United States.

5.2.2 American Depository Receipts

An **American depository receipt** (ADR) is a U.S. dollar-denominated security that trades like a common share on U.S. exchanges. First created in 1927, ADRs are the oldest type of depository receipts and are currently the most commonly traded depository receipts. They enable foreign companies to raise capital from U.S. investors. Note that an ADR is one form of a GDR; however, not all GDRs are ADRs because GDRs cannot be publicly traded in the United States. The term **American depository share** (ADS) is often used in tandem with the term ADR. A depository share is a security that is actually traded in the issuing company's domestic market. That is, while American depository receipts are the certificates that are traded on U.S. markets, American depository shares are the underlying shares on which these receipts are based.

---

28 Adapted from Japan Airlines Group's investor relations website (www.jal.com/en/press/2004/082301/img/ADRS.pdf).

There are four primary types of ADRs, with each type having different levels of corporate governance and filing requirements. Level I Sponsored ADRs trade in the over-the-counter (OTC) market and do not require full registration with the Securities and Exchange Commission (SEC). Level II and Level III Sponsored ADRs can trade on the New York Stock Exchange (NYSE), NASDAQ, and American Stock Exchange (AMEX). Level II and III ADRs allow companies to raise capital and make acquisitions using these securities. However, the issuing companies must fulfill all SEC requirements.

The fourth type of ADR, an SEC Rule 144A or a Regulation S depository receipt, does not require SEC registration. Instead, foreign companies are able to raise capital by privately placing these depository receipts with qualified institutional investors or to offshore non-U.S. investors. Exhibit 16 summarizes the main features of ADRs.

Exhibit 16	Summary of the Main Features of American Depository Receipts		
	Level I (Unlisted)	**Level II (Listed)**	**Level III (Listed)**	**Rule 144A (Unlisted)**
---	---	---	---	---
Objectives	Develop and broaden U.S. investor base with existing shares	Develop and broaden U.S. investor base with existing shares	Develop and broaden U.S. investor base with existing/new shares	Access qualified institutional buyers (QIBs)
Raising capital on U.S. markets?	No	No	Yes, through public offerings	Yes, through private placements to QIBs
SEC registration	Form F-6	Form F-6	Forms F-1 and F-6	None
Trading	Over the counter (OTC)	NYSE, NASDAQ, or AMEX	NYSE, NASDAQ, or AMEX	Private offerings, resales, and trading through automated linkages such as PORTAL
Listing fees	Low	High	High	Low
Size and earnings requirements	None	Yes	Yes	None

Source: Adapted from Boubakri, Cosset, and Samet (2008): Table 1.

More than 2,000 DRs, from over 80 countries, currently trade on U.S. exchanges. Based on current statistics, the total market value of DRs issued and traded is estimated at approximately US$2 trillion, or 15 percent of the total dollar value of equities traded in U.S. markets.[29]

5.2.3 *Global Registered Share*

A **global registered share** (GRS) is a common share that is traded on different stock exchanges around the world in different currencies. Currency conversions are not needed to purchase or sell them, because identical shares are quoted and traded in different currencies. Thus, the same share purchased on the Swiss exchange in Swiss francs can be sold on the Tokyo exchange for Japanese yen. As a result, GRSs offer more flexibility than depository receipts because the shares represent an actual ownership interest in the company that can be traded anywhere and currency conversions are not needed to purchase or sell them. GRSs were created and issued by Daimler Chrysler in 1998.

5.2.4 *Basket of Listed Depository Receipts*

Another type of global security is a **basket of listed depository receipts** (BLDR), which is an exchange-traded fund (ETF) that represents a portfolio of depository receipts. An ETF is a security that tracks an index but trades like an individual share on an exchange. An equity-ETF is a security that contains a portfolio of equities that tracks an index. It trades throughout the day and can be bought, sold, or sold short, just like an individual share. Like ordinary shares, ETFs can also be purchased on margin and used in hedging or arbitrage strategies. The BLDR is a specific class of ETF security that consists of an underlying portfolio of DRs and is designed to track the price performance of an underlying DR index. For example, the Asia 50 ADR Index Fund is a capitalization-weighted ETF designed to track the performance of 50 Asian market-based ADRs.

6   RISK AND RETURN CHARACTERISTICS OF EQUITY SECURITIES

Different types of equity securities have different ownership claims on a company's net assets. The type of equity security and its features affect its risk and return characteristics. The following sections discuss the different return and risk characteristics of equity securities.

6.1 Return Characteristics of Equity Securities

There are two main sources of equity securities' total return: price change (or capital gain) and dividend income. The price change represents the difference between the purchase price (P_{t-1}) and the sale price (P_t) of a share at the end of time $t - 1$ and t, respectively. Cash or stock dividends (D_t) represent distributions that the company makes to its shareholders during period t. Therefore, an equity security's total return is calculated as:

$$\text{Total return, } R_t = (P_t - P_{t-1} + D_t)/P_{t-1} \qquad\qquad (1)$$

For non-dividend-paying stocks, the total return consists of price appreciation only. Companies that are in the early stages of their life cycle generally do not pay dividends because earnings and cash flows are reinvested to finance the company's growth. In contrast, companies that are in the mature phase of their life cycle may not have as many profitable growth opportunities; therefore, excess cash flows are often returned to investors via the payment of regular dividends or through share repurchases.

For investors who purchase depository receipts or foreign shares directly, there is a third source of return: **foreign exchange gains** (or losses). Foreign exchange gains arise because of the change in the exchange rate between the investor's currency and the currency that the foreign shares are denominated in. For example, U.S. investors who purchase the ADRs of a Japanese company will earn an additional return if the yen appreciates relative to the U.S. dollar. Conversely, these investors will earn a lower total return if the yen depreciates relative to the U.S. dollar. For example, if the total return for a Japanese company was 10 percent in Japan and the yen depreciated by 10 percent against the U.S. dollar, the total return of the ADR would be (approximately) 0 percent. If the yen had instead appreciated by 10 percent against the U.S. dollar, the total return of the ADR would be (approximately) 20 percent.

Investors that only consider price appreciation overlook an important source of return: the compounding that results from reinvested dividends. Reinvested dividends are cash dividends that the investor receives and uses to purchase additional shares.

As Exhibit 17 shows, in the long run total returns on equity securities are dramatically influenced by the compounding effect of reinvested dividends. Between 1900 and 2008, US$1 invested in U.S. equities in 1900 would have grown in *real* terms to US$582 with dividends reinvested, but to just US$6 when taking only the price appreciation or capital gain into account. This corresponds to a real compounded return of 6 percent per year with dividends reinvested, versus only 1.7 percent per year without dividends reinvested. As a comparison, Exhibit 17 shows the ending real wealth for bonds and bills, which are US$9.90 and US$2.90, respectively. These ending real wealth figures correspond to annualized real compounded returns of 2.1 percent on bonds and 1.0 percent on bills. This exhibit also shows the various bear markets (the lower boxes) over these periods, which were described in detail in Exhibit 5. In addition, it shows that each bear market was followed by a significant upward trend in the U.S. (and other) equity markets (the upper boxes).

Exhibit 17	Impact of Reinvested Dividends on Cumulative Real Returns in the U.S. Equity Market: 1900–2008

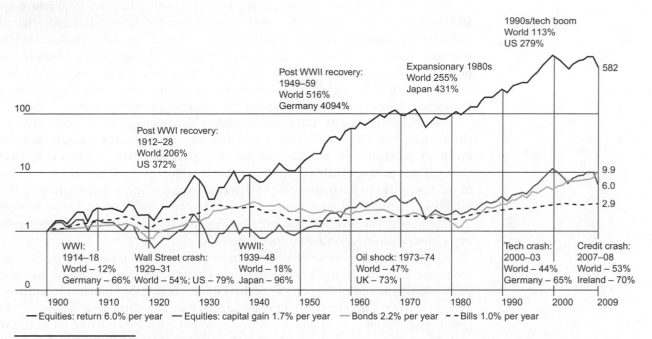

Source: Dimson, Marsh, and Staunton (2009).

6.2 Risk of Equity Securities

The risk of any security is based on the uncertainty of its future cash flows. The greater the uncertainty of its future cash flows, the greater the risk and the more variable or volatile the security's price. As discussed above, an equity security's total return is determined by its price change and dividends. Therefore, the risk of an equity security can be defined as the uncertainty of its expected (or future) total return. Risk is most often measured by calculating the standard deviation of the equity's expected total return.

A variety of different methods can be used to estimate an equity's expected total return and risk. One method uses the equity's average historical return and the standard deviation of this return as proxies for its expected future return and risk. Another method involves estimating a range of future returns over a specified period of time, assigning probabilities to those returns, and then calculating an expected return and a standard deviation of return based on this information.

The type of equity security, as well as its characteristics, affects the uncertainty of its future cash flows and therefore its risk. In general, preference shares are less risky than common shares for three main reasons:

1. Dividends on preference shares are known and fixed, and they account for a large portion of the preference shares' total return. Therefore, there is less uncertainty about future cash flows.

2. Preference shareholders receive dividends and other distributions before common shareholders.

3. The amount preference shareholders will receive if the company is liquidated is known and fixed as the par (or face) value of their shares. However, there is no guarantee that investors will receive that amount if the company experiences financial difficulty.

With common shares, however, a larger portion of shareholders' total return (or all of their total return for non-dividend shares) is based on future price appreciation and future dividends are unknown. If the company is liquidated, common shareholders will receive whatever amount (if any) is remaining after the company's creditors and preference shareholders have been paid. In summary, because the uncertainty surrounding the total return of preference shares is less than common shares, preference shares have lower risk and lower expected return than common shares.

It is important to note that some preference shares and common shares can be riskier than others because of their associated characteristics. For example, from an investor's point of view, putable common or preference shares are less risky than their callable or non-callable counterparts because they give the investor the option to sell the shares to the issuer at a pre-determined price. This pre-determined price establishes a minimum price that investors will receive and reduces the uncertainty associated with the security's future cash flow. As a result, putable shares generally pay a lower dividend than non-putable shares.

Because the major source of total return for preference shares is dividend income, the primary risk affecting all preference shares is the uncertainty of future dividend payments. Regardless of the preference shares' features (callable, putable, cumulative, etc.), the greater the uncertainty surrounding the issuer's ability to pay dividends, the greater risk. Because the ability of a company to pay dividends is based on its future cash flows and net income, investors try to estimate these amounts by examining past trends or forecasting future amounts. The more earnings and the greater amount of cash flow that the company has had, or is expected to have, the lower the uncertainty and risk associated with its ability to pay future dividends.

Callable common or preference shares are riskier than their non-callable counterparts because the issuer has the option to redeem the shares at a pre-determined price. Because the call price limits investors' potential future total return, callable shares generally pay a higher dividend to compensate investors for the risk that the shares could be called in the future. Similarly, putable preference shares have lower risk than non-putable preference shares. Cumulative preference shares have lower risk than non-cumulative preference shares because the cumulative feature gives investors the right to receive any unpaid dividends before any dividends can be paid to common shareholders.

EQUITY SECURITIES AND COMPANY VALUE   7

Companies issue equity securities on primary markets to raise capital and increase liquidity. This additional liquidity also provides the corporation an additional "currency" (its equity), which it can use to make acquisitions and provide stock option-based incentives to employees. The primary goal of raising capital is to finance the company's revenue-generating activities in order to increase its net income and maximize the wealth of its shareholders. In most cases, the capital that is raised is used to finance the purchase of long-lived assets, capital expansion projects, research and development, the entry into new product or geographic regions, and the acquisition of other companies. Alternatively, a company may be forced to raise capital to ensure that it continues to operate as a going concern. In these cases, capital is raised to fulfill regulatory requirements, improve capital adequacy ratios, or to ensure that debt covenants are met.

The ultimate goal of management is to increase the book value (shareholders' equity on a company's balance sheet) of the company and maximize the market value of its equity. Although management actions can directly affect the book value of the company (by increasing net income or by selling or purchasing its own shares), they can only indirectly affect the market value of its equity. The book value of a company's equity—the difference between its total assets and total liabilities—increases when the company retains its net income. The more net income that is earned and retained, the greater the company's book value of equity. Because management's decisions directly influence a company's net income, they also directly influence its book value of equity.

The market value of the company's equity, however, reflects the collective and differing expectations of investors concerning the amount, timing, and uncertainty of the company's future cash flows. Rarely will book value and market value be equal. Although management may be accomplishing its objective of increasing the company's book value, this increase may not be reflected in the market value of the company's equity because it does not affect investors' expectations about the company's future cash flows. A key measure that investors use to evaluate the effectiveness of management in increasing the company's book value is the accounting return on equity.

7.1 Accounting Return on Equity

Return on equity (ROE) is the primary measure that equity investors use to determine whether the management of a company is effectively and efficiently using the capital they have provided to generate profits. It measures the total amount of net income available to common shareholders generated by the total equity capital invested in the company. It is computed as net income available to ordinary shareholders (i.e., after preferred dividends have been deducted) divided by the average total book value of equity (BVE). That is:

$$\text{ROE}_t = \frac{\text{NI}_t}{\text{Average BVE}_t} = \frac{\text{NI}_t}{(\text{BVE}_t + \text{BVE}_{t-1})\,/\,2} \qquad (2)$$

where NI_t is the net income in year t and the average book value of equity is computed as the book values at the beginning and end of year t divided by 2. Return on equity assumes that the net income produced in the current year is generated by the equity existing at the beginning of the year and any new equity that was invested during the year. Note that some formulas only use shareholders' equity at the beginning of year t (that is, the end of year $t - 1$) in the denominator. This assumes that only the equity existing at the beginning of the year was used to generate the company's net income during the year. That is:

$$\text{ROE}_t = \frac{\text{NI}_t}{\text{BVE}_{t-1}}$$

(3)

Both formulas are appropriate to use as long as they are applied consistently. For example, using beginning of the year book value is appropriate when book values are relatively stable over time or when computing ROE for a company annually over a period of time. Average book value is more appropriate if a company experiences more volatile year-end book values or if the industry convention is to use average book values in calculating ROE.

One caveat to be aware of when computing and analyzing ROE is that net income and the book value of equity are directly affected by management's choice of accounting methods, such as those relating to depreciation (straight line versus accelerated methods) or inventories (first in, first out versus weighted average cost). Different accounting methods can make it difficult to compare the return on equity of companies even if they operate in the same industry. It may also be difficult to compare the ROE of the same company over time if its accounting methods have changed during that time.

Exhibit 18 contains information on the net income and total book value of shareholders' equity for three **blue chip** (widely held large market capitalization companies that are considered financially sound and are leaders in their respective industry or local stock market) pharmaceutical companies: Pfizer, Novartis AG, and GlaxoSmithKline. The data are for their financial years ending December 2006 through December 2008.[30]

Exhibit 18	Net Income and Book Value of Equity for Pfizer, Novartis AG, and GlaxoSmithKline (in Thousands of U.S. Dollars)		
	Financial Year Ending		
	31 Dec 2008	**31 Dec 2007**	**31 Dec 2006**
Pfizer			
Net income	$8,104,000	$8,144,000	$19,337,000
Total stockholders' equity	$57,556,000	$65,010,000	$71,358,000
Novartis AG			
Net income	$8,233,000	$11,968,000	$5,264,000
Total stockholders' equity	$50,437,000	$49,396,000	$41,670,000
GlaxoSmithKline			
Net income	$6,822,505	$10,605,663	$8,747,382
Total stockholders' equity	$11,483,295	$19,180,072	$67,888,692

Using the average book value of equity, the return on equity for Pfizer for the years ending December 2007 and 2008 can be calculated as:

Return on equity for the year ending December 2007

$$\text{ROE}_{2007} = \frac{\text{NI}_{2007}}{(\text{BVE}_{2006} + \text{BVE}_{2007})\,/\,2} = \frac{8,144,000}{(71,358,000 + 65,010,000)\,/\,2} = 11.9\%$$

---

[30] Pfizer uses U.S. GAAP to prepare its financial statements; Novartis and GlaxoSmithKline use International Financial Reporting Standards. Therefore, it would be inappropriate to compare the ROE of Pfizer to that of Novartis or GlaxoSmithKline.

Return on equity for the year ending December 2008

$$\text{ROE}_{2008} = \frac{\text{NI}_{2008}}{(\text{BVE}_{2007} + \text{BVE}_{2008}) / 2} = \frac{8,104,000}{(65,010,000 + 57,556,000) / 2} = 13.2\%$$

Exhibit 19 summarizes the return on equity for Novartis and GlaxoSmithKline in addition to Pfizer for 2007 and 2008.

Exhibit 19	Return on Equity for Pfizer, Novartis AG, and GlaxoSmithKline	
	31 Dec 2008 (%)	**31 Dec 2007 (%)**
Pfizer	13.2	11.9
Novartis AG	16.5	26.3
GlaxoSmithKline	44.5	24.4

In the case of Novartis, the ROE of 26.3 percent in 2007 indicates that the company was able to generate a return (profit) of US$0.263 on every US$1.00 of capital invested by shareholders. In 2008, its operating performance deteriorated because it was only able to generate a 16.5 percent return on its equity. In contrast, GlaxoSmithKline almost doubled its return on equity over this period, from 24.4 percent to 44.5 percent. Pfizer's ROE remained relatively unchanged.

ROE can increase if net income increases at a faster rate than shareholders' equity or if net income decreases at a slower rate than shareholders' equity. In the case of Novartis, ROE fell in 2008 because its net income decreased by over 30 percent while shareholders' equity remained relatively stable. Stated differently, Novartis was less effective in using its equity capital to generate profits in 2008 than in 2007. In the case of GlaxoSmithKline, its ROE increased dramatically from 24.4 percent to 44.5 percent in 2007 versus 2008 even though its net income fell over 35 percent because its average shareholder equity decreased dramatically from 2006–2007 to 2007–2008.

An important question to ask is whether an increasing ROE is always good. The short answer is, "it depends." One reason ROE can increase is if net income decreases at a slower rate than shareholders' equity, which is not a positive sign. In addition, ROE can increase if the company issues debt and then uses the proceeds to repurchase some of its outstanding shares. This action will increase the company's leverage and make its equity riskier. Therefore, it is important to examine the source of changes in the company's net income *and* shareholders' equity over time. The DuPont formula, which is discussed in a separate reading, can be used to analyze the sources of changes in a company's ROE.

The book value of a company's equity reflects the historical operating and financing decisions of its management. The market value of the company's equity reflects these decisions as well as investors' collective assessment and expectations about the company's future cash flows generated by its positive net present value investment opportunities. If investors believe that the company has a large number of these future cash flow-generating investment opportunities, the market value of the company's equity will exceed its book value. Exhibit 20 shows the market price per share, the total number of shares outstanding, and the total book value of shareholders' equity for Pfizer, Novartis AG, and GlaxoSmithKline at the end of December 2008. This exhibit also shows the total market value of equity (or market capitalization) computed as the number of shares outstanding multiplied by the market price per share.

Exhibit 20	Market Information for Pfizer, Novartis AG, and GlaxoSmithKline (in Thousands of U.S. Dollars except Market Price)		
	Pfizer	**Novartis AG**	**GlaxoSmithKline**
Market price	$16.97	$47.64	$35.84
Total shares outstanding	6,750,000	2,260,000	2,530,000
Total shareholders' equity	$57,556,000	$50,437,000	$11,483,295
Total market value of equity	$114,547,500	$107,666,400	$90,675,200

Note that in Exhibit 20, the total market value of equity for Pfizer is computed as:

Market value of equity = Market price per share × Shares outstanding

Market value of equity = US$16.97 × 6,750,000 = US$114,547,500.

The book value of equity per share for Pfizer can be computed as:

Book value of equity per share = Total shareholders' equity/Shares outstanding

Book value of equity per share = US$57,556,000/6,750,000 = US$8.53.

A useful ratio to compute is a company's price-to-book ratio, which is also referred to as the market-to-book ratio. This ratio provides an indication of investors' expectations about a company's future investment and cash flow-generating opportunities. The larger the price-to-book ratio (i.e., the greater the divergence between market value per share and book value per share), the more favorably investors will view the company's future investment opportunities. For Pfizer the price-to-book ratio is:

Price-to-book ratio = Market price per share/Book value of equity per share

Price-to-book ratio = US$16.97/US$8.53 = 1.99.

Exhibit 21 contains the market price per share, book value of equity per share, and price-to-book ratios for Novartis and GlaxoSmithKline in addition to Pfizer.

Exhibit 21	Pfizer, Novartis AG, and GlaxoSmithKline		
	Pfizer	**Novartis AG**	**GlaxoSmithKline**
Market price per share	$16.97	$47.64	$35.84
Book value of equity per share	$8.53	$22.32	$4.54
Price-to-book ratio	1.99	2.13	7.89

The market price per share of all three companies exceeds their respective book values, so their price-to-book ratios are all greater than 1.00. However, there are significant differences in the sizes of their price-to-book ratios. GlaxoSmithKline has the largest price-to-book ratio, while the price-to-book ratios of Pfizer and Novartis are similar to each other. This suggests that investors believe that GlaxoSmithKline has substantially higher future growth opportunities than either Pfizer or Novartis.

It is not appropriate to compare the price-to-book ratios of companies in different industries because their price-to-book ratios also reflect investors' outlook for the industry. Companies in high growth industries, such as technology, will generally have higher price-to-book ratios than companies in slower growth (i.e., mature) industries, such as heavy equipment. Therefore, it is more appropriate to compare the price-to-book ratios of companies in the same industry. A company with relatively high growth opportunities compared to its industry peers would likely have a higher price-to-book ratio than the average price-to-book ratio of the industry.

Book value and return on equity are useful in helping analysts determine value but can be limited as a primary means to estimate a company's true or intrinsic value, which is the present value of its future projected cash flows. In Exhibit 22, Warren Buffett, one of the most successful investors in the world and CEO of Berkshire Hathaway, provides an explanation of the differences between the book value of a company and its intrinsic value in a letter to shareholders. As discussed above, market value reflects the collective and differing expectations of investors concerning the amount, timing, and uncertainty of a company's future cash flows. A company's intrinsic value can only be estimated because it is impossible to predict the amount and timing of its future cash flows. However, astute investors—such as Buffett—have been able to profit from discrepancies between their estimates of a company's intrinsic value and the market value of its equity.

Exhibit 22	Book Value versus Intrinsic Value[31]

We regularly report our per-share book value, an easily calculable number, though one of limited use. Just as regularly, we tell you that what counts is intrinsic value, a number that is impossible to pinpoint but essential to estimate.

For example, in 1964, we could state with certitude that Berkshire's per-share book value was $19.46. However, that figure considerably overstated the stock's intrinsic value since all of the company's resources were tied up in a sub-profitable textile business. Our textile assets had neither going-concern nor liquidation values equal to their carrying values. In 1964, then, anyone inquiring into the soundness of Berkshire's balance sheet might well have deserved the answer once offered up by a Hollywood mogul of dubious reputation: "Don't worry, the liabilities are solid."

Today, Berkshire's situation has reversed: Many of the businesses we control are worth far more than their carrying value. (Those we don't control, such as Coca-Cola or Gillette, are carried at current market values.) We continue to give you book value figures, however, because they serve as a rough, understated, tracking measure for Berkshire's intrinsic value.

We define intrinsic value as the discounted value of the cash that can be taken out of a business during its remaining life. Anyone calculating intrinsic value necessarily comes up with a highly subjective figure that will change both as estimates of future cash flows are revised and as interest rates move. Despite its fuzziness, however, intrinsic value is all-important and is the only logical way to evaluate the relative attractiveness of investments and businesses.

To see how historical input (book value) and future output (intrinsic value) can diverge, let's look at another form of investment, a college education. Think of the education's cost as its "book value." If it is to be accurate, the cost should include the earnings that were foregone by the student because he chose college rather than a job.

(continued)

---

31 Extracts from Berkshire Hathaway's *2008 Annual Report* (www.berkshirehathaway.com).

| **Exhibit 22** | **Continued** |

For this exercise, we will ignore the important non-economic benefits of an education and focus strictly on its economic value. First, we must estimate the earnings that the graduate will receive over his lifetime and subtract from that figure an estimate of what he would have earned had he lacked his education. That gives us an excess earnings figure, which must then be discounted, at an appropriate interest rate, back to graduation day. The dollar result equals the intrinsic economic value of the education.

7.2 The Cost of Equity and Investors' Required Rates of Return

When companies issue debt (or borrow from a bank) or equity securities, there is a cost associated with the capital that is raised. In order to maximize profitability and shareholder wealth, companies attempt to raise capital efficiently so as to minimize these costs.

When a company issues debt, the cost it incurs for the use of these funds is called the cost of debt. The cost of debt is relatively easy to estimate because it reflects the periodic interest (or coupon) rate that the company is contractually obligated to pay to its bondholders (lenders). When a company raises capital by issuing equity, the cost it incurs is called the cost of equity. Unlike debt, however, the company is not contractually obligated to make any payments to its shareholders for the use of their funds. As a result, the cost of equity is more difficult to estimate.

Investors require a return on the funds they provide to the company. This return is called the investor's minimum required rate of return. When investors purchase the company's debt securities, their minimum required rate of return is the periodic rate of interest they charge the company for the use of their funds. Because all of the bondholders receive the same periodic rate of interest, their required rate of return is the same. Therefore, the company's cost of debt and the investors' minimum required rate of return on the debt are the same.

When investors purchase the company's equity securities, their minimum required rate of return is based on the future cash flows they expect to receive. Because these future cash flows are both uncertain and unknown, the investors' minimum required rate of return must be estimated. In addition, the minimum required return may differ across investors based on their expectations about the company's future cash flows. As a result, the company's cost of equity may be different from the investors' minimum required rate of return on equity.[32] Because companies try to raise capital at the lowest possible cost, the company's cost of equity is often used as a proxy for the investors' *minimum* required rate of return.

In other words, the cost of equity can be thought of as the minimum expected rate of return that a company must offer its investors to purchase its shares in the primary market and to maintain its share price in the secondary market. If this expected rate of return is not maintained in the secondary market, then the share price will adjust so that it meets the minimum required rate of return demanded by investors. For example, if investors require a higher rate of return on equity than the company's cost of equity, they would sell their shares and invest their funds elsewhere resulting in a decline in the company's share price. As the share price declined, the cost of equity would increase to reach the higher rate of return that investors require.

---

[32] Another important factor that can cause a firm's cost of equity to differ from investors' required rate of return on equity is the flotation cost associated with equity.

Two models commonly used to estimate a company's cost of equity (or investors' minimum required rate of return) are the dividend discount model (DDM) and the capital asset pricing model (CAPM). These models are discussed in detail in other curriculum readings.

The cost of debt (after tax) and the cost of equity (i.e., the minimum required rates of return on debt and equity) are integral components of the capital budgeting process because they are used to estimate a company's weighted average cost of capital (WACC). Capital budgeting is the decision-making process that companies use to evaluate potential long-term investments. The WACC represents the minimum required rate of return that the company must earn on its long-term investments to satisfy all providers of capital. The company then chooses among those long-term investments with expected returns that are greater than its WACC.

SUMMARY

Equity securities play a fundamental role in investment analysis and portfolio management. The importance of this asset class continues to grow on a global scale because of the need for equity capital in developed and emerging markets, technological innovation, and the growing sophistication of electronic information exchange. Given their absolute return potential and ability to impact the risk and return characteristics of portfolios, equity securities are of importance to both individual and institutional investors.

This reading introduces equity securities and provides an overview of global equity markets. A detailed analysis of their historical performance shows that equity securities have offered average real annual returns superior to government bills and bonds, which have provided average real annual returns that have only kept pace with inflation. The different types and characteristics of common and preference equity securities are examined, and the primary differences between public and private equity securities are outlined. An overview of the various types of equity securities listed and traded in global markets is provided, including a discussion of their risk and return characteristics. Finally, the role of equity securities in creating company value is examined as well as the relationship between a company's cost of equity, its accounting return on equity, investors' required rate of return, and the company's intrinsic value.

We conclude with a summary of the key components of this reading:

- Common shares represent an ownership interest in a company and give investors a claim on its operating performance, the opportunity to participate in the corporate decision-making process, and a claim on the company's net assets in the case of liquidation.

- Callable common shares give the issuer the right to buy back the shares from shareholders at a price determined when the shares are originally issued.

- Putable common shares give shareholders the right to sell the shares back to the issuer at a price specified when the shares are originally issued.

- Preference shares are a form of equity in which payments made to preference shareholders take precedence over any payments made to common stockholders.

- Cumulative preference shares are preference shares on which dividend payments are accrued so that any payments omitted by the company must be paid before another dividend can be paid to common shareholders. Non-cumulative preference shares have no such provisions, implying that the dividend payments are at the company's discretion and are thus similar to payments made to common shareholders.

- Participating preference shares allow investors to receive the standard preferred dividend plus the opportunity to receive a share of corporate profits above a pre-specified amount. Non-participating preference shares allow investors to simply receive the initial investment plus any accrued dividends in the event of liquidation.

- Callable and putable preference shares provide issuers and investors with the same rights and obligations as their common share counterparts.

- Private equity securities are issued primarily to institutional investors in private placements and do not trade in secondary equity markets. There are three types of private equity investments: venture capital, leveraged buyouts, and private investments in public equity (PIPEs).

- The objective of private equity investing is to increase the ability of the company's management to focus on its operating activities for long-term value creation. The strategy is to take the "private" company "public" after certain profit and other benchmarks have been met.

- Depository receipts are securities that trade like ordinary shares on a local exchange but which represent an economic interest in a foreign company. They allow the publicly listed shares of foreign companies to be traded on an exchange outside their domestic market.

- American depository receipts are U.S. dollar-denominated securities trading much like standard U.S. securities on U.S. markets. Global depository receipts are similar to ADRs but contain certain restrictions in terms of their ability to be resold among investors.

- Underlying characteristics of equity securities can greatly affect their risk and return.

- A company's accounting return on equity is the total return that it earns on shareholders' book equity.

- A company's cost of equity is the minimum rate of return that stockholders require the company to pay them for investing in its equity.

REFERENCES

Bailey, Elizabeth, Meg Wirth, and David Zapol. 2005. "Venture Capital and Global Health." *Financing Global Health Ventures*, Discussion Paper (September 2005): http://www.common-scapital.com/downloads/Venture_Capital_and_Global_Health.pdf.

Bary, Andrew. 2008. "Does Extreme Stress Signal an Economic Snapback?" *Barron's* (24 November 2008): online.barrons.com/article/SB122732177515750213.html.

Boubakri, Narjess, Jean-Claude Cosset, and Anis Samet. 2008. "The Choice of ADRs." Finance International Meeting AFFI – EUROFIDAI, December 2007. (http://ssrn.com/abstract=1006839).

Dimson, Elroy, Paul Marsh, and Mike Staunton. 2009. *Credit Suisse Global Investment Returns Yearbook 2009*. Credit Suisse Research Institute.

Henry, Peter Blair, and Anusha Chari. 2007. "Risk Sharing and Asset Prices: Evidence from a Natural Experiment." Working Paper; Center on Democracy, Development, and the Rule of Law.

Strömberg, Per. 2008. "The New Demography of Private Equity." *The Global Economic Impact of Private Equity Report 2008*, World Economic Forum.

PRACTICE PROBLEMS FOR READING 49

1. Which of the following is *not* a characteristic of common equity?

    A. It represents an ownership interest in the company.

    B. Shareholders participate in the decision-making process.

    C. The company is obligated to make periodic dividend payments.

2. The type of equity voting right that grants one vote for each share of equity owned is referred to as:

    A. proxy voting.

    B. statutory voting.

    C. cumulative voting.

3. All of the following are characteristics of preference shares *except*:

    A. They are either callable or putable.

    B. They generally do not have voting rights.

    C. They do not share in the operating performance of the company.

4. Participating preference shares entitle shareholders to:

    A. participate in the decision-making process of the company.

    B. convert their shares into a specified number of common shares.

    C. receive an additional dividend if the company's profits exceed a pre-determined level.

5. Which of the following statements about private equity securities is *incorrect*?

    A. They cannot be sold on secondary markets.

    B. They have market-determined quoted prices.

    C. They are primarily issued to institutional investors.

6. Venture capital investments:

    A. can be publicly traded.

    B. do not require a long-term commitment of funds.

    C. provide mezzanine financing to early-stage companies.

7. Which of the following statements *most accurately* describes one difference between private and public equity firms?

    A. Private equity firms are focused more on short-term results than public firms.

    B. Private equity firms' regulatory and investor relations operations are less costly than those of public firms.

    C. Private equity firms are incentivized to be more open with investors about governance and compensation than public firms.

8. Emerging markets have benefited from recent trends in international markets. Which of the following has *not* been a benefit of these trends?

    A. Emerging market companies do not have to worry about a lack of liquidity in their home equity markets.

    B. Emerging market companies have found it easier to raise capital in the markets of developed countries.

    C. Emerging market companies have benefited from the stability of foreign exchange markets.

9. When investing in unsponsored depository receipts, the voting rights to the shares in the trust belong to:

   A. the depository bank.

   B. the investors in the depository receipts.

   C. the issuer of the shares held in the trust.

10. With respect to Level III sponsored ADRs, which of the following is *least likely* to be accurate? They:

    A. have low listing fees.

    B. are traded on the NYSE, NASDAQ, and AMEX.

    C. are used to raise equity capital in U.S. markets.

11. A basket of listed depository receipts, or an exchange-traded fund, would *most likely* be used for:

    A. gaining exposure to a single equity.

    B. hedging exposure to a single equity.

    C. gaining exposure to multiple equities.

12. Calculate the total return on a share of equity using the following data:

    Purchase price: $50

    Sale price: $42

    Dividend paid during holding period: $2

    A. −12.0%

    B. −14.3%

    C. −16.0%

13. If a U.S.-based investor purchases a euro-denominated ETF and the euro subsequently depreciates in value relative to the dollar, the investor will have a total return that is:

    A. lower than the ETF's total return.

    B. higher than the ETF's total return.

    C. the same as the ETF's total return.

14. Which of the following is *incorrect* about the risk of an equity security? The risk of an equity security is:

    A. based on the uncertainty of its cash flows.

    B. based on the uncertainty of its future price.

    C. measured using the standard deviation of its dividends.

15. From an investor's point of view, which of the following equity securities is the *least* risky?

    A. Putable preference shares.

    B. Callable preference shares.

    C. Non-callable preference shares.

16. Which of the following is *least likely* to be a reason for a company to issue equity securities on the primary market?

    A. To raise capital.

    B. To increase liquidity.

    C. To increase return on equity.

17. Which of the following is *not* a primary goal of raising equity capital?

    A. To finance the purchase of long-lived assets.

    B. To finance the company's revenue-generating activities.

    C. To ensure that the company continues as a going concern.

18. Which of the following statements is *most accurate* in describing a company's book value?

    A. Book value increases when a company retains its net income.

    B. Book value is usually equal to the company's market value.

    C. The ultimate goal of management is to maximize book value.

19. Calculate the book value of a company using the following information:

Number of shares outstanding	100,000
Price per share	€52
Total assets	€12,000,000
Total liabilities	€7,500,000
Net Income	€2,000,000

    A. €4,500,000.

    B. €5,200,000.

    C. €6,500,000.

20. Which of the following statements is *least accurate* in describing a company's market value?

    A. Management's decisions do not influence the company's market value.

    B. Increases in book value may not be reflected in the company's market value.

    C. Market value reflects the collective and differing expectations of investors.

21. Calculate the 2009 return on equity (ROE) of a stable company using the following data:

Total sales	£2,500,000
Net income	£2,000,000
Beginning of year total assets	£50,000,000
Beginning of year total liabilities	£35,000,000
Number of shares outstanding at the end of 2009	1,000,000
Price per share at the end of 2009	£20

    A. 10.0%.

    B. 13.3%.

    C. 16.7%.

22. Holding all other factors constant, which of the following situations will *most likely* lead to an increase in a company's return on equity?

    A. The market price of the company's shares increases.

    B. Net income increases at a slower rate than shareholders' equity.

    C. The company issues debt to repurchase outstanding shares of equity.

23. Which of the following measures is the *most difficult* to estimate?

    A. The cost of debt.

    B. The cost of equity.

    C. Investors' required rate of return on debt.

24. A company's cost of equity is often used as a proxy for investors':

    A. average required rate of return.

    B. minimum required rate of return.

    C. maximum required rate of return.

SOLUTIONS FOR READING 49

1. C is correct. The company is not obligated to make dividend payments. It is at the discretion of the company whether or not it chooses to pay dividends.

2. B is correct. Statutory voting is the type of equity voting right that grants one vote per share owned.

3. A is correct. Preference shares do not have to be either callable or putable.

4. C is correct. Participating preference shares entitle shareholders to receive an additional dividend if the company's profits exceed a pre-determined level.

5. B is correct. Private equity securities do not have market-determined quoted prices.

6. C is correct. Venture capital investments can be used to provide mezzanine financing to companies in their early stage of development.

7. B is correct. Regulatory and investor relations costs are lower for private equity firms than for public firms. There are no stock exchange, regulatory, or shareholder involvements with private equity, whereas for public firms these costs can be high.

8. C is correct. The trends in emerging markets have not led to the stability of foreign exchange markets.

9. A is correct. In an unsponsored DR, the depository bank owns the voting rights to the shares. The bank purchases the shares, places them into a trust, and then sells shares in the trust—not the underlying shares—in other markets.

10. A is correct. The listing fees on Level III sponsored ADRs are high.

11. C is correct. An ETF is used to gain exposure to a basket of securities (equity, fixed income, commodity futures, etc.).

12. A is correct. The formula states $R_t = (P_t - P_{t-1} + D_t)/P_t$. Therefore, total return = $(42 - 50 + 2)/50 = -12.0\%$.

13. A is correct. The depreciated value of the euro will create an additional loss in the form of currency return that is lower than the ETF's return.

14. C is correct. Some equity securities do not pay dividends, and therefore the standard deviation of dividends cannot be used to measure the risk of all equity securities.

15. A is correct. Putable shares, whether common or preference, give the investor the option to sell the shares back to the issuer at a pre-determined price. This pre-determined price creates a floor for the share's price that reduces the uncertainty of future cash flows for the investor (i.e., lowers risk relative to the other two types of shares listed).

16. C is correct. Issuing shares in the primary (and secondary) market *reduces* a company's return on equity because it increases the total amount of equity capital invested in the company (i.e., the denominator in the ROE formula).

17. C is correct. Capital is raised to ensure the company's existence only when it is required. It is not a typical goal of raising capital.

18. A is correct. A company's book value increases when a company retains its net income.

19. A is correct. The book value of the company is equal to total assets minus total liabilities, which is €12,000,000 − €7,500,000 = €4,500,000.

20. A is correct. A company's market value is affected by management's decisions. Management's decisions can directly affect the company's *book* value, which can then affect its market value.

21. B is correct. A company's ROE is calculated as (NI_t/BVE_{t-1}). For 2009, the BVE_{t-1} is equal to the beginning total assets minus the beginning total liabilities, which equals £50,000,000 − £35,000,000 = £15,000,000. Therefore, ROE_{2009} = £2,000,000/£15,000,000 = 13.3%.

22. C is correct. A company's ROE will increase if it issues debt to repurchase outstanding shares of equity.

23. B is correct. The cost of equity is not easily determined. It is dependent on investors' required rate of return on equity, which reflects the different risk levels of investors and their expectations about the company's future cash flows.

24. B is correct. Companies try to raise funds at the lowest possible cost. Therefore, cost of equity is used as a proxy for the minimum required rate of return.

50

Introduction to Industry and Company Analysis

by Patrick W. Dorsey, CFA, Anthony M. Fiore, CFA, and Ian Rossa O'Reilly, CFA

LEARNING OUTCOMES

Mastery	The candidate should be able to:
☐	**a** explain the uses of industry analysis and the relation of industry analysis to company analysis;
☐	**b** compare methods by which companies can be grouped, current industry classification systems, and classify a company, given a description of its activities and the classification system;
☐	**c** explain the factors that affect the sensitivity of a company to the business cycle and the uses and limitations of industry and company descriptors such as "growth," "defensive," and "cyclical";
☐	**d** explain the relation of "peer group," as used in equity valuation, to a company's industry classification;
☐	**e** describe the elements that need to be covered in a thorough industry analysis;
☐	**f** describe the principles of strategic analysis of an industry;
☐	**g** explain the effects of barriers to entry, industry concentration, industry capacity, and market share stability on pricing power and return on capital;
☐	**h** describe product and industry life cycle models, classify an industry as to life cycle phase (e.g., embryonic, growth, shakeout, maturity, and decline) based on a description of it, and describe the limitations of the life-cycle concept in forecasting industry performance;
☐	**i** compare characteristics of representative industries from the various economic sectors;
☐	**j** describe demographic, governmental, social and technological influences on industry growth, profitability and risk;
☐	**k** describe the elements that should be covered in a thorough company analysis.

INTRODUCTION

Industry analysis is the analysis of a specific branch of manufacturing, service, or trade. Understanding the industry in which a company operates provides an essential framework for the analysis of the individual company—that is, **company analysis**. Equity analysis and credit analysis are often conducted by analysts who concentrate on one or several industries, which results in synergies and efficiencies in gathering and interpreting information.

Among the questions we address in this reading are the following:

■ What are the similarities and differences among industry classification systems?

■ How does an analyst go about choosing a peer group of companies?

■ What are the key factors to consider when analyzing an industry?

■ What advantages are enjoyed by companies in strategically well-positioned industries?

After discussing the uses of industry analysis in the next section, Sections 3 and 4 discuss, respectively, approaches to identifying similar companies and industry classification systems. Section 5 covers the description and analysis of industries. Also, Section 5, which includes an introduction to competitive analysis, provides a background to Section 6, which introduces company analysis. The reading ends with a summary, and practice problems follow the text.

USES OF INDUSTRY ANALYSIS

Industry analysis is useful in a number of investment applications that make use of fundamental analysis. Its uses include the following:

■ *Understanding a company's business and business environment.* Industry analysis is often a critical early step in stock selection and valuation because it provides insights into the issuer's growth opportunities, competitive dynamics, and business risks. For a credit analyst, industry analysis provides insights into the appropriateness of a company's use of debt financing and into its ability to meet its promised payments during economic contractions.

■ *Identifying active equity investment opportunities.* Investors taking a top-down investing approach use industry analysis to identify industries with positive, neutral, or negative outlooks for profitability and growth. Generally, investors will then overweight, market weight, or underweight those industries (as appropriate to their outlooks) relative to the investor's benchmark if the investor judges that the industry's perceived prospects are not fully incorporated in market prices. Apart from security selection, some investors attempt to outperform their benchmarks by industry or sector rotation—that is, timing investments in industries in relation to an analysis of industry fundamentals and/or business-cycle conditions (technical analysis may also play a role in such strategies). Several studies have underscored the importance of industry analysis by suggesting that the industry factor in stock returns is at least as important as the country factor (e.g., Cavaglia, Diermeier, Moroz, and De Zordo, 2004). In addition, industry membership has been found to account for about 20 percent of the variability of a company's profitability in the United States (McGahan and Porter 1995).

■ *Portfolio performance attribution.* Performance attribution, which addresses the sources of a portfolio's returns, usually in relation to the portfolio's benchmark, includes industry or sector selection. Industry classification schemes play a role in such performance attribution.

Later in this reading we explore the considerations involved in understanding a company's business and business environment. The next section addresses how companies may be grouped into industries.

APPROACHES TO IDENTIFYING SIMILAR COMPANIES   **3**

Industry classification attempts to place companies into groups on the basis of commonalities. In the following sections, we discuss the three major approaches to industry classification:

- products and/or services supplied;
- business-cycle sensitivities; and
- statistical similarities.

3.1 Products and/or Services Supplied

Modern classification schemes are most commonly based on grouping companies by similar products and/or services. According to this perspective, an **industry** is defined as a group of companies offering similar products and/or services. For example, major companies in the global heavy truck industry include Volvo, Daimler AG, Paccar, and Navistar, all of which make large commercial vehicles for the on-highway truck market. Similarly, some of the large players in the global automobile industry are Toyota, General Motors, Volkswagen, Ford, Honda, Nissan, PSA Peugeot Citroën, and Hyundai, all of which produce light vehicles that are close substitutes for one another.

Industry classification schemes typically provide multiple levels of aggregation. The term **sector** is often used to refer to a group of related industries. The health care sector, for example, consists of a number of related industries, including the pharmaceutical, biotechnology, medical device, medical supply, hospital, and managed care industries.

These classification schemes typically place a company in an industry on the basis of a determination of its principal business activity. A company's **principal business activity** is the source from which the company derives a majority of its revenues and/or earnings. For example, companies that derive a majority of their revenues from the sale of pharmaceuticals include Novartis AG, Pfizer Inc., Roche Holding AG, GlaxoSmithKline, and Sanofi-aventis S.A., all of which could be grouped together as part of the global pharmaceutical industry. Companies that engage in more than one significant business activity usually report the revenues (and, in many cases, operating profits) of the different business segments in their financial statements.[1]

Examples of classification systems based on products and/or services include the commercial classification systems that will be discussed later, namely, the Global Industry Classification Standard (GICS), Russell Global Sectors (RGS), and Industry Classification Benchmark. In addition to grouping companies by product and/or service, some of the major classification systems, including GICS and RGS, group consumer-related companies into cyclical and non-cyclical categories depending on the company's sensitivity to the business cycle. The next section addresses how companies can be categorized on the basis of economic sensitivity.

---

1 For more information, see International Financial Reporting Standard (IFRS) 8: Operating Segments. In IFRS 8, *business segments* are called *operating segments*.

3.2 Business-Cycle Sensitivities

Companies are sometimes grouped on the basis of their relative sensitivity to the business cycle. This method often results in two broad groupings of companies—cyclical and non-cyclical.

A **cyclical** company is one whose profits are strongly correlated with the strength of the overall economy. Such companies experience wider-than-average fluctuations in demand—high demand during periods of economic expansion and low demand during periods of economic contraction—and/or are subject to greater-than-average profit variability related to high operating leverage (i.e., high fixed costs). Concerning demand, cyclical products and services are often relatively expensive and/or represent purchases that can be delayed if necessary (e.g., because of declining disposable income). Examples of cyclical industries are autos, housing, basic materials, industrials, and technology. A **non-cyclical** company is one whose performance is largely independent of the business cycle. Non-cyclical companies produce goods or services for which demand remains relatively stable throughout the business cycle. Examples of non-cyclical industries are food and beverage, household and personal care products, health care, and utilities.

Although the classification systems we will discuss do not label their categories as cyclical or non-cyclical, certain sectors tend to experience greater economic sensitivity than others. Sectors that tend to exhibit a relatively high degree of economic sensitivity include consumer discretionary, energy, financials, industrials, technology, and materials. In contrast, sectors that exhibit relatively less economic sensitivity include consumer staples, health care, telecommunications, and utilities.

Example 1

Descriptions Related to the Cyclical/Noncyclical Distinction

Analysts commonly encounter a number of labels related to the cyclical/non-cyclical distinction. For example, non-cyclical industries have sometimes been sorted into defensive (or stable) versus growth. Defensive industries and companies are those whose revenues and profits are least affected by fluctuations in overall economic activity. These industries/companies tend to produce staple consumer goods (e.g., bread), to provide basic services (grocery stores, drug stores, fast food outlets), or to have their rates and revenues determined by contracts or government regulation (e.g., cost-of-service, rate-of-return regulated public utilities). Growth industries would include industries with specific demand dynamics that are so strong that they override the significance of broad economic or other external factors and generate growth regardless of overall economic conditions, although their rates of growth may slow during an economic downturn.[2]

The usefulness of industry and company labels such as cyclical, growth, and defensive is limited. Cyclical industries as well as growth industries often have growth companies within them. A cyclical industry itself, although exposed to the effects of fluctuations in overall economic activity, may grow at an above-average rate for periods spanning multiple business cycles.[3] Furthermore, when

---

2 Sometimes the "growth" label is attached to countries or regions in which economic growth is so strong that the fluctuations in local economic activity do not produce an actual decline in economic output, merely variation from high to low rates of real growth (e.g., China, India).

3 The label **growth cyclical** is sometimes used to describe companies that are growing rapidly on a long-term basis but that still experience above-average fluctuation in their revenues and profits over the course of a business cycle.

fluctuations in economic activity are large, as in the deep recession of 2008–2009, few companies escape the effects of the cyclical weakness in overall economic activity.

The defensive label is also problematic. Industries may include both companies that are growth and companies that are defensive in character, making the choice between a "growth" and a "defensive" label difficult. Moreover, "defensive" cannot be understood as necessarily being descriptive of investment characteristics. Food supermarkets, for example, would typically be described as defensive but can be subject to profit-damaging price wars. So-called defensive industries/companies may sometimes face industry dynamics that make them far from defensive in the sense of preserving shareholders' capital.

One limitation of the cyclical/non-cyclical classification is that business-cycle sensitivity is a continuous spectrum rather than an "either/or" issue, so placement of companies in one of the two major groups is somewhat arbitrary. The impact of severe recessions usually reaches all parts of the economy, so non-cyclical is better understood as a relative term.

Another limitation of a business-cycle classification for global investing is that different countries and regions of the world frequently progress through the various stages of the business cycle at different times. While one region of the world may be experiencing economic expansion, other regions or countries may be in recession, which complicates the application of a business-cycle approach to industry analysis. For example, a jewelry retailer (i.e., a cyclical company) that is selling domestically into a weak economy will exhibit markedly different fundamental performance relative to a jewelry company operating in an environment where demand is robust. Comparing these two companies—that is, similar companies that are currently exposed to different demand environments—could suggest investment opportunities. Combining fundamental data from such companies, however, to establish industry benchmark values would be misleading.

3.3 Statistical Similarities

Statistical approaches to grouping companies are typically based on the correlations of past securities' returns. For example, using the technique known as cluster analysis, companies are separated (on the basis of historical correlations of stock returns) into groups *in which* correlations are relatively high but *between which* correlations are relatively low. This method of aggregation often results in non-intuitive groups of companies, and the composition of the groups may vary significantly by time period and region of the world. Moreover, statistical approaches rely on historical data, but analysts have no guarantee that past correlation values will continue in the future. In addition, such approaches carry the inherent dangers of all statistical methods, namely, 1) falsely indicating a relationship that arose because of chance or 2) falsely excluding a relationship that actually is significant.

INDUSTRY CLASSIFICATION SYSTEMS   **4**

A well-designed classification system often serves as a useful starting point for industry analysis. It allows analysts to compare industry trends and relative valuations among companies in a group. Classification systems that take a global perspective enable portfolio managers and research analysts to make global comparisons of companies in the same industry. For example, given the global nature of the automobile industry, a thorough analysis of the industry would include auto companies from many different countries and regions of the world.

4.1 Commercial Industry Classification Systems

Major index providers, including Standard & Poor's, MSCI Barra, Russell Investments, Dow Jones, and FTSE, classify companies in their equity indices into industry groupings. Most classification schemes used by these index providers contain multiple levels of classification that start at the broadest level with a general sector grouping, then, in several further steps, subdivide or disaggregate the sectors into more "granular" (i.e., more narrowly defined) sub-industry groups.

4.1.1 *Global Industry Classification Standard*

GICS was jointly developed by Standard & Poor's and MSCI Barra, two of the largest providers of global equity indices, in 1999. As the name implies, GICS was designed to facilitate global comparisons of industries, and it classifies companies in both developed and developing economies. Each company is assigned to a sub-industry according to its principal business activity. Each sub-industry belongs to a particular industry; each industry belongs to an industry group; and each group belongs to a sector. In June 2009, the GICS classification structure comprised four levels of detail consisting of 154 sub-industries, 68 industries, 24 industry groups, and 10 sectors. The composition of GICS has historically been adjusted over time to reflect changes in the global equity markets.

4.1.2 *Russell Global Sectors*

The RGS classification system uses a three-tier structure to classify companies globally on the basis of the products or services a company produces. In June 2009, the RGS classification system consisted of 9 sectors, 32 subsectors, and 141 industries. Besides the number of tiers, another difference between the RGS and GICS classification systems is that the RGS system contains nine sectors, whereas GICS consists of ten. For example, the RGS system does not provide a separate sector for telecommunication service companies. Many companies that GICS classifies as "Telecommunication Services," including China Mobile Ltd., AT&T, and Telefonica, are assigned by RGS to its more broadly defined "Utilities" sector.

4.1.3 *Industry Classification Benchmark*

The Industry Classification Benchmark (ICB), which was jointly developed by Dow Jones and FTSE, uses a four-tier structure to categorize companies globally on the basis of the source from which a company derives the majority of its revenue. In June 2009, the ICB classification system consisted of 10 industries, 19 supersectors, 41 sectors, and 114 subsectors. Although the ICB is similar to GICS in the number of tiers and the method by which companies are assigned to particular groups, the two systems use significantly different nomenclature. For example, whereas GICS uses the term "sector" to describe its broadest grouping of companies, ICB uses the term "industry." Another difference between the two systems is that ICB distinguishes between consumer goods and consumer services companies, whereas both GICS and the RGS systems group consumer products companies and consumer services companies together into sectors on the basis of economic sensitivity. These stylistic distinctions tend to be less obvious at the more granular levels of the different hierarchies.

Despite these subtle differences, the three commercial classification systems use common methodologies for assigning companies to groups. Also, the broadest level of grouping for all three systems is quite similar. Specifically, GICS, the RGS, and the ICB each identify 9 or 10 broad groupings below which all other categories reside. Next, we describe sectors that are fairly representative of how the broadest level of industry classification is viewed by GICS, RGS, and ICB.

4.1.4 *Description of Representative Sectors*

Basic Materials and Processing: companies engaged in the production of building materials, chemicals, paper and forest products, containers and packaging, and metal, mineral, and mining companies.

Consumer Discretionary: companies that derive a majority of revenue from the sale of consumer-related products or services for which demand tends to exhibit a relatively high degree of economic sensitivity. Examples of business activities that frequently fall into this category are automotive, apparel, hotel, and restaurant businesses.

Consumer Staples: consumer-related companies whose business tends to exhibit less economic sensitivity than other companies; for example, manufacturers of food, beverage, tobacco, and personal care products.

Energy: companies whose primary line of business involves the exploration, production, or refining of natural resources used to produce energy; companies that derive a majority of revenue from the sale of equipment or through the provision of services to energy companies would also fall into this category.

Financial Services: companies whose primary line of business involves banking, finance, insurance, real estate, asset management, and/or brokerage services.

Health Care: manufacturers of pharmaceutical and biotech products, medical devices, health care equipment, and medical supplies and providers of health care services.

Industrial/Producer Durables: manufacturers of capital goods and providers of commercial services; for example, business activities would include heavy machinery and equipment manufacture, aerospace and defense, transportation services, and commercial services and supplies.

Technology: companies involved in the manufacture or sale of computers, software, semiconductors, and communications equipment; other business activities that frequently fall into this category are electronic entertainment, internet services, and technology consulting and services.

Telecommunications: companies that provide fixed-line and wireless communication services; some vendors prefer to combine telecommunication and utility companies together into a single "utilities" category.

Utilities: electric, gas, and water utilities; telecommunication companies are sometimes included in this category.

To classify a company accurately in a particular classification scheme requires definitions of the classification categories, a statement about the criteria used in classification, and detailed information about the subject company. Example 2 introduces an exercise in such classification. In addressing the question, the reader can make use of the widely applicable sector descriptions just given and familiarity with available business products and services.

Example 2

Classifying Companies into Industries

The text defines 10 representative sectors, repeated here in Exhibit 1. Suppose the classification system is based on the criterion of a company's principal business activity as judged primarily by source of revenue.

Exhibit 1	Ten Sectors

Sector

Basic Materials and Processing
Consumer Discretionary
Consumer Staples
Energy
Financial Services
Health Care
Industrial/Producer Durables
Technology
Telecommunications
Utilities

Based on the information given, determine an appropriate industry membership for each of the following hypothetical companies:

1. A natural gas transporter and marketer
2. A manufacturer of heavy construction equipment
3. A provider of regional telephone services
4. A semiconductor company
5. A manufacturer of medical devices
6. A chain of supermarkets
7. A manufacturer of chemicals and plastics
8. A manufacturer of automobiles
9. An investment management company
10. A manufacturer of luxury leather goods
11. A regulated supplier of electricity
12. A provider of wireless broadband services
13. A manufacturer of soaps and detergents
14. A software development company
15. An insurer
16. A regulated provider of water/wastewater services
17. A petroleum (oil) service company
18. A manufacturer of pharmaceuticals
19. A provider of rail transportation services
20. A metals mining company

Solution:

Sector	Company Number
Basic Materials and Processing	7, 20
Consumer Discretionary	8, 10
Consumer Staples	6, 13
Energy	1, 17
Financial Services	9, 15
Health Care	5, 18
Industrial/Producer Durables	2, 19
Technology	4, 14
Telecommunications	3, 12
Utilities	11, 16

Example 3 reviews some major concepts in industry classification.

Example 3

Industry Classification Schemes

1. The GICS classification system classifies companies on the basis of a company's primary business activity as measured primarily by:

   A. assets.

   B. income.

   C. revenue.

2. Which of the following is *least likely* to be accurately described as a cyclical company? A(n):

   A. automobile manufacturer.

   B. producer of breakfast cereals.

   C. apparel company producing the newest trendy clothes for teenage girls.

3. Which of the following is the *most accurate* statement? A statistical approach to grouping companies into industries:

   A. is based on historical correlations of the securities' returns.

   B. frequently produces industry groups whose composition is similar worldwide.

   C. emphasizes the descriptive statistics of industries consisting of companies producing similar products and/or services.

Solution to 1:

C is correct.

Solution to 2:

B is correct. A producer of staple foods such as cereals is a classic example of a non-cyclical company. Demand for automobiles is cyclical—that is, relatively high during economic expansions and relatively low during economic contractions.

> Also, demand for teenage fashions is likely to be more sensitive to the business cycle than demand for standard food items such as breakfast cereals. When budgets have been reduced, families may try to avoid expensive clothing or extend the life of existing wardrobes.
>
> **Solution to 3:**
>
> A is correct.

4.2 Governmental Industry Classification Systems

A number of classification systems in use by various governmental agencies today organize statistical data according to type of industrial or economic activity. A common goal of each government classification system is to facilitate the comparison of data—both over time and among countries that use the same system. Continuity of the data is critical to the measurement and evaluation of economic performance over time.

4.2.1 International Standard Industrial Classification of All Economic Activities

The International Standard Industrial Classification of All Economic Activities (ISIC) was adopted by the United Nations in 1948 to address the need for international comparability of economic statistics. ISIC classifies entities into various categories on the basis of the principal type of economic activity the entity performs. ISIC is organized into 11 categories, 21 sections, 88 divisions, 233 groups, and more than 400 classes. According to the United Nations, a majority of the countries around the world have either used ISIC as their national activity classification system or have developed national classifications derived from ISIC. Some of the organizations currently using the ISIC are the UN and its specialized agencies, the International Monetary Fund, the World Bank, and other international bodies.

4.2.2 Statistical Classification of Economic Activities in the European Community

Often regarded as the European version of ISIC, Statistical Classification of Economic Activities in the European Community (NACE) is the classification of economic activities that correspond to ISIC at the European level. Similar to ISIC, NACE classification is organized according to economic activity. NACE is composed of four levels—namely, sections (identified by alphabetical letters A through U), divisions (identified by two-digit numerical codes 01 through 99), groups (identified by three-digit numerical codes 01.1 through 99.0), and classes (identified by four-digit numerical codes 01.11 through 99.00).

4.2.3 Australian and New Zealand Standard Industrial Classification

The Australian and New Zealand Standard Industrial Classification (ANZSIC) was jointly developed by the Australian Bureau of Statistics and Statistics New Zealand in 1993 to facilitate the comparison of industry statistics of the two countries and comparisons with the rest of the world. International comparability was achieved by aligning ANZSIC with the international standards used by ISIC. ANZSIC has a structure comprising five levels—namely, divisions (the broadest level), subdivisions, groups, classes, and at the most granular level, subclasses (New Zealand only).

4.2.4 North American Industry Classification System

Jointly developed by the United States, Canada, and Mexico, the North American Industry Classification System (NAICS) replaced the Standard Industrial Classification (SIC) system in 1997. NAICS distinguishes between establishments and enterprises.

NAICS classifies establishments into industries according to the primary business activity of the establishment. In the NAICS system, an *establishment* is defined as "a single physical location where business is conducted or where services or industrial operations are performed" (e.g., factory, store, hotel, movie theater, farm, office). An *enterprise* may consist of more than one location performing the same or different types of economic activities. Each establishment of that enterprise is assigned a NAICS code on the basis of its own primary business activity.[4]

NAICS uses a two-digit through six-digit code to structure its categories into five levels of detail. The greater the number of digits in the code, the more narrowly defined the category. The five levels of categories, from broadest to narrowest, are sector (signified by the first two digits of the code), subsector (third digit of the code), industry group (fourth digit), NAICS industry (fifth digit), and national industry (sixth digit). The five-digit code is the level of greatest amount of comparability among countries; a six-digit code provides for more country-specific detail.

Although differences exist, the structures of ISIC, NACE, ANZSIC, and NAICS are similar enough that many of the categories from each of the different classification systems are compatible with one another. The U.S. Census Bureau has published tables showing how the various categories of the classification systems relate to one another.[5]

4.3 Strengths and Weaknesses of Current Systems

Unlike commercial classification systems, most government systems do not disclose information about a specific business or company, so an analyst cannot know all of the constituents of a particular category. For example, in the United States, federal law prohibits the Census Bureau from disclosing individual company activities, so, their NAICS and SIC codes are unknown.

Most government and commercial classification systems are reviewed and, if necessary, updated from time to time. Generally, commercial classification systems are adjusted more frequently than government classification systems, which may be updated only every five years or so. NAICS, for example, is reviewed for potential revisions every five years.

Government classification systems generally do not distinguish between small and large businesses, between for-profit and not-for-profit organizations, or between public and private companies. Many commercial classification systems have the ability to distinguish between large and small companies by virtue of association with a particular equity index, and these systems include only for-profit and publicly traded organizations.

Another limitation of current systems is that the narrowest classification unit assigned to a company generally cannot be assumed to be its peer group for the purposes of detailed fundamental comparisons or valuation. A **peer group** is a group of companies engaged in similar business activities whose economics and valuation are influenced by closely related factors. Comparisons of a company in relation to a well-defined peer group can provide valuable insights into the company's performance and its relative valuation.

4.4 Constructing a Peer Group

The construction of a peer group is a subjective process; the result often differs significantly from even the most narrowly defined categories given by the commercial classification systems. However, commercial classification systems do provide a starting

---

4 For more information, see www.census.gov/eos/www/naics/faqs/faqs.html#q2.

5 For more information, see www.census.gov/eos/www/naics/concordances/concordances.html.

point for the construction of a relevant peer group because, by using such systems, an analyst can quickly discover the public companies operating in the chosen industry.

In fact, one approach to constructing a peer group is to start by identifying other companies operating in the same industry. Analysts who subscribe to one or more of the commercial classification systems that were discussed in Section 4.1 can quickly generate a list of other companies in the industry in which the company operates according to that particular service provider's definition of the industry. An analyst can then investigate the business activities of these companies and make adjustments as necessary to ensure that the businesses truly are comparable. The following lists of suggested steps and questions are given as practical aids to analysts in identifying peer companies.

Steps in constructing a preliminary list of peer companies

- Examine commercial classification systems, if available to the analyst. These systems often provide a useful starting point for identifying companies operating in the same industry.
- Review the subject company's annual report for a discussion of the competitive environment. Companies frequently cite specific competitors.
- Review competitors' annual reports to identify other potential comparable companies.
- Review industry trade publications to identify comparable companies.
- Confirm that each comparable company derives a significant portion of its revenue and operating profit from a business activity similar to the primary business of the subject company.

Questions that may improve the list of peer companies

- What proportion of revenue and operating profit is derived from business activities similar to those of the subject company? In general, a higher percentage results in a more meaningful comparison.
- Does a potential peer company face a demand environment similar to that of the subject company? For example, a comparison of growth rates, margins, and valuations may be of limited value when comparing companies that are exposed to different stages of the business cycle. (As mentioned, such differences may be the result of conducting business in geographically different markets.)
- Does a potential company have a finance subsidiary? Some companies operate a finance division to facilitate the sale of their products (e.g., Caterpillar, Inc., and John Deere). To make a meaningful comparison of companies, the analyst should make adjustments to the financial statements to lessen the impact that the finance subsidiaries have on the various financial metrics being compared.

Example 4 illustrates the process of identifying a peer group of companies and shows some of the practical hurdles to determining a peer group.

Example 4

An Analyst Researches the Peer Group of Brink's Home Security

Suppose that an analyst needs to identify the peer group of companies for Brink's Home Security for use in the valuation section of a company report. Brink's is a provider of electronic security and alarm monitoring services primarily to residential customers in North America. The analyst starts by looking at Brink's industry classification according to GICS. As previously discussed, the most narrowly defined category that GICS uses is the sub-industry level, and in June 2009, Brink's was in the GICS sub-industry called Specialized Consumer Services, together with the companies listed here:

GICS Sector: Consumer Discretionary

  GICS Industry Group: Consumer Services

    GICS Industry: Diversified Consumer Services

      GICS Sub-Industry: Specialized Consumer Services

              Brink's Home Security Holdings, Inc.

              Coinstar, Inc.

              H&R Block, Inc.

              Hillenbrand Inc.

              Mathews International Corporation

              Pre-Paid Legal Services Inc.

              Regis Corporation

              Service Corporation International

              Sotheby's

After looking over the list of companies, the analyst quickly realizes that some adjustments need to be made to the list to end up with a peer group of companies that are comparable to Brink's. For example, Brink's has little in common with the hair care salon services of Regis or, for that matter, with the funeral service operations of Hillenbrand, Mathews, or Service Corporation. In fact, after careful inspection, the analyst concludes that none of the other companies included in the GICS sub-industry are particularly good "comparables" for Brink's.

Next, the analyst reviews the latest annual report for Brink's to find management statements concerning its competitors. On p. 6 of Brink's 2008 10-K, in the section titled "Industry Trends and Competition," is a list of other companies with comparable business activities: "We believe our primary competitors with national scope include: ADT Security Services, Inc., (part of Tyco International, Ltd.), Protection One, Inc., Monitronics International, Inc. and Stanley Security Solutions, (part of The Stanley Works)." The analyst notes that Protection One on this list is another publicly held security services company and a likely candidate for inclusion in the peer group for Brink's. Monitronics International is privately held, so the analyst excludes it from the peer group; up-to-date, detailed fundamental data are not available for it.

The analyst discovers that ADT represents a significant portion of Tyco International's sales and profits (more than 40 percent of 2008 sales and profits); therefore, an argument could be made to include Tyco International in the peer group. The analyst might also consider including Stanley Works in the peer group because that company derived roughly a third of its revenue and close to half of its operating profit from its security division in 2008. Just as the analyst reviewed the latest annual report for Brink's to identify additional potential comparables, the analyst should also scan the annual reports of the other companies listed to see if other comparables exist. In checking these three companies' annual reports, the analyst finds that Protection One is the only one that cites specific competitors; Tyco and Stanley Works discuss competition only broadly.

> After scanning all of the annual reports, the analyst finds no additional comparables.
>
> The analyst decides that Brink's peer group consists of ADT Security Services, Protection One, and Stanley Security Solutions but also decides to give extra weight to the comparison with Protection One in valuation because the comparison with Protection One has the fewest complicating factors.
>
> In connection with this discussion, note that International Financial Reporting Standards and U.S. GAAP require companies to disclose financial information about their operating segments (subject to certain qualifications). Such disclosures provide analysts with operational and financial information that can be helpful in peer-group determination.

Although companies with limited lines of business may neatly be categorized into a single peer group, companies with multiple divisions may be included in more than one category. For example, Belgium-based Anheuser-Busch InBev primarily makes and sells various brands of beer. It can easily be grouped together with other beverage companies (the theme park business constitutes a relatively immaterial part of total revenue). However, U.S.-based Hewlett-Packard Company (HP), a global provider of technology and software solutions, might reasonably be included in more than one category. Investors interested in the personal computer (PC) industry, for example, would probably include HP in their peer group, but investors constructing a peer group of providers of information technology services would probably include HP in that group also.

In summary, analysts must distinguish between a company's industry—as defined by one or more of the various classification systems—and its peer group. A company's peer group should consist of companies with similar business activities whose economic activity depends on similar drivers of demand and similar factors related to cost structure and access to financial capital. In practice, these necessities frequently result in a smaller group (even a different group) of companies than the most narrowly defined categories used by the common commercial classification systems. Example 5 illustrates various aspects of developing and using peer groups.

Example 5

The Semiconductor Industry: Business-Cycle Sensitivity and Peer-Group Determination

The GICS semiconductor and semiconductor equipment industry (453010) has two sub-industries—the semiconductor equipment sub-industry (45301010) and the semiconductors sub-industry (45301020). Members of the semiconductor equipment sub-industry include equipment suppliers such as Lam Research Corporation and ASML Holdings NV; the semiconductors sub-industry includes integrated circuit manufacturers Intel Corporation and Taiwan Semiconductor Manufacturing Company Ltd.

Lam Research is a leading supplier of wafer fabrication equipment and services to the world's semiconductor industry. Lam also offers wafer-cleaning equipment that is used after many of the individual steps required to manufacture a finished wafer. Often, the technical advances that Lam introduces in its wafer-etching and wafer-cleaning products are also available as upgrades to its installed base. This benefit provides customers with a cost-effective way to extend the performance and capabilities of their existing wafer fabrication lines.

ASML describes itself as the world's leading provider of lithography systems (etching and printing on wafers) for the semiconductor industry. ASML manufactures complex machines that are critical to the production of integrated circuits or microchips. ASML designs, develops, integrates, markets, and services these advanced systems, which help chip makers reduce the size and increase the functionality of microchips and consumer electronic equipment. The machines are costly and thus represent a substantial capital investment for a purchaser.

Based on revenue, Intel is the world's largest semiconductor chip maker and has the dominant share of microprocessors for the personal computer market. Intel has made significant investments in research and development (R&D) to introduce and produce new chips for new applications.

Established in 1987, Taiwan Semiconductor Manufacturing (TSM) is the world's largest dedicated semiconductor foundry (a semiconductor fabrication plant that executes the designs of other companies). TSM describes itself as offering cutting-edge process technologies, pioneering design services, manufacturing efficiency, and product quality. The company's revenues represent about 50 percent of the dedicated foundry segment in the semiconductor industry.

The questions that follow take the perspective of early 2009, when many economies around the world were in a recession. Based only on the information given, answer the following questions:

1. If the weak economy of early 2009 were to recover within the next 12–18 months, which of the two sub-industries of the semiconductor and semiconductor equipment industry would most likely be the first to experience a positive improvement in business?

2. Explain whether Intel and TSM should be considered members of the same peer group.

3. Explain whether Lam Research and ASML should be considered members of the same peer group.

Solution to 1:

In the most likely scenario, improvement in the business of the equipment makers (Lam and ASML) would lag that of semiconductor companies (Intel and TSM). Because of the weak economy of early 2009, excess manufacturing capacity should be available to meet increased demand for integrated circuits in the near term without additional equipment, which is a major capital investment. When semiconductor manufacturers believe the longer-term outlook has improved, they should begin to place orders for additional equipment.

Solution to 2:

Intel and TSM are not likely to be considered comparable members of the same peer group because they have different sets of customers and different business models. Intel designs and produces its own proprietary semiconductors for direct sale to customers, such as personal computer makers. TSM provides design and production services to a diverse group of integrated circuit suppliers that generally do not have their own in-house manufacturing capabilities. In mid-2009, Standard & Poor's did not group Intel and TSM in the same peer group; Intel was in the Semiconductors, Logic, Larger Companies group and TSM was in the Semiconductors, Foundry Services group.

Solution to 3:

Both Lam Research and ASML are leading companies that design and manufacture equipment to produce semiconductor chips. The companies are comparable because they both depend on the same economic factors that drive demand for their products. Their major customers are the semiconductor chip companies. In mid-2009, Standard & Poor's grouped both companies in the same peer group—Semiconductor Equipment, Larger Front End.

The next section addresses fundamental skills in describing and analyzing an industry.

5   DESCRIBING AND ANALYZING AN INDUSTRY

In their work, analysts study statistical relationships between industry trends and a range of economic and business variables. Analysts use economic, industry, and business publications and internet resources as sources of information. They also seek information from industry associations, from the individual subject companies they are analyzing, and from these companies' competitors, suppliers, and customers. An analyst with a superior knowledge about an industry's characteristics, conditions, and trends has a competitive edge in evaluating the investment merits of the companies in the industry.

Analysts attempt to develop practical, reliable industry forecasts by using various approaches to forecasting. They often estimate a range of projections for a variable reflecting various possible scenarios. Analysts may seek to compare their projections with the projections of other analysts, partly to study differences in methodology and conclusions but also to identify differences between their forecasts and consensus forecasts. These latter differences are extremely important for uncovering investment opportunities because, to be the basis for superior investment performance, the forecast for a value-relevant variable must be both correct and sufficiently different from the consensus reflected in the price of publicly traded securities. Note that, although some information on analysts' revenue projections, EPS estimates, and ratings are accessible in some markets, analysts may have limited access to details about other analysts' work and assumptions because such details are kept confidential for competitive reasons.

Investment managers and analysts also examine industry performance 1) in relation to other industries to identify industries with superior/inferior returns and 2) over time to determine the degree of consistency, stability, and risk in the returns in the industry over time. The objective of this analysis is to identify industries that offer the highest potential for investment returns on a risk-adjusted basis. The investment time horizon can be either long or short, as is the case for a rotation strategy in which portfolios are rotated into the industry groups that are expected to benefit from the next stage in the business cycle.

Often, analysts examine **strategic groups** (groups sharing distinct business models or catering to specific market segments in an industry) almost as separate industries within industries. Criteria for selecting a strategic group might include the complexity of the product or service, its mode of delivery, and "barriers to entry." For example, charter airlines form a strategic group among "airlines" that is quite distinct from scheduled airlines; full-service hotels form a strategic group that is separate from limited-service or budget hotels; and companies that sell proprietary drugs (which are protected by patents) would be in a separate group from companies that sell generic drugs (which do not have patent protection) partly because the two groups pursue different strategies and use different business models.

Analysts often consider and classify industries according to industry **life-cycle stage**. The analyst determines whether an industry is in the embryonic, growth, shake-out, mature, or declining stage of the industry life cycle. During the stages of the life cycle of a product or industry, its position on the experience curve is often analyzed. The **experience curve** shows direct cost per unit of good or service produced or delivered as a typically declining function of cumulative output. The curve declines 1) because as the utilization of capital equipment increases, fixed costs (administration, overhead, advertising, etc.) are spread over a larger number of units of production, 2) because of improvements in labor efficiency and management of facilities, and 3) because of advances in production methods and product design. Examples exist in virtually all industries, but the experience curve is especially important in industries with high fixed overhead costs and/or repetitive production operations, such as electronics and appliance, automobile, and aircraft manufacturing. The industry life cycle is discussed in depth later in this reading.

Exhibit 2 provides a framework designed to help analysts check that they have considered the range of forces that may affect the evolution of an industry. It shows, at the macro level, macroeconomic, demographic, governmental, social, and technological influences affecting the industry. It then depicts how an industry is affected by the forces driving industry competition (threat of new entrants, substitution threats, customer and supplier bargaining forces), the competitive forces in the industry, life-cycle issues, business-cycle considerations, and position of the industry on the experience curve. Exhibit 2 summarizes and brings together pictorially topics and concepts discussed in this section.

Exhibit 2	A Framework for Industry Analysis

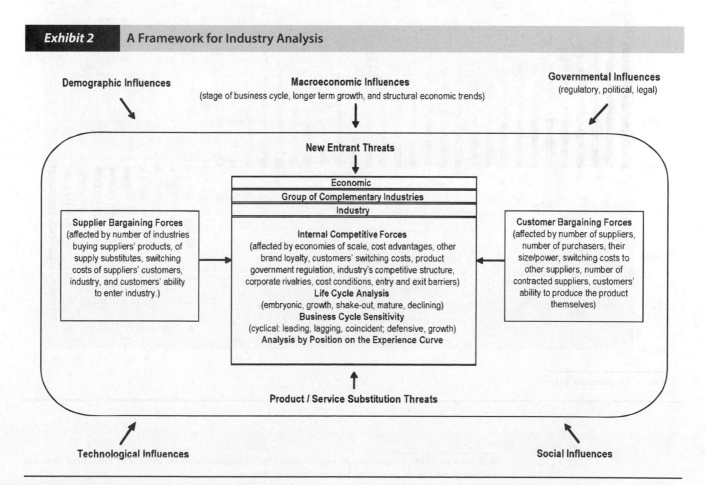

5.1 Principles of Strategic Analysis

When analyzing an industry, the analyst must recognize that the economic fundamentals can vary markedly among industries. Some industries are highly competitive, with most players struggling to earn adequate returns on capital, whereas other
industries have attractive characteristics that allow almost all industry participants
to generate healthy profits. Exhibit 3 makes this point graphically. It shows the average spread between return on invested capital (ROIC) and the cost of capital for 54
industries from 2006 through 2008.[6] Industries earning positive spreads appear to be
earning **economic profits**, in the sense that they are achieving returns on investment
above the opportunity cost of funds. This result should create value—that is, should
increase the wealth of the investors, who are the providers of capital. In contrast,
industries that are realizing negative spreads are destroying value. As can be seen,
some industries struggled to generate positive economic returns (i.e., to create value)
even during this period of synchronized global growth, while other industries did very
well in earning such returns.

Exhibit 3	Some Industries Create Value, Others Destroy It

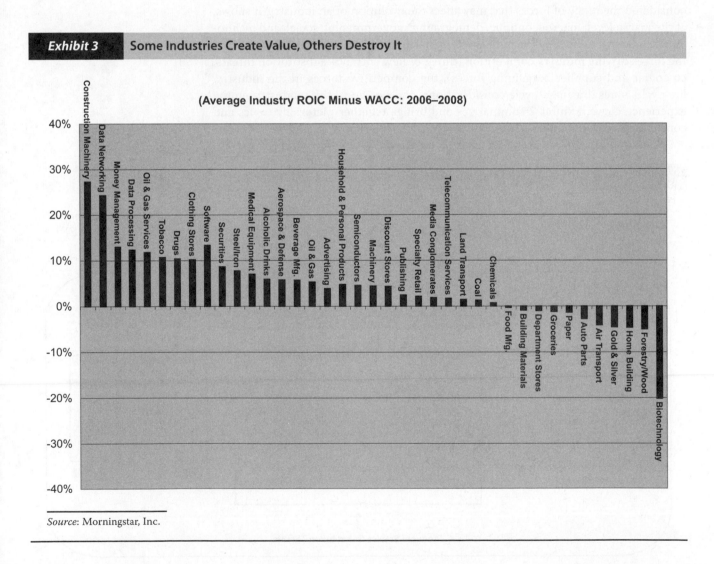

(Average Industry ROIC Minus WACC: 2006–2008)

Source: Morningstar, Inc.

---

6 Return on invested capital can be defined as net operating profit after tax divided by the sum of common
and preferred equity, long-term debt, and minority interests.

Differing competitive environments are often tied to the structural attributes of an industry, which is one reason industry analysis is a vital complement to company analysis. To thoroughly analyze a company itself, the analyst needs to understand the context in which the company operates. Needless to say, industry analysis must be forward looking. Many of the industries in Exhibit 3 were very different 10 or 15 years ago and would have been placed differently with respect to value creation; many will look very different 10 or 15 years from now. As analysts examine the competitive structure of an industry, they should always be thinking about what attributes could change in the future.

Analysis of the competitive environment with an emphasis on the implications of the environment for corporate strategy is known as **strategic analysis**. Michael Porter's "five forces" framework is the classic starting point for strategic analysis[7]; although it was originally aimed more at internal managers of businesses than at external security analysts, the framework is useful to both.[8]

Porter focused on five determinants of the intensity of competition in an industry:

- The **threat of substitute products**, which can negatively affect demand if customers choose other ways of satisfying their needs. For example, consumers may trade down from premium beers to discount brands during recessions. Low-priced brands may be close substitutes for premium brands, which, when consumer budgets are constrained, reduces the ability of premium brands to maintain or increase prices.

- The **bargaining power of customers**, which can affect the intensity of competition by exerting influence on suppliers regarding prices (and possibly other factors such as product quality). For example, auto parts companies generally sell to a small number of auto manufacturers, which allows those customers, the auto manufacturers, to be tough negotiators when it comes to setting prices.

- The **bargaining power of suppliers**, which may be able to raise prices or restrict the supply of key inputs to a company. For example, workers at a heavily unionized company may have greater bargaining power as suppliers of labor than workers at a comparable non-unionized company. Suppliers of scarce or limited parts or elements often possess significant pricing power.

- The **threat of new entrants** to the industry, which depends on barriers to entry, or how difficult it would be for new competitors to enter the industry. Industries that are easy to enter will generally be more competitive than industries with high barriers to entry.

- The **intensity of rivalry** among incumbent companies (i.e., the current companies in the industry), which is a function of the industry's competitive structure. Industries that are fragmented among many small competitors, have high fixed costs, provide undifferentiated (commodity-like) products, or have high exit barriers usually experience more intense rivalry than industries without these characteristics.

Although all five of these forces merit attention, the fourth and fifth are particularly recommended as a first focus for analysis. The two factors are broadly applicable because all companies have competitors and must worry about new entrants to their industries. Also, in investigating these two forces, the analyst may become familiar in detail with an industry's incumbents and potential entrants, and all these companies' relative competitive prospects.

---

7 See Porter (2008) for a recent presentation.

8 What aspects of a company are important may be different for internal and external analysts. Whether information about competitive positions is accurately reflected in market prices, for example, would be relatively more important to external analysts.

Addressing the following questions should help the analyst evaluate the threat of new entrants and the level of competition in an industry and thereby provide an effective base for describing and analyzing the industry:

■ What are the barriers to entry? Is it difficult or easy for a new competitor to challenge incumbents? Relatively high (low) barriers to entry imply that the threat of new entrants is relatively low (high).

■ How concentrated is the industry? Do a small number of companies control a relatively large share of the market, or does the industry have many players, each with a small market share?

■ What are capacity levels? That is, based on existing investment, how much of the goods or services can be delivered in a given time frame? Does the industry suffer chronic over- or under-capacity, or do supply and demand tend to come into balance reasonably quickly in the industry?

■ How stable are market shares? Do companies tend to rapidly gain or lose share, or is the industry stable?

■ Where is the industry in its life cycle? Does it have meaningful growth prospects, or is demand stagnant/declining?

■ How important is price to the customer's purchase decision?

The answers to these questions are elements of any thorough industry analysis.

5.1.1 Barriers to Entry

When a company is earning economic profits, the chances that it will be able to sustain them through time are greater, all else being equal, if the industry has high barriers to entry. The ease with which new competitors can challenge incumbents is often an important factor in determining the competitive landscape of an industry. If new competitors can easily enter the industry, the industry is likely to be highly competitive because high returns on invested capital will quickly be competed away by new entrants eager to grab their share of economic profits. As a result, industries with low barriers to entry often have little pricing power because price increases that raise companies' returns on capital will eventually attract new competitors to the industry.

If incumbents are protected by barriers to entry, the threat of new entrants is lower, and incumbents may enjoy a more benign competitive environment. Often, these barriers to entry can lead to greater pricing power, because potential competitors would find it difficult to enter the industry and undercut incumbents' prices. Of course, high barriers to entry do not guarantee pricing power, because incumbents may compete fiercely among each other.

A classic example of an industry with low barriers to entry is restaurants. Anyone with a modest amount of capital and some culinary skill can open a restaurant, and popular restaurants quickly attract competition. As a result, the industry is very competitive, and many restaurants fail in their first few years of business.

At the other end of the spectrum of barriers to entry are the global credit card networks such as MasterCard and Visa, both of which often post operating margins greater than 30 percent. Such high profits should attract competition, but the barriers to entry are extremely high. Capital costs are one hurdle; also, building a massive data-processing network would not be cheap. Imagine for a moment that a venture capitalist was willing to fund the construction of a network that would replicate the physical infrastructure of the incumbents—the new card-processing company would have to convince millions of consumers to use the new card and convince thousands of merchants to accept the card. Consumers would not want to use a card that merchants did not accept, and merchants would not want to accept a card that few consumers carried. This problem would be difficult to solve, which is why the barriers to entering this industry are quite high. The barriers help preserve the profitability of the incumbent players.

One way of understanding barriers to entry is simply by thinking about what it would take for new players to compete in an industry. How much money would they need to spend? What kind of intellectual capital would they need to acquire? How easy would it be to attract enough customers to become successful?

Another way to investigate the issue is by looking at historical data. How often have new companies tried to enter the industry? Is a list of industry participants today markedly different from what it was five or ten years ago? These kinds of data can be very helpful because the information is based on the real-world experience of many entrepreneurs and businesses making capital allocation decisions. If an industry has seen a flood of new entrants over the past several years, odds are good that the barriers are low; conversely, if the same ten companies that dominate an industry today dominated it ten years ago, barriers to entry are probably fairly high.

Do not confuse barriers to *entry*, however, with barriers to *success*. In some industries, entering may be easy but becoming successful enough to threaten the incumbents might be quite hard. For example, in the United States, starting a mutual fund requires a capital investment of perhaps US$150,000—not much of a barrier to an industry with historically high returns on capital. But once one has started a mutual fund, how does the company gather assets? Financial intermediaries are unlikely to sell a mutual fund with no track record. So, the fund may need to incur operational losses for a few years until it has established a good track record. Even with a track record, the fund will be competing in a crowded marketplace against companies with massive advertising budgets and well-paid salespeople. In this industry, good distribution can be even more valuable than good performance. So, although entering the asset management industry may be relatively easy, succeeding is another thing altogether.

Also, high barriers to entry do not automatically lead to good pricing power and attractive industry economics. Consider the cases of auto making, commercial aircraft manufacturing, and refining industries. Starting up a new company in any of these industries would be tremendously difficult. Aside from the massive capital costs, there would be significant other barriers to entry: A new automaker would need manufacturing expertise and a dealer network; an aircraft manufacturer would need a tremendous amount of intellectual capital; and a refiner would need process expertise and regulatory approvals.

Yet, all of these industries are quite competitive, with limited or nonexistent pricing power, and few industry participants reliably generate returns on capital in excess of their costs of capital. Among the reasons for this seeming paradox of high barriers to entry plus poor pricing power, two stand out.

- First, price is a large component of the customer's purchase decision when buying from these companies in these industries. In some cases, the reason is that the companies (e.g., refiners) sell a commodity; in some cases, the product is expensive but has easily available substitutes. For example, most airlines choose between purchasing Boeing and Airbus airplanes not on brand but on cost-related considerations: Airlines need to transport people and cargo at the lowest possible cost per mile because the airlines have limited ability to pass along higher costs to customers. That consideration makes price a huge component of their purchase decision. Most airlines purchase whichever plane is the most cost efficient at any point in time. The result is that the Boeing Company and Airbus have limited ability to price their planes at a level that generates good returns on invested capital.[9]

---

9 Neither company's commercial aircraft segment has reliably generated returns on capital comfortably in excess of the company's cost of capital for many years. Boeing's returns on capital have been respectable overall, but the company's military segment is much more profitable than its commercial aircraft segment.

■ Second, these industries all have high barriers to exit, which means they are prone to overcapacity. A refinery or automobile plant cannot be used for anything other than, respectively, refining oil or producing cars, which makes it hard to redeploy the capital elsewhere and exit the industry if conditions become unprofitable. This barrier gives owners of these types of assets a strong incentive to attempt to keep those loss-making plants operating, which, of course, prolongs conditions of overcapacity.

A final consideration when analyzing barriers to entry is that they can change over time. Years ago, a potential new entrant to the semiconductor industry would have needed the capital and expertise to build a "fab" (the industry term for a semiconductor manufacturing plant). Chip fabs are hugely expensive and technologically complex, which deterred potential new entrants. Starting in the mid-1990s, however, the outsourcing of chip making to contract semiconductor manufacturers became feasible, which meant that designers of chips could challenge the manufacturers without the need to build their own plants. As a result, the industry became much more fragmented through the late 1990s and into the first decade of the 21st century.

So, in general, high barriers to entry can lead to better pricing and less competitive industry conditions, but important exceptions are worth bearing in mind.

5.1.2 *Industry Concentration*

Much like industries with barriers to entry, industries that are concentrated among a relatively small number of players often experience relatively less price competition. Again, there are important exceptions, so the reader should not automatically assume that concentrated industries always have pricing power or that fragmented industries do not.

An analysis of industry concentration should start with market share: What percentage of the market does each of the largest players have, and how large are those shares relative to each other and relative to the remainder of the market? Often, the *relative* market shares of competitors matter as much as their *absolute* market shares.

For example, the global market for long-haul commercial aircraft is extremely concentrated—only Boeing and Airbus manufacture these types of planes. The two companies have roughly similar market shares, however, and control essentially the entire market. Because neither enjoys a scale advantage relative to its competitor and because any business gained by one is lost by the other, competition tends to be fierce.

This situation contrasts with the market for home improvement products in the United States, which is dominated by Home Depot and Lowe's. These two companies have 11 percent and 7 percent market share, respectively, which doesn't sound very large. However, the next largest competitor has only 2 percent of the market, and most market participants are tiny with miniscule market shares. Both Home Depot and Lowe's have historically posted high returns on invested capital, in part because they could profitably grow by targeting smaller competitors rather than engaging in fierce competition with each other.

Fragmented industries tend to be highly price competitive for several reasons. First, the large number of companies makes coordination difficult because there are too many competitors for each industry member to monitor effectively. Second, each player has such a small piece of the market that even a small gain in market share can make a meaningful difference to its fortunes, which increases the incentive of each company to undercut prices and attempt to steal share. Finally, the large number of players encourages industry members to think of themselves individualistically rather than as members of a larger group, which can lead to fierce competitive behavior.

In concentrated industries, in contrast, each player can relatively easily keep track of what its competitors are doing, which makes tacit coordination much more feasible. Also, leading industry members are large, which means they have more to lose—and proportionately less to gain—by destructive price behavior. Large companies are also more tied to the fortunes of the industry as a whole, making them more likely to consider the long-run effects of a price war on overall industry economics.

As with barriers to entry, the level of industry concentration is a guideline rather than a hard and fast rule when thinking about the level of pricing power in an industry. For example, Exhibit 4 shows a rough classification of industries compiled by Morningstar after asking its equity analysts whether industries were characterized by strong or weak pricing power and whether those industries were concentrated or fragmented. Examples of companies in industries are included in parentheses. In the upper right quadrant ("concentrated with weak pricing power"), those industries that are capital intensive and sell commodity-like products are shown in boldface.

Exhibit 4	A Two-Factor Analysis of Industries

Concentrated with Strong Pricing Power

Soft Drinks (Coca-Cola Co., PepsiCo)
Orthopedic Devices (Zimmer, Smith & Nephew)
Laboratory Services (Quest Diagnostics, LabCorp)
Biotech (Amgen, Genzyme)
Pharmaceuticals (Merck & Co., Novartis)
Microprocessors (Intel, Advanced Micro Devices)
Industrial Gases (Praxair, Air Products and Chemicals)
Enterprise Storage (EMC)
Enterprise Networking (Cisco Systems)
Integrated Shippers (UPS, FedEx, DHL International)
U.S. Railroads (Burlington Northern)
U.S. Defense (General Dynamics)
Heavy Construction Equipment (Caterpillar, Komatsu)
Seaborne Iron Ore (Vale, Rio Tinto)
Confections (Cadbury, Mars/Wrigley)
Credit Card Networks (MasterCard, Visa)
Custody & Asset Administration (BNY Mellon, State Street)
Investment Banking /Mergers &Acquisitions (Goldman Sachs, UBS)
Futures Exchanges (Chicago Mercantile Exchange, Intercontinental Exchange)
Canadian Banking (RBC Bank, TD Bank)
Australian Banking
Tobacco (Philip Morris, British American Tobacco)
Alcoholic Beverages (Diageo, Pernod Ricard)

Concentrated with Weak Pricing Power

Commercial Aircraft (Boeing, Airbus)
Automobiles (General Motors, Toyota, Daimler)
Memory (DRAM & Flash Product, Samsung, Hynix)
Semiconductor Equipment (Applied Materials, Tokyo Electron)
Generic Drugs (Teva Pharmaceutical Industries, Sandoz)
Consumer Electronics (Sony Electronics, Koninklijke Philips Electronics)
PCs (Dell, Acer, Lenovo)
Printers/Office Machines (HP, Lexmark)
Refiners (Valero, Marathon Oil)
Major Integrated Oil (BP, ExxonMobil)
Equity Exchanges (NYSE, Deutsche Börse Group)

Fragmented with Strong Pricing Power

Asset Management (BlackRock, Fidelity)
For-Profit Education (Apollo Group, DeVry University)
Analog Chips (Texas Instruments, STMicroelectronics)
Industrial Distribution (Fastenal, W.W. Grainger)
Propane Distribution (AmeriGas, Ferrellgas)
Private Banking (Northern Trust, Credit Suisse)

Fragmented with Weak Pricing Power

Consumer Packaged Goods (Procter & Gamble, Unilever)
Retail (Walmart, Carrefour Group)
Marine Transportation (Maersk Line, Frontline)
Solar Panels
Homebuilding
Airlines
Mining (metals)
Chemicals
Engineering & Construction
Metal Service Centers
Commercial Printing

(continued)

Exhibit 4	Continued

Fragmented with Strong Pricing Power	Fragmented with Weak Pricing Power
	Restaurants
	Radio Broadcasting
	Oil Services
	Life Insurance
	Reinsurance
	Exploration & Production (E&P)
	U.S. Banking
	Specialty Finance
	Property/Casualty Insurance
	Household and Personal Products

Source: Morningstar Equity Research.

The industries in the top right quadrant defy the "concentration is good for pricing" guideline. We discussed the commercial aircraft manufacturing example in the preceding section, but many other industries are dominated by a small number of players yet have difficult competitive environments and limited pricing power.

When we examine these concentrated-yet-competitive industries, a clear theme emerges: Many industries in this quadrant (the boldface ones) are highly capital intensive and sell commodity-like products. As we saw in the discussion of exit barriers, capital-intensive industries can be prone to overcapacity, which mitigates the benefits of industry concentration. Also, if the industry sells a commodity product that is difficult—or impossible—to differentiate, the incentive to compete on price increases because a lower price frequently results in greater market share.[10]

The computer memory market is a perfect example of a concentrated-yet-competitive industry. Dynamic random access memory (DRAM) is widely used in PCs, and the industry is concentrated, with about three-quarters of global market share held by the top four companies. The industry is also highly capital intensive; a new fab costs upwards of US$3 billion. But one DRAM chip is much like another, and players in this market have a huge economic incentive to capture market share because of the large scale economies involved in running a semiconductor manufacturing plant. As a result, price competition tends to be extremely fierce and industry concentration is essentially a moot point in the face of these other competitive dynamics.

The global soft drink market is also highly concentrated, of course, but capital requirements are relatively low and industry participants sell a differentiated product. Pepsi and Coca-Cola do not own their own bottling facilities, so a drop in market share does not affect them as much as it would a memory-chip maker. Moreover, although memory-chip companies are assured of gaining market share and increasing sales volumes by cutting prices, a sizable proportion of consumers would not switch from Pepsi to Coke (or vice-versa) even if one cost much less than the other.

Generally, industry concentration is a good indicator that an industry has pricing power and rational competition, but other factors may override the importance of concentration. Industry fragmentation is a much stronger signal that the industry is competitive with limited pricing power. Notice how few fragmented industries are in the bottom left quadrant in Exhibit 4.

---

10 There are a small number of concentrated and rational commodity industries, such as potash (a type of fertilizer) and seaborne iron ore. What sets these industries apart is that they are *hyper*-concentrated: The top two players control 60 percent of the global potash market, and the top three players control two-thirds of the global market for seaborne iron ore.

The industry characteristics discussed here are guidelines meant to steer the analyst in a particular direction, not rules that should cause the analyst to ignore other relevant analytical factors.

5.1.3 *Industry Capacity*

The effect on pricing of industry capacity (the maximum amount of a good or service that can be supplied in a given time period) is clear: Tight, or limited, capacity gives participants more pricing power as demand for the product or service exceeds supply, whereas overcapacity leads to price cutting and a very competitive environment as excess supply chases demand. An analyst should think about not only current capacity conditions but future changes in capacity levels. How quickly can companies in the industry adjust to fluctuations in demand? How flexible is the industry in bringing supply and demand into balance? What will be the effect of that process on industry pricing power or on industry margins?

Generally, capacity is fixed in the short term and variable in the long term because capacity can be increased—e.g., new factories can be built—if time is sufficient. What is considered "sufficient" time—and, therefore, the duration of the short term, in which capacity cannot be increased—may vary dramatically among industries. Sometimes, adding capacity takes years to complete, as in the case of the construction of a "greenfield" (new) manufacturing plant for pharmaceuticals or for paper, which is complex and subject to regulatory requirements (e.g., relating to the plant's waste). In other situations, capacity may be added or reduced relatively quickly, as is the case with service industries, such as advertising. In cyclical markets, such as commercial paper and paperboard, capacity conditions can change rapidly. Strong demand in the early stages of an economic recovery can result in the addition of supply. Given the long lead times to build manufacturing plants, new supply may reach the market just as demand slows, rapidly changing capacity conditions from tight to loose. Such considerations underscore the importance of forecasting long-term industry demand in evaluating industry investments in capacity.

One of the more dramatic examples of this process in recent years occurred in the market for maritime dry-bulk shipping during the commodity boom of 2003–2008. Rapid industrialization in China—combined with synchronized global economic growth—increased demand for cargo ships that could transport iron ore, coal, grains, and other high-volume/low-value commodities. Given that the supply of cargo ships could not be increased very quickly (because ships take time to build and large commercial shipyards typically have multi-year backlogs), shippers naturally raised prices to take advantage of the tight global cargo capacity. In fact, the price to charter the largest type of dry-bulk vessel—a Capesize-class ship too big to fit through the Panama Canal—increased more than fivefold in only a year, from approximately US$30,000 per day in early 2006 to almost US$160,000 per day by late 2007.

As one would expect, orders for new dry-bulk carriers skyrocketed during this period as the industry scrambled to add shipping capacity to take advantage of seemingly insatiable demand and very favorable pricing. In early 2006, the number of dry-bulk carriers on order from shipyards represented approximately 20 percent of the worldwide fleet. By late 2008, the number of bulk ships on order represented almost 70 percent of the global bulk fleet.[11] Of course, the prospect of this additional capacity, combined with a dramatic slump in aggregate global demand for commodities, caused a massive decline in shipping rates. Capesize charter rates plummeted from the US$160,000/day high of late 2007 to a low of under US$10,000 per day just one year later.

---

11 From "RS Platou Monthly" (November 2008): www.platou.com/loadfileservlet/loadfiledb?id=12289893 12093PUBLISHER&key=1228989321421.

In this example, the conditions of tight supply that were driving strong dry-bulk pricing were quite clear, and these high prices drove attractive returns on capital—and share-price performance—for dry-bulk-shipping companies. However, the careful analyst would have looked at future additions to supply in the form of new ships on order and would have forecasted that the tight supply conditions were not sustainable and thus that the pricing power of dry-bulk shippers was short-lived. These predictions are, in fact, precisely what occurred.

Note that capacity need not be physical. After Hurricane Katrina caused enormous damage to the southeastern United States in 2005, reinsurance rates quickly spiked as customers sought to increase their financial protection from future hurricanes. However, these high reinsurance rates enticed a flood of fresh capital into the reinsurance market, and a number of new reinsurance companies were founded, which brought rates back down.

Generally, if new capacity is physical—for example, an auto manufacturing plant or a massive cargo ship—it will take longer for new capacity to come on line to meet an increase in demand, resulting in a longer period of tight conditions. Unfortunately, capacity additions frequently overshoot long-run demand, and because physical capital is often hard to re-deploy, industries reliant on physical capacity may get stuck in conditions of excess capacity and diminished pricing power for an extended period.

Financial and human capital, in contrast, can be quickly shifted to new uses. In the reinsurance example, for instance, financial capital was quick to enter the reinsurance market and take advantage of tight capacity conditions, but if too much capital had entered the market, some portion of that capital could easily have left to seek higher returns elsewhere. Money can be used for many things, but massive bulk cargo vessels are not useful for much more than transporting heavy goods across oceans.

5.1.4 Market Share Stability

Examining the stability of industry market shares over time is similar to thinking about barriers to entry and the frequency with which new players enter an industry. In fact, barriers to entry and the frequency of new product introductions, together with such factors as product differentiation—all affect market shares. Stable market shares typically indicate less competitive industries; unstable market shares often indicate highly competitive industries that have limited pricing power.

A comparison of two non-commodity markets in the health care sector illustrates this point. Over the past decade, the orthopedic device industry—mainly artificial hips and knees—has been a relatively stable global oligopoly. As Exhibit 5 indicates, five companies control about 95 percent of the worldwide market, and the market shares of those companies have changed by only small amounts over the past several years.

Exhibit 5	Market Share Stability in Global Orthopedic Devices (Entries Are Market Share)			
Worldwide Knee/Hip Market Share	**2005 (%)**	**2006 (%)**	**2007 (%)**	**2008 (%)**
Zimmer	27.9	27.5	27.2	26.0
Johnson & Johnson (DePuy)	24.0	23.9	22.9	22.9
Stryker	21.6	21.4	21.5	21.3
Smith & Nephew	9.4	9.8	11.5	12.6
Biomet	11.5	10.9	10.9	11.3

Source: Company reports and Morningstar estimates.

In contrast, although the U.S. market for stents—small metal mesh devices used to prop open blocked arteries—is also controlled by a handful of companies, market shares recently have gone from being very stable to being marked by rapid change. Johnson & Johnson, which together with Boston Scientific, dominated the U.S. stent market for many years, went from having about half the market in 2007 to having only 15 percent in early 2009; over the same period, Abbott Laboratories increased its market share from zero to 25 percent. The reason for this change was the launch of new stents by Abbott and Medtronic, which took market share from Johnson & Johnson and Boston Scientific's established stents.

Orthopedic device companies have experienced more stability in their market shares for two reasons. First, artificial hips and knees are complicated to implant, and each manufacturer's products are slightly different. As a result, orthopedic surgeons become proficient at using one or several companies' devices and may be reluctant to incur the time and cost of learning how to implant products from a competing company. The second reason is the relatively slow pace of innovation in the orthopedic device industry, which tends to be evolutionary rather than revolutionary, making the benefit of switching among product lines relatively low. In addition, the number of orthopedic device companies has remained fairly static over many years.

In contrast, the U.S. stent market has experienced rapid shifts in market shares because of several factors. First, interventional cardiologists seem to be more open than orthopedic surgeons to implanting stents from different manufacturers; that tendency may reflect lower switching costs for stents relative to orthopedic devices. More importantly, however, the pace of innovation in the stent market has become quite rapid, giving cardiologists added incentive to switch to newer stents, with potentially better patient outcomes, as they became available.

Low switching costs plus a relatively high benefit from switching caused market shares to change quickly in the stent market. High switching costs for orthopedic devices coupled with slow innovation resulted in a lower benefit from switching, which led to greater market share stability in orthopedic devices.

5.1.5 *Industry Life Cycle*

An industry's life-cycle position often has a large impact on its competitive dynamics, making this position an important component of the strategic analysis of an industry.

5.1.5.1 Description of an Industry Life-Cycle Model   Industries, like individual companies, tend to evolve over time, and usually experience significant changes in the rate of growth and levels of profitability along the way. Just as an investment in an individual company requires careful monitoring, industry analysis is a continuous process to identify changes that may be occurring or be likely to occur. A useful framework for analyzing the evolution of an industry is an industry life-cycle model, which identifies the sequential stages that an industry typically goes through. The five stages of an industry life-cycle model are embryonic, growth, shakeout, mature, and decline. Each stage is characterized by different opportunities and threats.[12] Exhibit 6 shows the model as a curve illustrating the level and growth rate of demand at each stage.

---

12 Much of the discussion that follows regarding life-cycle stages owes a debt to the discussion in Hill and Jones (2008).

Exhibit 6	An Industry Life-Cycle Model

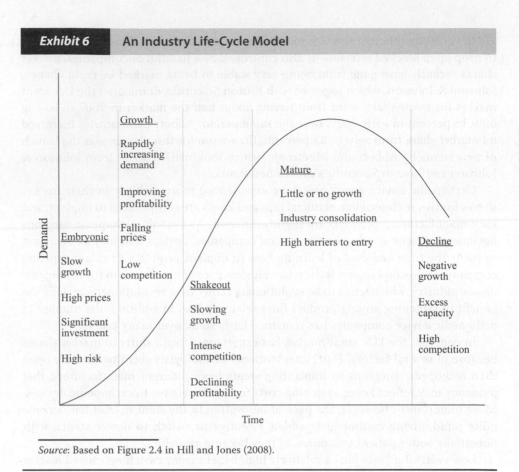

Source: Based on Figure 2.4 in Hill and Jones (2008).

Embryonic An embryonic industry is one that is just beginning to develop. For example, in the 1960s, the global semiconductor industry was in the embryonic stage (it has grown to become a US$249 billion industry in 2008)[13] and in the early 1980s, the global mobile phone industry was in the embryonic stage (it now produces and sells more than a billion handsets annually). Characteristics of the embryonic stage include slow growth and high prices because customers tend to be unfamiliar with the industry's product and volumes are not yet sufficient to achieve meaningful economies of scale. Increasing product awareness and developing distribution channels are key strategic initiatives of companies during this stage. Substantial investment is generally required, and the risk of failure is high. A majority of start-up companies do not succeed.

Growth A growth industry tends to be characterized by rapidly increasing demand, improving profitability, falling prices, and relativity low competition among companies in the industry. Demand is fueled by new customers entering the market, and prices fall as economies of scale are achieved and as distribution channels develop. The threat of new competitors entering the industry is usually highest during the growth stage, when barriers to entry are relatively low. Competition tends to be relatively limited, however, because rapidly expanding demand provides companies with an opportunity to grow without needing to capture market share from competitors. Industry profitability improves as volumes rise and economies of scale are attained.

Shakeout The shakeout stage is usually characterized by slowing growth, intense competition, and declining profitability. During the shakeout stage, demand approaches market saturation levels because few new customers are left to enter the market.

13 Semiconductor Industry Association Factsheet: www.sia-online.org/cs/industry_resources/industry_fact_sheet.

Competition is intense as growth becomes increasingly dependent on market share gains. Excess industry capacity begins to develop as the rate at which companies continue to invest exceeds the overall growth of industry demand. In an effort to boost volumes to fill excess capacity, companies often cut prices, so industry profitability begins to decline. During the shakeout stage, companies increasingly focus on reducing their cost structure (restructuring) and building brand loyalty. Marginal companies may fail or merge with others.

Mature Characteristics of a mature industry include little or no growth, industry consolidation, and relatively high barriers to entry. Industry growth tends to be limited to replacement demand and population expansion because the market at this stage is completely saturated. As a result of the shakeout, mature industries often consolidate and become oligopolies. The surviving companies tend to have brand loyalty and relatively efficient cost structures, both of which are significant barriers to entry. During periods of stable demand, companies in mature industries tend to recognize their interdependence and try to avoid price wars. Periodic price wars do occur, however, most notably during periods of declining demand (such as during economic downturns). Companies with superior products or services are likely to gain market share and experience above-industry-average growth and profitability.

Decline During the decline stage, industry growth turns negative, excess capacity develops, and competition increases. Industry demand at this stage may decline for a variety of reasons, including technological substitution (for example, the newspaper industry has been declining for years as more people turn to the internet and 24-hour cable news networks for information), social changes, and global competition (for example, low-cost foreign manufacturers pushing the U.S. textile industry into decline). As demand falls, excess capacity in the industry forms and companies respond by cutting prices, which often leads to price wars. The weaker companies often exit the industry at this point, merge, or redeploy capital into different products and services.

When overall demand for an industry's products or services is declining, the opportunity for individual companies to earn above-average returns on invested capital tends to be less than when demand is stable or increasing, because of price cutting and higher per-unit costs as production is cut back. Example 6 deals with industry life cycles.

Example 6

Industry Growth and Company Growth

U.S. shipments of prefabricated housing (precut, modular housing) declined sharply in 1999–2004 as the abundant availability of low-cost mortgage financing and other factors led individuals to purchase site-built housing. In 1998, however, some forecasts had projected that prefabricated housing would gain market share at the expense of site-built housing. What would have been the probable impact on market share of a typical company in the prefabricated housing industry under the 1998 optimistic forecast and under actual conditions?

Solution:

Increasing industry demand as forecasted in 1998 would have given companies in the prefabricated housing industry the opportunity to grow without taking market share from one another, mitigating the intensity of competition in this industry. Under actual industry circumstances of declining demand and a shrinking market, in contrast, revenue growth for a prefabricated housing company could happen only through market share gains from its competitors.

5.1.5.2 Using an Industry Life-Cycle Model   In general, new industries tend to be more competitive (with lots of players entering and exiting) than mature industries, which often have stable competitive environments and players that are more interested in protecting what they have than in gaining lots of market share. However, as industries move from maturity to decline, competitive pressures may increase again as industry participants perceive a zero-sum environment and fight over pieces of an ever-shrinking pie.

An important point for the analyst to think about is whether a company is "acting its age" relative to where its industry sits in the life cycle. Companies in growth industries should be building customer loyalty as they introduce consumers to new products or services, building scale, and reinvesting heavily in their operations to capitalize on increasing demand. They are probably not focusing strongly on internal efficiency. These companies are rather like young adults, who are reinvesting their human and financial capital with the goal of becoming more successful in life. Growth companies typically reinvest their cash flows in new products and product platforms rather than returning cash flows to shareholders because these companies still have many opportunities to deploy their capital to make positive returns. Although this analogy to the human life cycle is a helpful way to think about the model, the analyst should also be aware that the analogy is not exact in detail. Long-established companies sometimes find a way to accelerate growth through innovation or by expansion into new markets. Humans cannot really move back to the days of youth. So, a more precise formulation may be "acting its stage" rather than acting its age.

Companies in mature industries are likely to be pursuing replacement demand rather than new buyers and are probably focused on extending successful product lines rather than introducing revolutionary new products. They are also probably focusing on cost rationalization and efficiency gains rather than on taking lots of market share. Importantly, these companies have fewer growth opportunities than in the previous stage, and thus more limited avenues for profitably reinvesting capital, but they often have strong cash flows. Given their strong cash flows and relatively limited reinvestment opportunities, such companies should be, according to a common perspective, returning capital to shareholders via share repurchases or dividends. These companies are rather like middle-aged adults who are harvesting the fruits of their success earlier in life.

What can be a concern is a middle-aged company acting like a young, growth company and pouring capital into projects with low ROIC prospects in an effort to pursue size for its own sake. Many companies have a difficult time managing the transition from growth to maturity, and their returns on capital—and shareholder returns—may suffer until management decides to allocate capital in a manner more appropriate to the company's life-cycle stage.

For example, three large U.S. retailers—Walmart, Home Depot, and McDonalds—all went through the transition to maturity in the first decade of the 21st century. At various times between 2002 and 2005, these companies realized that their size and industry dominance meant that the days of double-digit growth that was driven largely by new store (restaurant) openings were a thing of the past. All three reallocated capital away from opening new stores to other areas—namely, increased inventory efficiency (Home Depot), improving the customer experience (McDonalds), and increased dividends and share repurchases (all three). As a result, returns on capital for each improved, as did shareholder returns.

5.1.5.3 Limitations of Industry Life-Cycle Analysis   Although models can provide a useful framework for thinking about an industry, the evolution of an industry does not always follow a predictable pattern. Various external factors may significantly affect the shape of the pattern, causing some stages to be longer or shorter than expected and, in certain cases, causing some stages to be skipped altogether.

Technological changes may cause an industry to experience an abrupt shift from growth to decline, thus skipping the shakeout and mature stages. For example, transistors replaced vacuum tubes in the 1960s at a time when the vacuum tube industry was still in its growth stage; word processors replaced typewriters in the 1980s; and today the movie rental industry is experiencing rapid change as consumers increasingly turn to on-demand services such as downloading movies from the internet or through their cable providers.

Regulatory changes can also have a profound impact on the structure of an industry. A prime example is the deregulation of the U.S. telecommunications industry in the 1990s, which transformed a monopolistic industry into an intensely competitive one. AT&T was broken into regional service providers, and many new long distance telephone service entrants, such as Sprint, emerged. The result was a wider range of product and service offerings and lower consumer prices. Changes in government reimbursement rates for health care products and services may (and have) affected the profitability of companies in the health care industry globally.

Social changes also have the ability to affect the profile of an industry. The casual dining industry has benefited over the past 30 years from the increase in the number of dual-income families, who often have more income but less time to cook meals to eat at home.

Demographics also play an important role. As the Baby Boom generation ages, for instance, industry demand for health care services is likely to increase.

Thus, life-cycle models tend to be most useful for analyzing industries during periods of relative stability. They are less practical when the industry may be experiencing rapid change because of external or other special circumstances.

Another limiting factor of models is that not all companies in an industry experience similar performances. The key objective for the analyst is to identify the potential winners while avoiding potential losers. Highly profitable companies can exist in competitive industries with below-average profitability—and vice versa. For example, Nokia has historically been able to use its scale to generate levels of profitability that are well above average despite operating in a highly competitive industry. In contrast, despite the historically above-average growth and profitability of the software industry, countless examples exist of software companies that failed to ever generate a profit and eventually went out of business.

Example 7

Industry Life Cycle

1. An industry experiencing slow growth and high prices is best characterized as being in the:

    A. mature stage.

    B. shakeout stage.

    C. embryonic stage.

2. Which of the following statements about the industry life-cycle model is *least* accurate?

    A. The model is more appropriately used during a period of rapid change than during a period of relative stability.

    B. External factors may cause some stages of the model to be longer or shorter than expected, and in certain cases, a stage may be skipped entirely.

    C. Not all companies in an industry will experience similar performance, and very profitable companies can exist in an industry with below-average profitability.

> **Solution to 1:**
>
> C is correct. Both slow growth and high prices are associated with the embryonic stage. High price is not a characteristic of the mature or shakeout stages.
>
> **Solution to 2:**
>
> A is correct. The statement is the least accurate. The model is best used during a period of relative stability rather than during a period of rapid change.

5.1.6 *Price Competition*

A highly useful tool for analyzing an industry is attempting to think like a customer of the industry. Whatever factor most influences customer purchase decisions is likely to also be the focus of competitive rivalry in the industry. In general, industries for which price is a large factor in customer purchase decisions tend to be more competitive than industries in which customers value other attributes more highly.

Although this depiction may sound like the description of a commodity industry versus a non-commodity industry, it is, in fact, a bit more subtle. Commercial aircraft and passenger cars are certainly more differentiated than lumps of coal or gallons of gasoline, but price nonetheless weighs heavily in the purchase decisions of buyers of aircraft and cars, because fairly good substitutes are easily available. If Airbus charges too much for an A320, an airline can buy a Boeing 737.[14] If BMW's price for a four-door luxury sedan rises too high, customers can switch to a Mercedes or other luxury brand with similar features. Similar switching can be expected as a result of a unilateral price increase in the case of most industries in the "Weak Pricing Power" column of Exhibit 4.

Contrast these industries with asset management, one of a handful of industries that is both fragmented and characterized by strong pricing power. Despite the well-documented impact of fees on future investment returns, the vast majority of asset management customers do not make decisions on the basis of price. Instead, asset management customers focus on historical returns, which allow this highly fragmented industry to maintain strong pricing power. Granted, the index fund arena is very price competitive, because any index fund is a perfect substitute for another fund tracking the same benchmark. But the active management segment of the industry has generally been able to price its products in an implicitly cooperative fashion that enables most players to generate consistently high returns on capital, presumably because price is not uppermost in the mind of a prospective mutual fund investor.

Returning to a more capital-intensive industry, consider heavy-equipment manufacturers, such as Caterpillar, Deere, and Komatsu. A large wheel loader or combine harvester requires a large capital outlay, so price certainly plays a part in the buyers' decisions. However, other factors are important enough to customers to allow these companies a small amount of pricing power. Construction equipment is typically used as a complement to other gear on a large project, which means that downtime for repairs increases costs because, for example, hourly laborers must wait for a bulldozer to be fixed. Broken equipment is also expensive for agricultural users, who may have only a few days in which to harvest a season's crop. Because of the importance to users of their products' reliability and their large service networks—which are important "differentiators" or factors bestowing a competitive advantage—Caterpillar, Komatsu, and Deere have historically been able to price their equipment at levels that have generated solid returns on invested capital.

---

14 A small amount of "path dependence" characterizes the airline industry, in that an airline with a large fleet of a particular Airbus model will be marginally more likely to stick with that model for a new purchase than it will be to buy a Boeing, but the aircraft manufacturers' ability to exploit this likelihood is minimal.

5.1.7 *Industry Comparison*

To illustrate how these elements might be applied, Exhibit 7 uses the factors discussed in this reading to examine three industries.

Exhibit 7	**Elements of a Strategic Analysis for Three Industries**		
	Branded Pharmaceuticals	**Oil Services**	**Confections/Candy**
Major Companies	Pfizer, Novartis, Merck, GlaxoSmithKline	Schlumberger, Baker Hughes, Halliburton	Cadbury, Hershey, Mars/Wrigley, Nestle
Barriers to Entry/ Success	*Very High*: Substantial financial and intellectual capital required to compete effectively. A potential new entrant would need to create a sizable R&D operation, a global distribution network, and large-scale manufacturing capacity.	*Medium*: Technological expertise is required, but high level of innovation allows niche companies to enter the industry and compete in specific areas.	*Very High*: Low financial or technological hurdles, but new players would lack the established brands that drive consumer purchase decisions.
Level of Concentration	*Concentrated*: A small number of companies control the bulk of the global market for branded drugs. Recent mergers have increased level of concentration.	*Fragmented*: Although only a small number of companies provide a full range of services, many smaller players compete effectively in specific areas. Service arms of national oil companies may control significant market share in their own countries, and some product lines are concentrated in the mature U.S. market.	*Very Concentrated*: Top four companies have a large proportion of global market share. Recent mergers have increased level of concentration.
Impact of Industry Capacity	*NA*: Pharmaceutical pricing is primarily determined by patent protection and regulatory issues, including government approvals of drugs and of manufacturing facilities. Manufacturing capacity is of little importance.	*Medium/High*: Demand can fluctuate quickly depending on commodity prices, and industry players often find themselves with too few (or too many) employees on the payroll.	*NA*: Pricing is driven primarily by brand strength. Manufacturing capacity has little effect.
Industry Stability	*Stable*: The branded pharmaceutical market is dominated by major companies and consolidation via mega-mergers. Market shares shift quickly, however, as new drugs are approved and gain acceptance or lose patent protection.	*Unstable*: Market shares may shift frequently depending on technology offerings and demand levels.	*Very Stable*: Market shares change glacially.
Life Cycle	*Mature*: Overall demand does not change greatly from year to year.	*Mature*: Demand does fluctuate with energy prices, but normalized revenue growth is only mid-single digits.	*Very Mature*: Growth is driven by population trends and pricing.

(continued)

Exhibit 7	Continued

	Branded Pharmaceuticals	**Oil Services**	**Confections/Candy**
Price Competition	*Low/Medium*: In the United States, price is a minimal factor because of consumer- and provider-driven, de-regulated health care system. Price is a larger part of the decision process in single-payer systems, where efficacy hurdles are higher.	*High*: Price is a major factor in purchasers' decisions. Some companies have modest pricing power because of a wide range of services or best-in-class technology, but primary customers (major oil companies) can usually substitute with in-house services if prices are too high. Also, innovation tends to diffuse quickly throughout the industry.	*Low*: A lack of private-label competition keeps pricing stable among established players, and brand/familiarity plays a much larger role in consumer purchase decisions than price.
Demographic Influences	*Positive*: Populations of developed markets are aging, which slightly increases demand.	*NA*	*NA*
Government & Regulatory Influences	*Very High*: All drugs must be approved for sale by national safety regulators. Patent regimes may differ among countries. Also, health care is heavily regulated in most countries.	*Medium*: Regulatory frameworks can affect energy demand at the margin. Also, governments play an important role in allocating exploration opportunities to E&P companies, which can indirectly affect the amount of work flowing down to service companies.	*Low*: Industry is not regulated, but childhood obesity concerns in developed markets are a low-level potential threat. Also, high-growth emerging markets may block entry of established players into their markets, possibly limiting growth.
Social Influences	*NA*	*NA*	*NA*
Technological Influences	*Medium/High*: Biologic (large-molecule) drugs are pushing new therapeutic boundaries, and many large pharmaceutical companies have a relatively small presence in biotech.	*Medium/High*: Industry is reasonably innovative, and players must re-invest in R&D to remain competitive. Temporary competitive advantages are possible via commercialization of new processes or exploitation of accumulated expertise.	*Very Low*: Innovation does not play a major role in the industry.
Growth vs. Defensive vs. Cyclical	*Defensive*: Demand for most health care services does not fluctuate with the economic cycle, but demand is not strong enough to be considered "growth."	*Cyclical*: Demand is highly variable and depends on oil prices, exploration budgets, and the economic cycle.	*Defensive*: Demand for candy and gum is extremely stable.

Note: "*NA*" in this exhibit stands for "not applicable."

Example 8 reviews some of the information presented in Exhibit 7.

Example 8

External Influences

1. Which of the following industries is *most* affected by government regulation?
   - **A.** Oil services.
   - **B.** Pharmaceuticals.
   - **C.** Confections and candy.

2. Which of the following industries is *least* affected by technological innovation?
   - **A.** Oil services.
   - **B.** Pharmaceuticals.
   - **C.** Confections and candy.

3. Which of the following statements about industry characteristics is *least* accurate?
   - **A.** Manufacturing capacity has little effect on pricing in the confections/candy industry.
   - **B.** The branded pharmaceutical industry is considered to be defensive rather than a growth industry.
   - **C.** With respect to the worldwide market, the oil services industry has a high level of concentration with a limited number of service providers.

Solution to 1:

B is correct. Exhibit 7 states that the pharmaceutical industry has high amount of government and regulatory influences.

Solution to 2:

C is correct. Exhibit 7 states that innovation does not play a large role in the candy industry.

Solution to 3:

C is correct; it is a false statement. From a worldwide perspective, the industry is considered fragmented. Although a small number of companies provide the full range of services, competition by many smaller players occurs in niche areas. In addition, national oil service companies control significant market share in their home çcountries.

5.2 External Influences on Industry Growth, Profitability, and Risk

External factors affecting an industry's growth include macroeconomic, technological, demographic, governmental, and social influences.

5.2.1 *Macroeconomic Influences*

Trends in overall economic activity generally have significant effects on the demand for an industry's products or services. These trends can be cyclical (i.e., related to the changes in economic activity caused by the business cycle) or structural (i.e., related to enduring changes in the composition or magnitude of economic activity). Among the economic variables that usually affect an industry's revenues and profits are the following:

- gross domestic product or the measure of the value of goods and services produced by an economy, either in current or constant currency (inflation-adjusted) terms;

- interest rates, which represent the cost of debt to consumers and businesses and are important ingredients in financial institutions' revenues and costs;

- the availability of credit, which affects business and consumer spending and financial solvency; and

- inflation, which reflects the changes in prices of goods and services and influences costs, interest rates, and consumer and business confidence.

5.2.2 *Technological Influences*

New technologies create new or improved products that can radically change an industry and can also change how other industries that use the products conduct their operations.

The computer hardware industry provides one of the best examples of how technological change can affect industries. The 1958 invention of the microchip (also known as an "integrated circuit," which is effectively a computer etched on a sliver of silicon) enabled the computer hardware industry to eventually create a new market of personal computing for the general public and radically extended the use of computers in business, government, and educational institutions.

Moore's law states that the number of transistors that can be inexpensively placed on an integrated circuit doubles approximately every two years. Several other measures of digital technology have improved at exponential rates related to Moore's law, including the size, cost, density and speed of components. As a result of these trends, the computer hardware industry encroached upon and, in time, came to dominate the fields of hardware for word processing and many forms of electronic communication and home entertainment. The computing industry's integrated circuit innovation increased economies of scale and erected large barriers to new entrants because the capital costs of innovation and production became very high. Intel capitalized on both factors which allowed it to garner an industry market leadership position and to become the dominant supplier of the PC industry's highest value component (the microprocessor). Thus, Intel became dominant because of its cost advantage, brand power, and access to capital.

Along the way, the computer hardware industry was supported and greatly assisted by the complementary industries of computer software and telecommunications (particularly in regard to development of the internet); also important were other industries—entertainment (television, movies, games), retailing, and the print media. Ever more powerful integrated circuits and advances in wireless technology, as well as the convergence of media, which the internet and new wireless technology have facilitated, continue to reshape the uses and the roles of PC hardware in business and personal life. In the middle of the 20th century, few people in the world would have imagined they would ever have any use for a home computer. Today, the estimate is that about 1.6 billion people, or almost a quarter of the world's population, have access to connected computing. For the United States, the estimate is at least 76 percent of the population; it is much less in emerging and underdeveloped countries. More than 4 billion mobile cellular telephone subscriptions exist in the world today,[15] and

---

15 See www.itu.int/newsroom/press_releases/2009/39.html.

the advances of mobile telephony appear poised to increase this figure dramatically in the years ahead as mobile phone and computer hardware technologies merge to provide new hand-held computing and communication capabilities.

Another example of the effects of technology on an industry is the impact of digital imaging technology on the photographic film industry. Digital imaging uses an electronic image sensor to record an image as electronic data rather than as chemical changes on film. This difference allows a much greater degree of image processing and transmission than in film photography. Since their invention in 1981, digital cameras have become extremely popular and now widely outsell traditional film cameras (although many professional photographers continue to use film for esthetic reasons for certain applications). Digital cameras include such features as video and audio recording. The effects of this major change in photographic technology have caused film and camera manufacturers—including Kodak, Fujifilm, Nikon Corporation, and Pentax Imaging Company—to completely restructure and redesign their products to adapt to the new technology's appeal to consumers.

5.2.3 Demographic Influences

Changes in population size, in the distributions of age and gender, and in other demographic characteristics may have significant effects on economic growth and on the amounts and types of goods and services consumed.

The effects of demographics on industries are well exemplified by the impact of the post–World War II Baby Boom in North America on demand for goods and services. Born between 1946 and 1964, this bulge of 76 million people in the North American population has influenced the composition of numerous products and services it needs in its passage from the cradle through childhood, adolescence, early adulthood, middle age, and into retirement. The teenage pop culture of the late 1950s and 1960s and all the products (records, movies, clothes, and fashions associated with it), the surge in demand for housing in the 1970s and 1980s, and the increasing demand for retirement-oriented investment products in the 1990s and early 2000s are all examples of the range of industries affected by this demographic bulge working its way through age categories of the population.

Another example of the effects of demographics on industries is the impact of an aging population in Japan, which has one of the highest percentages of elderly residents (21 percent over the age of 65) and a very low birth rate. Japan's ministry of health estimates that by 2055, the percentage of the population over 65 will rise to 40 percent and the total population will fall by 25 percent. These demographic changes are expected by some observers to have negative effects on the overall economy because, essentially, they imply a declining workforce. However, some sectors of the economy stand to benefit from these trends—for example, the heath care industry.

Example 9

The Post-World War II Baby Boom and Its Effects on the U.S. Housing Industry

In the United States, Canada, and Australia, the end of World War II marked the beginning of a sustained period of elevated birth rates per thousand in the population. This rise reflected the relief from the hardships of the Great Depression of the 1930s and WWII, increased levels of immigration (immigrants tend to be younger and hence more fertile than average) and a protracted period of postwar economic prosperity. The rate of births in the United States rose from 18.7 per thousand in 1935 and 20.4 per thousand in 1945 to 24.1 per thousand in 1950 and a peak of more than 25.0 per thousand in 1955–1957. Twenty years later, when the babies born during the period 1946–1964 entered adulthood, the housing industry experienced a surge in demand that led to a period of high sales of new homes. The rate of new housing starts in this period rose from 20.1 per thousand of population in 1966 to a peak of 35.3 per thousand in 1972 and remained elevated, except during the economic recession of 1974–1975, until the end of the 1970s.

Another demographic effect on the housing industry arising from the post-WWII Baby Boom came from the children of the Baby Boom generation (the so-called Echo Boomers). The Echo Boomers started to enter their most fertile years in the late 1970s and caused an increase in the number of births per thousand from a post-WWII low of 14.8 in 1975 to a peak of 16.7 in 1990. The Echo Boomers did not have as large an effect on housing demand 20 years later as their parents had had, but there was still a significant increase in new housing starts from 13.7 per thousand in 1995 to a high of 18.8 per thousand in 2005; easily available mortgage financing contributed to the increase.

5.2.4 *Governmental Influences*

Governmental influence on industries' revenues and profits is pervasive and important. In setting tax rates and rules for corporations and individuals, governments affect profits and incomes, which in turn, affect corporate and personal spending. Governments are also major purchasers of goods and services from a range of industries.

Example 10 illustrates the sudden shifts in wealth that can occur when governments step in to support or quash a securities market innovation. In the example, an **income trust** refers to a type of equity ownership vehicle established as a trust issuing ownership shares known as units. Income trusts became extremely popular among income-oriented investors in Canada in the late 1990s and early 2000s because under then-current regulation, such trusts could avoid taxation on income distributed to unit-holders (investors)—that is, avoid double taxation (once at the corporate level and once at the investor level). As Example 10 describes, the tax advantage that regulations permitted was eventually removed.

Example 10

The Effects of Tax Increases on Income Trusts in Canada

On 31 October 2006, in an effort to halt the rapid growth of income trust structures in the Canadian stock market, Canada's Minister of Finance James Flaherty announced that these tax-exempt flow-through entities would in the future be taxable on the income, with exemptions only for passive rent-collecting real estate investment trusts. A five year hiatus was established for existing trusts to adapt. He stated that the government needed to clamp down on trusts because too many companies were converting to the high-yield securities, primarily to save taxes. The S&P/TSX Capped Income Trust Index declined 12 percent on the day after the announcement, wiping out C$24 billion in market value.

Often, governments exert their influence indirectly by empowering other regulatory or self-regulatory organizations (e.g., stock exchanges, medical associations, utility rate setters, and other regulatory commissions) to govern the affairs of an industry. By setting the terms of entry into various sectors, such as financial services and health care, and the rules that companies and individuals must adhere to in these fields, governments control the supply, quality, and nature of many products and services and the public's access to them. For example, in the financial industry, the acceptance of savings deposits from and the issuance of securities to the investing public are usually tightly controlled by governments and their agencies. This control is imposed through rules designed to protect investors from fraudulent operators and to ensure that investors receive adequate disclosure about the nature and risks of their investments. Another example is that medical patients in most developed countries are treated by doctors who are trained according to standards set by medical associations acting as self-regulatory organizations empowered under government laws. In addition, the medications that patients receive must be approved by government agencies. In a somewhat different vein, users of tobacco products purchase items for which the marketing and sales taxes are heavily controlled by governments in most developed countries and for which warnings to consumers about the dangers of smoking are mandated by governments. In the case of industries that supply branches of government, such as the military, public works, and law enforcement departments, government contracts directly affect the revenues and profits of the suppliers.

Example 11

The Effects of Government Purchases on the Aerospace Industry

The aerospace, construction, and firearms industries are prime examples of industries for which governments are major customers and whose revenues and profits are significantly—in some cases, predominantly—affected by their sales to governments. An example is the European Aeronautic Defence and Space Company (EADS), a global leader in aerospace, defense, and related services with head offices in Paris and Ottobrunn, Germany. In 2008, EADS generated revenues of €43.3 billion and employed an international workforce of about 118,000. EADS includes Airbus, a leading manufacturer of commercial aircraft; Airbus Military, providing tanker, transport, and mission aircraft; Eurocopter, the world's largest helicopter supplier; and EADS Astrium, the European leader in space programs, including Ariane and Galileo. Its Defence & Security Division is a provider of comprehensive systems solutions and makes EADS the major partner in the Eurofighter consortium and a stakeholder in missile systems provider MBDA. On 3 March 2008, EADS shares rose 9.2 percent after the U.S. Air Force chose its Airbus A330 over Boeing's 767 for an airborne refueling plane contract worth as much as US$35 billion.

5.2.5 Social Influences

Societal changes involving how people work, spend their money, enjoy their leisure time, and conduct other aspects of their lives can have significant effects on the sales of various industries.

Tobacco consumption in the United Kingdom provides a good example of the effects of social influences on an industry. Although the role of government in curbing tobacco advertising, legislating health warnings on the purchases of tobacco products, and banning smoking in public places (such as restaurants, bars, public houses, and transportation vehicles) probably has been the most powerful apparent instrument of changes in tobacco consumption, the forces underlying that change have really been social in nature—namely, increasing consciousness on the part of the population of the damage to the health of tobacco users and those in their vicinity from smoking, the increasing cost to individuals and governments of the chronic illnesses caused by tobacco consumption, and the accompanying shift in public perception of smokers from socially correct to socially incorrect—even inconsiderate or reckless. As a result of these changes in society's views of smoking, cigarette consumption in the United Kingdom declined from 102.5 billion cigarettes in 1990 to less than 65.0 billion in 2009, placing downward pressure on tobacco companies' unit sales.

Example 12

The Effects on Various Industries of More Women Entering the Workforce

In 1870, women accounted for only 15 percent of the workforce in the United States outside the home. By 1950, after two world wars and the Great Depression, this figure had risen to 30 percent (it had been even higher temporarily during WWII because of high levels of war-mandated production) and by 2008, to 48 percent. Based on economic reasoning, identify four industries that should have benefitted from the social change that saw women shift from their most frequent historical roles in Western society as full-time homemakers to becoming more frequently full-time participants in the workforce.

Solution:

Industries include the following:

1. The restaurant business. The restaurant business stands to benefit from an increased demand given that women, because of their work responsibilities, may not have the time and energy to prepare meals. Restaurant industry growth was actually high in this period: From accounting for only 25 percent of every food dollar in the United States in 1950, the restaurant industry today consumes more than 44 percent of every food dollar, with 45 percent of current industry revenues arising from a category of restaurant that did not exist in 1950, namely, fast food.

2. Manufacturers of work clothing for women.

3. Home and child care services.

4. Automobile manufacturers. Extra vehicles became necessary to transport two members of the family to work, for instance, and children to school or day care.

5. Housing for the aging. With increasing workforce participation by women, aged family members requiring care or supervision became increasingly unable to rely on non-working female family members to provide care in their homes.

Example 13

The Airline Industry: A Case Study of Many Influences

The global airline industry exemplifies many of the concepts and influences we have discussed.

Life-Cycle Stage

The industry can be described as having some mature characteristics because average annual growth in global passenger traffic has remained relatively stable at 4.5 percent in the 2000s (compared with 4.7 percent in the 1990s). Some market segments in the industry, however, are still in their growth phase—notably, the markets of the Middle East and Asia, which are expected to grow at 6.5 percent compared with projected North American growth of 3.2 percent over the next 20 years.

Sensitivity to Business Cycle

The airline industry is a cyclical industry; global economic activity produces swings in revenues and, especially, profitability, because of the industry's high fixed costs and operating leverage. In 2009, for example, global passenger traffic is expected to have declined by approximately 8 percent and airlines are expected to report significant net losses—close to US$9.0 billion, which is down from a global industry profit of US$12.9 billion in 2007. The industry tends to respond early to upward and downward moves in economic cycles; depending on the region, air travel changes at 1.5 times to 2.0 times GDP growth. It is highly regulated, with governments and airport authorities playing a large role in allocating routes and airport slots. Government agencies and the International Airline Transport Association set rules for aircraft and flight safety. Airline customers tend to have low brand loyalty (except at the extremes of high and low prices and service); leisure travelers focus mainly on price, and business travelers focus mostly on schedules and service. Product and service differentiation at particular price points is low because aircraft, cabin configuration, and catering tend to be quite similar in most cases. For leisure travelers, the price competition is intense and is led by low-cost discount carriers, including Southwest Airlines in the United States, Ryanair in Europe, and Air Asia in Asia. For business travelers, the major scheduled airlines and a few service-quality specialists, such as Singapore Airlines, are the main contenders. Fuel costs (typically more than 25 percent of total costs and highly volatile) and labor costs (around 10 percent of total costs) have been the focus of management cost-reduction efforts. The airline industry is highly unionized, and labor strife has frequently been a source of costly disruptions to the industry. Technology has always played a major role in the airline industry, from its origins with small propeller-driven planes through the advent of the jet age to the drive for greater fuel efficiency since the oil price increases of the 1970s. Technology also poses a threat to the growth of business air travel in the form of improved telecommunications—notably, videoconferencing and webcasting. Arguably, the airline industry has been a great force in shaping demography by permitting difficult-to-access geographical areas to be settled with large populations. At the same time, large numbers of post-WWII Baby Boomers have been a factor in generating the growth in demand for air travel in the past half-century. In recent years, social issues have started to play a role in the airline industry; carbon emissions, for example, have come under scrutiny by environmentalists and governments.

COMPANY ANALYSIS

6

Company analysis includes an analysis of the company's financial position, products and/or services, and **competitive strategy** (its plans for responding to the threats and opportunities presented by the external environment). Company analysis takes place after the analyst has gained an understanding of a company's external environment— the macroeconomic, demographic, governmental, technological, and social forces influencing the industry's competitive structure. The analyst should seek to determine whether the strategy is primarily defensive or offensive in its nature and how the company intends to implement the strategy.

Porter identifies two chief competitive strategies: a low-cost strategy (cost leadership) and a product/service differentiation strategy.

In a low-cost strategy, companies strive to become the low-cost producers and to gain market share by offering their products and services at lower prices than their competition while still making a profit margin sufficient to generate a superior rate of return based on the higher revenues achieved. Low-cost strategies may be pursued defensively to protect market positions and returns or offensively to gain market share and increase returns. Pricing also can be defensive (when the competitive environment is one of low rivalry) or aggressive (when rivalry is intense). In the case of intense rivalry, pricing may even become predatory—that is, aimed at rapidly driving competitors out of business at the expense of near-term profitability. The hope in such a strategy is that having achieved a larger market share, the company can later increase prices to generate higher returns than before. For example, the predatory strategy has been alleged by some analysts to have been followed by major airlines trying to protect lucrative routes from discount airlines. Although laws concerning anti-competitive practices often prohibit predatory pricing to gain market share, in most cases, it is difficult to accurately ascribe the costs of products or services with sufficient precision to demonstrate that predatory pricing (as opposed to intense but fair price competition) is occurring. Companies seeking to follow low-cost strategies must have tight cost controls, efficient operating and reporting systems, and appropriate managerial incentives. In addition, they must commit themselves to painstaking scrutiny of production systems and their labor forces and to low-cost designs and product distribution. They must be able to invest in productivity-improving capital equipment and to finance that investment at a low cost of capital.

In differentiation strategies, companies attempt to establish themselves as the suppliers or producers of products and services that are unique either in quality, type, or means of distribution. To be successful, their price premiums must be above their costs of differentiation and the differentiation must be appealing to customers and sustainable over time. Corporate managers who successfully pursue differentiation strategies tend to have strong market research teams to identify and match customer needs with product development and marketing. Such a strategy puts a premium on employing creative and inventive people.

6.1 Elements that Should Be Covered in a Company Analysis

A thorough company analysis, particularly as presented in a research report, should

- provide an overview of the company (corporate profile), including a basic understanding of its businesses, investment activities, corporate governance, and perceived strengths and weaknesses;
- explain relevant industry characteristics;
- analyze the demand for the company's products and services;
- analyze the supply of products and services, which includes an analysis of costs;
- explain the company's pricing environment; and
- present and interpret relevant financial ratios, including comparisons over time and comparisons with competitors.

Company analysis often includes forecasting the company's financial statements, particularly when the purpose of the analysis is to use a discounted cash flow method to value the company's common equity.

Exhibit 8 provides a checklist of points to cover in a company analysis. The list may need to be adapted to serve the needs of a particular company analysis and is not exhaustive.

Exhibit 8	A Checklist for Company Analysis

Corporate Profile

- Identity of company's major products and services, current position in industry, and history
- Composition of sales
- Product life-cycle stages/experience curve effects[16]
- Research & development activities
- Past and planned capital expenditures
- Board structure, composition, electoral system, anti-takeover provisions, and other corporate governance issues
- Management strengths, weaknesses, compensation, turnover, and corporate culture
- Benefits, retirement plans, and their influence on shareholder value
- Labor relations
- Insider ownership levels and changes
- Legal actions and the company's state of preparedness
- Other special strengths or weaknesses

Industry Characteristics

- Stage in its life cycle
- Business-cycle sensitivity or economic characteristics
- Typical product life cycles in the industry (short and marked by technological obsolescence or long, such as pharmaceuticals protected by patents)
- Brand loyalty, customer switching costs, and intensity of competition
- Entry and exit barriers
- Industry supplier considerations (concentration of sources, ability to switch suppliers or enter suppliers' business)
- Number of companies in the industry and whether it is, as determined by market shares, fragmented or concentrated
- Opportunity to differentiate product/service and relative product/service price, cost, and quality advantages/disadvantages
- Technologies used
- Government regulation
- State and history of labor relations
- Other industry problems/opportunities

(continued)

---

16 A *product life cycle* relates to stages in the sales of a product. *Experience curve effects* refer to the tendency for the cost of producing a good or service to decline with cumulative output.

Exhibit 8	Continued

Analysis of Demand for Products/Services

- Sources of demand
- Product differentiation
- Past record, sensitivities, and correlations with social, demographic, economic, and other variables
- Outlook—short, medium, and long term, including new product and business opportunities

Analysis of Supply of Products/Services

- Sources (concentration, competition, and substitutes)
- Industry capacity outlook—short, medium, and long term
- Company's capacity and cost structure
- Import/export considerations
- Proprietary products or trademarks

Analysis of Pricing

- Past relationships among demand, supply, and prices
- Significance of raw material and labor costs and the outlook for their cost and availability
- Outlook for selling prices, demand, and profitability based on current and anticipated future trends

Financial Ratios and Measures
(in multi-year spreadsheets with historical and forecast data)

   I. Activity ratios, measuring how efficiently a company performs such functions as the collection of receivables and inventory management:

- Days of sales outstanding (DSO)
- Days of inventory on hand (DOH)
- Days of payables outstanding (DPO)

   II. Liquidity ratios, measuring a company's ability to meet its short-term obligations:

- Current ratio
- Quick ratio
- Cash ratio
- Cash conversion cycle (DOH + DSO – DPO)

   III. Solvency ratios, measuring a company's ability to meet its debt obligations. (In the following, "net debt" is the amount of interest-bearing liabilities after subtracting cash and cash equivalents.)

- Net debt to EBITDA (earnings before interest, taxes, depreciation, and amortization)
- Net debt to capital
- Debt to assets
- Debt to capital (at book and market values)
- Financial leverage ratio (Average total assets/Average total equity)

Exhibit 8	Continued

- Cash flow to debt
- Interest coverage ratio
- Off-balance-sheet liabilities and contingent liabilities
- Non-arm's-length financial dealings

IV. Profitability ratios, measuring a company's ability to generate profitable sales from its resources (assets).

- Gross profit margin
- Operating profit margin
- Pretax profit margin
- Net profit margin
- Return on invested capital or ROIC (Net operating profits after tax/ Average invested capital)
- Return on assets or ROA (Net income/Average total assets)
- Return on equity or ROE (Net income/Average total equity)

V. Financial statistics and related considerations, quantities and facts about a company's finances that an analyst should understand.

- Growth rate of net sales
- Growth rate of gross profit
- EBITDA
- Net income
- Operating cash flow
- EPS
- Operating cash flow per share
- Operating cash flow in relation to maintenance and total capital expenditures
- Expected rate of return on retained cash flow
- Debt maturities and ability of company to refinance and/or repay debt
- Dividend payout ratio (Common dividends/Net income available to common shareholders)
- Off-balance-sheet liabilities and contingent liabilities
- Non-arm's-length financial dealings

To evaluate a company's performance, the key measures presented in Exhibit 8 should be compared over time and between companies (particularly peer companies). The following formula can be used to analyze how and why a company's ROE differs from that of other companies or its own ROE in other periods by tracing the differences to changes in its profit margin, the productivity of its assets, or its financial leverage:

ROE = (Net profit margin: Net earnings/Net sales)

× (Asset turnover: Net sales/Average total assets)

× (Financial leverage: Average total assets/Average common equity)

The financial statements of a company over time provide numerous insights into the effects of industry conditions on its performance and the success or failure of its strategies. They also provide a framework for forecasting the company's operating performance when given the analyst's assumptions for numerous variables in the future. The financial ratios listed in Exhibit 8 are applicable to a wide range of companies and industries, but other statistics and ratios are often also used.

6.2 Spreadsheet Modeling

Spreadsheet modeling of financial statements to analyze and forecast revenues, operating and net income, and cash flows has become one of the most widely used tools in company analysis. Although spreadsheet models are a valuable tool for understanding past financial performance and forecasting future performance, the complexity of such models can at times be a problem. Because modeling requires the analyst to predict and input numerous items in financial statements, there is a risk of errors—either in assumptions made or in formulas in the model—which can compound, leading to erroneous forecasts. Yet, those forecasts may seem precise because of the sheer complexity of the model. The result is often a false sense of understanding and security on the part of those who rely on the models. To guard against this, before or after a model is completed, a "reality check" of the model is useful.

Such testing for reasonableness can be done by, first, asking what the few most important changes in income statement items are likely to be from last year to this year and the next year and, second, attempting to quantify the effects of these significant changes or "swing factors" on the bottom line. If an analyst cannot summarize in a few points what factors are realistically expected to change income from year to year and is not convinced that these assumptions are correct, then he or she does not really understand the output of the computer modeling efforts. In general, financial models should be in a format that matches the company's reporting of its financial results or supplementary disclosures or that can be accurately derived from these reports. Otherwise, there will be no natural reality check when the company issues its financial results and the analyst will not be able to compare his or her estimates with actual reported results.

SUMMARY

In this reading, we have provided an overview of industry analysis and illustrated approaches that are widely used by analysts to examine an industry.

- Company analysis and industry analysis are closely interrelated. Company and industry analysis together can provide insight into sources of industry revenue growth and competitors' market shares and thus the future of an individual company's top-line growth and bottom-line profitability.
- Industry analysis is useful for:
  - understanding a company's business and business environment;
  - identifying active equity investment opportunities;
  - formulating an industry or sector rotation strategy; and
  - portfolio performance attribution.
- The three main approaches to classifying companies are:
  - products and/or services supplied;
  - business-cycle sensitivities; and

- statistical similarities.
- Commercial industry classification systems include:
  - Global Industry Classification Standard;
  - Russell Global Sectors; and
  - Industry Classification Benchmark.
- Governmental industry classification systems include:
  - International Standard Industrial Classification of All Economic Activities;
  - Statistical Classification of Economic Activities in the European Community;
  - Australian and New Zealand Standard Industrial Classification; and
  - North American Industry Classification System.
- A limitation of current classification systems is that the narrowest classification unit assigned to a company generally cannot be assumed to constitute its peer group for the purposes of detailed fundamental comparisons or valuation.
- A peer group is a group of companies engaged in similar business activities whose economics and valuation are influenced by closely related factors.
- Steps in constructing a preliminary list of peer companies:
  - Examine commercial classification systems if available. These systems often provide a useful starting point for identifying companies operating in the same industry.
  - Review the subject company's annual report for a discussion of the competitive environment. Companies frequently cite specific competitors.
  - Review competitors' annual reports to identify other potential comparables.
  - Review industry trade publications to identify additional peer companies.
  - Confirm that each comparable or peer company derives a significant portion of its revenue and operating profit from a similar business activity as the subject company.
- Not all industries are created equal. Some are highly competitive, with many companies struggling to earn returns in excess of their cost of capital, and other industries have attractive characteristics that enable a majority of industry participants to generate healthy profits.
- Differing competitive environments are determined by the structural attributes of the industry. For this important reason, industry analysis is a vital complement to company analysis. The analyst needs to understand the context in which a company operates to fully understand the opportunities and threats that a company faces.
- The framework for strategic analysis known as "Porter's five forces" can provide a useful starting point. Porter maintains that the profitability of companies in an industry is determined by five forces: 1) The influence or threat of new entrants, which in turn is determined by economies of scale, brand loyalty, absolute cost advantages, customer switching costs, and government regulation; 2) the influence or threat of substitute products; 3) the bargaining power of customers, which is a function of switching costs among customers and the ability of customers to produce their own product; 4) the bargaining power of suppliers, which is a function of the feasibility of product substitution, the concentration of the buyer and supplier groups, and switching costs and entry costs in each case; and 5) the intensity of rivalry among established companies, which in turn is a function of industry competitive structure, demand conditions, cost conditions, and the height of exit barriers.

■ The concept of barriers to entry refers to the ease with which new competitors can challenge incumbents and can be an important factor in determining the competitive environment of an industry. If new competitors can easily enter the industry, the industry is likely to be highly competitive because incumbents that attempt to raise prices will be undercut by newcomers. As a result, industries with low barriers to entry tend to have low pricing power. Conversely, if incumbents are protected by barriers to entry, they may enjoy a more benign competitive environment that gives them greater pricing power over their customers because they do not have to worry about being undercut by upstarts.

■ Industry concentration is often, although not always, a sign that an industry may have pricing power and rational competition. Industry fragmentation is a much stronger signal, however, that the industry is competitive and pricing power is limited.

■ The effect of industry capacity on pricing is clear: Tight capacity gives participants more pricing power because demand for products or services exceeds supply; overcapacity leads to price cutting and a highly competitive environment as excess supply chases demand. The analyst should think about not only current capacity conditions but also future changes in capacity levels—how long it takes for supply and demand to come into balance and what effect that process has on industry pricing power and returns.

■ Examining the market share stability of an industry over time is similar to thinking about barriers to entry and the frequency with which new players enter an industry. Stable market shares typically indicate less competitive industries, whereas unstable market shares often indicate highly competitive industries with limited pricing power.

■ An industry's position in its life cycle often has a large impact on its competitive dynamics, so it is important to keep this positioning in mind when performing strategic analysis of an industry. Industries, like individual companies, tend to evolve over time and usually experience significant changes in the rate of growth and levels of profitability along the way. Just as an investment in an individual company requires careful monitoring, industry analysis is a continuous process that must be repeated over time to identify changes that may be occurring.

■ A useful framework for analyzing the evolution of an industry is an industry life-cycle model, which identifies the sequential stages that an industry typically goes through. The five stages of an industry life cycle according to the Hill and Jones model are:

- embryonic;
- growth;
- shakeout;
- mature; and
- decline.

■ Price competition and thinking like a customer are important factors that are often overlooked when analyzing an industry. Whatever factors most influence customer purchasing decisions are also likely to be the focus of competitive rivalry in the industry. Broadly, industries for which price is a large factor in customer purchase decisions tend to be more competitive than industries in which customers value other attributes more highly.

■ External influences on industry growth, profitability, and risk include:

- technology;
- demographics;

- government; and
- social factors.

■ Company analysis takes place after the analyst has gained an understanding of the company's external environment and includes answering questions about how the company will respond to the threats and opportunities presented by the external environment. This intended response is the individual company's competitive strategy. The analyst should seek to determine whether the strategy is primarily defensive or offensive in its nature and how the company intends to implement it.

■ Porter identifies two chief competitive strategies:
- A low-cost strategy (cost leadership) is one in which companies strive to become the low-cost producers and to gain market share by offering their products and services at lower prices than their competition while still making a profit margin sufficient to generate a superior rate of return based on the higher revenues achieved.

- A product/service differentiation strategy is one in which companies attempt to establish themselves as the suppliers or producers of products and services that are unique either in quality, type, or means of distribution. To be successful, the companies' price premiums must be above their costs of differentiation and the differentiation must be appealing to customers and sustainable over time.

■ A checklist for company analysis includes a thorough investigation of:
- corporate profile;
- industry characteristics;
- demand for products/services;
- supply of products/services;
- pricing; and
- financial ratios.

■ Spreadsheet modeling of financial statements to analyze and forecast revenues, operating and net income, and cash flows has become one of the most widely used tools in company analysis. Spreadsheet modeling can be used to quantify the effects of the changes in certain swing factors on the various financial statements. The analyst should be aware that the output of the model will depend significantly on the assumptions that are made.

REFERENCES

Cavaglia, Stefano, Jeffrey Diermeier, Vadim Moroz, and Sonia De Zordo. 2004. "Investing in Global Equities." *Journal of Portfolio Management*, vol. 30, no. 3 : 88–94.

Hill, Charles, and Gareth Jones. 2008. "External Analysis: The Identification of Opportunities and Threats." *Strategic Management: An Integrated Approach*. Boston, MA: Houghton Mifflin Co.

McGahan, Anita M., and Michael E. Porter. 1997. "How Much Does Industry Matter, Really?" *Strategic Management Journal*, vol. 18, no. S1: 15–30.

Porter, Michael E. 2008. "The Five Competitive Forces that Shape Strategy." *Harvard Business Review*, vol. 86, no. 1 : 78–93.

PRACTICE PROBLEMS FOR READING 50

1. Which of the following is *least likely* to involve industry analysis?
   A. Sector rotation strategy.
   B. Top-down fundamental investing.
   C. Tactical asset allocation strategy.

2. A sector rotation strategy involves investing in a sector by:
   A. making regular investments in it.
   B. investing in a pre-selected group of sectors on a rotating basis.
   C. timing investment to take advantage of business-cycle conditions.

3. Which of the following information about a company would *most likely* depend on an industry analysis? The company's:
   A. dividend policy.
   B. competitive environment.
   C. trends in corporate expenses.

4. Which industry classification system uses a three-tier classification system?
   A. Russell Global Sectors.
   B. Industry Classification Benchmark.
   C. Global Industry Classification Standard.

5. In which sector would a manufacturer of personal care products be classified?
   A. Health care.
   B. Consumer staples.
   C. Consumer discretionary.

6. Which of the following statements about commercial and government industry classification systems is *most* accurate?
   A. Many commercial classification systems include private for-profit companies.
   B. Both commercial and government classification systems exclude not-for-profit companies.
   C. Commercial classification systems are generally updated more frequently than government classification systems.

7. Which of the following is *not* a limitation of the cyclical/non-cyclical descriptive approach to classifying companies?
   A. A cyclical company may have a growth component in it.
   B. Business-cycle sensitivity is a discrete phenomenon rather than a continuous spectrum.
   C. A global company can experience economic expansion in one part of the world while experiencing recession in another part.

8. A company that is sensitive to the business cycle would *most likely*:
   A. not have growth opportunities.
   B. experience below-average fluctuation in demand.
   C. sell products that the customer can purchase at a later date if necessary.

9. Which of the following factors would *most likely* be a limitation of applying business-cycle analysis to global industry analysis?

   A. Some industries are relatively insensitive to the business cycle.

   B. Correlations of security returns between different world markets are relatively low.

   C. One region or country of the world may experience recession while another region experiences expansion.

10. Which of the following statements about peer groups is *most* accurate?

    A. Constructing a peer group for a company follows a standardized process.

    B. Commercial industry classification systems often provide a starting point for constructing a peer group.

    C. A peer group is generally composed of all the companies in the most narrowly defined category used by the commercial industry classification system.

11. With regard to forming a company's peer group, which of the following statements is *not* correct?

    A. Comments from the management of the company about competitors are generally not used when selecting the peer group.

    B. The higher the proportion of revenue and operating profit of the peer company derived from business activities similar to the subject company, the more meaningful the comparison.

    C. Comparing the company's performance measures with those for a potential peer-group company is of limited value when the companies are exposed to different stages of the business cycle.

12. When selecting companies for inclusion in a peer group, a company operating in three different business segments would:

    A. be in only one peer group.

    B. possibly be in more than one peer group.

    C. not be included in any peer group.

13. An industry that *most likely* has both high barriers to entry and high barriers to exit is the:

    A. restaurant industry.

    B. advertising industry.

    C. automobile industry.

14. Which factor is *most likely* associated with stable market share?

    A. Low switching costs.

    B. Low barriers to entry.

    C. Slow pace of product innovation.

15. Which of the following companies *most likely* has the greatest ability to quickly increase its capacity?

    A. Restaurant.

    B. Steel producer.

    C. Legal services provider.

16. A population that is rapidly aging would *most likely* cause the growth rate of the industry producing eye glasses and contact lenses to:

    A. decrease.

    B.   increase.

    C. not change.

17. If over a long period of time a country's average level of educational accomplishment increases, this development would *most likely* lead to the country's amount of income spent on consumer discretionary goods to:

    A. decrease.

    B. increase.

    C. not change.

18. If the technology for an industry involves high fixed capital investment, then one way to seek higher profit growth is by pursuing:

    A. economies of scale.

    B. diseconomies of scale.

    C. removal of features that differentiate the product or service provided.

19. Which of the following life-cycle phases is typically characterized by high prices?

    A. Mature.

    B. Growth.

    C. Embryonic.

20. In which of the following life-cycle phases are price wars *most likely* to be absent?

    A. Mature.

    B. Decline.

    C. Growth.

21. When graphically depicting the life-cycle model for an industry as a curve, the variables on the axes are:

    A. price and time.

    B. demand and time.

    C. demand and stage of the life cycle.

22. Which of the following is *most likely* a characteristic of a concentrated industry?

    A. Infrequent, tacit coordination.

    B. Difficulty in monitoring other industry members.

    C. Industry members attempting to avoid competition on price.

23. Which of the following industry characteristics is generally *least likely* to produce high returns on capital?

    A. High barriers to entry

    B. High degree of concentration

    C. Short lead time to build new plants

24. An industry with high barriers to entry and weak pricing power *most likely* has:

    A. high barriers to exit.

    B. stable market shares.

    C. significant numbers of issued patents.

25. Economic value is created for an industry's shareholders when the industry earns a return:

    A. below the cost of capital.

    B. equal to the cost of capital.

    C. above the cost of capital.

26. Which of the following is *not* one of Porter's five forces?

    A. Intensity of rivalry.

    B. Bargaining power of suppliers.

    C. Threat of government intervention.

27. Which of the following industries is *most likely* to be characterized as concentrated with strong pricing power?

    A. Asset management.

    B. Alcoholic beverages.

    C. Household and personal products.

28. Which of the following industries is *most likely* to be considered to have the lowest barriers to entry?

    A. Oil services.

    B. Confections and candy.

    C. Branded pharmaceuticals.

29. With respect to competitive strategy, a company with a successful cost leadership strategy is *most likely* characterized by:

    A. a low cost of capital.

    B. reduced market share.

    C. the ability to offer products at higher prices than competitors.

30. When conducting a company analysis, the analysis of demand for a company's product is *least likely* to consider the:

    A. company's cost structure.

    B. motivations of the customer base.

    C. product's differentiating characteristics.

31. Which of the following statements about company analysis is *most* accurate?

    A. The complexity of spreadsheet modeling ensures precise forecasts of financial statements.

    B. The interpretation of financial ratios should focus on comparing the company's results over time but not with competitors.

    C. The corporate profile would include a description of the company's business, investment activities, governance, and strengths and weaknesses.

SOLUTIONS FOR READING 50

1. C is correct. Tactical asset allocation involves timing investments in asset classes and does not make use of industry analysis.

2. C is correct. A sector rotation strategy is conducted by investors wishing to time investment in industries through an analysis of fundamentals and/or business-cycle conditions.

3. B is correct. Determination of a company's competitive environment depends on understanding its industry.

4. A is correct. The Russell system uses three tiers, whereas the other two systems are based on four tiers or levels.

5. B is correct. Personal care products are classified as consumer staples in the "Description of Representative Sectors."

6. C is correct. Commercial systems are generally updated more frequently than government systems, and include only publicly traded for-profit companies.

7. B is correct. Business-cycle sensitivity falls on a continuum and is not a discrete "either–or" phenomenon.

8. C is correct. Customers' flexibility as to when they purchase the product makes the product more sensitive to the business cycle.

9. C is correct. Varying conditions of recession or expansion around the world would affect the comparisons of companies with sales in different regions of the world.

10. B is correct. Constructing a peer group is a subjective process, and a logical starting point is to begin with a commercially available classification system. This system will identify a group of companies that may have properties comparable to the business activity of interest.

11. A is correct because it is a false statement. Reviewing the annual report to find management's discussion about the competitive environment and specific competitors is a suggested step in the process of constructing a peer group.

12. B is correct. The company could be in more than one peer group depending on the demand drivers for the business segments, although the multiple business segments may make it difficult to classify the company.

13. C is correct. For the automobile industry, the high capital requirements and other elements mentioned in the reading provide high barriers to entry, and recognition that auto factories are generally only of use for manufacturing cars implies a high barrier to exit.

14. C is correct. A slow pace of product innovation often means that customers prefer to stay with suppliers they know, implying stable market shares.

15. C is correct. Capacity increases in providing legal services would not involve several factors that would be important to the other two industries, including the need for substantial fixed capital investments or, in the case of a restaurant, outfitting rental or purchased space. These requirements would tend to slow down, respectively, steel production and restaurant expansion.

16. B is correct. Vision typically deteriorates at advanced ages. An increased number of older adults implies more eyewear products will be purchased.

17. B is correct. As their educational level increases, workers are able to perform more skilled tasks, earn higher wages, and as a result, have more income left for discretionary expenditures.

18. A is correct. Seeking economies of scale would tend to reduce per-unit costs and increase profit.

19. C is correct. The embryonic stage is characterized by slow growth and high prices.

20. C is correct. The growth phase is not likely to experience price wars because expanding industry demand provides companies the opportunity to grow even without increasing market share. When industry growth is stagnant, companies may only be able to grow by increasing market share, e.g., by engaging in price competition.

21. B is correct. The industry life-cycle model shows how demand evolves through time as an industry passes from the embryonic stage through the stage of decline.

22. C is correct. The relatively few members of the industry generally try to avoid price competition.

23. C is correct. With short lead times, industry capacity can be rapidly increased to satisfy demand, but it may also lead to overcapacity and lower profits.

24. A is correct. An industry that has high barriers to entry generally requires substantial physical capital and/or financial investment. With weak pricing power in the industry, finding a buyer for excess capacity (i.e., to exit the industry) may be difficult.

25. C is correct. Economic profit is earned and value created for shareholders when the company earns returns above the company's cost of capital.

26. C is correct. Although the threat of government intervention may be considered an element of some of Porter's five forces, it is not one of the listed forces.

27. B is correct. As displayed in Exhibit 4, the alcoholic beverage industry is concentrated and possesses strong pricing power.

28. A is correct. The oil services industry has medium barriers to entry because a company with a high level of technological innovation could obtain a niche market in a specific area of expertise.

29. A is correct. Companies with low cost strategies must be able to invest in productivity-improving equipment and finance that investment at a low cost of capital. Market share and pricing depend on whether the strategy is pursued defensively or offensively.

30. A is correct. The cost structure is an appropriate element when analyzing the supply of the product, but analysis of demand relies on the product's differentiating characteristics and the customers' needs and wants.

31. C is correct. The corporate profile would provide an understanding of these elements.

51

Equity Valuation: Concepts and Basic Tools

by John J. Nagorniak, CFA, and Stephen E. Wilcox, CFA

LEARNING OUTCOMES

Mastery	The candidate should be able to:
☐	**a** evaluate whether a security, given its current market price and a value estimate, is overvalued, fairly valued, or undervalued by the market;
☐	**b** describe major categories of equity valuation models;
☐	**c** explain the rationale for using present-value of cash flow models to value equity and describe the dividend discount and free-cash-flow-to-equity models;
☐	**d** calculate the intrinsic value of a non-callable, non-convertible preferred stock;
☐	**e** calculate and interpret the intrinsic value of an equity security based on the Gordon (constant) growth dividend discount model or a two-stage dividend discount model, as appropriate;
☐	**f** identify companies for which the constant growth or a multistage dividend discount model is appropriate;
☐	**g** explain the rationale for using price multiples to value equity and distinguish between multiples based on comparables versus multiples based on fundamentals;
☐	**h** calculate and interpret the following multiples: price to earnings, price to an estimate of operating cash flow, price to sales, and price to book value;
☐	**i** explain the use of enterprise value multiples in equity valuation and demonstrate the use of enterprise value multiples to estimate equity value;
☐	**j** explain asset-based valuation models and demonstrate the use of asset-based models to calculate equity value;
☐	**k** explain advantages and disadvantages of each category of valuation model.

1   INTRODUCTION

Analysts gather and process information to make investment decisions, including buy and sell recommendations. What information is gathered and how it is processed depend on the analyst and the purpose of the analysis. Technical analysis uses such information as stock price and trading volume as the basis for investment decisions. Fundamental analysis uses information about the economy, industry, and company as the basis for investment decisions. Examples of fundamentals are unemployment rates, gross domestic product (GDP) growth, industry growth, and quality of and growth in company earnings. Whereas technical analysts use information to predict price movements and base investment decisions on the direction of predicted change in prices, fundamental analysts use information to estimate the value of a security and to compare the estimated value to the market price and then base investment decisions on that comparison.

This reading introduces equity valuation models used to estimate the **intrinsic value** (synonym: **fundamental value**) of a security; intrinsic value is based on an analysis of investment fundamentals and characteristics. The fundamentals to be considered depend on the analyst's approach to valuation. In a top-down approach, an analyst examines the economic environment, identifies sectors that are expected to prosper in that environment, and analyzes securities of companies from previously identified attractive sectors. In a bottom-up approach, an analyst typically follows an industry or industries and forecasts fundamentals for the companies in those industries in order to determine valuation. Whatever the approach, an analyst who estimates the intrinsic value of an equity security is implicitly questioning the accuracy of the market price as an estimate of value. Valuation is particularly important in active equity portfolio management, which aims to improve on the return–risk trade-off of a portfolio's benchmark by identifying mispriced securities.

This reading is organized as follows. Section 2 discusses the implications of differences between estimated value and market price. Section 3 introduces three major categories of valuation model. Section 4 presents an overview of present value models with a focus on the dividend discount model. Section 5 describes and examines the use of multiples in valuation. Section 6 explains asset-based valuation and demonstrates how these models can be used to estimate value. Section 7 states conclusions and summarizes the reading.

2   ESTIMATED VALUE AND MARKET PRICE

By comparing estimates of value and market price, an analyst can arrive at one of three conclusions: The security is *undervalued*, *overvalued*, or *fairly valued* in the marketplace. For example, if the market price of an asset is $10 and the analyst estimates intrinsic value at $10, a logical conclusion is that the security is fairly valued. If the security is selling for $20, the security would be considered overvalued. If the security is selling for $5, the security would be considered undervalued. Basically, by estimating value, the analyst is assuming that the market price is not necessarily the best estimate of intrinsic value. If the estimated value exceeds the market price, the analyst infers the security is *undervalued*. If the estimated value equals the market price, the analyst infers the security is *fairly valued*. If the estimated value is less than the market price, the analyst infers the security is *overvalued*.

In practice, the conclusion is not so straightforward. Analysts must cope with uncertainties related to model appropriateness and the correct value of inputs. An analyst's final conclusion depends not only on the comparison of the estimated value and the market price but also on the analyst's confidence in the estimated value (i.e., in the model selected and the inputs used in it). One can envision a spectrum running from relatively high confidence in the valuation model *and* the inputs to relatively low confidence in the valuation model *and/or* the inputs. When confidence is relatively low, the analyst might demand a substantial divergence between his or her own value estimate and the market price before acting on an apparent mispricing. For instance, if the estimate of intrinsic value is $10 and the market price is $10.05, the analyst might reasonably conclude that the security is fairly valued and that the 1/2 of 1 percent market price difference from the estimated value is within the analyst's confidence interval.

Confidence in the convergence of the market price to the intrinsic value over the investment time horizon relevant to the objectives of the portfolio must also be taken into account before an analyst acts on an apparent mispricing or makes a buy, sell, or hold recommendation: The ability to benefit from identifying a mispriced security depends on the market price converging to the estimated intrinsic value.

In seeking to identify mispricing and attractive investments, analysts are treating market prices with skepticism, but they are also treating market prices with respect. For example, an analyst who finds that many securities examined appear to be overvalued will typically recheck models and inputs before acting on a conclusion of overvaluation. Analysts also often recognize and factor into recommendations that different market segments—such as securities closely followed by analysts versus securities relatively neglected by analysts—may differ in how common or persistent mispricing is. Mispricing may be more likely in securities neglected by analysts.

Example 1

Valuation and Analyst Response

1. An analyst finds that all the securities analyzed have estimated values higher than their market prices. The securities all appear to be:

   A. overvalued.

   B. undervalued.

   C. fairly valued.

2. An analyst finds that nearly all companies in a market segment have common shares which are trading at market prices above the analyst's estimate of the shares' values. This market segment is widely followed by analysts. Which of the following statements describes the analyst's *most appropriate* first action?

   A. Issue a sell recommendation for each share issue.

   B. Issue a buy recommendation for each share issue.

   C. Reexamine the models and inputs used for the valuations.

3. An analyst, using a number of models and a range of inputs, estimates a security's value to be between ¥250 and ¥270. The security is trading at ¥265. The security appears to be:

   A. overvalued.

   B. undervalued.

   C. fairly valued.

Solution to 1:

B is correct. The estimated intrinsic value for each security is greater than the market price. The securities all appear to be undervalued in the market. Note, however, that the analyst may wish to reexamine the model and inputs to check that the conclusion is valid.

Solution to 2:

C is correct. It seems improbable that all the share issues analyzed are overvalued, as indicated by market prices in excess of estimated value—particularly because the market segment is widely followed by analysts. Thus, the analyst will not issue a sell recommendation for each issue. The analyst will *most appropriately* reexamine the models and inputs prior to issuing any recommendations. A buy recommendation is not an appropriate response to an overvalued security.

Solution to 3:

C is correct. The security's market price of ¥265 is within the range estimated by the analyst. The security appears to be fairly valued.

Analysts often use a variety of models and inputs to achieve greater confidence in their estimates of intrinsic value. The use of more than one model and a range of inputs also helps the analyst understand the sensitivity of value estimates to different models and inputs.

3   MAJOR CATEGORIES OF EQUITY VALUATION MODELS

Three major categories of equity valuation models are as follows:

- **Present value models** (synonym: **discounted cash flow models**). These models estimate the intrinsic value of a security as the present value of the future benefits expected to be received from the security. In present value models, benefits are often defined in terms of cash expected to be distributed to shareholders (**dividend discount models**) or in terms of cash flows available to be distributed to shareholders after meeting capital expenditure and working capital needs (**free-cash-flow-to-equity models**). Many models fall within this category, ranging from the relatively simple to the very complex. In Section 4, we discuss in detail two of the simpler models, the Gordon (constant) growth model and the two-stage dividend discount models.

- **Multiplier models** (synonym: **market multiple models**). These models are based chiefly on share price multiples or enterprise value multiples. The former model estimates intrinsic value of a common share from a price multiple for some fundamental variable, such as revenues, earnings, cash flows, or book value. Examples of the multiples include price to earnings (P/E, share price divided by earnings per share) and price to sales (P/S, share price divided by sales per share). The fundamental variable may be stated on a forward basis (e.g., forecasted EPS for the next year) or a trailing basis (e.g., EPS for the past year), as long as the usage is consistent across companies being examined. Price multiples are also used to compare relative values. The use of the ratio of share price to EPS—that is, the P/E multiple—to judge relative value is an example of this approach to equity valuation.

  Enterprise value (EV) multiples have the form (Enterprise value)/(Value of a fundamental variable). Two possible choices for the denominator are earnings before interest, taxes, depreciation, and amortization (EBITDA) and total revenue. Enterprise value, the numerator, is a measure of a company's total market value from which cash and short-term investments have been subtracted (because an acquirer could use those assets to pay for acquiring the company). An estimate of common share value can be calculated indirectly from the EV multiple; the value of liabilities and preferred shares can be subtracted from the EV to arrive at the value of common equity.

- **Asset-based valuation models**. These models estimate intrinsic value of a common share from the estimated value of the assets of a corporation minus the estimated value of its liabilities and preferred shares. The estimated market value of the assets is often determined by making adjustments to the **book value** (synonym: **carrying value**) of assets and liabilities. The theory underlying the asset-based approach is that the value of a business is equal to the sum of the value of the business's assets.

As already mentioned, many analysts use more than one type of model to estimate value. Analysts recognize that each model is a simplification of the real world and that there are uncertainties related to model appropriateness and the inputs to the models. The choice of model(s) will depend on the availability of information to input into the model(s) and the analyst's confidence in the information and in the appropriateness of the model(s).

Example 2

Categories of Equity Valuation Models

1. An analyst is estimating the intrinsic value of a new company. The analyst has one year of financial statements for the company and has calculated the average values of a variety of price multiples for the industry in which the company operates. The analyst plans to use at least one model from each of the three categories of valuation models. The analyst is *least likely* to rely on the estimate(s) from the:

   A. multiplier model(s).

   B. present value model(s).

   C. asset-based valuation model(s).

2. Based on a company's EPS of €1.35, an analyst estimates the intrinsic value of a security to be €16.60. Which type of model is the analyst *most likely* to be using to estimate intrinsic value?

   A. Multiplier model.

   B. Present value model.

   C. Asset-based valuation model.

Solution to 1:

B is correct. Because the company has only one year of data available, the analyst is *least likely* to be confident in the inputs for a present value model. The values on the balance sheet, even before adjustment, are likely to be close to market values because the assets are all relatively new. The multiplier models are based on average multiples from the industry.

Solution to 2:

A is correct. The analyst is using a multiplier model based on the P/E multiple. The P/E multiple used was 16.60/1.35 = 12.3.

As you begin the study of specific equity valuation models in the next section, you must bear in mind that any model of value is, by necessity, a simplification of the real world. Never forget this simple fact! You may encounter models much more complicated than the ones discussed here, but even those models will be simplifications of reality.

4 PRESENT VALUE MODELS: THE DIVIDEND DISCOUNT MODEL

Present value models follow a fundamental tenet of economics stating that individuals defer consumption—that is, they invest—for the future benefits expected. Individuals and companies make an investment because they expect a rate of return over the investment period. Logically, the value of an investment should be equal to the present value of the expected future benefits. For common shares, an analyst can equate benefits to the cash flows to be generated by the investment. The simplest present value model of equity valuation is the dividend discount model (DDM), which specifies cash flows from a common stock investment to be dividends.[1] If the issuing company is assumed to be a going concern, the intrinsic value of a share is the present value of expected future dividends. If a constant required rate of return is also assumed, then the DDM expression for the intrinsic value of a share is Equation 1:

$$V_0 = \sum_{t=1}^{\infty} \frac{D_t}{(1+r)^t} \tag{1}$$

where

V_0 = value of a share of stock today, at $t = 0$
D_t = expected dividend in year t, assumed to be paid at the end of the year
r = required rate of return on the stock

At the shareholder level, cash received from a common stock investment includes any dividends received and the proceeds when shares are sold. If an investor intends to buy and hold a share for one year, the value of the share today is the present value of two cash flows—namely, the expected dividend *plus* the expected selling price in one year:

$$V_0 = \frac{D_1 + P_1}{(1+r)^1} = \frac{D_1}{(1+r)^1} + \frac{P_1}{(1+r)^1} \tag{2}$$

where P_1 = the expected price per share at $t = 1$.

To estimate the expected selling price, P_1, the analyst could estimate the price another investor with a one-year holding period would pay for the share in one year. If V_0 is based on D_1 and P_1, it follows that P_1 could be estimated from D_2 and P_2:

$$P_1 = \frac{D_2 + P_2}{(1+r)}$$

Substituting the right side of this equation for P_1 in Equation 2 results in V_0 estimated as

$$V_0 = \frac{D_1}{(1+r)} + \frac{D_2 + P_2}{(1+r)^2} = \frac{D_1}{(1+r)} + \frac{D_2}{(1+r)^2} + \frac{P_2}{(1+r)^2}$$

---

[1] Companies may also distribute cash to common shareholders by means of share repurchases.

Repeating this process, we find the value for n holding periods is the present value of the expected dividends for the n periods plus the present value of the expected price in n periods:

$$V_0 = \frac{D_1}{(1+r)^1} + \cdots + \frac{D_n}{(1+r)^n} + \frac{P_n}{(1+r)^n}$$

Using summation notation to represent the present value of the n expected dividends, we arrive at the general expression for an n-period holding period or investment horizon:

$$V_0 = \sum_{t=1}^{n} \frac{D_t}{(1+r)^t} + \frac{P_n}{(1+r)^n} \tag{3}$$

The expected value of a share at the end of the investment horizon—in effect, the expected selling price—is often referred to as the **terminal stock value** (or **terminal value**).

Example 3

Estimating Share Value for a Three-Year Investment Horizon

For the next three years, the annual dividends of a stock are expected to be €2.00, €2.10, and €2.20. The stock price is expected to be €20.00 at the end of three years. If the required rate of return on the shares is 10 percent, what is the estimated value of a share?

Solution:

The present values of the expected future cash flows can be written as follows:

$$V_0 = \frac{2.00}{(1.10)^1} + \frac{2.10}{(1.10)^2} + \frac{2.20}{(1.10)^3} + \frac{20.00}{(1.10)^3}$$

Calculating and summing these present values gives an estimated share value of $V_0 = 1.818 + 1.736 + 1.653 + 15.026 = $ €20.23.

The three dividends have a total present value of €5.207, and the terminal stock value has a present value of €15.026, for a total estimated value of €20.23.

Extending the holding period into the indefinite future, we can say that a stock's estimated value is the present value of all expected future dividends as shown in Equation 1.

Consideration of an indefinite future is valid because businesses established as corporations are generally set up to operate indefinitely. This general form of the DDM applies even in the case in which the investor has a finite investment horizon. For that investor, stock value today depends *directly* on the dividends the investor expects to receive before the stock is sold and depends *indirectly* on the expected dividends for periods subsequent to that sale, because those expected future dividends determine the expected selling price. Thus, the general expression given by Equation 1 holds irrespective of the investor's holding period.

In practice, many analysts prefer to use a free-cash-flow-to-equity (FCFE) valuation model. These analysts assume that dividend-paying *capacity* should be reflected in the cash flow estimates rather than *expected dividends*. FCFE is a measure of dividend-paying capacity. Analysts may also use FCFE valuation models for a non-dividend-paying stock. To use a DDM, the analyst needs to predict the timing and amount of the first dividend and all the dividends or dividend growth thereafter. Making these predictions for non-dividend-paying stock accurately is typically difficult, so in such cases, analysts often resort to FCFE models.

The calculation of FCFE starts with the calculation of cash flow from operations (CFO). CFO is simply defined as net income plus non-cash expenses minus investment in working capital. FCFE is a measure of cash flow generated in a period that is available for distribution to common shareholders. What does "available for distribution" mean? The entire CFO is *not* available for distribution; the portion of the CFO needed for fixed capital investment (FCInv) during the period to maintain the value of the company as a going concern is *not* viewed as available for distribution to common shareholders. Net amounts borrowed (borrowings minus repayments) are considered to be available for distribution to common shareholders. Thus, FCFE can be expressed as

$$FCFE = CFO - FCInv + Net\ borrowing \qquad (4)$$

The information needed to calculate historical FCFE is available from a company's statement of cash flows and financial disclosures. Frequently, under the assumption that management is acting in the interest of maintaining the value of the company as a going concern, reported capital expenditure is taken to represent FCInv. Analysts must make projections of financials to forecast future FCFE. Valuation obtained by using FCFE involves discounting expected future FCFE by the required rate of return on equity; the expression parallels Equation 1:

$$V_0 = \sum_{t=1}^{\infty} \frac{FCFE_t}{(1+r)^t}$$

Example 4

Present Value Models

1. An investor expects a share to pay dividends of $3.00 and $3.15 at the end of Years 1 and 2, respectively. At the end of the second year, the investor expects the shares to trade at $40.00. The required rate of return on the shares is 8 percent. If the investor's forecasts are accurate and the market price of the shares is currently $30, the *most likely* conclusion is that the shares are:

    A. overvalued.

    B. undervalued.

    C. fairly valued.

2. Two investors with different holding periods but the same expectations and required rate of return for a company are estimating the intrinsic value of a common share of the company. The investor with the shorter holding period will *most likely* estimate a:

    A. lower intrinsic value.

    B. higher intrinsic value.

    C. similar intrinsic value.

3. An equity valuation model that focuses on expected dividends rather than the capacity to pay dividends is the:

   A. dividend discount model.

   B. free cash flow to equity model.

   C. cash flow return on investment model.

Solution to 1:

B is correct.

$$V_0 = \frac{3.00}{(1.08)^1} + \frac{3.15}{(1.08)^2} + \frac{40.00}{(1.08)^2} = 39.77$$

The value estimate of $39.77 exceeds the market price of $30, so the conclusion is that the shares are undervalued.

Solution to 2:

C is correct. The intrinsic value of a security is independent of the investor's holding period.

Solution to 3:

A is correct. Dividend discount models focus on expected dividends.

How is the required rate of return for use in present value models estimated? To estimate the required rate of return on a share, analysts frequently use the capital asset pricing model (CAPM):

Required rate of return on share i =

Current expected risk − free rate of return

+ Beta$_i$[Market (equity) risk premium]

(5)

Equation 5 states that the required rate of return on a share is the sum of the current expected risk-free rate plus a risk premium that equals the product of the stock's beta (a measure of non-diversifiable risk) and the market risk premium (the expected return of the market in excess of the risk-free return, where in practice, the "market" is often represented by a broad stock market index). However, even if analysts agree that the CAPM is an appropriate model, their inputs into the CAPM may differ. Thus, there is no uniquely correct answer to the question: What is the required rate of return?

Other common methods for estimating the required rate of return for the stock of a company include adding a risk premium that is based on economic judgments, rather than the CAPM, to an appropriate risk-free rate (usually a government bond) and adding a risk premium to the yield on the company's bonds. Good business and economic judgment is paramount in estimating the required rate of return. In many investment firms, required rates of return are determined by firm policy.

4.1 Preferred Stock Valuation

General dividend discount models are relatively easy to apply to preferred shares. In its simplest form, **preferred stock** is a form of equity (generally, non-voting) that has priority over common stock in the receipt of dividends and on the issuer's assets in the event of a company's liquidation. It may have a stated maturity date at which time payment of the stock's par (face) value is made or it may be perpetual with no maturity date; additionally, it may be callable or convertible.

For a non-callable, non-convertible perpetual preferred share paying a level dividend D and assuming a constant required rate of return over time, Equation 1 reduces to the formula for the present value of a perpetuity. Its value is:

$$V_0 = \frac{D_0}{r} \qquad \qquad (6)$$

For example, a $100 par value non-callable perpetual preferred stock offers an annual dividend of $5.50. If its required rate of return is 6 percent, the value estimate would be $5.50/0.06 = $91.67.

For a non-callable, non-convertible preferred stock with maturity at time n, the estimated intrinsic value can be estimated by using Equation 3 but using the preferred stock's par value, F, instead of P_n:

$$V_0 = \sum_{t=1}^{n} \frac{D_t}{(1+r)^t} + \frac{F}{(1+r)^n} \qquad \qquad (7)$$

When Equation 7 is used, the most precise approach is to use values for n, r, and D that reflect the payment schedule of the dividends. This method is similar to the practice of fixed-income analysts in valuing a bond. For example, a non-convertible preferred stock with a par value of £20.00, maturity in six years, a nominal required rate of return of 8.20 percent, and semiannual dividends of £2.00 would be valued by using an n of 12, an r of 4.10 percent, a D of £2.00, and an F of £20.00. The result would be an estimated value of £31.01. Assuming payments are annual rather than semiannual (i.e., assuming that $n = 6$, $r = 8.20$ percent, and $D = £4.00$) would result in an estimated value of £30.84.

Preferred stock issues are frequently callable (redeemable) by the issuer at some point prior to maturity, often at par value or at prices in excess of par value that decline to par value as the maturity date approaches. Such call options tend to reduce the value of a preferred issue to an investor because the option to redeem will be exercised by the issuer when it is in the issuer's favor and ignored when it is not. For example, if an issuer can redeem shares at par value that would otherwise trade (on the basis of dividends, maturity, and required rate of return) above par value, the issuer has motivation to redeem the shares.

Preferred stock issues can also include a retraction option that enables the holder of the preferred stock to sell the shares back to the issuer prior to maturity on prespecified terms. Essentially, the holder of the shares has a put option. Such put options tend to increase the value of a preferred issue to an investor because the option to retract will be exercised by the investor when it is in the investor's favor and ignored when it is not. Although the precise valuation of issues with such embedded options is beyond the scope of this reading, Example 5 includes a case in which Equation 7 can be used to approximate the value of a callable, retractable preferred share.

Example 5

Preferred Share Valuation: Two Cases

Case 1: Non-callable, Non-convertible, Perpetual Preferred Shares

The following facts concerning the Union Electric Company 4.75 percent perpetual preferred shares (CUSIP identifier: 906548821) are as follows:

- Issuer: Union Electric Co. (owned by Ameren)
- Par value: US$100
- Dividend: US$4.75 per year
- Maturity: perpetual
- Embedded options: none
- Credit rating: Moody's Investors Service/Standard & Poor's Ba1/BB
- Required rate of return on Ba1/BB rated preferred shares as of valuation date: 7.5 percent.

A. Estimate the intrinsic value of this preferred share.

B. Explain whether the intrinsic value of this issue would be higher or lower if the issue were callable (with all other facts remaining unchanged).

Solution to 1A:

Basing the discount rate on the required rate of return on Ba1/BB rated preferred shares of 7.5 percent gives an intrinsic value estimate of US$4.75/0.075 = US$63.33.

Solution to 1B:

The intrinsic value would be lower if the issue were callable. The option to redeem or call the issue is valuable to the issuer because the call will be exercised when doing so is in the issuer's interest. The intrinsic value of the shares to the investor will typically be lower if the issue is callable. In this case, because the intrinsic value without the call is much less than the par value, the issuer would be unlikely to redeem the issue if it were callable; thus, callability would reduce intrinsic value, but only slightly.

Case 2: Retractable Term Preferred Shares

Retractable term preferred shares are a type of preferred share that has been issued by Canadian companies. This type of issue specifies a "retraction date" when the preferred shareholders have the option to sell back their shares to the issuer at par value (i.e., the shares are "retractable" or "putable" at that date).[2] At predetermined dates prior to the retraction date, the issuer has the option to redeem the preferred issue at predetermined prices (which are always at or above par value).

An example of a retractable term preferred share currently outstanding is YPG (Yellow Pages) Holdings, series 2, 5 percent first preferreds (TSX: YPG.PR.B). YPG Holdings is Canada's leading local commercial search provider and largest telephone directory publisher. The issue is in Canadian dollars. The shares have a $25 par value and pay a quarterly dividend of $0.3125 [= (5 percent × $25)/4]. As of 29 December 2008, shares were priced at $12.01 and carried ratings from Dominion Bond Rating Service (DBRS) and Standard & Poor's of Pfd-3H and P3, respectively. Thus, the shares are viewed by DBRS as having "adequate" credit quality, qualified by "H," which means relatively high quality within that group. The shares are redeemable at the option of YPG Holdings in June 2009 at $26.75, with redemption prices eventually declining to par value at later dates. The retraction date is 30 June 2017, or eight and half years (34 quarters) from

---

2 "Retraction" refers to this option, which is a put option. The terminology is not completely settled: The type of share being called "retractable term preferred" is also known as "hard retractable preferred," with "hard" referring to payment in cash rather than common shares at the retraction date. See the 2009 ScotiaMcLeod report http://www.ritceyteam.com/pdf/guide_to_preferred_shares.pdf.

the date (31 December 2008) the shares were being valued. Similarly rated preferred issues had an estimated nominal required rate of return of 15.5 percent (3.875 percent per quarter). Because the issue's market price is so far below the prices at which YPG could redeem or call the issue, redemption is considered to be unlikely and the redemption option is assumed here to have minimal value for an investor.

A. Assume that the issue will be retracted in June 2017; the holders of the shares will put the shares to the company in June 2017. Based on the information given, estimate the intrinsic value of a share.

Solution to 2A:

An intrinsic value estimate of a share of this preferred issue is $12.71:

$$V_0 = \left[\frac{\$0.3125}{(1 + 0.03875)} + \frac{\$0.3125}{(1 + 0.03875)^2} + \dots + \frac{\$0.3125}{(1 + 0.03875)^{34}} \right]$$
$$+ \frac{\$25}{(1 + 0.03875)^{34}} \approx \$12.71$$

4.2 The Gordon Growth Model

A rather obvious problem when one is trying to implement Equation 1 for common equity is that it requires the analyst to estimate an infinite series of expected dividends. To simplify this process, analysts frequently make assumptions about how dividends will grow or change over time. The Gordon (constant) growth model (Gordon, 1962) is a simple and well-recognized DDM. The model assumes dividends grow indefinitely at a constant rate.

Because of its assumption of a constant growth rate, the Gordon growth model is particularly appropriate for valuing the equity of dividend-paying companies that are relatively insensitive to the business cycle and in a mature growth phase. Examples might include an electric utility serving a slowly growing area or a producer of a staple food product (e.g., bread). A history of increasing the dividend at a stable growth rate is another practical criterion if the analyst believes that pattern will hold in the future.

With a constant growth assumption, Equation 1 can be written as Equation 8, where g is the constant growth rate:

$$V_0 = \sum_{t=1}^{\infty} \frac{D_0(1 + g)^t}{(1 + r)^t} = D_0 \left[\frac{(1 + g)}{(1 + r)} + \frac{(1 + g)^2}{(1 + r)^2} + \dots + \frac{(1 + g)^{\infty}}{(1 + r)^{\infty}} \right] \quad (8)$$

If required return r is assumed to be strictly greater than growth rate g, then the square-bracketed term in Equation 8 is an infinite geometric series and sums to $[(1 + g)/(r - g)]$. Substituting into Equation 8 produces the Gordon growth model as presented in Equation 9:

$$V_0 - \frac{D_0(1 + g)}{r - g} = \frac{D_1}{r - g} \quad (9)$$

For an illustration of the expression, suppose the current (most recent) annual dividend on a share is €5.00 and dividends are expected to grow at 4 percent per year. The required rate of return on equity is 8 percent. The Gordon growth model estimate of intrinsic value is, therefore, €5.00(1.04)/(0.08 − 0.04) = €5.20/0.04 = €130 per share. Note that the numerator is D_1 not D_0. (Using the wrong numerator is a common error.)

The Gordon growth model estimates intrinsic value as the present value of a growing perpetuity. If the growth rate, g, is assumed to be zero, Equation 8 reduces to the expression for the present value of a perpetuity, given earlier as Equation 6.

In estimating a long-term growth rate, analysts use a variety of methods, including assessing the growth in dividends or earnings over time, using the industry median growth rate, and using the relationship shown in Equation 10 to estimate the sustainable growth rate:

$$g = b \times ROE \tag{10}$$

where

g = dividend growth rate

b = earnings retention rate = $(1 - \text{Dividend payout ratio})$

ROE = return on equity

Example 6 illustrates the application of the Gordon growth model to the shares of an integrated petroleum company. The analyst believes it will not continue to grow at the relatively fast growth rate of its past but will moderate to a lower and stable growth rate in the future. The example asks how much the dividend growth assumption adds to the intrinsic value estimate. The question is relevant to valuation because if the amount is high on a percentage basis, a large part of the value of the share depends on the realization of the growth estimate. One can answer the question by subtracting from the intrinsic value estimate determined by Equation 9 the value determined by Equation 6, which assumes no dividend growth.[3]

Example 6

Applying the Gordon Growth Model

Total S.A. (Euronext Paris: FP), one of France's largest corporations and the world's fifth largest publicly traded integrated petroleum company, operates in more than 130 countries. Total engages in all aspects of the petroleum industry, produces base chemicals and specialty chemicals for the industrial and consumer markets, and has interests in the coal mining and power generation sectors. To meet growing energy needs on a long-term basis, Total considers sustainability when making decisions. Selected financial information for Total appears in Exhibit 1.

Exhibit 1	Selected Financial Information for Total S.A.				
Year	2008	2007	2006	2005	2004
EPS	€6.20	€5.37	€5.44	€5.08	€3.76
DPS	€2.28	€2.07	€1.87	€1.62	€1.35
Payout ratio	37%	39%	34%	32%	36%
ROE	32%	31%	33%	35%	33%
Share price					
(Paris Bourse)	€38.910	€56.830	€54.650	€52.367	€39.657

Note: DPS stands for "dividends per share."
Source: Company website: www.total.com.

---

3 A related concept, the present value of growth opportunities (PVGO), is discussed in more advanced readings.

The analyst estimates the growth rate to be approximately 14 percent based on the dividend growth rate over the period 2004 to 2008 [$1.35(1 + g)^4 = 2.28$, so $g = 14\%$]. To verify that the estimated growth rate of 14 percent is feasible in the future, the analyst also uses the average of Total's retention rate and ROE for the previous five years ($g \approx 0.64 \times 33\% \approx 21\%$) to estimate the sustainable growth rate.

Using a number of approaches, including adding a risk premium to a long-term French government bond and using the CAPM, the analyst estimates a required return of 19 percent. The most recent dividend of €2.28 is used for D_0.

1. Use the Gordon growth model to estimate Total's intrinsic value.

2. How much does the dividend growth assumption add to the intrinsic value estimate?

3. Based on the estimated intrinsic value, is a share of Total undervalued, overvalued, or fairly valued?

4. What is the intrinsic value if the growth rate estimate is lowered to 13 percent?

5. What is the intrinsic value if the growth rate estimate is lowered to 13 percent and the required rate of return estimate is increased to 20 percent?

Solution to 1:

$$V_0 = \frac{€2.28 \ (1 + 0.14)}{0.19 - 0.14} = €51.98$$

Solution to 2:

$$€51.98 - \frac{€2.28}{0.19} = €39.98$$

Solution to 3:

A share of Total appears to be undervalued. The analyst, before making a recommendation, might consider how realistic the estimated inputs are and check the sensitivity of the estimated value to changes in the inputs.

Solution to 4:

$$V_0 = \frac{€2.28 \ (1 + 0.13)}{0.19 - 0.13} = €42.94$$

Solution to 5:

$$V_0 = \frac{€2.28 \ (1 + 0.13)}{0.20 - 0.13} = €36.81$$

The Gordon growth model estimate of intrinsic value is extremely sensitive to the choice of required rate of return r and growth rate g. It is likely that the growth rate assumption and the required return assumption used initially were too high. Worldwide economic growth is typically in the low single digits, making it highly unlikely that Total's dividend can grow at 14 percent into perpetuity. Exhibit 2 presents a further sensitivity analysis of Total's intrinsic value to the required return and growth estimates.

Exhibit 2	Sensitivity Analysis of the Intrinsic-Value Estimate for Total S.A.				
	g = 2%	g = 5%	g = 8%	g = 11%	g = 14%
r = 7%	€46.512	€119.700	—	—	—
r = 10%	€29.070	€47.880	€123.120	—	—
r = 13%	€21.142	€29.925	€49.248	€126.540	—
r = 16%	€16.611	€21.764	€30.780	€50.616	€129.960
r = 19%	€13.680	€17.100	€22.385	€31.635	€51.984

Note that no value is shown when the growth rate exceeds the required rate of return. The Gordon growth model assumes that the growth rate cannot be greater than the required rate of return.

The assumptions of the Gordon model are as follows:

- Dividends are the correct metric to use for valuation purposes.
- The dividend growth rate is forever: It is perpetual and never changes.
- The required rate of return is also constant over time.
- The dividend growth rate is strictly less than the required rate of return.

An analyst might be dissatisfied with these assumptions for many reasons. The equities being examined might not currently pay a dividend. The Gordon assumptions might be too simplistic to reflect the characteristics of the companies being evaluated. Some alternatives to using the Gordon model are as follows:

- Use a more robust DDM that allows for varying patterns of growth.
- Use a cash flow measure other than dividends for valuation purposes.
- Use some other approach (such as a multiplier method) to valuation.

Applying a DDM is difficult if the company being analyzed is not currently paying a dividend. A company may not be paying a dividend if 1) the investment opportunities the company has are all so attractive that the retention and reinvestment of funds is preferable, from a return perspective, to the distribution of a dividend to shareholders or 2) the company is in such shaky financial condition that it cannot afford to pay a dividend. An analyst might still use a DDM to value such companies by assuming that dividends will begin at some future point in time. The analyst might further assume that constant growth occurs after that date and use the Gordon growth model for valuation. Extrapolating from no current dividend, however, generally yields highly uncertain forecasts. Analysts typically choose to use one or more of the alternatives instead of or as a supplement to the Gordon growth model.

Example 7

Gordon Growth Model in the Case of No Current Dividend

A company does not currently pay a dividend but is expected to begin to do so in five years (at $t = 5$). The first dividend is expected to be $4.00 and to be received five years from today. That dividend is expected to grow at 6 percent into perpetuity. The required return is 10 percent. What is the estimated current intrinsic value?

Solution:

The analyst can value the share in two pieces:

1. The analyst uses the Gordon growth model to estimate the value at $t = 5$; in the model, the year-ahead dividend is $\$4(1.06)$. Then the analyst finds the present value of this value as of $t = 0$.

2. The analyst finds the present value of the $\$4$ dividend not "counted" in the estimate in Piece 1 (which values dividends from $t = 6$ onward). Note that the statement of the problem implies that D_0, D_1, D_2, D_3, and D_4 are zero.

Piece 1: The value of this piece is $\$65.818$:

$$V_n = \frac{D_n(1 + g)}{r - g} = \frac{D_{n+1}}{r - g}$$

$$V_5 = \frac{\$4\,(1 + 0.06)}{0.10 - 0.06} = \frac{\$4.24}{0.04} = \$106$$

$$V_0 = \frac{\$106}{(1 + 0.10)^5} = \$65.818$$

Piece 2: The value of this piece is $\$2.484$:

$$V_0 = \frac{\$4}{(1 + 0.10)^5} = \$2.484$$

The sum of the two pieces is $\$65.818 + \$2.484 = \$68.30$.

Alternatively, the analyst could value the share at $t = 4$, the point at which dividends are expected to be paid in the following year and from which point they are expected to grow at a constant rate.

$$V_4 = \frac{\$4.00}{0.10 - 0.06} = \frac{\$4.00}{0.04} = \$100$$

$$V_0 = \frac{\$100}{(1 + 0.10)^4} = \$68.30$$

The next section addresses the application of the DDM with more flexible assumptions as to the dividend growth rate.

4.3 Multistage Dividend Discount Models

Multistage growth models are often used to model rapidly growing companies. The *two-stage DDM* assumes that at some point the company will begin to pay dividends that grow at a constant rate, but prior to that time the company will pay dividends that are growing at a higher rate than can be sustained in the long run. That is, the company is assumed to experience an initial, finite period of high growth, perhaps prior to the entry of competitors, followed by an infinite period of sustainable growth. The two-stage DDM thus makes use of two growth rates: a high growth rate for an initial, finite period followed by a lower, sustainable growth rate into perpetuity. The Gordon growth model is used to estimate a terminal value at time n that reflects the present value at time n of the dividends received during the sustainable growth period.

Equation 11 will be used here as the starting point for a two-stage valuation model. The two-stage valuation model is similar to Example 7 except that instead of assuming zero dividends for the initial period, the analyst assumes that dividends will exhibit a high rate of growth during the initial period. Equation 11 values the dividends over the short-term period of high growth and the terminal value at the end of the period of high growth. The short-term growth rate, g_S, lasts for n years. The intrinsic value per share in year n, V_n, represents the year n value of the dividends received during the sustainable growth period or the terminal value at time n. V_n can be estimated by using the Gordon growth model as shown in Equation 12, where g_L is the long-term or sustainable growth rate. The dividend in year $n+1$, D_{n+1}, can be determined by using Equation 13:

$$V_0 = \sum_{t=1}^{n} \frac{D_0(1 + g_S)^t}{(1 + r)^t} + \frac{V_n}{(1 + r)^n} \tag{11}$$

$$V_n = \frac{D_{n+1}}{r - g_L} \tag{12}$$

$$D_{n+1} = D_0(1 + g_S)^n (1 + g_L) \tag{13}$$

Example 8

Applying the Two-Stage Dividend Discount Model

The current dividend, D_0, is \$5.00. Growth is expected to be 10 percent a year for three years and then 5 percent thereafter. The required rate of return is 15 percent. Estimate the intrinsic value.

Solution:

$D_1 = \$5.00(1 + 0.10) = \$5.50$

$D_2 = \$5.00(1 + 0.10)^2 = \$6.05$

$D_3 = \$5.00(1 + 0.10)^3 = \$6.655$

$D_4 = \$5.00(1 + 0.10)^3 (1 + 0.05) = \$6.98775$

$V_3 = \dfrac{\$6.98775}{0.15 - 0.05} = \$69.8775$

$V_0 = \dfrac{\$5.50}{(1 + 0.15)} + \dfrac{\$6.05}{(1 + 0.15)^2} + \dfrac{\$6.655}{(1 + 0.15)^3} + \dfrac{\$69.8775}{(1 + 0.15)^3} \approx \$59.68$

The DDM can be extended to as many stages as deemed appropriate. For most publicly traded companies (that is, companies beyond the start-up stage), practitioners assume growth will ultimately fall into three stages[4]: 1) growth, 2) transition, and 3) maturity. This assumption supports the use of a *three-stage DDM*, which makes use of three growth rates: a high growth rate for an initial finite period, followed by a lower growth rate for a finite second period, followed by a lower, sustainable growth rate into perpetuity.

One can make the case that a three-stage DDM would be most appropriate for a fairly young company, one that is just entering the growth phase. The two-stage DDM would be appropriate to estimate the value of an older company that has already moved through its growth phase and is currently in the transition phase (a period with a higher growth rate than the sustainable growth rate) prior to moving to the maturity phase (the period with a lower, sustainable growth rate).

---

4 Sharpe, Alexander, and Bailey (1999).

However, the choice of a two-stage DDM need not rely solely on the age of a company. Long-established companies sometimes manage to restart above-average growth through, for example, innovation, expansion to new markets, or acquisitions. Or a company's long-run growth rate may be interrupted by a period of subnormal performance. If growth is expected to moderate (in the first case) or improve (in the second case) toward some long-term growth rate, a two-stage DDM may be appropriate. Thus, we chose a two-stage DDM to value Brown-Forman in Example 9.

Example 9

Two-Stage Dividend Discount Model: Brown-Forman

Brown-Forman Corporation (NYSE: BFB) is a diversified producer of wines and spirits. It was founded in 1870 by George Garvin Brown in Louisville, Kentucky, USA. His original brand, Old Forester Kentucky Straight Bourbon Whisky, was America's first bottled bourbon. Brown-Forman, one of the largest American-owned spirits and wine companies and among the top 10 largest global spirits companies, sells its brands in more than 135 countries and has offices in cities across the globe. In all, Brown-Forman has more than 35 brands in its portfolio of wines and spirits.

The 30 January 2009 *Value Line* report on Brown-Forman appears in Exhibit 3. Brown-Forman has increased its dividends every year except 2000, when the dividend remained at US$0.50 as it was in 1999. On the left side of the report, in the section titled "Annual Rates," dividend growth is shown as 7.5 percent for the past 10 years, 11 percent for the past 5 years, and estimated 5 percent for 2005–2007 to 2011–2013. After a period of growth through acquisition and merger, the pattern suggests that Brown-Forman may be transitioning to a mature growth phase.

The two-stage DDM is arguably a good choice for valuing Brown Forman because the company appears to be transitioning from a high-growth phase (note the 11 percent dividend growth for the past 5 years) to a lower-growth phase (note the forecast of 5 percent dividend growth to 2011–2013). The analyst discussion refers to the company facing "short-term obstacles" and states that the company's "capital appreciation potential for the 3- to 5-year time frame is well below average."

The CAPM can be used to estimate the required return, r, for Brown-Forman. The *Value Line* report (in the upper left corner) estimates beta to be 0.70. Using the yield of about 3.1 percent on 10-year U.S. Treasury notes as a proxy for the risk-free rate and assuming an equity risk premium of 5.0 percent, we find the estimate for r would be 6.6 percent [3.1% + 0.70(5.0%)].

To estimate the intrinsic value at the end of 2008, we use the 2008 dividend of US$1.08 from the *Value Line* report. The dividend is assumed to grow at a rate of 6.5 percent for two years and then 4.0 percent thereafter. The growth rate assumption for the first stage is consistent with the *Value Line* forecast for 2008 to 2009 growth. The assumption of a 4.0 percent perpetual growth rate produces a five-year growth rate assumption near 5 percent,[5] which is consistent with the *Value Line* forecast of 5 percent growth to 2011–2013. Thus:

$$D_{2009} = US\$1.08(1 + 0.065) = US\$1.1502$$

$$D_{2010} = US\$1.08(1 + 0.065)^2 = US\$1.224963$$

$$D_{2011} = US\$1.08(1 + 0.065)^2 (1 + 0.04) = US\$1.273962$$

$$V_{2010} = \frac{US\$1.273962}{0.066 - 0.04} = US\$48.99854$$

$$V_{2008} = \frac{US\$1.1502}{(1 + 0.066)} + \frac{US\$1.224963}{(1 + 0.066)^2} + \frac{US\$48.99854}{(1 + 0.066)^2} \approx US\$45.28$$

Given a recent price of US$47.88, as noted at the top of the *Value Line* report, the intrinsic-value estimate of US$45.28 suggests that Brown-Forman is modestly overvalued.

---

5 The exact geometric average annual growth rate can be determined as $[(1+0.065)\ (1+0.065)\ (1+0.04)\ (1+0.04)\ (1.04)]^{1/5} - 1 = 0.049929 \approx 5.0\%$.

Exhibit 3 | *Value Line* Report on Brown-Forman

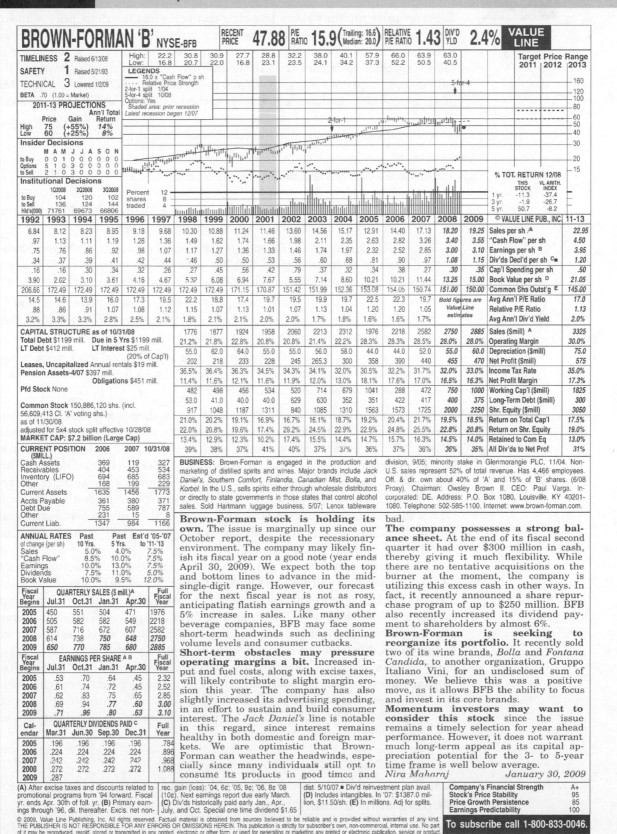

5   MULTIPLIER MODELS

The term **price multiple** refers to a ratio that compares the share price with some sort of monetary flow or value to allow evaluation of the relative worth of a company's stock. Some practitioners use price ratios as a screening mechanism. If the ratio falls below a specified value, the shares are identified as candidates for purchase, and if the ratio exceeds a specified value, the shares are identified as candidates for sale. Many practitioners use ratios when examining a group or sector of stocks and consider the shares for which the ratio is relatively low to be attractively valued securities.

Price multiples that are used by security analysts include the following:

- Price-to-earnings ratio (P/E). This measure is the ratio of the stock price to earnings per share. P/E is arguably the price multiple most frequently cited by the media and used by analysts and investors (Block 1999). The seminal works of McWilliams (1966), Miller and Widmann (1966), Nicholson (1968), Dreman (1977), and Basu (1977) presented evidence of a return advantage to low-P/E stocks.

- Price-to-book ratio (P/B). The ratio of the stock price to book value per share. Considerable evidence suggests that P/B multiples are inversely related to future rates of return (Fama and French 1995).

- Price-to-sales ratio (P/S). This measure is the ratio of stock price to sales per share. O'Shaughnessy (2005) provided evidence that a low P/S multiple is the most useful multiple for predicting future returns.

- Price-to-cash-flow ratio (P/CF). This measure is the ratio of stock price to some per-share measure of cash flow. The measures of cash flow include free cash flow (FCF) and operating cash flow (OCF).

A common criticism of all of these multiples is that they do not consider the future. This criticism is true if the multiple is calculated from trailing or current values of the divisor. Practitioners seek to counter this criticism by a variety of techniques, including forecasting fundamental values (the divisors) one or more years into the future. The resulting forward (leading or prospective) price multiples may differ markedly from the trailing price multiples. In the absence of an explicit forecast of fundamental values, the analyst is making an implicit forecast of the future when implementing such models. The choice of price multiple—trailing or forward—should be used consistently for companies being compared.

Besides the traditional price multiples used in valuation, just presented, analysts need to know how to calculate and interpret other ratios. Such ratios include those used to analyze business performance and financial condition based on data reported in financial statements. In addition, many industries have specialized measures of business performance that analysts covering those industries should be familiar with. In analyzing cable television companies, for example, the ratio of total market value of the company to the total number of subscribers is commonly used. Another common measure is revenue per subscriber. In the oil industry, a commonly cited ratio is proved reserves per common share. Industry-specific or sector-specific ratios such as these can be used to understand the key business variables in an industry or sector as well as to highlight attractively valued securities.

5.1 Relationships among Price Multiples, Present Value Models, and Fundamentals

Price multiples are frequently used independently of present value models. One price multiple valuation approach, the method of comparables, does not involve cash flow forecasts or discounting to present value. A price multiple is often related to fundamentals through a discounted cash flow model, however, such as the Gordon growth model. Understanding such connections can deepen the analyst's appreciation of the factors that affect the value of a multiple and often can help explain reasons for differences in multiples that do not involve mispricing. The expressions that are developed can be interpreted as the *justified value* of a multiple—that is, the value justified by (based on) fundamentals or a set of cash flow predictions. These expressions are an alternative way of presenting intrinsic-value estimates.

As an example, using the Gordon growth model identified previously in Equation 9 and assuming that price equals intrinsic value ($P_0 = V_0$), we can restate Equation 9 as follows:

$$P_0 = \frac{D_1}{r - g} \tag{9.1}$$

To arrive at the model for the justified forward P/E given in Equation 14, we divide both sides of Equation 9.1 by a forecast for next year's earnings, E_1. In Equation 14, the dividend payout ratio, p, is the ratio of dividends to earnings:

$$\frac{P_0}{E_1} = \frac{D_1 / E_1}{r - g} = \frac{p}{r - g} \tag{14}$$

Equation 14 indicates that the P/E is inversely related to the required rate of return and positively related to the growth rate; that is, as the required rate of return increases, the P/E declines, and as the growth rate increases, the P/E increases. The P/E and the payout ratio appear to be positively related. This relationship may not be true, however, because a higher payout ratio may imply a slower growth rate as a result of the company retaining a lower proportion of earnings for reinvestment. This phenomenon is referred to as the dividend displacement of earnings.

Example 10

Value Estimate Based on Fundamentals

Petroleo Brasileiro SA, commonly known as Petrobras (BOVESPA: PETR), was once labeled "the most expensive oil company" by Bloomberg.com. Data for Petrobras and the oil industry, including the trailing twelve-month (TTM) P/E and payout ratios, appear below.

	Petrobras	Industry
P/E ratio (TTM)	11.77	7.23
Payout ratio (TTM) (%)	24.40	21.66
EPS 5-year growth rate (%)	26.35	15.46
EPS (MRQ) vs. Qtr. 1 yr. ago (% change)	−41.44	−127.53

Note: MRQ stands for "most recent quarter."
Source: Reuters.

Explain how the information shown supports a higher P/E for Petrobras than for the industry.

Solution:

The data support a higher P/E for Petrobras because its payout ratio and five-year EPS growth rate exceed those of the industry. Equation 14 implies a positive relationship between the payout ratio and the P/E multiple. A higher payout ratio supports a higher P/E. Furthermore, to the extent that higher EPS growth implies a high growth rate in dividends, the high EPS growth rate supports a high P/E. Although the Petrobras quarterly EPS have declined relative to EPS of a year ago, the decline is less than that of the industry.

Example 11

Determining Justified Forward P/E

Heinrich Gladisch, CFA, is estimating the justified forward P/E for Nestlé (SIX: NESN), one of the world's leading nutrition and health companies. Gladisch notes that sales for 2008 were SFr109.9 billion (US$101.6 billion) and that net income was SFr18.0 billion (US$16.6 billion). He organizes the data for EPS, dividends per share, and the dividend payout ratio for the years 2004–2008 in the following table:

	2004	2005	2006	2007	2008
Earnings per share	SFr1.70	SFr2.08	SFr2.39	SFr2.78	SFr4.87
Year over year % change		22.4%	14.9%	16.3%	75.2%
Dividend per share	SFr0.80	SFr0.90	SFr1.04	SFr1.22	SFr1.40
Year over year % change		12.5%	15.6%	17.3%	14.8%
Dividend payout ratio	47.1%	43.3%	43.5%	43.9%	28.7%

Gladisch calculates that ROE averaged slightly more than 19 percent in the period 2004–2007 but jumped to about 35 percent in 2008. In 2008, however, Nestlé's reported net income included a large nonrecurring component. The company reported 2008 "underlying earnings," which it defined as net income "from continuing operations before impairments, restructuring costs, results on disposals and significant one-off items," to be SFr2.82. Predicting increasing pressure on Nestlé's profit margins from lower-priced goods, particularly in developed markets, Gladisch estimates a long-run ROE of 16 percent.

Gladisch decides that the dividend payout ratios of the 2004–2007 period— averaging 44.5 percent—are more representative of Nestlé's future payout ratio than is the low 2008 dividend payout ratio. The dividend payout ratio in 2008 was lower because management apparently based the 2008 dividend on the components of net income that were expected to continue into the future. Basing a dividend on net income including non-recurring items creates the potential need to reduce dividends in the future. Rounding up the 2004–2007 average, Gladisch settles on an estimate of 45 percent for the dividend payout ratio for use in calculating a justified forward P/E using Equation 14.

Gladisch's firm estimates that the required rate of return for Nestlé's shares is 12 percent per year. Gladisch also finds the following data in UBS and Credit Suisse analyst reports dated, respectively, 9 December 2009 and 16 October 2009:

	2009E	2010E
UBS forecast:		
EPS	SFr2.86	SFr3.10
Year over year % change	−41.3%	8.39%

	2009E	2010E
P/E (based on a price of SFr48.82)	17.1	15.6
Credit Suisse forecast:		
EPS	SFr2.82	SFr3.05
Year over year % change	−42.1%	8.16%
P/E (based on a price of SFr47.88)	16.9	15.6

1. Based only on information and estimates developed by Gladisch and his firm, estimate Nestlé's justified forward P/E.
2. Compare and contrast the justified forward P/E estimate from Question 1 to the estimates from UBS and Credit Suisse.

Solution to 1:

The estimate of the justified forward P/E is 14.1. The dividend growth rate can be estimated by using Equation 10 as (1 − Dividend payout ratio) × ROE = (1 − 0.45) × 0.16 = 0.088, or 8.8 percent. Therefore,

$$\frac{P_0}{E_1} = \frac{p}{r - g} = \frac{0.45}{0.12 - 0.088} = 14.1$$

Solution to 2:

The estimated justified forward P/E of 14.1 is lower than the 2009 P/E estimates of 17.1 by UBS and 16.9 by Credit Suisse. Using a required rate of return of 11.5 percent rather than 12 percent results in a justified forward P/E estimate of 16.7 = 0.45/(0.115 − 0.088). Using an ROE of 19 percent (the average ROE of the 2004–2007 period) rather than 16 percent results in a justified forward P/E estimate of 30.0 = 0.45/[0.12 − (0.55)(0.19)] = 0.45/(0.12 − 0.105). The justified forward P/E is very sensitive to changes in the inputs.

Justified forward P/E estimates can be sensitive to small changes in assumptions. Therefore, analysts can benefit from carrying out a sensitivity analysis, as shown in Exhibit 4, which is based on Example 11. Exhibit 4 shows how the justified forward P/E varies with changes in the estimates for the dividend payout ratio (columns) and return on equity. The dividend growth rate (rows) changes because of changes in the retention rate (1 − Payout rate) and ROE. Recall g = ROE times retention rate.

| Exhibit 4 | Estimates for Nestlé's Justified Forward P/E (Required Rate of Return = 12 Percent) |

Constant Dividend Growth Rate (%)	Dividend Payout Ratio				
	40.0%	42.5%	45.0%	47.5%	50.0%
7.0	8.0	8.5	9.0	9.5	10.0
7.5	8.9	9.4	10.0	10.6	11.1
8.0	10.0	10.6	11.3	11.9	12.5
8.5	11.4	12.1	12.9	13.6	14.3

(continued)

Exhibit 4	*Continued*				

Constant Dividend Growth Rate (%)	Dividend Payout Ratio				
	40.0%	42.5%	45.0%	47.5%	50.0%
9.0	13.3	14.2	15.0	15.8	16.7
9.5	16.0	17.0	18.0	19.0	20.0
10.0	20.0	21.3	22.5	23.8	25.0
10.5	26.7	28.3	30.0	31.7	33.3

5.2 The Method of Comparables

The method of comparables is the most widely used approach for analysts reporting valuation judgments on the basis of price multiples. This method essentially compares relative values estimated using multiples or the relative values of multiples. The economic rationale underlying the method of comparables is the **law of one price**: Identical assets should sell for the same price. The methodology involves using a price multiple to evaluate whether an asset is fairly valued, undervalued, or overvalued in relation to a benchmark value of the multiple. Choices for the benchmark multiple include the multiple of a closely matched individual stock or the average or median value of the multiple for the stock's industry. Some analysts perform trend or time-series analyses and use past or average values of a price multiple as a benchmark.

Identifying individual companies or even an industry as the "comparable" may present a challenge. Many large corporations operate in several lines of business, so the scale and scope of their operations can vary significantly. When identifying comparables (sometimes referred to as "comps"), the analyst should be careful to identify companies that are most similar according to a number of dimensions. These dimensions include (but are not limited to) overall size, product lines, and growth rate. The type of analysis shown in Section 5.1 relating multiples to fundamentals is a productive way to identify the fundamental variables that should be taken into account in identifying comparables.

Example 12

Method of Comparables (1)

As noted previously, P/E is a price multiple frequently used by analysts. Using P/E in the method of comparables can be problematic, however, as a result of business cycle effects on EPS. An alternative valuation tool that is useful during periods of economic slowdown or extraordinary growth is the P/S multiple. Although sales will decline during a recession and increase during a period of economic growth, the change in sales will be less than the change in earnings in percentage terms because earnings are heavily influenced by fixed operating and financing costs (operating and financial leverage).

The following data provide the P/S for most of the major automobile manufacturers in early 2009 (from the *Value Line* stock screener):

Company	P/S
General Motors	0.01

Company	P/S
Ford Motor	0.14
Daimler	0.27
Nissan Motor	0.32
Honda Motor	0.49
Toyota Motor	0.66

Which stock appears to be undervalued when compared with the others?

Solution:

The P/S analysis suggests that General Motors shares offer the best value. When the information shown was published, however, General Motors was on the brink of bankruptcy and had submitted several business plans to the U.S. government that included plant closings and elimination of the Pontiac brand. An analyst must be alert for potential explanations of apparently low or high multiples when performing comparables analysis, rather than just assuming a relative mispricing.

Example 13

Method of Comparables (2)

Incorporated in the Netherlands, the European Aeronautic Defense and Space Company, or EADS (Euronext Paris: EAD) is a dominant aerospace company in Europe. Its largest subsidiary, Airbus S.A.S., is an aircraft manufacturing company with bases in several European countries. The majority of EADS' profits arise from Airbus operations. Airbus and its primary competitor, Boeing (NYSE: BA), control most of the commercial airplane industry.

Comparisons are frequently made between EADS and Boeing. As noted in Exhibit 5, the companies are about equal in size as measured by total revenues in 2008. Converting total revenues from euros to U.S. dollars using the average daily exchange rate for 2008 of US$1.4726/€ results in a value of $64,242 million for EADS' total revenues. Thus, total revenues for EADS are only 5.5 percent higher than those for Boeing.

The companies do differ, however, in several important areas. EADS derives a greater share of its revenue from commercial aircraft production than does Boeing. Also, the book value of shareholders' equity was negative for Boeing at year-end 2008. Finally, the order backlog for EADS is much higher than that for Boeing. Converting the EADS order backlog from euros to U.S. dollars using the year-end rate for 2008 of $1.3919/€ results in a value of $557,105 million for EADS' order backlog. Thus, the order backlog for EADS is 72.0 percent higher than the backlog for Boeing.[6]

---

6 Exchange rate data are available from FRED (Federal Reserve Economic Data) at http://research.stlouisfed.org/fred2/.

Exhibit 5	Data for EADS and Boeing	
	EADS	**Boeing**
Total revenues (millions)	€43,625	$60,909
12-month revenue growth	10.6%	−8.3%
Percent of revenues from commercial aircraft	69.3%	46.4%
Debt ratio (Total liabilities/Equity)	85.4%	102.4%
Order backlog	€400,248	$323,860
Share price, 31/Dec/08	€12.03	$42.67
EPS (basic)	€1.95	$3.68
DPS	€0.20	$1.62
Dividend payout ratio	10.3%	44.0%
P/E ratio	6.2	11.6

Sources: Company websites: www.eads.com and www.boeing.com.

What data shown in Exhibit 5 support a higher P/E for Boeing than for EADS?

Solution:

Recall from Equation 14 and the discussion that followed it that P/E is directly related to the payout ratio and the dividend growth rate. The P/E is inversely related to the required rate of return. The only data presented in Exhibit 5 that support a higher P/E for Boeing is that company's higher dividend payout ratio (44.0 percent versus 10.3 percent for EADS).

The following implicitly supports a higher P/E for EADS: EADS has higher 12-month revenue growth and a higher backlog of orders, suggesting that it will have a higher future growth rate. Boeing also has a higher debt ratio, which implies greater financial risk and a higher required return.

Example 14

Method of Comparables (3)

Canon Inc. (TSE: 7751) is a leading worldwide manufacturer of business machines, cameras, and optical products. Canon was founded in 1937 as a camera manufacturer and is incorporated in Tokyo. The corporate philosophy of Canon is *kyosei* or "living and working together for the common good." The following data can be used to determine a P/E for Canon over the time period 2004–2008. Analyze the P/E of Canon over time and discuss the valuation of Canon.

Year	Price (a)	EPS (b)	P/E (a) ÷ (b)
2004	¥5,546	¥387.8	14.3
2005	¥6,883	¥432.9	15.9
2006	¥6,703	¥342.0	19.6

Year	Price (a)	EPS (b)	P/E (a) ÷ (b)
2007	¥5,211	¥377.6	13.8
2008	¥2,782	¥246.2	11.3

Sources: EPS and P/E data are from Canon's website: www.canon.com. P/E is based on share price data from the Tokyo Stock Exchange.

Solution:

Trend analysis of Canon's P/E reveals a peak of 19.6 in 2006. The 2008 P/E of 11.3 is the lowest of the five years reported. This finding suggests that Canon's share price may be underpriced as of year-end 2008. A bullish case for Canon's stock can be made if an analyst believes that P/E will return to its historical average (15.0 over this five-year period) or be higher. Such a bullish prediction requires that an increase in P/E not be offset by a decrease in EPS.

5.3 Illustration of a Valuation Based on Price Multiples

Telefónica S.A. (LSE: TDE), a world leader in the telecommunication sector, provides communication, information, and entertainment products and services in Europe, Africa, and Latin America. It has operated in its home country of Spain since 1924, but as of 2008, more than 60 percent of its business was outside its home market.

Deutsche Telekom AG (FWB: DTE) provides network access, communication services, and value-added services via fixed and mobile networks. It generates more than half of its revenues outside its home country, Germany.

Exhibit 6 provides comparable data for these two communication giants for 2006–2008.

Exhibit 6	Data for Telefónica and Deutsche Telekom

	Telefónica			Deutsche Telekom		
	2008	**2007**	**2006**	**2008**	**2007**	**2006**
(1) Total assets (€ billions)	99.9	105.9	109.0	123.1	120.7	130.2
Asset growth	−5.7%	−2.8%	—	2.0%	−7.3%	—
(2) Net revenues (€ billions)	57.9	56.4	52.9	61.7	62.5	61.3
Revenue growth	2.7%	6.6%	—	−1.3%	2.0%	—
(3) Net cash flow from operating activities (€ billions)	16.4	15.6	15.4	15.4	13.7	14.2
Cash flow growth	5.1%	1.3%	—	12.4%	−3.5%	—
(4) Book value of common shareholders' equity (€ billions)	19.6	22.9	20.0	43.1	45.2	49.7
Debt ratio: $1 - [(4) \div (1)]$	80.4%	78.4%	81.7%	65.0%	62.6%	61.8%
(5) Net profit (€ billions)	7.8	9.1	6.6	1.5	0.6	3.2
Earnings growth	−14.3%	37.9%	—	150.0%	−81.3%	—

(continued)

Exhibit 6	Continued						
		Telefónica			**Deutsche Telekom**		
		2008	**2007**	**2006**	**2008**	**2007**	**2006**
(6) Weighted average number of shares outstanding (millions)		4,646	4,759	4,779	4,340	4,339	4,353
(7) Price per share (€)		15.85	22.22	16.22	10.75	15.02	13.84
Price-to-revenue ratio (P/R): *(7) ÷ [(2) ÷ (6)]*		1.3	1.9	1.5	0.8	1.0	1.0
P/CF: *(7) ÷ [(3) ÷ (6)]*		4.5	6.8	5.0	3.0	4.8	4.2
P/B: *(7) ÷ [(4) ÷ (6)]*		3.8	4.6	3.9	1.1	1.4	1.2
P/E: *(7) ÷ [(5) ÷ (6)]*		9.4	11.6	11.7	31.1	108.6	18.8

Sources: Company websites: www.telefonica.es and www.deutschetelekom.com.

Time-series analysis of all price multiples in Exhibit 6 suggests that both companies are currently attractively valued. For example, the 2008 price-to-revenue ratio (P/R) of 1.3 for Telefónica is below the 2006–2008 average for this ratio of approximately 1.6. The 2008 P/CF of 3.0 for Deutsche Telekom is below the 2006–2008 average for this ratio of approximately 4.0.

A comparative analysis produces somewhat mixed results. The 2008 values for Deutsche Telekom for the P/R, P/CF, P/B multiples are lower than those for Telefónica. This result suggests that Deutsche Telekom is attractively valued when compared with Telefónica. The 2008 P/E for Telefónica, however, is much lower than for Deutsche Telekom.

An analyst investigating these contradictory results would look for information not reported in Exhibit 6. For example, the earnings before interest, taxes, depreciation, and amortization (EBITDA) for Telefónica was €22.9 billion in 2008. The EBITDA value for Deutsche Telekom was €18.0 billion in 2008. The 2008 price-to-EBITDA ratio for Telefónica is [(15.85 × 4,646)/22,900] or [15.85/(22,900/4,646)] = 3.2, whereas the 2008 price-to-EBITDA ratio for Deutsche Telekom is 2.6. Thus, the higher P/E for Deutsche Telekom may be explained by higher depreciation charges, higher interest costs, and/or a greater tax burden.

In summary, the major advantage of using price multiples is that they allow for relative comparisons, both cross-sectional (versus the market or another comparable) and in time series. The approach can be especially beneficial for analysts who are assigned to a particular industry or sector and need to identify the expected best performing stocks within that sector. Price multiples are popular with investors because the multiples can be calculated easily and many multiples are readily available from financial websites and newspapers.

Caution is necessary. A stock may be relatively undervalued when compared with its benchmarks but overvalued when compared with an estimate of intrinsic value as determined by one of the discounted cash flow methodologies. Furthermore, differences in reporting rules among different markets and in chosen accounting methods can result in revenues, earnings, book values, and cash flows that are not easily comparable. These differences can, in turn, result in multiples that are not easily comparable. Finally, the multiples for cyclical companies may be highly influenced by current economic conditions.

5.4 Enterprise Value

An alternative to estimating the value of equity is to estimate the value of the enterprise. Enterprise value is most frequently determined as market capitalization plus market value of preferred stock plus market value of debt minus cash and investments (cash equivalents and short-term investments). Enterprise value is often viewed as the cost of a takeover: In the event of a buyout, the acquiring company assumes the acquired company's debt but also receives its cash. Enterprise value is most useful when comparing companies with significant differences in capital structure.

Enterprise value (EV) multiples are widely used in Europe, with EV/EBITDA arguably the most common. EBITDA is a proxy for operating cash flow because it excludes depreciation and amortization. EBITDA may include other non-cash expenses, however, and non-cash revenues. EBITDA can be viewed as a source of funds to pay interest, dividends, and taxes. Because EBITDA is calculated prior to payment to any of the company's financial stakeholders, using it to estimate enterprise value is logically appropriate.

Using enterprise value instead of market capitalization to determine a multiple can be useful to analysts. Even where the P/E is problematic because of negative earnings, the EV/EBITDA multiple can generally be computed because EBITDA is usually positive. An alternative to using EBITDA in EV multiples is to use operating income.

In practice, analysts may have difficulty accurately assessing enterprise value if they do not have access to market quotations for the company's debt. When current market quotations are not available, bond values may be estimated from current quotations for bonds with similar maturity, sector, and credit characteristics. Substituting the book value of debt for the market value of debt provides only a rough estimate of the debt's market value. This is because market interest rates change and investors' perception of the issuer's credit risk may have changed since the debt was issued.

Example 15

Estimating the Market Value of Debt and Enterprise Value

Cameco Corporation (NYSE: CCJ) is one of the world's largest uranium producers; it accounts for 15 percent of world production from its mines in Canada and the United States. Cameco estimates it has about 226,796,185 kilograms of proven and probable reserves and holds premier land positions in the world's most promising areas for new uranium discoveries in Canada and Australia. Cameco is also a leading provider of processing services required to produce fuel for nuclear power plants. It generates 1,000 megawatts of electricity through a partnership in North America's largest nuclear generating station located in Ontario, Canada.

For simplicity of exposition in this example, we will present share counts in thousands and all dollar amounts in thousands of Canadian dollars. In 2008, Cameco had 350,130 shares outstanding. Its 2008 year-end share price was $20.99. Therefore, Cameco's 2008 year-end market capitalization was $7,349,229.

In its 2008 Annual Report (available at www.cameco.com), Cameco reported total debt and other liabilities of $2,716,475. The company presented the following schedule for long-term debt payments:

Year	Payment
2009	$10,175
2010	453,288

(continued)

Year	Payment
2011	13,272
2012	317,452
2013	16,325
Thereafter	412,645
Total	$1,223,157

Cameco's longest maturity debt matures in 2018. We will assume that the $412,645 to be paid "thereafter" will be paid in equal amounts of $82,529 over the 2014 to 2018 time period. A yield curve for zero-coupon Canadian government securities was available from the Bank of Canada. The yield-curve data and assumed risk premiums in Exhibit 7 were used to estimate the market value of Cameco's long-term debt:

Exhibit 7	Estimated Market Value				

Year	Yield on Zero-Coupon Government Security (%)	Assumed Risk Premium (%)	Discount Rate (%)	Book Value	Market Value
2009	0.89	0.50	1.39	$10,175	$10,036
2010	1.11	1.00	2.11	$453,288	$434,748
2011	1.39	1.50	2.89	$13,272	$12,185
2012	1.65	2.00	3.65	$317,452	$275,043
2013	1.88	2.50	4.38	$16,325	$13,175
2014	2.10	3.00	5.10	$82,529	$61,234
2015	2.30	3.50	5.80	$82,529	$55,617
2016	2.50	4.00	6.50	$82,529	$49,867
2017	2.71	4.50	7.21	$82,529	$44,105
2018	2.92	5.00	7.92	$82,529	$38,511
				$1,223,157	$994,521

Note from Exhibit 7 that the book value of long-term debt is $1,223,157 and its estimated market value is $994,521. The book value of total debt and liabilities of $2,716,475 minus the book value of long-term debt of $1,223,157 is $1,493,318. If we assume that the market value of that remaining debt is equal to its book value of $1,493,318, an estimate of the market value of total debt and liabilities is that amount plus the estimated market value of long-term debt of $994,521 or $2,487,839.

At the end of 2008, Cameco had cash and equivalents of $269,176. Enterprise value can be estimated as the $7,349,229 market value of stock plus the $2,487,839 market value of debt minus the $269,176 cash and equivalents, or $9,567,892. Cameco's 2008 EBITDA was $1,078,606; an estimate of EV/EBITDA is, therefore, $9,567,892 divided by $1,078,606, or 8.9.

Example 16

EV/Operating Income

Exhibit 8 presents data for nine major mining companies. Based on the information in Exhibit 8, which two mining companies seem to be the *most* undervalued?

Exhibit 8	Data for Nine Major Mining Companies			
Company	Ticker Symbol	EV (C$ millions)	Operating Income (OI) (C$ millions)	EV/OI
BHP Billiton	BHP	197,112.00	9,794.00	20.1
Rio Tinto	RIO	65,049.60	7,905.00	8.2
Anglo American	AAL	48,927.30	6,208.00	7.9
Barrick Gold	ABX	35,288.00	1,779.00	19.8
Goldcorp	G	28,278.00	616.66	45.9
Newmont Mining	NEM	22,040.80	1,385.00	15.9
AngloGold Ashanti	AU	19,918.30	−362.00	−55.0
Alcoa	AA	17,570.40	4,166.00	4.2
Freeport-McMoRan Copper & Gold	FCX	11,168.40	2,868.75	3.9

Source: www.miningnerds.com

Solution:

Alcoa and Freeport-McMoRan Copper & Gold have the lowest EV/OI and thus appear to be the *most* undervalued or favorably priced on the basis of the EV/OI. Note the negative ratio for AngloGold Ashanti. Negative ratios are difficult to interpret, so other means are used to evaluate companies with negative ratios.

ASSET-BASED VALUATION

6

An asset-based valuation of a company uses estimates of the market or fair value of the company's assets and liabilities. Thus, asset-based valuations work well for companies that do not have a high proportion of intangible or "off the books" assets and that do have a high proportion of current assets and current liabilities. The analyst may be able to value these companies' assets and liabilities in a reasonable fashion by starting with balance sheet items. For most companies, however, balance sheet values are different from market (fair) values, and the market (fair) values can be difficult to determine.

Asset-based valuation models are frequently used together with multiplier models to value private companies. As public companies increase reporting or disclosure of fair values, asset-based valuation may be increasingly used to supplement present value and multiplier models of valuation. Important facts that the practitioner should realize are as follows:

- Companies with assets that do not have easily determinable market (fair) values—such as those with significant property, plant, and equipment—are very difficult to analyze using asset valuation methods.

- Asset and liability fair values can be very different from the values at which they are carried on the balance sheet of a company.

- Some assets that are "intangible" are shown on the books of the company. Other intangible assets, such as the value from synergies or the value of a good business reputation, may not be shown on the books. Because asset-based valuation may not consider some intangibles, it can give a "floor" value for a situation involving a significant amount of intangibles. When a company has significant intangibles, the analyst should prefer a forward-looking cash flow valuation.

- Asset values may be more difficult to estimate in a hyper-inflationary environment.

We begin by discussing asset-based valuation for hypothetical nonpublic companies and then move on to a public company example. Analysts should consider the difficulties and rewards of using asset-based valuation for companies that are suited to this measure. Owners of small privately held businesses are familiar with valuations arrived at by valuing the assets of the company and then subtracting any relevant liabilities.

Example 17

An Asset-Based Valuation of a Family-Owned Laundry

A family owns a laundry and the real estate on which the laundry stands. The real estate is collateral for an outstanding loan of $100,000. How can asset-based valuation be used to value this business?

Solution:

The analyst should get at least two market appraisals for the real estate (building and land) and estimate the cost to extinguish the $100,000 loan. This information would provide estimated values for everything except the laundry as a going concern. That is, the analyst has market values for the building and land and the loan but needs to value the laundry business. The analyst can value the assets of the laundry: the equipment and inventory. The equipment can be valued at depreciated value, inflation-adjusted depreciated value, or replacement cost. Replacement cost in this case means the amount that would have to be spent to buy equivalent used machines. This amount is the market value of the used machines. The analyst will recognize that any intangible value of the laundry (prime location, clever marketing, etc.) is being excluded, which will result in an inaccurate asset-based valuation.

Example 17 shows some of the subtleties present in applying asset-based valuation to determine company value. It also shows how asset-based valuation does not deal with intangibles. Example 18 emphasizes this point.

Example 18

An Asset-Based Valuation of a Restaurant

The business being valued is a restaurant that serves breakfast and lunch. The owner/proprietor wants to sell the business and retire. The restaurant space is rented, not owned. This particular restaurant is hugely popular because of the proprietor's cooking skills and secret recipes. How can the analyst value this business?

Solution:

Because of the intangibles, setting a value on this business is challenging. A multiple of income or revenue might be considered. But even those approaches overlook the fact that the proprietor may not be selling his secret recipes and, furthermore, does not intend to continue cooking. Some (or all) of the intangible assets may vanish when the business is sold. Asset-based valuation for this restaurant would begin with estimating the value of the restaurant equipment and inventory and subtracting the value of any liabilities. This approach will provide only a good baseline, however, for a minimum valuation.

For public companies, the assets will typically be so extensive that a piece-by-piece analysis will be impossible, and the transition from book value to market value is a nontrivial task. The asset-based valuation approach is most applicable when the market value of the corporate assets is readily determinable and the intangible assets, which are typically difficult to value, are a relatively small proportion of corporate assets. Asset-based valuation has also been applied to financial companies, natural resource companies, and formerly going-concerns that are being liquidated. Even for other types of companies, however, asset-based valuation of tangible assets may provide a baseline for a minimal valuation.

Example 19

An Asset-Based Valuation of an Airline

Consider the value of an airline company that has few routes, high labor and other operating costs, has stopped paying dividends, and is losing millions of dollars each year. Using most valuation approaches, the company will have a negative value. Why might an asset-based valuation approach be appropriate for use by one of the company's competitors that is considering acquisition of this airline?

Solution:

The airline's routes, landing rights, leases of airport facilities, and ground equipment and airplanes may have substantial value to a competitor. An asset-based approach to valuing this company would value the company's assets separately and aside from the money-losing business in which they are presently being utilized.

Analysts recognizing the uncertainties related to model appropriateness and the inputs to the models frequently use more than one model or type of model in valuation to increase their confidence in their estimates of intrinsic value. The choice of models will depend on the availability of information to put into the models. Example 20 illustrates the use of three valuation methods.

Example 20

A Simple Example of the Use of Three Major Equity Valuation Models

Company data for dividend per share (DPS), earnings per share (EPS), share price, and price-to-earnings ratio (P/E) for the most recent five years are presented in

Exhibit 9. In addition, estimates (indicated by an "E" after the amount) of DPS and EPS for the next five years are shown. The valuation date is at the end of Year 5. The company has 1,000 shares outstanding.

Exhibit 9	Company DPS, EPS, Share Price, and P/E Data			
Year	**DPS**	**EPS**	**Share Price**	**TTM P/E**
10	$3.10E	$5.20E	—	—
9	$2.91E	$4.85E	—	—
8	$2.79E	$4.65E	—	—
7	$2.65E	$4.37E	—	—
6	$2.55E	$4.30E	—	—
5	$2.43	$4.00	$50.80	12.7
4	$2.32	$3.90	$51.48	13.2
3	$2.19	$3.65	$59.86	16.4
2	$2.14	$3.60	$54.72	15.2
1	$2.00	$3.30	$46.20	14.0

The company's balance sheet at the end of Year 5 is given in Exhibit 10.

Exhibit 10	Balance Sheet as of End of Year 5
Cash	$ 5,000
Accounts receivable	15,000
Inventories	30,000
Net fixed assets	50,000
Total assets	$100,000
Accounts payable	$ 3,000
Notes payable	17,000
Term loans	25,000
Common shareholders' equity	55,000
Total liabilities and equity	$100,000

1. Using a Gordon growth model, estimate intrinsic value. Use a discount rate of 10 percent and an estimate of growth based on growth in dividends over the next five years.

2. Using a multiplier approach, estimate intrinsic value. Assume that a reasonable estimate of P/E is the average trailing twelve-month (TTM) P/E ratio over Years 1 through 4.

3. Using an asset-based valuation approach, estimate value per share from adjusted book values. Assume that the market values of accounts receivable and inventories are as reported, the market value of net fixed assets is 110 percent of reported book value, and the reported book values of liabilities reflect their market values.

Solution to 1:

$$D_5 (1 + g)^5 = D_{10} 2.43(1 + g)^5 = 3.10$$

$$g \approx 5.0\%$$

Estimate of value $= V_5 = 2.55/ (0.10 - 0.05) = \$51.00$

Solution to 2:

Average P/E $= (14.0 + 15.2 + 16.4 + 13.2)/4 = 14.7$

Estimate of value $= \$4.00 \times 14.7 = \$58.80$

Solution to 3:

Market value of assets $= 5,000 + 15,000 + 30,000 + 1.1(50,000) = \$105,000$

Market value of liabilities $= \$3,000 + 17,000 + 25,000 = \$45,000$

Adjusted book value $= \$105,000 - 45,000 = \$60,000$

Estimated value (adjusted book value per share) $= \$60,000 \div 1,000$ shares $= \$60.00$

Given the current share price of $50.80, the multiplier and the asset-based valuation approaches indicate that the stock is undervalued. Given the intrinsic value estimated using the Gordon growth model, the analyst is likely to conclude that the stock is fairly priced. The analyst might examine the assumptions in the multiplier and the asset-based valuation approaches to determine why their estimated values differ from the estimated value provided by the Gordon growth model and the market price.

SUMMARY

The equity valuation models used to estimate intrinsic value—present value models, multiplier models, and asset-based valuation—are widely used and serve an important purpose. The valuation models presented here are a foundation on which to base analysis and research but must be applied wisely. Valuation is not simply a numerical analysis. The choice of model and the derivation of inputs require skill and judgment.

When valuing a company or group of companies, the analyst wants to choose a valuation model that is appropriate for the information available to be used as inputs. The available data will, in most instances, restrict the choice of model and influence the way it is used. Complex models exist that may improve on the simple valuation models described in this reading; but before using those models and assuming that complexity increases accuracy, the analyst would do well to consider the "law of parsimony:" A model should be kept as simple as possible in light of the available inputs. Valuation is a fallible discipline, and any method will result in an inaccurate forecast at some time. The goal is to minimize the inaccuracy of the forecast.

Among the points made in this reading are the following:

- An analyst estimating intrinsic value is implicitly questioning the market's estimate of value.

- If the estimated value exceeds the market price, the analyst infers the security is *undervalued*. If the estimated value equals the market price, the analyst infers the security is *fairly valued*. If the estimated value is less than the market price, the analyst infers the security is *overvalued*. Because of the uncertainties involved in valuation, an analyst may require that value estimates differ markedly from market price before concluding that a misvaluation exists.

■ Analysts often use more than one valuation model because of concerns about the applicability of any particular model and the variability in estimates that result from changes in inputs.

■ Three major categories of equity valuation models are present value, multiplier, and asset-based valuation models.

■ Present value models estimate value as the present value of expected future benefits.

■ Multiplier models estimate intrinsic value based on a multiple of some fundamental variable.

■ Asset-based valuation models estimate value based on the estimated value of assets and liabilities.

■ The choice of model will depend upon the availability of information to input into the model and the analyst's confidence in both the information and the appropriateness of the model.

■ In the dividend discount model, value is estimated as the present value of expected future dividends.

■ In the free cash flow to equity model, value is estimated as the present value of expected future free cash flow to equity.

■ The Gordon growth model, a simple DDM, estimates value as $D_1/(r - g)$.

■ The two stage dividend discount model estimates value as the sum of the present values of dividends over a short-term period of high growth and the present value of the terminal value at the end of the period of high growth. The terminal value is estimated using the Gordon growth model.

■ The choice of dividend model is based upon the patterns assumed with respect to future dividends.

■ Multiplier models typically use multiples of the form: P/ measure of fundamental variable or EV/ measure of fundamental variable.

■ Multiples can be based upon fundamentals or comparables.

■ Asset-based valuations models estimate value of equity as the value of the assets less the value of liabilities.

REFERENCES

Basu, S. 1977. "Investment Performance of Common Stocks in Relation to Their Price-Earnings Ratios: A Test of the Efficient Market Hypothesis." *Journal of Finance*, vol. 32, no. 3 : 663–682.

Block, S. 1999. "A Study of Financial Analysts: Practice and Theory." *Financial Analysts Journal*, vol. 55, no. 4 : 86–95.

Dreman, D. 1977. *Psychology of the Stock Market*. New York: AMACOM.

Fama, E., and K. French. 1995. "Size and Book-to-Market Factors in Earnings and Returns." *Journal of Finance*, vol. 50, no. 1 : 131–155.

McWilliams, J. 1966. "Prices, Earnings and P-E Ratios." *Financial Analysts Journal*, vol. 22, no. 3 : 137.

Miller, P., and E. Widmann. 1966. "Price Performance Outlook for High & Low P/E Stocks." *1966 Stock & Bond Issue, Commercial & Financial Chronicle*: 26–28.

Nicholson, S. 1968. "Price Ratios in Relation to Investment Results." *Financial Analysts Journal*, vol. 24, no. 1 : 105–109.

O'Shaughnessy, J. 2005. *What Works on Wall Street*. New York: McGraw-Hill.

Sharpe, W., G. Alexander, and J. Bailey. 1999. *Investments*. New Jersey: Prentice Hall, Inc.

PRACTICE PROBLEMS FOR READING 51

1. An analyst estimates the intrinsic value of a stock to be in the range of €17.85 to €21.45. The current market price of the stock is €24.35. This stock is *most likely*:

   A. overvalued.

   B. undervalued.

   C. fairly valued.

2. An analyst determines the intrinsic value of an equity security to be equal to $55. If the current price is $47, the equity is *most likely*:

   A. undervalued.

   B. fairly valued.

   C. overvalued.

3. In asset-based valuation models, the intrinsic value of a common share of stock is based on the:

   A. estimated market value of the company's assets.

   B. estimated market value of the company's assets plus liabilities.

   C. estimated market value of the company's assets minus liabilities.

4. Which of the following is *most likely* used in a present value model?

   A. Enterprise value.

   B. Price to free cash flow.

   C. Free cash flow to equity.

5. Book value is *least likely* to be considered when using:

   A. a multiplier model.

   B. an asset-based valuation model.

   C. a present value model.

6. An analyst is attempting to calculate the intrinsic value of a company and has gathered the following company data: EBITDA, total market value, and market value of cash and short-term investments, liabilities, and preferred shares. The analyst is *least likely* to use:

   A. a multiplier model.

   B. a discounted cash flow model.

   C. an asset-based valuation model.

7. An analyst who bases the calculation of intrinsic value on dividend-paying capacity rather than expected dividends will *most likely* use the:

   A. dividend discount model.

   B. free cash flow to equity model.

   C. cash flow from operations model.

8. An investor expects to purchase shares of common stock today and sell them after two years. The investor has estimated dividends for the next two years, D_1 and D_2, and the selling price of the stock two years from now, P_2. According to the dividend discount model, the intrinsic value of the stock today is the present value of:

   A. next year's dividend, D_1.

   B. future expected dividends, D_1 and D_2.

   C. future expected dividends and price—D_1, D_2 and P_2.

9. In the free cash flow to equity (FCFE) model, the intrinsic value of a share of stock is calculated as:

   A. the present value of future expected FCFE.

   B. the present value of future expected FCFE plus net borrowing.

   C. the present value of future expected FCFE minus fixed capital investment.

10. With respect to present value models, which of the following statements is *most accurate*?

    A. Present value models can be used only if a stock pays a dividend.

    B. Present value models can be used only if a stock pays a dividend or is expected to pay a dividend.

    C. Present value models can be used for stocks that currently pay a dividend, are expected to pay a dividend, or are not expected to pay a dividend.

11. A Canadian life insurance company has an issue of 4.80 percent, $25 par value, perpetual, non-convertible, non-callable preferred shares outstanding. The required rate of return on similar issues is 4.49 percent. The intrinsic value of a preferred share is *closest to*:

    A. $25.00.

    B. $26.75.

    C. $28.50.

12. Two analysts estimating the value of a non-convertible, non-callable, perpetual preferred stock with a constant dividend arrive at different estimated values. The *most likely* reason for the difference is that the analysts used different:

    A. time horizons.

    B. required rates of return.

    C. estimated dividend growth rates.

13. The Beasley Corporation has just paid a dividend of $1.75 per share. If the required rate of return is 12.3 percent per year and dividends are expected to grow indefinitely at a constant rate of 9.2 percent per year, the intrinsic value of Beasley Corporation stock is *closest* to:

    A. $15.54.

    B. $56.45.

    C. $61.65.

14. An investor is considering the purchase of a common stock with a $2.00 annual dividend. The dividend is expected to grow at a rate of 4 percent annually. If the investor's required rate of return is 7 percent, the intrinsic value of the stock is *closest* to:

    A. $50.00.

    B. $66.67.

    C. $69.33.

15. An analyst gathers or estimates the following information about a stock:

Current price per share	€22.56
Current annual dividend per share	€1.60
Annual dividend growth rate for Years 1–4	9.00%
Annual dividend growth rate for Years 5+	4.00%
Required rate of return	12%

Based on a dividend discount model, the stock is *most likely*:

A. undervalued.

B. fairly valued.

C. overvalued.

16. An analyst is attempting to value shares of the Dominion Company. The company has just paid a dividend of $0.58 per share. Dividends are expected to grow by 20 percent next year and 15 percent the year after that. From the third year onward, dividends are expected to grow at 5.6 percent per year indefinitely. If the required rate of return is 8.3 percent, the intrinsic value of the stock is *closest* to:

A. $26.00.

B. $27.00.

C. $28.00.

17. Hideki Corporation has just paid a dividend of ¥450 per share. Annual dividends are expected to grow at the rate of 4 percent per year over the next four years. At the end of four years, shares of Hideki Corporation are expected to sell for ¥9000. If the required rate of return is 12 percent, the intrinsic value of a share of Hideki Corporation is *closest* to:

A. ¥5,850.

B. ¥7,220.

C. ¥7,670.

18. The Gordon growth model can be used to value dividend-paying companies that are:

A. expected to grow very fast.

B. in a mature phase of growth.

C. very sensitive to the business cycle.

19. The best model to use when valuing a young dividend-paying company that is just entering the growth phase is *most likely* the:

A. Gordon growth model.

B. two-stage dividend discount model.

C. three-stage dividend discount model.

20. An equity analyst has been asked to estimate the intrinsic value of the common stock of Omega Corporation, a leading manufacturer of automobile seats. Omega is in a mature industry, and both its earnings and dividends are expected to grow at a rate of 3 percent annually. Which of the following is *most likely* to be the best model for determining the intrinsic value of an Omega share?

A. Gordon growth model.

B. Free cash flow to equity model.

C. Multistage dividend discount model.

21. A price earnings ratio that is derived from the Gordon growth model is inversely related to the:

   A. growth rate.

   B. dividend payout ratio.

   C. required rate of return.

22. The primary difference between P/E multiples based on comparables and P/E multiples based on fundamentals is that fundamentals-based P/Es take into account:

   A. future expectations.

   B. the law of one price.

   C. historical information.

23. An analyst makes the following statement: "Use of P/E and other multiples for analysis is not effective because the multiples are based on historical data and because not all companies have positive accounting earnings." The analyst's statement is *most likely*:

   A. inaccurate with respect to both historical data and earnings.

   B. accurate with respect to historical data and inaccurate with respect to earnings.

   C. inaccurate with respect to historical data and accurate with respect to earnings.

24. An analyst has prepared a table of the average trailing twelve-month price-to-earning (P/E), price-to-cash flow (P/CF), and price-to-sales (P/S) for the Tanaka Corporation for the years 2005 to 2008.

Year	P/E	P/CF	P/S
2005	4.9	5.4	1.2
2006	6.1	8.6	1.5
2007	8.3	7.3	1.9
2008	9.2	7.9	2.3

As of the date of the valuation in 2009, the trailing twelve-month P/E, P/CF, and P/S are, respectively, 9.2, 8.0, and 2.5. Based on the information provided, the analyst may reasonably conclude that Tanaka shares are *most likely*:

   A. overvalued.

   B. undervalued.

   C. fairly valued.

25. An analyst has gathered the following information for the Oudin Corporation:

   Expected earnings per share = €5.70

   Expected dividends per share = €2.70

   Dividends are expected to grow at 2.75 percent per year indefinitely

   The required rate of return is 8.35 percent

Based on the information provided, the price/earnings multiple for Oudin is *closest* to:

   A. 5.7.

   B. 8.5.

   C. 9.4.

26. An analyst gathers the following information about two companies:

	Alpha Corp.	Delta Co.
Current price per share	$57.32	$18.93
Last year's EPS	$3.82	$1.35
Current year's estimated EPS	$4.75	$1.40

Which of the following statements is *most accurate*?

A. Delta has the higher trailing P/E multiple and lower current estimated P/E multiple.

B. Alpha has the higher trailing P/E multiple and lower current estimated P/E multiple.

C. Alpha has the higher trailing P/E multiple and higher current estimated P/E multiple.

27. An analyst gathers the following information about similar companies in the banking sector:

	First Bank	Prime Bank	Pioneer Trust
P/B	1.10	0.60	0.60
P/E	8.40	11.10	8.30

Which of the companies is *most likely* to be undervalued?

A. First Bank.

B. Prime Bank.

C. Pioneer Trust.

28. The market value of equity for a company can be calculated as enterprise value:

A. minus market value of debt, preferred stock, and short-term investments.

B. plus market value of debt and preferred stock minus short-term investments.

C. minus market value of debt and preferred stock plus short-term investments.

29. Which of the following statements regarding the calculation of the enterprise value multiple is *most likely* correct?

A. Operating income may be used instead of EBITDA.

B. EBITDA may not be used if company earnings are negative.

C. Book value of debt may be used instead of market value of debt.

30. An analyst has determined that the appropriate EV/EBITDA for Rainbow Company is 10.2. The analyst has also collected the following forecasted information for Rainbow Company:

EBITDA = $22,000,000

Market value of debt = $56,000,000

Cash = $1,500,000

The value of equity for Rainbow Company is *closest* to:

A. $169 million.

B. $224 million.

C. $281 million.

31. Enterprise value is most often determined as market capitalization of common equity and preferred stock minus the value of cash equivalents plus the:

    A. book value of debt.

    B. market value of debt.

    C. market value of long-term debt.

32. Asset-based valuation models are best suited to companies where the capital structure does not have a high proportion of:

    A. debt.

    B. intangible assets.

    C. current assets and liabilities.

33. Which of the following is *most likely* a reason for using asset-based valuation?

    A. The analyst is valuing a privately held company.

    B. The company has a relatively high level of intangible assets.

    C. The market values of assets and liabilities are different from the balance sheet values.

34. A disadvantage of the EV method for valuing equity is that the following information may be difficult to obtain:

    A. Operating income.

    B. Market value of debt.

    C. Market value of equity.

35. Which type of equity valuation model is *most likely* to be preferable when one is comparing similar companies?

    A. A multiplier model.

    B. A present value model.

    C. An asset-based valuation model.

36. Which of the following is *most likely* considered a weakness of present value models?

    A. Present value models cannot be used for companies that do not pay dividends.

    B. Small changes in model assumptions and inputs can result in large changes in the computed intrinsic value of the security.

    C. The value of the security depends on the investor's holding period; thus, comparing valuations of different companies for different investors is difficult.

SOLUTIONS FOR READING 51

1. A is correct. The current market price of the stock exceeds the upper bound of the analyst's estimate of the intrinsic value of the stock.

2. A is correct. The market price is less than the estimated intrinsic, or fundamental, value.

3. C is correct. Asset-based valuation models calculate the intrinsic value of equity by subtracting liabilities from the market value of assets.

4. C is correct. It is a form of present value, or discounted cash flow, model. Both EV and FCFE are forms of multiplier models.

5. C is correct. Multiplier valuation models (in the form of P/B) and asset-based valuation models (in the form of adjustments to book value) use book value, whereas present value models typically discount future expected cash flows.

6. B is correct. To use a discounted cash flow model, the analyst will require FCFE or dividend data. In addition, the analyst will need data to calculate an appropriate discount rate.

7. B is correct. The FCFE model assumes that dividend-paying capacity is reflected in FCFE.

8. C is correct. According to the dividend discount model, the intrinsic value of a stock today is the present value of all future dividends. In this case, the intrinsic value is the present value of D_1, D_2, and P_2. Note that P_2 is the present value at Period 2 of all future dividends from Period 3 to infinity.

9. A is correct. In the FCFE model, the intrinsic value of stock is calculated by discounting expected future FCFE to present value. No further adjustments are required.

10. C is correct. Dividend discount models can be used for a stock that pays a current dividend or a stock that is expected to pay a dividend. FCFE can be used for both of those stocks and for stocks that do not, or are not expected to, pay dividends in the near future. Both of these models are forms of present value models.

11. B is correct. The expected annual dividend is 4.80% × $25 = $1.20. The value of a preferred share is $1.20/0.0449 = $26.73.

12. B is correct. The required rate of return, r, can vary widely depending on the inputs and is not unique. A preferred stock with a constant dividend would not have a growth rate to estimate, and the investor's time horizon would have no effect on the calculation of intrinsic value.

13. C is correct. $P_0 = D_1/(r - g) = 1.75(1.092)/(0.123 - 0.092) = 61.65.

14. C is correct. According to the Gordon growth model, $V_0 = D_1/(r - g)$. In this case, $D_1 = $2.00 \times 1.04 = 2.08, so $V_0 = $2.08/(0.07 - 0.04) = $69.3333 = 69.33.

15. A is correct. The current price of €22.56 is less than the intrinsic value (V_0) of €24.64; therefore, the stock appears to be currently undervalued. According to the two-stage dividend discount model:

$$V_0 = \sum_{t=1}^{n} \frac{D_0(1 + g_S)^t}{(1+r)^t} + \frac{V_n}{(1+r)^n} \text{ and } V_n = \frac{D_{n+1}}{r - g_L}$$

$$D_{n+1} = D_0(1 + g_S)^n(1 + g_L)$$

$$D_1 = €1.60 \times 1.09 = €1.744$$

$$D_2 = €1.60 \times (1.09)^2 = €1.901$$

$$D_3 = €1.60 \times (1.09)^3 = €2.072$$

$$D_4 = €1.60 \times (1.09)^4 = €2.259$$

$$D_5 = [€1.60 \times (1.09)^4](1.04) = €2.349$$

$$V_4 = €2.349/(0.12 - 0.04) = €29.363$$

$$V_0 = \frac{1.744}{(1.12)^1} + \frac{1.901}{(1.12)^2} + \frac{2.072}{(1.12)^3} + \frac{2.259}{(1.12)^4} + \frac{29.363}{(1.12)^4}$$

$$= 1.557 + 1.515 + 1.475 + 1.436 + 18.661$$

$$= €24.64 \text{ (which is greater than the current price of €22.56)}.$$

16. C is correct.

$$V_0 = \frac{D_1}{(1+r)} + \frac{D_2}{(1+r)^2} + \frac{P_2}{(1+r)^2}$$

$$= \frac{0.70}{(1.083)} + \frac{0.80}{(1.083)^2} + \frac{31.29}{(1.083)^2}$$

$$= \$28.01$$

Note that $D_1 = 0.58(1.20) = 0.70$, $D_2 = 0.58(1.20)(1.15) = 0.80$, and $P_2 = D_3/(k - g) = 0.80(1.056)/(0.083 - 0.056) = 31.29$

17. B is correct.

$$V_0 = \frac{D_1}{(1+r)} + \frac{D_2}{(1+r)^2} + \frac{D_3}{(1+r)^3} + \frac{D_4}{(1+r)^4} + \frac{P_4}{(1+r)^4}$$

$$= \frac{468}{(1.12)} + \frac{486.72}{(1.12)^2} + \frac{506.19}{(1.12)^3} + \frac{526.44}{(1.12)^4} + \frac{9000}{(1.12)^4}$$

$$= ¥7,220$$

18. B is correct. The Gordon growth model (also known as the constant growth model) can be used to value dividend-paying companies in a mature phase of growth. A stable dividend growth rate is often a plausible assumption for such companies.

19. C is correct. The Gordon growth model is best suited to valuing mature companies. The two-stage model is best for companies that are transitioning from a growth stage to a mature stage. The three-stage model is appropriate for young companies just entering the growth phase.

20. A is correct. The company is a mature company with a steadily growing dividend rate. The two-stage (or multistage) model is unnecessary because the dividend growth rate is expected to remain stable. Although an FCFE model could be used, that model is more often chosen for companies that currently pay no dividends.

21. C is correct. The justified forward P/E is calculated as follows:

$$\frac{P_0}{E_1} = \frac{\dfrac{D_1}{E_1}}{r - g}$$

P/E is inversely related to the required rate of return, r, and directly related to the growth rate, g, and the dividend payout ratio, D/E.

22. A is correct. Multiples based on comparables are grounded in the law of one price and take into account historical multiple values. In contrast, P/E multiples based on fundamentals can be based on the Gordon growth model, which takes into account future expected dividends.

23. A is correct. The statement is inaccurate in both respects. Although multiples can be calculated from historical data, forecasted values can be used as well. For companies without accounting earnings, several other multiples can be used. These multiples are often specific to a company's industry or sector and include price-to-sales and price-to-cash flow.

24. A is correct. Tanaka shares are most likely overvalued. As the table below shows, all the 2009 multiples are currently above their 2005–2008 averages.

Year	P/E	P/CF	P/R
2005	4.9	5.4	1.2
2006	6.1	8.6	1.5
2007	8.3	7.3	1.9
2008	9.2	7.9	2.3
Average	7.1	7.3	1.7

25. B is correct.

$$\frac{P_0}{E_1} = \frac{\dfrac{D_1}{E_1}}{r - g} = \frac{\dfrac{2.7}{5.7}}{0.0835 - 0.0275} = 8.5$$

26. B is correct. P/E = Current price/EPS, and Estimated P/E = Current price/Estimated EPS.

    Alpha P/E = $57.32/$3.82 = 15.01

    Alpha estimated P/E = $57.32/4.75 = 12.07

    Delta P/E = $18.93/$1.35 = 14.02

    Delta estimated P/E = $18.93/$1.40 = 13.52

27. C is correct. Relative to the others, Pioneer Trust has the lowest P/E multiple and the P/B multiple is tied for the lowest with Prime Bank. Given the law of one price, similar companies should trade at similar P/B and P/E levels. Thus, based on the information presented, Pioneer is most likely to be undervalued.

28. C is correct. Enterprise value is calculated as the market value of equity plus the market value of debt and preferred stock minus short-term investments. Therefore, the market value of equity is enterprise value minus the market value of debt and preferred stock plus short-term investments.

29. A is correct. Operating income may be used in place of EBITDA when calculating the enterprise value multiple. EBITDA may be used when company earnings are negative because EBITDA is usually positive. The book value of debt cannot be used in place of market value of debt.

30. A is correct.

    EV = 10.2 × 22,000,000 = $224,400,000

    Equity value = EV – Debt + Cash = 224,400,000 – 56,000,000
    + 1,500,000 = $169,900,000

31. B is correct. The market value of debt must be calculated and taken out of the enterprise value. Enterprise value, sometimes known as the cost of a takeover, is the cost of the purchase of the company, which would include the assumption of the company's debts at market value.

32. B is correct. Intangible assets are hard to value. Therefore, asset-based valuation models work best for companies that do not have a high proportion of intangible assets.

33. A is correct. Asset-based valuations are most often used when an analyst is valuing private enterprises. Both B and C are considerations in asset-based valuations but are more likely to be reasons to avoid that valuation model rather than reasons to use it.

34. B is correct. According to the reading, analysts may have not have access to market quotations for company debt.

35. A is correct. Although all models can be used to compare various companies, multiplier models have the advantage of reducing varying fundamental data points into a format that allows direct comparisons. As long as the analyst applies the data in a consistent manner for all the companies, this approach provides useful comparative data.

36. B is correct. Very small changes in inputs, such as required rate of return or dividend growth rate, can result in large changes to the valuation model output. Some present value models, such as FCFE models, can be used to value companies without dividends. Also, the intrinsic value of a security is independent of the investor's holding period.

Fixed Income

TOPIC LEVEL LEARNING OUTCOME

The candidate should be able to describe fixed income securities and their markets, yield measures, risk factors, and valuation measures and drivers. The candidate should also be able to calculate yields and values of fixed-income securities.

15

Fixed Income:

Basic Concepts

This study session presents the fundamentals of fixed-income investments, one of the largest segments of global financial markets. The first two readings introduce the basic features and characteristics of fixed-income securities and their associated risks. The third reading describes the primary issuers, sectors, and types of bonds. The final reading of the study session introduces yields and spreads and the effect of monetary policy on financial markets.

READING ASSIGNMENTS

Reading 52 Features of Debt Securities

*Fixed Income Analysis for the Chartered Financial Analyst®
Program*, Second Edition, by Frank J. Fabozzi, CFA

Reading 53 Risks Associated with Investing in Bonds

*Fixed Income Analysis for the Chartered Financial Analyst®
Program*, Second Edition, by Frank J. Fabozzi, CFA

Reading 54 Overview of Bond Sectors and Instruments

*Fixed Income Analysis for the Chartered Financial Analyst®
Program*, Second Edition, by Frank J. Fabozzi, CFA

Reading 55 Understanding Yield Spreads

*Fixed Income Analysis for the Chartered Financial Analyst®
Program*, Second Edition, by Frank J. Fabozzi, CFA

52

Features of Debt Securities

by Frank J. Fabozzi, CFA

LEARNING OUTCOMES

Mastery	The candidate should be able to:
☐	**a** explain the purposes of a bond's indenture and describe affirmative and negative covenants;
☐	**b** describe the basic features of a bond, the various coupon rate structures, and the structure of floating-rate securities;
☐	**c** define accrued interest, full price, and clean price;
☐	**d** explain the provisions for redemption and retirement of bonds;
☐	**e** identify common options embedded in a bond issue, explain the importance of embedded options, and identify whether an option benefits the issuer or the bondholder;
☐	**f** describe methods used by institutional investors in the bond market to finance the purchase of a security (i.e., margin buying and repurchase agreements).

INTRODUCTION

1

In investment management, the most important decision made is the allocation of funds among asset classes. The two major asset classes are equities and fixed income securities. Other asset classes such as real estate, private equity, hedge funds, and commodities are referred to as "alternative asset classes." Our focus in this reading is on one of the two major asset classes: fixed income securities.

While many people are intrigued by the exciting stories sometimes found with equities—who has not heard of someone who invested in the common stock of a small company and earned enough to retire at a young age?—we will find in our study of fixed income securities that the multitude of possible structures opens a fascinating field of study. While frequently overshadowed by the media prominence of the equity market, fixed income securities play a critical role in the portfolios of individual and institutional investors.

In its simplest form, a fixed income security is a financial obligation of an entity that promises to pay a specified sum of money at specified future dates. The entity that promises to make the payment is called the issuer of the security. Some examples of issuers are central governments such as the U.S. government and the French government, government-related agencies of a central government such as Fannie Mae and

Fixed Income Analysis for the Chartered Financial Analyst® Program, Second Edition, by Frank J. Fabozzi, CFA. Copyright © 2004 by CFA Institute.

Freddie Mac in the United States, a municipal government such as the state of New York in the United States and the city of Rio de Janeiro in Brazil, a corporation such as Coca-Cola in the United States and Yorkshire Water in the United Kingdom, and supranational governments such as the World Bank.

Fixed income securities fall into two general categories: debt obligations and preferred stock. In the case of a debt obligation, the issuer is called the borrower. The investor who purchases such a fixed income security is said to be the lender or creditor. The promised payments that the issuer agrees to make at the specified dates consist of two components: interest and principal (principal represents repayment of funds borrowed) payments. Fixed income securities that are debt obligations include bonds, mortgage-backed securities, asset-backed securities, and bank loans.

In contrast to a fixed income security that represents a debt obligation, preferred stock represents an ownership interest in a corporation. Dividend payments are made to the preferred stockholder and represent a distribution of the corporation's profit. Unlike investors who own a corporation's common stock, investors who own the preferred stock can only realize a contractually fixed dividend payment. Moreover, the payments that must be made to preferred stockholders have priority over the payments that a corporation pays to common stockholders. In the case of the bankruptcy of a corporation, preferred stockholders are given preference over common stockholders. Consequently, preferred stock is a form of equity that has characteristics similar to bonds.

Prior to the 1980s, fixed income securities were simple investment products. Holding aside default by the issuer, the investor knew how long interest would be received and when the amount borrowed would be repaid. Moreover, most investors purchased these securities with the intent of holding them to their maturity date. Beginning in the 1980s, the fixed income world changed. First, fixed income securities became more complex. There are features in many fixed income securities that make it difficult to determine when the amount borrowed will be repaid and for how long interest will be received. For some securities it is difficult to determine the amount of interest that will be received. Second, the hold-to-maturity investor has been replaced by institutional investors who actively trade fixed income securities.

We will frequently use the terms "fixed income securities" and "bonds" interchangeably. In addition, we will use the term "bonds" generically at times to refer collectively to mortgage-backed securities, asset-backed securities, and bank loans.

In this reading we will look at the various features of fixed income securities and in the next reading we explain how those features affect the risks associated with investing in fixed income securities. The majority of our illustrations throughout this volume use fixed income securities issued in the United States. While the U.S. fixed income market is the largest fixed income market in the world with a diversity of issuers and features, in recent years there has been significant growth in the fixed income markets of other countries as borrowers have shifted from funding via bank loans to the issuance of fixed income securities. This is a trend that is expected to continue.

2   INDENTURE AND COVENANTS

The promises of the issuer and the rights of the bondholders are set forth in great detail in a bond's indenture. Bondholders would have great difficulty in determining from time to time whether the issuer was keeping all the promises made in the indenture. This problem is resolved for the most part by bringing in a trustee as a third party to the bond or debt contract. The indenture identifies the trustee as a representative of the interests of the bondholders.

As part of the indenture, there are affirmative covenants and negative covenants. Affirmative covenants set forth activities that the borrower promises to do. The most common affirmative covenants are 1) to pay interest and principal on a timely basis, 2) to pay all taxes and other claims when due, 3) to maintain all properties used and useful in the borrower's business in good condition and working order, and 4) to submit periodic reports to a trustee stating that the borrower is in compliance with the loan agreement. Negative covenants set forth certain limitations and restrictions on the borrower's activities. The more common restrictive covenants are those that impose limitations on the borrower's ability to incur additional debt unless certain tests are satisfied.

MATURITY

The term to maturity of a bond is the number of years the debt is outstanding or the number of years remaining prior to final principal payment. The maturity date of a bond refers to the date that the debt will cease to exist, at which time the issuer will redeem the bond by paying the outstanding balance. The maturity date of a bond is always identified when describing a bond. For example, a description of a bond might state "due 12/1/2020."

The practice in the bond market is to refer to the "term to maturity" of a bond as simply its "maturity" or "term." As we explain below, there may be provisions in the indenture that allow either the issuer or bondholder to alter a bond's term to maturity.

Some market participants view bonds with a maturity between 1 and 5 years as "short-term." Bonds with a maturity between 5 and 12 years are viewed as "intermediate-term," and "long-term" bonds are those with a maturity of more than 12 years.

There are bonds of every maturity. Typically, the longest maturity is 30 years. However, Walt Disney Co. issued bonds in July 1993 with a maturity date of 7/15/2093, making them 100-year bonds at the time of issuance. In December 1993, the Tennessee Valley Authority issued bonds that mature on 12/15/2043, making them 50-year bonds at the time of issuance.

There are three reasons why the term to maturity of a bond is important:

Reason 1:	Term to maturity indicates the time period over which the bondholder can expect to receive interest payments and the number of years before the principal will be paid in full.
Reason 2:	The yield offered on a bond depends on the term to maturity. The relationship between the yield on a bond and maturity is called the yield curve and will be discussed in the reading on understanding yield spreads.
Reason 3:	The price of a bond will fluctuate over its life as interest rates in the market change. The price volatility of a bond is a function of its maturity (among other variables). More specifically, as explained in the reading on the measurement of interest rate risk, all other factors constant, the longer the maturity of a bond, the greater the price volatility resulting from a change in interest rates.

PAR VALUE

The par value of a bond is the amount that the issuer agrees to repay the bondholder at or by the maturity date. This amount is also referred to as the **principal value**, **face value**, redemption value, and **maturity value**. Bonds can have any par value.

Because bonds can have a different par value, the practice is to quote the price of a bond as a percentage of its par value. A value of "100" means 100% of par value. So, for example, if a bond has a par value of $1,000 and the issue is selling for $900, this bond would be said to be selling at 90. If a bond with a par value of $5,000 is selling for $5,500, the bond is said to be selling for 110.

When computing the dollar price of a bond in the United States, the bond must first be converted into a price per US$1 of par value. Then the price per $1 of par value is multiplied by the par value to get the dollar price. Here are examples of what the dollar price of a bond is, given the price quoted for the bond in the market, and the par amount involved in the transaction:[1]

Quoted Price	Price per $1 of Par Value (Rounded)	Par Value ($)	Dollar Price
90½	0.9050	1,000	905.00
102¾	1.0275	5,000	5,137.50
70⅝	0.7063	10,000	7,062.50
113¹¹⁄₃₂	1.1334	100,000	113,343.75

Notice that a bond may trade below or above its par value. When a bond trades below its par value, it is said to be trading at a discount. When a bond trades above its par value, it is said to be trading at a premium. The reason why a bond sells above or below its par value will be explained in the reading on risks associated with investing in bonds.

Practice Question 1

Given the information in the first and third columns for a U.S. investor, complete the information in the second and fourth columns:

Quoted Price	Price per $1 of Par Value	Par Value ($)	Dollar Price
103¼		1,000	
70⅛		5,000	
87⁵⁄₁₆		10,000	
117³⁄₃₂		100,000	

5 COUPON RATE

The coupon rate, also called the **nominal rate**, is the interest rate that the issuer agrees to pay each year. The annual amount of the interest payment made to bondholders during the term of the bond is called the coupon. The coupon is determined by multiplying the coupon rate by the par value of the bond. That is,

Coupon = Coupon rate × Par value

---

[1] You may not be able to precisely reproduce some of the results in these readings. Rounding practices vary depending on the spreadsheet or calculator, and differences may be particularly noticeable in examples involving several interim calculations.

For example, a bond with an 8% coupon rate and a par value of $1,000 will pay annual interest of $80 (= $1,000 × 0.08).

When describing a bond of an issuer, the coupon rate is indicated along with the maturity date. For example, the expression "6s of 12/1/2020" means a bond with a 6% coupon rate maturing on 12/1/2020. The "s" after the coupon rate indicates "coupon series." In our example, it means the "6% coupon series."

In the United States, the usual practice is for the issuer to pay the coupon in two semiannual installments. Mortgage-backed securities and asset-backed securities typically pay interest monthly. For bonds issued in some markets outside the United States, coupon payments are made only once per year.

The coupon rate also affects the bond's price sensitivity to changes in market interest rates. As illustrated in the reading on risks associated with investing in bonds, all other factors constant, the higher the coupon rate, the less the price will change in response to a change in market interest rates.

5.1 Zero-Coupon Bonds

Not all bonds make periodic coupon payments. Bonds that are not contracted to make periodic coupon payments are called zero-coupon bonds. The holder of a zero-coupon bond realizes interest by buying the bond substantially below its par value (i.e., buying the bond at a discount). Interest is then paid at the maturity date, with the interest being the difference between the par value and the price paid for the bond. So, for example, if an investor purchases a zero-coupon bond for 70, the interest is 30. This is the difference between the par value (100) and the price paid (70). The reason behind the issuance of zero-coupon bonds is explained in the reading on risks associated with investing in bonds.

5.2 Step-Up Notes

There are securities that have a coupon rate that increases over time. These securities are called step-up notes because the coupon rate "steps up" over time. For example, a 5-year step-up note might have a coupon rate that is 5% for the first two years and 6% for the last three years. Or, the step-up note could call for a 5% coupon rate for the first two years, 5.5% for the third and fourth years, and 6% for the fifth year. When there is only one change (or step up), as in our first example, the issue is referred to as a single step-up note. When there is more than one change, as in our second example, the issue is referred to as a multiple step-up note.

An example of an actual multiple step-up note is a 5-year issue of the Student Loan Marketing Association (Sallie Mae) issued in May 1994. The coupon schedule is as follows:

6.05%	from	5/3/94	to	5/2/95
6.50%	from	5/3/95	to	5/2/96
7.00%	from	5/3/96	to	5/2/97
7.75%	from	5/3/97	to	5/2/98
8.50%	from	5/3/98	to	5/2/99

5.3 Deferred Coupon Bonds

There are bonds whose interest payments are deferred for a specified number of years. That is, there are no interest payments during the deferred period. At the end of the deferred period, the issuer makes periodic interest payments until the bond matures. The interest payments that are made after the deferred period are higher than the interest payments that would have been made if the issuer had paid interest from the time the bond was issued. The higher interest payments after the deferred period are to compensate the bondholder for the lack of interest payments during the deferred period. These bonds are called deferred coupon bonds.

5.4 Floating-Rate Securities

The coupon rate on a bond need not be fixed over the bond's life. Floating-rate securities, sometimes called variable-rate securities, have coupon payments that reset periodically according to some reference rate. The typical formula (called the coupon formula) on certain determination dates when the coupon rate is reset is as follows:

Coupon rate = Reference rate + Quoted margin

The quoted margin is the additional amount that the issuer agrees to pay above the reference rate. For example, suppose that the reference rate is the 1-month London interbank offered rate (LIBOR).[2] Suppose that the quoted margin is 100 basis points.[3] Then the coupon formula is:

Coupon rate = 1-month LIBOR + 100 Basis points

So, if 1-month LIBOR on the coupon reset date is 5%, the coupon rate is reset for that period at 6% (5% plus 100 basis points).

The quoted margin need not be a positive value. The quoted margin could be subtracted from the reference rate. For example, the reference rate could be the yield on a 5-year Treasury security and the coupon rate could reset every six months based on the following coupon formula:

Coupon rate = 5-year Treasury yield – 90 Basis points

So, if the 5-year Treasury yield is 7% on the coupon reset date, the coupon rate is 6.1% (7% minus 90 basis points).

It is important to understand the mechanics for the payment and the setting of the coupon rate. Suppose that a floater pays interest semiannually and further assume that the coupon reset date is today. Then, the coupon rate is determined via the coupon formula and this is the interest rate that the issuer agrees to pay at the next interest payment date six months from now.

A floater may have a restriction on the maximum coupon rate that will be paid at any reset date. The maximum coupon rate is called a **cap**. For example, suppose for a floater whose coupon formula is the 3-month Treasury bill rate plus 50 basis points, there is a cap of 9%. If the 3-month Treasury bill rate is 9% at a coupon reset date, then the coupon formula would give a coupon rate of 9.5%. However, the cap restricts the coupon rate to 9%. Thus, for our hypothetical floater, once the 3-month Treasury bill rate exceeds 8.5%, the coupon rate is capped at 9%. Because a cap restricts the coupon rate from increasing, a cap is an unattractive feature for the investor. In contrast, there could be a minimum coupon rate specified for a floater. The minimum coupon rate is called a **floor**. If the coupon formula produces a coupon rate that is below the floor, the floor rate is paid instead. Thus, a floor is an attractive feature for the investor. As we explain in Section 10, caps and floors are effectively embedded options.

---

2 LIBOR is the interest rate which major international banks offer each other on Eurodollar certificates of deposit.

3 In the fixed income market, market participants refer to changes in interest rates or differences in interest rates in terms of basis points. A basis point is defined as 0.0001, or equivalently, 0.01%. Consequently, 100 basis points are equal to 1%. (In our example the coupon formula can be expressed as 1-month LIBOR + 1%.) A change in interest rates from, say, 5.0% to 6.2% means that there is a 1.2% change in rates or 120 basis points.

While the reference rate for most floaters is an interest rate or an interest rate index, a wide variety of reference rates appear in coupon formulas. The coupon for a floater could be indexed to movements in foreign exchange rates, the price of a commodity (e.g., crude oil), the return on an equity index (e.g., the S&P 500), or movements in a bond index. In fact, through financial engineering, issuers have been able to structure floaters with almost any reference rate. In several countries, there are government bonds whose coupon formula is tied to an inflation index.

Practice Question 2

A floating-rate issue has the following coupon formula:

6-month Treasury rate + 50 basis points with a cap of 7%

The coupon rate is set every six months. Suppose that at the reset date the 6-month Treasury rate is as shown below. Compute the coupon rate for the next 6-month period:

	6-Month Treasury Rate (%)	Coupon Rate
First reset date	5.5	?
Second reset date	5.8	?
Third reset date	6.3	?
Fourth reset date	6.8	?
Fifth reset date	7.3	?
Sixth reset date	6.1	?

The U.S. Department of the Treasury in January 1997 began issuing inflation-adjusted securities. These issues are referred to as Treasury Inflation Protection Securities (TIPS). The reference rate for the coupon formula is the rate of inflation as measured by the Consumer Price Index for All Urban Consumers (i.e., CPI-U). (The mechanics of the payment of the coupon will be explained in the reading on bond sectors and instruments where these securities are discussed.) Corporations and agencies in the United States issue inflation-linked (or inflation-indexed) bonds. For example, in February 1997, JPMorgan & Company issued a 15-year bond that pays the CPI plus 400 basis points. In the same month, the Federal Home Loan Bank issued a 5-year bond with a coupon rate equal to the CPI plus 315 basis points and a 10-year bond with a coupon rate equal to the CPI plus 337 basis points.

Typically, the coupon formula for a floater is such that the coupon rate increases when the reference rate increases, and decreases when the reference rate decreases. There are issues whose coupon rate moves in the opposite direction from the change in the reference rate. Such issues are called **inverse floaters** or reverse floaters.[4] It is not too difficult to understand why an investor would be interested in an inverse floater. It gives an investor who believes interest rates will decline the opportunity to obtain a higher coupon interest rate. The issuer isn't necessarily taking the opposite view because it can hedge the risk that interest rates will decline.[5]

---

4 In the agency, corporate, and municipal markets, inverse floaters are created as structured notes. We discuss structured notes in the reading on bond sectors and instruments. Inverse floaters in the mortgage-backed securities market are common and are created through a process that will be discussed at Level II.
5 The issuer hedges by using financial instruments known as derivatives, which we cover at Level II.

The coupon formula for an inverse floater is:

Coupon rate = $K - L \times$ (Reference Rate)

where K and L are values specified in the prospectus for the issue.

For example, suppose that for a particular inverse floater, K is 20% and L is 2. Then the coupon reset formula would be:

Coupon rate = 20% − 2 × (Reference Rate)

Suppose that the reference rate is the 3-month Treasury bill rate, then the coupon formula would be:

Coupon rate = 20% − 2 × (3-month Treasury bill rate)

If at the coupon reset date the 3-month Treasury bill rate is 6%, the coupon rate for the next period is:

Coupon rate = 20% − 2 × 6% = 8%

If at the next reset date the 3-month Treasury bill rate declines to 5%, the coupon rate increases to:

Coupon rate = 20% − 2 × 5% = 10%

Notice that if the 3-month Treasury bill rate exceeds 10%, then the coupon formula would produce a negative coupon rate. To prevent this, there is a floor imposed on the coupon rate. There is also a cap on the inverse floater. This occurs if the 3-month Treasury bill rate is zero. In that unlikely event, the maximum coupon rate is 20% for our hypothetical inverse floater.

There is a wide range of coupon formulas that we will encounter in our study of fixed income securities.[6] These are discussed below. The reason why issuers have been able to create floating-rate securities with offbeat coupon formulas is due to derivative instruments. It is too early in our study of fixed income analysis and portfolio management to appreciate why some of these offbeat coupon formulas exist in the bond market. Suffice it to say that some of these offbeat coupon formulas allow the investor to take a view on either the movement of some interest rate (i.e., for speculating on an interest rate movement) or to reduce exposure to the risk of some interest rate movement (i.e., for interest rate risk management). The advantage to the issuer is that it can lower its cost of borrowing by creating offbeat coupon formulas for investors.[7] While it may seem that the issuer is taking the opposite position to the investor, this is not the case. What in fact happens is that the issuer can hedge its risk exposure by using derivative instruments so as to obtain the type of financing it seeks (i.e., fixed rate borrowing or floating rate borrowing). These offbeat coupon formulas are typically found in "structured notes," a form of medium-term note that will be discussed in the reading on bond sectors and instruments.

Practice Question 3

Identify the following types of bonds based on their coupon structures:

A. Coupon formula:

Coupon rate = 32% − 2 × (5-year Treasury rate)

---

6 In the reading on bond sectors and instruments, we will describe other types of floating-rate securities.
7 These offbeat coupon bond formulas are actually created as a result of inquiries from clients of dealer firms. That is, a salesperson will be approached by fixed income portfolio managers requesting a structure be created that provides the exposure sought. The dealer firm will then notify the investment banking group of the dealer firm to contact potential issuers.

B. Coupon structure:

Years 1–3	5.1%
Years 4–9	5.7%
Years 10–20	6.2%

C. Coupon formula:

Coupon rate = Change in the consumer price index + 3.1%

5.5 Accrued Interest

Bond issuers do not disburse coupon interest payments every day. Instead, typically in the United States coupon interest is paid every six months. In some countries, interest is paid annually. For mortgage-backed and asset-backed securities, interest is usually paid monthly. The coupon payment is made to the bondholder of record. Thus, if an investor sells a bond between coupon payments and the buyer holds it until the next coupon payment, then the entire coupon interest earned for the period will be paid to the buyer of the bond since the buyer will be the holder of record. The seller of the bond gives up the interest from the time of the last coupon payment to the time until the bond is sold. The amount of interest over this period that will be received by the buyer even though it was earned by the seller is called accrued interest. We will see how to calculate **accrued interest** in the reading introducing the valuation of debt securities.

In the United States and in many countries, the bond buyer must pay the bond seller the accrued interest. The amount that the buyer pays the seller is the agreed upon price for the bond plus accrued interest. This amount is called the **full price**. (Some market participants refer to this as the dirty price.) The agreed upon bond price without accrued interest is simply referred to as the price. (Some refer to it as the clean price.)

A bond in which the buyer must pay the seller accrued interest is said to be trading *cum-coupon* ("with coupon"). If the buyer forgoes the next coupon payment, the bond is said to be trading *ex-coupon* ("without coupon"). In the United States, bonds are always traded *cum-coupon*. There are bond markets outside the United States where bonds are traded *ex-coupon* for a certain period before the coupon payment date.

There are exceptions to the rule that the bond buyer must pay the bond seller accrued interest. The most important exception is when the issuer has not fulfilled its promise to make the periodic interest payments. In this case, the issuer is said to be in default. In such instances, the bond is sold without accrued interest and is said to be traded flat.

PROVISIONS FOR PAYING OFF BONDS   6

The issuer of a bond agrees to pay the principal by the stated maturity date. The issuer can agree to pay the entire amount borrowed in one lump sum payment at the maturity date. That is, the issuer is not required to make any principal repayments prior to the maturity date. Such bonds are said to have a bullet maturity. The bullet maturity structure has become the most common structure in the United States and Europe for both corporate and government issuers.

Fixed income securities backed by pools of loans (mortgage-backed securities and asset-backed securities) often have a schedule of partial principal payments. Such fixed income securities are said to be amortizing securities. For many loans, the payments are structured so that when the last loan payment is made, the entire amount owed is fully paid.

Another example of an amortizing feature is a bond that has a sinking fund provision. This provision for repayment of a bond may be designed to pay all of an issue by the maturity date, or it may be arranged to repay only a part of the total by the maturity date. We discuss this provision later in this section.

An issue may have a call provision granting the issuer an option to retire all or part of the issue prior to the stated maturity date. Some issues specify that the issuer must retire a predetermined amount of the issue periodically. Various types of call provisions are discussed below.

6.1 Call and Refunding Provisions

An issuer generally wants the right to retire a bond issue prior to the stated maturity date. The issuer recognizes that at some time in the future interest rates may fall sufficiently below the issue's coupon rate so that redeeming the issue and replacing it with another lower coupon rate issue would be economically beneficial. This right is a disadvantage to the bondholder since proceeds received must be reinvested in the lower interest rate issue. As a result, an issuer who wants to include this right as part of a bond offering must compensate the bondholder when the issue is sold by offering a higher coupon rate, or equivalently, accepting a lower price than if the right is not included.

The right of the issuer to retire the issue prior to the stated maturity date is referred to as a call provision. If an issuer exercises this right, the issuer is said to "call the bond." The price which the issuer must pay to retire the issue is referred to as the call price or redemption price.

When a bond is issued, typically the issuer may not call the bond for a number of years. That is, the issue is said to have a deferred call. The date at which the bond may first be called is referred to as the first call date. The first call date for the Walt Disney 7.55s due 7/15/2093 (the 100-year bonds) is 7/15/2023. For the 50-year Tennessee Valley Authority 6⅞ due 12/15/2043, the first call date is 12/15/2003.

Bonds can be called in whole (the entire issue) or in part (only a portion). When less than the entire issue is called, the certificates to be called are either selected randomly or on a pro rata basis. When bonds are selected randomly, a computer program is used to select the serial number of the bond certificates called. The serial numbers are then published in the *Wall Street Journal* and major metropolitan dailies. Pro rata redemption means that all bondholders of the issue will have the same percentage of their holdings redeemed (subject to the restrictions imposed on minimum denominations). Pro rata redemption is rare for publicly issued debt but is common for debt issues directly or privately placed with borrowers.

A bond issue that permits the issuer to call an issue prior to the stated maturity date is referred to as a callable bond. At one time, the callable bond structure was common for corporate bonds issued in the United States. However, since the mid-1990s, there has been significantly less issuance of callable bonds by corporate issuers of high credit quality. Instead, as noted above, the most popular structure is the bullet bond. In contrast, corporate issuers of low credit quality continue to issue callable bonds.[8] In Europe, historically the callable bond structure has not been as popular as in the United States.

---

8 As explained in the reading on the risks associated with investing in bonds, high credit quality issuers are referred to as "investment grade" issuers, and low credit quality issuers are referred to as "non-investment grade" issuers. The reason why high credit quality issuers have reduced their issuance of callable bonds while it is still the more popular structure for low credit quality issuers is explained at Level III.

6.1.1 *Call (Redemption) Price*

When the issuer exercises an option to call an issue, the call price can be either 1) fixed regardless of the call date, 2) based on a price specified in the call schedule, or 3) based on a make-whole premium provision. We will use various debt issues of Anheuser-Busch Companies to illustrate these three ways by which the call price is specified.

6.1.1.1 Single Call Price Regardless of Call Date   On 6/10/97, Anheuser-Busch Companies issued $250 million of notes with a coupon rate of 7.1% due June 15, 2007. The prospectus stated that:

> ...The Notes will be redeemable at the option of the Company at any time on or after June 15, 2004, as set forth herein.
>
> The Notes will be redeemable at the option of the Company at any time on or after June 15, 2004, in whole or in part, upon not fewer than 30 days' nor more than 60 days' notice, at a Redemption Price equal to 100% of the principal amount thereof, together with accrued interest to the date fixed for redemption.

This issue had a deferred call of seven years at issuance and a first call date of June 15, 2004. Regardless of the call date, the call price is par plus accrued interest.

6.1.1.2 Call Price Based on Call Schedule   With a call schedule, the call price depends on when the issuer calls the issue. As an example of an issue with a call schedule, in July 1997 Anheuser-Busch Companies issued $250 million of debentures with a coupon rate of 7⅛ due July 1, 2017. (We will see what a debt instrument referred to as a "debenture" is in the reading on an overview of bond sectors and instruments.) The provision dealing with the call feature of this issue states:

> The Debentures will be redeemable at the option of the Company at any time on or after July 1, 2007, in whole or in part, upon not fewer than 30 days' nor more than 60 days' notice, at Redemption Prices equal to the percentages set forth below of the principal amount to be redeemed for the respective 12-month periods beginning July 1 of the years indicated, together in each case with accrued interest to the Redemption Date:

12 Months Beginning July 1	Redemption Price (%)	12 Months Beginning July 1	Redemption Price (%)
2007	103.026	2012	101.513
2008	102.723	2013	101.210
2009	102.421	2014	100.908
2010	102.118	2015	100.605
2011	101.816	2016	100.303

This issue had a deferred call of 10 years from the date of issuance, and the call price begins at a premium above par value and declines over time toward par value. Notice that regardless of when the issue is called, the issuer pays a premium above par value.

A second example of a call schedule is provided by the $150 million Anheuser-Busch Companies' 8⅝s due 12/1/2016 issued November 20, 1986. This issue had a 10-year deferred call (the first call date was December 1, 1996) and the following call schedule:

If Redeemed during the 12 Months Beginning December 1:	Call Price	If Redeemed during the 12 Months Beginning December 1:	Call Price
1996	104.313	2002	101.725
1997	103.881	2003	101.294
1998	103.450	2004	100.863
1999	103.019	2005	100.431
2000	102.588	2006 and thereafter	100.000
2001	102.156		

Notice that for this issue the call price begins at a premium, but after 2006 the call price declines to par value. The first date at which an issue can be called at par value is the first par call date.

6.1.1.3 Call Price Based on Make-Whole Premium

A make-whole premium provision, also called a yield-maintenance premium provision, provides a formula for determining the premium that an issuer must pay to call an issue. The purpose of the make-whole premium is to protect the yield of those investors who purchased the issue at issuance. A make-whole premium does so by setting an amount for the premium, such that when added to the principal amount and reinvested at the redemption date in U.S. Treasury securities having the same remaining life, it would provide a yield equal to the original issue's yield. The premium plus the principal at which the issue is called is referred to as the make-whole redemption price.

We can use an Anheuser-Busch Companies' issue to illustrate a make-whole premium provision—the $250 million 6% debentures due 11/1/2041 issued on 1/5/2001. The prospectus for this issue states:

> We may redeem the Debentures, in whole or in part, at our option at any time at a redemption price equal to the greater of i) 100% of the principal amount of such Debentures and ii) as determined by a Quotation Agent (as defined below), the sum of the present values of the remaining scheduled payments of principal and interest thereon (not including any portion of such payments of interest accrued as of the date of redemption) discounted to the date of redemption on a semi-annual basis (assuming a 360-day year consisting of twelve 30-day months) at the Adjusted Treasury Rate (as defined below) plus 25 basis points plus, in each case, accrued interest thereon to the date of redemption.

The prospectus defined what is meant by a "Quotation Agent" and the "Adjusted Treasury Rate." For our purposes here, it is not necessary to go into the definitions, only that there is some mechanism for determining a call price that reflects current market conditions as measured by the yield on Treasury securities. (Treasury securities are explained in the reading on bond sectors and instruments.)

6.1.2 Noncallable versus Nonrefundable Bonds

If a bond issue does not have any protection against early call, then it is said to be a currently callable issue. But most new bond issues, even if currently callable, usually have some restrictions against certain types of early redemption. The most common restriction is that of prohibiting the refunding of the bonds for a certain number of years or for the issue's life. Bonds that are noncallable for the issue's life are more common than bonds that are nonrefundable for life but otherwise callable.

Many investors are confused by the terms noncallable and nonrefundable. Call protection is much more robust than refunding protection. While there may be certain exceptions to absolute or complete call protection in some cases (such as sinking funds and the redemption of debt under certain mandatory provisions discussed later), call protection still provides greater assurance against premature and unwanted redemption than refunding protection. Refunding protection merely prevents redemption from certain sources, namely the proceeds of other debt issues sold at a lower cost of money. The holder is protected only if interest rates decline and the borrower can obtain lower-cost money to pay off the debt.

For example, Anheuser-Busch Companies issued on 6/23/88 10% coupon bonds due 7/1/2018. The issue was immediately callable. However, the prospectus specified in the call schedule that

> prior to July 1, 1998, the Company may not redeem any of the Debentures pursuant to such option, directly or indirectly, from or in anticipation of the proceeds of the issuance of any indebtedness for money borrowed having an interest cost of less than 10% per annum.

Thus, this Anheuser-Busch bond issue could not be redeemed prior to July 2, 1998, if the company raised the money from a new issue with an interest cost lower than 10%. There is nothing to prevent the company from calling the bonds within the 10-year refunding protected period from debt sold at a higher rate (although the company normally wouldn't do so) or from money obtained through other means. And that is exactly what Anheuser-Busch did. Between December 1993 and June 1994, it called $68.8 million of these relatively high-coupon bonds at 107.5% of par value (the call price) with funds from its general operations. This was permitted because funds from the company's general operations are viewed as more expensive than the interest cost of indebtedness. Thus, Anheuser-Busch was allowed to call this issue prior to July 1, 1998.

6.1.3 *Regular versus Special Redemption Prices*

The call prices for the various issues cited above are called the regular redemption prices or general redemption prices. Notice that the regular redemption prices are above par until the first par call date. There are also special redemption prices for bonds redeemed through the sinking fund and through other provisions, and the proceeds from the confiscation of property through the right of eminent domain or the forced sale or transfer of assets due to deregulation. The special redemption price is usually par value. Thus, there is an advantage to the issuer of being able to redeem an issue prior to the first par call date at the special redemption price (usually par) rather than at the regular redemption price.

A concern of an investor is that an issuer will use all means possible to maneuver a call so that the special redemption price applies. This is referred to as the par call problem. There have been ample examples, and subsequent litigation, where corporations have used the special redemption price and bondholders have challenged the use by the issuer.

6.2 Prepayments

For amortizing securities that are backed by loans that have a schedule of principal payments, individual borrowers typically have the option to pay off all or part of their loan prior to a scheduled principal payment date. Any principal payment prior to a scheduled principal payment date is called a prepayment. The right of borrowers to prepay principal is called a prepayment option.

Basically, the prepayment option is the same as a call option. However, unlike a call option, there is not a call price that depends on when the borrower pays off the issue. Typically, the price at which a loan is prepaid is par value. Prepayments will be discussed when mortgage-backed and asset-backed securities are discussed at Level II.

6.3 Sinking Fund Provision

An indenture may require the issuer to retire a specified portion of the issue each year. This is referred to as a sinking fund requirement. The alleged purpose of the sinking fund provision is to reduce credit risk (discussed in the reading on risks associated with investing in bonds). This kind of provision for debt payment may be designed to retire all of a bond issue by the maturity date, or it may be designed to pay only a portion of the total indebtedness by the end of the term. If only a portion is paid, the remaining principal is called a balloon maturity.

An example of an issue with a sinking fund requirement that pays the entire principal by the maturity date is the $150 million Ingersoll Rand 7.20s issue due 6/1/2025. This bond, issued on 6/5/1995, has a sinking fund schedule that begins on 6/1/2006. Each year the issuer must retire $7.5 million.

Generally, the issuer may satisfy the sinking fund requirement by either 1) making a cash payment to the trustee equal to the par value of the bonds to be retired; the trustee then calls the bonds for redemption using a lottery, or 2) delivering to the trustee bonds purchased in the open market that have a total par value equal to the amount to be retired. If the bonds are retired using the first method, interest payments stop at the redemption date.

Usually, the periodic payments required for a sinking fund requirement are the same for each period. Selected issues may permit variable periodic payments, where payments change according to certain prescribed conditions set forth in the indenture. Many bond issue indentures include a provision that grants the issuer the option to retire more than the sinking fund requirement. This is referred to as an accelerated sinking fund provision. For example, the Anheuser Busch 8⅝s due 12/1/2016, whose call schedule was presented earlier, has a sinking fund requirement of $7.5 million each year beginning on 12/1/1997. The issuer is permitted to retire up to $15 million each year.

Usually the sinking fund call price is the par value if the bonds were originally sold at par. When issued at a premium, the call price generally starts at the issuance price and scales down to par as the issue approaches maturity.

7   CONVERSION PRIVILEGE

A convertible bond is an issue that grants the bondholder the right to convert the bond for a specified number of shares of common stock. Such a feature allows the bondholder to take advantage of favorable movements in the price of the issuer's common stock. An exchangeable bond allows the bondholder to exchange the issue for a specified number of shares of common stock of a corporation different from the issuer of the bond. These bonds are discussed at Level II where a framework for analyzing them is also provided.

8   PUT PROVISION

An issue with a put provision included in the indenture grants the bondholder the right to sell the issue back to the issuer at a specified price on designated dates. The specified price is called the put price. Typically, a bond is putable at par if it is issued at or close to par value. For a zero-coupon bond, the put price is below par.

The advantage of a put provision to the bondholder is that if, after the issuance date, market rates rise above the issue's coupon rate, the bondholder can force the issuer to redeem the bond at the put price and then reinvest the put bond proceeds at the prevailing higher rate.

CURRENCY DENOMINATION

9

The payments that the issuer makes to the bondholder can be in any currency. For bonds issued in the United States, the issuer typically makes coupon payments and principal repayments in U.S. dollars. However, there is nothing that forces the issuer to make payments in U.S. dollars. The indenture can specify that the issuer may make payments in some other specified currency.

An issue in which payments to bondholders are in U.S. dollars is called a dollar-denominated issue. A nondollar-denominated issue is one in which payments are not denominated in U.S. dollars. There are some issues whose coupon payments are in one currency and whose principal payment is in another currency. An issue with this characteristic is called a dual-currency issue.

EMBEDDED OPTIONS

10

As we have seen, it is common for a bond issue to include a provision in the indenture that gives the issuer and/or the bondholder an option to take some action against the other party. These options are referred to as embedded options to distinguish them from stand alone options (i.e., options that can be purchased on an exchange or in the over-the-counter market). They are referred to as embedded options because the option is embedded in the issue. In fact, there may be more than one embedded option in an issue.

10.1 Embedded Options Granted to Issuers

The most common embedded options that are granted to issuers or borrowers discussed in the previous section include:

- the right to call the issue;
- the right of the underlying borrowers in a pool of loans to prepay principal above the scheduled principal payment;
- the accelerated sinking fund provision; and
- the cap on a floater.

The accelerated sinking fund provision is an embedded option because the issuer can call more than is necessary to meet the sinking fund requirement. An issuer usually takes this action when interest rates decline below the issue's coupon rate even if there are other restrictions in the issue that prevent the issue from being called.

The cap of a floater can be thought of as an option requiring no action by the issuer to take advantage of a rise in interest rates. Effectively, the bondholder has granted to the issuer the right not to pay more than the cap.

Notice that whether or not the first three options are exercised by the issuer or borrower depends on the level of interest rates prevailing in the market relative to the issue's coupon rate or the borrowing rate of the underlying loans (in the case of mortgage-backed and asset-backed securities). These options become more valuable when interest rates fall. The cap of a floater also depends on the prevailing level of rates. But here the option becomes more valuable when interest rates rise.

10.2 Embedded Options Granted to Bondholders

The most common embedded options granted to bondholders are:

- conversion privilege;
- the right to put the issue;
- floor on a floater.

The value of the conversion privilege depends on the market price of the stock relative to the embedded purchase price held by the bondholder when exercising the conversion option. The put privilege benefits the bondholder if interest rates rise above the issue's coupon rate. While a cap on a floater benefits the issuer if interest rates rise, a floor benefits the bondholder if interest rates fall since it fixes a minimum coupon rate payable.

10.3 Importance of Understanding Embedded Options

At the outset of this reading, we stated that fixed income securities have become more complex. One reason for this increased complexity is that embedded options make it more difficult to project the cash flows of a security. The cash flow for a fixed income security is defined as its interest and the principal payments.

To value a fixed income security with embedded options, it is necessary to:

1. model the factors that determine whether or not an embedded option will be exercised over the life of the security; and

2. in the case of options granted to the issuer/borrower, model the behavior of issuers and borrowers to determine the conditions necessary for them to exercise an embedded option.

For example, consider a callable bond issued by a corporation. Projecting the cash flow requires 1) modeling interest rates (over the life of the security) at which the issuer can refund an issue and 2) developing a rule for determining the economic conditions necessary for the issuer to benefit from calling the issue. In the case of mortgage-backed or asset-backed securities, again it is necessary to model how interest rates will influence borrowers to refinance their loan over the life of the security. Models for valuing bonds with embedded options will be covered at Level II.

It cannot be overemphasized that embedded options affect not only the value of a bond but also the total return of a bond. In the next reading, the risks associated with the presence of an embedded option will be explained. What is critical to understand is that due to the presence of embedded options it is necessary to develop models of interest rate movements and rules for exercising embedded options. Any analysis of securities with embedded options exposes an investor to **modeling risk**. Modeling risk is the risk that the model analyzing embedded options produces the wrong value because the assumptions are not correct or the assumptions were not realized. This risk will become clearer at Level II when we describe models for valuing bonds with embedded options.

11   BORROWING FUNDS TO PURCHASE BONDS

At Level II, we will discuss investment strategies an investor uses to borrow funds to purchase securities. The expectation of the investor is that the return earned by investing in the securities purchased with the borrowed funds will exceed the borrowing cost. There are several sources of funds available to an investor when borrowing funds.

When securities are purchased with borrowed funds, the most common practice is to use the securities as collateral for the loan. In such instances, the transaction is referred to as a collateralized loan. Two collateralized borrowing arrangements are used by investors—margin buying and repurchase agreements.

11.1 Margin Buying

In a margin buying arrangement, the funds borrowed to buy the securities are provided by the broker and the broker gets the money from a bank. The interest rate banks charge brokers for these transactions is called the call money rate (or broker loan rate). The broker charges the investor the call money rate plus a service charge. The broker is not free to lend as much as it wishes to the investor to buy securities. In the United States, the Securities and Exchange Act of 1934 prohibits brokers from lending more than a specified percentage of the market value of the securities. The 1934 Act gives the Board of Governors of the Federal Reserve the responsibility to set initial margin requirements, which it does under Regulations T and U. While margin buying is the most common collateralized borrowing arrangement for common stock investors (both retail investors and institutional investors) and retail bond investors (i.e., individual investors), it is not the common for institutional bond investors.

11.2 Repurchase Agreement

The collateralized borrowing arrangement used by institutional investors in the bond market is the repurchase agreement. We will discuss this arrangement in more detail at Level III. However, it is important to understand the basics of the repurchase agreement because it affects how some bonds in the market are valued.

A repurchase agreement is the sale of a security with a commitment by the seller to buy the same security back from the purchaser at a specified price at a designated future date. The repurchase price is the price at which the seller and the buyer agree that the seller will repurchase the security on a specified future date called the repurchase date. The difference between the repurchase price and the sale price is the dollar interest cost of the loan; based on the dollar interest cost, the sales price, and the length of the repurchase agreement, an implied interest rate can be computed. This implied interest rate is called the repo rate. The advantage to the investor of using this borrowing arrangement is that the interest rate is less than the cost of bank financing. When the term of the loan is one day, it is called an overnight repo (or overnight RP); a loan for more than one day is called a term repo (or term RP). As will be explained at Level III, there is not one repo rate. The rate varies from transaction to transaction depending on a variety of factors.

SOLUTIONS FOR PRACTICE QUESTIONS

1.

Quoted Price	Price per $1 Par Value (Rounded)	Par Value ($)	Dollar Price
103 ¼	1.0325	1,000	1,032.50
70 ⅛	0.7013	5,000	3,506.25
87 ⁵⁄₁₆	0.8731	10,000	8,731.25
117 ⁷⁄₃₂	1.1709	100,000	117,093.75

2.

	6-Month Treasury Rate (%)	Coupon Rate (%)
First reset date	5.5	6.0
Second reset date	5.8	6.3
Third reset date	6.3	6.8
Fourth reset date	6.8	7.0
Fifth reset date	7.3	7.0
Sixth reset date	6.1	6.6

3. **A.** Inverse floater.

  B. Step-up note (or multiple step-up note).

  C. Inflation-linked bond.

SUMMARY

- A fixed income security is a financial obligation of an entity (the issuer) who promises to pay a specified sum of money at specified future dates.

- Fixed income securities fall into two general categories: debt obligations and preferred stock.

- The promises of the issuer and the rights of the bondholders are set forth in the indenture.

- The par value (principal, face value, redemption value, or maturity value) of a bond is the amount that the issuer agrees to repay the bondholder at or by the maturity date.

- Bond prices are quoted as a percentage of par value, with par value equal to 100.

- The interest rate that the issuer agrees to pay each year is called the coupon rate; the coupon is the annual amount of the interest payment and is found by multiplying the par value by the coupon rate.

- Zero-coupon bonds do not make periodic coupon payments; the bondholder realizes interest at the maturity date equal to the difference between the maturity value and the price paid for the bond.

- A floating-rate security is an issue whose coupon rate resets periodically based on some formula; the typical coupon formula is some reference rate plus a quoted margin.

- A floating-rate security may have a cap, which sets the maximum coupon rate that will be paid, and/or a floor, which sets the minimum coupon rate that will be paid.

- A cap is a disadvantage to the bondholder while a floor is an advantage to the bondholder.

- A step-up note is a security whose coupon rate increases over time.

- Accrued interest is the amount of interest accrued since the last coupon payment; in the United States (as well as in many countries), the bond buyer must pay the bond seller the accrued interest.

- The full price (or dirty price) of a security is the agreed upon price plus accrued interest; the price (or clean price) is the agreed upon price without accrued interest.

- An amortizing security is a security for which there is a schedule for the repayment of principal.

- Many issues have a call provision granting the issuer an option to retire all or part of the issue prior to the stated maturity date.

- A call provision is an advantage to the issuer and a disadvantage to the bondholder.

- When a callable bond is issued, if the issuer cannot call the bond for a number of years, the bond is said to have a deferred call.

- The call or redemption price can be either fixed regardless of the call date or based on a call schedule or based on a make-whole premium provision.

- With a call schedule, the call price depends on when the issuer calls the issue.

- A make-whole premium provision sets forth a formula for determining the premium that the issuer must pay to call an issue, with the premium designed to protect the yield of those investors who purchased the issue.

- The call prices are regular or general redemption prices; there are special redemption prices for debt redeemed through the sinking fund and through other provisions.

- A currently callable bond is an issue that does not have any protection against early call.

- Most new bond issues, even if currently callable, usually have some restrictions against refunding.

- Call protection is much more absolute than refunding protection.

- For an amortizing security backed by a pool of loans, the underlying borrowers typically have the right to prepay the outstanding principal balance in whole or in part prior to the scheduled principal payment dates; this provision is called a prepayment option.

- A sinking fund provision requires that the issuer retire a specified portion of an issue each year.

- An accelerated sinking fund provision allows the issuer to retire more than the amount stipulated to satisfy the periodic sinking fund requirement.

- A putable bond is one in which the bondholder has the right to sell the issue back to the issuer at a specified price on designated dates.

- A convertible bond is an issue giving the bondholder the right to exchange the bond for a specified number of shares of common stock at a specified price.

- The presence of embedded options makes the valuation of fixed income securities complex and requires the modeling of interest rates and issuer/borrower behavior in order to project cash flows.

- An investor can borrow funds to purchase a security by using the security itself as collateral.

- There are two types of collateralized borrowing arrangements for purchasing securities: margin buying and repurchase agreements.

- Typically, institutional investors in the bond market do not finance the purchase of a security by buying on margin; rather, they use repurchase agreements.

- A repurchase agreement is the sale of a security with a commitment by the seller to repurchase the security from the buyer at the repurchase price on the repurchase date.

- The borrowing rate for a repurchase agreement is called the repo rate and while this rate is less than the cost of bank borrowing, it varies from transaction to transaction based on several factors.

PRACTICE PROBLEMS FOR READING 52

1. Consider the following two bond issues.

   Bond A: 5% 15-year bond

   Bond B: 5% 30-year bond

   Neither bond has an embedded option. Both bonds are trading in the market at the same yield.

   Which bond will fluctuate *more* in price when interest rates change? Why?

2. Given the information in the first and third columns, complete the table in the second and fourth columns:

Quoted Price	Price per $1 of Par Value	Par Value ($)	Dollar Price
96¼		1,000	
102⅞		5,000	
109%₁₆		10,000	
68¹¹⁄₃₂		100,000	

3. A floating-rate issue has the following coupon formula:

   1-year Treasury rate + 30 basis points with a cap of 7% and a floor of 4.5%

   The coupon rate is reset every year. Suppose that at the reset date the 1-year Treasury rate is as shown below. Compute the coupon rate for the next year:

	1-Year Treasury Rate (%)	Coupon Rate
First reset date	6.1	?
Second reset date	6.5	?
Third reset date	6.9	?
Fourth reset date	6.8	?
Fifth reset date	5.7	?
Sixth reset date	5.0	?
Seventh reset date	4.1	?
Eighth reset date	3.9	?
Ninth reset date	3.2	?
Tenth reset date	4.4	?

4. An excerpt from the prospectus of a $200 million issue by Becton, Dickinson and Company for the 7.15% Notes due October 1, 2009, states:

   Optional Redemption We may, at our option, redeem all or any part of the notes. If we choose to do so, we will mail a notice of redemption to you not less than 30 days and not more than 60 days before this redemption occurs. The redemption price will be equal to the greater of: 1) 100% of the principal amount of the notes to be redeemed; and 2) the sum of the present values of the Remaining Scheduled Payments on the notes, discounted to the redemption

Practice Problems and Solutions: 1–11 taken from *Fixed Income Analysis for the Chartered Financial Analyst® Program*, Second Edition, by Frank J. Fabozzi, CFA. Copyright © 2004 by CFA Institute. All other problems and solutions copyright © CFA Institute.

date on a semiannual basis, assuming a 360-day year consisting of twelve 30-day months, at the Treasury Rate plus 15 basis points.

A. What type of call provision is this?

B. What is the purpose of this type of call provision?

5. An excerpt from Cincinnati Gas & Electric Company's prospectus for the 10⅛% First Mortgage Bonds due in 2020 states:

> The Offered Bonds are redeemable (though CG&E does not contemplate doing so) prior to May 1, 1995 through the use of earnings, proceeds from the sale of equity securities and cash accumulations other than those resulting from a refunding operation such as hereinafter described. The Offered Bonds are not redeemable prior to May 1, 1995 as a part of, or in anticipation of, any refunding operation involving the incurring of indebtedness by CG&E having an effective interest cost (calculated to the second decimal place in accordance with generally accepted financial practice) of less than the effective interest cost of the Offered Bonds (similarly calculated) or through the operation of the Maintenance and Replacement Fund.

What does this excerpt tell the investor about provisions of this issuer to pay off this issue prior to the stated maturity date?

6. An assistant portfolio manager reviewed the prospectus of a bond that will be issued next week on January 1 of 2000. The call schedule for this $200 million, 7.75% coupon 20-year issue specifies the following:

> The Bonds will be redeemable at the option of the Company at any time in whole or in part, upon not fewer than 30 nor more than 60 days' notice, at the following redemption prices (which are expressed in percentages of principal amount) in each case together with accrued interest to the date fixed for redemption:

> If redeemed during the 12 months beginning January 1,

2000 through 2005	104.00%
2006 through 2010	103.00%
2011 through 2012	101.00%
from 2013 on	100.00%

> provided, however, that prior to January 1, 2006, the Company may not redeem any of the Bonds pursuant to such option, directly or indirectly, from or in anticipation of the proceeds of the issuance of any indebtedness for money borrowed having an interest cost of less than 7.75% per annum.

The prospectus further specifies that:

> The Company will provide for the retirement by redemption of $10 million of the principal amount of the Bonds each of the years 2010 to and including 2019 at the principal amount thereof, together with accrued interest to the date of redemption. The Company may also provide for the redemption of up to an additional $10 million principal amount . . . annually, . . . such optional right being non-cumulative.

The assistant portfolio manager made the following statements to a client after reviewing this bond issue. Comment on each statement. *(When answering this question, remember that the assistant portfolio manager is responding to statements just before the bond is issued in 2000.)*

A. "My major concern is that if rates decline significantly in the next few years, this issue will be called by the Company in order to replace it with a bond issue with a coupon rate less than 7.75%."

B. "One major advantage of this issue is that if the Company redeems it *for any reason* in the first five years, investors are guaranteed receiving a price of 104, a premium over the initial offering price of 100."

C. "A beneficial feature of this issue is that it has a sinking fund provision that reduces the risk that the Company won't have enough funds to pay off the issue at the maturity date."

D. "A further attractive feature of this issue is that the Company can accelerate the payoff of the issue via the sinking fund provision, reducing the risk that funds will not be available at the maturity date."

E. In response to a client question about what will be the interest and principal that the client can depend on if $5 million par value of the issue is purchased, the assistant portfolio manager responded: "I can construct a schedule that shows every six months for the next 20 years the dollar amount of the interest and the principal repayment. It is quite simple to compute—basically it is just multiplying two numbers."

7. There are some securities that are backed by a pool of loans. These loans have a schedule of interest and principal payments every month and give each borrower whose loan is in the pool the right to pay off their respective loan at any time at par. Suppose that a portfolio manager purchased one of these securities. Can the portfolio manager rely on the schedule of interest and principal payments in determining the cash flow that will be generated by such securities (assuming no borrowers default)? Why or why not?

8. A. What is an accelerated sinking fund provision?

   B. Why can an accelerated sinking fund provision be viewed as an embedded call option granted to the issuer?

9. The importance of knowing the terms of bond issues, especially those relating to redemption, cannot be overemphasized. Yet there have appeared numerous instances of investors, professional and others, who acknowledge that they don't read the documentation. For example, in an August 14, 1983 article published in the *New York Times* titled "The Lessons of a Bond Failure," the following statements were attributed to some stockbrokers: "But brokers in the field say they often don't spend much time reading these [official] statements," "I can be honest and say I never look at the prospectus. . . . Generally, you don't have time to do that," and "There are some clients who really don't know what they buy. . . . They just say, 'That's a good interest rate.'" Why is it important to understand the redemption features of a bond issue?

10. What is meant by an embedded option?

11. A. What is the typical arrangement used by institutional investors in the bond market: bank financing, margin buying, or repurchase agreement?

   B. What is the difference between a term repo and an overnight repo?

12. Do embedded options designed to benefit bondholders (investors) include:

	an accelerated sinking fund provision?	a cap on a floater?
A.	No	No
B.	No	Yes
C.	Yes	No

13. The quoted price of a corporate bond is 90½. The par value is $5,000. The dollar price is *closest* to:
    A. $4,500.
    B. $4,525.
    C. $4,750.

14. An analyst is reviewing a corporate bond with the following coupon structure:

    Coupon rate = 40% −2 × (10-year Treasury rate)

    This corporate bond is *most* appropriately classified as a(n):
    A. step-up note.
    B. inverse floater.
    C. deferred coupon bond.

15. Which of the following is *not* an embedded option that benefits the bondholder?
    A. A floor on a floater.
    B. A conversion privilege.
    C. An accelerated sinking fund provision.

16. Consider the following statements.

    Statement 1: "Callable bonds are more likely to be called if interest rates have increased since issuance of the bonds."

    Statement 2: "In the United States, when trading bonds with coupons, the bond seller must pay a portion of the next coupon, representing accrued interest, to the bond buyer."

    Are the statements *most likely* correct or incorrect?
    A. Both statements are incorrect.
    B. Statement 1 is incorrect and Statement 2 is correct.
    C. Statement 1 is correct and Statement 2 is incorrect.

17. Sinking funds are *most likely* to:
    A. reduce credit risk (default risk).
    B. never allow issuers to retire more than the sinking fund requirement.
    C. always reduce the outstanding balance of the bond issue to zero prior to maturity.

18. "The sale of a security with a commitment by the seller to buy the same security back at a specified price at a designated future date" *best* describes:
    A. prepayment risk.
    B. a repurchase agreement.
    C. an adjustable price issue.

SOLUTIONS FOR READING 52

1. All other factors constant, the longer the maturity, the greater the price change when interest rates change. So, Bond B is the answer.

2.

Quoted Price	Price per $1 Par Value (Rounded)	Par Value ($)	Dollar Price
96¼	0.9625	1,000	962.50
102⅞	1.0288	5,000	5,143.75
109⁹⁄₁₆	1.0956	10,000	10,956.25
68¹¹⁄₃₂	0.6834	100,000	68,343.75

3.

	1-Year Treasury Rate (%)	Coupon Rate (%)
First reset date	6.1	6.4
Second reset date	6.5	6.8
Third reset date	6.9	7.0
Fourth reset date	6.8	7.0
Fifth reset date	5.7	6.0
Sixth reset date	5.0	5.3
Seventh reset date	4.1	4.5
Eighth reset date	3.9	4.5
Ninth reset date	3.2	4.5
Tenth reset date	4.4	4.7

4. **A.** This provision is a make-whole redemption provision (also called a yield maintenance premium provision).

   B. A make-whole premium provision provides a formula for determining the redemption price, called the make-whole redemption price. The purpose of the provision is to protect the yield of those investors who purchased the issue at its original offering.

5. For this bond the excerpt tells us that the issue may be redeemed prior to May 1, 1995 but they may not be refunded—that is, they cannot be called using a lower cost of funds than the issue itself. After May 1, 1995, the issue may be redeemed via a refunding. The issue can be called using any source of funds such as a new bond issue with a lower coupon rate than the issue itself.

6. **A.** While it may be true that the Company can call the issue if rates decline, there is a nonrefunding restriction prior to January 1, 2006. The Company may not refund the issue with a source of funds that costs less than 7.75% until after that date.

   B. This is only true if the issuer redeems the issue as permitted by the call schedule. In that case the premium is paid. However, there is a sinking fund provision. If the issuer calls in the particular certificates of the issue held by the investor in order to satisfy the sinking fund provision, the issue is called at par value. So, there is no guarantee that the issue will be paid off at a premium at any time if the issue is called to satisfy the sinking fund provision.

   C. It is commonly thought that the presence of a sinking fund provision reduces the risk that the issuer will not have sufficient funds to pay off the amount due at the maturity date. But this must be balanced against the fact that a bondholder might have his or her bonds taken away at par value when the issuer calls a part of the issue to satisfy the sinking fund provision. If the issue is trading above par value, the bondholder only receives par. So, for example, if the issue is trading at 115 and it is called by the Company to satisfy the sinking fund provision, the investor receives par value (100), realizing a loss of 15.

D. As in part C, while it may seem that the right of the issuer to make additional payments beyond the required amount of the sinking fund will reduce the likelihood that the issuer will have insufficient funds to pay off the issue at the maturity date, there is still the potential loss if the issue is called at par. Moreover, the issuer is likely to make additional payments permitted to retire the issue via the sinking fund special call price of 100 when the bond is trading at a premium, because that is when interest rates in the market are less than the coupon rate on the issue.

E. The assistant portfolio manager cannot know for certain how long the bond issue will be outstanding because it can be called per the call schedule. Moreover, because of the sinking fund provision, a portion of their particular bonds might be called to satisfy the sinking fund requirement. (One of the major topics in fixed income analysis is that because of the uncertainty about the cash flow of a bond due to the right to call an issue, sophisticated analytical techniques and valuation models are needed.)

7. The borrowers whose loans are included in the pool can at lower interest rates refinance their loans if interest rates decline below the rate on their loans. Consequently, the security holder cannot rely on the schedule of principal and interest payments of the pool of loans to determine with certainty future cash flow.

8. A. An accelerated sinking fund provision grants the issuer the right to redeem more than the minimum amount necessary to satisfy the sinking fund requirement.

B. An accelerated sinking fund provision is an embedded option granted to an issuer because it allows the issuer to retire the issue at par value when interest rates have declined. The issuer can do this even if the issue is nonrefundable or noncallable at that time.

9. When an investor is considering the purchase of a bond, he or she should evaluate any provision granted to the issuer that may affect their expected return over their desired time horizon. Moreover, when a bond is purchased in the secondary market at a price above par value, the concern is that the issue may be paid off prior to the maturity date. The result would be the loss of the premium. So, for example, if an investor believes that a bond is noncallable but the issue has a sinking fund requirement, it is possible that the issue held by an investor can be called at the special redemption price of 100 when the issue is trading at a premium.

10. An investor can purchase a stand alone option on an exchange or in the over-the-counter market. When an investor purchases a bond, there are choices or "options" provided for in the indenture that grants either the bondholder or the issuer the right or option to do something. These choices are commonly referred to as embedded options.

11. A. Institutional investors typically use a repurchase agreement to finance the purchase of a bond.

B. A term repo is a repurchase agreement where the borrowing is for more than one day; an overnight repo involves borrowing for only one day.

12. A is correct. An accelerated sinking fund provision benefits the issuer (borrower) by granting the borrower the option to retire a portion of the debt that is greater than the sinking fund requirement. A cap on a floater benefits the issuer (borrower) by limiting the level of interest that may be paid on a floating rate security. Thus, neither embedded option benefits the bondholder (investor).

13. B is correct. The dollar price of the bond can be calculated as follows:

    $0.905 \times \$5,000 = \$4,525$

14. B is correct. The coupon formula for an inverse floater is:

    Coupon rate = $K - L \times$ (Reference rate)

    where K and L are values specified in the prospectus. The coupon rate is inversely related to the reference rate.

15. C is correct. An accelerated sinking fund provision is an example of an option that benefits the bond issuer.

16. A is correct. Both statements are incorrect. Bonds are more likely to be called if interest rates fall, allowing the issuer to refund the issue at a lower coupon rate. Accrued interest is paid by the buyer of a bond to the seller.

17. A is correct. Sinking funds are designed to reduce default risk (the crisis-at-maturity). If present in the indenture, sinking funds must be met. They are not optional. Some sinking funds allow for accelerated sinking funds provisions. Some sinking funds pay only part of the outstanding balance, leaving a balloon payment at maturity.

18. B is correct. The statement is the definition of a repurchase agreement.

Risks Associated with Investing in Bonds

by Frank J. Fabozzi, CFA

LEARNING OUTCOMES

Mastery	The candidate should be able to:
☐	**a** explain the risks associated with investing in bonds;
☐	**b** identify the relations among a bond's coupon rate, the yield required by the market, and the bond's price relative to par value (i.e., discount, premium, or equal to par);
☐	**c** explain how a bond maturity, coupon, embedded options and yield level affect its interest rate risk;
☐	**d** identify the relation of the price of a callable bond to the price of an option-free bond and the price of the embedded call option;
☐	**e** explain the interest rate risk of a floating-rate security and why its price may differ from par value;
☐	**f** calculate and interpret the duration and dollar duration of a bond;
☐	**g** describe yield-curve risk and explain why duration does not account for yield-curve risk;
☐	**h** explain the disadvantages of a callable or prepayable security to an investor;
☐	**i** identify the factors that affect the reinvestment risk of a security and explain why prepayable amortizing securities expose investors to greater reinvestment risk than nonamortizing securities;
☐	**j** describe types of credit risk and the meaning and role of credit ratings;
☐	**k** explain liquidity risk and why it might be important to investors even if they expect to hold a security to the maturity date;
☐	**l** describe the exchange rate risk an investor faces when a bond makes payments in a foreign currency;
☐	**m** explain inflation risk;
☐	**n** explain how yield volatility affects the price of a bond with an embedded option and how changes in volatility affect the value of a callable bond and a putable bond;
☐	**o** describe sovereign risk and types of event risk.

Fixed Income Analysis for the Chartered Financial Analyst® Program, Second Edition, by Frank J. Fabozzi, CFA. Copyright © 2004 by CFA Institute.

1 INTRODUCTION

Armed with an understanding of the basic features of bonds, we now turn to the risks associated with investing in bonds. These risks include:

- interest rate risk;
- call and prepayment risk;
- yield curve risk;
- reinvestment risk;
- credit risk;
- liquidity risk;
- exchange-rate risk;
- volatility risk;
- inflation or purchasing power risk;
- event risk;
- sovereign risk.

We will see how features of a bond that we described in the reading on features of debt securities—coupon rate, maturity, embedded options, and currency denomination—affect several of these risks.

2 INTEREST RATE RISK

As we will demonstrate in the reading on the valuation of debt securities, the price of a typical bond will change in the opposite direction to the change in interest rates or yields.[1] That is, when interest rates rise, a bond's price will fall; when interest rates fall, a bond's price will rise. For example, consider a 6% 20-year bond. If the yield investors require to buy this bond is 6%, the price of this bond would be $100. However, if the required yield increased to 6.5%, the price of this bond would decline to $94.4479. Thus, for a 50 basis point increase in yield, the bond's price declines by 5.55%. If, instead, the yield declines from 6% to 5.5%, the bond's price will rise by 6.02% to $106.0195.

Since the price of a bond fluctuates with market interest rates, the risk that an investor faces is that the price of a bond held in a portfolio will decline if market interest rates rise. This risk is referred to as interest rate risk and is the major risk faced by investors in the bond market.

2.1 Reason for the Inverse Relationship between Changes in Interest Rates and Price

The reason for this inverse relationship between a bond's price change and the change in interest rates (or change in market yields) is as follows. Suppose investor X purchases our hypothetical 6% coupon 20-year bond at a price equal to par (100). As explained in the reading on yield measures, spot rates, and forward rates, the yield for this bond is 6%. Suppose that immediately after the purchase of this bond two things happen. First, market interest rates rise to 6.50% so that if a bond issuer wishes to sell a bond priced at par, it will require a 6.50% coupon rate to attract investors to purchase the bond. Second, suppose investor X wants to sell the bond with a 6% coupon rate. In

---

[1] At this stage, we will use the terms interest rate and yield interchangeably. We'll see in the reading on yield measures, spot rates, and forward rates how to compute a bond's yield.

attempting to sell the bond, investor X would not find an investor who would be willing to pay par value for a bond with a coupon rate of 6%. The reason is that any investor who wanted to purchase this bond could obtain a similar 20-year bond with a coupon rate 50 basis points higher, 6.5%.

What can the investor do? The investor cannot force the issuer to change the coupon rate to 6.5%. Nor can the investor force the issuer to shorten the maturity of the bond to a point where a new investor might be willing to accept a 6% coupon rate. The only thing that the investor can do is adjust the price of the bond to a new price where a buyer would realize a yield of 6.5%. This means that the price would have to be adjusted down to a price below par. It turns out, the new price must be 94.4479.[2] While we assumed in our illustration an initial price of par value, the principle holds for any purchase price. Regardless of the price that an investor pays for a bond, an instantaneous increase in market interest rates will result in a decline in a bond's price.

Suppose that instead of a rise in market interest rates to 6.5%, interest rates decline to 5.5%. Investors would be more than happy to purchase the 6% coupon 20-year bond at par. However, investor X realizes that the market is only offering investors the opportunity to buy a similar bond at par with a coupon rate of 5.5%. Consequently, investor X will increase the price of the bond until it offers a yield of 5.5%. That price turns out to be 106.0195.

Let's summarize the important relationships suggested by our example.

1. A bond will trade at a price equal to par when the coupon rate is equal to the yield required by market. That is,[3]

   Coupon rate = Yield required by market → Price = Par value

2. A bond will trade at a price below par (sell at a discount) or above par (sell at a premium) if the coupon rate is different from the yield required by the market. Specifically,

   Coupon rate < Yield required by market → Price < Par value (discount)

   Coupon rate > Yield required by market → Price > Par value (premium)

3. The price of a bond changes in the opposite direction to the change in interest rates. So, for an instantaneous change in interest rates the following relationship holds:

   If interest rates increase → Price of a bond decreases
   If interest rates decrease → Price of a bond increases

Practice Question 1

The following information is reported in the business section of a newspaper:

Issue	Coupon (%)	Maturity	Yield Required by Market (%)	Price
A	$7\frac{3}{8}$	16 years	6.00	114.02
B	$6\frac{3}{4}$	4 years	7.00	99.14

---

2 We'll see how to compute the price of a bond in the reading on yield measures, spot rates, and forward rates.

3 The arrow symbol in the expressions means "therefore."

Issue	Coupon (%)	Maturity	Yield Required by Market (%)	Price
C	0	10 years	5.00	102.10
D	$5\frac{1}{2}$	20 years	5.90	104.15
E	$8\frac{1}{2}$	18 years	8.50	100.00
F	$4\frac{1}{2}$	6 years	4.00	96.50
G	$6\frac{1}{4}$	25 years	6.25	103.45

Which issues have an error in their reported price? (No calculations are required.)

2.2 Bond Features that Affect Interest Rate Risk

A bond's price sensitivity to changes in market interest rates (i.e., a bond's interest rate risk) depends on various features of the issue, such as maturity, coupon rate, and embedded options.[4] While we discuss these features in more detail in the reading on the measurement of interest rate risk, we provide a brief discussion below.

2.2.1 The Impact of Maturity

All other factors constant, *the longer the bond's maturity, the greater the bond's price sensitivity to changes in interest rates.* For example, we know that for a 6% 20-year bond selling to yield 6%, a rise in the yield required by investors to 6.5% will cause the bond's price to decline from 100 to 94.4479, a 5.55% price decline. Similarly for a 6% 5-year bond selling to yield 6%, the price is 100. A rise in the yield required by investors from 6% to 6.5% would decrease the price to 97.8944. The decline in the bond's price is only 2.11%.

2.2.2 The Impact of Coupon Rate

A property of a bond is that all other factors constant, *the lower the coupon rate, the greater the bond's price sensitivity to changes in interest rates.* For example, consider a 9% 20-year bond selling to yield 6%. The price of this bond would be 134.6722. If the yield required by investors increases by 50 basis points to 6.5%, the price of this bond would fall by 5.13% to 127.7605. This decline is less than the 5.55% decline for the 6% 20-year bond selling to yield 6% discussed above.

An implication is that zero-coupon bonds have greater price sensitivity to interest rate changes than same-maturity bonds bearing a coupon rate and trading at the same yield.

2.2.3 The Impact of Embedded Options

In the reading on features of debt securities, we discussed the various embedded options that may be included in a bond issue. As we continue our study of fixed income analysis, we will see that the value of a bond with embedded options will change depending on how the value of the embedded options changes when interest

---

[4] Recall from the reading on features of debt securities that an embedded option is the feature in a bond issue that grants either the issuer or the investor an option. Examples include call option, put option, and conversion option.

rates change. For example, we will see that as interest rates decline, the price of a callable bond may not increase as much as an otherwise option-free bond (that is, a bond with no embedded options).

For now, to understand why, let's decompose the price of a callable bond into two components, as shown below:

Price of callable bond = Price of option-free bond − Price of embedded call option

The reason for subtracting the price of the embedded call option from the price of the option-free bond is that the call option is a benefit to the issuer and a disadvantage to the bondholder. This reduces the price of a callable bond relative to an option-free bond.

Now, when interest rates decline, the price of an option-free bond increases. However, the price of the embedded call option in a callable bond also increases because the call option becomes more valuable to the issuer. So, when interest rates decline both price components increase in value, *but* the change in the price of the callable bond depends on the relative price change between the two components. Typically, a decline in interest rates will result in an increase in the price of the callable bond but not by as much as the price change of an otherwise comparable option-free bond.

Similarly, when interest rates rise, the price of a callable bond will not fall as much as an otherwise option-free bond. The reason is that the price of the embedded call option declines. So, when interest rates rise, the price of the option-free bond declines, but this is partially offset by the decrease in the price of the embedded call option component.

Practice Question 2

All of the issues below are option-free bonds and the yield required by the market for each bond is the same. Which issue has the greatest interest rate risk and which has the least interest rate risk? (No calculations are required.)

Issue	Coupon Rate (%)	Maturity
1	$5\frac{1}{4}$	15 years
2	$6\frac{1}{2}$	12 years
3	$4\frac{3}{4}$	20 years
4	$8\frac{1}{2}$	10 years

2.3 The Impact of the Yield Level

Because of credit risk (discussed later), different bonds trade at different yields, even if they have the same coupon rate, maturity, and embedded options. How, then, holding other factors constant, does the level of interest rates affect a bond's price sensitivity to changes in interest rates? As it turns out, the higher a bond's yield, the lower the price sensitivity.

To see this, we compare a 6% 20-year bond initially selling at a yield of 6%, and a 6% 20-year bond initially selling at a yield of 10%. The former is initially at a price of 100, and the latter 65.68. Now, if the yield for both bonds increases by 100 basis points, the first bond trades down by 10.68 points (10.68%) to a price of 89.32. The second bond will trade down to a price of 59.88, for a price decline of only 5.80 points (or 8.83%). Thus, we see that the bond that trades at a lower yield is more volatile in both percentage price change and absolute price change, as long as the other bond characteristics are the same. An implication of this is that, for a given change in interest rates, price sensitivity is lower when the level of interest rates in the market is high, and price sensitivity is higher when the level of interest rates is low.

Practice Question 3

The following four issues are all option-free bonds; which has the greatest interest rate risk? (No calculations are required.)

Issue	Coupon Rate (%)	Maturity	Required Yield by the Market (%)
4	$6\frac{1}{2}$	12 years	7.00
5	$7\frac{1}{4}$	12 years	7.40
6	$6\frac{1}{2}$	12 years	7.20
7	$7\frac{1}{2}$	11 years	8.00

2.4 Interest Rate Risk for Floating-Rate Securities

The change in the price of a fixed-rate coupon bond when market interest rates change is due to the fact that the bond's coupon rate differs from the prevailing market interest rate. For a floating-rate security, the coupon rate is reset periodically based on the prevailing market interest rate used as the reference rate plus a quoted margin. The quoted margin is set for the life of the security. The price of a floating-rate security will fluctuate depending on three factors.

First, the longer the time to the next coupon reset date, the greater the potential price fluctuation.[5] For example, consider a floating-rate security whose coupon resets every six months and suppose the coupon formula is the 6-month Treasury rate plus 20 basis points. Suppose that on the coupon reset date the 6-month Treasury rate is 5.8%. If on the day after the coupon reset date, the 6-month Treasury rate rises to 6.1%, this security is paying a 6-month coupon rate that is less than the prevailing 6-month rate for the next six months. The price of the security must decline to reflect this lower coupon rate. Suppose instead that the coupon resets every month at the 1-month Treasury rate and that this rate rises immediately after the coupon rate is reset. In this case, while the investor would be realizing a submarket 1-month coupon rate, it is only for one month. The 1-month coupon bond's price decline will be less than the 6-month coupon bond's price decline.

The second reason why a floating-rate security's price will fluctuate is that the required margin that investors demand in the market changes. For example, consider once again the security whose coupon formula is the 6-month Treasury rate plus 20 basis points. If market conditions change such that investors want a margin of 30 basis points rather than 20 basis points, this security would be offering a coupon rate that is 10 basis points below the market rate. As a result, the security's price will decline.

Finally, a floating-rate security will typically have a cap. Once the coupon rate as specified by the coupon reset formula rises above the cap rate, the coupon will be set at the cap rate and the security will then offer a below-market coupon rate and its price will decline. In fact, once the cap is reached, the security's price will react much the same way to changes in market interest rates as that of a fixed-rate coupon security. This risk for a floating-rate security is called cap risk.

---

5 As explained in the reading on features of debt securities, the coupon reset formula is set at the reset date at the beginning of the period but is not paid until the end of the period.

Reading 22 ▪ Risk Associated with ...

Practice Question 4

A floating-rate issue of NotReal.com has the following coupon formula that is reset every six months:

Coupon rate = 6-month Treasury rate + 120 Basis points with a cap of 8.5%

A. Assume that subsequent to the issuance of this floater, the market wants a higher margin than 120 basis points for purchasing a similar issue to NotReal.com. What will happen to the price of this issue?

B. Assume that the 6-month Treasury rate was 4% when this issue was purchased by an investor but today the 6-month Treasury rate is 7%. What risk has increased since the time the NotReal.com issue was purchased?

2.5 Measuring Interest Rate Risk

Investors are interested in estimating the price sensitivity of a bond to changes in market interest rates. We will spend a good deal of time looking at how to quantify a bond's interest rate risk in the reading on the measurement of interest rate risk, as well as other readings. For now, let's see how we can get a rough idea of how to quantify the interest rate risk of a bond.

What we are interested in is a first approximation of how a bond's price will change when interest rates change. We can look at the price change in terms of 1) the percentage price change from the initial price or 2) the dollar price change from the initial price.

2.5.1 *Approximate Percentage Price Change*

The most straightforward way to calculate the percentage price change is to average the percentage price change resulting from an increase and a decrease in interest rates of the same number of basis points. For example, suppose that we are trying to estimate the sensitivity of the price of bond ABC that is currently selling for 90 to yield 6%. Now, suppose that interest rates increase by 25 basis points from 6% to 6.25%. The change in yield of 25 basis points is referred to as the "rate shock." The question is, how much will the price of bond ABC change due to this rate shock? To determine what the new price will be if the yield increases to 6.25%, *it is necessary to have a valuation model.* A valuation model provides an estimate of what the value of a bond will be for a given yield level. We will discuss the various models for valuing simple bonds and complex bonds with embedded options in later readings.

For now, we will assume that the valuation model tells us that the price of bond ABC will be 88 if the yield is 6.25%. This means that the price will decline by 2 points or 2.22% of the initial price of 90. If we divide the 2.22% by 25 basis points, the resulting number tells us that the price will decline by 0.0889% per 1 basis point change in yield.

Now suppose that the valuation model tells us that if yields decline from 6% to 5.75%, the price will increase to 92.7. This means that the price increases by 2.7 points or 3.00% of the initial price of 90. Dividing the 3.00% by 25 basis points indicates that the price will change by 0.1200% per 1 basis point change in yield.

We can average the two percentage price changes for a 1 basis point change in yield up and down. The average percentage price change is 0.1044% [=(0.0889% + 0.1200%)/2]. This means that for a 100 basis point change in yield, the average percentage price change is 10.44% (100 times 0.1044%).

A formula for estimating the *approximate percentage price change for a 100 basis point change in yield is*:

$$\frac{\text{Price if yields decline} - \text{Price if yields rise}}{2 \times (\text{Initial price}) \times (\text{Change in yield in decimal})}$$

In our illustration,

Price if yields decline by 25 basis points = 92.7

Price if yields rise by 25 basis points = 88.0

Initial price = 90

Change in yield in decimal = 0.0025

Substituting these values into the formula we obtain the approximate percentage price change for a 100 basis point change in yield to be:

$$\frac{92.7 - 88.0}{2 \times (90) \times (0.0025)} = 10.44$$

There is a special name given to this estimate of the percentage price change for a 100 basis point change in yield. It is called **duration**. As can be seen, duration is a measure of the price sensitivity of a bond to a change in yield. So, for example, if the duration of a bond is 10.44, this means that the approximate percentage price change if yields change by 100 basis points is 10.44%. For a 50 basis point change in yields, the approximate percentage price change is 5.22% (10.44% divided by 2). For a 25 basis point change in yield, the approximate percentage price change is 2.61% (10.44% divided by 4).

Notice that the approximate percentage is assumed to be the same for a rise and decline in yield. When we discuss the properties of the price volatility of a bond to changes in yield in the reading on the measurement of interest rate risk, we will see that the percentage price change is not symmetric, and we will discuss the implication for using duration as a measure of interest rate risk. *It is important to note that the computed duration of a bond is only as good as the valuation model used to get the prices when the yield is shocked up and down. If the valuation model is unreliable, then the duration is a poor measure of the bond's price sensitivity to changes in yield.*

2.5.2 Approximating the Dollar Price Change

It is simple to move from duration, which measures the approximate percentage price change, to the approximate dollar price change of a position in a bond given the market value of the position and its duration. For example, consider again bond ABC with a duration of 10.44. Suppose that the market value of this bond is $5 million. Then for a 100 basis point change in yield, the approximate dollar price change is equal to 10.44% times $5 million, or $522,000. For a 50 basis point change in yield, the approximate dollar price change is $261,000; for a 25 basis point change in yield the approximate dollar price change is $130,500.

The approximate dollar price change for a 100 basis point change in yield is sometimes referred to as the dollar duration.

Practice Question 5

A. A portfolio manager wants to estimate the interest rate risk of a bond using duration. The current price of the bond is 106. A valuation model employed by the manager found that if interest rates decline by 25 basis points, the price will increase to 108.5 and if interest rates increase by the same number of basis points, the price will decline to 104. What is the duration of this bond?

> **B.** If the portfolio manager purchased $10 million in market value of this bond, using duration to estimate the percentage price change, how much will the value of the bond change if interest rates change by 50 basis points?

YIELD CURVE RISK

3

We know that if interest rates or yields in the market change, the price of a bond will change. One of the factors that will affect how sensitive a bond's price is to changes in yield is the bond's maturity. A portfolio of bonds is a collection of bond issues typically with different maturities. So, when interest rates change, the price of each bond issue in the portfolio will change and the portfolio's value will change.

As you will see in the reading on understanding yield spreads, there is not one interest rate or yield in the economy. There is a structure of interest rates. One important structure is the relationship between yield and maturity. The graphical depiction of this relationship is called the yield curve. As we will see in the reading on understanding yield spreads, when interest rates change, they typically do not change by an equal number of basis points for all maturities.

For example, suppose that a $65 million portfolio contains the four bonds shown in Exhibit 1. All bonds are trading at a price equal to par value.

If we want to know how much the value of the portfolio changes if interest rates change, typically it is assumed that all yields change by the same number of basis points. Thus, if we wanted to know how sensitive the portfolio's value is to a 25 basis point change in yields, we would increase the yield of the four bond issues by 25 basis points, determine the new price of each bond, the market value of each bond, and the new value of the portfolio. Panel (a) of Exhibit 2 illustrates the 25 basis point increase in yield. For our hypothetical portfolio, the value of each bond issue changes as shown in panel (a) of Exhibit 1. The portfolio's value decreases by $1,759,003 from $65 million to $63,240,997.

Suppose that, instead of an equal basis point change in the yield for all maturities, the 20-year yield changes by 25 basis points, but the yields for the other maturities change as follows: 1) 2-year maturity changes by 10 basis points (from 5% to 5.1%), 2) 5-year maturity changes by 20 basis points (from 5.25% to 5.45%), and 3) 30-year maturity changes by 45 basis points (from 5.75% to 6.2%). Panel (b) of Exhibit 2 illustrates these yield changes. We will see at Level II that this type of movement (or shift) in the yield curve is referred to as a "steepening of the yield curve." For this type of yield curve shift, the portfolio's value is shown in panel (b) of Exhibit 1. The decline in the portfolio's value is $2,514,375 (from $65 million to $62,485,625).

Exhibit 1	Illustration of Yield Curve Risk Composition of the Portfolio			
Bond	**Coupon (%)**	**Maturity (Years)**	**Yield (%)**	**Par Value ($)**
A	5.00	2	5.00	5,000,000
B	5.25	5	5.25	10,000,000
C	5.50	20	5.50	20,000,000
D	5.75	30	5.75	30,000,000
Total				65,000,000

(continued)

Exhibit 1	Continued

A. Parallel Shift in Yield Curve of +25 Basis Points

Bond	Coupon (%)	Maturity (Years)	Original Yield (%)	Par Value ($)	New Yield (%)	New Bond Price	Value
A	5.00	2	5.00	5,000,000	5.25	99.5312	4,976,558
B	5.25	5	5.25	10,000,000	5.50	98.9200	9,891,999
C	5.50	20	5.50	20,000,000	5.75	97.0514	19,410,274
D	5.75	30	5.75	30,000,000	6.00	96.5406	28,962,166
Total				65,000,000			63,240,997

B. Nonparallel Shift of the Yield Curve

Bond	Coupon (%)	Maturity (Years)	Original Yield (%)	Par Value ($)	New Yield (%)	New Bond Price	Value
A	5.00	2	5.00	5,000,000	5.10	99.8121	4,990,606
B	5.25	5	5.25	10,000,000	5.45	99.1349	9,913,488
C	5.50	20	5.50	20,000,000	5.75	97.0514	19,410,274
D	5.75	30	5.75	30,000,000	6.20	93.9042	28,171,257
Total				65,000,000			62,485,625

C. Nonparallel Shift of the Yield Curve

Bond	Coupon (%)	Maturity (Years)	Original Yield (%)	Par Value ($)	New Yield (%)	New Bond Price	Value
A	5.00	2	5.00	5,000,000	5.05	99.9060	4,995,300
B	5.25	5	5.25	10,000,000	5.40	99.3503	9,935,033
C	5.50	20	5.50	20,000,000	5.75	97.0514	19,410,274
D	5.75	30	5.75	30,000,000	6.10	95.2082	28,562,467
Total				65,000,000			62,903,074

Suppose, instead, that if the 20-year yield changes by 25 basis points, the yields for the other three maturities change as follows: 1) 2-year maturity changes by 5 basis points (from 5% to 5.05%), 2) 5-year maturity changes by 15 basis points (from 5.25% to 5.40%), and 3) 30-year maturity changes by 35 basis points (from 5.75% to 6.1%). Panel (c) of Exhibit 2 illustrates this shift in yields. The new value for the portfolio based on this yield curve shift is shown in panel (c) of Exhibit 1. The decline in the portfolio's value is $2,096,926 (from $65 million to $62,903,074). The yield curve shift in the third illustration does not steepen as much as in the second, when the yield curve steepens considerably.

The point here is that portfolios have different exposures to how the yield curve shifts. This risk exposure is called yield curve risk. The implication is that any measure of interest rate risk that assumes that the interest rates change by an equal number of basis points for all maturities (referred to as a "parallel yield curve shift") is only an approximation.

Exhibit 2	Shifts of the Yield Curve

A. Parallel Shift in Yield Curve of +25 Basis Points

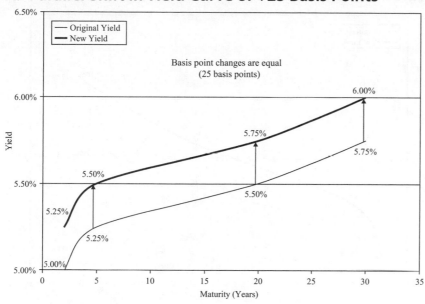

B. Nonparallel Shift of the Yield Curve

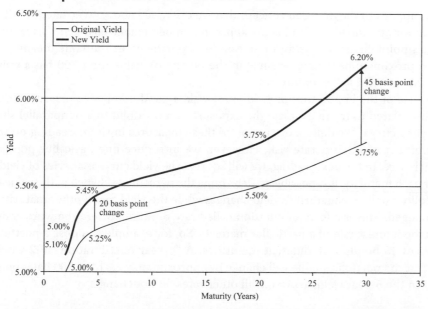

(continued)

Exhibit 2	Continued

C. Another Nonparallel Shift of the Yield Curve

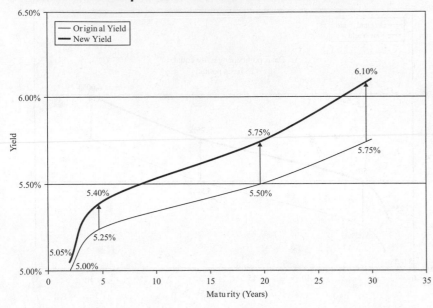

This applies to the duration concept that we discussed above. We stated that the duration for an individual bond is the approximate percentage change in price for a 100 basis point change in yield. A duration for a portfolio has the same meaning: it is the approximate percentage change in the portfolio's value for a 100 basis point change in the yield *for all maturities*.

Because of the importance of yield curve risk, a good number of measures have been formulated to try to estimate the exposure of a portfolio to a nonparallel shift in the yield curve. We defer a discussion of these measures until the reading on the measurement of interest rate risk. However, we introduce one basic but popular approach here. In the next reading, we will see that the yield curve is a series of yields, one for each maturity. It is possible to determine the percentage change in the value of a portfolio if only one maturity's yield changes while the yield for all other maturities is unchanged. This is a form of duration called rate duration, where the word "rate" means the interest rate of a particular maturity. So, for example, suppose a portfolio consists of 40 bonds with different maturities. A "5-year rate duration" of 2 would mean that the portfolio's value will change by approximately 2% for a 100 basis point change in the 5-year yield, assuming all other rates do not change.

Practice Question 6

Suppose that an $85 million portfolio consists of the following five issues:

Issue	Maturity	Market Value ($)
1	2 years	20 million
2	5 years	15 million
3	10 years	30 million
4	15 years	5 million
5	28 years	15 million

A. The portfolio manager computed a duration for the portfolio of 5. Approximately how much will the value of the portfolio decline if interest rates increase by 50 basis points?

B. In your calculation in part A, what is the assumption made in using the duration of 5 to compute the decline in the portfolio's value?

C. Suppose that the portfolio manager computes a 5-year rate duration of 1.5. What does that mean?

Consequently, in theory, there is not one rate duration but a rate duration for each maturity. In practice, a rate duration is not computed for all maturities. Instead, the rate duration is computed for several key maturities on the yield curve and this is referred to as key rate duration. Key rate duration is therefore simply the rate duration with respect to a change in a "key" maturity sector. Vendors of analytical systems report key rate durations for the maturities that in their view are the key maturity sectors. Key rate duration will be discussed further at Level II.

CALL AND PREPAYMENT RISK   4

As explained in the reading on features of debt securities, a bond may include a provision that allows the issuer to retire, or call, all or part of the issue before the maturity date. From the investor's perspective, there are three disadvantages to call provisions:

Disadvantage 1:   The cash flow pattern of a callable bond is not known with certainty because it is not known when the bond will be called.

Disadvantage 2:   Because the issuer is likely to call the bonds when interest rates have declined below the bond's coupon rate, the investor is exposed to reinvestment risk, i.e., the investor will have to reinvest the proceeds when the bond is called at interest rates lower than the bond's coupon rate.

Disadvantage 3:   The price appreciation potential of the bond will be reduced relative to an otherwise comparable option-free bond. (This is called price compression.)

We explained the third disadvantage in Section 2 when we discussed how the price of a callable bond may not rise as much as an otherwise comparable option-free bond when interest rates decline.

Because of these three disadvantages faced by the investor, a callable bond is said to expose the investor to call risk. The same disadvantages apply to mortgage-backed and asset-backed securities where the borrower can prepay principal prior to scheduled principal payment dates. This risk is referred to as prepayment risk.

REINVESTMENT RISK   5

Reinvestment risk is the risk that the proceeds received from the payment of interest and principal (i.e., scheduled payments, called proceeds, and principal prepayments) that are available for reinvestment must be reinvested at a lower interest rate than the security that generated the proceeds. We already saw how reinvestment risk is present when an investor purchases a callable or principal prepayable bond. When the issuer calls a bond, it is typically done to lower the issuer's interest expense because interest rates have declined after the bond is issued. The investor faces the problem of having to reinvest the called bond proceeds received from the issuer in a lower interest rate environment.

Reinvestment risk also occurs when an investor purchases a bond and relies on the yield of that bond as a measure of return. We have not yet explained how to compute the "yield" for a bond. When we do, it will be demonstrated that for the yield computed at the time of purchase to be realized, the investor must be able to reinvest any coupon payments at the computed yield. So, for example, if an investor purchases a 20-year bond with a yield of 6%, to realize the yield of 6%, every time a coupon interest payment is made, it is necessary to reinvest the payment at an interest rate of 6% until maturity. So, it is assumed that the first coupon payment can be reinvested for the next 19.5 years at 6%; the second coupon payment can be reinvested for the next 19 years at 6%, and so on. The risk that the coupon payments will be reinvested at less than 6% is also reinvestment risk.

When dealing with amortizing securities (i.e., securities that repay principal periodically), reinvestment risk is even greater. Typically, amortizing securities pay interest and principal monthly and permit the borrower to prepay principal prior to scheduled payment dates. Now the investor is more concerned with reinvestment risk due to principal prepayments usually resulting from a decline in interest rates, just as in the case of a callable bond. However, since payments are monthly, the investor has to make sure that the interest and principal can be reinvested at no less than the computed yield every month as opposed to semiannually.

This reinvestment risk for an amortizing security is important to understand. Too often it is said by some market participants that securities that pay both interest and principal monthly are advantageous because the investor has the opportunity to reinvest more frequently and to reinvest a larger amount (because principal is received) relative to a bond that pays only semiannual coupon payments. This is not the case in a declining interest rate environment, which will cause borrowers to accelerate their principal prepayments and force the investor to reinvest at lower interest rates.

With an understanding of reinvestment risk, we can now appreciate why zero-coupon bonds may be attractive to certain investors. Because there are no coupon payments to reinvest, there is no reinvestment risk. That is, zero-coupon bonds eliminate reinvestment risk. Elimination of reinvestment risk is important to some investors. That's the plus side of the risk equation. The minus side is that, as explained in Section 2, the lower the coupon rate the greater the interest rate risk for two bonds with the same maturity. Thus, zero-coupon bonds of a given maturity expose investors to the greatest interest rate risk.

Once we cover our basic analytical tools in later readings, we will see how to quantify a bond issue's reinvestment risk.

6   CREDIT RISK

An investor who lends funds by purchasing a bond issue is exposed to credit risk. There are three types of credit risk:

1. default risk
2. credit spread risk
3. downgrade risk

We discuss each type below.

6.1 Default Risk

Default risk is defined as the risk that the issuer will fail to satisfy the terms of the obligation with respect to the timely payment of interest and principal.

Studies have examined the probability of issuers defaulting. The percentage of a population of bonds that is expected to default is called the default rate. If a default occurs, this does not mean the investor loses the entire amount invested. An investor can expect to recover a certain percentage of the investment. This is called the recovery rate. Given the default rate and the recovery rate, the estimated expected loss due to a default can be computed. We will explain the findings of studies on default rates and recovery rates in the reading on bond sectors and instruments.

6.2 Credit Spread Risk

Even in the absence of default, an investor is concerned that the market value of a bond will decline and/or the price performance of a bond will be worse than that of other bonds. To understand this, recall that the price of a bond changes in the opposite direction to the change in the yield required by the market. Thus, if yields in the economy increase, the price of a bond declines, and vice versa.

As we will see in the reading on bond sectors and instruments, the yield on a bond is made up of two components: 1) the yield on a similar default-free bond issue and 2) a premium above the yield on a default-free bond issue necessary to compensate for the risks associated with the bond. The risk premium is referred to as a **yield spread**. In the United States, Treasury issues are the benchmark yields because they are believed to be default free, they are highly liquid, and they are not callable (with the exception of some old issues). The part of the risk premium or yield spread attributable to default risk is called the credit spread.

The price performance of a non-Treasury bond issue and the return over some time period will depend on how the credit spread changes. If the credit spread increases, investors say that the spread has "widened," and the market price of the bond issue will decline (assuming U.S. Treasury rates have not changed). The risk that an issuer's debt obligation will decline due to an increase in the credit spread is called credit spread risk.

This risk exists for an individual issue, for issues in a particular industry or economic sector, and for all non-Treasury issues in the economy. For example, in general during economic recessions, investors are concerned that issuers will face a decline in cash flows that would be used to service their bond obligations. As a result, the credit spread tends to widen for U.S. non-Treasury issuers, and the prices of all such issues throughout the economy will decline.

6.3 Downgrade Risk

While portfolio managers seek to allocate funds among different sectors of the bond market to capitalize on anticipated changes in credit spreads, an analyst investigating the credit quality of an individual issue is concerned with the prospects of the credit spread increasing for that particular issue. But how does the analyst assess whether he or she believes the market will change the credit spread associated with an individual issue?

One tool investors use to gauge the default risk of an issue is the credit ratings assigned to issues by rating companies, popularly referred to as rating agencies. There are three rating agencies in the United States: Moody's Investors Service, Inc., Standard & Poor's Corporation, and Fitch Ratings.

A credit rating is an indicator of the potential default risk associated with a particular bond issue or issuer. It represents in a simplistic way the credit rating agency's assessment of an issuer's ability to meet the payment of principal and interest in accordance with the terms of the indenture. Credit rating symbols or characters are uncomplicated representations of more complex ideas. In effect, they are summary opinions. Exhibit 3 identifies the ratings assigned by Moody's, S&P, and Fitch for bonds and the meaning of each rating.

In all systems, the term high grade means low credit risk, or conversely, a high probability of receiving future payments is promised by the issuer. The highest-grade bonds are designated by Moody's by the symbol Aaa, and by S&P and Fitch by the symbol AAA. The next highest grade is denoted by the symbol Aa (Moody's) or AA (S&P and Fitch); for the third grade, all three rating companies use A. The next three grades are Baa or BBB, Ba or BB, and B, respectively. There are also C grades. Moody's uses 1, 2, or 3 to provide a narrower credit quality breakdown within each class, and S&P and Fitch use plus and minus signs for the same purpose.

Bonds rated triple A (AAA or Aaa) are said to be prime grade; double A (AA or Aa) are of high quality grade; single A issues are called upper medium grade, and triple B are lower medium grade. Lower-rated bonds are said to have speculative grade elements or to be distinctly speculative grade.

Bond issues that are assigned a rating in the top four categories (that is, AAA, AA, A, and BBB) are referred to as investment-grade bonds. Issues that carry a rating below the top four categories are referred to as noninvestment-grade bonds or speculative bonds, or more popularly as high yield bonds or junk bonds. Thus, the bond market can be divided into two sectors: the investment grade and non-investment grade markets as summarized below:

Investment grade bonds	AAA, AA, A, and BBB
Non-investment grade bonds (speculative/high yield)	Below BBB

Once a credit rating is assigned to a debt obligation, a rating agency monitors the credit quality of the issuer and can reassign a different credit rating. An improvement in the credit quality of an issue or issuer is rewarded with a better credit rating, referred to as an upgrade; a deterioration in the credit rating of an issue or issuer is penalized by the assignment of an inferior credit rating, referred to as a downgrade. An unanticipated downgrading of an issue or issuer increases the credit spread and results in a decline in the price of the issue or the issuer's bonds. This risk is referred to as downgrade risk and is closely related to credit spread risk.

As we have explained, the credit rating is a measure of potential default risk. An analyst must be aware of how rating agencies gauge default risk for purposes of assigning ratings in order to understand the other aspects of credit risk. The agencies' assessment of potential default drives downgrade risk, and in turn, both default potential and credit rating changes drive credit spread risk.

A popular tool used by managers to gauge the prospects of an issue being downgraded or upgraded is a rating transition matrix. This is simply a table constructed by the rating agencies that shows the percentage of issues that were downgraded or upgraded in a given time period. So, the table can be used to approximate downgrade risk and default risk.

Exhibit 3	Bond Rating Symbols and Summary Description		
Moody's	**S&P**	**Fitch**	**Summary Description**
Investment Grade—High Credit-Worthiness			
Aaa	AAA	AAA	Gilt edge, prime, maximum safety
Aa1	AA+	AA+	
Aa2	AA	AA	High grade, high-credit quality
Aa3	AA−	AA−	

Exhibit 3	**Continued**		

Moody's	S&P	Fitch	Summary Description
A1	A+	A+	
A2	A	A	Upper medium grade
A3	A–	A–	
Baa1	BBB+	BBB+	
Baa2	BBB	BBB	Lower medium grade
Baa3	BBB–	BBB–	

Speculative—Lower Credit-Worthiness

Moody's	S&P	Fitch	Summary Description
Ba1	BB+	BB+	
Ba2	BB	BB	Low grade, speculative
Ba3	BB–	BB–	
B1		B+	
B2	B	B	Highly speculative
B3		B–	

Predominantly Speculative, Substantial Risk, or in Default

Moody's	S&P	Fitch	Summary Description
Caa	CCC+ CCC	CCC+ CCC	Substantial risk, in poor standing
Ca	CC	CC	May be in default, very speculative
C	C	C	Extremely speculative
	CI		Income bonds—no interest being paid
		DDD	
		DD	Default
	D	D	

Exhibit 4 shows a hypothetical rating transition matrix for a 1-year period. The first column shows the ratings at the start of the year and the top row shows the rating at the end of the year. Let's interpret one of the numbers. Look at the cell where the rating at the beginning of the year is AA and the rating at the end of the year is AA. This cell represents the percentage of issues rated AA at the beginning of the year that did not change their rating over the year. That is, there were no downgrades or upgrades. As can be seen, 92.75% of the issues rated AA at the start of the year were rated AA at the end of the year. Now look at the cell where the rating at the beginning of the year is AA and at the end of the year is A.

| Exhibit 4 | Hypothetical 1-Year Rating Transition Matrix |

Rating at Start of Year	Rating at End of Year								
	AAA	AA	A	BBB	BB	B	CCC	D	Total
AAA	93.20	6.00	0.60	0.12	0.08	0.00	0.00	0.00	100
AA	1.60	92.75	5.07	0.36	0.11	0.07	0.03	0.01	100
A	0.18	2.65	91.91	4.80	0.37	0.02	0.02	0.05	100
BBB	0.04	0.30	5.20	87.70	5.70	0.70	0.16	0.20	100
BB	0.03	0.11	0.61	6.80	81.65	7.10	2.60	1.10	100
B	0.01	0.09	0.55	0.88	7.90	75.67	8.70	6.20	100
CCC	0.00	0.01	0.31	0.84	2.30	8.10	62.54	25.90	100

This shows the percentage of issues rated AA at the beginning of the year that were downgraded to A by the end of the year. In our hypothetical 1-year rating transition matrix, this percentage is 5.07%. One can view these percentages as probabilities. There is a probability that an issue rated AA will be downgraded to A by the end of the year and it is 5.07%. One can estimate total downgrade risk as well. Look at the row that shows issues rated AA at the beginning of the year. The cells in the columns A, BBB, BB, B, CCC, and D all represent downgrades from AA. Thus, if we add all of these columns in this row (5.07%, 0.36%, 0.11%, 0.07%, 0.03%, and 0.01%), we get 5.65% which is an estimate of the probability of an issue being downgraded from AA in one year. Thus, 5.65% can be viewed as an estimate of downgrade risk.

A rating transition matrix also shows the potential for upgrades. Again, using Exhibit 4 look at the row that shows issues rated AA at the beginning of the year. Looking at the cell shown in the column AAA rating at the end of the year, one finds 1.60%. This is the percentage of issues rated AA at the beginning of the year that were upgraded to AAA by the end of the year.

Finally, look at the D rating category. These are issues that go into default. We can use the information in the column with the D rating at the end of the year to estimate the probability that an issue with a particular rating will go into default at the end of the year. Hence, this would be an estimate of default risk. So, for example, the probability that an issue rated AA at the beginning of the year will go into default by the end of the year is 0.01%. In contrast, the probability of an issue rated CCC at the beginning of the year will go into default by the end of the year is 25.9%.

7   LIQUIDITY RISK

When an investor wants to sell a bond prior to the maturity date, he or she is concerned with whether or not the bid price from broker/dealers is close to the indicated value of the issue. For example, if recent trades in the market for a particular issue have been between $90 and $90.5 and market conditions have not changed, an investor would expect to sell the bond somewhere in the $90 to $90.5 range.

Liquidity risk is the risk that the investor will have to sell a bond below its indicated value, where the indication is revealed by a recent transaction. The primary measure of liquidity is the size of the spread between the bid price (the price at which a dealer is willing to buy a security) and the ask price (the price at which a dealer is willing to sell a security). The wider the bid-ask spread, the greater the liquidity risk.

A liquid market can generally be defined by "small bid-ask spreads which do not materially increase for large transactions."[6] How to define the bid-ask spread in a multiple dealer market is subject to interpretation. For example, consider the bid-ask prices for four dealers. Each quote is for $92 plus the number of 32nds shown in Exhibit 5. The bid-ask spread shown in the exhibit is measured relative to a specific dealer. The best bid-ask spread is for $\frac{2}{32}$ Dealers 2 and 3.

From the perspective of the overall market, the bid-ask spread can be computed by looking at the best bid price (high price at which a broker/dealer is willing to buy a security) and the lowest ask price (lowest offer price at which a broker/dealer is willing to sell the same security). This liquidity measure is called the market bid-ask spread. For the four dealers, the highest bid price is $92\frac{2}{32}$ and the lowest ask price is $92\frac{3}{32}$. Thus, the market bid-ask spread is $\frac{1}{32}$.

Exhibit 5	Broker/Dealer Bid-Ask Spreads for a Specific Security

	Dealer			
	1	2	3	4
Bid price	1	1	2	2
Ask price	4	3	4	5

Bid-ask spread for each dealer (in 32nds):

	Dealer			
	1	2	3	4
Bid-ask spread	3	2	2	3

7.1 Liquidity Risk and Marking Positions to Market

For investors who plan to hold a bond until maturity and need *not* mark the position to market, liquidity risk is not a major concern. An institutional investor who plans to hold an issue to maturity but is periodically marked to market is concerned with liquidity risk. By marking a position to market, the security is revalued in the portfolio based on its current market price. For example, mutual funds are required to mark to market at the end of each day the investments in their portfolio in order to compute the mutual fund's net asset value (NAV). While other institutional investors may not mark to market as frequently as mutual funds, they are marked to market when reports are periodically sent to clients or the board of directors or trustees.

Where are the prices obtained to mark a position to market? Typically, a portfolio manager will solicit bids from several broker/dealers and then use some process to determine the bid price used to mark (i.e., value) the position. The less liquid the issue, the greater the variation there will be in the bid prices obtained from broker/dealers. With an issue that has little liquidity, the price may have to be determined from a pricing service (i.e., a service company that employs models to determine the fair value of a security) rather than from dealer bid prices.

In the reading on features of debt securities we discussed the use of repurchase agreements as a form of borrowing funds to purchase bonds. The bonds purchased are used as collateral. The bonds purchased are marked to market periodically in

6 Robert I. Gerber, "A User's Guide to Buy-Side Bond Trading," Chapter 16 in Frank J. Fabozzi (ed.), *Managing Fixed Income Portfolios* (New Hope, PA: Frank J. Fabozzi Associates, 1997), p. 278.

order to determine whether or not the collateral provides adequate protection to the lender for funds borrowed (i.e., the dealer providing the financing). When liquidity in the market declines, a portfolio manager who has borrowed funds must rely solely on the bid prices determined by the dealer lending the funds.

7.2 Changes in Liquidity Risk

Bid-ask spreads, and therefore liquidity risk, change over time. Changing market liquidity is a concern to portfolio managers who are contemplating investing in new complex bond structures. Situations such as an unexpected change in interest rates might cause a widening of the bid-ask spread, as investors and dealers are reluctant to take new positions until they have had a chance to assess the new market level of interest rates.

Here is another example of where market liquidity may change. While there are opportunities for those who invest in a new type of bond structure, there are typically few dealers making a market when the structure is so new. If subsequently the new structure becomes popular, more dealers will enter the market and liquidity improves. In contrast, if the new bond structure turns out to be unappealing, the initial buyers face a market with less liquidity because some dealers exit the market and others offer bids that are unattractive because they do not want to hold the bonds for a potential new purchaser.

Thus, we see that the liquidity risk of an issue changes over time. An actual example of a change in market liquidity occurred during the Spring of 1994. One sector of the mortgage-backed securities market, called the derivative mortgage market, saw the collapse of an important investor (a hedge fund) and the resulting exit from the market of several dealers. As a result, liquidity in the market substantially declined and bid-ask spreads widened dramatically.

8   EXCHANGE RATE OR CURRENCY RISK

A bond whose payments are not in the domestic currency of the portfolio manager has unknown cash flows in his or her domestic currency. The cash flows in the manager's domestic currency are dependent on the exchange rate at the time the payments are received from the issuer. For example, suppose a portfolio manager's domestic currency is the U.S. dollar and that manager purchases a bond whose payments are in Japanese yen. If the yen depreciates relative to the U.S. dollar at the time a payment is made, then fewer U.S. dollars can be exchanged.

As another example, consider a portfolio manager in the United Kingdom. This manager's domestic currency is the pound. If that manager purchases a U.S. dollar denominated bond, then the manager is concerned that the U.S. dollar will depreciate relative to the British pound when the issuer makes a payment. If the U.S. dollar does depreciate, then fewer British pounds will be received on the foreign exchange market.

The risk of receiving less of the domestic currency when investing in a bond issue that makes payments in a currency other than the manager's domestic currency is called exchange rate risk or currency risk.

9   INFLATION OR PURCHASING POWER RISK

Inflation risk or purchasing power risk arises from the decline in the value of a security's cash flows due to inflation, which is measured in terms of purchasing power. For example, if an investor purchases a bond with a coupon rate of 5%, but the inflation rate is 3%, the purchasing power of the investor has not increased by 5%. Instead, the investor's purchasing power has increased by only about 2%.

For all but inflation protection bonds, an investor is exposed to inflation risk because the interest rate the issuer promises to make is fixed for the life of the issue.

VOLATILITY RISK

10

In our discussion of the impact of embedded options on the interest rate risk of a bond in Section 2, we said that a change in the factors that affect the value of the embedded options will affect how the bond's price will change. Earlier, we looked at how a change in the level of interest rates will affect the price of a bond with an embedded option. But there are other factors that will affect the price of an embedded option.

While we discuss these other factors at Level II, we can get an appreciation of one important factor from a general understanding of option pricing. A major factor affecting the value of an option is "expected volatility." In the case of an option on common stock, expected volatility refers to "expected price volatility." The relationship is as follows: the greater the expected price volatility, the greater the value of the option. The same relationship holds for options on bonds. However, instead of expected price volatility, for bonds it is the "expected yield volatility." The greater the expected yield volatility, the greater the value (price) of an option. The interpretation of yield volatility and how it is estimated are explained at Level II.

Now let us tie this into the pricing of a callable bond. We repeat the formula for the components of a callable bond below:

Price of callable bond = Price of option-free bond − Price of embedded call option

If expected yield volatility increases, holding all other factors constant, the price of the embedded call option will increase. As a result, the price of a callable bond will decrease (because the former is subtracted from the price of the option-free bond).

To see how a change in expected yield volatility affects the price of a putable bond, we can write the price of a putable bond as follows:

Price of putable bond = Price of option-free bond + Price of embedded put option

A decrease in expected yield volatility reduces the price of the embedded put option and therefore will decrease the price of a putable bond. Thus, the volatility risk of a putable bond is that expected yield volatility will decrease.

This risk that the price of a bond with an embedded option will decline when expected yield volatility changes is called volatility risk. Below is a summary of the effect of changes in expected yield volatility on the price of callable and putable bonds:

Type of Embedded Option	Volatility Risk Due to
Callable bonds	An increase in expected yield volatility
Putable bonds	A decrease in expected yield volatility

EVENT RISK

11

Occasionally the ability of an issuer to make interest and principal payments changes dramatically and unexpectedly because of factors including the following:

1. a natural disaster (such as an earthquake or hurricane) or an industrial accident that impairs an issuer's ability to meet its obligations

2. a takeover or corporate restructuring that impairs an issuer's ability to meet its obligations

3. a regulatory change

These factors are commonly referred to as event risk.

11.1 Corporate Takeover/Restructurings

The first type of event risk results in a credit rating downgrade of an issuer by rating agencies and is therefore a form of downgrade risk. However, downgrade risk is typically confined to the particular issuer whereas event risk from a natural disaster usually affects more than one issuer.

The second type of event risk also results in a downgrade and can also impact other issuers. An excellent example occurred in the fall of 1988 with the leveraged buyout (LBO) of RJR Nabisco, Inc. The entire industrial sector of the bond market suffered as bond market participants withdrew from the market, new issues were postponed, and secondary market activity came to a standstill as a result of the initial LBO bid announcement. The yield that investors wanted on Nabisco's bonds increased by about 250 basis points. Moreover, because the RJR LBO demonstrated that size was not an obstacle for an LBO, other large industrial firms that market participants previously thought were unlikely candidates for an LBO were fair game. The spillover effect to other industrial companies of the RJR LBO resulted in required yields increasing dramatically.

11.2 Regulatory Risk

The third type of risk listed above is **regulatory risk**. This risk comes in a variety of forms. Regulated entities include investment companies, depository institutions, and insurance companies. Pension funds are regulated by ERISA. Regulation of these entities is in terms of the acceptable securities in which they may invest and/or the treatment of the securities for regulatory accounting purposes.

Changes in regulations may require a regulated entity to divest itself from certain types of investments. A flood of the divested securities on the market will adversely impact the price of similar securities.

12 SOVEREIGN RISK

When an investor acquires a bond issued by a foreign entity (e.g., a French investor acquiring a Brazilian government bond), the investor faces sovereign risk. This is the risk that, as a result of actions of the foreign government, there may be either a default or an adverse price change even in the absence of a default. This is analogous to the forms of credit risk described in Section 6—credit risk spread and downgrade risk. That is, even if a foreign government does not default, actions by a foreign government can increase the credit risk spread sought by investors or increase the likelihood of a downgrade. Both of these will have an adverse impact on a bond's price.

Sovereign risk consists of two parts. First is the unwillingness of a foreign government to pay. A foreign government may simply repudiate its debt. The second is the inability to pay due to unfavorable economic conditions in the country. Historically, most foreign government defaults have been due to a government's inability to pay rather than unwillingness to pay.

SOLUTIONS FOR PRACTICE QUESTIONS

1. **A.** The price for Issue A should be a premium since the coupon rate is greater than the yield required by the market. So, there is no error for Issue A.

   B. The price for Issue B should be a discount since the coupon rate is less than the yield required by the market. So, there is no error for Issue B.

   C. Issue C's coupon rate (0%) is less than the yield required by the market (5%). So, Issue C should be selling at a discount but the reported price is above par value. Hence, the reported price for Issue C is wrong.

   D. Issue D's coupon rate (5.5%) is less than the yield required by the market (5.9%). So, Issue D should be selling at a discount but the reported price is above par value. Hence, the reported price for Issue D is wrong.

   E. The price for Issue E should be par value since the coupon rate is equal to the yield required by the market. So, there is no error for Issue E.

   F. Issue F's coupon rate (4½%) is greater than the yield required by the market (4.0%). So, Issue F should be selling at a premium but the reported price is below par value. Hence, the reported price for Issue F is wrong.

   G. The coupon rate for Issue G and the yield required by the market are equal. So, the price should be par value. Since the reported price is above par value, Issue G's reported price is wrong.

2. Interest rate risk is the exposure of an issue to a change in the yield required by the market or to a change in interest rates. For option-free bonds selling at the same yield, maturity and coupon rate determine the interest rate risk of an issue. Since Issue 3 has both the longest maturity and the lowest coupon, it will have the greatest price sensitivity to changes in interest rates. The issue with the least interest rate risk is Issue 4 since it has the shortest maturity and the highest coupon rate.

3. Issues 5 and 7 have a higher coupon rate and a maturity less than or equal to Issues 4 and 6 and are trading at a higher yield. Thus, Issues 5 and 7 must have less interest rate risk. Issues 4 and 6 have the same maturity and coupon rate. However, Issue 4 is trading at a lower yield relative to issue 6 (7.00% versus 7.20%). Consequently, Issue 4 has the greatest interest rate risk.

4. **A.** If the market wants a higher margin than 120 basis points for similar issues to NotReal.com after issuance, the price will decline because the quoted margin for the issue (120 basis points) is a below-market margin. Even when the coupon rate is reset it will be less than the market required rate for similar issues.

   B. At the time NotReal.com was purchased by an investor, the coupon rate based on the 6-month Treasury rate of 4% was 5.2% (4% plus 120 basis points) considerably below the cap of 8.5%. With the assumed 6-month Treasury rate at 7.0%, the coupon rate is 8.2% (7% plus 120 basis points). Obviously, this is much closer to the cap of 8.5%. While cap risk was present at the time of purchase of this issue, the cap risk was low. With the rise in the 6-month Treasury rate to 7%, cap risk is considerably greater.

5. **A.** In our illustration,

   Price if yields decline by 25 basis points = 108.50

   Price if yields rise by 25 basis points = 104.00

   Initial price = 106.00

Change in yield in decimal = 0.0025

$$\text{Duration} = \frac{108.50 - 104.00}{2(106.00)(0.0025)} = 8.49$$

B. For a 100 basis point change and a duration of 8.49, the price will change by approximately 8.49%. For a 50 basis point change it would change by approximately 4.245%. Since the current market value is $10 million, the market value will change by approximately $10 million times 4.245% or $424,500.

6. A. The portfolio will change by approximately 5% for a 100 basis point change in interest rates and 2.5% for a 50 basis point change. Since the current market value is $85 million, the portfolio's value will change by approximately 2.5% times $85 million, or $2,125,000.

B. The five bonds in the portfolio have different maturities, ranging from 2 years to 28 years. The assumption when using duration is that if interest rates change, the interest rate for all the maturities changes by the same number of basis points.

C. A 5-year rate duration of 1.5 means that if all other key rates are unchanged but the 5-year rate increases by 100 basis points, the value of the portfolio will change by approximately 1.5%.

SUMMARY

- The price of a bond changes inversely with a change in market interest rates.
- Interest rate risk refers to the adverse price movement of a bond as a result of a change in market interest rates; for the bond investor typically it is the risk that interest rates will rise.
- A bond's interest rate risk depends on the features of the bond—maturity, coupon rate, yield, and embedded options.
- All other factors constant, the longer the bond's maturity, the greater is the bond's price sensitivity to changes in interest rates.
- All other factors constant, the lower the coupon rate, the greater the bond's price sensitivity to changes in interest rates.
- The price of a callable bond is equal to the price of an option-free bond minus the price of any embedded call option.
- When interest rates rise, the price of a callable bond will not fall by as much as an otherwise comparable option-free bond because the price of the embedded call option decreases.
- The price of a putable bond is equal to the price of an option-free bond plus the price of the embedded put option.
- All other factors constant, the higher the level of interest rate at which a bond trades, the lower is the price sensitivity when interest rates change.
- The price sensitivity of a bond to changes in interest rates can be measured in terms of 1) the percentage price change from initial price or 2) the dollar price change from initial price.
- The most straightforward way to calculate the percentage price change is to average the percentage price change due to the same increase and decrease in interest rates.

- Duration is a measure of interest rate risk; it measures the price sensitivity of a bond to interest rate changes.

- Duration can be interpreted as the approximate percentage price change of a bond for a 100 basis point change in interest rates.

- The computed duration is only as good as the valuation model used to obtain the prices when interest rates are shocked up and down by the same number of basis points.

- There can be substantial differences in the duration of complex bonds because valuation models used to obtain prices can vary.

- Given the duration of a bond and its market value, the dollar price change can be computed for a given change in interest rates.

- Yield curve risk for a portfolio occurs when, if interest rates increase by different amounts at different maturities, the portfolio's value will be different than if interest rates had increased by the same amount.

- A portfolio's duration measures the sensitivity of the portfolio's value to changes in interest rates assuming the interest rates for all maturities change by the same amount.

- Any measure of interest rate risk that assumes interest rates change by the same amount for all maturities (referred to as a "parallel yield curve shift") is only an approximation.

- One measure of yield curve risk is rate duration, which is the approximate percentage price change for a 100 basis point change in the interest rate for one maturity, holding all other maturity interest rates constant.

- Call risk and prepayment risk refer to the risk that a security will be paid prior to the scheduled principal payment dates.

- Reinvestment risk is the risk that interest and principal payments (scheduled payments, called proceeds, or prepayments) available for reinvestment must be reinvested at a lower interest rate than the security that generated the proceeds.

- From an investor's perspective, the disadvantages to call and prepayment provisions are 1) the cash flow pattern is uncertain, 2) reinvestment risk increases because proceeds received will have to be reinvested at a relatively lower interest rate, and 3) the capital appreciation potential of a bond is reduced.

- Reinvestment risk for an amortizing security can be significant because of the right to prepay principal and the fact that interest and principal are repaid monthly.

- A zero-coupon bond has no reinvestment risk but has greater interest rate risk than a coupon bond of the same maturity.

- There are three forms of credit risk: default risk, credit spread risk, and downgrade risk.

- Default risk is the risk that the issuer will fail to satisfy the terms of indebtedness with respect to the timely payment of interest and principal.

- Credit spread risk is the risk that the price of an issuer's bond will decline due to an increase in the credit spread.

- Downgrade risk is the risk that one or more of the rating agencies will reduce the credit rating of an issue or issuer.

- There are three rating agencies in the United States: Standard & Poor's Corporation, Moody's Investors Service, Inc., and Fitch.

- A credit rating is an indicator of the potential default risk associated with a particular bond issue that represents in a simplistic way the credit rater's assessment of an issuer's ability to pay principal and interest in accordance with the terms of the debt contract.

- A rating transition matrix is prepared by rating agencies to show the change in credit ratings over some time period.

- A rating transition matrix can be used to estimate downgrade risk and default risk.

- Liquidity risk is the risk that the investor will have to sell a bond below its indicated value.

- The primary measure of liquidity is the size of the spread between the bid and ask price quoted by dealers.

- A market bid-ask spread is the difference between the highest bid price and the lowest ask price from among dealers.

- The liquidity risk of an issue changes over time.

- Exchange rate risk arises when interest and principal payments of a bond are not denominated in the domestic currency of the investor.

- Exchange rate risk is the risk that the currency in which the interest and principal payments are denominated will decline relative to the domestic currency of the investor.

- Inflation risk or purchasing power risk arises from the decline in value of a security's cash flows due to inflation, which is measured in terms of purchasing power.

- Volatility risk is the risk that the price of a bond with an embedded option will decline when expected yield volatility changes.

- For a callable bond, volatility risk is the risk that expected yield volatility will increase; for a putable bond, volatility risk is the risk that expected yield volatility will decrease.

- Event risk is the risk that the ability of an issuer to make interest and principal payments changes dramatically and unexpectedly because of certain events such as a natural catastrophe, corporate takeover, or regulatory changes.

- Sovereign risk is the risk that a foreign government's actions cause a default or an adverse price decline on its bond issue.

PRACTICE PROBLEMS FOR READING 53

1. For each of the following issues, indicate whether the price of the issue should be par value, above par value, or below par value:

Issue	Coupon Rate (%)	Yield Required by Market (%)
A	A	5¼	7.25
B	B	6⅝	7.15
C	C	0	6.20
D	D	5⅞	5.00
E	E	4½	4.50

2. Explain why a callable bond's price would be expected to decline less than an otherwise comparable option-free bond when interest rates rise.

3. **A.** Short-term investors such as money market mutual funds invest in floating-rate securities having maturities greater than 1 year. Suppose that the coupon rate is reset everyday. Why is the interest rate risk small for such issues?

   B. Why would it be improper to say that a floating-rate security whose coupon rate resets every day has no interest rate risk?

4. John Smith and Jane Brody are assistant portfolio managers. The senior portfolio manager has asked them to consider the acquisition of one of two option-free bond issues with the following characteristics:

   Issue 1 has a lower coupon rate than Issue 2

   Issue 1 has a shorter maturity than Issue 2

   Both issues have the same credit rating.

   Smith and Brody are discussing the interest rate risk of the two issues. Smith argues that Issue 1 has greater interest rate risk than Issue 2 because of its lower coupon rate. Brody counters by arguing that Issue 2 has greater interest rate risk because it has a longer maturity than Issue 1.

   A. Which assistant portfolio manager is correct with respect to their selection to the issue with the greater interest rate risk?

   B. Suppose that you are the senior portfolio manager. How would you suggest that Smith and Brody determine which issue has the greater interest rate risk?

5. A portfolio manager wants to estimate the interest rate risk of a bond using duration. The current price of the bond is 82. A valuation model found that if interest rates decline by 30 basis points, the price will increase to 83.50 and if interest rates increase by 30 basis points, the price will decline to 80.75. What is the duration of this bond?

6. A portfolio manager purchased $8 million in market value of a bond with a duration of 5. For this bond, determine the estimated change in its market value for the change in interest rates shown below:

   A. 100 basis points.

   B. 50 basis points.

   C. 25 basis points.

   D. 10 basis points.

7. A portfolio manager of a bond fund is considering the acquisition of an extremely complex bond issue. It is complex because it has multiple embedded options. The manager wants to estimate the interest rate risk of the bond issue so that he can determine the impact of including it in his current portfolio. The portfolio manager contacts the dealer who created the bond issue to obtain an estimate for the issue's duration. The dealer estimates the duration to be 7. The portfolio manager solicited his firm's in-house quantitative analyst and asked her to estimate the issue's duration. She estimated the duration to be 10. Explain why there is such a dramatic difference in the issue's duration as estimated by the dealer's analysts and the firm's in-house analyst.

8. Duration is commonly used as a measure of interest rate risk. However, duration does not consider yield curve risk. Why?

9. What measure can a portfolio manager use to assess the interest rate risk of a portfolio to a change in the 5-year yield?

10. For the investor in a callable bond, what are the two forms of reinvestment risk?

11. Investors are exposed to credit risk when they purchase a bond. However, even if an issuer does not default on its obligation prior to its maturity date, there is still a concern about how credit risk can adversely impact the performance of a bond. Why?

12. Using the hypothetical rating transition matrix shown in Exhibit 4 of the reading, answer the following questions:

    A. What is the probability that a bond rated BBB will be downgraded?

    B. What is the probability that a bond rated BBB will go into default?

    C. What is the probability that a bond rated BBB will be upgraded?

    D. What is the probability that a bond rated B will be upgraded to investment grade?

    E. What is the probability that a bond rated A will be downgraded to noninvestment grade?

    F. What is the probability that a AAA rated bond will *not* be downgraded at the end of one year?

13. Suppose that the bid and ask prices of five dealers for Issue XYX is 96 plus the number of 32nds shown:

	Dealer				
	1	2	3	4	5
Bid price	14	14	15	15	13
Ask price	18	17	18	20	19

    What is the market bid-ask spread for Issue XYX?

14. A portfolio manager is considering the purchase of a new type of bond. The bond is extremely complex in terms of its embedded options. Currently, there is only one dealer making a market in this type of bond. In addition, the manager plans to finance the purchase of this bond by using the bond as collateral. The bond matures in five years and the manager plans to hold the bond for five years. Because the manager plans to hold the bond to its maturity, he has indicated that he is not concerned with liquidity risk. Explain why you agree or disagree with the manager's view that he is not concerned with liquidity risk.

15. Identify the difference in the major risks associated with the following investment alternatives:

A. For an investor who plans to hold a security for one year, purchasing a Treasury security that matures in one year versus purchasing a Treasury security that matures in 30 years.

B. For an investor who plans to hold an investment for 10 years, purchasing a Treasury security that matures in 10 years versus purchasing an AAA corporate security that matures in 10 years.

C. For an investor who plans to hold an investment for two years, purchasing a zero-coupon Treasury security that matures in one year versus purchasing a zero-coupon Treasury security that matures in two years.

D. For an investor who plans to hold an investment for five years, purchasing an AA sovereign bond (with dollar denominated cash flow payments) versus purchasing a U.S. corporate bond with a B rating.

E. For an investor who plans to hold an investment for four years, purchasing a less actively traded 10-year AA rated bond versus purchasing a 10-year AA rated bond that is actively traded.

F. For a U.S. investor who plans to hold an investment for six years, purchasing a Treasury security that matures in six years versus purchasing an Italian government security that matures in six years and is denominated in lira.

16. Sam Stevens is the trustee for the Hole Punchers Labor Union (HPLU). He has approached the investment management firm of IM Associates (IMA) to manage its $200 million bond portfolio. IMA assigned Carol Peters as the portfolio manager for the HPLU account. In their first meeting, Mr. Stevens told Ms. Peters:

> "We are an extremely conservative pension fund. We believe in investing in only investment grade bonds so that there will be minimal risk that the principal invested will be lost. We want at least 40% of the portfolio to be held in bonds that will mature within the next three years. I would like your thoughts on this proposed structure for the portfolio."

How should Ms. Peters respond?

17. **A.** A treasurer of a municipality with a municipal pension fund has required that its in-house portfolio manager invest all funds in the highest investment grade securities that mature in one month or less. The treasurer believes that this is a safe policy. Comment on this investment policy.

B. The same treasurer requires that the in-house portfolio municipality's operating fund (i.e., fund needed for day-to-day operations of the municipality) follow the same investment policy. Comment on the appropriateness of this investment policy for managing the municipality's operating fund.

18. In January 1994, General Electric Capital Corporation (GECC) had outstanding $500 million of Reset Notes due March 15, 2018. The reset notes were floating-rate securities. In January 1994, the bonds had an 8% coupon rate for three years that ended March 15, 1997. On January 26, 1994, GECC notified the noteholders that it would redeem the issue on March 15th at par value. This was within the required 30 to 60 day prior notice period. Investors who sought investments with very short-term instruments (e.g., money market investors) bought the notes after GECC's planned redemption announcement. The notes were viewed as short-term because they would be redeemed in six weeks or so. In early February, the Federal Reserve started to boost interest rates and on February 15th, GECC canceled the proposed redemption. Instead, it decided to reset the new interest rate based on the indenture at 108% of the

three-year Treasury rate in effect on the tenth day preceding the date of the new interest period of March 15th. The *Wall Street Journal* reported that the notes dropped from par to 98 ($1,000 to $980 per note) after the cancellation of the proposed redemption.[1]

Why did the price decline?

19. A British portfolio manager is considering investing in Japanese government bonds denominated in yen. What are the major risks associated with this investment?

20. Explain how certain types of event risk can result in downgrade risk.

21. Comment on the following statement: "Sovereign risk is the risk that a foreign government defaults on its obligation."

22. All else equal, will an increase in expected yield volatility increase the price of a bond with an embedded:

	call option?	put option?
A.	No	No
B.	No	Yes
C.	Yes	No

23. An analyst stated that a callable bond has less reinvestment risk and more price appreciation potential than an otherwise identical option-free bond. The analyst's statement *most likely* is:

    A. incorrect with respect to both reinvestment risk and price appreciation potential.

    B. incorrect with respect to reinvestment risk, but correct with respect to price appreciation potential.

    C. correct with respect to reinvestment risk, but incorrect with respect to price appreciation potential.

24. An analyst stated that an amortizing security typically has more reinvestment risk and more interest rate risk than an otherwise identical zero-coupon bond. The analyst's statement *most likely* is:

    A. correct with respect to both reinvestment risk and interest rate risk.

    B. incorrect with respect to reinvestment risk, but correct with respect to interest rate risk.

    C. correct with respect to reinvestment risk, but incorrect with respect to interest rate risk.

25. An analyst made the following statement: "We expect interest rates to be very volatile for the foreseeable future. I think we should buy floating-rate securities because they have less interest rate risk than fixed-rate securities and the price will always reset to par value." Is the analyst's statement *most likely* correct with respect to:

	relative interest rate risk?	price reset?
A.	No	No
B.	No	Yes
C.	Yes	No

---

1 To complete this story, investors were infuriated and they protested to GECC. On March 8th the new interest rate of 5.61% was announced in the financial press. On the very next day GECC announced a tender offer for the notes commencing March 17th. It would buy them back at par plus accrued interest on April 15th. This bailed out many investors who had faith in GECC's original redemption announcement.

26. Changes in the *slope* of the yield curve:

    A. have little effect on the value of a well-diversified portfolio of bonds.

    B. highlight the need for risk measures such as rate duration and key rate duration.

    C. impact the value of floating-rate securities more than they impact the value of fixed-coupon securities.

27. Consider the following statements about credit risk and liquidity risk:

    Statement 1   "Investment-grade bonds include bonds rated BBB (by S&P) or Baa (by Moody's) or higher."

    Statement 2   "Bonds financed by repurchase agreements have less liquidity risk than bonds held as part of a 'buy-and-hold' strategy."

    Are the statements *most likely* correct or incorrect?

    A. Neither statement is correct.

    B. Statement 1 is incorrect, but Statement 2 is correct.

    C. Statement 1 is correct, but Statement 2 is incorrect.

28. A bond portfolio manager gathered the following information about a bond issue:

Par value	$10,000,000
Current market value	$9,850,000
Duration	4.8

    If yields are expected to decline by 75 basis points, which of the following would provide the *most* appropriate estimate of the price change for the bond issue?

    A. 3.6% of $9,850,000.

    B. 3.6% of $10,000,000.

    C. 4.8% of $9,850,000.

SOLUTIONS FOR READING 53

1. **A.** Below par value since the coupon rate is less than the yield required by the market.

   B. Below par value since the coupon rate is less than the yield required by the market.

   C. Below par value since the coupon rate is less than the yield required by the market.

   D. Above par value since the coupon rate is greater than the yield required by the market.

   E. Par value since the coupon rate is equal to the yield required by the market.

	Issue	Coupon Rate (%)	Yield Required by the Market (%)	Price
A	A	5¼	7.25	Below par
B	B	6⅝	7.15	Below par
C	C	0	6.20	Below par
D	D	5⅞	5.00	Above par
E	E	4½	4.50	Par

2. The price of a callable bond can be expressed as follows:

   Price of callable bond = Price of option-free bond

   − Price of embedded call option

   An increase in interest rates will reduce the price of the option-free bond. However, to partially offset that price decline of the option-free bond, the price of the embedded call option will decrease. This is because as interest rates rise the value of the embedded call option to the issuer is worth less. Since a lower price for the embedded call option is subtracted from the lower price of the option-free bond, the price of the callable bond does not fall as much as that of an option-free bond.

3. **A.** A floating-rate security's exposure to interest rate risk is affected by the time to the next reset date. The shorter the time, the less likely the issue will offer a below-market interest rate until the next reset date. So, a daily reset will not expose the investor of this floater to interest rate risk due to this factor. However, there is interest rate risk, which we will see in part B.

   B. The reason there is still interest rate risk with a daily reset floating-rate security is that the margin required by the market may change. And, if there is a cap on the floater, there is cap risk.

4. **A.** While both assistant portfolio managers are correct in that they have identified two features of an issue that will impact interest rate risk, it is the interaction of the two that will affect an issue's interest rate risk. From the information provided in the question, it cannot be determined which has the greater interest rate risk.

   B. You, as the senior portfolio manager, might want to suggest that the two assistant portfolio managers compute the duration of the two issues.

5. The information for computing duration:

   Price if yields decline by 30 basis points = 83.50

   Price if yields rise by 30 basis points = 80.75

Initial price = 82.00

Change in yield in decimal = 0.0030

Then,

$$\text{Duration} = \frac{83.50 - 80.75}{2(82.00)(0.0030)} = 5.59$$

6. Since the duration is the approximate percentage price change for a 100 basis point change in interest rates, a bond with a duration of 5 will change by approximately 5% for a 100 basis point change in interest rates. Since the market value of the bond is $8 million, the change in the market value for a 100 basis point change in interest rates is found by multiplying 5% by $8 million. Therefore, the change in market value per 100 basis point change in interest rates is $400,000. To get an estimate of the change in the market value for any other change in interest rates, it is only necessary to scale the change in market value accordingly.

    A. For 100 basis points = $400,000.

    B. For 50 basis points = $200,000 (=$400,000/2).

    C. For 25 basis points = $100,000 ($400,000/4).

    D. For 10 basis points = $40,000 ($400,000/10).

7. To calculate duration, the price must be estimated for an increase and decrease (i.e., a rate shock) of the same number of basis points. A valuation model must be employed to obtain the two prices. With an extremely complex bond issue, the valuation models by different analysts can produce substantially different prices when rates are shocked. This will result in differences in estimates of duration.

8. For an individual bond, duration is an estimate of the price sensitivity of a bond to changes in interest rates. A portfolio duration can be estimated from the duration of the individual bond holdings in the portfolio. To use the portfolio's duration as an estimate of interest rate risk it is assumed that when interest rates change, the interest rate for all maturities change by the same number of basis points. That is, it does not consider non-parallel changes of the yield curve.

9. The approach briefly discussed in this reading for doing so is *rate duration*. Specifically, the 5-year rate duration indicates the approximate percentage change in the value of the portfolio if the yield on all maturities are unchanged but the yield for the 5-year maturity changes by 100 basis points.

10. The first form of reinvestment risk is due to the likelihood the proceeds from the called issue will be reinvested at a lower interest rate. The second form of reinvestment risk is the typical risk faced by an investor when purchasing a bond with a coupon. It is necessary to reinvest all the coupon payments at the computed yield in order to realize the yield at the time the bond is purchased.

11. Credit risk includes default risk, credit spread risk, and downgrade risk. While an investor holds a bond in his or her portfolio, if the issuer does not default there is still 1) the risk that credit spreads in the market will increase (credit spread risk) causing the price of the bond to decline and 2) the risk that the issue will be downgraded by the rating agencies causing the price to decline or not perform as well as other issues (downgrade risk).

12. A. The probability that a bond rated BBB will be downgraded is equal to the sum of the probabilities of a downgrade to BB, B, CCC or D. From the corresponding cells in the exhibit: 5.70% + 0.70% + 0.16% + 0.20% = 6.76%. Therefore, the probability of a downgrade is 6.76%.

    B. The probability that a bond rated BBB will go into default is the probability that it will fall into the D rating. From the exhibit we see that the probability is 0.20%.

C. The probability that a bond rated BBB will be upgraded is equal to the sum of the probabilities of an upgrade to AAA, AA, or A. From the corresponding cells in the exhibit: 0.04% + 0.30% + 5.20% = 5.54%. Therefore, the probability of an upgrade is 5.54%.

D. The probability that a bond rated B will be upgraded to investment grade is the sum of the probabilities that the bond will be rated AAA, AA, A or BBB at the end of the year. (Remember that the first four rating categories are investment grade.) From the exhibit: 0.01% + 0.09% + 0.55% + 0.88% = 1.53%. Therefore, the probability that a bond rated B will be upgraded to investment grade is 1.53%.

E. The probability that a bond rated A will be downgraded to noninvestment grade is the sum of the probabilities that the bond will be downgraded to below BBB. From the exhibit: 0.37% + 0.02% + 0.02% + 0.05% = 0.46%, therefore, the probability that a bond rated A will be downgraded to noninvestment grade is 0.46%.

F. The probability that a bond rated AAA will not be downgraded is 93.2%.

13. The market bid–ask spread is the difference between the highest bid price and the lowest ask price. Dealers 3 and 4 have the best bid price ($96^{15}\!/\!_{32}$). Dealer 2 has the lowest ask price ($96^{17}\!/\!_{32}$). The market bid–ask spread is therefore $^{2}\!/\!_{32}$.

14. If this manager's portfolio is marked-to-market, the manager must be concerned with the bid prices provided to mark the position to market. With only one dealer, there is concern that if this dealer decides to discontinue making a market in this issue, bids must be obtained from a different source. Finally, this manager intends to finance the purchase. The lender of the funds (the dealer financing the purchase) will mark the position to market based on the price it determines and this price will reflect the liquidity risk. Consequently, this manager should be concerned with the liquidity risk even if the manager intends to hold the security to the maturity date.

15. A. The purchase of a 30-year Treasury exposes the investor to interest rate risk since at the end of one year, the security is a 29-year instrument. Its price at the end of one year depends on what happens to interest rates one year later.

B. The major difference in risk is with respect to credit risk. Specifically, the AAA issue exposes the investor to credit risk.

C. There is reinvestment risk for the 1-year zero-coupon Treasury issue because the principal must be reinvested at the end of one year.

D. The major difference is the quantity of credit risk exposure of both issues. The U.S. corporate bond issue has greater credit risk. (Note that the sovereign issue is dollar denominated so that there is no exchange rate risk.)

E. The less actively traded issue will have greater liquidity risk.

F. There are two differences in risk. First, there is the greater credit risk of investing in Italian government bonds relative to U.S. Treasury bonds. Second, investing in the Italian government bonds denominated in lira exposes a U.S. investor to exchange rate risk.

16. Probably the first thing that Ms. Peters should ask is what the investment objectives are of HPLU. Addressing directly the two statements Mr. Stevens made, consider the first. Mr. Stevens believes that by buying investment grade bonds the portfolio will not be exposed to a loss of principal. However, all bonds—investment grade and non-investment grade—are exposed to the potential loss of principal if interest rates rise (i.e., interest rate risk) if an issue must be sold prior to its maturity date. If a callable bond is purchased, there can be a loss of principal if the call price is less than the purchase price (i.e., call risk). The issue can also be downgraded (i.e., downgrade risk) or the market can require a higher spread (i.e., credit spread risk), both resulting in a decline in the price of an issue. This will result in a loss of principal if the issue must be sold prior to the maturity date.

The request that the bond portfolio have 40% in issues that mature within three years will reduce the interest rate risk of the portfolio. However, it will expose the HPLU to reinvestment risk (assuming the investment horizon for HPLU is greater than three years) since when the bonds mature there is the risk that the proceeds received may have to be reinvested at a lower interest rate than the coupon rate of the maturing issues.

17. **A.** It is reasonable to assume that the municipality will not need to redeem proceeds from the pension fund to make current payments to beneficiaries. Instead, the investment objective is to have the fund grow in order to meet future payments that must be made to retiring employees. Investing in just high investment grade securities that mature in one month or less exposes the pension fund to substantial reinvestment risk. So, while the fund reduces its interest rate risk by investing in such securities, it increases exposure to reinvestment risk. In the case of a pension fund, it would be expected that it can absorb some level of interest rate risk but would not want to be exposed to substantial reinvestment risk. So, this investment strategy may not make sense for the municipality's pension fund.

    B. The opposite is true for the operating fund. The municipality can be expected to need proceeds on a shorter term basis. It should be less willing to expose the operating fund to interest rate risk but willing to sacrifice investment income (i.e., willing to accept reinvestment risk).

18. When the proposed redemption was announced, the securities were treated as short-term investments with a maturity of about six weeks—from the announcement date of January 26th to the redemption date of March 15th. When GECC canceled the proposed redemption issue and set the coupon rate as allowed by the indenture, the price of the issue declined because the new coupon rate was not competitive with market rates for issues with GECC's rating with the same time to the next reset date in three years.

19. A major risk is foreign exchange risk. This is the risk that the Japanese yen will depreciate relative to the British pound when a coupon payment or principal repayment is received. There is still the interest rate risk associated with the Japanese government bond that results from a rise in Japanese interest rates. There is reinvestment risk. There is also credit risk, although this risk is minimal. Sovereign risk is also a minimal concern.

20. Certain events can impair the ability of an issue or issuer to repay its debt obligations. For example, a corporate takeover that increases the issuer's debt can result in a downgrade. Regulatory changes that reduce revenues or increase expenses of a regulated company or a company serving a market that is adversely affected by the regulation will be downgraded if it is viewed by the rating agency that the ability to satisfy obligations has been impaired.

21. This statement about sovereign risk is incomplete. There are actions that can be taken by a foreign government other than a default that can have an adverse impact on a bond's price. These actions can result in an increase in the credit spread risk or an increase in downgrade risk.

22. B is correct. An increase in expected yield volatility increases the price of both embedded call and put options. The price of the embedded call option is subtracted from the price of a comparable option-free bond, therefore, the price of the callable bond *decreases*. In the case of an embedded put option, the price of the embedded option is added to the price of a comparable option-free bond, causing the price of the bond to *increase*. Whether the value of the option is added to or subtracted from the price of an option-free bond is dependent upon who benefits from the option, the issuer or the holder.

23. A is correct. Both statements are incorrect. An issuer is more likely to call a bond when rates have declined, thereby increasing the reinvestment risk relative to an option-free bond. Because of the call provision, the callable bond has less price appreciation potential than an identical option-free bond (termed price compression).

24. C is correct. An amortizing security includes payments of both interest and principal that must be reinvested. A zero-coupon bond has no reinvestment risk prior to maturity because no cash flows are received that must be reinvested. Because zero-coupon bonds do not have periodic cash flows, they have the highest interest rate risk for a given maturity and given change in market yields.

25. C is correct. Floating rate securities generally have less interest rate risk than fixed coupon rate securities. Reasons that the security might not reset to par include a change in the required margin that investors demand (spread) or the security may have a cap on the floating interest rate.

26. B is correct. Yield curve changes are rarely parallel. Non-parallel shifts in the yield curve affect the various bonds held in a portfolio differently, depending on their coupon rate, time to maturity, embedded options, etc. Therefore, additional risk measures have been developed. Two widely used measures are rate duration, which refers to the duration of a particular maturity (e.g., five-year rate duration), and key rate duration, which is rate duration for the most important (key) rates that impact a portfolio.

27. C is correct. Statement 1 correctly defines investment-grade bonds. Statement 2 is incorrect because repurchase agreements expose investors to liquidity risk as the collateral used in the repo is marked-to-market periodically.

28. A is correct. A duration of 4.8 means that the approximate percentage price change for a 100 basis point change in yield will be 4.8%. A 75 basis point change would be 4.8(0.75) = 3.6%. The price change would be 3.6% of the market value.

54

Overview of Bond Sectors and Instruments

by Frank J. Fabozzi, CFA

LEARNING OUTCOMES

Mastery	The candidate should be able to:
☐	**a** describe features, credit risk characteristics, and distribution methods for government securities;
☐	**b** describe the types of securities issued by the U.S. Department of the Treasury (e.g., bills, notes, bonds, and inflation protection securities), and distinguish between on-the-run and off-the-run Treasury securities;
☐	**c** describe how stripped Treasury securities are created and distinguish between coupon strips and principal strips;
☐	**d** describe the types and characteristics of securities issued by U.S. federal agencies;
☐	**e** describe the types and characteristics of mortgage-backed securities and explain the cash flow and prepayment risk for each type;
☐	**f** explain the motivation for creating a collateralized mortgage obligation;
☐	**g** describe the types of securities issued by municipalities in the United States and distinguish between tax-backed debt and revenue bonds;
☐	**h** describe the characteristics and motivation for the various types of debt issued by corporations (including corporate bonds, medium-term notes, structured notes, commercial paper, negotiable CDs, and bankers acceptances);
☐	**i** define an asset-backed security, describe the role of a special purpose vehicle in an asset-backed security's transaction, state the motivation for a corporation to issue an asset-backed security, and describe the types of external credit enhancements for asset-backed securities;
☐	**j** describe collateralized debt obligations;
☐	**k** describe the mechanisms available for placing bonds in the primary market and distinguish between the primary and secondary markets for bonds.

1   INTRODUCTION

Thus far we have covered the general features of bonds and the risks associated with investing in bonds. In this reading, we will review the major sectors of a country's bond market and the securities issued. This includes sovereign bonds, semi-government bonds, municipal or province securities, corporate debt securities, mortgage-backed securities, asset-backed securities, and collateralized debt obligations. Our coverage in this reading describes the instruments found in these sectors.

2   SECTORS OF THE BOND MARKET

While there is no uniform system for classifying the sectors of the bond markets throughout the world, we will use the classification shown in Exhibit 1. From the perspective of a given country, the bond market can be classified into two markets: an internal bond market and an external bond market.

2.1 Internal Bond Market

The internal bond market of a country is also called the national bond market. It is divided into two parts: the domestic bond market and the foreign bond market. The domestic bond market is where issuers domiciled in the country issue bonds and where those bonds are subsequently traded.

The foreign bond market of a country is where bonds of issuers not domiciled in the country are issued and traded. For example, in the United States, the foreign bond market is the market where bonds are issued by non-U.S. entities and then subsequently traded in the United States. In the U.K., a sterling-denominated bond issued by a Japanese corporation and subsequently traded in the U.K. bond market is part of the U.K. foreign bond market. Bonds in the foreign sector of a bond market have nicknames. For example, foreign bonds in the U.S. market are nicknamed "Yankee bonds" and sterling-denominated bonds in the U.K. foreign bond market are nicknamed "Bulldog bonds." Foreign bonds can be denominated in any currency. For example, a foreign bond issued by an Australian corporation in the United States can be denominated in U.S. dollars, Australian dollars, or euros.

Exhibit 1	Overview of the Sectors of the Bond Market

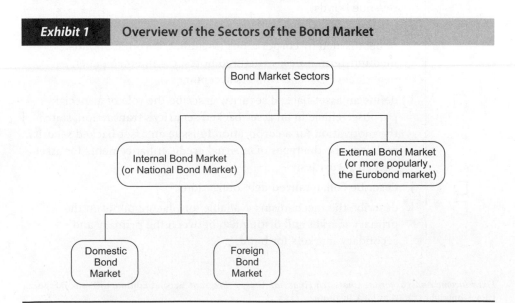

Issuers of foreign bonds include central governments and their subdivisions, corporations, and supranationals. A supranational is an entity that is formed by two or more central governments through international treaties. Supranationals promote economic development for the member countries. Two examples of supranationals are the International Bank for Reconstruction and Development, popularly referred to as the World Bank, and the Inter-American Development Bank.

2.2 External Bond Market

The external bond market includes bonds with the following distinguishing features:

- they are underwritten by an international syndicate;
- at issuance, they are offered simultaneously to investors in a number of countries;
- they are issued outside the jurisdiction of any single country; and
- they are in unregistered form.

The external bond market is referred to as the international bond market, the offshore bond market, or, more popularly, the Eurobond market.[1] Throughout this reading we will use the term Eurobond market to describe this sector of the bond market.

Eurobonds are classified based on the currency in which the issue is denominated. For example, when Eurobonds are denominated in U.S. dollars, they are referred to as Eurodollar bonds. Eurobonds denominated in Japanese yen are referred to as Euroyen bonds.

A global bond is a debt obligation that is issued and traded in the foreign bond market of one or more countries and the Eurobond market.

SOVEREIGN BONDS

3

In many countries that have a bond market, the largest sector is often bonds issued by a country's central government. These bonds are referred to as sovereign bonds. A government can issue securities in its national bond market which are subsequently traded within that market. A government can also issue bonds in the Eurobond market or the foreign sector of another country's bond market. While the currency denomination of a government security is typically the currency of the issuing country, a government can issue bonds denominated in any currency.

3.1 Credit Risk

An investor in any bond is exposed to credit risk. The perception throughout the world is that bonds issued by the U.S. government are virtually free of credit risk. Consequently, the market views these bonds as default-free bonds. Sovereign bonds of non-U.S. central governments are rated by the credit rating agencies. These ratings are referred to as sovereign ratings. Standard & Poor's and Moody's rate sovereign debt. We will discuss the factors considered in rating sovereign bonds at Level II.

The rating agencies assign two types of ratings to sovereign debt. One is a local currency debt rating and the other is a foreign currency debt rating. The reason for assigning two ratings is that historically, the default frequency differs by the currency

---

[1] It should be noted that the classification used here is by no means universally accepted. Some market observers refer to the external bond market as consisting of the foreign bond market and the Eurobond market.

denomination of the debt. Specifically, defaults have been greater on foreign currency denominated debt. The reason for the difference in default rates for local currency debt and foreign currency debt is that if a government is willing to raise taxes and control its domestic financial system, it can generate sufficient local currency to meet its local currency debt obligation. This is not the case with foreign currency denominated debt. A central government must purchase foreign currency to meet a debt obligation in that foreign currency and therefore has less control with respect to its exchange rate. Thus, a significant depreciation of the local currency relative to a foreign currency denominated debt obligation will impair a central government's ability to satisfy that obligation.

3.2 Methods of Distributing New Government Securities

Four methods have been used by central governments to distribute new bonds that they issue: 1) regular auction cycle/multiple-price method, 2) regular auction cycle/single-price method, 3) ad hoc auction method, and 4) tap method.

With the regular auction cycle/multiple-price method, there is a regular auction cycle, and winning bidders are allocated securities at the yield (price) they bid. For the regular auction cycle/single-price method, there is a regular auction cycle, and all winning bidders are awarded securities at the highest yield accepted by the government. For example, if the highest yield for a single-price auction is 7.14% and someone bid 7.12%, that bidder would be awarded the securities at 7.14%. In contrast, with a multiple-price auction that bidder would be awarded securities at 7.12%. U.S. government bonds are currently issued using a regular auction cycle/single-price method.

In the ad hoc auction system, governments announce auctions when prevailing market conditions appear favorable. It is only at the time of the auction that the amount to be auctioned and the maturity of the security to be offered is announced. This is one of the methods used by the Bank of England in distributing British government bonds. In a tap system, additional bonds of a previously outstanding bond issue are auctioned. The government announces periodically that it is adding this new supply. The tap system has been used in the United Kingdom, the United States, and the Netherlands.

3.2.1 *United States Treasury Securities*

U.S. Treasury securities are issued by the U.S. Department of the Treasury and are backed by the full faith and credit of the U.S. government. As noted above, market participants throughout the world view U.S. Treasury securities as having no credit risk. Because of the importance of the U.S. government securities market, we will take a close look at this market.

Treasury securities are sold in the primary market through sealed-bid auctions on a regular cycle using a single-price method. Each auction is announced several days in advance by means of a Treasury Department press release or press conference. The auction for Treasury securities is conducted on a competitive bid basis.

The secondary market for Treasury securities is an over-the-counter market where a group of U.S. government securities dealers offer continuous bid and ask prices on outstanding Treasuries. There is virtually 24-hour trading of Treasury securities. The most recently auctioned issue for a maturity is referred to as the on-the-run issue or the current issue. Securities that are replaced by the on-the-run issue are called off-the-run issues.

Exhibit 2 provides a summary of the securities issued by the U.S. Department of the Treasury. U.S. Treasury securities are categorized as fixed-principal securities or inflation-indexed securities.

| Exhibit 2 | Overview of U.S. Treasury Debt Instruments |

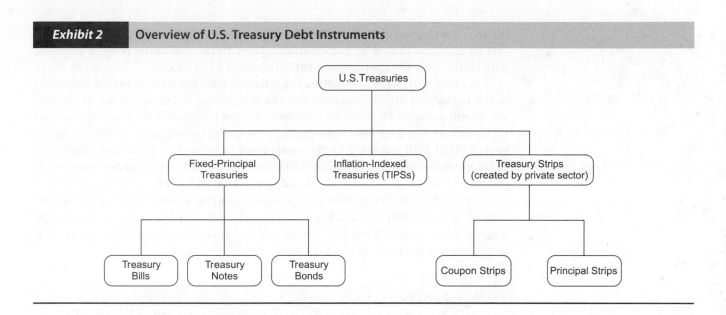

3.2.1.1 Fixed-Principal Treasury Securities

Fixed-principal securities include Treasury bills, Treasury notes, and Treasury bonds. Treasury bills are issued at a discount to par value, have no coupon rate, mature at par value, and have a maturity date of less than 12 months. As discount securities, Treasury bills do not pay coupon interest; the return to the investor is the difference between the maturity value and the purchase price. We will explain how the price and the yield for a Treasury bill are computed in the reading on yield measures, spot rates, and forward rates.

Treasury coupon securities issued with original maturities of more than one year and no more than 10 years are called **Treasury notes**. Coupon securities are issued at approximately par value and mature at par value. Treasury coupon securities with original maturities greater than 10 years are called **Treasury bonds**. While a few issues of the outstanding bonds are callable, the U.S. Treasury has not issued callable Treasury securities since 1984. As of this writing, the U.S. Department of the Treasury has stopped issuing Treasury bonds.

3.2.1.2 Inflation-Indexed Treasury Securities

The U.S. Department of the Treasury issues Treasury notes and bonds that provide protection against inflation. These securities are popularly referred to as Treasury inflation protection securities or TIPS. (The Treasury refers to these securities as Treasury inflation indexed securities, TIIS.)

TIPS work as follows. The coupon rate on an issue is set at a fixed rate. That rate is determined via the auction process described later in this section. The coupon rate is called the "real rate" because it is the rate that the investor ultimately earns above the inflation rate. The inflation index that the government uses for the inflation adjustment is the non-seasonally adjusted U.S. City Average All Items Consumer Price Index for All Urban Consumers (CPI-U).

The principal that the Treasury Department will base both the dollar amount of the coupon payment and the maturity value on is adjusted semiannually. This is called the inflation-adjusted principal. The adjustment for inflation is as follows. Suppose that the coupon rate for a TIPS is 3.5% and the annual inflation rate is 3%. Suppose further that an investor purchases on January 1, $100,000 of par value (principal) of this issue. The semiannual inflation rate is 1.5% (3% divided by 2). The inflation-adjusted principal at the end of the first six-month period is found by multiplying the original par value by (1 + the semiannual inflation rate). In our example, the inflation-adjusted principal at the end of the first six-month period is $101,500. It is this inflation-adjusted principal that is the basis for computing the coupon interest for the first six-month period. The coupon payment is then 1.75% (one half the real rate of 3.5%) multiplied by the inflation-adjusted principal at the coupon payment date ($101,500). The coupon payment is therefore $1,776.25.

Let's look at the next six months. The inflation-adjusted principal at the beginning of the period is $101,500. Suppose that the semiannual inflation rate for the second six-month period is 1%. Then the inflation-adjusted principal at the end of the second six-month period is the inflation-adjusted principal at the beginning of the six-month period ($101,500) increased by the semiannual inflation rate (1%). The adjustment to the principal is $1,015 (1% times $101,500). So, the inflation-adjusted principal at the end of the second six-month period (December 31 in our example) is $102,515 ($101,500 + $1,015). The coupon interest that will be paid to the investor at the second coupon payment date is found by multiplying the inflation-adjusted principal on the coupon payment date ($102,515) by one-half the real rate (i.e., one-half of 3.5%). That is, the coupon payment will be $1,794.01.

Practice Question 1

Suppose an investor purchases $10,000 of par value of a Treasury inflation protection security. The real rate (determined at the auction) is 3.8%.

A. Assume that at the end of the first six months the CPI-U is 2.4% (annual rate). Compute the i) inflation adjustment to principal at the end of the first six months, ii) the inflation-adjusted principal at the end of the first six months, and iii) the coupon payment made to the investor at the end of the first six months.

B. Assume that at the end of the second six months the CPI-U is 2.8% (annual rate). Compute the i) inflation adjustment to principal at the end of the second six months, ii) the inflation-adjusted principal at the end of the second six months, and iii) the coupon payment made to the investor at the end of the second six months.

As can be seen, part of the adjustment for inflation comes in the coupon payment since it is based on the inflation-adjusted principal. However, the U.S. government taxes the adjustment each year. This feature reduces the attractiveness of TIPS as investments for tax-paying entities.

Because of the possibility of deflation (i.e., price declines), the inflation-adjusted principal at maturity may turn out to be less than the initial par value. However, the Treasury has structured TIPS so that they are redeemed at the greater of the inflation-adjusted principal and the initial par value.

An inflation-adjusted principal must be calculated for a settlement date. The inflation-adjusted principal is defined in terms of an index ratio, which is the ratio of the reference CPI for the settlement date to the reference CPI for the issue date. The reference CPI is calculated with a 3-month lag. For example, the reference CPI for May 1 is the CPI-U reported in February. The U.S. Department of the Treasury publishes and makes available on its website (www.publicdebt.treas.gov) a daily index ratio for an issue.

3.2.1.3 Treasury STRIPS The Treasury does not issue zero-coupon notes or bonds. However, because of the demand for zero-coupon instruments with no credit risk and a maturity greater than one year, the private sector has created such securities.

To illustrate the process, suppose $100 million of a Treasury note with a 10-year maturity and a coupon rate of 10% is purchased to create zero-coupon Treasury securities (see Exhibit 3). The cash flows from this Treasury note are 20 semiannual payments of $5 million each ($100 million times 10% divided by 2) and the repayment of principal ("corpus") of $100 million 10 years from now. As there are 21 different payments to be made by the Treasury, a receipt representing a single payment claim on each payment is issued at a discount, creating 21 zero-coupon instruments. The amount of the maturity value for a receipt on a particular payment, whether coupon or principal, depends on the amount of the payment to be made by the Treasury on the underlying Treasury note. In our example, 20 coupon receipts each have a maturity value of $5 million, and one receipt, the principal, has a maturity value of $100 million. The maturity dates for the receipts coincide with the corresponding payment dates for the Treasury security.

Exhibit 3	Coupon Stripping: Creating Zero-Coupon Treasury Securities

Security

Par: $100 million
Coupon: 10%, semiannual
Maturity: 10 years

Security

| Coupon:
$5 million
Receipt in:
6 months | Coupon:
$5 million
Receipt in:
1 year | Coupon:
$5 million
Receipt in:
1.5 years | .... | Coupon:
$5 million
Receipt in:
10 years | Principal:
$100 million
Receipt in:
10 years |

Zero-coupon securities created

| Maturity value:
$5 million
Maturity:
6 months | Maturity value:
$5 million
Maturity:
1 year | Maturity value:
$5 million
Maturity:
1.5 years | .... | Maturity value:
$5 million
Maturity:
10 years | Maturity value:
$100 million
Maturity:
10 years |

Zero-coupon instruments are issued through the Treasury's Separate Trading of Registered Interest and Principal Securities (STRIPS) program, a program designed to facilitate the stripping of Treasury securities. The zero-coupon Treasury securities created under the STRIPS program are direct obligations of the U.S. government.

Stripped Treasury securities are simply referred to as Treasury strips. Strips created from coupon payments are called coupon strips, and those created from the principal payment are called principal strips. The reason why a distinction is made between coupon strips and the principal strips has to do with the tax treatment by non-U.S. entities as discussed below.

A disadvantage of a taxable entity investing in Treasury coupon strips is that accrued interest is taxed each year even though interest is not paid until maturity. Thus, these instruments have negative cash flows until the maturity date because tax payments must be made on interest earned but not received in cash. One reason for distinguishing between strips created from the principal and coupon is that some foreign buyers have a preference for the strips created from the principal (i.e., the principal strips). This preference is due to the tax treatment of the interest in their home country. Some countries' tax laws treat the interest as a capital gain if the principal strip is purchased. The capital gain receives a preferential tax treatment (i.e., lower tax rate) compared to ordinary income.

3.2.2 Non-U.S. Sovereign Bond Issuers

It is not possible to discuss the bonds/notes of all governments in the world. Instead, we will take a brief look at a few major sovereign issuers.

The German government issues bonds (called *Bunds*) with maturities from 8–30 years and notes (*Bundesobligationen*, Bobls) with a maturity of five years. Ten-year Bunds are the largest sector of the German government securities market in terms of amount outstanding and secondary market turnover. Bunds and Bobls have fixed-rate coupons and are bullet structures.

The bonds issued by the United Kingdom are called "gilt-edged stocks" or simply *gilts*. There are more types of gilts than there are types of issues in other government bond markets. The largest sector of the gilt market is straight fixed-rate coupon bonds. The second major sector of the gilt market is index-linked issues, referred to as "linkers." There are a few issues of outstanding gilts called "irredeemables." These are issues with no maturity date and are therefore called "undated gilts." Government-designated gilt issues may be stripped to create gilt strips, a process that began in December 1997.

The French Treasury issues long-dated bonds, *Obligation Assimilable du Trésor* (OATs), with maturities up to 30 years and notes, *Bons du Trésor á Taux Fixe et á Intérét Annuel* (BTANs), with maturities between 2 and 5 years. OATs are not callable. While most OAT issues have a fixed-rate coupon, there are some special issues with a floating-rate coupon. Long-dated OATs can be stripped to create OAT strips. The French government was one of the first countries after the United States to allow stripping.

The Italian government issues 1) bonds, *Buoni del Tresoro Poliennali* (BTPs), with a fixed-rate coupon that are issued with original maturities of 5, 10, and 30 years, 2) floating-rate notes, *Certificati di Credito del Tresoro* (CCTs), typically with a 7-year maturity and referenced to the Italian Treasury bill rate, 3) 2-year zero-coupon notes, *Certificati di Tresoro a Zero Coupon* (CTZs), and 4) bonds with put options, *Certificati del Tresoro con Opzione* (CTOs). The putable bonds are issued with the same maturities as the BTPs. The investor has the right to put the bond to the Italian government halfway through its stated maturity date. The Italian government has not issued CTOs since 1992.

The Canadian government bond market has been closely related to the U.S. government bond market and has a similar structure, including types of issues. Bonds have a fixed coupon rate except for the inflation protection bonds (called "real return bonds"). All new Canadian bonds are in "bullet" form; that is, they are not callable or putable.

About three-quarters of the Australian government securities market consists of fixed-rate bonds and inflation protections bonds called "Treasury indexed bonds." Treasury indexed bonds have either interest payments or capital linked to the Australian Consumer Price Index. The balance of the market consists of floating-rate issues, referred to as "Treasury adjustable bonds," that have a maturity between 3 to 5 years, and the reference rate is the Australian Bank Bill Index.

There are two types of Japanese government securities (referred to as JGBs) issued publicly: 1) medium-term bonds and 2) long-dated bonds. There are two types of medium-term bonds: bonds with coupons and zero-coupon bonds. Bonds with coupons have maturities of 2, 3, and 4 years. The other type of medium-term bond is the 5-year zero-coupon bond. Long-dated bonds are interest bearing.

The financial markets of Latin America, Asia (with the exception of Japan), and Eastern Europe are viewed as "emerging markets." Investing in the government bonds of emerging market countries entails considerably more credit risk than investing in the government bonds of major industrialized countries. A good amount of secondary trading of government debt of emerging markets is in Brady bonds, which represent a restructuring of nonperforming bank loans to emerging market governments into marketable securities. There are two types of Brady bonds. The first type covers the interest due on these loans ("past-due interest bonds"). The second type covers the principal amount owed on the bank loans ("principal bonds").

SEMI-GOVERNMENT/AGENCY BONDS

4

A central government can establish an agency or organization that issues bonds. The bonds of such entities are not issued directly by the central government but may have either a direct or implied government guarantee. These bonds are generically referred to as semi-government bonds or government agency bonds. In some countries, semi-government bonds include bonds issued by regions of the country.

Here are a few examples of semi-government bonds. In Australia, there are the bonds issued by Telstra or a State electric power supplier such as Pacific Power. These bonds are guaranteed by the full faith and credit of the Commonwealth of Australia. Government agency bonds are issued by Germany's Federal Railway (*Bundesbahn*) and the Post Office (*Bundespost*) with the full faith and credit of the central government.

In the United States, semi-government bonds are referred to as federal agency securities. They are further classified by the types of issuer—those issued by federally related institutions and those issued by government-sponsored enterprises. Our focus in the remainder of this section is on U.S. federal agency securities. Exhibit 4 provides an overview of the U.S. federal agency securities market.

Exhibit 4	Overview of U.S. Federal Agency Securities

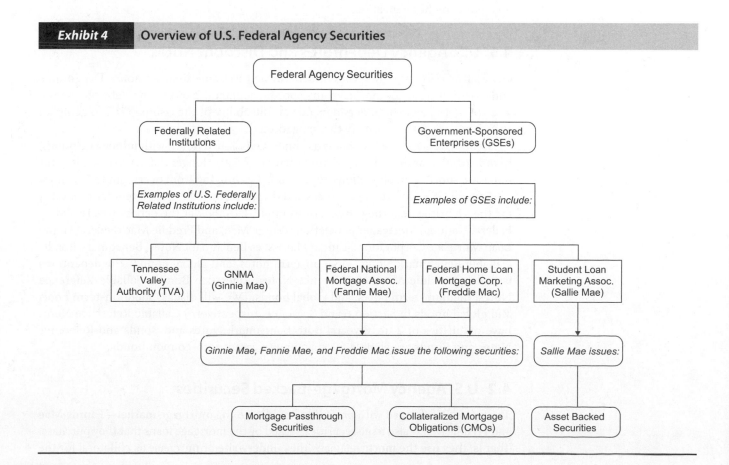

Federally related institutions are arms of the federal government. They include the Export-Import Bank of the United States, the Tennessee Valley Authority (TVA), the Commodity Credit Corporation, the Farmers Housing Administration, the General Services Administration, the Government National Mortgage Association (Ginnie Mae), the Maritime Administration, the Private Export Funding Corporation, the Rural Electrification Administration, the Rural Telephone Bank, the Small Business Administration, and the Washington Metropolitan Area Transit Authority. With the exception of securities of the TVA and the Private Export Funding Corporation, the securities are backed by the full faith and credit of the U.S. government. In recent years, the TVA has been the only issuer of securities directly into the marketplace.

Government-sponsored enterprises (GSEs) are privately owned, publicly chartered entities. They were created by Congress to reduce the cost of capital for certain borrowing sectors of the economy deemed to be important enough to warrant assistance. The entities in these sectors include farmers, homeowners, and students. The enabling legislation dealing with a GSE is reviewed periodically. GSEs issue securities directly in the marketplace. The market for these securities, while smaller than that of Treasury securities, has in recent years become an active and important sector of the bond market.

Today there are six GSEs that currently issue securities: Federal National Mortgage Association (Fannie Mae), Federal Home Loan Mortgage Corporation (Freddie Mac), Federal Agricultural Mortgage Corporation (Farmer Mac), Federal Farm Credit System, Federal Home Loan Bank System, and Student Loan Marketing Association (Sallie Mae). Fannie Mae, Freddie Mac, and the Federal Home Loan Bank are responsible for providing credit to the residential housing sector. Farmer Mac provides the same function for farm properties. The Federal Farm Credit Bank System is responsible for the credit market in the agricultural sector of the economy. Sallie Mae provides funds to support higher education.

4.1 U.S. Agency Debentures and Discount Notes

Generally, GSEs issue two types of debt: debentures and discount notes. Debentures and discount notes do not have any specific collateral backing the debt obligation. The ability to pay debtholders depends on the ability of the issuing GSE to generate sufficient cash flows to satisfy the obligation.

Debentures can be either notes or bonds. GSE-issued notes, with minor exceptions, have 1- to 20-year maturities and bonds have maturities longer than 20 years. Discount notes are short-term obligations, with maturities ranging from overnight to 360 days.

Several GSEs are frequent issuers and therefore have developed regular programs for the securities that they issue. For example, let's look at the debentures issued by Federal National Mortgage Association (Fannie Mae) and Freddie Mac (Federal Home Loan Mortgage Corporation). Fannie Mae issues Benchmark Notes, Benchmark Bonds, Callable Benchmark Notes, medium-term notes, and global bonds. The debentures issued by Freddie Mac are Reference Notes, Reference Bonds, Callable Reference Notes, medium-term notes, and global bonds. (We will discuss medium-term notes and global bonds in Section 6 and Section 8, respectively.) Callable Reference Notes have maturities of 2 to 10 years. Both Benchmark Notes and Bonds and Reference Notes and Bonds are eligible for stripping to create zero-coupon bonds.

4.2 U.S. Agency Mortgage-Backed Securities

The two GSEs charged with providing liquidity to the mortgage market—Fannie Mae and Freddie Mac—also issue securities backed by the mortgage loans that they purchase. That is, they use the mortgage loans they underwrite or purchase as collateral for the securities they issue. These securities are called agency mortgage-backed securities and include mortgage passthrough securities, collateralized mortgage obligations (CMOs), and stripped mortgage-backed securities. The latter two mortgage-backed securities are referred to as derivative mortgage-backed securities because they are created from mortgage passthrough securities.

While we confine our discussion to the U.S. mortgage-backed securities market, most developed countries have similar mortgage products.

4.2.1 *Mortgage Loans*

A mortgage loan is a loan secured by the collateral of some specified real estate property which obliges the borrower to make a predetermined series of payments. The mortgage gives the lender the right, if the borrower defaults, to "foreclose" on the loan and seize the property in order to ensure that the debt is paid off. The interest rate on the mortgage loan is called the mortgage rate or contract rate.

There are many types of mortgage designs available in the United States. A mortgage design is a specification of the mortgage rate, term of the mortgage, and the manner in which the borrowed funds are repaid. For now, we will use the most common mortgage design to explain the characteristics of a mortgage-backed security: a fixed-rate, level-payment, fully amortizing mortgage.

The basic idea behind this mortgage design is that each monthly mortgage payment is the same dollar amount and includes interest and principal payment. The monthly payments are such that at the end of the loan's term, the loan has been fully amortized (i.e., there is no mortgage principal balance outstanding).

Each monthly mortgage payment for this mortgage design is due on the first of each month and consists of:

1. interest of ¹⁄₁₂ of the fixed annual interest rate times the amount of the outstanding mortgage balance at the end of the previous month; and

2. a payment of a portion of the outstanding mortgage principal balance.

The difference between the monthly mortgage payment and the portion of the payment that represents interest equals the amount that is applied to reduce the outstanding mortgage principal balance. This amount is referred to as the **amortization**. We shall also refer to it as the scheduled principal payment.

To illustrate this mortgage design, consider a 30-year (360-month), $100,000 mortgage with an 8.125% mortgage rate. The monthly mortgage payment would be $742.50.[2] Exhibit 5 shows for selected months how each monthly mortgage payment is divided between interest and scheduled principal payment. At the beginning of month 1, the mortgage balance is $100,000, the amount of the original loan. The mortgage payment for month 1 includes interest on the $100,000 borrowed for the

---

2 The calculation of the monthly mortgage payment is simply an application of the present value of an annuity. The formula as applied to mortgage payments is as follows:

$$MP = B\left[\frac{r(1+r)^n}{(1+r)^n - 1}\right]$$

where

MP = monthly mortgage payment
B = amount borrowed (i.e., original loan balance)
r = monthly mortgage rate (annual rate divided by 12)
n = number of months of the mortgage loan

In our example,

B = $100,000   r = 0.0067708 (0.08125/12)   n = 360

Then

$$MP = \$100,000\left[\frac{0.0067708(1.0067708)^{360}}{(1.0067708)^{360} - 1}\right] = \$742.50$$

month. Since the interest rate is 8.125%, the monthly interest rate is 0.0067708 (0.08125 divided by 12). Interest for month 1 is therefore $677.08 ($100,000 times 0.0067708). The $65.41 difference between the monthly mortgage payment of $742.50[2] and the interest of $677.08 is the portion of the monthly mortgage payment that represents the scheduled principal payment (i.e., amortization). This $65.41 in month 1 reduces the mortgage balance.

Exhibit 5	Amortization Schedule for a Level-Payment, Fixed-Rate, Fully Amortized Mortgage (Selected Months)

Mortgage loan:	$100,000	Monthly payment:	$742.50
Mortgage rate:	8.125%	Term of loan:	30 years (360 months)

(1)	(2)	(3)	(4)	(5)	(6)
Month	Beginning of Month Mortgage Balance	Mortgage Payment	Interest	Scheduled Principal Repayment	End of Month Mortgage Balance
1	$100,000.00	$742.50	$677.08	$65.41	$99,934.59
2	99,934.59	742.50	676.64	65.86	99,868.73
3	99,868.73	742.50	676.19	66.30	99,802.43
4	99,802.43	742.50	675.75	66.75	99,735.68
...	...	...	...	...	...
25	98,301.53	742.50	665.58	76.91	98,224.62
26	98,224.62	742.50	665.06	77.43	98,147.19
27	98,147.19	742.50	664.54	77.96	98,069.23
...	...	...	...	...	...
184	76,446.29	742.50	517.61	224.89	76,221.40
185	76,221.40	742.50	516.08	226.41	75,994.99
186	75,994.99	742.50	514.55	227.95	75,767.04
...	...	...	...	...	...
289	42,200.92	742.50	285.74	456.76	41,744.15
290	41,744.15	742.50	282.64	459.85	41,284.30
291	41,284.30	742.50	279.53	462.97	40,821.33
...	...	...	...	...	...
358	2,197.66	742.50	14.88	727.62	1,470.05
359	1,470.05	742.50	9.95	732.54	737.50
360	737.50	742.50	4.99	737.50	0.00

The mortgage balance at the end of month 1 (beginning of month 2) is then $99,934.59 ($100,000 minus $65.41). The interest for the second monthly mortgage payment is $676.64, the monthly interest rate (0.0066708) times the mortgage balance at the beginning of month 2 ($99,934.59). The difference between the $742.50 monthly mortgage payment and the $676.64 interest is $65.86, representing the amount of the mortgage balance paid off with that monthly mortgage payment. Notice that the mortgage payment in month 360—the final payment—is sufficient to pay off the remaining mortgage principal balance.

As Exhibit 5 clearly shows, the portion of the monthly mortgage payment applied to interest declines each month and the portion applied to principal repayment increases. The reason for this is that as the mortgage balance is reduced with each monthly mortgage payment, the interest on the mortgage balance declines. Since the monthly mortgage payment is a fixed dollar amount, an increasingly larger portion of the monthly payment is applied to reduce the mortgage principal balance outstanding in each subsequent month.

To an investor in a mortgage loan (or a pool of mortgage loans), the monthly mortgage payments as described above do not equal an investor's cash flow. There are two reasons for this: 1) servicing fees and 2) prepayments.

Every mortgage loan must be serviced. Servicing of a mortgage loan involves collecting monthly payments and forwarding proceeds to owners of the loan; sending payment notices to mortgagors; reminding mortgagors when payments are overdue; maintaining records of principal balances; administering an escrow balance for real estate taxes and insurance; initiating foreclosure proceedings if necessary; and, furnishing tax information to mortgagors when applicable. The servicing fee is a portion of the mortgage rate. If the mortgage rate is 8.125% and the servicing fee is 50 basis points, then the investor receives interest of 7.625%. The interest rate that the investor receives is said to be the net interest.

Our illustration of the cash flow for a level-payment, fixed-rate, fully amortized mortgage assumes that the homeowner does not pay off any portion of the mortgage principal balance prior to the scheduled payment date. But homeowners do pay off all or part of their mortgage balance prior to the scheduled payment date. A payment made in excess of the monthly mortgage payment is called a prepayment. The prepayment may be for the entire principal outstanding principal balance or a partial additional payment of the mortgage principal balance. When a prepayment is not for the entire amount, it is called a curtailment. Typically, there is no penalty for prepaying a mortgage loan.

Thus, the cash flows for a mortgage loan are monthly and consist of three components: 1) net interest, 2) scheduled principal payment, and 3) prepayments. The effect of prepayments is that the amount and timing of the cash flow from a mortgage is not known with certainty. This is the risk that we referred to as prepayment risk in the reading on risks associated with investing in bonds.[3]

For example, all that the investor in a $100,000, 8.125% 30-year mortgage knows is that as long as the loan is outstanding and the borrower does not default, interest will be received and the principal will be repaid at the scheduled date each month; then at the end of the 30 years, the investor would have received $100,000 in principal payments. What the investor does not know—the uncertainty—is for how long the loan will be outstanding, and therefore what the timing of the principal payments will be. This is true for all mortgage loans, not just the level-payment, fixed-rate, fully amortized mortgage.

Practice Question 2

Suppose that a mortgage loan for $100,000 is obtained for 30 years. The mortgage is a level-payment, fixed-rate, fully amortized mortgage. The mortgage rate is 7.5% and the monthly mortgage payment is $699.21. Compute an amortization schedule as shown in Exhibit 5 for the first six months.

---

3 Factors affecting prepayments will be discussed at Level II.

4.2.2 *Mortgage Passthrough Securities*

A mortgage passthrough security, or simply passthrough, is a security created when one or more holders of mortgages form a collection (pool) of mortgages and sell shares or participation certificates in the pool. A pool may consist of several thousand or only a few mortgages. When a mortgage is included in a pool of mortgages that is used as collateral for a passthrough, the mortgage is said to be securitized.

The cash flow of a passthrough depends on the cash flow of the underlying pool of mortgages. As we just explained, the cash flow consists of monthly mortgage payments representing net interest, the scheduled principal payment, and any principal prepayments. Payments are made to security holders each month. Because of prepayments, the amount of the cash flow is uncertain in terms of the timing of the principal receipt.

To illustrate the creation of a passthrough look at Exhibits 6 and 7. Exhibit 6 shows 2,000 mortgage loans and the cash flows from these loans. For the sake of simplicity, we assume that the amount of each loan is $100,000 so that the aggregate value of all 2,000 loans is $200 million.

Exhibit 6	Mortgage Loans

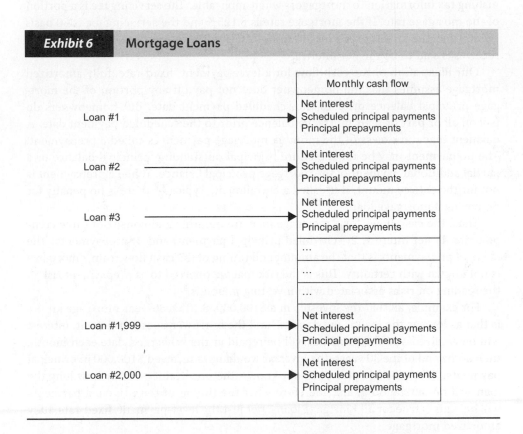

An investor who owns any one of the individual mortgage loans shown in Exhibit 6 faces prepayment risk. In the case of an individual loan, it is particularly difficult to predict prepayments. If an individual investor were to purchase all 2,000 loans, however, prepayments might become more predictable based on historical prepayment experience. However, that would call for an investment of $200 million to buy all 2,000 loans.

Suppose, instead, that some entity purchases all 2,000 loans in Exhibit 6 and pools them. The 2,000 loans can be used as collateral to issue a security whose cash flow is based on the cash flow from the 2,000 loans, as depicted in Exhibit 7. Suppose that 200,000 certificates are issued. Thus, each certificate is initially worth $1,000 ($200 million divided by 200,000). Each certificate holder would be entitled to 0.0005% (1/200,000) of the cash flow. The security created is a mortgage passthrough security.

Exhibit 7	Creation of a Passthrough Security

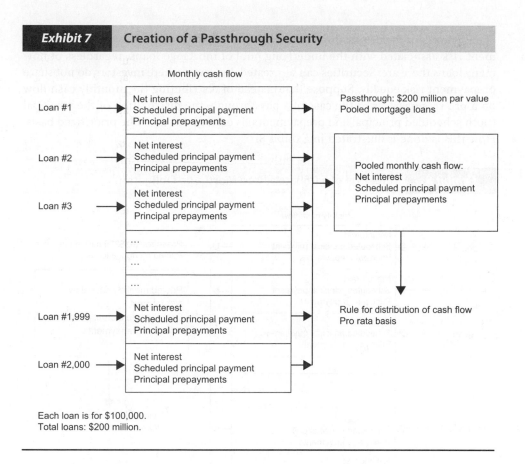

Each loan is for $100,000.
Total loans: $200 million.

Let's see what has been accomplished by creating the passthrough. The total amount of prepayment risk has not changed. Yet, the investor is now exposed to the prepayment risk spread over 2,000 loans rather than one individual mortgage loan and for an investment of less than $200 million.

Let's compare the cash flow for a mortgage passthrough security (an amortizing security) to that of a noncallable coupon bond (a nonamortizing security). For a standard coupon bond, there are no principal payments prior to maturity while for a mortgage passthrough security the principal is paid over time. Unlike a standard coupon bond that pays interest semiannually, a mortgage passthrough makes monthly interest and principal payments. Mortgage passthrough securities are similar to coupon bonds that are callable in that there is uncertainty about the cash flows due to uncertainty about when the entire principal will be paid.

Passthrough securities are issued by Ginnie Mae, Fannie Mae, and Freddie Mac. They are guaranteed with respect to the timely payment of interest and principal.[4] The loans that are permitted to be included in the pool of mortgage loans issued by Ginnie Mae, Fannie Mae, and Freddie Mac must meet the underwriting standards that have been established by these entities. Loans that satisfy the underwriting requirements are referred to as conforming loans. Mortgage-backed securities not issued by agencies are backed by pools of nonconforming loans.

4.2.3 Collateralized Mortgage Obligations

Now we will show how one type of agency mortgage derivative security is created—a collateralized mortgage obligation (CMO). The motivation for creation of a CMO is to distribute prepayment risk among different classes of bonds.

---

4 Freddie Mac previously issued passthrough securities that guaranteed the timely payment of interest but guaranteed only the eventual payment of principal (when it is collected or within one year).

The investor in our passthrough in Exhibit 7 remains exposed to the total prepayment risk associated with the underlying pool of mortgage loans, regardless of how many loans there are. Securities can be created, however, where investors do not share prepayment risk equally. Suppose that instead of distributing the monthly cash flow on a pro rata basis, as in the case of a passthrough, the distribution of the principal (both scheduled principal and prepayments) is carried out on some prioritized basis. How this is done is illustrated in Exhibit 8.

Exhibit 8	**Creation of a Collateralized Mortgage Obligation**

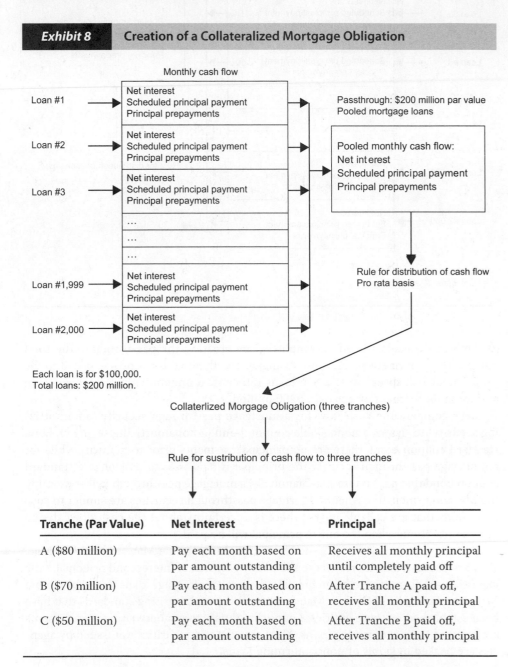

Tranche (Par Value)	Net Interest	Principal
A ($80 million)	Pay each month based on par amount outstanding	Receives all monthly principal until completely paid off
B ($70 million)	Pay each month based on par amount outstanding	After Tranche A paid off, receives all monthly principal
C ($50 million)	Pay each month based on par amount outstanding	After Tranche B paid off, receives all monthly principal

The exhibit shows the cash flow of our original 2,000 mortgage loans and the passthrough. Also shown are three classes of bonds, commonly referred to as tranches,[5] the par value of each tranche, and a set of payment rules indicating how the principal from the passthrough is to be distributed to each tranche. Note that the sum of the

---

5 "Tranche" is from an old French word meaning "slice." (The pronunciation of tranche rhymes with the English word "launch," as in launch a ship or a rocket.)

par value of the three tranches is equal to $200 million. Although it is not shown in the exhibit, for each of the three tranches, there will be certificates representing a proportionate interest in a tranche. For example, suppose that for Tranche A, which has a par value of $80 million, there are 80,000 certificates issued. Each certificate would receive a proportionate share (0.00125%) of payments received by Tranche A.

The rule for the distribution of principal shown in Exhibit 8 is that Tranche A will receive all principal (both scheduled and prepayments) until that tranche's remaining principal balance is zero. Then, Tranche B receives all principal payments until its remaining principal balance is zero. After Tranche B is completely paid, Tranche C receives principal payments. The rule for the distribution of the cash flows in Exhibit 8 indicates that each of the three tranches receives interest on the basis of the amount of the par value outstanding.

The mortgage-backed security that has been created is called a CMO. The collateral for a CMO issued by the agencies is a pool of passthrough securities which is placed in a trust. The ultimate source for the CMO's cash flow is the pool of mortgage loans.

Let's look now at what has been accomplished. Once again, the total prepayment risk for the CMO is the same as the total prepayment risk for the 2,000 mortgage loans. However, the prepayment risk has been distributed differently across the three tranches of the CMO. Tranche A absorbs prepayments first, then Tranche B, and then Tranche C. The result of this is that Tranche A effectively is a shorter term security than the other two tranches; Tranche C will have the longest maturity. Different institutional investors will be attracted to the different tranches, depending on the nature of their liabilities and the effective maturity of the CMO tranche. Moreover, there is less uncertainty about the maturity of each tranche of the CMO than there is about the maturity of the pool of passthroughs from which the CMO is created. Thus, redirection of the cash flow from the underlying mortgage pool creates tranches that satisfy the asset/liability objectives of certain institutional investors better than a passthrough. Stated differently, the rule for distributing principal repayments redistributes prepayment risk among the tranches.

The CMO we describe in Exhibit 8 has a simple set of rules for the distribution of the cash flow. Today, much more complicated CMO structures exist. The basic objective is to provide certain CMO tranches with less uncertainty about prepayment risk. Note, of course, that this can occur only if the reduction in prepayment risk for some tranches is absorbed by other tranches in the CMO structure. A good example is one type of CMO tranche called a planned amortization class tranche or PAC tranche. This is a tranche that has a schedule for the repayment of principal (hence the name "planned amortization") if prepayments are realized at a certain prepayment rate.[6] As a result, the prepayment risk is reduced (not eliminated) for this type of CMO tranche. The tranche that realizes greater prepayment risk in order for the PAC tranche to have greater prepayment protection is called the support tranche.

We will describe in much more detail PAC tranches and supports tranches, as well as other types of CMO tranches at Level II.

STATE AND LOCAL GOVERNMENTS

5

Non-central government entities also issue bonds. In the United States, this includes state and local governments and entities that they create. These securities are referred to as municipal securities or municipal bonds. Because the U.S. bond market has the largest and most developed market for non-central government bonds, we will focus on municipal securities in this market.

---

6 We will explain what is meant by "prepayment rate" at Level II.

In the United States, there are both tax-exempt and taxable municipal securities. "Tax-exempt" means that interest on a municipal security is exempt from federal income taxation. The tax-exemption of municipal securities applies to interest income, not capital gains. The exemption may or may not extend to taxation at the state and local levels. Each state has its own rules as to how interest on municipal securities is taxed. Most municipal securities that have been issued are tax-exempt. Municipal securities are commonly referred to as tax-exempt securities despite the fact that there are taxable municipal securities that have been issued and are traded in the market. Municipal bonds are traded in the over-the-counter market supported by municipal bond dealers across the country.

Like other non-Treasury fixed income securities, municipal securities expose investors to credit risk. The nationally recognized rating organizations rate municipal securities according to their credit risk. In Level II, we look at the factors rating agencies consider in assessing credit risk.

There are basically two types of municipal security structures: tax-backed debt and revenue bonds. We describe each below, as well as some variants.

5.1 Tax-Backed Debt

Tax-backed debt obligations are instruments issued by states, counties, special districts, cities, towns, and school districts that are secured by some form of tax revenue. Exhibit 9 provides an overview of the types of tax-backed debt issued in the U.S. municipal securities market. Tax-backed debt includes general obligation debt, appropriation-backed obligations, and debt obligations supported by public credit enhancement programs. We discuss each below.

Exhibit 9   Tax-Backed Debt Issues in the U.S. Municipal Securities Market

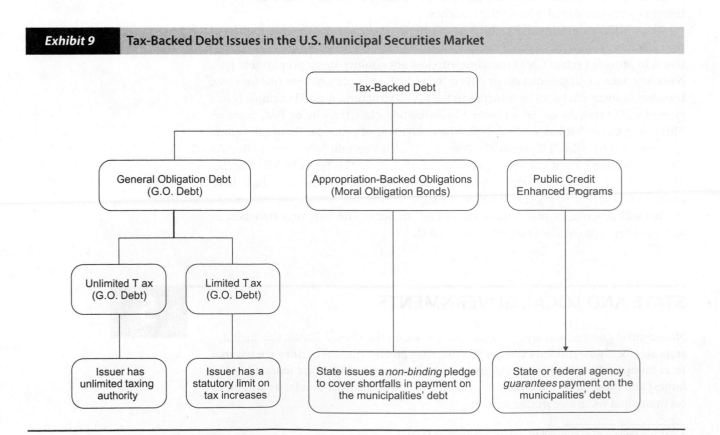

5.1.1 *General Obligation Debt*

The broadest type of tax-backed debt is general obligation debt. There are two types of general obligation pledges: unlimited and limited. An unlimited tax general obligation debt is the stronger form of general obligation pledge because it is secured by the issuer's unlimited taxing power. The tax revenue sources include corporate and individual income taxes, sales taxes, and property taxes. Unlimited tax general obligation debt is said to be secured by the full faith and credit of the issuer. A limited tax general obligation debt is a limited tax pledge because, for such debt, there is a statutory limit on tax rates that the issuer may levy to service the debt.

Certain general obligation bonds are secured not only by the issuer's general taxing powers to create revenues accumulated in a general fund, but also by certain identified fees, grants, and special charges, which provide additional revenues from outside the general fund. Such bonds are known as double-barreled in security because of the dual nature of the revenue sources. For example, the debt obligations issued by special purpose service systems may be secured by a pledge of property taxes, a pledge of special fees/operating revenue from the service provided, or a pledge of both property taxes and special fees/operating revenues. In the last case, they are double-barreled.

5.1.2 *Appropriation-Backed Obligations*

Agencies or authorities of several states have issued bonds that carry a potential state liability for making up shortfalls in the issuing entity's obligation. The appropriation of funds from the state's general tax revenue must be approved by the state legislature. However, the state's pledge is not binding. Debt obligations with this nonbinding pledge of tax revenue are called moral obligation bonds. Because a moral obligation bond requires legislative approval to appropriate the funds, it is classified as an appropriation-backed obligation. The purpose of the moral obligation pledge is to enhance the credit-worthiness of the issuing entity. However, the investor must rely on the best efforts of the state to approve the appropriation.

5.1.3 *Debt Obligations Supported by Public Credit Enhancement Programs*

While a moral obligation is a form of credit enhancement provided by a state, it is not a legally enforceable or legally binding obligation of the state. There are entities that have issued debt that carries some form of public credit enhancement that is legally enforceable. This occurs when there is a guarantee by the state or a federal agency or when there is an obligation to automatically withhold and deploy state aid to pay any defaulted debt service by the issuing entity. Typically, the latter form of public credit enhancement is used for debt obligations of a state's school systems.

Some examples of state credit enhancement programs include Virginia's bond guarantee program that authorizes the governor to withhold state aid payments to a municipality and divert those funds to pay principal and interest to a municipality's general obligation holders in the event of a default. South Carolina's constitution requires mandatory withholding of state aid by the state treasurer if a school district is not capable of meeting its general obligation debt. Texas created the Permanent School Fund to guarantee the timely payment of principal and interest of the debt obligations of qualified school districts. The fund's income is obtained from land and mineral rights owned by the state of Texas.

More recently, states and local governments have issued increasing amounts of bonds where the debt service is to be paid from so-called "dedicated" revenues such as sales taxes, tobacco settlement payments, fees, and penalty payments. Many are structured to mimic the asset-backed bonds that are discussed later in this reading (Section 7).

5.2 Revenue Bonds

The second basic type of security structure is found in a revenue bond. Revenue bonds are issued for enterprise financings that are secured by the revenues generated by the completed projects themselves, or for general public-purpose financings in which the issuers pledge to the bondholders the tax and revenue resources that were previously part of the general fund. This latter type of revenue bond is usually created to allow issuers to raise debt outside general obligation debt limits and without voter approval.

Revenue bonds can be classified by the type of financing. These include utility revenue bonds, transportation revenue bonds, housing revenue bonds, higher education revenue bonds, health care revenue bonds, sports complex and convention center revenue bonds, seaport revenue bonds, and industrial revenue bonds.

5.3 Special Bond Structures

Some municipal securities have special security structures. These include insured bonds and prerefunded bonds.

5.3.1 *Insured Bonds*

Insured bonds, in addition to being secured by the issuer's revenue, are also backed by insurance policies written by commercial insurance companies. Insurance on a municipal bond is an agreement by an insurance company to pay the bondholder principal and/or coupon interest that is due on a stated maturity date but that has not been paid by the bond issuer. Once issued, this municipal bond insurance usually extends for the term of the bond issue and cannot be canceled by the insurance company.

5.3.2 *Prerefunded Bonds*

Although originally issued as either revenue or general obligation bonds, municipals are sometimes prerefunded and thus called prerefunded municipal bonds. A prerefunding usually occurs when the original bonds are escrowed or collateralized by direct obligations guaranteed by the U.S. government. By this, it is meant that a portfolio of securities guaranteed by the U.S. government is placed in a trust. The portfolio of securities is assembled such that the cash flows from the securities match the obligations that the issuer must pay. For example, suppose that a municipality has a 7% $100 million issue with 12 years remaining to maturity. The municipality's obligation is to make payments of $3.5 million every six months for the next 12 years and $100 million 12 years from now. If the issuer wants to prerefund this issue, a portfolio of U.S. government obligations can be purchased that has a cash flow of $3.5 million every six months for the next 12 years and $100 million 12 years from now.

Once this portfolio of securities whose cash flows match those of the municipality's obligation is in place, the prerefunded bonds are no longer secured as either general obligation or revenue bonds. The bonds are now supported by cash flows from the portfolio of securities held in an escrow fund. Such bonds, if escrowed with securities guaranteed by the U.S. government, have little, if any, credit risk. They are the safest municipal bonds available.

The escrow fund for a prerefunded municipal bond can be structured so that the bonds to be refunded are to be called at the first possible call date or a subsequent call date established in the original bond indenture. While prerefunded bonds are usually retired at their first or subsequent call date, some are structured to match the debt obligation to the maturity date. Such bonds are known as escrowed-to-maturity bonds.

CORPORATE DEBT SECURITIES

6

Corporations throughout the world that seek to borrow funds can do so through either bank borrowing or the issuance of debt securities. The securities issued include bonds (called corporate bonds), medium term notes, asset-backed securities, and commercial paper. Exhibit 10 provides an overview of the structures found in the corporate debt market. In many countries throughout the world, the principal form of borrowing is via bank borrowing and, as a result, a well-developed market for non-bank borrowing has not developed or is still in its infancy stage. However, even in countries where the market for corporate debt securities is small, large corporations can borrow outside of their country's domestic market.

Exhibit 10	Overview of Corporate Debt Securities

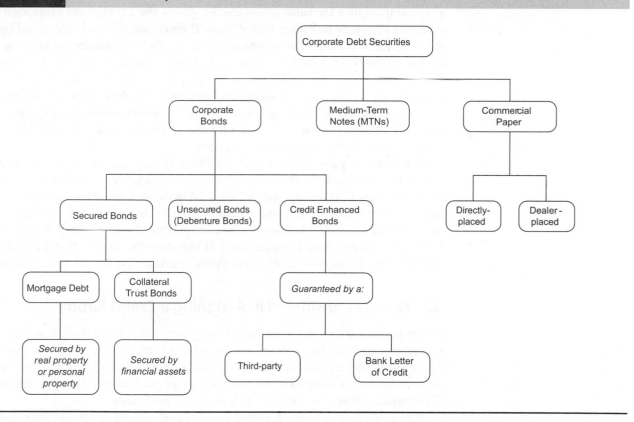

Because in the United States there is a well-developed market for corporations to borrow via the public issuance of debt obligations, we will look at this market. Before we describe the features of corporate bonds in the United States, we will discuss the rights of bondholders in a bankruptcy and the factors considered by rating agencies in assigning a credit rating.

6.1 Bankruptcy and Bondholder Rights in the United States

Every country has securities laws and contract laws that govern the rights of bondholders and a bankruptcy code that covers the treatment of bondholders in the case of a bankruptcy. There are principles that are common in the legal arrangements throughout the world. Below we discuss the features of the U.S. system.

The holder of a U.S. corporate debt instrument has priority over the equity owners in a bankruptcy proceeding. Moreover, there are creditors who have priority over other creditors. The law governing bankruptcy in the United States is the Bankruptcy Reform Act of 1978 as amended from time to time. One purpose of the act is to set forth the rules for a corporation to be either liquidated or reorganized when filing bankruptcy.

The **liquidation** of a corporation means that all the assets will be distributed to the claim holders of the corporation and no corporate entity will survive. In a **reorganization**, a new corporate entity will emerge at the end of the bankruptcy proceedings. Some security holders of the bankrupt corporation will receive cash in exchange for their claims, others may receive new securities in the corporation that results from the reorganization, and others may receive a combination of both cash and new securities in the resulting corporation.

Another purpose of the bankruptcy act is to give a corporation time to decide whether to reorganize or liquidate and then the necessary time to formulate a plan to accomplish either a reorganization or liquidation. This is achieved because when a corporation files for bankruptcy, the act grants the corporation protection from creditors who seek to collect their claims. The petition for bankruptcy can be filed either by the company itself, in which case it is called a voluntary bankruptcy, or be filed by its creditors, in which case it is called an involuntary bankruptcy. A company that files for protection under the bankruptcy act generally becomes a "debtor-in-possession" and continues to operate its business under the supervision of the court.

The bankruptcy act is comprised of 15 chapters, each chapter covering a particular type of bankruptcy. Chapter 7 deals with the liquidation of a company; Chapter 11 deals with the reorganization of a company.

When a company is liquidated, creditors receive distributions based on the absolute priority rule to the extent assets are available. The absolute priority rule is the principle that senior creditors are paid in full before junior creditors are paid anything. For secured and unsecured creditors, the absolute priority rule guarantees their seniority to equity holders. In liquidations, the absolute priority rule generally holds. In contrast, there is a good body of literature that argues that strict absolute priority typically has not been upheld by the courts or the SEC in reorganizations.

6.2 Factors Considered in Assigning a Credit Rating

In the previous reading, we explained that there are companies that assign credit ratings to corporate issues based on the prospects of default. These companies are called rating agencies. In conducting a credit examination, each rating agency, as well as credit analysts employed by investment management companies, consider the four C's of credit—character, capacity, collateral, and covenants.

It is important to understand that a credit analysis can be for an entire company or a particular debt obligation of that company. Consequently, a rating agency may assign a different rating to the various issues of the same corporation depending on the level of seniority of the bondholders of each issue in the case of bankruptcy. For example, we will explain below that there is senior debt and subordinated debt. Senior debtholders have a better position relative to subordinated debtholders in the case of a bankruptcy for a given issuer. So, a rating agency, for example, may assign a rating of "A" to the senior debt of a corporation and a lower rating, "BBB," to the subordinated debt of the same corporation.

Character analysis involves the analysis of the quality of management. In discussing the factors it considers in assigning a credit rating, Moody's Investors Service notes the following regarding the quality of management:

> Although difficult to quantify, management quality is one of the most impor-
> tant factors supporting an issuer's credit strength. When the unexpected

occurs, it is a management's ability to react appropriately that will sustain the company's performance.[7]

In assessing management quality, the analysts at Moody's, for example, try to understand the business strategies and policies formulated by management. Moody's considers the following factors: 1) strategic direction, 2) financial philosophy, 3) conservatism, 4) track record, 5) succession planning, and 6) control systems.[8]

In assessing the ability of an issuer to pay (i.e., capacity), the analysts conduct financial statement analysis as discussed at Level II. In addition to financial statement analysis, the factors examined by analysts at Moody's are 1) industry trends, 2) the regulatory environment, 3) basic operating and competitive position, 4) financial position and sources of liquidity, 5) company structure (including structural subordination and priority of claim), 6) parent company support agreements, and 7) special event risk.[9]

The third C, collateral, is looked at not only in the traditional sense of assets pledged to secure the debt, but also to the quality and value of those unpledged assets controlled by the issuer. Unpledged collateral is capable of supplying additional sources of funds to support payment of debt. Assets form the basis for generating cash flow which services the debt in good times as well as bad. We discuss later the various types of collateral used for a corporate debt issue and features that analysts should be cognizant of when evaluating an investor's secured position.

Covenants deal with limitations and restrictions on the borrower's activities. Affirmative covenants call upon the debtor to make promises to do certain things. Negative covenants are those which require the borrower not to take certain actions. Negative covenants are usually negotiated between the borrower and the lender or their agents. Borrowers want the least restrictive loan agreement available, while lenders should want the most restrictive, consistent with sound business practices. But lenders should not try to restrain borrowers from accepted business activities and conduct. A borrower might be willing to include additional restrictions (up to a point) if it can get a lower interest rate on the debt obligation. When borrowers seek to weaken restrictions in their favor, they are often willing to pay more interest or give other consideration. We will see examples of positive and negative covenants later in this reading.

6.3 Corporate Bonds

In the reading on features of debt securities, we discussed the features of bonds including the wide range of coupon types, the provisions for principal payments, provisions for early retirement, and other embedded options. Also, in the reading on risks associated with investing in bonds, we reviewed the various forms of credit risk and the ratings assigned by rating agencies. In our discussion of corporate bonds here, we will discuss secured and unsecured debt and information about default and recovery rates.

6.3.1 *Secured Debt, Unsecured Debt, and Credit Enhancements*

A corporate debt obligation may be secured or unsecured. Secured debt means that there is some form of collateral pledged to ensure payment of the debt. Remove the pledged collateral and we have unsecured debt.

It is important to recognize that while a superior legal status will strengthen a bondholder's chance of recovery in case of default, it will not absolutely prevent bondholders from suffering financial loss when the issuer's ability to generate sufficient

---

7 "Industrial Company Rating Methodology," *Moody's Investors Service: Global Credit Research* (July 1998), p. 6.
8 "Industrial Company Rating Methodology," p. 7.
9 "Industrial Company Rating Methodology," p. 3.

cash flow to pay its obligations is seriously eroded. Claims against a weak borrower are often satisfied for less than par value.

6.3.1.1 Secured Debt   Either real property or personal property may be pledged as security for secured debt. With mortgage debt, the issuer grants the bondholders a lien against pledged assets. A lien is a legal right to sell mortgaged property to satisfy unpaid obligations to bondholders. In practice, foreclosure and sale of mortgaged property is unusual. If a default occurs, there is usually a financial reorganization of the issuer in which provision is made for settlement of the debt to bondholders. The mortgage lien is important, though, because it gives the mortgage bondholders a strong bargaining position relative to other creditors in determining the terms of a reorganization.

Some companies do not own fixed assets or other real property and so have nothing on which they can give a mortgage lien to secure bondholders. Instead, they own securities of other companies; they are holding companies and the other companies are subsidiaries. To satisfy the desire of bondholders for security, the issuer grants investors a lien on stocks, notes, bonds or other kind of financial asset they own. Bonds secured by such assets are called collateral trust bonds. The eligible collateral is periodically marked to market by the trustee to ensure that the market value has a liquidation value in excess of the amount needed to repay the entire outstanding bonds and accrued interest. If the collateral is insufficient, the issuer must, within a certain period, bring the value of the collateral up to the required amount. If the issuer is unable to do so, the trustee would then sell collateral and redeem bonds.

Mortgage bonds have many different names. The following names have been used: first mortgage bonds (most common name), first and general mortgage bonds, first refunding mortgage bonds, and first mortgage and collateral trusts. There are instances (excluding prior lien bonds as mentioned above) when a company might have two or more layers of mortgage debt outstanding with different priorities. This situation usually occurs because companies cannot issue additional first mortgage debt (or the equivalent) under the existing indentures. Often this secondary debt level is called general and refunding mortgage bonds (G&R). In reality, this is mostly second mortgage debt. Some issuers may have third mortgage bonds.

Although an indenture may not limit the total amount of bonds that may be issued with the same lien, there are certain issuance tests that usually have to be satisfied before the company may sell more bonds. Typically there is an earnings test that must be satisfied before additional bonds may be issued with the same lien.

6.3.1.2 Unsecured Debt   Unsecured debt is commonly referred to as debenture bonds. Although a debenture bond is not secured by a specific pledge of property, that does not mean that bondholders have no claim on property of issuers or on their earnings. Debenture bondholders have the claim of general creditors on all assets of the issuer not pledged specifically to secure other debt. And they even have a claim on pledged assets to the extent that these assets generate proceeds in liquidation that are greater than necessary to satisfy secured creditors. Subordinated debenture bonds are issues that rank after secured debt, after debenture bonds, and often after some general creditors in their claim on assets and earnings.

One of the important protective provisions for unsecured debt holders is the negative pledge clause. This provision, found in most senior unsecured debt issues and a few subordinated issues, prohibits a company from creating or assuming any lien to secure a debt issue without equally securing the subject debt issue(s) (with certain exceptions).

6.3.1.3 Credit Enhancements   Some debt issuers have other companies guarantee their loans. This is normally done when a subsidiary issues debt and the investors want the added protection of a third-party guarantee. The use of guarantees makes it easier and more convenient to finance special projects and affiliates, although guarantees are also extended to operating company debt.

An example of a third-party (but related) guarantee was US West Capital Funding, Inc. 8% Guaranteed Notes that were due October 15, 1996 (guaranteed by US West, Inc.). The principal purpose of Capital Funding was to provide financing to US West and its affiliates through the issuance of debt guaranteed by US West. PepsiCo, Inc. has guaranteed the debt of its financing affiliate, PepsiCo Capital Resources, Inc., and The Standard Oil Company (an Ohio Corporation) has unconditionally guaranteed the debt of Sohio Pipe Line Company.

Another credit enhancing feature is the letter of credit (LOC) issued by a bank. A LOC requires the bank to make payments to the trustee when requested so that monies will be available for the bond issuer to meet its interest and principal payments when due. Thus the credit of the bank under the LOC is substituted for that of the debt issuer. Specialized insurance companies also lend their credit standing to corporate debt, both new issues and outstanding secondary market issues. In such cases, the credit rating of the bond is usually no better than the credit rating of the guarantor.

While a guarantee or other type of credit enhancement may add some measure of protection to a debtholder, caution should not be thrown to the wind. In effect, one's job may even become more complex as an analysis of both the issuer and the guarantor should be performed. In many cases, only the latter is needed if the issuer is merely a financing conduit without any operations of its own. However, if both concerns are operating companies, it may very well be necessary to analyze both, as the timely payment of principal and interest ultimately will depend on the stronger party. Generally, a downgrade of the credit enhancer's claims-paying ability reduces the value of the credit-enhanced bonds.

6.3.2 Default Rates and Recovery Rates

Now we turn our attention to the various aspects of the historical performance of corporate issuers with respect to fulfilling their obligations to bondholders. Specifically, we will review two aspects of this performance. First, we will review the default rate of corporate borrowers. Second, we will review the default loss rate of corporate borrowers. From an investment perspective, default rates by themselves are not of paramount significance: it is perfectly possible for a portfolio of bonds to suffer defaults and to outperform Treasuries at the same time, provided the yield spread of the portfolio is sufficiently high to offset the losses from default. Furthermore, because holders of defaulted bonds typically recover some percentage of the face amount of their investment, the default loss rate is substantially lower than the default rate. Therefore, it is important to look at default loss rates or, equivalently, recovery rates.

6.3.2.1 Default Rates   A default rate can be measured in different ways. A simple way to define a default rate is to use the issuer as the unit of study. A default rate is then measured as the number of issuers that default divided by the total number of issuers at the beginning of the year. This measure—referred to as the issuer default rate—gives no recognition to the amount defaulted nor the total amount of issuance. Moody's, for example, uses this default rate statistic in its study of default rates. The rationale for ignoring dollar amounts is that the credit decision of an investor does not increase with the size of the issuer. The second measure—called the dollar default rate—defines the default rate as the par value of all bonds that defaulted in a given calendar year, divided by the total par value of all bonds outstanding during the year. With either default rate statistic, one can measure the default for a given year or an average annual default rate over a certain number of years.

There have been several excellent studies of corporate bond default rates. All of the studies found that the lower the credit rating, the greater the probability of a corporate issuer defaulting.

There have been extensive studies focusing on default rates for non-investment grade corporate bonds (i.e., speculative-grade issuer or high yield bonds). Studies by Edward Altman suggest that the annual default rate for speculative-grade corporate debt has been between 2.15% and 2.4% per year.[10] Asquith, Mullins, and Wolff, however, found that nearly one out of every three speculative-grade bonds defaults.[11] The large discrepancy arises because researchers use three different definitions of "default rate"; even if applied to the same universe of bonds (which they are not), the results of these studies could be valid simultaneously.[12]

Altman defines the default rate as the dollar default rate. His estimates (2.15% and 2.40%) are simple averages of the annual dollar default rates over a number of years. Asquith, Mullins, and Wolff use a cumulative dollar default rate statistic. While both measures are useful indicators of bond default propensity, they are not directly comparable. Even when restated on an annualized basis, they do not all measure the same quantity. The default statistics reported in both studies, however, are surprisingly similar once cumulative rates have been annualized. A majority of studies place the annual dollar default rates for all original issue high-yield bonds between 3% and 4%.

6.3.2.2 Recovery Rates　There have been several studies that have focused on recovery rates or default loss rates for corporate debt. Measuring the amount recovered is not a simple task. The final distribution to claimants when a default occurs may consist of cash and securities. Often it is difficult to track what was received and then determine the present value of any non-cash payments received.

Here we review recovery information as reported in a study by Moody's which uses the trading price at the time of default as a proxy for the amount recovered.[13] The recovery rate is the trading price at that time divided by the par value. Moody's found that the recovery rate was 38% for all bonds. Moreover, the study found that the higher the level of seniority, the greater the recovery rate.

6.4 Medium-Term Notes

A medium-term note (MTN) is a debt instrument, with the unique characteristic that notes are offered continuously to investors by an agent of the issuer. Investors can select from several maturity ranges: 9 months to 1 year, more than 1 year to 18 months, more than 18 months to 2 years, and so on up to 30 years. Medium-term notes are registered with the Securities and Exchange Commission under Rule 415 (the shelf registration rule) which gives a borrower (corporation, agency, sovereign, or supranational) the maximum flexibility for issuing securities on a continuous basis. As with corporate bonds, MTNs are rated by the nationally recognized statistical rating organizations.

The term "medium-term note" used to describe this debt instrument is misleading. Traditionally, the term "note" or "medium-term" was used to refer to debt issues with a maturity greater than one year but less than 15 years. Certainly this is not a characteristic of MTNs since they have been sold with maturities from nine months to 30 years, and even longer. For example, in July 1993, Walt Disney Corporation issued a security with a 100-year maturity off its medium-term note shelf registration. From

---

10 Edward I. Altman and Scott A. Nammacher, *Investing in Junk Bonds* (New York: John Wiley, 1987) and Edward I. Altman, "Research Update: Mortality Rates and Losses, Bond Rating Drift," unpublished study prepared for a workshop sponsored by Merrill Lynch Merchant Banking Group, High Yield Sales and Trading, 1989.

11 Paul Asquith, David W. Mullins, Jr., and Eric D. Wolff, "Original Issue High Yield Bonds: Aging Analysis of Defaults, Exchanges, and Calls," *Journal of Finance* (September 1989), pp. 923–952.

12 As a parallel, we know that the mortality rate in the United States is currently less than 1% per year, but we also know that 100% of all humans (eventually) die.

13 Moody's Investors Service, *Corporate Bond Defaults and Default Rates: 1970–1994*, Moody's Special Report, January 1995, p. 13.

the perspective of the borrower, the initial purpose of the MTN was to fill the funding gap between commercial paper and long-term bonds. It is for this reason that they are referred to as "medium term."

Borrowers have flexibility in designing MTNs to satisfy their own needs. They can issue fixed- or floating-rate debt. The coupon payments can be denominated in U.S. dollars or in a foreign currency. MTNs have been designed with the same features as corporate bonds.

6.4.1 *The Primary Market*

Medium-term notes differ from bonds in the manner in which they are distributed to investors when they are initially sold. Although some corporate bond issues are sold on a "best-efforts basis" (i.e., the underwriter does not purchase the securities from the issuer but only agrees to sell them),[14] typically corporate bonds are underwritten by investment bankers. When "underwritten," the investment banker purchases the bonds from the issuer at an agreed upon price and yield and then attempts to sell them to investors. This is discussed further in Section 9. MTNs have been traditionally distributed on a best-efforts basis by either an investment banking firm or other broker/dealers acting as agents. Another difference between bonds and MTNs is that when offered, MTNs are usually sold in relatively small amounts on either a continuous or an intermittent basis, while bonds are sold in large, discrete offerings.

An entity that wants to initiate a MTN program will file a shelf registration[15] with the SEC for the offering of securities. While the SEC registration for MTN offerings are between $100 million and $1 billion, once completely sold, the issuer can file another shelf registration for a new MTN offering. The registration will include a list of the investment banking firms, usually two to four, that the borrower has arranged to act as agents to distribute the MTNs.

The issuer then posts rates over a range of maturities: for example, nine months to one year, one year to 18 months, 18 months to two years, and annually thereafter. In an offering rate schedule, an issuer will post rates as a spread over a Treasury security of comparable maturity. Rates will not be posted for maturity ranges that the issuer does not desire to sell.

The agents will then make the offering rate schedule available to their investor base interested in MTNs. An investor who is interested in the offering will contact the agent. In turn, the agent contacts the issuer to confirm the terms of the transaction. Since the maturity range in an offering rate schedule does not specify a specific maturity date, the investor can choose the final maturity subject to approval by the issuer.

The rate offering schedule can be changed at any time by the issuer either in response to changing market conditions or because the issuer has raised the desired amount of funds at a given maturity. In the latter case, the issuer can either not post a rate for that maturity range or lower the rate.

6.4.2 *Structured MTNs*

At one time, the typical MTN was a fixed-rate debenture that was noncallable. It is common today for issuers of MTNs to couple their offerings with transactions in the derivative markets (options, futures/forwards, swaps, caps, and floors) so they may create debt

---

14 The primary market for bonds is described in Section 9.1.

15 SEC Rule 415 permits certain issuers to file a single registration document indicating that it intends to sell a certain amount of a certain class of securities at one or more times within the next two years. Rule 415 is popularly referred to as the "shelf registration rule" because the securities can be viewed as sitting on the issuer's "shelf" and can be taken off that shelf and sold to the public without obtaining additional SEC approval. In essence, the filing of a single registration document allows the issuer to come to market quickly because the sale of the security has been preapproved by the SEC. Prior to establishment of Rule 415, there was a lengthy period required before a security could be sold to the public. As a result, in a fast-moving market, issuers could not come to market quickly with an offering to take advantage of what it perceived to be attractive financing opportunities.

obligations with more complex risk/return features than are available in the corporate bond market. Specifically, an issue can have a floating-rate over all or part of the life of the security and the coupon formula can be based on a benchmark interest rate, equity index, individual stock price, foreign exchange rate, or commodity index. There are MTNs with inverse floating coupon rates, and they can include various embedded options.

MTNs created when the issuer simultaneously transacts in the derivative markets are called **structured notes**. The most common derivative instrument used in creating structured notes is a swap, an instrument described at Level II. By using the derivative markets in combination with an offering, issuers are able to create investment vehicles that are more customized for institutional investors to satisfy their investment objectives, but who are forbidden from using swaps for hedging or speculating. Moreover, it allows institutional investors who are restricted to investing in investment grade debt issues the opportunity to participate in other asset classes such as the equity market. Hence, structured notes are sometimes referred to as "rule busters." For example, an investor who buys an MTN whose coupon rate is tied to the performance of the S&P 500 (the reference rate) is participating in the equity market without owning common stock. If the coupon rate is tied to a foreign stock index, the investor is participating in the equity market of a foreign country without owning foreign common stock. In exchange for creating a structured note product, issuers can reduce their funding costs.

Common structured notes include: step-up notes, inverse floaters, deleveraged floaters, dual-indexed floaters, range notes, and index amortizing notes.

6.4.2.1 Deleveraged Floaters

A deleveraged floater is a floater that has a coupon formula where the coupon rate is computed as a fraction of the reference rate plus a quoted margin. The general formula for a deleveraged floater is:

Coupon rate = b × (Reference rate) + Quoted margin

where b is a value between zero and one.

6.4.2.2 Dual-Indexed Floaters

The coupon rate for a dual-indexed floater is typically a fixed percentage plus the difference between two reference rates. For example, the Federal Home Loan Bank System issued a floater whose coupon rate (reset quarterly) as follows:

(10-year **Constant Maturity Treasury** rate) – (3-month LIBOR) + 160 Basis points

6.4.2.3 Range Notes

A range note is a type of floater whose coupon rate is equal to the reference rate as long as the reference rate is within a certain range at the reset date. If the reference rate is outside of the range, the coupon rate is zero for that period. For example, a 3-year range note might specify that the reference rate is the 1-year Treasury rate and that the coupon rate resets every year. The coupon rate for the year is the Treasury rate as long as the Treasury rate at the coupon reset date falls within the range as specified below:

	Year 1 (%)	Year 2 (%)	Year 3 (%)
Lower limit of range	4.5	5.25	6.00
Upper limit of range	6.5	7.25	8.00

If the 1-year Treasury rate is outside of the range, the coupon rate is zero. For example, if in year 1 the 1-year Treasury rate is 5% at the coupon reset date, the coupon rate for the year is 5%. However, if the 1-year Treasury rate is 7%, the coupon rate for the year is zero since the 1-year Treasury rate is greater than the upper limit for year 1 of 6.5%.

6.4.2.4 Index Amortizing Notes

An index amortizing note (IAN) is a structured note with a fixed coupon rate but whose principal payments are made prior to the stated maturity date based on the prevailing value for some reference interest rate. The principal payments are structured so that the time to maturity of an IAN increases when the reference interest rate increases and the maturity decreases when the reference interest rate decreases.

From our understanding of reinvestment risks, we can see the risks associated with investing in an IAN. Since the coupon rate is fixed, when interest rates rise, an investor would prefer to receive principal back faster in order to reinvest the proceeds received at the prevailing higher rate. However, with an IAN, the rate of principal repayment is decreased. In contrast, when interest rates decline, an investor does not want principal repaid quickly because the investor would then be forced to reinvest the proceeds received at the prevailing lower interest rate. With an IAN, when interest rates decline, the investor will, in fact, receive principal back faster.

6.5 Commercial Paper

Commercial paper is a short-term unsecured promissory note that is issued in the open market and represents the obligation of the issuing corporation. Typically, commercial paper is issued as a zero-coupon instrument. In the United States, the maturity of commercial paper is typically less than 270 days, and the most common maturity is 50 days or less.

To pay off holders of maturing paper, issuers generally use the proceeds obtained from selling new commercial paper. This process is often described as "rolling over" short-term paper. The risk that the investor in commercial paper faces is that the issuer will be unable to issue new paper at maturity. As a safeguard against this "roll-over risk," commercial paper is typically backed by unused bank credit lines.

There is very little secondary trading of commercial paper. Typically, an investor in commercial paper is an entity that plans to hold it until maturity. This is understandable since an investor can purchase commercial paper in a direct transaction with the issuer, which will issue paper with the specific maturity the investor desires.

Corporate issuers of commercial paper can be divided into financial companies and nonfinancial companies. There has been significantly greater use of commercial paper by financial companies compared to nonfinancial companies. There are three types of financial companies: captive finance companies, bank-related finance companies, and independent finance companies. Captive finance companies are subsidiaries of manufacturing companies. Their primary purpose is to secure financing for the customers of the parent company. For example, U.S. automobile manufacturers have captive finance companies. Furthermore, a bank holding company may have a subsidiary that is a finance company, providing loans to enable individuals and businesses to acquire a wide range of products. Independent finance companies are those that are not subsidiaries of equipment manufacturing firms or bank holding companies.

Commercial paper is classified as either directly placed paper or dealer-placed paper. Directly placed paper is sold by the issuing firm to investors without the help of an agent or an intermediary. A large majority of the issuers of directly placed paper are financial companies. These entities require continuous funds in order to provide loans to customers. As a result, they find it cost-effective to establish a sales force to sell their commercial paper directly to investors. General Electric Capital Corporation (GE Capital)—the principal financial services arm of General Electric Company—is the largest and most active direct issuer of commercial paper in the United States. Dealer-placed commercial paper requires the services of an agent to sell an issuer's paper.

The three nationally recognized statistical rating organizations that rate corporate bonds and medium-term notes also rate commercial paper. The ratings are shown in Exhibit 11. Commercial paper ratings, as with the ratings on other securities, are categorized as either investment grade or noninvestment grade.

| Exhibit 11 | Commercial Paper Ratings | | |

| Category | Commercial Rating Company | | |
	Fitch	Moody's	S&P
Investment grade	F-1 +		A-1 +
	F-1	P-1	A-1
	F-2	P-2	A-2
	F-3	P-3	A-3
Noninvestment grade	F-S	NP (Not Prime)	B
			C
In default	D		D

6.6 Bank Obligations

Commercial banks are special types of corporations. Larger banks will raise funds using the various debt obligations described earlier. In this section, we describe two other debt obligations of banks—negotiable certificates of deposit and bankers acceptances—that are used by banks to raise funds.

6.6.1 Negotiable CDs

A certificate of deposit (CD) is a financial asset issued by a bank (or other deposit-accepting entity) that indicates a specified sum of money has been deposited at the issuing depository institution. A CD bears a maturity date and a specified interest rate; it can be issued in any denomination. In the United States, CDs issued by most banks are insured by the Federal Deposit Insurance Corporation (FDIC), but only for amounts up to $100,000. There is no limit on the maximum maturity. A CD may be nonnegotiable or negotiable. In the former case, the initial depositor must wait until the maturity date of the CD to obtain the funds. If the depositor chooses to withdraw funds prior to the maturity date, an early withdrawal penalty is imposed. In contrast, a negotiable CD allows the initial depositor (or any subsequent owner of the CD) to sell the CD in the open market prior to the maturity date. Negotiable CDs are usually issued in denominations of $1 million or more. Hence, an investor in a negotiable CD issued by an FDIC insured bank is exposed to the credit risk for any amount in excess of $100,000.

An important type of negotiable CD is the Eurodollar CD, which is a U.S. dollar-denominated CD issued primarily in London by U.S., European, Canadian, and Japanese banks. The interest rates paid on Eurodollar CDs play an important role in the world financial markets because they are viewed globally as the cost of bank borrowing. This is due to the fact that these interest rates represent the rates at which major international banks offer to pay each other to borrow money by issuing a Eurodollar CD with given maturities. The interest rate paid is called the **London interbank offered rate (LIBOR)**. The maturities for the Eurodollar CD range from overnight to five years. So, references to "3-month LIBOR" indicate the interest rate that major international banks are offering to pay to other such banks on a Eurodollar CD that matures in three months. During the 1990s, LIBOR has increasingly become the reference rate of choice for borrowing arrangements—loans and floating-rate securities.

6.6.2 Bankers Acceptances

Simply put, a bankers acceptance is a vehicle created to facilitate commercial trade transactions. The instrument is called a bankers acceptance because a bank accepts the ultimate responsibility to repay a loan to its holder. The use of bankers acceptances to finance a commercial transaction is referred to as "acceptance financing." In the United States, the transactions in which bankers acceptances are created include 1) the importing of goods; 2) the exporting of goods to foreign entities; 3) the storing and shipping of goods between two foreign countries where neither the importer nor the exporter is a U.S. firm; and 4) the storing and shipping of goods between two U.S. entities in the United States. Bankers acceptances are sold on a discounted basis just as Treasury bills and commercial paper.

The best way to explain the creation of a bankers acceptance is by an illustration. Several entities are involved in our hypothetical transaction:

■ Luxury Cars USA (Luxury Cars), a firm in Pennsylvania that sells automobiles.

■ Italian Fast Autos, Inc. (IFA), a manufacturer of automobiles in Italy.

■ First Doylestown Bank (Doylestown Bank), a commercial bank in Doylestown, Pennsylvania.

■ *Banco di Francesco*, a bank in Naples, Italy.

■ The Izzabof Money Market Fund, a U.S. mutual fund.

Luxury Cars and IFA are considering a commercial transaction. Luxury Cars wants to import 45 cars manufactured by IFA. IFA is concerned with the ability of Luxury Cars to make payment on the 45 cars when they are received.

Acceptance financing is suggested as a means for facilitating the transaction. Luxury Cars offers $900,000 for the 45 cars. The terms of the sale stipulate payment to be made to IFA 60 days after it ships the 45 cars to Luxury Cars. IFA determines whether it is willing to accept the $900,000. In considering the offering price, IFA must calculate the present value of the $900,000, because it will not be receiving payment until 60 days after shipment. Suppose that IFA agrees to these terms.

Luxury Cars arranges with its bank, Doylestown Bank, to issue a letter of credit. The letter of credit indicates that Doylestown Bank will make good on the payment of $900,000 that Luxury Cars must make to IFA 60 days after shipment. The letter of credit, or time draft, will be sent by Doylestown Bank to IFA's bank, *Banco di Francesco*. Upon receipt of the letter of credit, *Banco di Francesco* will notify IFA, which will then ship the 45 cars. After the cars are shipped, IFA presents the shipping documents to *Banco di Francesco* and receives the present value of $900,000. IFA is now out of the picture.

Banco di Francesco presents the time draft and the shipping documents to Doylestown Bank. The latter will then stamp "accepted" on the time draft. By doing so, Doylestown Bank has created a bankers acceptance. This means that Doylestown Bank agrees to pay the holder of the bankers acceptance $900,000 at the maturity date. Luxury Cars will receive the shipping documents so that it can procure the 45 cars once it signs a note or some other type of financing arrangement with Doylestown Bank.

At this point, the holder of the bankers acceptance is *Banco di Francesco*. It has two choices. It can continue to hold the bankers acceptance as an investment in its loan portfolio, or it can request that Doylestown Bank make a payment of the present value of $900,000. Let's assume that *Banco di Francesco* requests payment of the present value of $900,000. Now the holder of the bankers acceptance is Doylestown Bank. It has two choices: retain the bankers acceptance as an investment as part of its loan portfolio or sell it to an investor. Suppose that Doylestown Bank chooses the latter, and that The Izzabof Money Market Fund is seeking a high-quality investment with the same maturity as that of the bankers acceptance. Doylestown Bank sells the bankers acceptance to the money market fund at the present value of $900,000. Rather than sell the instrument directly to an investor, Doylestown Bank could sell it to a dealer, who would then resell it to an investor such as a money market fund. In either case, at the maturity date, the money market fund presents the bankers acceptance to Doylestown Bank, receiving $900,000, which the bank in turn recovers from Luxury Cars.

Investing in bankers acceptances exposes the investor to credit risk and liquidity risk. Credit risk arises because neither the borrower nor the accepting bank may be able to pay the principal due at the maturity date. When the bankers acceptance market was growing in the early 1980s, there were over 25 dealers. By 1989, the decline in the amount of bankers acceptances issued drove many one-time major dealers out of the business. Today, there are only a few major dealers and therefore bankers acceptances are considered illiquid. Nevertheless, since bankers acceptances are typically purchased by investors who plan to hold them to maturity, liquidity risk is not a concern to such investors.

7   ASSET-BACKED SECURITIES

In Section 4.2 we described how residential mortgage loans have been securitized. While residential mortgage loans is by far the largest type of asset that has been securitized, the major types of assets that have been securitized in many countries have included the following:

- auto loans and leases;
- consumer loans;
- commercial assets (e.g., including aircraft, equipment leases, trade receivables);
- credit cards;
- home equity loans;
- manufactured housing loans.

Asset-backed securities are securities backed by a pool of loans or receivables. Our objective in this section is to provide a brief introduction to asset-backed securities.

7.1 The Role of the Special Purpose Vehicle

The key question for investors first introduced to the asset-backed securities market is why doesn't a corporation simply issue a corporate bond or medium-term note rather than an asset-backed security? To understand why, consider a triple B rated corporation that manufactures construction equipment. We will refer to this corporation as XYZ Corp. Some of its sales are for cash and others are on an installment sales basis. The installment sales are assets on the balance sheet of XYZ Corp., shown as "installment sales receivables."

Suppose XYZ Corp. wants to raise $75 million. If it issues a corporate bond, for example, XYZ Corp.'s funding cost would be whatever the benchmark Treasury yield is plus a yield spread for BBB issuers. Suppose, instead, that XYZ Corp. has installment sales receivables that are more than $75 million. XYZ Corp. can use the installment sales receivables as collateral for a bond issue. What will its funding cost be? It will probably be the same as if it issued a corporate bond. The reason is if XYZ Corp. defaults on any of its obligations, the creditors will have claim on all of its assets, including the installment sales receivables to satisfy payment of their bonds.

However, suppose that XYZ Corp. can create another corporation or legal entity and sell the installment sales receivables to that entity. We'll refer to this entity as SPV Corp. If the transaction is done properly, SPV Corp. owns the installment sales receivables, not XYZ Corp. It is important to understand that SPV Corp. is *not* a subsidiary of XYZ Corp.; therefore, the assets in SPV Corp. (i.e., the installment sales receivables) are not owned by XYZ Corp. This means that if XYZ Corp. is forced into bankruptcy, its creditors cannot claim the installment sales receivables because they are owned by SPV Corp. What are the implications?

Suppose that SPV Corp. sells securities backed by the installment sales receivables. Now creditors will evaluate the credit risk associated with collecting the receivables independent of the credit rating of XYZ Corp. What credit rating will be received for the securities issued by SPV Corp.? Whatever SPV Corp. wants the rating to be! It may seem strange that the issuer (SPV Corp.) can get any rating it wants, but that is the case. The reason is that SPV Corp. will show the characteristics of the collateral for the security (i.e., the installment sales receivables) to a rating agency. In turn, the rating agency will evaluate the credit quality of the collateral and inform the issuer what must be done to obtain specific ratings.

More specifically, the issuer will be asked to "credit enhance" the securities. There are various forms of credit enhancement. Basically, the rating agencies will look at the potential losses from the pool of installment sales receivables and make a determination of how much credit enhancement is needed for it to issue a specific rating. The higher the credit rating sought by the issuer, the greater the credit enhancement. Thus, XYZ Corp. which is BBB rated can obtain funding using its installment sales receivables as collateral to obtain a better credit rating for the securities issued. In fact, with enough credit enhancement, it can issue a AAA-rated security.

The key to a corporation issuing a security with a higher credit rating than the corporation's own credit rating is using SPV Corp. as the issuer. Actually, this legal entity that a corporation sells the assets to is called a **special purpose vehicle** or special purpose corporation. It plays a critical role in the ability to create a security—an asset-backed security—that separates the assets used as collateral from the corporation that is seeking financing.

Why doesn't a corporation always seek the highest credit rating (AAA) for its securities backed by collateral? The answer is that credit enhancement does not come without a cost. Credit enhancement mechanisms increase the costs associated with a securitized borrowing via an asset-backed security. So, the corporation must monitor the trade-off when seeking a higher rating between the additional cost of credit enhancing the security versus the reduction in funding cost by issuing a security with a higher credit rating.

Additionally, if bankruptcy occurs, there is the risk that a bankruptcy judge may decide that the assets of the special purpose vehicle are assets that the creditors of the corporation seeking financing (XYZ Corp. in our example) may claim after all. This is an important but unresolved legal issue in the United States. Legal experts have argued that this is unlikely. In the prospectus of an asset-backed security, there will be a legal opinion addressing this issue. This is the reason why special purpose vehicles in the United States are referred to as "bankruptcy remote" entities.

7.2 Credit Enhancement Mechanisms

In Level II, we will review how rating agencies analyze collateral in order to assign ratings. What is important to understand is that the amount of credit enhancement will be determined relative to a particular rating. There are two general types of credit enhancement structures: external and internal.

External credit enhancements come in the form of third-party guarantees. The most common forms of external credit enhancements are 1) a corporate guarantee, 2) a letter of credit, and 3) bond insurance. A corporate guarantee could be from the issuing entity seeking the funding (XYZ Corp. in our illustration above) or its parent company. Bond insurance provides the same function as in municipal bond structures and is referred to as an insurance "wrap."

A disadvantage of an external credit enhancement is that it is subject to the credit risk of the third-party guarantor. Should the third-party guarantor be downgraded, the issue itself could be subject to downgrade even if the collateral is performing as expected. This is based on the "weak link" test followed by rating agencies. According to this test, when evaluating a proposed structure, the credit quality of the issue is only as good as the weakest link in credit enhancement regardless of the quality of the underlying loans. Basically, an external credit enhancement exposes the investor to event risk since the downgrading of one entity (the third-party guarantor) can result in a downgrade of the asset-backed security.

Internal credit enhancements come in more complicated forms than external credit enhancements. The most common forms of internal credit enhancements are reserve funds, over collateralization, and senior/subordinate structures. We discuss each of these at Level II.

8 COLLATERALIZED DEBT OBLIGATIONS

A fixed income product that is also classified as part of the asset-backed securities market is the collateralized debt obligation (CDO). CDOs deserve special attention because of their growth since 2000. Moreover, while a CDO is backed by various assets, it is managed in a way that is not typical in other asset-backed security transactions. CDOs have been issued in both developed and developing countries.

A CDO is a product backed by a diversified pool of one or more of the following types of debt obligations:

- U.S. domestic investment-grade and high-yield corporate bonds;
- U.S. domestic bank loans;
- emerging market bonds;
- special situation loans and distressed debt;
- foreign bank loans;
- asset-backed securities;
- residential and commercial mortgage-backed securities;
- other CDOs.

When the underlying pool of debt obligations consists of bond-type instruments (corporate and emerging market bonds), a CDO is referred to as a collateralized bond obligation (CBO). When the underlying pool of debt obligations are bank loans, a CDO is referred to as a collateralized loan obligation (CLO).

In a CDO structure, an asset manager is responsible for managing the portfolio of assets (i.e., the debt obligations in which it invests). The funds to purchase the underlying assets (i.e., the bonds and loans) are obtained from the issuance of a CDO. The CDO is structured into notes or *tranches* similar to a CMO issue. The tranches are assigned ratings by a rating agency. There are restrictions as to how the manager manages the CDO portfolio, usually in the form of specific tests that must be satisfied. If any of the restrictions are violated by the asset manager, the notes can be downgraded, and it is possible that the trustee begin paying principal to the senior noteholders in the CDO structure.

CDOs are categorized based on the motivation of the sponsor of the transaction. If the motivation of the sponsor is to earn the spread between the yield offered on the fixed income products held in the portfolio of the underlying pool (i.e., the collateral) and the payments made to the noteholders in the structure, then the transaction is referred to as an arbitrage transaction. (Moreover, a CDO is a vehicle for a sponsor that is an investment management firm to gather additional assets to manage and thereby generate additional management fees.) If the motivation of the sponsor is to remove debt instruments (primarily loans) from its balance sheet, then the transaction is referred to as a balance sheet transaction. Sponsors of balance sheet transactions are typically financial institutions such as banks and insurance companies seeking to reduce their capital requirements by removing loans due to their higher risk-based capital requirements.

PRIMARY MARKET AND SECONDARY MARKET FOR BONDS

9

Financial markets can be categorized as those dealing with financial claims that are newly issued, called the primary market, and those for exchanging financial claims previously issued, called the secondary market.

9.1 Primary Market

The primary market for bonds involves the distribution to investors of newly issued securities by central governments, its agencies, municipal governments, and corporations. Investment bankers work with issuers to distribute newly issued securities. The traditional process for issuing new securities involves investment bankers performing one or more of the following three functions: 1) advising the issuer on the terms and the timing of the offering, 2) buying the securities from the issuer, and 3) distributing the issue to the public. The advisor role may require investment bankers to design a security structure that is more palatable to investors than a particular traditional instrument.

In the sale of new securities, investment bankers need not undertake the second function—buying the securities from the issuer. An investment banker may merely act as an advisor and/or distributor of the new security. The function of buying the securities from the issuer is called underwriting. When an investment banking firm buys the securities from the issuer and accepts the risk of selling the securities to investors at a lower price, it is referred to as an underwriter. When the investment banking firm agrees to buy the securities from the issuer at a set price, the underwriting arrangement is referred to as a firm commitment. In contrast, in a best efforts arrangement, the investment banking firm only agrees to use its expertise to sell the securities—it does not buy the entire issue from the issuer. The fee earned from the initial offering of a security is the difference between the price paid to the issuer and the price at which the investment bank reoffers the security to the public (called the reoffering price).

9.1.1 *Bought Deal and Auction Process*

Not all bond issues are underwritten using the traditional firm commitment or best effort process we just described. Variations in the United States, the Euromarkets, and foreign markets for bonds include the bought deal and the auction process. The mechanics of a bought deal are as follows. The underwriting firm or group of underwriting firms offers a potential issuer of debt securities a firm bid to purchase a specified amount of securities with a certain coupon rate and maturity. The issuer is given a day or so (maybe even a few hours) to accept or reject the bid. If the bid is accepted, the underwriting firm has "bought the deal." It can, in turn, sell the securities to other investment banking firms for distribution to their clients and/or distribute the securities to its clients. Typically, the underwriting firm that buys the deal will have presold most of the issue to its institutional clients. Thus, the risk of capital loss for the underwriting firm in a bought deal may not be as great as it first appears. There are some deals that are so straightforward that a large underwriting firm may have enough institutional investor interest to keep the risks of distributing the issue at the reoffering price quite small. Moreover, hedging strategies using interest rate risk control tools can reduce or eliminate the risk of realizing a loss of selling the bonds at a price below the reoffering price.

In the auction process, the issuer announces the terms of the issue and interested parties submit bids for the entire issue. This process is more commonly referred to as a competitive bidding underwriting. For example, suppose that a public utility wishes to issue $400 million of bonds. Various underwriters will form syndicates and bid on the issue. The syndicate that bids the lowest yield (i.e., the lowest cost to the issuer) wins the entire $400 million bond issue and then reoffers it to the public.

9.1.2 *Private Placement of Securities*

Public and private offerings of securities differ in terms of the regulatory requirements that must be satisfied by the issuer. For example, in the United States, the Securities Act of 1933 and the Securities Exchange Act of 1934 require that all securities offered to the general public must be registered with the SEC, unless there is a specific exemption. The Securities Acts allow certain exemptions from federal registration. Section 4(2) of the 1933 Act exempts from registration "transactions by an issuer not involving any public offering."

The exemption of an offering does not mean that the issuer need not disclose information to potential investors. The issuer must still furnish the same information deemed material by the SEC. This is provided in a private placement memorandum, as opposed to a prospectus for a public offering. The distinction between the private placement memorandum and the prospectus is that the former does not include information deemed by the SEC as "non-material," whereas such information is required in a prospectus. Moreover, unlike a prospectus, the private placement memorandum is not subject to SEC review.

In the United States, one restriction that was imposed on buyers of privately placed securities is that they may not be sold for two years after acquisition. Thus, there was no liquidity in the market for that time period. Buyers of privately placed securities must be compensated for the lack of liquidity, which raises the cost to the issuer of the securities. SEC Rule 144A, which became effective in 1990, eliminates the two-year holding period by permitting large institutions to trade securities acquired in a private placement among themselves without having to register these securities with the SEC. Private placements are therefore now classified as Rule 144A offerings or non-Rule 144A offerings. The latter are more commonly referred to as traditional private placements. Rule 144A offerings are underwritten by investment bankers.

9.2 Secondary Market

In the secondary market, an issuer of a bond—whether it is a corporation or a governmental unit—may obtain regular information about the bond's value. The periodic trading of a bond reveals to the issuer the consensus price that the bond commands in an open market. Thus, issuers can discover what value investors attach to their bonds and the implied interest rates investors expect and demand from them. Bond investors receive several benefits from a secondary market. The market obviously offers them liquidity for their bond holdings as well as information about fair or consensus values. Furthermore, secondary markets bring together many interested parties and thereby reduces the costs of searching for likely buyers and sellers of bonds.

A bond can trade on an exchange or in an over-the-counter market. Traditionally, bond trading has taken place predominately in the over-the-counter market where broker-dealer trading desks take principal positions to fill customer buy and sell orders. In recent years, however, there has been an evolution away from this form of traditional bond trading and toward electronic bond trading. This evolution toward electronic bond trading is likely to continue.

There are several related reasons for the transition to the electronic trading of bonds. First, because the bond business has been a principal business (where broker-dealer firms risk their own capital) rather than an agency business (where broker-dealer firms act merely as an agent or broker), the capital of the market makers is critical. The amount of capital available to institutional investors to invest throughout the world has placed significant demands on the capital of broker-dealer firms. As a result, making markets in bonds has become more risky for broker-dealer firms. Second, the increase in bond market volatility has increased the capital required of broker-dealer firms in the bond business. Finally, the profitability of bond market trading has declined since many of the products have become more commodity-like and their bid-offer spreads have decreased.

The combination of the increased risk and the decreased profitability of bond market trading has induced the major broker-dealer firms to deemphasize this business in the allocation of capital. Broker-dealer firms have determined that it is more efficient to employ their capital in other activities such as underwriting and asset management, rather than in principal-type market-making businesses. As a result, the liquidity of the traditionally principal-oriented bond markets has declined, and this decline in liquidity has opened the way for other market-making mechanisms. This retreat by traditional market-making firms opened the door for electronic trading. In fact, the major broker-dealer firms in bonds have supported electronic trading in bonds.

Electronic trading in bonds has helped fill this developing vacuum and provided liquidity to the bond markets. In addition to the overall advantages of electronic trading in providing liquidity to the markets and price discovery (particularly for less liquid markets) is the resulting trading and portfolio management efficiencies that have been realized. For example, portfolio managers can load their buy/sell orders into a website, trade from these orders, and then clear these orders.

There are a variety of types of electronic trading systems for bonds. The two major types of electronic trading systems are dealer-to-customer systems and exchange systems. Dealer-to-customer systems can be a single-dealer system or multiple-dealer system. Single-dealer systems are based on a customer dealing with a single, identified dealer over the computer. The single-dealer system simply computerizes the traditional customer-dealer market-making mechanism. Multi-dealer systems provide some advancement over the single-dealer method. A customer can select from any of several identified dealers whose bids and offers are provided on a computer screen. The customer knows the identity of the dealer.

In an exchange system, dealer and customer bids and offers are entered into the system on an anonymous basis, and the clearing of the executed trades is done through a common process. Two different major types of exchange systems are those based on continuous trading and call auctions. Continuous trading permits trading at continuously changing market-determined prices throughout the day and is appropriate for liquid bonds, such as Treasury and agency securities. Call auctions provide for fixed price auctions (that is, all the transactions or exchanges occur at the same "fixed" price) at specific times during the day and are appropriate for less liquid bonds such as corporate bonds and municipal bonds.

SOLUTIONS FOR PRACTICE QUESTIONS FOUND IN READING

1. **A.** Since the inflation rate (as measured by the CPI-U) is 2.4%, the semiannual inflation rate for adjusting the principal is 1.2%.

   i. The inflation adjustment to the principal is

   $10,000 × 0.012 = $120.00

   ii. The inflation-adjusted principal is

   $10,000 + Inflation adjustment to the principal = $10,000 + $120 = $10,120

   iii. The coupon payment is equal to

   Inflation-adjusted principal × (Real rate/2) = $10,120 × (0.038/2) = $192.28

   B. Since the inflation rate is 2.8%, the semiannual inflation rate for adjusting the principal is 1.4%.

   i. The inflation adjustment to the principal is

   $10,120 × 0.014 = $141.68

   ii. The inflation-adjusted principal is

   $10,120 + Inflation adjustment to the principal = $10,120 + $141.68 = $10,261.68

   iii. The coupon payment is equal to

   Inflation-adjusted principal × (Real rate/2) = $10,261.68 × (0.038/2) = $194.97

2. Monthly mortgage payment = $699.21

   Monthly mortgage rate = 0.00625 (0.075/12)

Month	Beginning of Month Mortgage Balance	Mortgage Payment	Interest	Scheduled Principal Repayment	End of Month Mortgage Balance
1	100,000.00	699.21	625.00	74.21	99,925.79
2	99,925.79	699.21	624.54	74.68	99,851.11
3	99,851.11	699.21	624.07	75.15	99,775.96
4	99,775.96	699.21	623.60	75.61	99,700.35
5	99,700.35	699.21	623.13	76.09	99,624.26
6	99,624.26	699.21	622.65	76.56	99,547.70

SUMMARY

▪ The bond market of a country consists of an internal bond market (also called the national bond market) and an external bond market (also called the international bond market, the offshore bond market, or, more popularly, the Eurobond market).

- A country's national bond market consists of the domestic bond market and the foreign bond market.

- Eurobonds are bonds which generally have the following distinguishing features: 1) they are underwritten by an international syndicate, 2) at issuance they are offered simultaneously to investors in a number of countries, 3) they are issued outside the jurisdiction of any single country, and 4) they are in unregistered form.

- Sovereign debt is the obligation of a country's central government.

- Sovereign credits are rated by Standard & Poor's and Moody's.

- There are two ratings assigned to each central government: a local currency debt rating and a foreign currency debt rating.

- Historically, defaults have been greater on foreign currency denominated debt.

- There are various methods of distribution that have been used by central governments when issuing securities: regular auction cycle/single-price system; regular auction cycle/multiple-price system, ad hoc auction system, and the tap system.

- In the United States, government securities are issued by the Department of the Treasury and include fixed-principal securities and inflation-indexed securities.

- The most recently auctioned Treasury issue for a maturity is referred to as the on-the-run issue or current coupon issue; off-the-run issues are issues auctioned prior to the current coupon issue.

- Treasury discount securities are called bills and have a maturity of one year or less.

- A Treasury note is a coupon-bearing security which when issued has an original maturity between two and 10 years; a Treasury bond is a coupon-bearing security which when issued has an original maturity greater than 10 years.

- The Treasury issues inflation-protection securities (TIPS) whose principal and coupon payments are indexed to the Consumer Price Index.

- Zero-coupon Treasury instruments are created by dealers stripping the coupon payments and principal payment of a Treasury coupon security.

- Strips created from the coupon payments are called coupon strips; those created from the principal payment are called principal strips.

- A disadvantage for a taxable entity investing in Treasury strips is that accrued interest is taxed each year even though interest is not received.

- The bonds of an agency or organization established by a central government are called semi-government bonds or government agency bonds and may have either a direct or implied credit guarantee by the central government.

- In the U.S. bond market, federal agencies are categorized as either federally related institutions or government-sponsored enterprises.

- Federally related institutions are arms of the U.S. government and, with the exception of securities of the Tennessee Valley Authority and the Private Export Funding Corporation, are backed by the full faith and credit of the U.S. government.

- Government-sponsored enterprises (GSEs) are privately owned, publicly chartered entities that were created by Congress to reduce the cost of capital for certain borrowing sectors of the economy deemed to be important enough to warrant assistance.

- A mortgage loan is a loan secured by the collateral of some specified real estate property.

- Mortgage loan payments consist of interest, scheduled principal payment, and prepayments.

- Prepayments are any payments in excess of the required monthly mortgage payment.

- Prepayment risk is the uncertainty about the cash flows due to prepayments.

- Loans included in an agency issued mortgage-backed security are conforming loans—loans that meet the underwriting standards established by the issuing entity.

- For a mortgage passthrough security the monthly payments are passed through to the certificate holders on a pro rata basis.

- In a collateralized mortgage obligation (CMO), there are rules for the payment of interest and principal (scheduled and prepaid) to the bond classes (tranches) in the CMO.

- The payment rules in a CMO structure allow for the redistribution of prepayment risk to the tranches comprising the CMO.

- In the U.S. bond market, municipal securities are debt obligations issued by state governments, local governments, and entities created by state and local governments.

- There are both tax-exempt and taxable municipal securities, where "tax-exempt" means that interest is exempt from federal income taxation; most municipal securities that have been issued are tax-exempt.

- There are basically two types of municipal security structures: tax-backed debt and revenue bonds.

- Tax-backed debt obligations are instruments secured by some form of tax revenue.

- Tax-backed debt includes general obligation debt (the broadest type of tax-backed debt), appropriation-backed obligations, and debt obligations supported by public credit enhancement programs.

- Revenue bonds are issued for enterprise financings that are secured by the revenues generated by the completed projects themselves, or for general public-purpose financings in which the issuers pledge to the bondholders the tax and revenue resources that were previously part of the general fund.

- Insured bonds, in addition to being secured by the issuer's revenue, are backed by insurance policies written by commercial insurance companies.

- Prerefunded bonds are supported by a portfolio of Treasury securities held in an escrow fund.

- In the United States, the Bankruptcy Reform Act of 1978 as amended governs the bankruptcy process.

- Chapter 7 of the bankruptcy act deals with the liquidation of a company; Chapter 11 of the bankruptcy act deals with the reorganization of a company.

- In theory, creditors should receive distributions based on the absolute priority rule to the extent assets are available; this rule means that senior creditors are paid in full before junior creditors are paid anything.

- Generally, the absolute priority rule holds in the case of liquidations and is typically violated in reorganizations.

- In analyzing a corporate bond, a credit analyst must consider the four C's of credit—character, capacity, collateral, and covenants.

- Character relates to the ethical reputation as well as the business qualifications and operating record of the board of directors, management, and executives responsible for the use of the borrowed funds and their repayment.

- Capacity deals with the ability of an issuer to pay its obligations.

- Collateral involves not only the traditional pledging of assets to secure the debt, but also the quality and value of unpledged assets controlled by the issuer.

- Covenants impose restrictions on how management operates the company and conducts its financial affairs.

- A corporate debt issue is said to be secured debt if there is some form of collateral pledged to ensure payment of the debt.

- Mortgage debt is debt secured by real property such as land, buildings, plant, and equipment.

- Collateral trust debentures, bonds, and notes are secured by financial assets such as cash, receivables, other notes, debentures or bonds, and not by real property.

- Unsecured debt, like secured debt, comes in several different layers or levels of claim against the corporation's assets.

- Some debt issues are credit enhanced by having other companies guarantee their payment.

- One of the important protective provisions for unsecured debt holders is the negative pledge clause which prohibits a company from creating or assuming any lien to secure a debt issue without equally securing the subject debt issue(s) (with certain exceptions).

- Investors in corporate bonds are interested in default rates and, more importantly, default loss rates or recovery rates.

- There is ample evidence to suggest that the lower the credit rating, the higher the probability of a corporate issuer defaulting.

- Medium-term notes are corporate debt obligations offered on a continuous basis and are offered through agents.

- The rates posted for medium-term notes are for various maturity ranges, with maturities as short as nine months to as long as 30 years.

- MTNs have been issued simultaneously with transactions in the derivatives market to create structured MTNs allowing issuers greater flexibility in creating MTNs that are attractive to investors who seek to hedge or take a market position that they might otherwise be prohibited from doing.

- Common structured notes include: step-up notes, inverse floaters, deleveraged floaters, dual-indexed floaters, range notes, and index amortizing notes.

- Commercial paper is a short-term unsecured promissory note issued in the open market that is an obligation of the issuing entity.

- Commercial paper is sold on a discount basis and has a maturity less than 270 days.

- Bank obligations in addition to the traditional corporate debt instruments include certificates of deposits and bankers acceptances.

- Asset-backed securities are securities backed by a pool of loans or receivables.

- The motivation for issuers to issue an asset-backed security rather than a traditional debt obligation is that there is the opportunity to reduce funding cost by separating the credit rating of the issuer from the credit quality of the pool of loans or receivables.

- The separation of the pool of assets from the issuer is accomplished by means of a special purpose vehicle or special purpose corporation.

- In obtaining a credit rating for an asset-backed security, the rating agencies require that the issue be credit enhanced; the higher the credit rating sought, the greater the credit enhancement needed.

- There are two general types of credit enhancement structures: external and internal.

- A collateralized debt obligation is a product backed by a pool of one or more of the following types of fixed income securities: bonds, asset-backed securities, mortgage-backed securities, bank loans, and other CDOs.

- The asset manager in a collateralized debt obligation is responsible for managing the portfolio of assets (i.e., the debt obligations backing the transaction) and there are restrictions imposed on the activities of the asset manager.

- The funds to purchase the underlying assets in a collateral debt obligation are obtained from the CDO issuance with ratings assigned by a rating agency.

- Collateralized debt obligations are categorized as either arbitrage transactions or balance sheet transactions, the classification being based on the motivation of the sponsor of the transaction.

- Bonds have traditionally been issued via an underwriting as a firm commitment or on a best efforts basis; bonds are also underwritten via a bought deal or an auction process.

- A bond can be placed privately with an institutional investor rather than issued via a public offering.

- In the United States, private placements are now classified as Rule 144A offerings (underwritten by an investment bank) and non-Rule 144A offerings (a traditional private placement).

- Bonds typically trade in the over-the-counter market.

- The two major types of electronic trading systems for bonds are the dealer-to-customer systems and the exchange systems.

PRACTICE PROBLEMS FOR READING 54

1. Explain whether you agree or disagree with each of the following statements:

   A. "The foreign bond market sector of the Japanese bond market consists of bonds of Japanese entities that are issued outside of Japan."

   B. "Because bonds issued by central governments are backed by the full faith and credit of the issuing country, these bonds are not rated."

   C. "A country's semi-government bonds carry the full faith and credit of the central government."

   D. "In the United States, all federal agency bonds carry the full faith and credit of the U.S. government."

2. Why do rating agencies assign two types of ratings to the debt of a sovereign entity?

3. When issuing bonds, a central government can select from several distribution methods.

   A. What is the difference between a single-price auction and a multiple-price auction?

   B. What is a tap system?

4. Suppose a portfolio manager purchases $1 million of par value of a Treasury inflation protection security. The real rate (determined at the auction) is 3.2%.

   A. Assume that at the end of the first six months the CPI-U is 3.6% (annual rate). Compute the i) inflation adjustment to principal at the end of the first six months, ii) the inflation-adjusted principal at the end of the first six months, and iii) the coupon payment made to the investor at the end of the first six months.

   B. Assume that at the end of the second six months the CPI-U is 4.0% (annual rate). Compute the i) inflation adjustment to principal at the end of the second six months, ii) the inflation-adjusted principal at the end of the second six months, and iii) the coupon payment made to the investor at the end of the second six months.

5. A. What is the measure of the rate of inflation selected by the U.S. Treasury to determine the inflation adjustment for Treasury inflation protection securities?

   B. Suppose that there is deflation over the life of a Treasury inflation protection security resulting in an inflation-adjusted principal at the maturity date that is less than the initial par value. How much will the U.S. Treasury pay at the maturity date to redeem the principal?

   C. Why is it necessary for the U.S. Treasury to report a daily index ratio for each TIPS issue?

6. What is a U.S. federal agency debenture?

7. Suppose that a 15-year mortgage loan for $200,000 is obtained. The mortgage is a level-payment, fixed-rate, fully amortized mortgage. The mortgage rate is 7.0% and the monthly mortgage payment is $1,797.66.

   A. Compute an amortization schedule for the first six months.

   B. What will the mortgage balance be at the end of the 15th year?

Practice Problems and Solutions: 1–28 taken from *Fixed Income Analysis for the Chartered Financial Analyst® Program*, Second Edition, by Frank J. Fabozzi, CFA. Copyright © 2004 by CFA Institute. All other problems and solutions copyright © CFA Institute.

    C. If an investor purchased this mortgage, what will the timing of the cash flow be assuming that the borrower does not default?

8. **A.** What is a prepayment?

    B. What do the monthly cash flows of a mortgage-backed security consist of?

    C. What is a curtailment?

9. What is prepayment risk?

10. **A.** What is the difference between a mortgage passthrough security and a collateralized mortgage obligation?

    B. Why is a collateralized mortgage obligation created?

11. Name two U.S. government-sponsored enterprises that issue mortgage-backed securities.

12. What is the difference between a limited and unlimited general obligation bond?

13. What is a moral obligation bond?

14. What is an insured municipal bond?

15. **A.** What is a prerefunded bond?

    B. Why does a properly structured prerefunded municipal bond have no credit risk?

16. **A.** What is the difference between a liquidation and a reorganization?

    B. What is the principle of absolute priority?

    C. Comment on the following statement: "An investor who purchases a mortgage bond issued by a corporation knows that should the corporation become bankrupt, mortgage bondholders will be paid in full before the stockholders receive any proceeds."

17. **A.** What is a subordinated debenture corporate bond?

    B. What is negative pledge clause?

18. **A.** Why is the default rate alone not an adequate measure of the potential performance of corporate bonds?

    B. One study of default rates for speculative grade corporate bonds has found that one-third of all such issues default. Other studies have found that the default rate is between 2.15% and 2.4% for speculative grade corporate bonds. Why is there such a difference in these findings for speculative grade corporate bonds?

    C. Comment on the following statement: "Most studies have found that recovery rates are less than 15% of the trading price at the time of default and the recovery rate does not vary with the level of seniority."

19. **A.** What is the difference between a medium-term note and a corporate bond?

    B. What is a structured note?

    C. What factor determines the principal payment for an index amortizing note and what is the risk of investing in this type of structured note?

20. **A.** What is the risk associated with investing in a negotiable certificate of deposit issued by a U.S. bank?

    B. What is meant by "1-month LIBOR"?

21. What are the risks associated with investing in a bankers acceptance?

22. A financial corporation with a BBB rating has a consumer loan portfolio. An investment banker has suggested that this corporation consider issuing an

asset-backed security where the collateral for the security is the consumer loan portfolio. What would be the advantage of issuing an asset-backed security rather than a straight offering of corporate bonds?

23. What is the role played by a special purpose vehicle in an asset-backed security structure?

24. A. What are the various forms of external credit enhancement for an asset-backed security?

B. What is the disadvantage of using an external credit enhancement in an asset-backed security structure?

25. A. What is a collateralized debt obligation?

B. Explain whether you agree or disagree with the following statement: "The asset manager in a collateralized debt obligation is free to manage the portfolio as aggressively or passively as he or she deems appropriate."

C. What distinguishes an arbitrage transaction from a balance sheet transaction?

26. What is a bought deal?

27. How are private placements classified?

28. Explain the two major types of electronic bond trading systems.

29. Which of the following is *least likely* a type of collateral for asset-backed securities?

A. Credit cards.

B. Home equity.

C. Negotiable CDs.

30. A U.S. Treasury note with exactly four years to maturity *most likely* can be broken into as many as:

A. four Treasury STRIPS.

B. eight Treasury STRIPS.

C. nine Treasury STRIPS.

31. Consider the following statements about mortgages and mortgage securities:

Statement 1:	"Prepayments of mortgages generally increase as interest rates increase."
Statement 2:	"Mortgage passthrough securities eliminate prepayment risk."

Are the statements *most likely* correct or incorrect?

A. Both statements are incorrect.

B. Statement 1 is incorrect, but Statement 2 is correct.

C. Statement 1 is correct, but Statement 2 is incorrect.

32. Which of the following is *least likely* an example of secured debt?

A. Collateral trust bonds.

B. Subordinated debenture bonds.

C. General and refunding mortgage bonds.

33. Which of the following is *least likely* an example of an asset-backed security?

A. Commercial paper.

B. Collateralized debt obligations.

C. Mortgage passthrough securities.

34. Consider the following statements about bond markets:

Statement 1: "In addition to firm commitment and best efforts approaches to underwriting bonds, corporate bond issues in the United States can also be brought to the public using the 'solid block' convention."

Statement 2: "Privately placed corporate bonds issued under SEC Rule 144A cannot be traded for two years following their initial issue."

Are the statements *most likely* correct or incorrect?

A. Both statements are incorrect.

B. Statement 1 is incorrect, but Statement 2 is correct.

C. Statement 1 is correct, but Statement 2 is incorrect.

SOLUTIONS FOR READING 54

1. None of the statements is correct and therefore one must disagree with each statement for the following reasons:

   A. The foreign bond market sector of the Japanese bond market consists of non-Japanese entities that issue bonds in Japan.

   B. All but U.S. government bonds are rated.

   C. The guarantee of semi-government bonds varies from country to country. Some may carry the full faith and credit of the central government while others may have an implied or indirect guarantee.

   D. In the United States, federally related agency securities (with some exceptions) carry the full faith and credit of the U.S. government. Government-sponsored enterprises (with some exceptions) have an implied guarantee.

2. The reason for assigning two types of ratings is that historically the default frequency for government issues denominated in a foreign currency is different from that of government issues denominated in the local currency.

3. **A.** In a single-price auction, all winning bidders are awarded securities at the highest yield bid. In a multiple-price auction, all winning bidders are awarded securities at the yield they bid.

   B. In a tap system, a government issues additional bonds of a previously outstanding bond issue via an auction.

4. **A.** Since the inflation rate (as measured by the CPI-U) is 3.6%, the semiannual inflation rate for adjusting the principal is 1.8%.

   i. The inflation adjustment to the principal is

   $1,000,000 \times 0.018 = \$18,000$

   ii. The inflation-adjusted principal is

   $1,000,000 +$ Inflation adjustment to the principal $= \$1,000,000 + \$18,000 = \$1,018,000$

   iii. The coupon payment is equal to

   Inflation-adjusted principal $\times$ (Real rate/2) $= \$1,018,000 \times (0.032/2) = \$16,288.00$

   B. Since the inflation rate is 4.0%, the semiannual inflation rate for adjusting the principal is 2.0%.

   i. The inflation adjustment to the principal is

   $1,018,000 \times 0.02 = \$20,360$

   ii. The inflation-adjusted principal is

   $1,018,000 +$ Inflation adjustment to the principal $= \$1,018,000 + \$20,360 = \$1,038,360$

   iii. The coupon payment is equal to

   Inflation-adjusted principal $\times$ (Real rate/2) $= \$1,038,360 \times (0.032/2) = \$16,613.76$

5. **A.** The inflation rate selected is the non-seasonally adjusted U.S. City Average All Items Consumer Price Index for All Urban Consumers (denoted CPI-U).

    B. The Treasury has agreed that if the inflation-adjusted principal is less than the initial par value, the par value will be paid at maturity.

    C. When a TIPS issue is purchased between coupon payments, the price paid by the buyer has to be adjusted for the inflation up to the settlement date. That is why the Treasury reports a daily index ratio for an issue.

6. Agency debentures are securities issued by government-sponsored enterprises that do not have any specific collateral securing the bond. The ability to pay bondholders depends on the ability of the issuing GSE to generate sufficient cash flow to satisfy the obligation.

7. **A.** Monthly mortgage payment = \$1,797.66

       Monthly mortgage rate = 0.00583333 (0.07/12)

Month	Beginning of Month Mortgage Balance	Mortgage Payment	Interest	Scheduled Principal Repayment	End of Month Mortgage Balance
1	200,000.00	1,797.66	1,166.67	630.99	199,369.01
2	199,369.01	1,797.66	1,162.99	634.67	198,734.34
3	198,734.34	1,797.66	1,159.28	638.37	198,095.97
4	198,095.97	1,797.66	1,155.56	642.10	197,453.87
5	197,453.87	1,797.66	1,151.81	645.84	196,808.03
6	196,808.03	1,797.66	1,148.05	649.61	196,158.42

    B. In the last month (month 180), after the final monthly mortgage payment is made, the ending mortgage balance will be zero. That is, the mortgage will be fully paid.

    C. The cash flow is unknown even if the borrower does not default. This is because the borrower has the right to prepay in whole or in part the mortgage balance at any time.

8. **A.** A prepayment is additional principal paid by the borrower in excess of the monthly mortgage payment.

    B. The monthly cash flow of a mortgage-backed security is made up of three elements: 1) net interest (i.e., interest less servicing and other fees), 2) scheduled principal repayments (amortization), and 3) prepayments.

    C. A curtailment is a form of prepayment. Rather than prepaying the entire outstanding mortgage balance, a curtailment is a pay off of only part of the outstanding balance—it shortens (or "curtails") the life of the loan.

9. Prepayment risk is the uncertainty regarding the receipt of cash flows due to prepayments. Because of prepayments the investor does not know when principal payments will be received even if borrowers do not default on their mortgage loan.

10. **A.** In a mortgage passthrough security, the monthly cash flow from the underlying pool of mortgages is distributed on a pro rata basis to all the certificate holders. In contrast, for a collateralized mortgage obligation, there are rules for the distribution of the interest (net interest) and the principal (scheduled and prepaid) to different tranches.

    B. The rules for the distribution of interest and rules for the distribution of principal to the different tranches in a CMO structure effectively redistribute prepayment risk among the tranches.

11. Two government-sponsored enterprises that issue mortgage-backed securities are Fannie Mae and Freddie Mac.

12. An unlimited tax general obligation bond is a stronger form of a general obligation bond than a limited tax general obligation bond. The former is secured by the issuer's unlimited taxing power. The latter is a limited tax pledge because for such debt there is a statutory limit on tax rates that the issuer may levy to service the debt.

13. A moral obligation bond is a municipal bond that in the case of default of an issuer allows the state where the issuer is located to appropriate funds that are scheduled to be paid to the defaulted issuer and use those funds to meet the defaulted issuer's obligation. This is a nonbinding obligation that depends on the best efforts of the state to appropriate the funds to satisfy the defaulted issuer's obligation.

14. An insured municipal bond is an issue that is backed by an insurance policy written by a commercial insurance company such that the insurer agrees to pay bondholders any principal and/or coupon interest that the municipal issuer fails to pay.

15. **A.** A prerefunded bond is a municipal bond that may have originally been a general obligation bond or a revenue bond that is effectively refunded by creating a portfolio of Treasury securities that generates a cash flow equal to the debt service payments on the issue.

    B. Regardless of the credit rating of the issue prior to prerefunding, after prerefunding the issue is effectively collateralized by a portfolio of Treasury obligations such that the cash flow of the Treasury portfolio matches the payments on the issue when they are due. Hence, a prerefunded issue has no credit risk if properly structured.

16. **A.** In a liquidation, all the assets of a corporation will be distributed to the holders of claims and no corporate entity will survive. In a reorganization, a new corporate entity will be created and some security holders will receive in exchange for their claims cash and/or new securities in the new corporation.

    B. The absolute priority principle is that senior creditors are paid in full before junior creditors are paid anything.

    C. The statement is true in a liquidation; however, this is not necessarily the case in a reorganization. In fact, studies suggest that the principle of absolute priority is the exception rather than the rule in a reorganization.

17. **A.** An unsecured bond is called a debenture. Subordinated debenture bonds are issues that rank after secured debt, after debenture bonds, and often after some general creditors in their claim on assets and earnings.

    B. A negative pledge clause prohibits a corporation from creating or assuming any lien to secure a debt issue at the expense of existing creditors. This is an important provision for unsecured creditors.

18. **A.** The performance of corporate bonds will depend not only on the default rate, but the recovery rate as well as the spread over Treasury securities.

    B. The reason for the discrepancy is that these studies are measuring defaults over different periods. Studies that find that one-third default look at cumulative default rates over a period of time. The 2.15% to 2.4% figure is an annual default rate.

    C. The comment is wrong for two reasons. First, studies have found that the recovery rate is about 38% of the trading price at the time of default. Second, studies have found that the higher the level of seniority, the greater the recovery rate.

19. **A.** A medium-term note and corporate bond differ as to how they are distributed to investors when they are initially sold. For a MTN, an issuer offers securities on a continuous basis via an investment banking firm or a broker/dealer acting as an agent by posting rates daily as to the rate it is willing to pay for specific maturities. In contrast, a corporate bond is issued on a discrete basis—it is issued at a given point in time by an investment banker.

B. An issuer can couple a medium-term note offering with one or more positions in derivative instruments to create an instrument that has a coupon rate customized with respect to risk-return characteristics for an institutional investor. Such medium-term notes are called structured notes.

C. With an index amortizing note (IAN), the coupon rate is fixed and the principal payments are made prior to the stated maturity date based on the prevailing value for some reference interest rate. Specifically, the principal payments decrease when the reference interest rate increases (hence the maturity increases) and increases when the reference interest rate decreases (hence the maturity decreases). The risk faced by the investor is that an IAN will be outstanding for a longer period when interest rates rise, just when the investor would like proceeds to reinvest at a higher interest rate; there is reinvestment risk when interest rates fall because more principal is paid as rates decline, just when the investor would not want to receive principal.

20. **A.** Since negotiable certificates of deposit issued by U.S. banks typically exceed the federally insured amount of $100,000, there is credit risk for the amount invested in excess of $100,000.

B. LIBOR refers to the London interbank offered rate and it is the interest rate paid on Eurodollar certificates of deposit. "1-month LIBOR" is the interest rate that major international banks are offering to pay to each other on a Eurodollar CD that matures in one month.

21. Investing in bankers acceptances exposes the investor to the risk that neither the borrower nor the accepting bank will be able to pay the principal due at the maturity date; that is, the investor faces credit risk. On the surface, there is liquidity risk because there are few dealers who make a market in bankers acceptances. However, investors typically purchase bankers acceptances with the intent of holding them to maturity. Consequently, in practice, liquidity risk is not a concern to such investors.

22. The advantage is that depending on the quality of the consumer loan portfolio, this BBB rated issuer may be able to issue an asset-backed security with a higher rating than BBB and thereby reduce its borrowing costs, net of the cost of credit enhancement.

23. A special purpose vehicle allows a corporation seeking funds to issue a security backed by collateral such that the security will be rated based on the credit quality of the collateral rather than the entity seeking funds. Effectively, the special purpose vehicle is the owner of the collateral so that the creditors of the entity seeking funds cannot claim the collateral should the entity default.

24. **A.** External credit enhancement includes corporate guarantees, a letter of credit, and bond insurance.

B. A disadvantage of an external credit enhancement is that it exposes the asset-backed security structure to a credit downgrading should the third-party guarantor be downgraded.

25. **A.** A collateralized debt obligation is a structure backed by a portfolio of one or more fixed income products—corporate bonds, asset-backed securities, mortgage-backed securities, bank loans, and other CDOs. Funds are raised to purchase the assets by the sale of the CDO. An asset manager manages the assets.

    B. The statement is incorrect. When a CDO is issued, the notes are rated. Restrictions are imposed on the asset manager in order to avoid a downgrading of the tranches or the possibility that the trustee must begin paying off the principal to the senior tranches.

    C. The distinction between an arbitrage transaction from a balance sheet transaction is based on the motivation of the sponsor of the CDO. Arbitrage transactions are motivated by the objective to capture the spread between the yield offered on the pool of assets underlying the CDO and the cost of borrowing which is the yield offered to sell the CDO. In balance sheet transactions, typically undertaken by financial institutions such as banks and insurance companies, the motivation is to remove assets from the balance sheet, thereby obtaining capital relief in the form of lower risk-based capital requirements.

26. A bought deal is a form of a bond underwriting. The underwriting firm or group of underwriting firms offers an issuer a firm bid to purchase a specified amount of the bonds with a certain coupon rate and maturity. The issuer is given a short time period to accept or reject the bid. If the bid is accepted, the underwriting firm has bought the deal.

27. In the United States, SEC Rule 144A eliminates the two-year holding period requirement for privately placed securities by permitting large institutions to trade securities acquired in a private placement among themselves without having to register these securities with the SEC. As a result, private placements are classified in two types. The first type are Rule 144A offerings which are underwritten securities. The second type are the traditional private placements which are referred to as non-Rule 144A offerings.

28. The two major types of electronic bond trading systems are the dealer-to-customer systems and exchange systems. The former are further divided into single-dealer systems and multiple-dealer systems. Single-dealer systems are based on a customer dealing with a single, identified dealer over the computer. In multi-dealer systems a customer can select from any of several identified dealers whose bids and offers are provided on a computer screen.

    The second type of electronic system for bonds is the exchange system. In this system, dealer and customer bids and offers are entered into the system on an anonymous basis, and the clearing of the executed trades is done through a common process. Exchange systems can be further divided into continuous trading and call auction systems. Continuous trading permits trading at continuously changing market determined prices throughout the day. Call auctions provide for fixed price auctions at specific times during the day.

29. C is correct. Negotiable CDs are a financial asset issued by a bank and are not collateralized. Both credit card receivables and home equity loans are types of collateral used to support asset-backed securities.

30. C is correct. Each of the eight coupons could be a Treasury STRIP and the principal could form the basis of a ninth STRIP.

31. A is correct. Prepayments increase as interest rates *decrease*. Mortgage passthrough securities show some reduction in prepayment risk due to diversification, but prepayment risk is not eliminated.

32. B is correct. Debentures are unsecured.

33. A is correct. Commercial paper is a short-term unsecured promissory note.

34. A is correct. Statement 1 is incorrect. There is no "solid block" convention. Primary market conventions for bonds *do* include "bought deal" and "auction process" approaches. Statement 2 is also incorrect. Rule 144A issues can be traded between qualified large institutions even though two years have not passed since their initial issue.

55

Understanding Yield Spreads

by Frank J. Fabozzi, CFA

LEARNING OUTCOMES

Mastery	The candidate should be able to:
☐	**a** identify the interest rate policy tools available to a central bank;
☐	**b** describe a yield curve and the various shapes of the yield curve;
☐	**c** explain the basic theories of the term structure of interest rates and describe the implications of each theory for the shape of the yield curve;
☐	**d** define a spot rate;
☐	**e** calculate and compare yield spread measures;
☐	**f** describe credit spreads and relationships between credit spreads and economic conditions;
☐	**g** describe how embedded options affect yield spreads;
☐	**h** explain how liquidity and issue-size affects the yield spread of a bond relative to other similar securities;
☐	**i** calculate the after-tax yield of a taxable security and the tax-equivalent yield of a tax-exempt security;
☐	**j** define LIBOR and explain its importance to funded investors who borrow short term.

INTRODUCTION

1

The interest rate offered on a particular bond issue depends on the interest rate that can be earned on 1) risk-free instruments and 2) the perceived risks associated with the issue. We refer to the interest rates on risk-free instruments as the "level of interest rates." The actions of a country's central bank influence the level of interest rates as does the state of the country's economy. In the United States, the level of interest rates depends on the state of the economy, the interest rate policies implemented by the Board of Governors of the Federal Reserve Board, and the government's fiscal policies.

A casual examination of the financial press and dealer quote sheets shows a wide range of interest rates reported at any given point in time. Why are there differences in interest rates among debt instruments? We provided information on this topic in the readings on features of debt securities and risks associated with investing in bonds. In the reading on features of debt securities, we explained the various features of a bond, and in the reading on risks associated with investing in bonds, we explained how those features affect the risk characteristics of a bond relative to bonds without that feature.

In this reading, we look more closely at the differences in yields offered by bonds in different sectors of the bond market and within a sector of the bond market. This information is used by investors in assessing the "relative value" of individual securities within a bond sector, or among sectors of the bond market. Relative value analysis is a process of ranking individual securities or sectors with respect to expected return potential. We will continue to use the terms "interest rate" and "yield" interchangeably.

2 INTEREST RATE DETERMINATION

Our focus in this reading is on 1) the relationship between interest rates offered on different bond issues at a point in time and 2) the relationships among interest rates offered in different sectors of the economy at a given point in time. We will provide a brief discussion of the role of the U.S. Federal Reserve (the Fed), the policy-making body whose interest rate policy tools directly influence short-term interest rates and indirectly influence long-term interest rates.

Once the Fed makes a policy decision, it immediately announces the policy in a statement issued at the close of its meeting. The Fed also communicates its future intentions via public speeches or its Chairman's testimony before Congress. Managers who pursue an active strategy of positioning a portfolio to take advantage of expected changes in interest rates watch closely the same key economic indicators that the Fed watches in order to anticipate a change in the Fed's monetary policy and to assess the expected impact on short-term interest rates. The indicators that are closely watched by the Fed include non-farm payrolls, industrial production, housing starts, motor vehicle sales, durable good orders, National Association of Purchasing Management supplier deliveries, and commodity prices.

In implementing monetary policy, the Fed uses the following interest rate policy tools:

1. open market operations

2. the discount rate

3. bank reserve requirements

4. verbal persuasion to influence how bankers supply credit to businesses and consumers

Engaging in open market operations and changing the discount rate are the tools most often employed. Together, these tools can raise or lower the cost of funds in the economy. Open market operations do this through the Fed's buying and selling of U.S. Treasury securities. This action either adds funds to the market (when Treasury securities are purchased) or withdraws funds from the market (when Treasury securities are sold). Fed open market operations influence the federal funds rate, the rate at which banks borrow and lend funds from each other. The discount rate is the interest rate at which banks can borrow on a collateralized basis at the Fed's discount window. Increasing the discount rate makes the cost of funds more expensive for banks; the cost of funds is reduced when the discount rate is lowered. Changing bank reserve requirements is a less frequently used policy, as is the use of verbal persuasion to influence the supply of credit.

U.S. TREASURY RATES

3

The securities issued by the U.S. Department of the Treasury are backed by the full faith and credit of the U.S. government. Consequently, market participants throughout the world view these securities as being "default risk-free" securities. However, there are risks associated with owning U.S. Treasury securities.

The Treasury issues the following securities:

Treasury bills: Zero-coupon securities with a maturity at issuance of one year or less. The Treasury currently issues 1-month, 3-month, and 6-month bills.

Treasury notes: Coupon securities with maturity at issuance greater than 1 year but not greater than 10 years. The Treasury currently issues 2-year, 5-year, and 10-year notes.

Treasury bonds: Coupon securities with maturity at issuance greater than 10 years. Treasury bonds have traditionally been issued with maturities up to 30 years.

Inflation-protection securities: Coupon securities whose principal's reference rate is the Consumer Price Index.

The on-the-run issue or current issue is the most recently auctioned issue of Treasury notes and bonds of each maturity. The off-the-run issues are securities that were previously issued and are replaced by the on-the-run issue. Issues that have been replaced by several more recent issues are said to be "well off-the-run issues."

The secondary market for Treasury securities is an over-the-counter market where a group of U.S. government securities dealers provides continuous bids and offers on specific outstanding Treasuries. This secondary market is the most liquid financial market in the world. Off-the-run issues are less liquid than on-the-run issues.

3.1 Risks of Treasury Securities

With this brief review of Treasury securities, let's look at their risks. We listed the general risks in the reading on risks associated with investing in bonds and repeat them here: 1) interest rate risk, 2) call and prepayment risk, 3) yield curve risk, 4) reinvestment risk, 5) credit risk, 6) liquidity risk, 7) exchange-rate risk, 8) volatility risk, 9) inflation or purchasing power risk, and 10) event risk.

All fixed income securities, including Treasury securities, expose investors to interest rate risk.[1] However, the degree of interest rate risk is not the same for all securities. The reason is that maturity and coupon rate affect how much the price changes when interest rates change. One measure of a security's interest rate risk is its *duration*.[2] Since Treasury securities, like other fixed income securities, have different durations, they have different exposures to interest rate risk as measured by duration.

Technically, yield curve risk and volatility risk are risks associated with Treasury securities. However, at this early stage of our understanding of fixed income analysis, we will not attempt to explain these risks. It is not necessary to understand these risks at this point in order to appreciate the material that follows in this section.

---

1 Interest rate risk is the risk of an adverse movement in the price of a bond due to changes in interest rates.
2 Duration is a measure of a bond's price sensitivity to a change in interest rates.

Because Treasury securities are noncallable, there is no reinvestment risk due to an issue being called.[3] Treasury coupon securities carry reinvestment risk because in order to realize the yield offered on the security, the investor must reinvest the coupon payments received at an interest rate equal to the computed yield. So, all Treasury coupon securities are exposed to reinvestment risk. Treasury bills are not exposed to reinvestment risk because they are zero-coupon instruments.

As for credit risk, the perception in the global financial community is that Treasury securities have no credit risk. In fact, when market participants and the popular press state that Treasury securities are "risk free," they are referring to credit risk.

Treasury securities are highly liquid. However, on-the-run and off-the-run Treasury securities trade with different degrees of liquidity. Consequently, the yields offered by on-the-run and off-the-run issues reflect different degrees of liquidity.

Since U.S. Treasury securities are dollar denominated, there is no exchange-rate risk for an investor whose domestic currency is the U.S. dollar. However, non-U.S. investors whose domestic currency is not the U.S. dollar are exposed to exchange-rate risk.

Fixed-rate Treasury securities are exposed to inflation risk. Treasury inflation protection securities (TIPS) have a coupon rate that is effectively adjusted for the rate of inflation and therefore have protection against inflation risk.

Finally, the yield on Treasury securities is impacted by a myriad of events that can be classified as political risk, a form of event risk. The actions of monetary and fiscal policy in the United States, as well as the actions of other central banks and governments, can have an adverse or favorable impact on U.S. Treasury yields.

3.2 The Treasury Yield Curve

Given that Treasury securities do not expose investors to credit risk, market participants look at the yield offered on an on-the-run Treasury security as the minimum interest rate required on a non-Treasury security with the same maturity. The relationship between yield and maturity of on-the-run Treasury securities on February 8, 2002 is displayed in Exhibit 1 in tabular form. The relationship shown in Exhibit 1 is called the Treasury yield curve—even though the "curve" shown in the exhibit is presented in tabular form.

The information presented in Exhibit 1 indicates that the longer the maturity the higher the yield and is referred to as an upward sloping yield curve. Since this is the most typical shape for the Treasury yield curve, it is also referred to as a normal yield curve. Other relationships have been observed. An inverted yield curve indicates that the longer the maturity, the lower the yield. For a flat yield curve the yield is approximately the same regardless of maturity.

Exhibit 2 provides a graphic example of the variants of these shapes and also shows how a yield curve can change over time. In the exhibit, the yield curve at the beginning of 2001 was inverted up to the 5-year maturity but was upward sloping beyond the 5-year maturity. By December 2001, all interest rates had declined. As seen in the exhibit, interest rates less than the 10-year maturity dropped substantially more than longer-term rates resulting in an upward sloping yield curve.

---

3 The Treasury no longer issues callable bonds. The Treasury issued callable bonds in the early 1980s and all of these issues will mature no later than November 2014 (assuming that they are not called before then). Moreover, as of 2004, the longest maturity of these issues is 10 years. Consequently, while outstanding callable issues of the Treasury are referred to as "bonds," based on their current maturity these issues would not be compared to long-term bonds in any type of relative value analysis. Therefore, because the Treasury no longer issues callable bonds and the outstanding issues do not have the maturity characteristics of a long-term bond, we will ignore these callable issues and simply treat Treasury bonds as noncallable.

Exhibit 1	Relationship between Yield and Maturity for On-the-Run Treasury Issues on February 8, 2002

Issue (Maturity)	Yield (%)
1 month	1.68
3 months	1.71
6 months	1.81
1 year[a]	2.09
2 years	2.91
5 years	4.18
10 years	4.88
30 years[b]	5.38

[a] The 1-year issue is based on the 2-year issue closest to maturing in one year.

[b] The 30-year issue shown is based on the last 30-year issue before the Treasury suspended issuance in October 2001. Issuance resumed in February 2006.

Source: *Global Relative Value*, Lehman Brothers, Fixed Income Research, February 11, 2002, p. 128.

The number of on-the-run securities available in constructing the yield curve has decreased over the last two decades. While the 1-year and 30-year yields are shown in the February 8, 2002 yield curve, as of this writing there is no 1-year Treasury bill, and the maturity of the 30-year Treasury bond (the last one issued before suspension of the issuance of 30-year Treasury bonds) will decline over time. To get a yield for maturities where no on-the-run Treasury issue exists, it is necessary to interpolate from the yield of two on-the-run issues. Several methodologies are used in practice. (The simplest is just a linear interpolation.) Thus, when market participants talk about a yield on the Treasury yield curve that is not one of the available on-the-run maturities—for example, the 8-year yield—it is only an approximation.

Exhibit 2	U.S. Treasury Yield Curve: December 2000 and December 2001

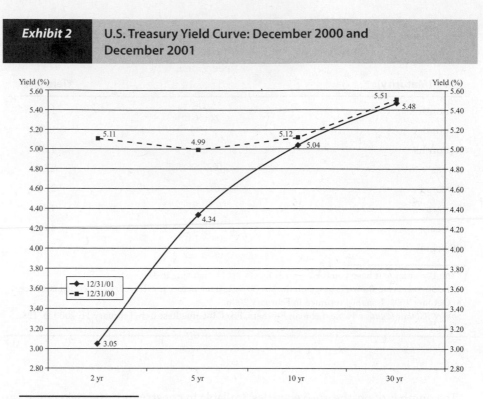

Source: Lehman Brothers Fixed Income Research, *Global Fixed Income Strategy "Playbook,"* January 2002.

It is critical to understand that any non-Treasury issue must offer a premium above the yield offered for the same maturity on-the-run Treasury issue. For example, if a corporation wanted to offer a 10-year noncallable issue on February 8, 2002, the issuer must offer a yield greater than 4.88% (the yield for the 10-year on-the-run Treasury issue). How much greater depends on the additional risks associated with investing in the 10-year corporate issue compared to investors in the 10-year on-the-run Treasury issue. Even off-the-run Treasury issues must offer a premium to reflect differences in liquidity.

Two factors complicate the relationship between maturity and yield as portrayed by the yield curve. The first is that the yield for on-the-run issues may be distorted by the fact that purchase of these securities can be financed at lower rates, and as a result these issues offer artificially low yields. To clarify, some investors purchase securities with borrowed funds and use the securities purchased as collateral for the loan. This type of collateralized borrowing is called a repurchase agreement. Since dealers want to obtain use of these securities for their own trading activities, they are willing to lend funds to investors at a lower interest rate than is otherwise available for borrowing in the market. Consequently, incorporated into the price of an on-the-run Treasury security is the cheaper financing available, resulting in a lower yield for an on-the-run issue than would prevail in the absence of this financing advantage.

The second factor complicating the comparison of on-the-run and off-the-run Treasury issues (in addition to liquidity differences) is that they have different interest rate risks and different reinvestment risks. So, for example, if the coupon rate for the 5-year on-the-run Treasury issue in February 2002 is 4.18% and an off-the-run Treasury issue with just less than 5 years to maturity has a 5.25% coupon rate, the two bonds have different degrees of interest rate risk. Specifically, the on-the-run issue has greater interest rate risk (duration) because of the lower coupon rate. However, it has less reinvestment risk because the coupon rate is lower.

Because of this, when market participants talk about interest rates in the Treasury market and use these interest rates to value securities, they look at another relationship in the Treasury market: the relationship between yield and maturity for zero-coupon Treasury securities. But wait, we said that the Treasury only issues three zero-coupon securities—1-month, 3-month, and 6-month Treasury bills. Where do we obtain the relationship between yield and maturity for zero-coupon Treasury securities? We discuss this next.

3.2.1 Theories of the Term Structure of Interest Rates

What information does the yield curve reveal? How can we explain and interpret changes in the yield curve? These questions are of great interest to anyone concerned with such tasks as the valuation of multiperiod securities, economic forecasting, and risk management. Theories of the term structure of interest rates[4] address these questions. Here we introduce the three main theories or explanations of the term structure. We shall present these theories intuitively.[5]

The three main term structure theories are:

- the pure expectations theory (unbiased expectations theory);
- the liquidity preference theory (or liquidity premium theory); and
- the market segmentation theory.

Each theory is explained below.

3.2.1.1 Pure Expectations Theory   The pure expectations theory makes the simplest and most direct link between the yield curve and investors' expectations about future interest rates, and, because long-term interest rates are plausibly linked to investor expectations about future inflation, it also opens the door to some interesting economic interpretations.

The pure expectations theory explains the term structure in terms of expected future short-term interest rates. According to the pure expectations theory, the market sets the yield on a two-year bond so that the return on the two-year bond is approximately equal to the return on a one-year bond plus the expected return on a one-year bond purchased one year from today.

Under this theory, a rising term structure indicates that the market expects short-term rates to rise in the future. For example, if the yield on the two-year bond is higher than the yield on the one-year bond, according to this theory, investors expect the one-year rate a year from now to be sufficiently higher than the one-year rate available now so that the two ways of investing for two years have the same expected return. Similarly, a flat term structure reflects an expectation that future short-term rates will be unchanged from today's short-term rates, while a falling term structure reflects an expectation that future short-term rates will decline. This is summarized below:

Shape of Term Structure	Implication According to Pure Expectations Theory
upward sloping (normal)	rates expected to rise
downward sloping (inverted)	rates expected to decline
flat	rates not expected to change

The implications above are the broadest interpretation of the theory.

---

4 Term structure means the same as maturity—structure a description of how a bond's yield changes as the bond's maturity changes. In other words, term structure asks the question: Why do long-term bonds have a different yield than short-term bonds?

5 At Level II, we provide a more mathematical treatment of these theories in terms of forward rates that we will discuss in the reading on yield measures, spot rates, and forward rates.

How does the pure expectations theory explain a humped yield curve? According to the theory, this can result when investors expect the returns on one-year securities to rise for a number of years, then fall for a number of years.

The relationships that the table above illustrates suggest that the shape of the yield curve contains information regarding investors' expectations about future inflation. A pioneer of the theory of interest rates (the economist Irving Fisher) asserted that interest rates reflect the sum of a relatively stable real rate of interest plus a premium for expected inflation. Under this hypothesis, if short-term rates are expected to rise, investors expect inflation to rise as well. An upward (downward) sloping term structure would mean that investors expected rising (declining) future inflation. Much economic discussion in the financial press and elsewhere is based on this interpretation of the yield curve.

The shortcoming of the pure expectations theory is that it assumes investors are indifferent to interest rate risk and any other risk factors associated with investing in bonds with different maturities.

3.2.1.2 Liquidity Preference Theory

The liquidity preference theory asserts that market participants want to be compensated for the interest rate risk associated with holding longer-term bonds. The longer the maturity, the greater the price volatility when interest rates change and investors want to be compensated for this risk. According to the liquidity preference theory, the term structure of interest rates is determined by 1) expectations about future interest rates and 2) a yield premium for interest rate risk.[6] Because interest rate risk increases with maturity, the liquidity preference theory asserts that the yield premium increases with maturity.

Consequently, based on this theory, an upward-sloping yield curve may reflect expectations that future interest rates either 1) will rise, or 2) will be unchanged or even fall, but with a yield premium increasing with maturity fast enough to produce an upward sloping yield curve. Thus, for an upward sloping yield curve (the most frequently observed type), the liquidity preference theory by itself has nothing to say about expected future short-term interest rates. For flat or downward sloping yield curves, the liquidity preference theory is consistent with a forecast of declining future short-term interest rates, given the theory's prediction that the yield premium for interest rate risk increases with maturity.

Because the liquidity preference theory argues that the term structure is determined by both expectations regarding future interest rates and a yield premium for interest rate risk, it is referred to as biased expectations theory.

3.2.1.3 Market Segmentation Theory

Proponents of the market segmentation theory argue that within the different maturity sectors of the yield curve the supply and demand for funds determine the interest rate for that sector. That is, each maturity sector is an independent or segmented market for purposes of determining the interest rate in that maturity sector. Thus, positive sloping, inverted, and humped yield curves are all possible. In fact, the market segmentation theory can be used to explain any shape that one might observe for the yield curve.

Let's understand why proponents of this theory view each maturity sector as independent or segmented. In the bond market, investors can be divided into two groups based on their return needs: investors that manage funds versus a broad-based bond market index and those that manage funds versus their liabilities. The easiest case is for those that manage funds against liabilities. Investors managing funds where

---

6 In the liquidity preference theory, "liquidity" is measured in terms of interest rate risk. Specifically, the more interest rate risk, the less the liquidity.

liabilities represent the benchmark will restrict their activities to the maturity sector that provides the best match with the maturity of their liabilities.[7] This is the basic principle of asset-liability management. If these investors invest funds outside of the maturity sector that provides the best match against liabilities, they are exposing themselves to the risks associated with an asset-liability mismatch. For example, consider the manager of a defined benefit pension fund. Since the liabilities of a defined benefit pension fund are long-term, the manager will invest in the long-term maturity sector of the bond market. Similarly, commercial banks whose liabilities are typically short-term focus on short-term fixed-income investments. Even if the rate on long-term bonds were considerably more attractive than that on short-term investments, according to the market segmentation theory, commercial banks will restrict their activities to investments at the short end of the yield curve. Reinforcing this notion of a segmented market are restrictions imposed on financial institutions that prevent them from mismatching the maturity of assets and liabilities.

A variant of the market segmentation theory is the preferred habitat theory. This theory argues that investors prefer to invest in particular maturity sectors as dedicated by the nature of their liabilities. However, proponents of this theory do not assert that investors would be unwilling to shift out of their preferred maturity sector; instead, it is argued that if investors are given an inducement to do so in the form of a yield premium, they will shift out of their preferred habitat. The implication of the preferred habitat theory for the shape of the yield curve is that any shape is possible.

3.3 Treasury STRIPS

Although the U.S. Department of the Treasury does not issue zero-coupon Treasury securities with maturity greater than one year, government dealers can synthetically create zero-coupon securities, which are effectively guaranteed by the full faith and credit of the U.S. government, with longer maturities. They create these securities by separating the coupon payments and the principal payment of a coupon-bearing Treasury security and selling them off separately. The process, referred to as stripping a Treasury security, results in securities called Treasury STRIPS. The Treasury STRIPS created from coupon payments are called Treasury coupon STRIPS, and those created from the principal payment are called Treasury principal STRIPS. We explained the process of creating Treasury STRIPS in the reading on bond sectors and instruments.

Because zero-coupon instruments have no reinvestment risk, Treasury STRIPS for different maturities provide a superior relationship between yield and maturity than do securities on the on-the-run Treasury yield curve. The lack of reinvestment risk eliminates the bias resulting from the difference in reinvestment risk for the securities being compared. Another advantage is that the duration of a zero-coupon security is approximately equal to its maturity. Consequently, when comparing bond issues against Treasury STRIPS, we can compare them on the basis of duration.

The yield on a zero-coupon security has a special name: the spot rate. In the case of a Treasury security, the yield is called a Treasury spot rate. The relationship between maturity and Treasury spot rates is called the term structure of interest rates. Sometimes discussions of the term structure of interest rates in the Treasury market get confusing. The Treasury yield curve and the Treasury term structure of interest rates are often used interchangeably. While there is a technical difference between the two, the context in which these terms are used should be understood.

---

7 One of the principles of finance is the "matching principle:" short-term assets should be financed with (or matched with) short-term liabilities; long-term assets should be financed with (or matched with) long-term sources of financing.

4 YIELDS ON NON-TREASURY SECURITIES

Despite the imperfections of the Treasury yield curve as a benchmark for the minimum interest rate that an investor requires for investing in a non-Treasury security, it is commonplace to refer to the additional yield over the benchmark Treasury issue of the same maturity as the **yield spread**. In fact, because non-Treasury sectors of the fixed-income market offer a yield spread to Treasury securities, non-Treasury sectors are commonly referred to as spread sectors, and non-Treasury securities in these sectors are referred to as spread products.

4.1 Measuring Yield Spreads

While it is common to talk about spreads relative to a Treasury security of the same maturity, a yield spread between any two bond issues can be easily computed. In general, the yield spread between any two bond issues, bond X and bond Y, is computed as follows:

Yield spread = Yield on bond X − Yield on bond Y

where bond Y is considered the reference bond (or benchmark) against which bond X is measured.

When a yield spread is computed in this manner, it is referred to as an absolute yield spread and it is measured in basis points. For example, on February 8, 2002, the yield on the 10-year on-the-run Treasury issue was 4.88%, and the yield on a single A rated 10-year industrial bond was 6.24%. If bond X is the 10-year industrial bond and bond Y is the 10-year on-the-run Treasury issue, the absolute yield spread was:

Yield spread = 6.24% − 4.88% = 1.36% or 136 Basis points

Unless otherwise specified, yield spreads are typically measured in this way. Yield spreads can also be measured on a relative basis by taking the ratio of the yield spread to the yield of the reference bond. This is called a relative yield spread and is computed as shown below, assuming that the reference bond is bond Y:

$$\text{Relative yield spread} = \frac{\text{Yield on bond X} - \text{Yield on bond Y}}{\text{Yield on bond Y}}$$

Sometimes bonds are compared in terms of a yield ratio, the quotient of two bond yields, as shown below:

$$\text{Yield ratio} = \frac{\text{Yield on bond X}}{\text{Yield on bond Y}}$$

Typically, in the U.S. bond market when these measures are computed, bond Y (the reference bond) is a Treasury issue. In that case, the equations for the yield spread measures are as follows:

Absolute yield spread = Yield on bond X − Yield of on-the-run Treasury

$$\text{Relative yield spread} = \frac{\text{Yield on bond X} - \text{Yield of on-the-run Treasury}}{\text{Yield of on-the-run Treasury}}$$

$$\text{Yield ratio} = \frac{\text{Yield on bond X}}{\text{Yield of on-the-run Treasury}}$$

For the above example comparing the yields on the 10-year single A-rated industrial bond and the 10-year on-the-run Treasury, the relative yield spread and yield ratio are computed below:

Absolute yield spread $= 6.24\% - 4.88\% = 1.36\% = 136$ Basis points

Relative yield spread $= \dfrac{6.24\% - 4.88\%}{4.88\%} = 0.279 = 27.9\%$

Yield ratio $= \dfrac{6.24\%}{4.88\%} = 1.279$

The reason for computing yield spreads in terms of a relative yield spread or a yield ratio is that the magnitude of the yield spread is affected by the level of interest rates. For example, in 1957 the yield on Treasuries was about 3%. At that time, the absolute yield spread between triple B rated utility bonds and Treasuries was 40 basis points. This was a relative yield spread of 13% (0.40% divided by 3%). However, when the yield on Treasuries exceeded 10% in 1985, an absolute yield spread of 40 basis points would have meant a relative yield spread of only 4% (0.40% divided by 10%). Consequently, in 1985 an absolute yield spread greater than 40 basis points would have been required in order to produce a similar relative yield spread.

In this reading, we will focus on the yield spread as most commonly measured, the absolute yield spread. So, when we refer to yield spread, we mean absolute yield spread.

Whether we measure the yield spread as an absolute yield spread, a relative yield spread, or a yield ratio, the question to answer is what causes the yield spread between two bond issues. Basically, active bond portfolio strategies involve assessing the factors that cause the yield spread, forecasting how that yield spread may change over an investment horizon, and taking a position to capitalize on that forecast.

Practice Question 1

The following table gives the yield for the 5-year Treasury and for two 5-year corporate bonds as of February 8, 2002.

Issue	Yield (%)
5-year on-the-run Treasury issue	4.18
5-year yield for GE (Aaa/AAA)	4.93
5-year yield for Verizon Communications (A1/A+)	5.11

A. Compute the following yield spread measures between the 5-year GE yield and the 5-year on-the-run Treasury yield: absolute yield spread, relative yield spread, and yield ratio.

B. Compute the following yield spread measures between the 5-year Verizon Communications yield and the 5-year on-the-run Treasury yield: absolute yield spread, relative yield spread, and yield ratio.

4.2 Intermarket Sector Spreads and Intramarket Spreads

The bond market is classified into sectors based on the type of issuer. In the United States, these sectors include the U.S. government sector, the U.S. government agencies sector, the municipal sector, the corporate sector, the mortgage-backed securities sector, the asset-backed securities sector, and the foreign (sovereign, supranational, and corporate) sector. Different sectors are generally perceived as offering different risks and rewards.

The major market sectors are further divided into sub-sectors reflecting common economic characteristics. For example, within the corporate sector, the sub-sectors are: 1) industrial companies, 2) utility companies, 3) finance companies, and 4) banks. In the market for asset-backed securities, the sub-sectors are based on the type of collateral backing the security. The major types are securities backed by pools of 1) credit card receivables, 2) home equity loans, 3) automobile loans, 4) manufactured housing loans, and 5) student loans. Excluding the Treasury market sector, the other market sectors have a wide range of issuers, each with different abilities to satisfy their contractual obligations. Therefore, a key feature of a debt obligation is the nature of the issuer.

The yield spread between the yields offered in two sectors of the bond market with the same maturity is referred to as an intermarket sector spread. The most common intermarket sector spread calculated by market participants is the yield spread between a non-Treasury sector and Treasury securities with the same maturity.

The yield spread between two issues within a market sector is called an intramarket sector spread. As with Treasury securities, a yield curve can be estimated for a given issuer. The yield spread typically increases with maturity. The yield spreads for a given issuer can be added to the yield for the corresponding maturity of the on-the-run Treasury issue. The resulting yield curve is then an issuer's on-the-run yield curve.

The factors other than maturity that affect the intermarket and intramarket yield spreads are 1) the relative credit risk of the two issues, 2) the presence of embedded options, 3) the liquidity of the two issues, and 4) the taxability of interest received by investors.

4.3 Credit Spreads

The yield spread between non-Treasury securities and Treasury securities that are identical in all respects except for credit rating is referred to as a credit spread or quality spread. "Identical in all respects except credit rating" means that the maturities are the same and that there are no embedded options.

For example, Exhibit 3 shows information on the yield spread within the corporate sector by credit rating and maturity, for the 90-day period ending February 8, 2002. The high, low, and average spreads for the 90-day period are reported. Note that the lower the credit rating, the higher the credit spread. Also note that, for a given sector of the corporate market and a given credit rating, the credit spread increases with maturity.

Exhibit 3	**Credit Spreads (in Basis Points) in the Corporate Sector on February 8, 2002**								
	AA—90-Day			A—90-Day			BBB—90-Day		
Maturity (Years)	**High**	**Low**	**Avg**	**High**	**Low**	**Avg**	**High**	**Low**	**Avg**
Industrials									
5	87	58	72	135	85	112	162	117	140
10	102	73	90	158	109	134	180	133	156
30	114	93	106	170	132	152	199	154	175
Utilities									
5	140	0	103	153	112	134	200	163	184
10	160	0	121	168	132	153	220	182	204
30	175	0	132	188	151	171	240	200	222

| Exhibit 3 | Continued |

	AA—90-Day			A—90-Day			BBB—90-Day		
Maturity (Years)	High	Low	Avg	High	Low	Avg	High	Low	Avg
Finance									
5	103	55	86	233	177	198			
10	125	78	103	253	170	209			
30	148	100	130	253	207	228			
Banks									
5	97	60	81	113	83	100			
10	120	78	95	127	92	110			
30	138	105	121	170	127	145			

Source: Abstracted from *Global Relative Value*, Lehman Brothers, Fixed Income Research, February 11, 2002, p. 133.

It is argued that credit spreads between corporates and Treasuries change systematically with changes in the economy. Credit spreads widen (i.e., become larger) in a declining or contracting economy and narrow (i.e., become smaller) during economic expansion. The economic rationale is that, in a declining or contracting economy, corporations experience declines in revenue and cash flow, making it more difficult for corporate issuers to service their contractual debt obligations. To induce investors to hold spread products as credit quality deteriorates, the credit spread widens. The widening occurs as investors sell off corporates and invest the proceeds in Treasury securities (popularly referred to as a "flight to quality"). The converse is that, during economic expansion and brisk economic activity, revenue and cash flow increase, increasing the likelihood that corporate issuers will have the capacity to service their contractual debt obligations.

Exhibit 4 provides evidence of the impact of the business cycle on credit spreads since 1919. The credit spread in the exhibit is the difference between Baa-rated and Aaa-rated corporate bonds; the shaded areas in the exhibit represent periods of economic recession as defined by the National Bureau of Economic Research (NBER). In general, corporate credit spreads tightened during the early stages of economic expansion, and spreads widened sharply during economic recessions. In fact, spreads typically begin to widen before the official beginning of an economic recession.[8]

Some market observers use the yield spread between issuers in cyclical and non-cyclical industry sectors as a proxy for yield spreads due to expected economic conditions. The rationale is as follows. While companies in both cyclical and non-cyclical industries are adversely affected by expectations of a recession, the impact is greater for cyclical industries. As a result, the yield spread between issuers in cyclical, and non-cyclical industry sectors will widen with expectations of a contracting economy.

---

8 For a further discussion and evidence regarding business cycles and credit spreads, see Chapter 10 in Leland E. Crabbe and Frank J. Fabozzi, *Managing a Corporate Portfolio* (Hoboken, NJ: John Wiley & Sons, 2002).

| Exhibit 4 | Credit Spreads between Baa and Aaa Corporate Bonds over the Business Cycle since 1919 |

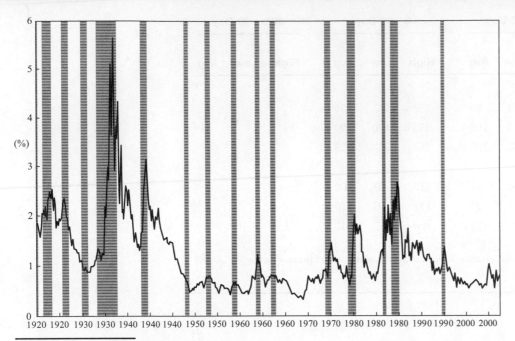

Note: Shaded areas = economic recession as defined by the NBER.
Source: Exhibit 1 in Leland E. Crabbe and Frank J. Fabozzi, *Managing a Corporate Portfolio* (Hoboken, NJ: John Wiley & Sons, 2002), p. 154.

4.4 Including Embedded Options

It is not uncommon for a bond issue to include a provision that gives either the issuer and/or the bondholder an option to take some action against the other party. The most common type of option in a bond issue is the call provision that grants the issuer the right to retire the debt, fully or partially, before the scheduled maturity date.

The presence of an embedded option has an effect on both the yield spread of an issue relative to a Treasury security and the yield spread relative to otherwise comparable issues that do not have an embedded option. In general, investors require a larger yield spread to a comparable Treasury security for an issue with an embedded option that is favorable to the issuer (e.g., a call option) than for an issue without such an option. In contrast, market participants require a smaller yield spread to a comparable Treasury security for an issue with an embedded option that is favorable to the investor (e.g., put option or conversion option). In fact, for a bond with an option favorable to an investor, the interest rate may be less than that on a comparable Treasury security.

Even for callable bonds, the yield spread depends on the type of call feature. For a callable bond with a deferred call, the longer the deferred call period, the greater the call protection provided to the investor. Thus, all other factors equal, the longer the deferred call period, the lower the yield spread attributable to the call feature.

A major part of the bond market is the mortgage-backed securities sector.[9] These securities expose an investor to prepayment risk, and the yield spread between a mortgage-backed security and a comparable Treasury security reflects this prepayment risk. To see this, consider a basic mortgage-backed security called a Ginnie Mae passthrough security. This security is backed by the full faith and credit of the U.S. government. Consequently, the yield spread between a Ginnie Mae passthrough security

---

9 The mortgage-backed securities sector is often referred to as simply the "mortgage sector."

and a comparable Treasury security is not due to credit risk. Rather, it is primarily due to prepayment risk. For example, Exhibit 5 reports the yield on 30-year Ginnie Mae passthrough securities with different coupon rates. The first issue to be addressed is the maturity of the comparable Treasury issue against which the Ginnie Mae should be benchmarked in order to calculate a yield spread. This is an issue because a mortgage passthrough security is an amortizing security that repays principal over time rather than just at the stated maturity date (30 years in our illustration). Consequently, while the stated maturity of a Ginnie Mae passthrough is 30 years, its yield should not be compared to the yield on a 30-year Treasury issue. For now, you can see that the Treasury benchmark in Exhibit 5 depends on the coupon rate. The yield spread, shown in the second column, depends on the coupon rate.

Exhibit 5	Yield Spreads and Option-Adjusted Spread (OAS) for Ginnie Mae 30-Year Passthrough Securities (February 8, 2002)

Coupon Rate (%)	Yield Spread (bps)	Benchmark Treasury	OAS on 2/8/02 (bps)	90-Day OAS (bps)		
				High	Low	Avg
6.5	203	5 year	52	75	46	59
7.0	212	5 year	57	83	54	65
7.5	155	3 year	63	94	62	74
8.0	105	3 year	73	108	73	88
9.0	244	2 year	131	160	124	139

Source: Abstracted from *Global Relative Value*, Lehman Brothers, Fixed Income Research, February 11, 2002, p.132.

Practice Question 2

Below are the yield spreads estimated between 10-year federal agency securities and the 10-year on-the-run Treasury issue on June 30, 1998 as reported in the July 20, 1998 issue of *Spread Talk* published by Prudential Securities (p. 7):

Issue	Yield Spread (bps)
noncallable	40
callable, 1 year deferred call	110
callable, 2 year deferred call	95
callable, 3 year deferred call	75

A. Why is the yield spread for the noncallable issue less than for the three callable issues?

B. Why is it that, for the callable issues, the longer the deferred call period, the smaller the yield spread?

In general, when a yield spread is cited for an issue that is callable, part of the spread reflects the risk associated with the embedded option. Reported yield spreads do not adjust for embedded options. The raw yield spreads are sometimes referred to as nominal spreads—nominal in the sense that the value of embedded options has not been removed in computing an adjusted yield spread. The yield spread that adjusts for the embedded option is OAS.

The last four columns in Exhibit 5 show Lehman Brothers' estimate of the option-adjusted spread for the 30-year Ginnie Mae passthroughs shown in the exhibit—the option-adjusted spread on February 8, 2002 and for the prior 90-day period (high, low, and average). The nominal spread is the yield spread shown in the second column. Notice that the option-adjusted spread is considerably less than the nominal spread. For example, for the 7.5% coupon issue the nominal spread is 155 basis points. After adjusting for the prepayment risk (i.e., the embedded option), the spread as measured by the option-adjusted spread is considerably less, 63 basis points.

4.5 Liquidity

Even within the Treasury market, a yield spread exists between off-the-run Treasury issues and on-the-run Treasury issues of similar maturity due to differences in liquidity and the effects of the repo market. Similarly, in the spread sectors, generic on-the-run yield curves can be estimated, and the liquidity spread due to an off-the-run issue can be computed.

A Lehman Brothers' study found that one factor that affects liquidity (and therefore the yield spread) is the size of an issue—the larger the issue, the greater the liquidity relative to a smaller issue, and the greater the liquidity, the lower the yield spread.[10]

4.6 Taxability of Interest Income

In the United States, unless exempted under the federal income tax code, interest income is taxable at the federal income tax level. In addition to federal income taxes, state and local taxes may apply to interest income.

The federal tax code specifically exempts interest income from qualified municipal bond issues from taxation.[11] Because of the tax-exempt feature of these municipal bonds, the yield on municipal bonds is less than that on Treasuries with the same maturity. Exhibit 6 shows this relationship on February 12, 2002, as reported by Bloomberg Financial Markets. The yield ratio shown for municipal bonds is the ratio of AAA general obligation bond yields to yields for the same maturity on-the-run Treasury issue.[12]

The difference in yield between tax-exempt securities and Treasury securities is typically measured not in terms of the absolute yield spread but as a yield ratio. More specifically, it is measured as the quotient of the yield on a tax-exempt security relative to the yield on a comparable Treasury security. This is reported in Exhibit 6. The yield ratio has changed over time due to changes in tax rates, as well as other factors. The higher the tax rate, the more attractive the tax-exempt feature and the lower the yield ratio.

The U.S. municipal bond market is divided into two bond sectors: general obligation bonds and revenue bonds. For the tax-exempt bond market, the benchmark for calculating yield spreads is not Treasury securities, but rather a generic AAA general obligation yield curve constructed by dealer firms active in the municipal bond market and by data/analytics vendors.

---

10 *Global Relative Value*, Lehman Brothers, Fixed Income Research, June 28, 1999, COR-2 AND 3.

11 As explained in the reading on bond sectors and instruments, some municipal bonds are taxable.

12 Some maturities for Treasury securities shown in the exhibit are not on-the-run issues. These are estimates for the market yields.

	Yield on AAA General	Yield on U.S.	
Maturity	Obligation (%)	Treasury (%)	Yield Ratio
3 months	1.29	1.72	0.75
6 months	1.41	1.84	0.77
1 year	1.69	2.16	0.78
2 years	2.20	3.02	0.73
3 years	2.68	3.68	0.73
4 years	3.09	4.13	0.75
5 years	3.42	4.42	0.77
7 years	3.86	4.84	0.80
10 years	4.25	4.95	0.86
15 years	4.73	5.78	0.82
20 years	4.90	5.85	0.84
30 years	4.95	5.50	0.90

Exhibit 6 Yield Ratio for AAA General Obligation Municipal Bonds to U.S. Treasuries of the Same Maturity (February 12, 2002)

Source: Bloomberg Financial Markets.

4.6.1 *After-Tax Yield and Taxable-Equivalent Yield*

The yield on a taxable bond issue after federal income taxes are paid is called the after-tax yield and is computed as follows:

$$\text{After-tax yield} = \text{Pre-tax yield} \times (1 - \text{Marginal tax rate})$$

Of course, the marginal tax rate[13] varies among investors. For example, suppose a taxable bond issue offers a yield of 5% and is acquired by an investor facing a marginal tax rate of 31%. The after-tax yield would then be:

$$\text{After-tax yield} = 0.05 \times (1 - 0.31) = 0.0345 = 3.45\%$$

Alternatively, we can determine the yield that must be offered on a taxable bond issue to give the same after-tax yield as a tax-exempt issue. This yield is called the taxable-equivalent yield or tax-equivalent yield and is computed as follows:

$$\text{Taxable-equivalent yield} = \frac{\text{Tax-exempt yield}}{(1 - \text{Marginal tax rate})}$$

For example, consider an investor facing a 31% marginal tax rate who purchases a tax-exempt issue with a yield of 4%. The taxable-equivalent yield is then:

$$\text{Taxable-equivalent yield} = \frac{0.04}{(1 - 0.31)} = 0.058 = 5.80\%$$

Notice that the higher the marginal tax rate, the higher the taxable-equivalent yield. For instance, in our last example if the marginal tax rate is 40% rather than 31%, the taxable-equivalent yield would be 6.67% rather than 5.80%, as shown below:

$$\text{Taxable-equivalent yield} = \frac{0.04}{(1 - 0.40)} = 0.0667 = 6.67\%$$

---

13 The marginal tax rate is the tax rate at which an additional dollar is taxed.

Practice Question 3

Following is information about two investors, Ms. High and Mr. Low:

	Marginal Tax Bracket (%)
Ms. High	40
Mr. Low	15

A. Suppose that these two investors are considering investing in a taxable bond that offers a yield of 6.8%. What is the after-tax yield for each investor?

B. Suppose that these two investors can purchase a tax-exempt security offering a yield of 4.8%. What is the taxable-equivalent yield for each investor?

Some state and local governments tax interest income from bond issues that are exempt from federal income taxes. Some municipalities exempt interest income from all municipal issues from taxation, while others do not. Some states exempt interest income from bonds issued by municipalities within the state but tax the interest income from bonds issued by municipalities outside of the state. The implication is that two municipal securities with the same credit rating and the same maturity may trade at different yield spreads because of the relative demand for bonds of municipalities in different states. For example, in a high income tax state such as New York, the demand for bonds of New York municipalities drives down their yields relative to bonds issued by municipalities in a zero income tax state such as Texas.

4.7 Technical Factors

At times, deviations from typical yield spreads are caused by temporary imbalances between supply and demand. For example, in the second quarter of 1999, issuers became concerned that the Fed would pursue a policy to increase interest rates. In response, a record issuance of corporate securities resulted in an increase in the yield spread between corporates and Treasuries.

In the municipal market, yield spreads are affected by the temporary oversupply of issues within a market sector. For example, a substantial new issue volume of high-grade state general obligation bonds may tend to decrease the yield spread between high-grade and low-grade revenue bonds. In a weak market environment, it is easier for high-grade municipal bonds to come to market than for weaker credits. So at times high grades flood weak markets even when there is a relative scarcity of medium- and low-grade municipal bond issues.

Since technical factors cause temporary misalignments of the yield spread relationship, some investors look at the forward calendar of planned offerings to project the impact on future yield spreads. Some corporate analysts identify the risk of yield spread changes due to the supply of new issues when evaluating issuers or sectors.

NON-U.S. INTEREST RATES

The same factors that affect yield spreads in the United States are responsible for yield spreads in other countries and between countries. Major non-U.S. bond markets have a government benchmark yield curve similar to that of the U.S. Treasury yield curve. Exhibit 7 shows the government yield curve as of the beginning and end of 2001 for Germany, Japan, the U.K., and France. These yield curves are presented to illustrate the different shapes and the way in which they can change. Notice that only the Japanese yield curve shifted in an almost parallel fashion (i.e., the rate for all maturities changed by approximately the same number of basis points).

The German bond market is the largest market for publicly issued bonds in Europe. The yields on German government bonds are viewed as benchmark interest rates in Europe. Because of the important role of the German bond market, nominal spreads are typically computed relative to German government bonds (German bunds).

Exhibit 7	Yield Curves in Germany, Japan, the U.K., and France: 2001

A. German Bund Yield Curve

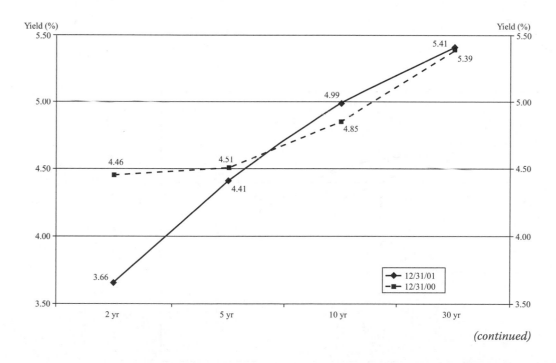

(continued)

Exhibit 7   *Continued*

B. Japanese Government Bond Yield Curve

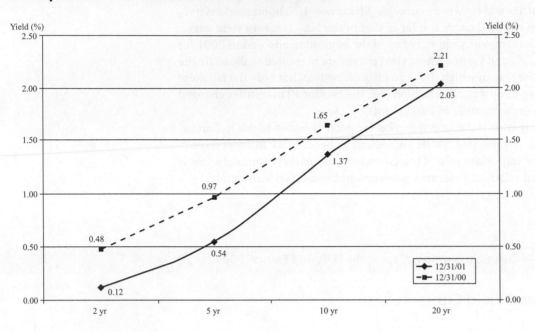

C. U.K. Gilt Yield Curve

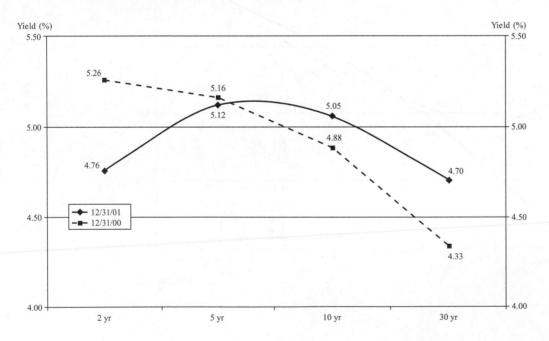

Exhibit 7	Continued

D. French OAT Yield Curve

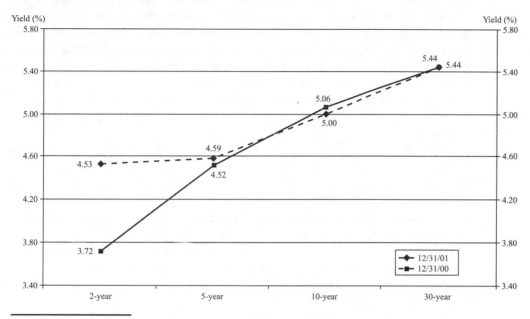

Source: Lehman Brothers Fixed Income Research, *Global Fixed Income Strategy "Playbook,"* January 2002.

Institutional investors who borrow funds on a short-term basis to invest (referred to as "funded investors") obviously desire to earn an amount in excess of their borrowing cost. The most popular borrowing cost reference rate is the **London interbank offered rate (LIBOR)**. LIBOR is the interest rate at which banks pay to borrow funds from other banks in the London interbank market. The borrowing occurs via a cash deposit of one bank (the lender) into a certificate of deposit (CD) in another bank (the borrower). The maturity of the CD can be from overnight to five years. So, 3-month LIBOR represents the interest rate paid on a CD that matures in three months. The CD can be denominated in one of several currencies. The currencies for which LIBOR is reported are the U.S. dollar, the British pound, the Euro, the Canadian dollar, the Australian dollar, the Japanese yen, and Swiss francs. When it is denominated in U.S. dollars, it is referred to as a Eurodollar CD. LIBOR is determined for every London business day by the British Bankers' Association (BBA) by maturity and for each currency and is reported by various services.

Entities seeking to borrow funds pay a spread over LIBOR and seek to earn a spread over that funding cost when they invest the borrowed funds. So, for example, if the 3-month borrowing cost for a funded investor is 3-month LIBOR plus 25 basis points and the investor can earn 3-month LIBOR plus 125 basis points for three months, then the investor earns a spread of 100 basis points for three months (125 basis points – 25 basis points).

SWAP SPREADS

6

Another important spread measure is the **swap spread**.

6.1 Interest Rate Swap and the Swap Spread

In an interest rate swap, two parties (called counterparties) agree to exchange periodic interest payments. The dollar amount of the interest payments exchanged is based on a predetermined dollar principal, which is called the notional principal or notional amount. The dollar amount each counterparty pays to the other is the agreed-upon periodic interest rate times the notional principal. The only dollars exchanged between the parties are the interest payments, not the notional principal. In the most common type of swap, one party agrees to pay the other party fixed interest payments at designated dates for the life of the swap. This party is referred to as the fixed-rate payer. The fixed rate that the fixed-rate payer pays is called the swap rate. The other party, who agrees to make interest rate payments that float with some reference rate, is referred to as the fixed-rate receiver.

The reference rates used for the floating rate in an interest rate swap is one of various money market instruments: LIBOR (the most common reference rate used in swaps), Treasury bill rate, commercial paper rate, bankers' acceptance rate, federal funds rate, and prime rate.

The convention that has evolved for quoting a swap rate is that a dealer sets the floating rate equal to the reference rate and then quotes the fixed rate that will apply. The fixed rate has a specified "spread" above the yield for a Treasury with the same term to maturity as the swap. This specified spread is called the swap spread. The swap rate is the sum of the yield for a Treasury with the same maturity as the swap plus the swap spread.

To illustrate an interest rate swap in which one party pays fixed and receives floating, assume the following:

- term of swap: 5 years;
- swap spread: 50 basis points;
- reference rate: 3-month LIBOR;
- notional amount: $50 million;
- frequency of payments: every three months.

Suppose also that the 5-year Treasury rate is 5.5% at the time the swap is entered into. Then the swap rate will be 6%, found by adding the swap spread of 50 basis points to the 5-year Treasury yield of 5.5%.

This means that the fixed-rate payer agrees to pay a 6% annual rate for the next five years with payments made quarterly and receive from the fixed-rate receiver 3-month LIBOR with the payments made quarterly. Since the notional amount is $50 million, this means that every three months, the fixed-rate payer pays $750,000 (6% times $50 million divided by 4). The fixed-rate receiver pays 3-month LIBOR times $50 million divided by 4. The table below shows the payment made by the fixed-rate receiver to the fixed-rate payer for different values of 3-month LIBOR[14]:

If 3-Month LIBOR Is	Annual Dollar Amount	Quarterly Payment
4%	$2,000,000	$500,000
5	2,500,000	625,000
6	3,000,000	750,000
7	3,500,000	875,000
8	4,000,000	1,000,000

---

14 The amount of the payment is found by dividing the annual dollar amount by four because payments are made quarterly. In a real world application, both the fixed-rate and floating-rate payments are adjusted for the number of days in a quarter, but it is unnecessary for us to deal with this adjustment here.

In practice, the payments are netted out. For example, if 3-month LIBOR is 4%, the fixed-rate receiver would receive $750,000 and pay to the fixed-rate payer $500,000. Netting the two payments, the fixed-rate payer pays the fixed-rate receiver $250,000 ($750,000 − $500,000).

6.2 Role of Interest Rate Swaps

Interest rate swaps have many important applications in fixed income portfolio management and risk management. They tie together the fixed-rate and floating-rate sectors of the bond market. As a result, investors can convert a fixed-rate asset into a floating-rate asset with an interest rate swap.

Suppose a financial institution has invested in 5-year bonds with a $50 million par value and a coupon rate of 9% and that this bond is selling at par value. Moreover, this institution borrows $50 million on a quarterly basis (to fund the purchase of the bonds) and its cost of funds is 3-month LIBOR plus 50 basis points. The "income spread" between its assets (i.e., 5-year bonds) and its liabilities (its funding cost) for any 3-month period depends on 3-month LIBOR. The following table shows how the annual spread varies with 3-month LIBOR:

Asset Yield (%)	3-Month LIBOR (%)	Funding Cost (%)	Annual Income Spread (%)
9.00	4.00	4.50	4.50
9.00	5.00	5.50	3.50
9.00	6.00	6.50	2.50
9.00	7.00	7.50	1.50
9.00	8.00	8.50	0.50
9.00	8.50	9.00	0.00
9.00	9.00	9.50	−0.50
9.00	10.00	10.50	−1.50
9.00	11.00	11.50	−2.50

As 3-month LIBOR increases, the income spread decreases. If 3-month LIBOR exceeds 8.5%, the income spread is negative (i.e., it costs more to borrow than is earned on the bonds in which the borrowed funds are invested).

This financial institution has a mismatch between its assets and its liabilities. An interest rate swap can be used to hedge this mismatch. For example, suppose the manager of this financial institution enters into a 5-year swap with a $50 million notional amount in which it agrees to pay a fixed rate (i.e., to be the fixed-rate payer) in exchange for 3-month LIBOR. Suppose further that the swap rate is 6%. Then the annual income spread taking into account the swap payments is as follows for different values of 3-month LIBOR:

Asset Yield (%)	3-Month LIBOR (%)	Funding Cost (%)	Fixed Rate Paid in Swap (%)	3-Month LIBOR Rec. in Swap (%)	Annual Income Spread (%)
9.00	4.00	4.50	6.00	4.00	2.50
9.00	5.00	5.50	6.00	5.00	2.50
9.00	6.00	6.50	6.00	6.00	2.50
9.00	7.00	7.50	6.00	7.00	2.50

(continued)

Asset Yield (%)	3-Month LIBOR (%)	Funding Cost (%)	Fixed Rate Paid in Swap (%)	3-Month LIBOR Rec. in Swap (%)	Annual Income Spread (%)
9.00	8.00	8.50	6.00	8.00	2.50
9.00	8.50	9.00	6.00	8.50	2.50
9.00	9.00	9.50	6.00	9.00	2.50
9.00	10.00	10.50	6.00	10.00	2.50
9.00	11.00	11.50	6.00	11.00	2.50

Assuming the bond does not default and is not called, the financial institution has locked in a spread of 250 basis points.

Effectively, the financial institution using this interest rate swap converted a fixed-rate asset into a floating-rate asset. The reference rate for the synthetic floating-rate asset is 3-month LIBOR and the liabilities are in terms of 3-month LIBOR. Alternatively, the financial institution could have converted its liabilities to a fixed-rate by entering into a 5-year $50 million notional amount swap by being the fixed-rate payer and the results would have been the same.

Practice Question 4

Assume that the asset yield in the illustration is 8.6% instead of 9% and the funding cost is 3-month LIBOR plus 60 basis points. Demonstrate the spread that has been locked in by the interest rate swap (assuming the issuer of the assets does not default) by completing the following table:

Asset Yield (%)	3-Month LIBOR (%)	Funding Cost (%)	Fixed Rate Paid in Swap (%)	3-Month LIBOR Rec. in Swap (%)	Annual Income Spread (%)
	4.00				
	5.00				
	6.00				
	7.00				
	8.00				
	8.50				
	9.00				
	10.00				
	11.00				

This simple illustration shows the critical importance of an interest rate swap. Investors and issuers with a mismatch of assets and liabilities can use an interest rate swap to better match assets and liabilities, thereby reducing their risk.

6.3 Determinants of the Swap Spread

Market participants throughout the world view the swap spread as the appropriate spread measure for valuation and relative value analysis. Here we discuss the determinants of the swap spread.

We know that

Swap rate = Treasury rate + Swap spread

where Treasury rate is equal to the yield on a Treasury with the same maturity as the swap. Since the parties are swapping the future reference rate for the swap rate, then:

Reference rate = Treasury rate + Swap spread

Solving for the swap spread we have:

Swap spread = Reference rate − Treasury rate

Since the most common reference rate is LIBOR, we can substitute this into the above formula getting:

Swap spread = LIBOR − Treasury rate

Thus, the swap spread is a spread of the global cost of short-term borrowing over the Treasury rate.

Exhibit 8	Three-Year Trailing Correlation between Swap Spreads and Credit Spreads (AA, A, and BB): June 1992 to December 2001

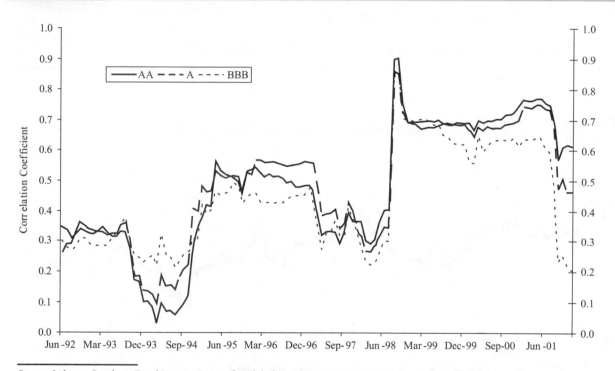

Source: Lehman Brothers Fixed Income Research, *Global Fixed Income Strategy "Playbook,"* January 2002.

The swap spread primarily reflects the credit spreads in the corporate bond market.[15] Studies have found a high correlation between swap spreads and credit spreads in various sectors of the fixed income market. This can be seen in Exhibit 8 which shows the 3-year trailing correlation from June 1992 to December 2001 between swap spreads and AA, A, and BBB credit spreads. Note from the exhibit that the highest correlation is with AA credit spreads.

---

15 We say primarily because there are also technical factors that affect the swap spread. For a discussion of these factors, see Richard Gordon, "The Truth about Swap Spreads," in Frank J. Fabozzi (ed.), *Professional Perspectives on Fixed Income Portfolio Management: Volume 1* (New Hope, PA: Frank J. Fabozzi Associates, 2000), pp. 97–104.

6.4 Swap Spread Curve

A swap spread curve shows the relationship between the swap rate and swap maturity. A swap spread curve is available by country. The swap spread is the amount added to the yield of the respective country's government bond with the same maturity as the maturity of the swap. Exhibit 9 shows the swap spread curves for Germany, Japan, the U.K., and the U.S. for January 2001 and December 2001. The swap spreads move together. For example, Exhibit 10 shows the daily 5-year swap spreads from December 2000 to December 2001 for the U.S. and Germany.

Exhibit 9	January and December 2001 Swap Spread Curves for Germany, Japan, U.K., and U.S.															
	Germany				**Japan**				**U.K.**				**U.S.**			
	2-Year	5-Year	10-Year	30-Year	2-Year	5-Year	10-Year	30-Year	2-Year	5-Year	10-Year	30-Year	2-Year	5-Year	10-Year	30-Year
Jan-01	23	40	54	45	8	10	14	29	40	64	83	91	63	82	81	73
Dec-01	22	28	28	14	3	(2)	(1)	8	36	45	52	42	46	76	77	72

Source: Lehman Brothers Fixed Income Research, *Global Fixed Income Strategy "Playbook,"* January 2002.

Exhibit 10	Daily 5-Year Swap Spreads in Germany and the United States: 2001

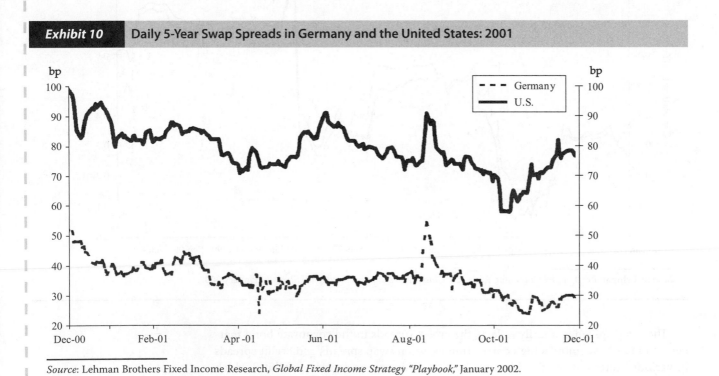

Source: Lehman Brothers Fixed Income Research, *Global Fixed Income Strategy "Playbook,"* January 2002.

END OPTIONAL SEGMENT

SOLUTIONS FOR PRACTICE QUESTIONS

1. In the computation, we will treat the Treasury issue as Bond B and the corporate issue as Bond A.

   A. GE versus Treasury

   $$\text{Absolute yield spread} = 4.93\% - 4.18\% = 0.75\% = 75 \text{ Basis points}$$

   $$\text{Relative yield spread} = \frac{4.93\% - 4.18\%}{4.18\%} = 0.179 = 17.9\%$$

   $$\text{Yield ratio} = \frac{4.93\%}{4.18\%} = 1.179$$

   B. Verizon versus Treasury

   $$\text{Absolute yield spread} = 5.11\% - 4.18\% = 0.93\% = 93 \text{ Basis points}$$

   $$\text{Relative yield spread} = \frac{5.11\% - 4.18\%}{4.18\%} = 0.222 = 22.2\%$$

   $$\text{Yield ratio} = \frac{5.11\%}{4.18\%} = 1.222$$

2. **A.** Since the call feature is unattractive to an investor because it results in call risk, the callable issues must offer higher yield spreads.

   B. The longer the protection against the issue being called, the lower the call risk. Consequently, the longer the deferred call period, the lower the yield spread.

3. **A.** After-tax yield for Ms. High = $0.068(1 - 0.40) = 0.0408 = 4.08\%$ After-tax yield for Mr. Low = $0.068(1 - 0.15) = 0.0578 = 5.78\%$

   B. Taxable equivalent yield for Ms. High $= \dfrac{0.048}{1 - 0.40} = 0.0800 = 8.00\%$

   Taxable equivalent yield for Mr. Low $= \dfrac{0.048}{1 - 0.15} = 0.0565 = 5.65\%$

4. The annual income spread locked in is 2% or 200 basis points.

Asset Yield (%)	3-Month LIBOR (%)	Funding Cost (%)	Fixed Rate Paid in Swap (%)	3-Month LIBOR Rec. in Swap (%)	Annual Income Spread[a] (%)
8.60	4.00	4.60	6.00	4.00	2.00
8.60	5.00	5.60	6.00	5.00	2.00
8.60	6.00	6.60	6.00	6.00	2.00
8.60	7.00	7.60	6.00	7.00	2.00
8.60	8.00	8.60	6.00	8.00	2.00
8.60	8.50	9.10	6.00	8.50	2.00
8.60	9.00	9.60	6.00	9.00	2.00
8.60	10.00	10.60	6.00	10.00	2.00
8.60	11.00	11.60	6.00	11.00	2.00

[a] Annual income spread = Asset yield − Funding cost − Fixed rate paid in swap + 3-month LIBOR received in swap.

SUMMARY

- The interest rate offered on a particular bond issue depends on the interest rate that can be earned on risk-free instruments and the perceived risks associated with the issue.

- The U.S. Federal Reserve Board is the policy-making body whose interest rate policy tools directly influence short-term interest rates and indirectly influence long-term interest rates in the United States.

- The Fed's most frequently employed interest rate policy tools are open market operations and changing the discount rate; less frequently used tools are changing bank reserve requirements and verbal persuasion to influence how bankers supply credit to businesses and consumers.

- Because Treasury securities have no credit risk, market participants look at the interest rate or yield offered on an on-the-run Treasury security as the minimum interest rate required on a non-Treasury security with the same maturity.

- The Treasury yield curve shows the relationship between yield and maturity of on-the-run Treasury issues.

- The typical shape for the Treasury yield curve is upward sloping—yield increases with maturity—which is referred to as a normal yield curve.

- Inverted yield curves (yield decreasing with maturity) and flat yield curves (yield roughly the same regardless of maturity) have been observed for the yield curve.

- Two factors complicate the relationship between maturity and yield as indicated by the Treasury yield curve: 1) the yield for on-the-run issues is distorted since these securities can be financed at cheaper rates and, as a result, offer a lower yield than in the absence of this financing advantage and 2) on-the-run Treasury issues and off-the-run issues have different interest rate reinvestment risks.

- The yields on Treasury STRIPS of different maturities provide a superior relationship between yield and maturity compared to the on-the-run Treasury yield curve.

- The yield on a zero-coupon or stripped Treasury security is called the Treasury spot rate.

- The term structure of interest rates is the relationship between maturity and Treasury spot rates.

- Three theories have been offered to explain the shape of the yield curve: pure expectations theory, liquidity preference theory, and market segmentation theory.

- The pure expectations theory asserts that the market sets yields based solely on expectations for future interest rates.

- According to the pure expectations theory: 1) a rising term structure reflects an expectation that future short-term rates will rise, 2) a flat term structure reflects an expectation that future short-term rates will be mostly constant, and 3) a falling term structure reflects an expectation that future short-term rates will decline.

- The liquidity preference theory asserts that market participants want to be compensated for the interest rate risk associated with holding longer-term bonds.

- The market segmentation theory asserts that there are different maturity sectors of the yield curve and that each maturity sector is independent or segmented from the other maturity sectors. Within each maturity sector, the interest rate is determined by the supply and demand for funds.

- According to the market segmentation theory, any shape is possible for the yield curve.

- Despite the imperfections of the Treasury yield curve as a benchmark for the minimum interest rate that an investor requires for investing in a non-Treasury security, it is common to refer to a non-Treasury security's additional yield over the nearest maturity on-the-run Treasury issue as the "yield spread."

- The yield spread can be computed in three ways: 1) the difference between the yield on two bonds or bond sectors (called the absolute yield spread), 2) the difference in yields as a percentage of the benchmark yield (called the relative yield spread), and 3) the ratio of the yield relative to the benchmark yield (called the yield ratio).

- An intermarket yield spread is the yield spread between two securities with the same maturity in two different sectors of the bond market.

- The most common intermarket sector spread calculated is the yield spread between the yield on a security in a non-Treasury market sector and a Treasury security with the same maturity.

- An intramarket sector spread is the yield spread between two issues within the same market sector.

- An issuer specific yield curve can be computed given the yield spread, by maturity, for an issuer and the yield for on-the-run Treasury securities.

- The factors other than maturity that affect the intermarket and intramarket yield spreads are 1) the relative credit risk of the two issues; 2) the presence of embedded options; 3) the relative liquidity of the two issues; and, 4) the taxability of the interest.

- A credit spread or quality spread is the yield spread between a non-Treasury security and a Treasury security that are "identical in all respects except for credit rating."

- Some market participants argue that credit spreads between corporates and Treasuries change systematically because of changes in economic prospects—widening in a declining economy ("flight to quality") and narrowing in an expanding economy.

- Generally investors require a larger spread to a comparable Treasury security for issues with an embedded option favorable to the issuer, and a smaller spread for an issue with an embedded option favorable to the investor.

- For mortgage-backed securities, one reason for the increased yield spread relative to a comparable Treasury security is exposure to prepayment risk.

- The option-adjusted spread of a security seeks to measure the yield spread after adjusting for embedded options.

- A yield spread exists due to the difference in the perceived liquidity of two issues.

- One factor that affects liquidity (and therefore the yield spread) is the size of an issue—the larger the issue, the greater the liquidity relative to a smaller issue, and the greater the liquidity, the lower the yield spread.

- Because of the tax-exempt feature of municipal bonds, the yield on municipal bonds is less than that on Treasuries with the same maturity.

- The difference in yield between tax-exempt securities and Treasury securities is typically measured in terms of a yield ratio—the yield on a tax-exempt security as a percentage of the yield on a comparable Treasury security.

- The after-tax yield is computed by multiplying the pre-tax yield by one minus the marginal tax rate.

- In the tax-exempt bond market, the benchmark for calculating yield spreads is a generic AAA general obligation bond with a specified maturity.

- Technical factors having to do with temporary imbalances between the supply of and demand for new issues affect yield spreads.

- The same factors that affect yield spreads in the United States affect yield spreads in other countries and between countries.

- Major non-U.S. bond markets have government benchmark yield curves similar to the U.S. Treasury yield curve.

- Because of the important role of the German bond market, nominal spreads in the European bond market are typically computed relative to German government bonds.

- Funded investors who borrow short term typically measure the relative value of a security using borrowing rates rather than the Treasury rate.

- The most popular borrowing cost reference rate is the London interbank offered rate (LIBOR), which is the interest rate banks pay to borrow funds from other banks in the London interbank market.

- Funded investors typically pay a spread over LIBOR and seek to earn a spread over that funding cost when they invest the borrowed funds.

PRACTICE PROBLEMS FOR READING 55

1. The following statement appears on page 2 of the August 2, 1999 issue of Prudential Securities' *Spread Talk*.

   > The market appears to be focusing all of its energy on predicting whether or not the Fed will raise rates again at the August and/or October FOMC [Federal Open Market Committee] meetings.

   How do market observers try to predict "whether or not the Fed will raise rates"?

2. Ms. Peters is a financial advisor. One of her clients called and asked about a recent change in the shape of the yield curve from upward sloping to downward sloping. The client told Ms. Peters that she thought that the market was signaling that interest rates were expected to decline in the future. What should Ms. Peters' response be to her client?

3. How does the liquidity preference theory differ from the pure expectations theory?

4. According to the pure expectations theory, what does a humped yield curve suggest about the expectations of future interest rates?

5. Assume the following information pertaining to federal agency spreads was reported:

Agency Spreads versus Benchmark Treasury (Basis Points)

		Last 12 Months		
	Yield Spread	High	Low	Average
Noncallable				
3-year	70	70	28	44.1
5-year	80	80	32	55.4
10-year	95	95	45	71.2
Callable				
3-year (NC1)	107	107	50	80.2
5-year (NC1)	145	145	77	112.1
5-year (NC2)	132	132	65	96.9
5-year (NC3)	124	124	—	33.6
10-year (NC3)	178	178	99	132.9
10-year (NC5)	156	156	79	112.5

(continued)

Practice Problems and Solutions: 1–13 taken from *Fixed Income Analysis for the Chartered Financial Analyst® Program*, Second Edition, by Frank J. Fabozzi, CFA. Copyright © 2004 by CFA Institute. All other problems and solutions copyright © CFA Institute.

	Continued			
		Last 12 Months		
	Yield Spread	**High**	**Low**	**Average**
Callable OAS (Volatility = 14%)				
3-year (NC1)	75	75	20	50.0
5-year (NC1)	100	100	20	63.8
5-year (NC2)	100	100	23	60.7
5-year (NC3)	100	100	29	59.6
10-year (NC3)	115	115	34	77.0
10-year (NC5)	115	115	36	77.4

Note: NCX = *X*-year deferred call; — = not available

A. Relative to the previous 12 months, what does the yield spread data above indicate about yield spreads?

B. Explain what causes the yield spread relationship between callable and noncallable issues for a given maturity.

C. Explain what causes the yield spread relationship among the different callable issues for a given maturity.

D. Why are the yield spreads shown in the second panel referred to as nominal spreads?

E. Explain what causes the yield spread relationship between the callable yield spread and the callable OAS for a given maturity and given deferred call.

6. Comment on the following statement by a representative of an investment management firm who is working with a client in selecting sectors in which the manager for the account will be permitted to invest:

> Mortgage-backed securities give our managers the opportunity to increase yield because these securities offer a higher yield than comparable Treasury securities. In particular, our managers prefer Ginnie Mae mortgage-backed securities because they have no credit risk since they are backed by the full faith and credit of the U.S. government. Therefore, our managers can pick up additional yield with no additional credit risk. While Ginnie Mae mortgage-backed securities may not be as liquid as U.S. Treasury securities, the yield spread is more than adequate to compensate for the lesser liquidity.

7. A. Why is the yield spread between a bond with an embedded option and an otherwise comparable Treasury security referred to as a "nominal spread"?

B. What is an option-adjusted spread and why is it superior to a nominal spread as a yield spread measure for a bond with an embedded option?

8. Suppose that the yield on a 10-year noncallable corporate bond is 7.25% and the yield for the on-the-run 10-year Treasury is 6.02%. Compute the following:

A. the absolute yield spread.

B. the relative yield spread.

C. the yield ratio.

9. Following is a quote that appeared in the May 19, 1999 *Global Relative Value* by Lehman Brothers (COR-1):

As we have written in the past, percent yield spreads (spread as a percent of Treasury yields) are still cheap on an historical basis. As an illustration, the average single A 10-year industrial percent yield spread was 17% on April 30 compared to a 10 year monthly average of 12%.

A. What is another name for the yield spread measure cited in the quote?

B. Why would the analysts at Lehman Brothers focus on "percent yield spreads" rather than absolute yield spread?

10. If proposals are being considered by Congress to reduce tax rates and the market views that passage of such legislation is likely, what would you expect to happen to municipal bond yields?

11. A. Why isn't the Treasury yield curve used as a benchmark in measuring yield spreads between different sectors of the municipal bond market?

B. What benchmark is used?

12. A. What is the after-tax yield for an investor in the 40% tax bracket if the taxable yield is 5%?

B. What is the taxable-equivalent yield for an investor in the 39% tax bracket if the tax-exempt yield on an investment is 3.1%?

13. Why are funded investors who borrow short term interested in a LIBOR yield curve rather than the Treasury yield curve?

14. All other factors being equal, would bond yield spreads from Treasury securities *most likely* be larger (wider):

	for bond issues that are liquid or illiquid?	for bonds issued with put options or with call options?
A.	Liquid	Call options
B.	Illiquid	Put options
C.	Illiquid	Call options

15. An analyst made the following statement: "We should purchase Treasury notes because they are risk-free. Default risk is essentially non-existent." Is the analyst's statement correct with respect to:

	risk-free?	default risk?
A.	No	No
B.	No	Yes
C.	Yes	No

16. In a normal yield curve environment, the relationship between yield and maturity can be *best* described as:

A. the longer the maturity, the lower the yield.

B. the longer the maturity, the higher the yield.

C. maturity and yield are independent of each other.

17. An investor is considering purchasing a five-year corporate bond. The yield on the bond is 6.25%, the rate of inflation is 3%, the yield on the on-the-run Treasury is 4.80%, and the price of the bond is par (or $100.00). The absolute yield spread, relative yield spread, and yield ratio, respectively, are:

A. 3.25%, 108.33%, 2.08.

B. 1.45%, 1.30, 30.21%.

C. 1.45%, 30.21%, 1.30.

18. Frieda Wannamaker is a taxable investor who is currently in the 28% income-tax bracket. She is considering purchasing a tax-exempt bond with a yield of 3.75%. The taxable equivalent yield on this bond is *closest* to:
    A. 1.46%.
    B. 5.21%.
    C. 7.47%.

19. Wayne Sewage and Sanitation District has $10,000,000 of 4.85% coupon tax-exempt municipal bonds outstanding. All else held constant, if the marginal tax rate of an individual investor holding $10,000 worth of these bonds is reduced to 20% from a starting value of 35%:
    A. the taxable-equivalent yield for that investor will not change.
    B. the taxable-equivalent yield increases from 6.0625% to 7.4615%.
    C. the investor will be more inclined to purchase equivalent risk corporate bonds.

20. Can an inverted (i.e., downward sloping) yield curve occur with the three theories of the term structure of interest rates? (Pure expectations theory, liquidity preference theory, and market segmentation theory.)
    A. Yes.
    B. All except pure expectations.
    C. All except liquidity preference.

21. The nominal yield spread for a callable bond will be, in general:
    A. solely dependent on the default risk of the bond.
    B. solely dependent on the slope of the term structure of interest rates.
    C. greater than the nominal yield spread for a comparable noncallable bond.

22. Acme Industries bonds have a yield-to-maturity (YTM) of 7.45%. If a similar maturity U.S. Treasury bond exhibits a YTM of 6.90%:
    A. the yield ratio is 1.08 and the relative yield spread is 0.08.
    B. the absolute yield spread is 55 basis points and the relative yield spread is 1.08.
    C. the absolute yield spread is 55 basis points and the relative yield spread is 0.93.

SOLUTIONS FOR READING 55

1. Market participants look at the key indicators watched by the Fed in order to try to predict how the Fed will react to the movement in those indicators.

2. Ms. Peters should inform her client that under one theory of the term structure of interest rates, the pure expectations theory, a downward sloping yield curve does suggest that short-term interest rates in the future will decline. According to the liquidity preference theory a downward sloping yield curve suggests that rates are expected to decline. But it should be noted that the liquidity preference theory does not view a positive yield curve as one where rates may be expected to rise. This is because the yield premium for liquidity can be large enough so that even if expected future rates are expected to decline, the yield curve would be upward sloping. A downward sloping yield curve according to the market segmentation theory cannot be interpreted in terms of the market's expectations regarding future rates.

3. The pure expectations theory asserts that the only factor affecting the shape of the yield curve is expectations about future interest rates. The liquidity preference theory asserts that there are two factors that affect the shape of the yield curve: expectations about future interest rate and a yield premium to compensate for interest rate risk.

4. According to the pure expectations theory, a humped yield curve means that short-term interest rates are expected to rise for a time and then begin to fall.

5. **A.** The data clearly indicate that yield spreads are at their 12-month highs.

    B. A callable agency issue offers a higher yield spread than a noncallable agency issue because of the call risk faced by investors in the former.

    C. For a given maturity, the longer the deferred call period the lower the call risk. Hence, the yield spread for a callable issue is less the longer the deferred call period.

    D. Because yield spreads are not adjusted for call risk, they are referred to as nominal spreads.

    E. The compensation for credit risk, liquidity risk, and call risk are lumped together in the nominal spreads (i.e., yield spreads shown in the second panel). The OAS is an estimate of the yield spread after adjusting for the call (or option) risk. So, the OAS is less than the nominal yield spread.

6. While it is true that a Ginnie Mae mortgage-backed security has no credit risk and that part of the yield spread between a Ginnie Mae mortgage-backed security and a U.S. Treasury security is due to differences in liquidity, the major reason for the yield spread is the prepayment risk of a mortgage-backed security. This risk is ignored in the statement made by the representative of the investment management firm.

7. **A.** Part of the yield spread between a non-Treasury bond with an embedded option and a Treasury security (which is an option-free security) is due to the value of the embedded option. For example, for a callable non-Treasury bond, the yield spread relative to a Treasury security represents compensation for the following: 1) credit risk, 2) liquidity risk, and 3) call risk. When a spread measure includes all three forms of compensation, it is called a "nominal spread." However, investors want to know the yield spread after adjusting for the value of the embedded options (the call option in our illustration).

B. The option-adjusted spread seeks to measure the part of the yield spread between a non-Treasury security and a Treasury security once the portion attributed to the call risk is removed. So, the option-adjusted spread is less than the nominal spread. The option-adjusted spread allows an investor to better compare the yield spread on bonds with and without embedded options.

8. **A.** Absolute yield spread = 7.25% − 6.02% = 1.23% = 123 Basis points.

   B. Relative yield spread $= \dfrac{7.25\% - 6.02\%}{6.02\%} = 0.204 = 20.4\%.$

   C. Yield ratio $= \dfrac{7.25\%}{6.02\%} = 1.204.$

9. **A.** The percent yield spread is the relative yield spread.

   B. Analysts recognize that historical comparisons of the absolute yield spread for assessing how yield spreads are changing do not take into account the level of yields. For example, a 40 basis point absolute yield spread in a 5% interest rate environment is quite different from a 40 basis point absolute yield spread in a 10% yield environment.

10. Tax-exempt municipal securities offer a lower yield than Treasury securities because of the value of the tax-exempt feature. This feature is more attractive to high tax bracket investors than to low tax bracket investors. A reduction in marginal tax rates makes the tax-exempt feature less attractive to investors. This would require that tax-exempt municipals offer higher yields compared to yields prior to the reduction.

    Anticipating a reduction in tax rates would affect municipal yields. The extent of this effect would depend on the market's assessment of the probability the proposal would be enacted.

11. **A.** Because municipals are tax-exempt, their return or yield spread depends on each investor's marginal tax rate. Treasuries are subject to federal income tax so comparing the two yields to calculate a yield spread would be different for various investors.

    B. The AAA rated municipal general obligation yield curve is used because it offers a similar tax-exempt status to compare its yield against when considering other tax-exempt municipal bonds.

12. **A.** The after-tax yield is

    $$0.05 \times (1 - 0.40) = 0.03 = 3\%$$

    B. The taxable-equivalent yield is

    $$\frac{0.031}{(1 - 0.39)} = 0.0508 = 5.08\%$$

13. A funded investor who borrows short term is interested in the spread above the borrowing cost. Since LIBOR is the global cost of borrowing, a LIBOR yield curve is a more appropriate measure for assessing the potential return than the Treasury yield curve.

14. C is correct. Yield spreads tend to be wider if issues are illiquid because the investor demands a higher spread to compensate for the illiquidity. Bonds with call options tend to have a wider yield spread because the option favors the issuer and the investor demands a higher spread in compensation.

15. B is correct. For practical purposes, the default risk on Treasury securities is considered zero; however, other risks associated in investing in Treasury securities include interest rate risk, yield risk, reinvestment risk, inflation risk, and event risk.

16. B is correct. A normal yield curve (or upward sloping yield curve) is defined as one where the longer the maturity, the higher the yield.

17. C is correct.

$$\text{The yield spread} = \text{Yield on bond X} - \text{Yield on bond Y (or treasury)}$$
$$= (0.0625 - 0.048) = 0.0145 \text{ or } 1.45\%$$

$$\text{The relative yield spread} = (\text{Yield on bond X} - \text{Yield on bond Y})/$$
$$\text{Yield on bond Y}$$
$$= (0.0625 - 0.048)/(0.048) = 0.3021 \text{ or } 30.21\%$$

$$\text{The yield ratio} = \text{Yield on Bond X}/\text{Yield on bond Y}$$
$$= 6.25\%/4.80\% = 1.30$$

18. B is correct.

$$\text{The taxable equivalent yield} = \text{Tax-exempt}/(1 - \text{Marginal tax rate})$$
$$= (0.0375)/(1 - 0.28) = 0.0521 \text{ or } 5.21\%$$

19. C is correct. All else held constant, lower tax rates reduce the relative attractiveness of tax-exempt municipal bonds over taxable corporate bonds.

20. A is correct. An inverted yield curve can occur under all three of the theories.

21. C is correct. To compensate the investor for the risk of a call, the nominal yield spread will generally be greater for a callable bond than for an equivalent non-callable bond.

22. A is correct. The absolute yield spread is 7.45 − 6.90 = 55 bps. The relative yield spread is (7.45 − 6.90) / 6.90 = 0.08. The yield ratio is 7.45 / 6.90 = 1.08.

16

Fixed Income

Analysis and Valuation

This study session explains tools for valuation and analysis of fixed-income securities and markets. The first reading is an introduction to the valuation of bonds. The other two readings provide additional coverage of valuation-related topics.

READING ASSIGNMENTS

Reading 56 *Introduction to the Valuation of Debt Securities*

Fixed Income Analysis for the Chartered Financial Analyst®
Program, Second Edition, by Frank J. Fabozzi, CFA

Reading 57 *Yield Measures, Spot Rates, and Forward Rates*

Fixed Income Analysis for the Chartered Financial Analyst®
Program, Second Edition, by Frank J. Fabozzi, CFA

Reading 58 *Introduction to the Measurement of Interest Rate Risk*

Fixed Income Analysis for the Chartered Financial Analyst®
Program, Second Edition, by Frank J. Fabozzi, CFA

Reading 59 *Fundamentals of Credit Analysis*

By Christopher L. Gootkind, CFA

Introduction to the Valuation of Debt Securities

by Frank J. Fabozzi, CFA

LEARNING OUTCOMES

Mastery	The candidate should be able to:
☐	**a** explain steps in the bond valuation process;
☐	**b** describe types of bonds for which estimating the expected cash flows is difficult;
☐	**c** calculate the value of a bond (coupon and zero-coupon);
☐	**d** explain how the price of a bond changes if the discount rate changes and as the bond approaches its maturity date;
☐	**e** calculate the change in value of a bond given a change in its discount rate;
☐	**f** explain and demonstrate the use of the arbitrage-free valuation approach and describe how a dealer can generate an arbitrage profit if a bond is mispriced.

INTRODUCTION

1

Valuation is the process of determining the fair value of a financial asset. The process is also referred to as "valuing" or "pricing" a financial asset. In this reading, we will explain the general principles of fixed income security valuation. In this reading, we will limit our discussion to the valuation of option-free bonds.

GENERAL PRINCIPLES OF VALUATION

2

The fundamental principle of financial asset valuation is that its value is equal to the present value of its expected cash flows. This principle applies regardless of the financial asset. Thus, the valuation of a financial asset involves the following three steps:

Step 1: Estimate the expected cash flows.

Step 2: Determine the appropriate interest rate or interest rates that should be used to discount the cash flows.

Step 3:   Calculate the present value of the expected cash flows found in step 1 using the interest rate or interest rates determined in step 2.

2.1 Estimating Cash Flows

Cash flow is simply the cash that is expected to be received in the future from an investment. In the case of a fixed income security, it does not make any difference whether the cash flow is interest income or payment of principal. The cash flows of a security are the collection of each period's cash flow. Holding aside the risk of default, the cash flows for few fixed income securities are simple to project. Noncallable U.S. Treasury securities have known cash flows. For Treasury coupon securities, the cash flows are the coupon interest payments every six months up to and including the maturity date and the principal payment at the maturity date.

At times, investors will find it difficult to estimate the cash flows when they purchase a fixed income security. For example, if:

1. the issuer or the investor has the option to change the contractual due date for the payment of the principal, or

2. the coupon payment is reset periodically by a formula based on some value or values of reference rates, prices, or exchange rates, or

3. the investor has the choice to convert or exchange the security into common stock.

Callable bonds, putable bonds, mortgage-backed securities, and asset-backed securities are examples of 1). Floating-rate securities are an example of 2). Convertible bonds and exchangeable bonds are examples of 3).

For securities that fall into the first category, future interest rate movements are the key factor to determine if the option will be exercised. Specifically, if interest rates fall far enough, the issuer can sell a new issue of bonds at the lower interest rate and use the proceeds to pay off (call) the older bonds that have the higher coupon rate. (This assumes that the interest savings are larger than the costs involved in refunding.) Similarly, for a loan, if rates fall enough that the interest savings outweigh the refinancing costs, the borrower has an incentive to refinance. For a putable bond, the investor will put the issue if interest rates rise enough to drive the market price below the put price (i.e., the price at which it must be repurchased by the issuer).

What this means is that to properly estimate the cash flows of a fixed income security, it is necessary to incorporate into the analysis how, in the future, changes in interest rates and other factors affecting the embedded option may affect cash flows.

2.2 Determining the Appropriate Rate or Rates

Once the cash flows for a fixed income security are estimated, the next step is to determine the appropriate interest rate to be used to discount the cash flows. As we did in the previous reading, we will use the terms *interest rate* and *yield* interchangeably. The minimum interest rate that an investor should require is the yield available in the marketplace on a default-free cash flow. In the United States, this is the yield on a U.S. Treasury security. This is *one* of the reasons that the Treasury market is closely watched. What is the *minimum* interest rate U.S. investors demand? At this point, we can assume it is the yield on the on-the-run Treasury security with the same maturity as the security being valued.[1] We qualify this shortly.

---

[1] As explained in the overview of bond sectors and instruments reading, the on-the-run Treasury issues are the most recently auctioned Treasury issues.

For a security that is not issued by the U.S. government, investors will require a yield premium over the yield available on an on-the-run Treasury issue. This yield premium reflects the additional risks that the investor accepts.

For each cash flow estimated, the same interest rate can be used to calculate the present value. However, since each cash flow is unique, it is more appropriate to value each cash flow using an interest rate specific to that cash flow's maturity. In the traditional approach to valuation a single interest rate is used. In Section 4, we will see that the proper approach to valuation uses multiple interest rates, each specific to a particular cash flow. In that section, we will also demonstrate why this must be the case.

2.3 Discounting the Expected Cash Flows

Given expected (estimated) cash flows and the appropriate interest rate or interest rates to be used to discount the cash flows, the final step in the valuation process is to value the cash flows.

What is the value of a single cash flow to be received in the future? It is the amount of money that must be invested today to generate that future value. The resulting value is called the **present value** of a cash flow. (It is also called the discounted value.) The present value of a cash flow will depend on 1) when a cash flow will be received (i.e., the timing of a cash flow) and 2) the interest rate used to calculate the present value. The interest rate used is called the **discount rate**.

First, we calculate the present value for each expected cash flow. Then, to determine the value of the security, we calculate the sum of the present values (i.e., for all of the security's expected cash flows).

If a discount rate i can be earned on any sum invested today, the present value of the expected cash flow to be received t years from now is:

$$\text{Present value}_t = \frac{\text{Expected cash flow in period } t}{\left(1 + i\right)^t} \tag{1}$$

The value of a financial asset is then the sum of the present value of all the expected cash flows. That is, assuming that there are N expected cash flows:

$$\text{Value} = \text{Present value}_1 + \text{Present value}_2 + \ldots + \text{Present value}_N \tag{2}$$

To illustrate the present value formula, consider a simple bond that matures in four years, has a coupon rate of 10%, and has a maturity value of $100. For simplicity, let's assume the bond pays interest annually and a discount rate of 8% should be used to calculate the present value of each cash flow. The cash flow for this bond is:

Year	Cash Flow
1	$10
2	10
3	10
4	110

The present value of each cash flow is:

$$Year\ 1:\ present\ value_1 = \frac{\$10}{(1.08)^1} = \$9.2593$$

$$Year\ 2:\ present\ value_2 = \frac{\$10}{(1.08)^2} = \$8.5734$$

$$Year\ 3:\ present\ value_3 = \frac{\$10}{(1.08)^3} = \$7.9383$$

$$Year\ 4:\ present\ value_4 = \frac{\$110}{(1.08)^4} = \$80.8533$$

The value of this security is then the sum of the present values of the four cash flows. That is, the present value is $106.6243 ($9.2593 + $8.5734 + $7.9383 + $80.8533).

Practice Question 1

A. What is the present value of a 5-year security with a coupon rate of 7% that pays annually assuming a discount rate of 5% and a par value of $100?

B. A 5-year amortizing security with a par value of $10,000 and a coupon rate of 5% has an expected cash flow of $2,309.75 per year, assuming there are no principal prepayments. The annual cash flow includes interest and principal payment. What is the present value of this amortizing security assuming a discount rate of 6%?

2.3.1　*Present Value Properties*

An important property about the present value can be seen from the above illustration. For the first three years, the cash flow is the same ($10) and the discount rate is the same (8%). The present value decreases as we go further into the future. *This is an important property of the present value: for a given discount rate, the further into the future a cash flow is received, the lower its present value.* This can be seen in the present value formula. As t increases, present value$_t$ decreases.

Suppose that instead of a discount rate of 8%, a 12% discount rate is used for each cash flow. Then, the present value of each cash flow is:

$$Year\ 1:\ present\ value_1 = \frac{\$10}{(1.12)^1} = \$8.9286$$

$$Year\ 2:\ present\ value_2 = \frac{\$10}{(1.12)^2} = \$7.9719$$

$$Year\ 3:\ present\ value_3 = \frac{\$10}{(1.12)^3} = \$7.1178$$

$$Year\ 4:\ present\ value_4 = \frac{\$110}{(1.12)^4} = \$69.9070$$

Exhibit 1	Price Discount Rate Relationship for an Option-Free Bond

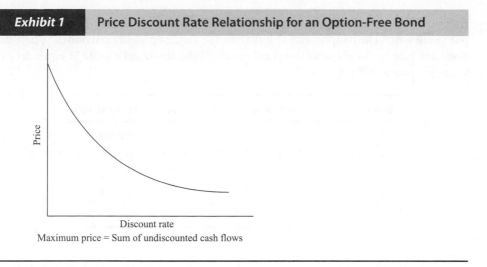

Maximum price = Sum of undiscounted cash flows

The value of this security is then $93.9253 ($8.9286 + $7.9719 + $7.1178 + $69.9070). The security's value is lower if a 12% discount rate is used compared to an 8% discount rate ($93.9253 versus $106.6243). This is another general property of present value: *the higher the discount rate, the lower the present value.* Since the value of a security is the present value of the expected cash flows, this property carries over to the value of a security: *the higher the discount rate, the lower a security's value.* The reverse is also true: *the lower the discount rate, the higher a security's value.*

Exhibit 1 shows, for an option-free bond, this inverse relationship between a security's value and the discount rate. The shape of the curve in Exhibit 1 is referred to as convex. By convex, it is meant the curve is bowed in from the origin. As we will see in the reading on the measurement of interest rate risk, this convexity or bowed shape has implications for the price volatility of a bond when interest rates change. What is important to understand is that the relationship is not linear.

Practice Question 2

What is the present value of the cash flow of the 5-year 7% coupon security in Practice Question 1 assuming a discount rate of 4% rather than 5%?

2.3.2 *Relationship between Coupon Rate, Discount Rate, and Price Relative to Par Value*

In the reading on risks associated with investing in bonds, we described the relationship between a bond's coupon rate, required market yield, and price relative to its par value (i.e., premium, discount, or equal to par). The required yield is equivalent to the discount rate discussed above. We stated the following relationship:

Coupon rate = Yield required by market, *therefore* Price = Par value

Coupon rate < Yield required by market, *therefore* Price < Par value (discount)

Coupon rate > Yield required by market, *therefore* Price > Par value (premium)

Now that we know how to value a bond, we can demonstrate the relationship. The coupon rate on our hypothetical bond is 10%. When an 8% discount rate is used, the bond's value is $106.6243. That is, the price is greater than par value (premium). This is because the coupon rate (10%) is greater than the required yield (the 8% discount rate). We also showed that when the discount rate is 12% (i.e., greater than the coupon rate of 10%), the price of the bond is $93.9253. That is, the bond's value is less than par value when the coupon rate is less than the required yield (discount). When the discount rate is the same as the coupon rate, 10%, the bond's value is equal to par value as shown below:

Year	Cash Flow	Present Value at 10%
1	$10	$9.0909
2	10	8.2645
3	10	7.5131
4	110	75.1315
	Total	$100.0000

Practice Question 3

A. What is the value of a 5-year 7% coupon bond per $100 of par value when the discount rate is i) 6%, ii) 7%, and iii) 8%?

B. Show that the results obtained in part A are consistent with the relationship between the coupon rate, discount rate, and price relative to par value given in the text.

2.3.3 *Change in a Bond's Value as It Moves toward Maturity*

As a bond moves closer to its maturity date, its value changes. More specifically, assuming that the discount rate does not change, a bond's value:

1. decreases over time if the bond is selling at a premium

2. increases over time if the bond is selling at a discount

3. is unchanged if the bond is selling at par value

At the maturity date, the bond's value is equal to its par value. So, over time as the bond moves toward its maturity date, its price will move to its par value—a characteristic sometimes referred to as a "pull to par value."

To illustrate what happens to a bond selling at a premium, consider once again the 4-year 10% coupon bond. When the discount rate is 8%, the bond's price is 106.6243. Suppose that one year later, the discount rate is still 8%. There are only three cash flows remaining since the bond is now a 3-year security. The cash flow and the present value of the cash flows are given below:

Year	Cash Flow	Present Value at 8%
1	$10	$9.2593
2	10	8.5734
3	110	87.3215
	Total	$105.1542

The price has declined from $106.6243 to $105.1542.

Now suppose that the bond's price is initially below par value. For example, as stated earlier, if the discount rate is 12%, the 4-year 10% coupon bond's value is $93.9253. Assuming the discount rate remains at 12%, one year later the cash flow and the present value of the cash flow would be as shown below:

Year	Cash Flow	Present Value at 12%
1	$10	$8.9286
2	10	7.9719
3	110	78.2958
	Total	$95.1963

The bond's price increases from $93.9253 to $95.1963.

To understand how the price of a bond changes as it moves towards maturity, consider the following three 20-year bonds for which the yield required by the market is 8%: a premium bond (10% coupon), a discount bond (6% coupon), and a par bond (8% coupon). To simplify the example, it is assumed that each bond pays interest annually. Exhibit 2 shows the price of each bond as it moves toward maturity, assuming that the 8% yield required by the market does not change. The premium bond with an initial price of 119.6363 decreases in price until it reaches par value at the maturity date. The discount bond with an initial price of 80.3637 increases in price until it reaches par value at the maturity date.

In practice, over time the discount rate will change. So, the bond's value will change due to both the change in the discount rate and the change in the cash flow as the bond moves toward maturity. For example, again suppose that the discount rate for the 4-year 10% coupon is 8%, so that the bond is selling for $106.6243. One year later, suppose that the discount rate appropriate for a 3-year 10% coupon bond increases from 8% to 9%. Then the cash flow and present value of the cash flows are shown below:

Year	Cash Flow	Present Value at 9%
1	$10	$9.1743
2	10	8.4168
3	110	84.9402
	Total	$102.5313

The bond's price will decline from $106.6243 to $102.5313. As shown earlier, if the discount rate did not increase, the price would have declined to only $105.1542. The price decline of $4.0930 ($106.6243 – $102.5313) can be decomposed as follows:

Price change attributable to moving to maturity (no change in discount rate)	$1.4701	(106.6243 – 105.1542)
Price change attributable to an increase in the discount rate from 8% to 9%	$2.6229	(105.1542 – 102.5313)
Total price change	$4.0930	

Exhibit 2	Movement of a Premium, Discount, and Par Bond as a Bond Moves toward Maturity

Information about the three bonds:
All bonds mature in 20 years and have a yield required by the market of 8%
Coupon payments are annual
Premium bond = 10% coupon selling for 119.6363
Discount bond = 6% coupon selling for 80.3637
Par bond = 8% coupon selling at par value

(continued)

Exhibit 2	Continued

Assumption: The yield required by the market is unchanged over the life of the bond at 8%.

Time to Maturity in Years	Premium Bond	Discount Bond	Par Bond
20	119.6363	80.3637	100.0000
19	119.2072	80.7928	100.0000
18	118.7438	81.2562	100.0000
17	118.2433	81.7567	100.0000
16	117.7027	82.2973	100.0000
15	117.1190	82.8810	100.0000
14	116.4885	83.5115	100.0000
13	115.8076	84.1924	100.0000
12	115.0722	84.9278	100.0000
11	114.2779	85.7221	100.0000
10	113.4202	86.5798	100.0000
9	112.4938	87.5062	100.0000
8	111.4933	88.5067	100.0000
7	110.4127	89.5873	100.0000
6	109.2458	90.7542	100.0000
5	107.9854	92.0146	100.0000
4	106.6243	93.3757	100.0000
3	105.1542	94.8458	100.0000
2	103.5665	96.4335	100.0000
1	101.8519	98.1481	100.0000
0	100.0000	100.0000	100.0000

The Effect of Time on a Bond's Price

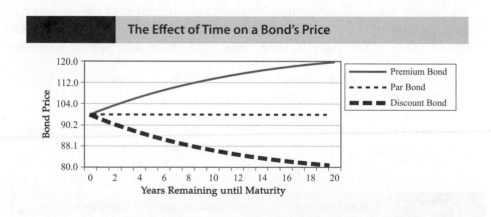

2.4 Valuation Using Multiple Discount Rates

Thus far, we have used one discount rate to compute the present value of each cash flow. As we will see shortly, the proper way to value the cash flows of a bond is to use a different discount rate that is unique to the time period in which a cash flow will be received. So, let's look at how we would value a security using a different discount rate for each cash flow.

Suppose that the appropriate discount rates are as follows:

Year 1	6.8%
Year 2	7.2%
Year 3	7.6%
Year 4	8.0%

Then, for the 4-year 10% coupon bond, the present value of each cash flow is:

Year 1: present value$_1$ $= \dfrac{\$10}{(1.068)^1} = \$9.3633$

Year 2: present value$_2$ $= \dfrac{\$10}{(1.072)^2} = \$8.7018$

Year 3: present value$_3$ $= \dfrac{\$10}{(1.076)^3} = \$8.0272$

Year 4: present value$_4$ $= \dfrac{\$110}{(1.080)^4} = \$80.8533$

The present value of this security, assuming the above set of discount rates, is $106.9456.

Practice Question 4

Compute the value per $100 of par value of a 5-year 7% coupon bond, assuming the payments are annual and the discount rate for each year is as follows:

Year	Discount Rate (%)
1	3.5
2	3.9
3	4.2
4	4.5
5	5.0

2.5 Valuing Semiannual Cash Flows

In our illustrations, we assumed coupon payments are paid once per year. For most bonds, the coupon payments are semiannual. This does not introduce any complexities into the calculation. The procedure is to simply adjust the coupon payments by dividing the annual coupon payment by 2 and adjust the discount rate by dividing the annual discount rate by 2. The time period t in the present value formula is treated in terms of 6-month periods rather than years.

For example, consider once again the 4-year 10% coupon bond with a maturity value of $100. The cash flow for the first 3.5 years is equal to $5 ($10/2). The last cash flow is equal to the final coupon payment ($5) plus the maturity value ($100). So the last cash flow is $105.

Now the tricky part. If an annual discount rate of 8% is used, how do we obtain the semiannual discount rate? We will simply use one-half the annual rate, 4% (or 8%/2). The reader should have a problem with this: a 4% semiannual rate is not an 8% effective annual rate. That is correct. However, as we will see in the next reading, the *convention* in the bond market is to quote annual interest rates that are just double semiannual rates. This will be explained more fully in the next reading. Don't let this throw you off here. For now, just accept the fact that one-half an annual discount rate is used to obtain a semiannual discount rate in the balance of the reading.

Given the cash flows and the semiannual discount rate of 4%, the present value of each cash flow is shown below:

$$\textit{Period 1: } \text{present value}_1 = \frac{\$5}{(1.04)^1} = \$4.8077$$

$$\textit{Period 2: } \text{present value}_2 = \frac{\$5}{(1.04)^2} = \$4.6228$$

$$\textit{Period 3: } \text{present value}_3 = \frac{\$5}{(1.04)^3} = \$4.4450$$

$$\textit{Peried 4: } \text{present value}_4 = \frac{\$5}{(1.04)^4} = \$4.2740$$

$$\textit{Peried 5: } \text{present value}_5 = \frac{\$5}{(1.04)^5} = \$4.1096$$

$$\textit{Peried 6: } \text{present value}_6 = \frac{\$5}{(1.04)^6} = \$3.9516$$

$$\textit{Peried 7: } \text{present value}_7 = \frac{\$5}{(1.04)^7} = \$3.7996$$

$$\textit{Peried 8: } \text{present value}_8 = \frac{\$105}{(1.04)^8} = \$76.7225$$

The security's value is equal to the sum of the present value of the eight cash flows, \$106.7327. Notice that this price is greater than the price when coupon payments are annual (\$106.6243). This is because one-half the annual coupon payment is received six months sooner than when payments are annual. This produces a higher present value for the semiannual coupon payments relative to the annual coupon payments.

The value of a non-amortizing bond can be divided into two components: 1) the present value of the coupon payments and 2) the present value of the maturity value. For a fixed-rate coupon bond, the coupon payments represent an annuity. A short-cut formula can be used to compute the value of a bond when using a single discount rate: compute the present value of the annuity and then add the present value of the maturity value.[2]

The present value of an annuity is equal to:

$$\text{Annuity payment} \times \left[\frac{1 - \dfrac{1}{(1+i)^{\text{no. of periods}}}}{i} \right]$$

For a bond with annual interest payments, i is the annual discount rate and the "no. of periods" is equal to the number of years.

---

[2] Note that in our earlier illustration, we computed the present value of the semiannual coupon payments before the maturity date and then added the present value of the last cash flow (last semiannual coupon payment plus the maturity value). In the presentation of how to use the short-cut formula, we are computing the present value of all the semiannual coupon payments and then adding the present value of the maturity value. Both approaches will give the same answer for the value of a bond.

Applying this formula to a semiannual-pay bond, the annuity payment is one-half the annual coupon payment and the number of periods is double the number of years to maturity. So, the present value of the coupon payments can be expressed as:

$$\text{Semiannual coupon payment} \times \left[\frac{1 - \dfrac{1}{(1+i)^{\text{no. of periods} \times 2}}}{i} \right]$$

where i is the semiannual discount rate (annual rate/2). Notice that in the formula, we use the number of years multiplied by 2 since a period in our illustration is six months. The present value of the maturity value is equal to

$$\text{Present value of maturity value} = \frac{\$100}{(1+i)^{\text{no. of years} \times 2}}$$

To illustrate this computation, consider once again the 4-year 10% coupon bond with an annual discount rate of 8% and a semiannual discount rate of one-half this rate (4%) for the reason cited earlier. Then:

Semiannual coupon payment = $5

Semiannual discount rate (i) = 4%

Number of years = 4

then the present value of the coupon payments is

$$\$5 \times \left[\frac{1 - \dfrac{1}{(1.04)^{4 \times 2}}}{0.04} \right] = \$33.6637$$

To determine the price, the present value of the maturity value must be added to the present value of the coupon payments. The present value of the maturity value is

$$\text{Present value of maturity value} = \frac{\$100}{(1.04)^{4 \times 2}} = \$73.0690$$

The price is then $106.7327 ($33.6637 + $73.0690). This agrees with our previous calculation for the price of this bond.

Practice Question 5

What is the value of a 5-year 7% coupon bond that pays interest semiannually assuming that the annual discount rate is 5%?

2.6 Valuing a Zero-Coupon Bond

For a zero-coupon bond, there is only one cash flow—the maturity value. The value of a zero-coupon bond that matures N years from now is

$$\frac{\text{Maturity value}}{(1+i)^{\text{no. of years} \times 2}}$$

where i is the semiannual discount rate.

It may seem surprising that the number of periods is double the number of years to maturity. In computing the value of a zero-coupon bond, the number of 6-month periods (i.e., "no. of years × 2") is used in the denominator of the formula. The rationale is that the pricing of a zero-coupon bond should be consistent with the pricing of a semiannual coupon bond. Therefore, the use of 6-month periods is required in order to have uniformity between the present value calculations.

To illustrate the application of the formula, the value of a 5-year zero-coupon bond with a maturity value of $100 discounted at an 8% interest rate is $67.5564, as shown below:

$$i = 0.04 (= 0.08/2)$$

$$N = 5$$

$$\frac{\$100}{(1.04)^{5 \times 2}} = \$67.5564$$

Practice Question 6

A. Complete the following table for a 10-year zero-coupon bond with a maturity value of $1,000 for each of the following *annual* discount rates.

Annual Rate (%)	Semiannual Rate (%)	Price
1		
2		
3		
4		
5		
6		
7		
8		
9		
10		
11		
12		
13		
14		

B. Given the prices for the bond in part A, draw a graph of the price/yield relationship. On the horizontal axis (*x*-axis) should be the annual rate and on the vertical axis (*y*-axis) should be the price.

2.7 Valuing a Bond between Coupon Payments

For coupon-paying bonds, a complication arises when we try to price a bond between coupon payments. The amount that the buyer pays the seller in such cases is the present value of the cash flow. But one of the cash flows, the very next cash flow, encompasses two components as shown below:

1. interest earned by the seller

2. interest earned by the buyer

$$\text{interest earned by seller} \qquad\qquad \text{interest earned by buyer}$$

| last coupon | settlement | next coupon |
| payment date | date | payment date |

The interest earned by the seller is the interest that has accrued[3] between the last coupon payment date and the settlement date.[4] This interest is called **accrued interest**. At the time of purchase, the buyer must compensate the seller for the accrued interest. The buyer recovers the accrued interest when the next coupon payment is received.

When the price of a bond is computed using the present value calculations described earlier, it is computed with accrued interest embodied in the price. This price is referred to as the **full price**. (Some market participants refer to it as the dirty price.) It is the full price that the buyer pays the seller. From the full price, the accrued interest must be deducted to determine the price of the bond, sometimes referred to as the clean price.

Below, we show how the present value formula is modified to compute the full price when a bond is purchased between coupon periods.

2.7.1 Computing the Full Price

To compute the full price, it is first necessary to determine the fractional periods between the settlement date and the next coupon payment date. This is determined as follows:

$$w \text{ periods} = \frac{\text{Days between settlement date and next coupon payment date}}{\text{Days in coupon period}}$$

Then the present value of the expected cash flow to be received t periods from now using a discount rate i assuming the first coupon payment is w periods from now is:

$$\text{Present value}_t = \frac{\text{Expected cash flow}}{(1 + i)^{t-1+w}}$$

This procedure for calculating the present value when a security is purchased between coupon payments is called the "Street method."

To illustrate the calculation, suppose that there are five semiannual coupon payments remaining for a 10% coupon bond. Also assume the following:

1. 78 days between the settlement date and the next coupon payment date

2. 182 days in the coupon period

Then w is 0.4286 periods (= 78/182). The present value of each cash flow assuming that each is discounted at 8% annual discount rate is

$$\textit{Period 1}: \quad \text{Present value}_1 = \frac{\$5}{(1.04)^{0.4286}} = \$4.9167$$

$$\textit{Period 2}: \quad \text{Present value}_2 = \frac{\$5}{(1.04)^{1.4286}} = \$4.7276$$

$$\textit{Period 3}: \quad \text{Present value}_3 = \frac{\$5}{(1.04)^{2.4286}} = \$4.5457$$

$$\textit{Period 4}: \quad \text{Present value}_4 = \frac{\$5}{(1.04)^{3.4286}} = \$4.3709$$

$$\textit{Period 5}: \quad \text{Present value}_5 = \frac{\$105}{(1.04)^{4.4286}} = \$88.2583$$

---

3 "Accrued" means that the interest is earned but not distributed to the bondholder.
4 The settlement date is the date a transaction is completed.

The full price is the sum of the present value of the cash flows, which is $106.8192. Remember that the full price includes the accrued interest that the buyer is paying the seller.

Practice Question 7

Suppose that a bond is purchased between coupon periods. The days between the settlement date and the next coupon period is 58. There are 183 days in the coupon period. Suppose that the bond purchased has a coupon rate of 7% and there are 10 semiannual coupon payments remaining. What is the full price for this bond if a 5% annual discount rate is used?

2.7.2 *Computing the Accrued Interest and the Clean Price*

To find the price without accrued interest, called the clean price or simply price, the accrued interest must be computed. To determine the accrued interest, it is first necessary to determine the number of days in the accrued interest period. The number of days in the accrued interest period is determined as follows:

> Days in accrued interest period = Days in coupon period – Days between settlement and next coupon payment

The percentage of the next semiannual coupon payment that the seller has earned as accrued interest is found as follows:

> $$\frac{\text{Day in accrued interest period}}{\text{Days in coupon period}}$$

So, for example, returning to our illustration where the full price was computed, since there are 182 days in the coupon period and there are 78 days from the settlement date to the next coupon payment, the days in the accrued interest period is 182 minus 78, or 104 days. Therefore, the percentage of the coupon payment that is accrued interest is:

$$\frac{104}{182} = 0.5714 = 57.14\%$$

This is the same percentage found by simply subtracting w from 1. In our illustration, w was 0.4286. Then $1 - 0.4286 = 0.5714$.

Given the value of w, the amount of accrued interest (AI) is equal to:

> AI = Semiannual coupon payment $\times (1 - w)$

So, for the 10% coupon bond whose full price we computed, since the semiannual coupon payment per $100 of par value is $5 and w is 0.4286, the accrued interest is:

> $\$5 \times (1 - 0.4286) = \$2.8570$

The clean price is then:

> Full price – Accrued interest

In our illustration, the clean price is[5]

> $\$106.8192 - \$2.8570 = \$103.9622$

---

[5] Notice that in computing the full price the present value of the next coupon payment is computed. However, the buyer pays the seller the accrued interest now despite the fact that it will be recovered at the next coupon payment date.

2.7.3 *Day Count Conventions*

The practice for calculating the number of days between two dates depends on *day count conventions* used in the bond market. The convention differs by the type of security. Day count conventions are also used to calculate the number of days in the numerator and denominator of the ratio *w*.

The accrued interest (AI) assuming semiannual payments is calculated as follows:

$$AI = \frac{\text{Annual coupon}}{2} \times \frac{\text{Days in AI period}}{\text{Days in coupon period}}$$

In calculating the number of days between two dates, the actual number of days is not always the same as the number of days that should be used in the accrued interest formula. The number of days used depends on the day count convention for the particular security. Specifically, day count conventions differ for Treasury securities and government agency securities, municipal bonds, and corporate bonds.

For coupon-bearing Treasury securities, the day count convention used is to determine the actual number of days between two dates. This is referred to as the "actual/actual" day count convention. For example, consider a coupon-bearing Treasury security whose previous coupon payment was March 1. The next coupon payment would be on September 1. Suppose this Treasury security is purchased with a settlement date of July 17. The actual number of days between July 17 (the settlement date) and September 1 (the date of the next coupon payment) is 46 days, as shown below:

July 17 to July 31	14 days
August	31 days
September 1	1 day
	46 days

Note that the settlement date (July 17) is not counted. The number of days in the coupon period is the actual number of days between March 1 and September 1, which is 184 days. The number of days between the last coupon payment (March 1) through July 17 is therefore 138 days (184 days – 46 days).

For coupon-bearing agency, municipal, and corporate bonds, a different day count convention is used. It is assumed that every month has 30 days, that any 6-month period has 180 days, and that there are 360 days in a year. This day count convention is referred to as "30/360." For example, consider once again the Treasury security purchased with a settlement date of July 17, the previous coupon payment on March 1, and the next coupon payment on September 1. If the security is an agency, municipal, or corporate bond, the number of days until the next coupon payment is 44 days as shown below:

July 17 to July 31	13 days
August	30 days
September 1	1 day
	44 days

Note that the settlement date, July 17, is not counted. Since July is treated as having 30 days, there are 13 days (30 days minus the first 17 days in July). The number of days from March 1 to July 17 is 136, which is the number of days in the accrued interest period.

3   TRADITIONAL APPROACH TO VALUATION

The traditional approach to valuation has been to discount every cash flow of a fixed income security by the same interest rate (or discount rate). For example, consider the three hypothetical 10-year Treasury securities shown in Exhibit 3: a 12% coupon bond, an 8% coupon bond, and a zero-coupon bond. The cash flows for each bond are shown in the exhibit. Since the cash flows of all three bonds are viewed as default free, the traditional practice is to use the same discount rate to calculate the present value of all three bonds and use the same discount rate for the cash flow for each period. The discount rate used is the yield for the on-the-run issue obtained from the Treasury yield curve. For example, suppose that the yield for the 10-year on-the-run Treasury issue is 10%. Then, the practice is to discount each cash flow for each bond using a 10% discount rate.

Exhibit 3	Cash Flows for Three 10-Year Hypothetical Treasury Securities per $100 of Par Value		
Each Period Is Six Months			
	Coupon Rate		
Period	**12%**	**8%**	**0%**
1–19	$6	$4	$0
20	106	104	100

For a non-Treasury security, a yield premium or yield spread is added to the on-the-run Treasury yield. The yield spread is the same regardless of when a cash flow is to be received in the traditional approach. For a 10-year non-Treasury security, suppose that 90 basis points is the appropriate yield spread. Then all cash flows would be discounted at the yield for the on-the-run 10-year Treasury issue of 10% plus 90 basis points.

4   THE ARBITRAGE-FREE VALUATION APPROACH

The fundamental flaw of the traditional approach is that it views each security as the same package of cash flows. For example, consider a 10-year U.S. Treasury issue with an 8% coupon rate. The cash flows per $100 of par value would be 19 payments of $4 every six months and $104 twenty 6-month periods from now. The traditional practice would discount each cash flow using the same discount rate.

The proper way to view the 10-year 8% coupon Treasury issue is as a package of zero-coupon bonds whose maturity value is equal to the amount of the cash flow and whose maturity date is equal to each cash flow's payment date. Thus, the 10-year 8% coupon Treasury issue should be viewed as 20 zero-coupon bonds. The reason this is the proper way to value a security is that it does not allow arbitrage profit by taking apart or "stripping" a security and selling off the stripped securities at a higher aggregate value than it would cost to purchase the security in the market.

We'll illustrate this later. We refer to this approach to valuation as the arbitrage-free valuation approach.[6]

By viewing any financial asset as a package of zero-coupon bonds, a consistent valuation framework can be developed. Viewing a financial asset as a package of zero-coupon bonds means that any two bonds would be viewed as different packages of zero-coupon bonds and valued accordingly.

The difference between the traditional valuation approach and the arbitrage-free approach is illustrated in Exhibit 4, which shows how the three bonds whose cash flows are depicted in Exhibit 3 should be valued. With the traditional approach, the discount rate for all three bonds is the yield on a 10-year U.S. Treasury security. With the arbitrage-free approach, the discount rate for a cash flow is the theoretical rate that the U.S. Treasury would have to pay if it issued a zero-coupon bond with a maturity date equal to the maturity date of the cash flow.

| Exhibit 4 | Comparison of Traditional Approach and Arbitrage-Free Approach in Valuing a Treasury Security |

	Each Period Is Six Months				
	Discount (Base Interest) Rate		**Cash Flows for**[a]		
Period	**Traditional Approach**	**Arbitrage-Free Approach**	**12%**	**8%**	**0%**
1	10-year Treasury rate	1-period Treasury spot rate	$6	$4	$0
2	10-year Treasury rate	2-period Treasury spot rate	6	4	0
3	10-year Treasury rate	3-period Treasury spot rate	6	4	0
4	10-year Treasury rate	4-period Treasury spot rate	6	4	0
5	10-year Treasury rate	5-period Treasury spot rate	6	4	0
6	10-year Treasury rate	6-period Treasury spot rate	6	4	0
7	10-year Treasury rate	7-period Treasury spot rate	6	4	0
8	10-year Treasury rate	8-period Treasury spot rate	6	4	0
9	10-year Treasury rate	9-period Treasury spot rate	6	4	0
10	10-year Treasury rate	10-period Treasury spot rate	6	4	0
11	10-year Treasury rate	11-period Treasury spot rate	6	4	0
12	10-year Treasury rate	12-period Treasury spot rate	6	4	0
13	10-year Treasury rate	13-period Treasury spot rate	6	4	0
14	10-year Treasury rate	14-period Treasury spot rate	6	4	0
15	10-year Treasury rate	15-period Treasury spot rate	6	4	0
16	10-year Treasury rate	16-period Treasury spot rate	6	4	0
17	10-year Treasury rate	17-period Treasury spot rate	6	4	0
18	10-year Treasury rate	18-period Treasury spot rate	6	4	0
19	10-year Treasury rate	19-period Treasury spot rate	6	4	0
20	10-year Treasury rate	20-period Treasury spot rate	106	104	100

[a] Per $100 of par value.

6 In its simple form, arbitrage is the simultaneous buying and selling of an asset at two different prices in two different markets. The arbitrageur profits without risk by buying cheap in one market and simultaneously selling at the higher price in the other market. Such opportunities for arbitrage are rare. Less obvious arbitrage opportunities exist in situations where a package of assets can produce a payoff (expected return) identical to an asset that is priced differently. This arbitrage relies on a fundamental principle of finance called the "law of one price," which states that a given asset must have the same price regardless of the means by which one goes about creating that asset. The law of one price implies that if the payoff of an asset can be synthetically created by a package of assets, the price of the package and the price of the asset whose payoff it replicates must be equal.

Therefore, to implement the arbitrage-free approach, it is necessary to determine the theoretical rate that the U.S. Treasury would have to pay on a zero-coupon Treasury security for each maturity. As explained in the previous reading, the name given to the zero-coupon Treasury rate is the Treasury spot rate. In the reading on yield measures, spot rates, and forward rates, we will explain how the Treasury spot rate can be calculated. The spot rate for a Treasury security is the interest rate that should be used to discount a default-free cash flow with the same maturity. We call the value of a bond based on spot rates the arbitrage-free value.

4.1 Valuation Using Treasury Spot Rates

For the purposes of our discussion, we will take the Treasury spot rate for each maturity as given. To illustrate how Treasury spot rates are used to compute the arbitrage-free value of a Treasury security, we will use the hypothetical Treasury spot rates shown in the fourth column of Exhibit 5 to value an 8% 10-year Treasury security. The present value of each period's cash flow is shown in the last column. The sum of the present values is the arbitrage-free value for the Treasury security. For the 8% 10-year Treasury, it is $115.2619.

Exhibit 5	Determination of the Arbitrage-Free Value of an 8% 10-Year Treasury			
Period	**Years**	**Cash Flow ($)**	**Spot Rate (%)[a]**	**Present Value ($)[b]**
1	0.5	4	3.0000	3.9409
2	1.0	4	3.3000	3.8712
3	1.5	4	3.5053	3.7968
4	2.0	4	3.9164	3.7014
5	2.5	4	4.4376	3.5843
6	3.0	4	4.7520	3.4743
7	3.5	4	4.9622	3.3694
8	4.0	4	5.0650	3.2747
9	4.5	4	5.1701	3.1791
10	5.0	4	5.2772	3.0829
11	5.5	4	5.3864	2.9861
12	6.0	4	5.4976	2.8889
13	6.5	4	5.6108	2.7916
14	7.0	4	5.6643	2.7055
15	7.5	4	5.7193	2.6205
16	8.0	4	5.7755	2.5365
17	8.5	4	5.8331	2.4536
18	9.0	4	5.9584	2.3581
19	9.5	4	6.0863	2.2631
20	10.0	104	6.2169	56.3830
			Total	$115.2621

[a] The spot rate is an annual discount rate. The convention to obtain a semiannual discount rate is to take one-half the annual discount rate. So, for period 6 (i.e., 3 years), the spot rate is 4.7520%. The semiannual discount rate is 2.376%.

[b] The present value for the cash flow is equal to: $\dfrac{\text{Cash flow}}{(1+\text{Spot rate}/2)^{\text{period}}}$

As a second illustration, suppose that a 4.8% coupon 10-year Treasury bond is being valued based on the Treasury spot rates shown in Exhibit 5. The arbitrage-free value of this bond is $90.8428 as shown in Exhibit 6.

Exhibit 6		Determination of the Arbitrage-Free Value of a 4.8% 10-Year Treasury		
Period	Years	Cash Flow ($)	Spot Rate (%)[a]	Present Value ($)[b]
1	0.5	2.4	3.0000	2.3645
2	1.0	2.4	3.3000	2.3227
3	1.5	2.4	3.5053	2.2781
4	2.0	2.4	3.9164	2.2209
5	2.5	2.4	4.4376	2.1506
6	3.0	2.4	4.7520	2.0846
7	3.5	2.4	4.9622	2.0216
8	4.0	2.4	5.0650	1.9648
9	4.5	2.4	5.1701	1.9075
10	5.0	2.4	5.2772	1.8497
11	5.5	2.4	5.3864	1.7916
12	6.0	2.4	5.4976	1.7334
13	6.5	2.4	5.6108	1.6750
14	7.0	2.4	5.6643	1.6233
15	7.5	2.4	5.7193	1.5723
16	8.0	2.4	5.7755	1.5219
17	8.5	2.4	5.8331	1.4722
18	9.0	2.4	5.9584	1.4149
19	9.5	2.4	6.0863	1.3578
20	10.0	102.4	6.2169	55.5156
			Total	90.8430

[a] The spot rate is an annual discount rate. The convention to obtain a semiannual discount rate is to take one-half the annual discount rate. So, for period 6 (i.e., 3 years), the spot rate is 4.7520%. The semiannual discount rate is 2.376%.
[b] The present value for the cash flow is equal to: $\dfrac{\text{Cash flow}}{(1+\ \text{Spot rate}/2)^{\text{period}}}$

In the next reading, we discuss yield measures. The yield to maturity is a measure that would be computed for this bond. We won't show how it is computed in this reading, but simply state the result. The yield for the 4.8% coupon 10-year Treasury bond is 6.033%. Notice that the spot rates are used to obtain the price, and the price is then used to compute a conventional yield measure. *It is important to understand that there are an infinite number of spot rate curves that can generate the same price of $90.8428 and therefore the same yield.*

Practice Question 9

A. Using the Treasury spot rates shown in Exhibit 5, what is the arbitrage-free value of a 7.4% coupon 8-year Treasury security?

B. Using the Treasury spot rates shown in Exhibit 5, what is the arbitrage-free value of a 4% coupon 8-year Treasury security?

4.2 Reason for Using Treasury Spot Rates

Thus far, we simply asserted that the value of a Treasury security should be based on discounting each cash flow using the corresponding Treasury spot rate. But what if market participants value a security using the yield for the on-the-run Treasury with a maturity equal to the maturity of the Treasury security being valued? (In other words, what if participants use the yield on coupon-bearing securities rather than the yield on zero-coupon securities?) Let's see why a Treasury security will have to trade close to its arbitrage-free value.

4.2.1 Stripping and the Arbitrage-Free Valuation

The key in the process is the existence of the Treasury strips market. As explained in the reading on bond sectors and instruments, a dealer has the ability to take apart the cash flows of a Treasury coupon security (i.e., strip the security) and create zero-coupon securities. These zero-coupon securities, which we called Treasury strips, can be sold to investors. At what interest rate or yield can these Treasury strips be sold to investors? They can be sold at the Treasury spot rates. If the market price of a Treasury security is less than its value using the arbitrage-free valuation approach, then a dealer can buy the Treasury security, strip it, and sell off the Treasury strips so as to generate greater proceeds than the cost of purchasing the Treasury security. The resulting profit is an arbitrage profit. Since, as we will see, the value determined by using the Treasury spot rates does not allow for the generation of an arbitrage profit, this is the reason why the approach is referred to as an "arbitrage-free" approach.

To illustrate this, suppose that the yield for the on-the-run 10-year Treasury issue is 6%. (We will see in the reading on yield measures, spot rates, and forward rates that the Treasury spot rate curve in Exhibit 5 was generated from a yield curve where the on-the-run 10-year Treasury issue was 6%.) Suppose that the 8% coupon 10-year Treasury issue is valued using the traditional approach based on 6%. Exhibit 7 shows the value based on discounting all the cash flows at 6% is $114.8775.

Exhibit 7		Price of an 8% 10-Year Treasury Valued at a 6% Discount Rate		
Period	**Years**	**Cash Flow ($)**	**Discount Rate (%)**[a]	**Present Value ($)**[b]
1	0.5	4	6.0000	3.8835
2	1.0	4	6.0000	3.7704
3	1.5	4	6.0000	3.6606
4	2.0	4	6.0000	3.5539
5	2.5	4	6.0000	3.4504
6	3.0	4	6.0000	3.3499
7	3.5	4	6.0000	3.2524
8	4.0	4	6.0000	3.1576
9	4.5	4	6.0000	3.0657
10	5.0	4	6.0000	2.9764
11	5.5	4	6.0000	2.8897
12	6.0	4	6.0000	2.8055
13	6.5	4	6.0000	2.7238
14	7.0	4	6.0000	2.6445
15	7.5	4	6.0000	2.5674

Exhibit 7	Continued			
Period	Years	Cash Flow ($)	Discount Rate (%)[a]	Present Value ($)[b]
16	8.0	4	6.0000	2.4927
17	8.5	4	6.0000	2.4201
18	9.0	4	6.0000	2.3496
19	9.5	4	6.0000	2.2811
20	10.0	104	6.0000	57.5823
			Total	$114.8775

[a] The spot rate is an annual discount rate. The convention to obtain a semiannual discount rate is to take one-half the annual discount rate. So, since the discount rate for each period is 6%, the semiannual discount rate is 3%.

[b] The present value for the cash flow is equal to: $\dfrac{\text{Cash flow}}{(1.03)^{\text{period}}}$

Consider what would happen if the market priced the security at $114.8775. The value based on the Treasury spot rates (Exhibit 5) is $115.2621. What can the dealer do? The dealer can buy the 8% 10-year issue for $114.8775, strip it, and sell the Treasury strips at the spot rates shown in Exhibit 5. By doing so, the proceeds that will be received by the dealer are $115.2621. This results in an arbitrage profit of $0.3846 (= $115.2621 − $114.8775).[7] Dealers recognizing this arbitrage opportunity will bid up the price of the 8% 10-year Treasury issue in order to acquire it and strip it. At what point will the arbitrage profit disappear? When the security is priced at $115.2621, the value that we said is the arbitrage-free value.

To understand in more detail where this arbitrage profit is coming from, look at Exhibit 8. The third column shows how much each cash flow can be sold for by the dealer if it is stripped. The values in the third column are simply the present values in Exhibit 5 based on discounting the cash flows at the Treasury spot rates. The fourth column shows how much the dealer is effectively purchasing the cash flow if each cash flow is discounted at 6%. This is the last column in Exhibit 7. The sum of the arbitrage profit from each cash flow stripped is the total arbitrage profit.

Exhibit 8	Arbitrage Profit from Stripping the 8% 10-Year Treasury			
Period	Years	Sell for	Buy for	Arbitrage Profit
1	0.5	3.9409	3.8835	0.0574
2	1.0	3.8712	3.7704	0.1008
3	1.5	3.7968	3.6606	0.1363
4	2.0	3.7014	3.5539	0.1475
5	2.5	3.5843	3.4504	0.1339
6	3.0	3.4743	3.3499	0.1244
7	3.5	3.3694	3.2524	0.1170
8	4.0	3.2747	3.1576	0.1170
9	4.5	3.1791	3.0657	0.1134
10	5.0	3.0829	2.9764	0.1065

(continued)

7 This may seem like a small amount, but remember that this is for a single $100 par value bond. Multiply this by thousands of bonds and you can see a dealer's profit potential.

Exhibit 8	Continued			
Period	Years	Sell for	Buy for	Arbitrage Profit
11	5.5	2.9861	2.8897	0.0964
12	6.0	2.8889	2.8055	0.0834
13	6.5	2.7916	2.7238	0.0678
14	7.0	2.7055	2.6445	0.0611
15	7.5	2.6205	2.5674	0.0531
16	8.0	2.5365	2.4927	0.0439
17	8.5	2.4536	2.4201	0.0336
18	9.0	2.3581	2.3496	0.0086
19	9.5	2.2631	2.2811	−0.0181
20	10.0	56.3830	57.5823	−1.1993
		115.2621	114.8775	0.3846

4.2.2 Reconstitution and Arbitrage-Free Valuation

We have just demonstrated how coupon stripping of a Treasury issue will force its market value to be close to the value determined by arbitrage-free valuation when the market price is less than the arbitrage-free value. What happens when a Treasury issue's market price is greater than the arbitrage-free value? Obviously, a dealer will not want to strip the Treasury issue since the proceeds generated from stripping will be less than the cost of purchasing the issue.

When such situations occur, the dealer will follow a procedure called reconstitution.[8] Basically, the dealer can purchase a package of Treasury strips so as to create a synthetic (i.e., artificial) Treasury coupon security that is worth more than the same maturity and same coupon Treasury issue.

To illustrate this, consider the 4.8% 10-year Treasury issue whose arbitrage-free value was computed in Exhibit 6. The arbitrage-free value is $90.8430. Exhibit 9 shows the price assuming the traditional approach where all the cash flows are discounted at a 6% interest rate. The price is $91.0735. What the dealer can do is purchase the Treasury strip for each 6-month period at the prices shown in Exhibit 6 and sell short the 4.8% 10-year Treasury coupon issue whose cash flows are being replicated. By doing so, the dealer has the cash flow of a 4.8% coupon 10-year Treasury security at a cost of $90.8430, thereby generating an arbitrage profit of $0.2305 ($91.0735 − $90.8430). The cash flows from the package of Treasury strips purchased are used to make the payments for the Treasury coupon security shorted. Actually, in practice, this can be done in a more efficient manner using a procedure for reconstitution provided for by the Department of the Treasury.

Exhibit 9	Price of a 4.8% 10-Year Treasury Valued at a 6% Discount Rate			
Period	Years	Cash Flow ($)	Discount Rate (%)	Present Value ($)
1	0.5	2.4	6.0000	2.3301
2	1.0	2.4	6.0000	2.2622

---

8 The definition of *reconstitute* is to provide with a new structure, often by assembling various parts into a whole. *Reconstitution* then, as used here, means to assemble the parts (the Treasury strips) in such a way that a new whole (a Treasury coupon bond) is created. That is, it is the opposite of *stripping* a coupon bond.

	Exhibit 9	Continued			
Period	**Years**	**Cash Flow ($)**	**Discount Rate (%)**	**Present Value ($)**	
3	1.5	2.4	6.0000	2.1963	
4	2.0	2.4	6.0000	2.1324	
5	2.5	2.4	6.0000	2.0703	
6	3.0	2.4	6.0000	2.0100	
7	3.5	2.4	6.0000	1.9514	
8	4.0	2.4	6.0000	1.8946	
9	4.5	2.4	6.0000	1.8394	
10	5.0	2.4	6.0000	1.7858	
11	5.5	2.4	6.0000	1.7338	
12	6.0	2.4	6.0000	1.6833	
13	6.5	2.4	6.0000	1.6343	
14	7.0	2.4	6.0000	1.5867	
15	7.5	2.4	6.0000	1.5405	
16	8.0	2.4	6.0000	1.4956	
17	8.5	2.4	6.0000	1.4520	
18	9.0	2.4	6.0000	1.4097	
19	9.5	2.4	6.0000	1.3687	
20	10.0	102.4	6.0000	56.6964	
			Total	91.0735	

What forces the market price to the arbitrage-free value of $90.8430? As dealers sell short the Treasury coupon issue (4.8% 10-year issue), the price of the issue decreases. When the price is driven down to $90.8430, the arbitrage profit no longer exists.

This process of stripping and reconstitution assures that the price of a Treasury issue will not depart materially from its arbitrage-free value. In other countries, as governments permit the stripping and reconstitution of their issues, the value of non-U.S. government issues has also moved toward their arbitrage-free value.

4.3 Credit Spreads and the Valuation of Non-Treasury Securities

The Treasury spot rates can be used to value any default-free security. For a non-Treasury security, the theoretical value is not as easy to determine. The value of a non-Treasury security is found by discounting the cash flows by the Treasury spot rates plus a yield spread to reflect the additional risks.

The spot rate used to discount the cash flow of a non-Treasury security can be the Treasury spot rate plus a constant credit spread. For example, suppose the 6-month Treasury spot rate is 3% and the 10-year Treasury spot rate is 6%. Also suppose that a suitable credit spread is 90 basis points. Then a 3.9% spot rate is used to discount a 6-month cash flow of a non-Treasury bond and a 6.9% discount rate to discount a 10-year cash flow. (Remember that when each semiannual cash flow is discounted, the discount rate used is one-half the spot rate—1.95% for the 6-month spot rate and 3.45% for the 10-year spot rate.)

The drawback of this approach is that there is no reason to expect the credit spread to be the same regardless of when the cash flow is received. We actually observed this in the previous reading when we saw how credit spreads increase with maturity. Consequently, it might be expected that credit spreads increase with the maturity of the bond. That is, there is a term structure of credit spreads.

Dealer firms typically estimate a term structure for credit spreads for each credit rating and market sector. Generally, the credit spread increases with maturity. This is a typical shape for the term structure of credit spreads. In addition, the shape of the term structure is not the same for all credit ratings. Typically, the lower the credit rating, the steeper the term structure of credit spreads.

When the credit spreads for a given credit rating and market sector are added to the Treasury spot rates, the resulting term structure is used to value bonds with that credit rating in that market sector. This term structure is referred to as the benchmark spot rate curve or benchmark zero-coupon rate curve.

For example, Exhibit 10 reproduces the Treasury spot rate curve in Exhibit 5. Also shown in the exhibit is a hypothetical credit spread for a non-Treasury security. The resulting benchmark spot rate curve is in the next-to-the-last column. It is this spot rate curve that is used to value the securities that have the same credit rating and are in the same market sector. This is done in Exhibit 10 for a hypothetical 8% 10-year issue. The arbitrage-free value is $108.4616. Notice that the theoretical value is less than that for an otherwise comparable Treasury security. The arbitrage-free value for an 8% 10-year Treasury is $115.2621 (see Exhibit 5).

Exhibit 10	Calculation of Arbitrage-Free Value of a Hypothetical 8% 10-Year Non-Treasury Security Using Benchmark Spot Rate Curve

Period	Years	Cash Flow ($)	Treasury Spot Rate (%)	Credit Spread (%)	Benchmark Spot (%)	Present Value ($)
1	0.5	4	3.0000	0.20	3.2000	3.9370
2	1.0	4	3.3000	0.20	3.5000	3.8636
3	1.5	4	3.5053	0.25	3.7553	3.7829
4	2.0	4	3.9164	0.30	4.2164	3.6797
5	2.5	4	4.4376	0.35	4.7876	3.5538
6	3.0	4	4.7520	0.35	5.1020	3.4389
7	3.5	4	4.9622	0.40	5.3622	3.3237
8	4.0	4	5.0650	0.45	5.5150	3.2177
9	4.5	4	5.1701	0.45	5.6201	3.1170
10	5.0	4	5.2772	0.50	5.7772	3.0088
11	5.5	4	5.3864	0.55	5.9364	2.8995
12	6.0	4	5.4976	0.60	6.0976	2.7896
13	6.5	4	5.6108	0.65	6.2608	2.6794
14	7.0	4	5.6643	0.70	6.3643	2.5799
15	7.5	4	5.7193	0.75	6.4693	2.4813
16	8.0	4	5.7755	0.80	6.5755	2.3838
17	8.5	4	5.8331	0.85	6.6831	2.2876
18	9.0	4	5.9584	0.90	6.8584	2.1801
19	9.5	4	6.0863	0.95	7.0363	2.0737
20	10.0	104	6.2169	1.00	7.2169	51.1835
					Total	$108.4616

VALUATION MODELS

A valuation model provides the fair value of a security. Thus far, the two valuation approaches we have presented have dealt with valuing simple securities. By simple we mean that it assumes the securities do not have an embedded option. A Treasury security and an option-free non-Treasury security can be valued using the arbitrage-free valuation approach.

More general valuation models handle securities with embedded options. In the fixed income area, two common models used are the **binomial model** and the **Monte Carlo simulation model**. The former model is used to value callable bonds, putable bonds, floating-rate notes, and structured notes in which the coupon formula is based on an interest rate. The Monte Carlo simulation model is used to value mortgage-backed securities and certain types of asset-backed securities.[9]

In very general terms, the following five features are common to the binomial and Monte Carlo simulation valuation models:

1. Each model begins with the yields on the on-the-run Treasury securities and generates Treasury spot rates.

2. Each model makes an assumption about the expected volatility of short-term interest rates. This is a critical assumption in both models since it can significantly affect the security's fair value.

3. Based on the volatility assumption, different "branches" of an interest rate tree (in the case of the binomial model) and interest rate "paths" (in the case of the Monte Carlo model) are generated.

4. The model is calibrated to the Treasury market. This means that if an "on-the-run" Treasury issue is valued using the model, the model will produce the observed market price.

5. Rules are developed to determine when an issuer/borrower will exercise embedded options—a call/put rule for callable/putable bonds and a prepayment model for mortgage-backed and certain asset-backed securities.

The user of any valuation model is exposed to modeling risk. This is the risk that the output of the model is incorrect because the assumptions upon which it is based are incorrect. Consequently, it is imperative the results of a valuation model be stress-tested for modeling risk by altering assumptions.

SOLUTIONS FOR PRACTICE QUESTIONS

1. **A.** The cash flow per $100 of par value for this security is:

Year	Cash Flow
1	$7
2	7
3	7
4	7
5	107

The present value for each cash flow assuming a discount rate of 5% is:

---

9 A short summary reason is: mortgage-backed securities and certain asset-backed securities are interest rate path dependent securities, and the binomial model cannot value such securities.

$$\text{Year 1: Present value}_1 = \frac{\$7}{(1.05)^1} = \$6.6667$$

$$\text{Year 2: Present value}_2 = \frac{\$7}{(1.05)^2} = \$6.3492$$

$$\text{Year 3: Present value}_3 = \frac{\$7}{(1.05)^3} = \$6.0469$$

$$\text{Year 4: Present value}_4 = \frac{\$7}{(1.05)^4} = \$5.7589$$

$$\text{Year 5: Present value}_5 = \frac{\$107}{(1.05)^5} = \$83.8373$$

The present value is the sum of the five present values above, $108.6590.

B. The cash flow for this security is $2,309.75 for each year. The present value of each cash flow assuming a discount rate of 6% is:

$$\text{Year 1: Present value}_1 = \frac{\$2,309.75}{(1.06)^1} = \$2,179.0094$$

$$\text{Year 2: Present value}_2 = \frac{\$2,309.75}{(1.06)^2} = \$2,055.6693$$

$$\text{Year 3: Present value}_3 = \frac{\$2,309.75}{(1.06)^3} = \$1,939.3106$$

$$\text{Year 4: Present value}_4 = \frac{\$2,309.75}{(1.06)^4} = \$1,829.5383$$

$$\text{Year 5: Present value}_5 = \frac{\$2,309.75}{(1.06)^5} = \$1,725.9796$$

The present value of the five cash flows is $9,729.5072.

2. The present value for each cash flow assuming a discount rate of 4% is:

$$\text{Year 1: Present value}_1 = \frac{\$7}{(1.04)^1} = \$6.7308$$

$$\text{Year 2: Present value}_2 = \frac{\$7}{(1.04)^2} = \$6.4719$$

$$\text{Year 3: Present value}_3 = \frac{\$7}{(1.04)^3} = \$6.2230$$

$$\text{Year 4: Present value}_4 = \frac{\$7}{(1.04)^4} = \$5.9836$$

$$\text{Year 5: Present value}_5 = \frac{\$107}{(1.04)^5} = \$87.9462$$

The present value is the sum of the five present values above, $113.3555. A 4% discount produced a present value of $113.3555, which is greater than the present value of $108.6590 when the higher discount rate of 5% is used.

3. A. The value of the bond for the three discount rates is provided below:

Year	Present Value at 6%	Present Value at 7%	Present Value at 8%
1	$6.6038	$6.5421	$6.4815
2	6.2300	6.1141	6.0014
3	5.8773	5.7141	5.5568
4	5.5447	5.3403	5.1452
5	79.9566	76.2895	72.8224
	$104.2124	$100.0000	$96.0073

B. The following relationship holds:

- When the coupon rate is greater than the discount rate (7% versus 6%), the bond's value is a premium to par value ($104.2124).
- When the coupon rate is equal to the discount rate, the bond's value is par value.
- When the coupon rate is less than the discount rate (7% versus 8%), the bond's value is a discount to par value ($96.0073).

4. The cash flow per $100 of par value for this security is:

Year	Cash Flow
1	$7
2	7
3	7
4	7
5	107

The present value of each cash flow is:

$$\text{Year 1: Present value}_1 = \frac{\$7}{(1.035)^1} = \$6.7633$$

$$\text{Year 2: Present value}_2 = \frac{\$7}{(1.039)^2} = \$6.4844$$

$$\text{Year 3: Present value}_3 = \frac{\$7}{(1.042)^3} = \$6.1872$$

$$\text{Year 4: Present value}_4 = \frac{\$7}{(1.045)^4} = \$5.8699$$

$$\text{Year 5: Present value}_5 = \frac{\$107}{(1.050)^5} = \$83.8373$$

The sum of the present values is $109.1421.

5. The semiannual cash flows for the first 9 six-month periods per $100 of par value is $3.50. For the last period, the cash flow is $103.50. The semiannual discount rate is 2.5%. The present value of each cash flow discounted at 2.5% is shown below:

$$Year\ 1:\ Present\ value_1 = \frac{\$3.5}{(1.025)^1} = \$3.4146$$

$$Year\ 2:\ Present\ value_2 = \frac{\$3.5}{(1.025)^2} = \$3.3314$$

$$Year\ 3:\ Present\ value_3 = \frac{\$3.5}{(1.025)^3} = \$3.2501$$

$$Year\ 4:\ Present\ value_4 = \frac{\$3.5}{(1.025)^4} = \$3.1708$$

$$Year\ 5:\ Present\ value_5 = \frac{\$3.5}{(1.025)^5} = \$3.0935$$

$$Year\ 6:\ Present\ value_6 = \frac{\$3.5}{(1.025)^6} = \$3.0180$$

$$Year\ 7:\ Present\ value_7 = \frac{\$3.5}{(1.025)^7} = \$2.9444$$

$$Year\ 8:\ Present\ value_8 = \frac{\$3.5}{(1.025)^8} = \$2.8726$$

$$Year\ 9:\ Present\ value_9 = \frac{\$3.5}{(1.025)^9} = \$2.8025$$

$$Year\ 10:\ Present\ value_{10} = \frac{\$103.5}{(1.025)^{10}} = \$80.8540$$

The value of this bond is the sum of the present values, $108.7519.

Alternatively, the short-cut formula can be used. The present value of the coupon payments is:

$$\$3.5 \times \left[\frac{1 - \dfrac{1}{(1.025)^{5 \times 2}}}{0.025} \right] = \$30.6322$$

The present value of the maturity value is:

$$Present\ value\ of\ maturity = \frac{\$100}{(1.025)^{5 \times 2}} = \$78.1198$$

The price is then $108.7520 (= $30.6322 + $78.1198), the same value as computed above.

6. **A.** The value given the semiannual discount rate i (one-half the annual discount rate) is found by the following formula:

$$\frac{\$1,000}{(1 + i)^{20}}$$

The solutions follow:

Annual Rate (%)	Semiannual Rate (%)	Price
1	0.5	905.0629
2	1.0	819.5445

Annual Rate (%)	Semiannual Rate (%)	Price
3	1.5	742.4704
4	2.0	672.9713
5	2.5	610.2709
6	3.0	553.6758
7	3.5	502.5659
8	4.0	456.3869
9	4.5	414.6429
10	5.0	376.8895
11	5.5	342.7290
12	6.0	311.8047
13	6.5	283.7970
14	7.0	258.4190

B.

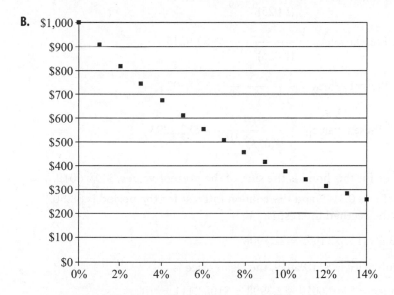

7. First, w must be calculated. We know that

Days between settlement date and next coupon payment   58

Days in the coupon period   183

Therefore,

$$w \text{ periods} = \frac{58}{183} = 0.3169$$

Since the discount rate is 5%, the semiannual rate is 2.5%. The present value of each cash flow is:

$$\textit{Year 1}: \text{Present value}_1 = \frac{\$3.5}{(1.025)^{0.3169}} = \$3.4727$$

$$\textit{Year 2}: \text{Present value}_2 = \frac{\$3.5}{(1.025)^{1.3169}} = \$3.3880$$

$$\textit{Year 3}: \text{Present value}_3 = \frac{\$3.5}{(1.025)^{2.3169}} = \$3.3054$$

$$\textit{Year 4}: \text{Present value}_4 = \frac{\$3.5}{(1.025)^{3.3169}} = \$3.2248$$

$$\textit{Year 5}: \text{Present value}_5 = \frac{\$3.5}{(1.025)^{4.3169}} = \$3.1461$$

$$\textit{Year 6}: \text{Present value}_6 = \frac{\$3.5}{(1.025)^{5.3169}} = \$3.0694$$

$$\textit{Year 7}: \text{Present value}_7 = \frac{\$3.5}{(1.025)^{6.3169}} = \$2.9945$$

$$\textit{Year 8}: \text{Present value}_8 = \frac{\$3.5}{(1.025)^{7.3169}} = \$2.9215$$

$$\textit{Year 9}: \text{Present value}_9 = \frac{\$3.5}{(1.025)^{8.3169}} = \$2.8502$$

$$\textit{Year 10}: \text{Present value}_{10} = \frac{\$103.5}{(1.025)^{9.3169}} = \$82.2293$$

The full price for this bond is the sum of the present values, $110.6019.

8. The value of w is 0.3169 and the coupon interest for the period is $3.50. Therefore, the accrued interest is:

$$AI = \$3.5 \times (1 - 0.3169) = \$2.3908$$

Since the full price is $110.6019, the clean price is

$$\text{Clean price} = \$110.6019 - \$2.3908 = \$108.2111$$

9. **A.** The value for the 7.4% coupon 8-year Treasury security is $111.3324 as shown below:

Period	Years	Cash Flow ($)	Spot Rate (%)	Present Value ($)
1	0.5	3.7	3.0000	3.6453
2	1.0	3.7	3.3000	3.5809
3	1.5	3.7	3.5053	3.5121
4	2.0	3.7	3.9164	3.4238
5	2.5	3.7	4.4376	3.3155
6	3.0	3.7	4.7520	3.2138
7	3.5	3.7	4.9622	3.1167
8	4.0	3.7	5.0650	3.0291
9	4.5	3.7	5.1701	2.9407
10	5.0	3.7	5.2772	2.8516

Period	Years	Cash Flow ($)	Spot Rate (%)	Present Value ($)
11	5.5	3.7	5.3864	2.7621
12	6.0	3.7	5.4976	2.6723
13	6.5	3.7	5.6108	2.5822
14	7.0	3.7	5.6643	2.5026
15	7.5	3.7	5.7193	2.4240
16	8.0	103.7	5.7755	65.7597
		Total		111.3324

B. The value for the 4% coupon 8-year Treasury security is $89.3155 as shown below:

Period	Years	Cash Flow ($)	Spot Rate (%)	Present Value ($)
1	0.5	2	3.0000	1.9704
2	1.0	2	3.3000	1.9356
3	1.5	2	3.5053	1.8984
4	2.0	2	3.9164	1.8507
5	2.5	2	4.4376	1.7922
6	3.0	2	4.7520	1.7372
7	3.5	2	4.9622	1.6847
8	4.0	2	5.0650	1.6373
9	4.5	2	5.1701	1.5895
10	5.0	2	5.2772	1.5414
11	5.5	2	5.3864	1.4930
12	6.0	2	5.4976	1.4445
13	6.5	2	5.6108	1.3958
14	7.0	2	5.6643	1.3528
15	7.5	2	5.7193	1.3103
16	8.0	102	5.7755	64.6817
		Total		89.3155

SUMMARY

- Valuation is the process of determining the fair value of a financial asset.
- The fundamental principle of valuation is that the value of any financial asset is the present value of the expected cash flows, where a cash flow is the amount of cash expected to be received at some future periods.
- The valuation process involves three steps: 1) estimating the expected cash flows, 2) determining the appropriate interest rate or interest rates to be used to discount the cash flows, and 3) calculating the present value of the expected cash flows.

■ For any fixed income security which neither the issuer nor the investor can alter the payment of the principal before its contractual due date, the cash flows can easily be determined assuming that the issuer does not default.

■ The difficulty in determining cash flows arises for securities where either the issuer or the investor can alter the cash flows, or the coupon rate is reset by a formula dependent on some reference rate, price, or exchange rate.

■ On-the-run Treasury yields are viewed as the minimum interest rate an investor requires when investing in a bond.

■ The risk premium or yield spread over the interest rate on a Treasury security investors require reflects the additional risks in a security that is not issued by the U.S. government.

■ For a given discount rate, the present value of a single cash flow received in the future is the amount of money that must be invested today that will generate that future value.

■ The present value of a cash flow will depend on when a cash flow will be received (i.e., the timing of a cash flow) and the discount rate (i.e., interest rate) used to calculate the present value.

■ The sum of the present values for a security's expected cash flows is the value of the security.

■ The present value is lower the further into the future the cash flow will be received.

■ The higher the discount rate, the lower a cash flow's present value and since the value of a security is the sum of the present value of the cash flows, the higher the discount rate, the lower a security's value.

■ The price/yield relationship for an option-free bond is convex.

■ The value of a bond is equal to the present value of the coupon payments plus the present value of the maturity value.

■ When a bond is purchased between coupon periods, the buyer pays a price that includes accrued interest, called the full price or dirty price.

■ The clean price or simply price of a bond is the full price minus accrued interest.

■ In computing accrued interest, day count conventions are used to determine the number of days in the coupon payment period and the number of days since the last coupon payment date.

■ The traditional valuation methodology is to discount every cash flow of a security by the same interest rate (or discount rate), thereby incorrectly viewing each security as the same package of cash flows.

■ The arbitrage-free approach values a bond as a package of cash flows, with each cash flow viewed as a zero-coupon bond and each cash flow discounted at its own unique discount rate.

■ The Treasury zero-coupon rates are called Treasury spot rates.

■ The Treasury spot rates are used to discount the cash flows in the arbitrage-free valuation approach.

■ To value a security with credit risk, it is necessary to determine a term structure of credit rates.

■ Adding a credit spread for an issuer to the Treasury spot rate curve gives the benchmark spot rate curve used to value that issuer's security.

- Valuation models seek to provide the fair value of a bond and accommodate securities with embedded options.

- The common valuation models used to value bonds with embedded options are the binomial model and the Monte Carlo simulation model.

- The binomial model is used to value callable bonds, putable bonds, floating-rate notes, and structured notes in which the coupon formula is based on an interest rate.

- The Monte Carlo simulation model is used to value mortgage-backed and certain asset-backed securities.

- The user of a valuation model is exposed to modeling risk and should test the sensitivity of the model to alternative assumptions.

PRACTICE PROBLEMS FOR READING 56

1. Compute the value of a 5-year 7.4% coupon bond that pays interest annually assuming that the appropriate discount rate is 5.6%.

2. A 5-year amortizing security with a par value of $100,000 and a coupon rate of 6.4% has an expected cash flow of $23,998.55 per year assuming no prepayments. The annual cash flow includes interest and principal payment. What is the value of this amortizing security assuming no principal prepayments and a discount rate of 7.8%?

3. **A.** Assuming annual interest payments, what is the value of a 5-year 6.2% coupon bond when the discount rate is i) 4.5%, ii) 6.2%, and iii) 7.3%?

   B. Show that the results obtained in part A are consistent with the relationship between the coupon rate, discount rate, and price relative to par value.

4. A client is reviewing a year-end portfolio report. Since the beginning of the year, market yields have increased slightly. In comparing the beginning-of-the-year price for the bonds selling at a discount from par value to the end-of-year prices, the client observes that all the prices are higher. The client is perplexed since he expected that the price of all bonds should be lower since interest rates increased. Explain to the client why the prices of the bonds in the portfolio selling at discount have increased in value.

5. A 4-year 5.8% coupon bond is selling to yield 7%. The bond pays interest annually. One year later interest rates decrease from 7% to 6.2%.

   A. What is the price of the 4-year 5.8% coupon bond selling to yield 7%?

   B. What is the price of this bond one year later assuming the yield is unchanged at 7%?

   C. What is the price of this bond one year later if instead of the yield being unchanged the yield decreases to 6.2%?

   D. Complete the following:

      i. Price change attributable to moving to maturity (no change in discount rate).

      ii. Price change attributable to a decrease in the discount rate from 7% to 6.2%.

      iii. Total price change.

6. What is the value of a 5-year 5.8% annual coupon bond if the appropriate discount rate for discounting each cash flow is as follows:

Year	Discount Rate (%)
1	5.90
2	6.40
3	6.60
4	6.90
5	7.30

7. What is the value of a 5-year 7.4% coupon bond selling to yield 5.6% assuming the coupon payments are made semiannually?

8. What is the value of a zero-coupon bond paying semiannually that matures in 20 years, has a maturity of $1 million, and is selling to yield 7.6%?

9. Suppose that a bond is purchased between coupon periods. The days between the settlement date and the next coupon period are 115. There are 183 days in the coupon period. Suppose that the bond purchased has a coupon rate of 7.4% and there are 10 semiannual coupon payments remaining.

   A. What is the dirty price for this bond if a 5.6% discount rate is used?

   B. What is the accrued interest for this bond?

   C. What is the clean price?

10. Suppose that the prevailing Treasury spot rate curve is the one shown in Exhibit 5.

   A. What is the value of a 7.4% 8-year Treasury issue?

   B. Suppose that the 7.4% 8-year Treasury issue is priced in the market based on the on-the-run 8-year Treasury yield. Assume further that yield is 5.65%, so that each cash flow is discounted at 5.65% divided by 2. What is the price of the 7.4% 8-year Treasury issue based on a 5.65% discount rate?

   C. Given the arbitrage-free value found in part A and the price in part B, what action would a dealer take and what would the arbitrage profit be if the market priced the 7.4% 8-year Treasury issue at the price found in part B?

   D. What process assures that the market price will not differ materially from the arbitrage-free value?

11. Suppose that the prevailing Treasury spot rate curve is the one shown in Exhibit 5.

   A. What is the value of a 4% 8-year Treasury issue?

   B. Suppose that the 4% 8-year Treasury issue is priced in the market based on the on-the-run 8-year Treasury yield. Assume further that yield is 5.65%, so that each cash flow is discounted at 5.65% divided by 2. What is the price of the 4% 8-year Treasury issue based on a 5.65% discount rate?

   C. Given the arbitrage-free value found in part A and the price in part B, what action would a dealer take and what would the arbitrage profit be if the market priced the 4% 8-year Treasury issue at the price found in part B?

   D. What process assures that the market price will not differ materially from the arbitrage-free value?

12. The present value of a 3-year, $1,000 par value bond with a coupon rate of 5 percent that pays interest annually assuming a discount rate of 3 percent is *closest* to:

   A. $943.43.

   B. $1,056.57.

   C. $1,182.91.

13. Assuming that the discount rate remains constant as a bond approaches maturity, the price of a premium bond *most likely* will:

   A. increase.

   B. decrease.

   C. remain constant.

14. The present value of a $1,000 par value, zero-coupon bond with a three-year maturity assuming an annual discount rate of 6 percent compounded semiannually is *closest* to:

    A. $837.48.

    B. $839.62.

    C. $943.40.

15. Assume a $1,000,000 par value, semiannual coupon U.S. Treasury note with two years to maturity and a coupon rate of 10 percent. Using the following Treasury spot rates and ignoring accrued interest and transactions costs, the arbitrage-free value of the Treasury note is *closest* to:

Maturity	Spot Rate (%)
Six months	6.00
Twelve months	7.50
Eighteen months	9.00
Twenty-four months	10.00

    A. $846,210.

    B. $1,000,000.

    C. $1,002,647.

16. Given the following U.S. Treasury spot rates and ignoring transactions costs, the value of a $1,000,000 par value, zero-coupon U.S. Treasury bond with exactly three years left to maturity is *closest* to:

Maturity	Spot Rate (%)
Six months	6.00
Twelve months	7.00
Eighteen months	8.00
Twenty-four months	9.00
Thirty months	10.00
Thirty-six months	11.00

    A. $534,640.

    B. $725,246.

    C. $731,914.

17. A bond with 14 years to maturity and a coupon rate of 6.375 percent has a yield-to-maturity (YTM) of 4.5 percent. Assuming the bond's YTM remains constant, the bond's value as it approaches maturity will *most likely*:

    A. increase.

    B. decrease.

    C. remain constant.

18. A $1,000 par value, semiannual coupon bond has a coupon rate of 5 percent and is quoted at 101 + 12/32nds percent of par with settlement on April 8. The next coupon will be paid on July 15 (98 days after the settlement date). Given there are 181 days between January 15 and July 15 and using an "actual days/actual days" convention, the bond's full invoice price (dirty price) is *closest* to:

    A. $1,022.66.

    B. $1,025.21.

    C. $1,027.29.

19. If the price of a U.S. Treasury bond moves above the value that is consistent with the spot rate curve, dealers initiate a process of buying Treasury STRIPS and packaging them so as to reproduce the mispriced bond. This dealer activity is *best* described as:

    A. rehabilitation.

    B. reaffirmation.

    C. reconstitution.

20. Each of the option-free bonds listed below has a par value of $1,000:

	Bond 1	Bond 2
Time to maturity	10 years	10 years
Annual coupon rate	5.0%	7.0%
Discount rate today	6.5%	6.5%

Which of the following statements about the two bonds is *most* accurate? If the discount rate for each of the bonds remains at 6.5 percent for ten years, the passage of time will result in a decrease in value for:

    A. Bond 1 only.

    B. Bond 2 only.

    C. both of the bonds.

SOLUTIONS FOR READING 56

1. The value is $107.6655 as shown below:

Year	Cash Flow	PV at 5.6%
1	$ 7.4	$ 7.0076
2	7.4	6.6360
3	7.4	6.2841
4	7.4	5.9508
5	107.4	81.7871
	Total	107.6655

2. The value is $96,326.46 as shown below:

Year	Cash Flow	PV at 7.8%
1	$23,998.55	$22,262.11
2	23,998.55	20,651.30
3	23,998.55	19,157.05
4	23,998.55	17,770.92
5	23,998.55	16,485.09
	Total	96,326.47

3. **A.** The present value of the cash flows for the three discount rates is provided below:

Year	Cash Flow	PV at 4.5%	Cash Flow	PV at 6.2%	Cash Flow	PV at 7.3%
1	$6.2	$5.9330	$6.2	$5.8380	$6.2	$5.7782
2	6.2	5.6775	6.2	5.4972	6.2	5.3851
3	6.2	5.4330	6.2	5.1763	6.2	5.0187
4	6.2	5.1991	6.2	4.8741	6.2	4.6773
5	106.2	85.2203	106.2	78.6144	106.2	74.6665
	Total	107.4630	Total	100.0000	Total	95.5258

   B. The following relationship holds:

   ▪ When the coupon rate (6.2%) is greater than the discount rate (4.5%), the bond's value is a premium to par value ($107.4630).

   ▪ When the coupon rate is equal to the discount rate, the bond's value is par value.

   ▪ When the coupon rate (6.2%) is less than the discount rate (7.3%), the bond's value is a discount to par value ($95.5258).

4. A basic property of a discount bond is that its price increases as it moves toward maturity assuming that interest rates do not change. Over the one year that the portfolio is being reviewed, while market yields have increased slightly, the bonds selling at a discount at the beginning of the year can increase despite a slight increase in the market yield since the beginning of the year.

5. A. The price is $95.9353 as shown below:

Year	Cash Flow	PV at 7%
1	5.8	5.4206
2	5.8	5.0659
3	5.8	4.7345
4	105.8	80.7143
	Total	$95.9353

B. The price of the 3-year 5.8% coupon bond assuming the yield is unchanged at 7% is $96.8508, as shown below:

Year	Cash Flow	PV at 7%
1	5.8	5.4206
2	5.8	5.0659
3	105.8	86.3643
	Total	$96.8508

C. The price is $98.9347 as shown below:

Year	Cash Flow	PV at 6.2%
1	5.8	5.4614
2	5.8	5.1426
3	105.8	88.3308
	Total	$98.9347

D.

Price change attributable to moving to maturity (no change in discount rate)	$0.9155	(96.8508 – 95.9353)
Price change attribute to a decrease in the discount rate from 7% to 6.2%	$2.0839	(98.9347 – 96.8508)
Total price change	$2.9994	

6. The value is $94.2148 as shown below:

Year	Discount Rate (%)	Cash Flow	PV
1	5.90	$ 5.8	$ 5.4769
2	6.40	5.8	5.1232
3	6.60	5.8	4.7880
4	6.90	5.8	4.4414
5	7.30	105.8	74.3853
		Total	94.2148

7. The value is $107.7561 as shown below:

Period	Discount Rate	Cash Flow	PV at 2.8%
1	0.028	$ 3.7	$ 3.5992
2	0.028	3.7	3.5012

(continued)

Period	Discount Rate	Cash Flow	PV at 2.8%
3	0.028	3.7	3.4058
4	0.028	3.7	3.3131
5	0.028	3.7	3.2228
6	0.028	3.7	3.1350
7	0.028	3.7	3.0496
8	0.028	3.7	2.9666
9	0.028	3.7	2.8858
10	0.028	103.7	78.6770
		Total	107.7561

Alternatively, the short-cut formula can be used

> Semiannual coupon payment = $3.70
>
> Semiannual discount rate = 2.8%
>
> Number of years = 5

then

$$\$3.70 \times \left[\frac{1 - \dfrac{1}{(1.028)^{5 \times 2}}}{0.028} \right] = \$31.8864$$

To determine the price, the present value of the maturity value must be added to the present value of the coupon payments. The present value of the maturity value is

$$\text{Present value of maturity value} = \frac{\$100}{(1.028)^{5 \times 2}} = \$75.8698$$

The price is then $107.7561 ($31.8864 + $75.8698). This agrees with our previous calculation for the price of this bond.

8. $\dfrac{\$1,000,000}{(1.038)^{40}} = \$224,960.29$

9. A. First, w must be calculated. We know that

> Days between settlement date and next coupon payment   115
>
> Days in the coupon period   183

Therefore,

$$w \text{ periods} = \frac{115}{183} = 0.6284$$

Since the discount rate is 5.6%, the semiannual rate is 2.8%. The present value of the cash flows is $108.8676 and is therefore the full price.

Period	Cash Flow	PV at 2.8%
1	$ 3.7	$ 3.6363
2	3.7	3.5373
3	3.7	3.4410

Period	Cash Flow	PV at 2.8%
4	3.7	3.3472
5	3.7	3.2561
6	3.7	3.1674
7	3.7	3.0811
8	3.7	2.9972
9	3.7	2.9155
10	103.7	79.4885
	Total	108.8676

Alternative Approach

The dirty price or full price is the clean price plus accrued interest.

The accrued interest earned to date is approximately 3.7(68/183) = 1.375

Solving for the clean price can be approached in a number of alternative ways including using a financial calculator.

N = 9.6284
I/Y = 2.8
PMT = 3.7
FV = 100
Solving PV = −107.50 = clean price
Full or dirty price 107.50 + 1.38 = 108.88

B. The accrued interest is

$$AI = \text{Semiannual coupon payment} \times (1 - w)$$
$$AI = \$3.7 \times (1 - 0.6284) = 1.3749$$

C. The clean price is

$$\text{Clean price} = \text{Full price} - \text{Accrued interest}$$
$$\$108.8676 - \$1.3749 = \$107.4927$$

10. A. The arbitrage-free value was found in Practice Question 9A to be $111.3324.

B. The price based on single discount rate of 5.65% is $111.1395 as shown below:

Period	Years	Cash Flow	PV at 2.825%
1	0.5	3.7	3.5983
2	1.0	3.7	3.4995
3	1.5	3.7	3.4033
4	2.0	3.7	3.3098
5	2.5	3.7	3.2189
6	3.0	3.7	3.1305
7	3.5	3.7	3.0445
8	4.0	3.7	2.9608

(continued)

Period	Years	Cash Flow	PV at 2.825%
9	4.5	3.7	2.8795
10	5.0	3.7	2.8004
11	5.5	3.7	2.7234
12	6.0	3.7	2.6486
13	6.5	3.7	2.5758
14	7.0	3.7	2.5051
15	7.5	3.7	2.4362
16	8.0	103.7	66.4048
		Total	111.1395

C. Dealers would buy the 7.4% 8-year issue for $111.1395, strip it, and sell the Treasury strips for $111.3324. The arbitrage profit is $0.1929 ($111.3324 – $111.1395). The table below shows how that arbitrage profit is realized.

Period	Years	Sell for	Buy for	Arbitrage Profit
1	0.5	3.6453	3.5983	0.0470
2	1.0	3.5809	3.4995	0.0814
3	1.5	3.5121	3.4033	0.1087
4	2.0	3.4238	3.3098	0.1140
5	2.5	3.3155	3.2189	0.0966
6	3.0	3.2138	3.1305	0.0833
7	3.5	3.1167	3.0445	0.0722
8	4.0	3.0291	2.9608	0.0683
9	4.5	2.9407	2.8795	0.0612
10	5.0	2.8516	2.8004	0.0513
11	5.5	2.7621	2.7234	0.0387
12	6.0	2.6723	2.6486	0.0237
13	6.5	2.5822	2.5758	0.0064
14	7.0	2.5026	2.5051	−0.0024
15	7.5	2.4240	2.4362	−0.0123
16	8.0	65.7597	66.4048	−0.6451
Total		111.3324	111.1395	0.1929

D. The process of bidding up the price of the 7.4% 8-year Treasury issue by dealers in order to strip it will increase the price until no material arbitrage profit is available—the arbitrage-free value of $111.3324.

11. A. The arbitrage-free value was found in Practice Question 9B to be $89.3155.

B. The price based on a single discount rate of 5.65% is as shown below to be $89.4971.

Period	Years	Cash Flow	PV at 2.825%
1	0.5	$ 2	$ 1.9451
2	1.0	2	1.8916
3	1.5	2	1.8396
4	2.0	2	1.7891

Period	Years	Cash Flow	PV at 2.825%
5	2.5	2	1.7399
6	3.0	2	1.6921
7	3.5	2	1.6457
8	4.0	2	1.6004
9	4.5	2	1.5565
10	5.0	2	1.5137
11	5.5	2	1.4721
12	6.0	2	1.4317
13	6.5	2	1.3923
14	7.0	2	1.3541
15	7.5	2	1.3169
16	8.0	102	65.3162
		Total	89.4971

C. The dealer will buy a package of Treasury strips such that the cash flow from the package will replicate the cash flow of a 4% 8-year Treasury issue and sell the overvalued Treasury issue. The cost of buying the package of Treasury strips is $89.3155. The value of selling the Treasury issue or, if reconstituted, the value of the synthetic coupon Treasury created is $89.4971. The arbitrage profit is therefore $0.1816 ($89.4971 − $89.3155).

D. The process of dealers selling the Treasury issue will drive down its prices until the market price is close to the arbitrage-free value of $89.3154.

12. B is correct. The present value of the bond is the sum of the present values of the bond's future cash flows:

Year 1: Present value$_1$ = $50/(1.03) = $48.5437

Year 2: Present value$_2$ = $50/(1.03)^2$ = $47.1298

Year 3: Present value$_3$ = $1,050/(1.03)^3$ = $960.8987

PV = ($48.5437 + $47.1298 + $960.8987) = $1,056.57

13. B is correct. Assuming that the discount rate remains constant, a bond that is selling at a premium (greater than par) will decrease in price as it moves toward maturity.

14. A is correct.

The present value of the bond = Maturity value / $(1 + i)^{\text{Years to maturity} \times 2}$

Where: i = semiannual discount rate = 6% / 2 = 3%

$$PV = \$1,000/(1.03)^6 = \$837.48$$

15. C is correct. Note that the four cash flows are, in percent of par terms, 5, 5, 5, and 105. Adjust the spot rates for semiannual compounding. Solve (5 / 1.03) + (5 / (1.0375)^2) + (5 / (1.045)^3) + (105 / (1.05)^4) = 100.2647 percent of par. As par is $1,000,000, the correct answer is $1,002,647.

16. B is correct. Use semiannual compounding. Solve $1,000,000 / (1.055)^6 = $725,246.

17. B is correct. The bond is selling at a premium (coupon rate > YTM). As it approaches maturity, the bond's value will decrease towards par value.

18. B is correct. The invoice price equals 101 + (12/32) + (83 / 181 × (5 / 2)) = 102.5214 percent of par. As par is $1,000, the invoice price is $1,025.21.

19. C is correct. Reconstitution is the opposite process of stripping a coupon bond.

20. B is correct. Bond 1 is currently selling at a discount to par and Bond 2 is selling at a premium to par. If the discount rate does not change for either bond, Bond 1 will increase in price and Bond 2 will decrease in price because all bonds are expected to mature at par value.

57

Yield Measures, Spot Rates, and Forward Rates

by Frank J. Fabozzi, CFA

LEARNING OUTCOMES

Mastery	The candidate should be able to:
☐	**a** describe the sources of return from investing in a bond;
☐	**b** calculate and interpret traditional yield measures for fixed-rate bonds and explain their limitations and assumptions;
☐	**c** explain the reinvestment assumption implicit in calculating yield to maturity and describe the factors that affect reinvestment risk;
☐	**d** calculate and interpret the bond equivalent yield of an annual-pay bond and the annual-pay yield of a semiannual-pay bond;
☐	**e** describe the calculation of the theoretical Treasury spot rate curve and calculate the value of a bond using spot rates;
☐	**f** explain nominal, zero-volatility, and option-adjusted spreads and the relations among these spreads and option cost;
☐	**g** explain a forward rate and calculate spot rates from forward rates, forward rates from spot rates, and the value of a bond using forward rates.

INTRODUCTION

1

Frequently, investors assess the relative value of a security by some yield or yield spread measure quoted in the market. These measures are based on assumptions that limit their use to gauge relative value. This reading explains the various yield and yield spread measures and their limitations.

In this reading, we will see a basic approach to computing the spot rates from the on-the-run Treasury issues. We will see the limitations of the nominal spread measure and explain two measures that overcome these limitations—zero-volatility spread and option-adjusted spread.

Fixed Income Analysis for the Chartered Financial Analyst Program, Second Edition, by Frank J. Fabozzi, CFA. Copyright © 2004 by CFA Institute.

2 SOURCES OF RETURN

When an investor purchases a fixed income security, he or she can expect to receive a dollar return from one or more of the following sources:

1. the coupon interest payments made by the issuer

2. any capital gain (or capital loss—a negative dollar return) when the security matures, is called, or is sold

3. income from reinvestment of interim cash flows (interest and/or principal payments prior to stated maturity)

Any yield measure that purports to measure the potential return from a fixed income security should consider all three sources of return described above.

2.1 Coupon Interest Payments

The most obvious source of return on a bond is the periodic coupon interest payments. For zero-coupon instruments, the return from this source is zero. By purchasing a security below its par value and receiving the full par value at maturity, the investor in a zero-coupon instrument is effectively receiving interest in a lump sum.

2.2 Capital Gain or Loss

An investor receives cash when a bond matures, is called, or is sold. If these proceeds are greater than the purchase price, a capital gain results. For a bond held to maturity, there will be a capital gain if the bond is purchased below its par value. For example, a bond purchased for $94.17 with a par value of $100 will generate a capital gain of $5.83 ($100 − $94.17) if held to maturity. For a callable bond, a capital gain results if the price at which the bond is called (i.e., the call price) is greater than the purchase price. For example, if the bond in our previous example is callable and subsequently called at $100.50, a capital gain of $6.33 ($100.50 − $94.17) will be realized. If the same bond is sold prior to its maturity or before it is called, a capital gain will result if the proceeds exceed the purchase price. So, if our hypothetical bond is sold prior to the maturity date for $103, the capital gain would be $8.83 ($103 − $94.17).

Similarly, for all three outcomes, a capital loss is generated when the proceeds received are less than the purchase price. For a bond held to maturity, there will be a capital loss if the bond is purchased for more than its par value (i.e., purchased at a premium). For example, a bond purchased for $102.50 with a par value of $100 will generate a capital loss of $2.50 ($102.50 − $100) if held to maturity. For a callable bond, a capital loss results if the price at which the bond is called is less than the purchase price. For example, if the bond in our example is callable and subsequently called at $100.50, a capital loss of $2 ($102.50 − $100.50) will be realized. If the same bond is sold prior to its maturity or before it is called, a capital loss will result if the sale price is less than the purchase price. So, if our hypothetical bond is sold prior to the maturity date for $98.50, the capital loss would be $4 ($102.50 − $98.50).

2.3 Reinvestment Income

Prior to maturity, with the exception of zero-coupon instruments, fixed income securities make periodic interest payments that can be reinvested. Amortizing securities (such as mortgage-backed securities and asset-backed securities) make periodic principal payments that can be reinvested prior to final maturity. The interest earned from reinvesting the interim cash flows (interest and/or principal payments) prior to final or stated maturity is called reinvestment income.

TRADITIONAL YIELD MEASURES

3

Yield measures cited in the bond market include current yield, yield to maturity, yield to call, yield to put, yield to worst, and cash flow yield. These yield measures are expressed as a percent return rather than a dollar return. Below we explain how each measure is calculated and its limitations.

3.1 Current Yield

The current yield relates the annual dollar coupon interest to a bond's market price. The formula for the current yield is:

$$\text{Current yield} = \frac{\text{Annual dollar coupon interest}}{\text{Price}}$$

For example, the current yield for a 7% 8-year bond whose price is $94.17 is 7.43% as shown below:

Annual dollar coupon interest $= 0.07 \times \$100 = \$7$

Price $= \$94.17$

$$\text{Current yield} = \frac{\$7}{\$94.17} = 0.0743 \text{ or } 7.43\%$$

The current yield will be greater than the coupon rate when the bond sells at a discount; the reverse is true for a bond selling at a premium. For a bond selling at par, the current yield will be equal to the coupon rate.

The drawback of the current yield is that it considers only the coupon interest and no other source for an investor's return. No consideration is given to the capital gain an investor will realize when a bond purchased at a discount is held to maturity; nor is there any recognition of the capital loss an investor will realize if a bond purchased at a premium is held to maturity. No consideration is given to reinvestment income.

3.2 Yield to Maturity

The most popular measure of yield in the bond market is the **yield to maturity**. The yield to maturity is the interest rate that will make the present value of a bond's cash flows equal to its market price plus accrued interest. To find the yield to maturity, we first determine the expected cash flows and then search, by trial and error, for the interest rate that will make the present value of cash flows equal to the market price plus accrued interest. (This is simply a special case of an **internal rate of return (IRR)** calculation where the cash flows are those received if the bond is held to the maturity date.) In the illustrations presented in this reading, we assume that the next coupon payment will be six months from now so that there is no accrued interest.

To illustrate, consider a 7% 8-year bond selling for $94.17. The cash flows for this bond are 1) 16 payments every 6-months of $3.50 and 2) a payment sixteen 6-month periods from now of $100. The present value using various *semiannual* discount (interest) rates is:

Semiannual Interest Rate	3.5%	3.6%	3.7%	3.8%	3.9%	4.0%
Present Value	100.00	98.80	97.62	96.45	95.30	94.17

When a 4.0% interest rate is used, the present value of the cash flows is equal to $94.17, which is the price of the bond. Hence, 4.0% is the *semiannual* yield to maturity.

The market convention adopted to annualize the semiannual yield to maturity is to double it and call that the yield to maturity. Thus, the yield to maturity for the above bond is 8% (2 times 4.0%). The yield to maturity computed using this convention—doubling the semiannual yield—is called a **bond-equivalent yield**.

The following relationships between the price of a bond, coupon rate, current yield, and yield to maturity hold:

Bond Selling at	Relationship
Par	Coupon rate = Current yield = Yield to maturity
Discount	Coupon rate < Current yield < Yield to maturity
Premium	Coupon rate > Current yield > Yield to maturity

Practice Question 1

Determine whether the yield to maturity of a 6% 15-year bond selling for $84.25 is either 7.2%, 7.6%, or 7.8%.

3.2.1 The Bond-Equivalent Yield Convention

The *convention* developed in the bond market to move from a semiannual yield to an annual yield is to simply double the semiannual yield. As just noted, this is called the bond-equivalent yield. In general, when one doubles a semiannual yield (or a semiannual return) to obtain an annual measure, one is said to be computing the measure on a **bond-equivalent basis**.

Students of the bond market are troubled by this convention. The two questions most commonly asked are: First, why is the practice of simply doubling a semiannual yield followed? Second, wouldn't it be more appropriate to compute the effective annual yield by compounding the semiannual yield?[1]

The answer to the first question is that it is simply a convention. There is no danger with a convention unless you use it improperly. The fact is that market participants recognize that a yield (or return) is computed on a semiannual basis by convention and adjust accordingly when using the number. So, if the bond-equivalent yield on a security purchased by an investor is 6%, the investor knows the semiannual yield is 3%. Given that, the investor can use that semiannual yield to compute an effective annual yield or any other annualized measure desired. For a manager comparing the yield on a security as an asset purchased to a yield required on a liability to satisfy, the yield figure will be measured in a manner consistent with that of the yield required on the liability.

The answer to the second question is that it is true that computing an effective annual yield would be better. But so what? Once we discover the limitations of yield measures in general, we will question whether or not an investor should use a bond-equivalent yield measure or an effective annual yield measure in making investment decisions. That is, when we identify the major problems with yield measures, the doubling of a semiannual yield is the least of our problems.

So, don't lose any sleep over this convention. Just make sure that you use a bond-equivalent yield measure properly.

---

1 By compounding the semiannual yield it is meant that the annual yield is computed as follows:
Effective annual yield $= (1 + \text{Semiannual yield})^2 - 1$

3.2.2 *Limitations of Yield-to-Maturity Measure*

The yield to maturity considers not only the coupon income but any capital gain or loss that the investor will realize by holding the bond to maturity. The yield to maturity also considers the timing of the cash flows. *It does consider reinvestment income; however, it assumes that the coupon payments can be reinvested at an interest rate equal to the yield to maturity.* So, if the yield to maturity for a bond is 8%, for example, to earn that yield the coupon payments must be reinvested at an interest rate equal to 8%.

The illustrations below clearly demonstrate this. In the illustrations, the analysis will be in terms of dollars. Be sure you keep in mind the difference between the total future dollars, which is equal to all the dollars an investor expects to receive (including the recovery of the principal), and the total dollar return, which is equal to the dollars an investor expects to realize from the three sources of return (coupon payments, capital gain/loss, and reinvestment income).

Suppose an investor has $94.17 and places the funds in a certificate of deposit (CD) that matures in 8 years. Let's suppose that the bank agrees to pay 4% interest every six months. This means that the bank is agreeing to pay 8% on a bond-equivalent basis (i.e., doubling the semiannual yield). We can translate all of this into the total future dollars that will be generated by this investment at the end of 8 years. From the standard formula for the future value of an investment today, we can determine the total future dollars as:

$$\$94.17 \times (1.04)^{16} = \$176.38$$

So, to an investor who invests $94.17 for 8 years at an 8% yield on a bond-equivalent basis and interest is paid semiannually, the investment will generate $176.38. Decomposing the total future dollars we see that:

Total future dollars	=	$176.38
Return of principal	=	$94.17
Total interest from CD	=	$82.21

Thus, any investment that promises a yield of 8% on a bond-equivalent basis for 8 years on an investment of $94.17 must generate total future dollars of $176.38 or equivalently a return from all sources of $82.21. That is, if we look at the three sources of a bond return that offered an 8% yield with semiannual coupon payments and sold at a price of $94.17, the following would have to hold:

	Coupon interest
+	Capital gain
+	Reinvestment income
=	Total dollar return = Total interest from CD = $82.21

Now, instead of a certificate of deposit, suppose that an investor purchases a bond with a coupon rate of 7% that matures in 8 years. We know that the three sources of return are coupon income, capital gain/loss, and reinvestment income. Suppose that the price of this bond is $94.17. The yield to maturity for this bond (on a bond-equivalent basis) is 8%. Notice that this is the same type of investment as the certificate of deposit—the bank offered an 8% yield on a bond-equivalent basis for 8 years and made payments semiannually. So, what should the investor in this bond expect in terms of *total future dollars*? As we just demonstrated, an investment of $94.17 must generate $176.38 in order to say that it provided a yield of 8%. Or equivalently, the total dollar return that must be generated is $82.21. Let's look at what in fact is generated in terms of dollar return.

The coupon is $3.50 every six months. So the dollar return from the coupon interest is $3.50 for 16 six-month periods, or $56. When the bond matures, there is a capital gain of $5.83 ($100 – $94.17). Therefore, based on these two sources of return we have:

Coupon interest	=	$56.00
Capital gain	=	$5.83
Dollar return *without reinvestment income*	=	$61.83

Something's wrong here. Only $61.83 is generated from the bond, whereas $82.21 is needed in order to say that this bond provided an 8% yield. That is, there is a dollar return shortfall of $20.38 ($82.21 – $61.83). How is this dollar return shortfall generated?

Recall that in the case of the certificate of deposit, the bank does the reinvesting of the principal and interest, and pays 4% every six months or 8% on a bond equivalent basis. In contrast, for the bond, the investor has to reinvest any coupon interest until the bond matures. It is the reinvestment income that must generate the dollar return shortfall of $20.38. But at what yield will the investor have to reinvest the coupon payments in order to generate the $20.38? The answer is: the yield to maturity.[2] That is, the reinvestment income will be $20.38 if each semiannual coupon payment of $3.50 can be reinvested at a semiannual yield of 4% (one half the yield to maturity). The reinvestment income earned on a given coupon payment of $3.50, if it is invested from the time of receipt in period t to the maturity date (16 periods in our example) at a 4% semiannual rate, is:

$$\$3.50(1.04)^{16-t} - \$3.50$$

The first coupon payment ($t = 1$) can be reinvested for 15 periods. Applying the formula above we find the reinvestment income earned on the first coupon payment is:

$$\$3.50(1.04)^{16-1} - \$3.50 = \$2.80$$

Similarly, the reinvestment income for all coupon payments is shown below:

Period	Periods Reinvested	Coupon Payment	Reinvestment Income
1	15	$3.5	$2.80
2	14	3.5	2.56
3	13	3.5	2.33
4	12	3.5	2.10
5	11	3.5	1.89
6	10	3.5	1.68
7	9	3.5	1.48

---

2 This can be verified by using the future value of an annuity. The future of an annuity is given by the following formula:

$$\text{Annuity payment}\left[\frac{(1+i)^n - 1}{i}\right]$$

where i is the interest rate and n is the number of periods.
In our example, i is 4%, n is 16, and the amount of the annuity is the semiannual coupon of $3.50. Therefore, the future value of the coupon payment is

$$\$3.50\left[\frac{(1.04)^{16} - 1}{0.04}\right] = \$76.38$$

Since the coupon payments are $56, the reinvestment income is $20.38 ($76.38 – $56). This is the amount that is necessary to produce the dollar return shortfall in our example.

Period	Periods Reinvested	Coupon Payment	Reinvestment Income
8	8	3.5	1.29
9	7	3.5	1.11
10	6	3.5	0.93
11	5	3.5	0.76
12	4	3.5	0.59
13	3	3.5	0.44
14	2	3.5	0.29
15	1	3.5	0.14
16	0	3.5	0.00
		Total	$20.39

The total reinvestment income is $20.39 (differing from $20.38 due to rounding).

So, with the reinvestment income of $20.38 at 4% semiannually (i.e., one-half the yield to maturity on a bond-equivalent basis), the total dollar return is

Coupon interest	=	$56.00
Capital gain	=	$5.83
Reinvestment income	=	$20.38
Total dollar return	=	$82.21

In our illustration, we used an investment in a certificate of deposit to show what the total future dollars will have to be in order to obtain a yield of 8% on an investment of $94.17 for 8 years when interest payments are semiannual. However, this holds for any type of investment, not just a certificate of deposit. For example, if an investor is told that he or she can purchase a debt instrument for $94.17 that offers an 8% yield (on a bond-equivalent basis) for 8 years and makes interest payments semiannually, then the investor should translate this yield into the following:

I should be receiving total future dollars of $176.38.

I should be receiving a total dollar return of $82.21.

It is always important to think in terms of dollars (or pound sterling, yen, or other currency) because "yield measures" are misleading.

We can also see that the reinvestment income can be a significant portion of the total dollar return. In our example, the total dollar return is $82.21, and the total dollar return from reinvestment income to make up the shortfall is $20.38. This means that reinvestment income is about 25% of the total dollar return.

This is such an important point that we should go through this one more time for another bond. Suppose an investor purchases a 15-year 8% coupon bond at par value ($100). The yield for this bond is simple to determine since the bond is trading at par. The yield is equal to the coupon rate, 8%. Let's translate this into dollars. We know that if an investor makes an investment of $100 for 15 years that offers an 8% yield and the interest payments are semiannual, the total future dollars will be:

$$\$100 \times (1.04)^{30} = 324.34$$

Decomposing the total future dollars we see that:

Total future dollars	=	$324.34
Return of principal	=	$100.00
Total dollar return	=	$224.34

Without reinvestment income, the dollar return is:

Coupon interest	=	$120
Capital gain	=	$ 0
Dollar return *without reinvestment income*	=	$120

Note that the capital gain is $0 because the bond is purchased at par value.

The dollar return shortfall is therefore $104.34 ($224.34 − $120). This shortfall is made up if the coupon payments can be reinvested at a yield of 8% (the yield on the bond at the time of purchase). For this bond, the reinvestment income is 46.5% of the total dollar return needed to produce a yield of 8% ($104.34/$224.34).[3]

Clearly, the investor will only realize the yield to maturity stated at the time of purchase if the following two assumptions hold:

Assumption 1:	The coupon payments can be reinvested at the yield to maturity.
Assumption 2:	The bond is held to maturity.

With respect to the first assumption, the risk that an investor faces is that future interest rates will be less than the yield to maturity at the time the bond is purchased, known as reinvestment risk. If the bond is not held to maturity, the investor faces the risk that he may have to sell for less than the purchase price, resulting in a return that is less than the yield to maturity, known as interest rate risk.

Practice Question 2

A. Suppose that an investor purchases a 6% coupon bond with 20 years to maturity at a price of $89.32 per $100 par value. The yield to maturity for this bond is 7%. Determine the dollar return that must be generated from reinvestment income in order to generate a yield of 7% and the percentage of the reinvestment income relative to the total dollar return needed to generate a 7% yield.

B. Suppose that a zero-coupon bond that matures in 10 years is selling to yield 7%. Determine the dollar return that must be generated from reinvestment income in order to generate a yield of 7% and the percentage of the reinvestment income relative to the total dollar return needed to generate a 7% yield.

3.2.3 *Factors Affecting Reinvestment Risk*

There are two characteristics of a bond that affect the degree of reinvestment risk:

Characteristic 1:	For a given yield to maturity and a given non-zero coupon rate, the longer the maturity, the more the bond's total dollar return depends on reinvestment income to realize the yield to maturity at the time of purchase—that is, the greater the reinvestment risk.

---

3 The future value of the coupon payments of $4 for 30 six-month periods is:

$$\$4.00 \left[\frac{(1.04)^{30} - 1}{0.04} \right] = \$224.34$$

Since the coupon payments are $120 and the capital gain is $0, the reinvestment income is $104.34. This is the amount that is necessary to produce the dollar return shortfall in our example.

The implication is the yield to maturity measure for long-term maturity coupon bonds tells little about the potential return that an investor may realize if the bond is held to maturity. For long-term bonds, in high interest rate environments, the reinvestment income component may be as high as 70% of the bond's total dollar return.

Characteristic 2:   For a coupon paying bond, for a given maturity and a given yield to maturity, the higher the coupon rate, the more dependent the bond's total dollar return will be on the reinvestment of the coupon payments in order to produce the yield to maturity at the time of purchase.

This means that holding maturity and yield to maturity constant, bonds selling at a premium will be more dependent on reinvestment income than bonds selling at par. This is because the reinvestment income has to make up the capital loss due to amortizing the price premium when holding the bond to maturity. In contrast, a bond selling at a discount will be less dependent on reinvestment income than a bond selling at par because a portion of the return is coming from the capital gain due to accrediting the price discount when holding the bond to maturity. For zero-coupon bonds, none of the bond's total dollar return is dependent on reinvestment income. So, a zero-coupon bond has no reinvestment risk if held to maturity.

The dependence of the total dollar return on reinvestment income for bonds with different coupon rates and maturities is shown in Exhibit 1.

Exhibit 1	Percentage of Total Dollar Return from Reinvestment Income for a Bond to Generate an 8% Yield (BEY)				
	Years to Maturity				
	2	**3**	**5**	**8**	**15**
Bond with a 7% Coupon					
Price	98.19	97.38	95.94	94.17	91.35
% of total	5.2%	8.6%	15.2%	24.8%	44.5%
Bond with an 8% Coupon					
Price	100.00	100.00	100.00	100.00	100.00
% of total	5.8%	9.5%	16.7%	26.7%	46.5%
Bond with a 12% Coupon					
Price	107.26	110.48	116.22	122.30	134.58
% of total	8.1%	12.9%	21.6%	31.0%	51.8%

3.2.4 *Comparing Semiannual-Pay and Annual-Pay Bonds*

In our yield calculations, we have been dealing with bonds that pay interest semiannually. A non-U.S. bond may pay interest annually rather than semiannually. This is the case for many government bonds in Europe and Eurobonds. In such instances, an adjustment is required to make a direct comparison between the yield to maturity on a U.S. fixed-rate bond and that on an annual-pay non-U.S. fixed-rate bond.

Given the yield to maturity on an annual-pay bond, its bond-equivalent yield is computed as follows:

Bond-equivalent yield of an annual-pay bond

$$= 2\left[(1 + \text{Yield on annual-pay bond})^{0.5} - 1\right]$$

The term in the square brackets involves determining what semiannual yield, when compounded, produces the yield on an annual-pay bond. Doubling this semiannual yield (i.e., multiplying the term in the square brackets by 2) gives the bond-equivalent yield.

For example, suppose that the yield to maturity on an annual-pay bond is 6%. Then the bond-equivalent yield is:

$$2\left[(1.06)^{0.5} - 1\right] = 5.91\%$$

Notice that the bond-equivalent yield will always be less than the annual-pay bond's yield to maturity.

To convert the bond-equivalent yield of a U.S. bond issue to an annual-pay basis so that it can be compared to the yield on an annual-pay bond, the following formula can be used:

Yield on an annual-pay basis

$$= \left[\left(1 + \frac{\text{Yield on a bond-equivalent basis}}{2}\right)^2 - 1\right]$$

By dividing the yield on a bond-equivalent basis by 2 in the above expression, the semiannual yield is computed. The semiannual yield is then compounded to get the yield on an annual-pay basis.

For example, suppose that the yield of a U.S. bond issue quoted on a bond-equivalent basis is 6%. The yield to maturity on an annual-pay basis would be:

$$\left[(1.03)^2 - 1\right] = 6.09\%$$

The yield on an annual-pay basis is always greater than the yield on a bond-equivalent basis because of compounding.

Practice Question 3

A. If the yield to maturity on an annual-pay bond is 4.8%, what is the bond-equivalent yield?

B. If the yield of a U.S. bond issue quoted on a bond-equivalent basis is 4.8%, what is the yield to maturity on an annual-pay basis?

3.3 Yield to Call

When a bond is callable, the practice has been to calculate a yield to call as well as a yield to maturity. A callable bond may have a call schedule.[4] The yield to call assumes the issuer will call a bond on some assumed call date and that the call price is the price specified in the call schedule. Typically, investors calculate a yield to first call or yield to next call, a yield to first par call, and a yield to refunding. The yield to first call is computed for an issue that is not currently callable, while the yield to next call is computed for an issue that is currently callable.

---

4 A call schedule shows the call price that the issuer must pay based on the date when the issue is called. An example of a call schedule is provided in the reading on understanding yield spreads.

Yield to refunding is used when bonds are currently callable but have some restrictions on the source of funds used to buy back the debt when a call is exercised. Namely, if a debt issue contains some refunding protection, bonds cannot be called for a certain period of time with the proceeds of other debt issues sold at a lower cost of money. As a result, the bondholder is afforded some protection if interest rates decline and the issuer can obtain lower-cost funds to pay off the debt. It should be stressed that the bonds can be called with funds derived from other sources (e.g., cash on hand) during the refunded-protected period. The refunding date is the first date the bond can be called using lower-cost debt.

The procedure for calculating any yield to call measure is the same as for any yield to maturity calculation: determine the interest rate that will make the present value of the expected cash flows equal to the price plus accrued interest. In the case of yield to first call, the expected cash flows are the coupon payments to the first call date and the call price. For the yield to first par call, the expected cash flows are the coupon payments to the first date at which the issuer can call the bond at par and the par value. For the yield to refunding, the expected cash flows are the coupon payments to the first refunding date and the call price at the first refunding date.

To illustrate the computation, consider a 7% 8-year bond with a maturity value of $100 selling for $106.36. Suppose that the first call date is three years from now and the call price is $103. The cash flows for this bond if it is called in three years are 1) 6 coupon payments of $3.50 every six months and 2) $103 in six 6-month periods from now.

The present value for several semiannual interest rates is shown in Exhibit 2. Since a semiannual interest rate of 2.8% makes the present value of the cash flows equal to the price, 2.8% is the yield to first call. Therefore, the yield to first call on a bond-equivalent basis is 5.6%.

For our 7% 8-year callable bond, suppose that the first par call date is 5 years from now. The cash flows for computing the first par call are then: 1) a total 10 coupon payments of $3.50 each paid every six months and 2) $100 in ten 6-month periods. The yield to par call is 5.53%. Let's verify that this is the case. The semiannual yield is 2.765% (one-half of 5.53%). The present value of the 10 coupon payments of $3.50 every six months when discounted at 2.765% is $30.22. The present value of $100 (the call price of par) at the end of five years (10 semiannual periods) is $76.13. The present value of the cash flow is then $106.35 (= $30.22 + $76.13). Since the price of the bond is $106.36 and since using a yield of 5.53% produces a value for this callable bond that differs from $106.36 by only 1 penny, 5.53% is the yield to first par call.

Let's take a closer look at the yield to call as a measure of the potential return of a security. The yield to call considers all three sources of potential return from owning a bond. However, as in the case of the yield to maturity, it assumes that all cash flows can be reinvested at the yield to call until the assumed call date. As we just demonstrated, this assumption may be inappropriate. Moreover, the yield to call assumes that

Assumption 1:   The investor will hold the bond to the assumed call date.

Assumption 2:   The issuer will call the bond on that date.

| Exhibit 2 | Yield to Call for an 8-Year 7% Coupon Bond with a Maturity Value of $100, First Call Date Is the End of Year 3, and Call Price of $103 |

Annual Interest Rate (%)	Semiannual Interest Rate (%)	Present Value of 6 Payments of $3.5	Present Value of $103 6 Periods from Now	Present Value of Cash Flows
5.0	2.5	$19.28	$88.82	$108.10
5.2	2.6	19.21	88.30	107.51
5.4	2.7	19.15	87.78	106.93
5.6	2.8	19.09	87.27	106.36

These assumptions underlying the yield to call are unrealistic. Moreover, comparison of different yields to call with the yield to maturity are meaningless because the cash flows stop at the assumed call date. For example, consider two bonds, M and N. Suppose that the yield to maturity for bond M, a 5-year noncallable bond, is 7.5% while for bond N the yield to call, assuming the bond will be called in three years, is 7.8%. Which bond is better for an investor with a 5-year investment horizon? It's not possible to tell from the yields cited. If the investor intends to hold the bond for five years and the issuer calls bond N after three years, the total dollar return that will be available at the end of five years will depend on the interest rate that can be earned from investing funds from the call date to the end of the investment horizon.

Practice Question 4

Suppose that a 9% 10-year bond has the following call structure:

not callable for the next 5 years

first callable at beginning of year 6 (i.e., at the end of the fifth year) at $104.50

first par call date at beginning of year 9 (i.e., at the end of the eighth year)

The price of the bond is $123.04.

A. Is the yield to first call for this bond 4.4%, 4.6%, or 4.8%?

B. Is the yield to first par call for this bond 5.41%, 5.62%, or 5.75%?

3.4 Yield to Put

When a bond is putable, the yield to the first put date is calculated. The yield to put is the interest rate that will make the present value of the cash flows to the first put date equal to the price plus accrued interest. As with all yield measures (except the current yield), yield to put assumes that any interim coupon payments can be reinvested at the yield calculated. Moreover, the yield to put assumes that the bond will be put on the first put date.

For example, suppose that a 6.2% coupon bond maturing in 8 years is putable at par in 3 years. The price of this bond is $102.19. The cash flows for this bond if it is put in three years are: 1) a total of 6 coupon payments of $3.10 each paid every six months and 2) the $100 put price in six 6-month periods from now. The semiannual interest rate that will make the present value of the cash flows equal to the price of $102.19 is 2.7%. Therefore, 2.7% is the semiannual yield to put and 5.4% is the yield to put on a bond equivalent basis.

3.5 Yield to Worst

A yield can be calculated for every possible call date and put date. In addition, a yield to maturity can be calculated. The lowest of all these possible yields is called the yield to worst. For example, suppose that there are only four possible call dates for a callable bond, that the yield to call assuming each possible call date is 6%, 6.2%, 5.8%, and 5.7%, and that the yield to maturity is 7.5%. Then the yield to worst is the minimum of these yields, 5.7% in our example.

The yield to worst measure holds little meaning as a measure of potential return. It supposedly states that this is the worst possible yield that the investor will realize. However, as we have noted about any yield measure, it does not identify the potential return over some investment horizon. Moreover, the yield to worst does not recognize that each yield calculation used in determining the yield to worst has different exposures to reinvestment risk.

3.6 Cash Flow Yield

Mortgage-backed securities and asset-backed securities are backed by a pool of loans or receivables. The cash flows for these securities include principal payment as well as interest. The complication that arises is that the individual borrowers whose loans make up the pool typically can prepay their loan in whole or in part prior to the scheduled principal payment dates. Because of principal prepayments, in order to project cash flows it is necessary to make an assumption about the rate at which principal prepayments will occur. This rate is called the prepayment rate or prepayment speed.

Given cash flows based on an assumed prepayment rate, a yield can be calculated. The yield is the interest rate that will make the present value of the projected cash flows equal to the price plus accrued interest. The yield calculated is commonly referred to as a cash flow yield.[5]

3.6.1 *Bond-Equivalent Yield*

Typically, the cash flows for mortgage-backed and asset-backed securities are monthly. Therefore the interest rate that will make the present value of projected principal and interest payments equal to the market price plus accrued interest is a monthly rate. The monthly yield is then annualized as follows.

First, the semiannual effective yield is computed from the monthly yield by compounding it for six months as follows:

$$\text{Effective semiannual yield} = (1 + \text{Monthly yield})^6 - 1$$

Next, the effective semiannual yield is doubled to get the annual cash flow yield on a bond-equivalent basis. That is,

$$\text{Cash flow yield} = 2 \times \text{Effective semiannual yield}$$

$$= 2\left[(1 + \textit{Monthly yield})^6 - 1\right]$$

For example, if the monthly yield is 0.5%, then:

$$\text{Cash flow yield on a bond-equivalent basis} = 2\left[(1.005)^6 - 1\right] = 6.08\%$$

The calculation of the cash flow yield may seem strange because it first requires the computing of an effective semiannual yield given the monthly yield and then doubling. This is simply a market convention. Of course, the student of the bond market

---

5 Some firms such as Prudential Securities refer to this yield as yield to maturity rather than cash flow yield.

can always ask the same two questions as with the yield to maturity: Why it is done? Isn't it better to just compound the monthly yield to get an effective annual yield? The answers are the same as given earlier for the yield to maturity. Moreover, as we will see next, this is the least of our problems in using a cash flow yield measure for an asset-backed and mortgage-backed security.

3.6.2 *Limitations of Cash Flow Yield*

As we have noted, the yield to maturity has two shortcomings as a measure of a bond's potential return: 1) it is assumed that the coupon payments can be reinvested at a rate equal to the yield to maturity and 2) it is assumed that the bond is held to maturity. These shortcomings are equally present in application of the cash flow yield measure: 1) the projected cash flows are assumed to be reinvested at the cash flow yield and 2) the mortgage-backed or asset-backed security is assumed to be held until the final payoff of all the loans, based on some prepayment assumption. The significance of reinvestment risk—the risk that the cash flows will be reinvested at a rate less than the cash flow yield—is particularly important for mortgage-backed and asset-backed securities since payments are typically monthly and include principal payments (scheduled and prepaid) and interest. Moreover, the cash flow yield is dependent on realizing the projected cash flows according to some prepayment rate. If actual prepayments differ significantly from the prepayment rate assumed, the cash flow yield will not be realized.

3.7 Spread/Margin Measures for Floating-Rate Securities

The coupon rate for a floating-rate security (or floater) changes periodically according to a reference rate (such as LIBOR or a Treasury rate). Since the future value for the reference rate is unknown, it is not possible to determine the cash flows. This means that a yield to maturity cannot be calculated. Instead, "margin" measures are computed. Margin is simply some spread above the floater's reference rate.

Several spread or margin measures are routinely used to evaluate floaters. Two margin measures commonly used are spread for life and discount margin.[6]

3.7.1 *Spread for Life*

When a floater is selling at a premium/discount to par, investors consider the premium or discount as an additional source of dollar return. Spread for life (also called simple margin) is a measure of potential return that accounts for the accretion (amortization) of the discount (premium) as well as the constant quoted margin over the security's remaining life. Spread for life (in basis points) is calculated using the following formula:

$$\text{Spread for life} = \left[\frac{100(100 - \text{Price})}{\text{Maturity}} + \text{Quoted margin} \right] \times \left(\frac{100}{\text{Price}} \right)$$

where

$\qquad$ Price = market price per \$100 of par value
$\qquad$ Maturity = number of years to maturity
$\qquad$ Quoted margin = quoted margin in the coupon reset formula measured in basis
$\qquad\qquad\qquad\qquad\qquad$ points

For example, suppose that a floater with a quoted margin of 80 basis points is selling for 99.3098 and matures in 6 years. Then,

---

6 For a discussion of other traditional measures, see Chapter 3 in Frank J. Fabozzi and Steven V. Mann, *Floating Rate Securities* (New Hope, PA; Frank J. Fabozzi Associates, 2000).

$$\text{Price} = 99.3098$$
$$\text{Maturity} = 6$$
$$\text{Quoted margin} = 80$$

$$\text{Spread for life} = \left[\frac{100(100 - 99.3098)}{6} + 80\right] \times \left(\frac{100}{99.3098}\right)$$

$$= 92.14 \text{ Basis points}$$

The limitations of the spread for life are that it considers only the accretion/amortization of the discount/premium over the floater's remaining term to maturity and does not consider the level of the coupon rate or the time value of money.

3.7.2 Discount Margin

Discount margin estimates the average margin over the reference rate that the investor can expect to earn over the life of the security. The procedure for calculating the discount margin is as follows:

Step 1   Determine the cash flows assuming that the reference rate does *not* change over the life of the security.

Step 2   Select a margin.

Step 3   Discount the cash flows found in Step 1 by the current value of the reference rate plus the margin selected in Step 2.

Step 4   Compare the present value of the cash flows as calculated in Step 3 to the price plus accrued interest. If the present value is equal to the security's price plus accrued interest, the discount margin is the margin assumed in Step 2. If the present value is not equal to the security's price plus accrued interest, go back to Step 2 and try a different margin.

For a security selling at par, the discount margin is simply the quoted margin in the coupon reset formula.

To illustrate the calculation, suppose that the coupon reset formula for a 6-year floating-rate security selling for $99.3098 is 6-month LIBOR plus 80 basis points. The coupon rate is reset every 6 months. Assume that the current value for the reference rate is 10%.

Exhibit 3 shows the calculation of the discount margin for this security. The second column shows the current value for 6-month LIBOR. The third column sets forth the cash flows for the security. The cash flow for the first 11 periods is equal to one-half the current 6-month LIBOR (5%) plus the semiannual quoted margin of 40 basis points multiplied by $100. At the maturity date (i.e., period 12), the cash flow is $5.4 plus the maturity value of $100. The column headings of the last five columns show the assumed margin. The rows below the assumed margin show the present value of each cash flow. The last row gives the total present value of the cash flows.

Exhibit 3	**Calculation of the Discount Margin for a Floating-Rate Security**

Floating rate security:

Maturity	=	6 years
Price	=	99.3098
Coupon formula	=	LIBOR + 80 basis points
		Reset every six months

(continued)

| Exhibit 3 | Continued |

Period	LIBOR (%)	Cash Flow ($)[a]	Present Value ($) at Assumed Margin of[b]				
			80 bps	84 bps	88 bps	96 bps	100 bps
1	10	5.4	5.1233	5.1224	5.1214	5.1195	5.1185
2	10	5.4	4.8609	4.8590	4.8572	4.8535	4.8516
3	10	5.4	4.6118	4.6092	4.6066	4.6013	4.5987
4	10	5.4	4.3755	4.3722	4.3689	4.3623	4.3590
5	10	5.4	4.1514	4.1474	4.1435	4.1356	4.1317
6	10	5.4	3.9387	3.9342	3.9297	3.9208	3.9163
7	10	5.4	3.7369	3.7319	3.7270	3.7171	3.7122
8	10	5.4	3.5454	3.5401	3.5347	3.5240	3.5186
9	10	5.4	3.3638	3.3580	3.3523	3.3409	3.3352
10	10	5.4	3.1914	3.1854	3.1794	3.1673	3.1613
11	10	5.4	3.0279	3.0216	3.0153	3.0028	2.9965
12	10	105.4	56.0729	55.9454	55.8182	55.5647	55.4385
		Present value	100.0000	99.8269	99.6541	99.3098	99.1381

[a] For periods 1–11: Cash flow = $100 (0.5) (LIBOR + Assumed margin) For period 12: Cash flow = $100 (0.5) (LIBOR + Assumed margin) + $100

[b] The discount rate is found as follows. To LIBOR of 10%, the assumed margin is added. Thus, for an 80 basis point assumed margin, the discount rate is 10.80%. This is an annual discount rate on a bond-equivalent basis. The semiannual discount rate is then half this amount, 5.4%. It is this discount rate that is used to compute the present value of the cash flows for an assumed margin of 80 basis points.

For the five assumed margins, the present value is equal to the price of the floating-rate security ($99.3098) when the assumed margin is 96 basis points. Therefore, the discount margin is 96 basis points. Notice that the discount margin is 80 basis points, the same as the quoted margin, when this security is selling at par.

There are two drawbacks of the discount margin as a measure of the potential return from investing in a floating-rate security. First, the measure assumes that the reference rate will not change over the life of the security. Second, if the floating-rate security has a cap or floor, this is not taken into consideration.

Practice Question 5

Suppose that the price of the floater in our illustration was 99.8269 rather than 99.3098. Without doing any calculation, determine what the discount margin would be.

3.8 Yield on Treasury Bills

Treasury bills are zero-coupon instruments with a maturity of one year or less. The convention in the Treasury bill market is to calculate a bill's yield on a discount basis. This yield is determined by two variables:

1. the settlement price per $1 of maturity value (denoted by p)

2. the number of days to maturity, which is calculated as the number of days between the settlement date and the maturity date (denoted by N_{SM})

The yield on a discount basis (denoted by d) is calculated as follows:

$$d = (1 - p)\left(\frac{360}{N_{SM}}\right)$$

We will use two actual Treasury bills to illustrate the calculation of the yield on a discount basis assuming a settlement date in both cases of 8/6/97. The first bill has a maturity date of 1/8/98 and a price of 0.97769722. For this bill, the number of days from the settlement date to the maturity date, N_{SM}, is 155. Therefore, the yield on a discount basis is

$$d = (1 - 0.97769722)\left(\frac{360}{155}\right) = 5.18\%$$

For our second bill, the maturity date is 7/23/98 and the price is 0.9490075. Assuming a settlement date of 8/6/97, the number of days from the settlement date to the maturity date is 351. The yield on a discount basis for this bill is

$$d = (1 - 0.9490075)\left(\frac{360}{351}\right) = 5.23\%$$

Given the yield on a discount basis, the price of a bill (per $1 of maturity value) is computed as follows:

$$p = 1 - d(N_{SM}/360)$$

For the 155-day bill selling for a yield on a discount basis of 5.18%, the price per $1 of maturity value is

$$p = 1 - 0.0518(155/360) = 0.97769722$$

For the 351-day bill selling for a yield on a discount basis of 5.23%, the price per $1 of maturity value is

$$p = 1 - 0.0523(351/360) = 0.9490075$$

The quoted yield on a discount basis is not a meaningful measure of the return from holding a Treasury bill for two reasons. First, the measure is based on a maturity value investment rather than on the actual dollar amount invested. Second, the yield is annualized according to a 360-day year rather than a 365-day year, making it difficult to compare yields on Treasury bills with Treasury notes and bonds which pay interest based on the actual number of days in a year. The use of 360 days for a year is a convention for money market instruments. Despite its shortcomings as a measure of return, this is the method dealers have adopted to quote Treasury bills.

Market participants recognize this limitation of yield on a discount basis and consequently make adjustments to make the yield quoted on a Treasury bill comparable to that on a Treasury coupon security. For investors who want to compare the yield on Treasury bills to that of other money market instruments (i.e., debt obligations with a maturity that does not exceed one year), there is a formula to convert the yield on a discount basis to that of a money market yield. The key point is that while the convention is to quote the yield on a Treasury bill in terms of a yield on a discount basis, no one uses that yield measure other than to compute the price given the quoted yield.

Practice Question 6

A. A Treasury bill with 115 days from settlement to maturity is selling for $0.9825 per $1 of maturity value. What is the yield on a discount basis?

> **B.** A Treasury bill with 162 days from settlement to maturity is quoted as having a yield on a discount basis of 5.9%. What is the price of this Treasury bill?

4   THEORETICAL SPOT RATES

The theoretical spot rates for Treasury securities represent the appropriate set of interest rates that should be used to value default-free cash flows. A default-free theoretical spot rate curve can be constructed from the observed Treasury yield curve. There are several approaches that are used in practice. The approach that we describe below for creating a theoretical spot rate curve is called bootstrapping. (The bootstrapping method described here is also used in constructing a theoretical spot rate curve for LIBOR.)

4.1 Bootstrapping

Bootstrapping begins with the yield for the on-the-run Treasury issues because there is no credit risk and no liquidity risk. In practice, however, there is a problem of obtaining a sufficient number of data points for constructing the U.S. Treasury yield curve. In the United States, the U.S. Department of the Treasury currently issues 3-month and 6-month Treasury bills and 2-year, 5-year, 10-year Treasury notes and 30-year Treasury bonds. Issuance of the 30-year bond was suspended October 2001 to February 2006. Treasury bills are zero-coupon instruments and Treasury notes are coupon-paying instruments. Hence, there are not many data points from which to construct a Treasury yield curve, particularly after two years.

On September 5, 2003, Lehman Brothers reported the following values for these four yields:

2 year	1.71%
5 year	3.25%
10 year	4.35%
30 year	5.21%

To fill in the yield for the 25 missing whole year maturities (3 year, 4 year, 6 year, 7 year, 8 year, 9 year, 11 year, and so on to the 29-year maturity), the yield for the 25 whole year maturities are interpolated from the yield on the surrounding maturities. The simplest interpolation, and the one most commonly used in practice, is simple linear interpolation.

For example, suppose that we want to fill in the gap for each one year of maturity. To determine the amount to add to the on-the-run Treasury yield as we go from the lower maturity to the higher maturity, the following formula is used:

$$\frac{\text{Yield at higher maturity} - \text{Yield at lower maturity}}{\text{Number of years between two observed maturity points}}$$

The estimated on-the-run yield for all intermediate whole-year maturities is found by adding the amount computed from the above formula to the yield at the lower maturity.

For example, using the September 5, 2003 yields, the 5-year yield of 3.25% and the 10-year yield of 4.35% are used to obtain the interpolated 6-year, 7-year, 8-year, and 9-year yields by first calculating:

$$\frac{4.35\% - 3.25\%}{5} = 0.22\%$$

Then,

interpolated 6-year yield	=	3.25% + 0.22%	=	3.47%
interpolated 7-year yield	=	3.47% + 0.22%	=	3.69%
interpolated 8-year yield	=	3.69% + 0.22%	=	3.91%
interpolated 9-year yield	=	3.91% + 0.22%	=	4.13%

Thus, when market participants talk about a yield on the Treasury yield curve that is not one of the on-the-run maturities—for example, the 8-year yield—it is only an approximation. Notice that there is a large gap between maturity points. This may result in misleading yields for the interim maturity points when estimated using the linear interpolation method, a point that we return to later in this reading.

To illustrate bootstrapping, we will use the Treasury yields shown in Exhibit 4 for maturities up to 10 years using 6-month periods.[7] Thus, there are 20 Treasury yields shown. The yields shown are assumed to have been interpolated from the on-the-run Treasury issues. Exhibit 5 shows the Treasury yield curve based on the yields shown in Exhibit 4. Our objective is to show how the values in the last column of Exhibit 4 (labeled "Spot Rate") are obtained.

Exhibit 4	Hypothetical Treasury Yields (Interpolated)			
Period	**Years**	**Annual Par Yield to Maturity (BEY) (%)**[a]	**Price**	**Spot Rate (BEY) (%)**[a]
1	0.5	3.00	—	3.0000
2	1.0	3.30	—	3.3000
3	1.5	3.50	100.00	3.5053
4	2.0	3.90	100.00	3.9164
5	2.5	4.40	100.00	4.4376
6	3.0	4.70	100.00	4.7520
7	3.5	4.90	100.00	4.9622
8	4.0	5.00	100.00	5.0650
9	4.5	5.10	100.00	5.1701
10	5.0	5.20	100.00	5.2772
11	5.5	5.30	100.00	5.3864
12	6.0	5.40	100.00	5.4976
13	6.5	5.50	100.00	5.6108
14	7.0	5.55	100.00	5.6643
15	7.5	5.60	100.00	5.7193
16	8.0	5.65	100.00	5.7755
17	8.5	5.70	100.00	5.8331

(continued)

---

7 Two points should be noted about the yields reported in Exhibit 4. First, the yields are unrelated to our earlier Treasury yields on September 5, 2003 that we used to show how to calculate the yield on interim maturities using linear interpolation. Second, the Treasury yields in our illustration after the first year are all shown at par value. Hence the Treasury yield curve in Exhibit 4 is called a *par yield curve*.

Exhibit 4	Continued			
Period	Years	Annual Par Yield to Maturity (BEY) (%)[a]	Price	Spot Rate (BEY) (%)[a]
18	9.0	5.80	100.00	5.9584
19	9.5	5.90	100.00	6.0863
20	10.0	6.00	100.00	6.2169

[a] The yield to maturity and the spot rate are annual rates. They are reported as bond-equivalent yields. To obtain the semiannual yield or rate, one half the annual yield or annual rate is used.

Exhibit 5	Treasury Par Yield Curve

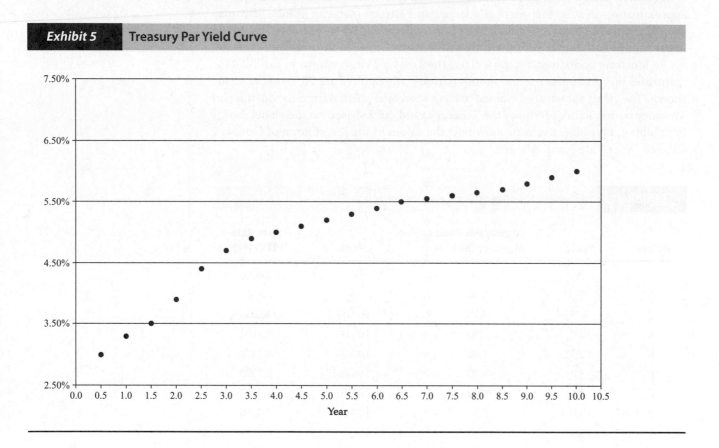

Throughout the analysis and illustrations to come, it is important to remember that the basic principle is the value of the Treasury coupon security should be equal to the value of the package of zero-coupon Treasury securities that duplicates the coupon bond's cash flows. We saw this in the reading on the valuation of debt securities when we discussed arbitrage-free valuation.

Consider the 6-month and 1-year Treasury securities in Exhibit 4. As we explained in the reading on the valuation of debt securities, these two securities are called Treasury bills, and they are issued as zero-coupon instruments. Therefore, the annualized yield (not the discount yield) of 3.00% for the 6-month Treasury security is equal to the 6-month spot rate.[8] Similarly, for the 1-year Treasury security, the cited yield of 3.30% is the 1-year spot rate. Given these two spot rates, we can compute the spot

---

8 We will assume that the annualized yield for the Treasury bill is computed on a bond-equivalent basis. Earlier in this reading, we saw how the yield on a Treasury bill is quoted. The quoted yield can be converted into a bond-equivalent yield; we assume this has already been done in Exhibit 4.

rate for a theoretical 1.5-year zero-coupon Treasury. The value of a theoretical 1.5-year Treasury should equal the present value of the three cash flows from the 1.5-year coupon Treasury, where the yield used for discounting is the spot rate corresponding to the time of receipt of each six-month cash flow. Since all the coupon bonds are selling at par, as explained in the previous section, the yield to maturity for each bond is the coupon rate. Using $100 par, the cash flows for the 1.5-year coupon Treasury are:

0.5 year	0.035	×	$100	×	0.5		=	$1.75
1.0 year	0.035	×	$100	×	0.5		=	$1.75
1.5 years	0.035	×	$100	×	0.5	+ 100	=	$101.75

The present value of the cash flows is then:

$$\frac{1.75}{\left(1 + z_1\right)^1} + \frac{1.75}{\left(1 + z_2\right)^2} + \frac{101.75}{\left(1 + z_3\right)^3}$$

where

z_1 = one-half the annualized 6-month theoretical spot rate
z_2 = one-half the 1-year theoretical spot rate
z_3 = one-half the 1.5-year theoretical spot rate

Since the 6-month spot rate is 3% and the 1-year spot rate is 3.30%, we know that:

$z_1 = 0.0150$ and $z_2 = 0.0165$

We can compute the present value of the 1.5-year coupon Treasury security as:

$$\frac{1.75}{\left(1 + z_1\right)^1} + \frac{1.75}{\left(1 + z_2\right)^2} + \frac{101.75}{\left(1 + z_3\right)^3} = \frac{1.75}{\left(1.015\right)^1} + \frac{1.75}{\left(1.0165\right)^2} + \frac{101.75}{\left(1 + z_3\right)^3}$$

Since the price of the 1.5-year coupon Treasury security is par value (see Exhibit 4), the following relationship must hold[9]:

$$\frac{1.75}{\left(1.015\right)^1} + \frac{1.75}{\left(1.0165\right)^2} + \frac{101.75}{\left(1 + z_3\right)^3} = 100$$

We can solve for the theoretical 1.5-year spot rate as follows:

$$1.7241 + 1.6936 + \frac{101.75}{\left(1 + z_3\right)^3} = 100$$

$$\frac{101.75}{\left(1 + z_3\right)^3} = 96.5822$$

$$\left(1 + z_3\right)^3 = \frac{101.75}{96.5822}$$

$$z_3 = 0.0175265 = 1.7527\%$$

Doubling this yield, we obtain the bond-equivalent yield of 3.5053%, which is the theoretical 1.5-year spot rate. That rate is the rate that the market would apply to a 1.5-year zero-coupon Treasury security if, in fact, such a security existed. In other words, all Treasury cash flows to be received 1.5 years from now should be valued (i.e., discounted) at 3.5053%.

---

9 If we had not been working with a par yield curve, the equation would have been set equal to whatever the market price for the 1.5-year issue is.

Given the theoretical 1.5-year spot rate, we can obtain the theoretical 2-year spot rate. The cash flows for the 2-year coupon Treasury in Exhibit 4 are:

0.5 year	0.039	×	$100	×	0.5		=	$1.95
1.0 year	0.039	×	$100	×	0.5		=	$1.95
1.5 years	0.039	×	$100	×	0.5		=	$1.95
2.0 years	0.039	×	$100	×	0.5	+ 100	=	$101.95

The present value of the cash flows is then:

$$\frac{1.95}{\left(1+z_1\right)^1} + \frac{1.95}{\left(1+z_2\right)^2} + \frac{1.95}{\left(1+z_3\right)^3} + \frac{101.95}{\left(1+z_4\right)^4}$$

where z_4 = one-half the 2-year theoretical spot rate.

Since the 6-month spot rate, 1-year spot rate, and 1.5-year spot rate are 3.00%, 3.30%, and 3.5053%, respectively, then:

$$z_1 = 0.0150 \quad z_2 = 0.0165 \quad z_3 = 0.017527$$

Therefore, the present value of the 2-year coupon Treasury security is:

$$\frac{1.95}{\left(1.0150\right)^1} + \frac{1.95}{\left(1.0165\right)^2} + \frac{1.95}{\left(1.017527\right)^3} + \frac{101.95}{\left(1+z_4\right)^4}$$

Since the price of the 2-year coupon Treasury security is par, the following relationship must hold:

$$\frac{1.95}{\left(1.0150\right)^1} + \frac{1.95}{\left(1.0165\right)^2} + \frac{1.95}{\left(1.017527\right)^3} + \frac{101.95}{\left(1+z_4\right)^4} = 100$$

We can solve for the theoretical 2-year spot rate as follows:

$$\frac{101.95}{\left(1+z_4\right)^4} = 94.3407$$

$$\left(1+z_4\right)^4 = \frac{101.95}{94.3407}$$

$$z_4 = 0.019582 = 1.9582\%$$

Doubling this yield, we obtain the theoretical 2-year spot rate bond-equivalent yield of 3.9164%.

One can follow this approach sequentially to derive the theoretical 2.5-year spot rate from the calculated values of z_1, z_2, z_3, and z_4 (the 6-month, 1-year, 1.5-year, and 2-year rates), and the price and coupon of the 2.5-year bond in Exhibit 4. Further, one could derive theoretical spot rates for the remaining 15 half-yearly rates.

The spot rates thus obtained are shown in the last column of Exhibit 4. They represent the term structure of default-free spot rate for maturities up to 10 years at the particular time to which the bond price quotations refer. In fact, it is the default-free spot rates shown in Exhibit 4 that were used in our illustrations in the previous reading.

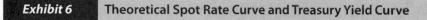

| **Exhibit 6** | Theoretical Spot Rate Curve and Treasury Yield Curve |

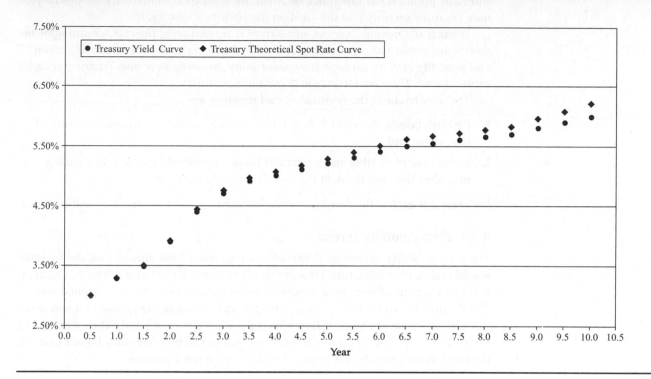

Exhibit 6 shows a plot of the spot rates. The graph is called the theoretical spot rate curve. Also shown on Exhibit 6 is a plot of the par yield curve from Exhibit 5. Notice that the theoretical spot rate curve lies above the par yield curve. This will always be the case when the par yield curve is upward sloping. When the par yield curve is downward sloping, the theoretical spot rate curve will lie below the par yield curve.

Practice Question 7

Show how the 2.5-year spot rate reported in Exhibit 4 is obtained.

4.2 Yield Spread Measures Relative to a Spot Rate Curve

Traditional analysis of the yield spread for a non-Treasury bond involves calculating the difference between the bond's yield and the yield to maturity of a benchmark Treasury coupon security. The latter is obtained from the Treasury yield curve. For example, consider the following 10-year bonds:

Issue	Coupon (%)	Price	Yield to Maturity (%)
Treasury	6	100.00	6.00
Non-Treasury	8	104.19	7.40

The yield spread for these two bonds as traditionally computed is 140 basis points (7.4% minus 6%). We have referred to this traditional yield spread as the nominal spread.

Exhibit 7 shows the Treasury yield curve from Exhibit 5. The nominal spread of 140 basis points is the difference between the 7.4% yield to maturity for the 10-year non-Treasury security and the yield on the 10-year Treasury, 6%.

What is the nominal spread measuring? It is measuring the compensation for the additional credit risk, option risk (i.e., the risk associated with embedded options),[10] *and liquidity risk an investor is exposed to by investing in a non-Treasury security rather than a Treasury security with the same maturity.*

The drawbacks of the nominal spread measure are:

1. for both bonds, the yield fails to take into consideration the term structure of spot rates; and

2. in the case of callable and/or putable bonds, expected interest rate volatility may alter the cash flows of the non-Treasury bond.

Let's examine each of the drawbacks and alternative spread measures for handling them.

4.2.1 *Zero-Volatility Spread*

The zero-volatility spread or Z-spread is a measure of the spread that the investor would realize over the entire Treasury spot rate curve if the bond is held to maturity. It is not a spread off one point on the Treasury yield curve, as is the nominal spread. The Z-spread, also called the static spread, is calculated as the spread that will make the present value of the cash flows from the non-Treasury bond, when discounted at the Treasury spot rate plus the spread, equal to the non-Treasury bond's price. A trial-and-error procedure is required to determine the Z-spread.

Exhibit 7	Illustration of the Nominal Spread

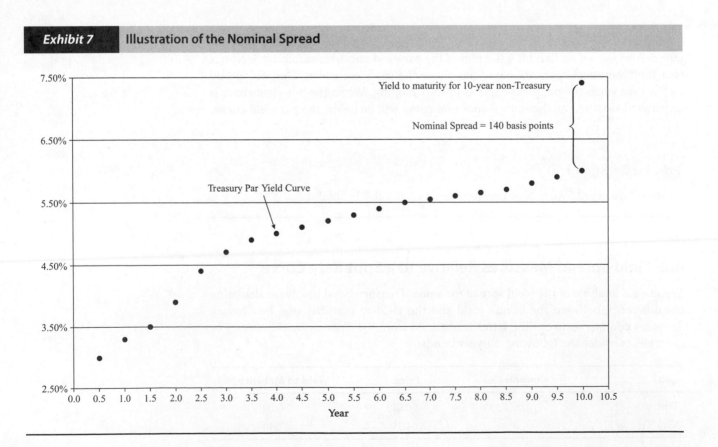

---

10 Option risk includes prepayment and call risk.

Exhibit 8	Determining Z-Spread for an 8% Coupon, 10-Year Non-Treasury Issue Selling at $104.19 to Yield 7.4%

Period	Years	Cash Flow ($)	Spot Rate (%)[a]	Present Value ($) Assuming a Spread of[b]		
				100 bps	125 bps	146 bps
1	0.5	4.00	3.0000	3.9216	3.9168	3.9127
2	1.0	4.00	3.3000	3.8334	3.8240	3.8162
3	1.5	4.00	3.5053	3.7414	3.7277	3.7163
4	2.0	4.00	3.9164	3.6297	3.6121	3.5973
5	2.5	4.00	4.4376	3.4979	3.4767	3.4590
6	3.0	4.00	4.7520	3.3742	3.3497	3.3293
7	3.5	4.00	4.9622	3.2565	3.2290	3.2061
8	4.0	4.00	5.0650	3.1497	3.1193	3.0940
9	4.5	4.00	5.1701	3.0430	3.0100	2.9825
10	5.0	4.00	5.2772	2.9366	2.9013	2.8719
11	5.5	4.00	5.3864	2.8307	2.7933	2.7622
12	6.0	4.00	5.4976	2.7255	2.6862	2.6536
13	6.5	4.00	5.6108	2.6210	2.5801	2.5463
14	7.0	4.00	5.6643	2.5279	2.4855	2.4504
15	7.5	4.00	5.7193	2.4367	2.3929	2.3568
16	8.0	4.00	5.7755	2.3472	2.3023	2.2652
17	8.5	4.00	5.8331	2.2596	2.2137	2.1758
18	9.0	4.00	5.9584	2.1612	2.1148	2.0766
19	9.5	4.00	6.0863	2.0642	2.0174	1.9790
20	10.0	104.00	6.2169	51.1835	49.9638	48.9632
			Total	107.5416	105.7165	104.2146

[a] The spot rate is an annual rate.

[b] The discount rate used to compute the present value of each cash flow in the third column is found by adding the assumed spread to the spot rate and then dividing by 2. For example, for period 4 the spot rate is 3.9164%. If the assumed spread is 100 basis points, then 100 basis points is added to 3.9164% to give 4.9164%. Dividing this rate by 2 gives the semiannual rate of 2.4582%. The present value is then

$$\frac{\text{Cash flow in period } t}{(1.024582)^t}$$

To illustrate how this is done, let's use the non-Treasury bond in our previous illustration and the Treasury spot rates in Exhibit 4. These spot rates are repeated in Exhibit 8. The third column in Exhibit 8 shows the cash flows for the 8% 10-year non-Treasury issue. The goal is to determine the spread that, when added to all the Treasury spot rates, will produce a present value for the cash flows of the non-Treasury bond equal to its market price of $104.19.

Suppose we select a spread of 100 basis points. To each Treasury spot rate shown in the fourth column of Exhibit 8, 100 basis points is added. So, for example, the 5-year (period 10) spot rate is 6.2772% (5.2772% plus 1%). The spot rate plus 100 basis points is then used to calculate the present values as shown in the fifth column. The total present value of the fifth column is $107.5414. Because the present value is not equal to the non-Treasury issue's price ($104.19), the Z-spread is not 100 basis points. If a spread of 125 basis points is tried, it can be seen from the next-to-the-last column of

Exhibit 8 that the present value is \$105.7165; again, because this is not equal to the non-Treasury issue's price, 125 basis points is not the Z-spread. The last column of Exhibit 8 shows the present value when a 146 basis point spread is tried. The present value is equal to the non-Treasury issue's price. Therefore 146 basis points is the Z-spread, compared to the nominal spread of 140 basis points.

A graphical presentation of the Z-spread is shown in Exhibit 9. Since the benchmark for computing the Z-spread is the theoretical spot rate curve, that curve is shown in the exhibit. Above each yield at each maturity on the theoretical spot rate curve is a yield that is 146 basis points higher. This is the Z-spread. It is a spread over the entire spot rate curve.

What should be clear is that the difference between the nominal spread and the Z-spread is the benchmark that is being used: the nominal spread is a spread off of one point on the Treasury yield curve (see Exhibit 7) while the Z-spread is a spread over the entire theoretical Treasury spot rate curve.

What does the Z-spread represent for this non-Treasury security? Since the Z-spread is measured relative to the Treasury spot rate curve, it represents a spread to compensate for the non-Treasury security's credit risk, liquidity risk, and any option risk (i.e., the risks associated with any embedded options).

Exhibit 9	Illustration of the Z-Spread

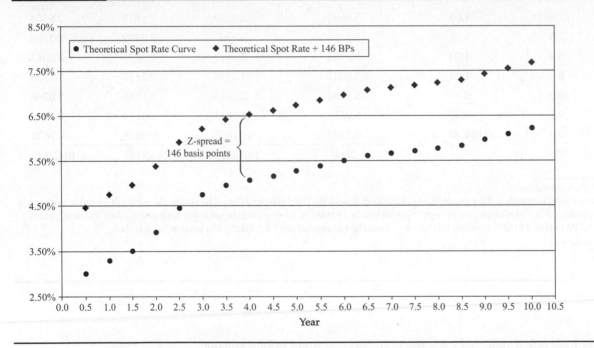

Practice Question 8

Suppose the price of the non-Treasury issue in our example is 105.7165 instead of 104.2145. Without doing computations, what would the Z-spread be?

4.2.1.1 Divergence between Z-Spread and Nominal Spread Typically, for standard coupon-paying bonds with a bullet maturity (i.e., a single payment of principal) the Z-spread and the nominal spread will not differ significantly. In our example, it is only 6 basis points. In general terms, the divergence (i.e., amount of difference) is a function of 1) the shape of the term structure of interest rates and 2) the characteristics of the security (i.e., coupon rate, time to maturity, and type of principal payment provision—non-amortizing versus amortizing).

For short-term issues, there is little divergence. The main factor causing any difference is the shape of the Treasury spot rate curve. The steeper the spot rate curve, the greater the difference. To illustrate this, consider the two spot rate curves shown in Exhibit 10. The yield for the longest maturity of both spot rate curves is 6%. The first curve is steeper than the one used in Exhibit 8; the second curve is flat, with the yield for all maturities equal to 6%. For our 8% 10-year non-Treasury issue, it can be shown that for the first spot rate curve in Exhibit 10 the Z-spread is 192 basis points. Thus, with this steeper spot rate curve, the difference between the Z-spread and the nominal spread is 52 basis points. For the flat curve the Z-spread is 140 basis points, the same as the nominal spread. This will always be the case because the nominal spread assumes that the same yield is used to discount each cash flow and, with a flat yield curve, the same yield is being used to discount each flow. Thus, the nominal yield spread and the Z-spread will produce the same value for this security.

Exhibit 10	Two Hypothetical Spot Rate Curves		
Period	**Years**	**Steep Curve (%)**	**Flat Curve (%)**
1	0.5	2.00	6.00
2	1.0	2.40	6.00
3	1.5	2.80	6.00
4	2.0	2.90	6.00
5	2.5	3.00	6.00
6	3.0	3.10	6.00
7	3.5	3.30	6.00
8	4.0	3.80	6.00
9	4.5	3.90	6.00
10	5.0	4.20	6.00
11	5.5	4.40	6.00
12	6.0	4.50	6.00
13	6.5	4.60	6.00
14	7.0	4.70	6.00
15	7.5	4.90	6.00
16	8.0	5.00	6.00
17	8.5	5.30	6.00
18	9.0	5.70	6.00
19	9.5	5.80	6.00
20	10.0	6.00	6.00

The difference between the Z-spread and the nominal spread is greater for issues in which the principal is repaid over time rather than only at maturity. Thus the difference between the nominal spread and the Z-spread will be considerably greater for mortgage-backed and asset-backed securities in a steep yield curve environment. We can see this intuitively if we think in terms of a 10-year zero-coupon bond and a 10-year amortizing security with equal semiannual cash flows (that includes interest and principal payment). The Z-spread for the zero-coupon bond will not be affected by the shape of the term structure but the amortizing security will be.

4.2.1.2 Z-Spread Relative to Any Benchmark　In the same way that a Z-spread relative to a Treasury spot rate curve can be calculated, a Z-spread to any benchmark spot rate curve can be calculated. To illustrate, suppose that a hypothetical non-Treasury security with a coupon rate of 8% and a 10-year maturity is trading at $105.5423. Assume that the *benchmark spot rate curve for this issuer* is the one given in Exhibit 10 of the previous reading. The Z-spread relative to that issuer's benchmark spot rate curve is the spread that must be added to the spot rates shown in the next-to-last column of that exhibit that will make the present value of the cash flows equal to the market price. In our illustration, the Z-spread relative to this benchmark is 40 basis points.

What does the Z-spread mean when the benchmark is not the Treasury spot rate curve (i.e., default-free spot rate curve)? When the Treasury spot rate curve is the benchmark, we said that the Z-spread for a non-Treasury issue embodies credit risk, liquidity risk, and any option risk. When the benchmark is the spot rate curve for the issuer, the Z-spread is measuring the spread attributable to the liquidity risk of the issue and any option risk.

Thus, when a Z-spread is cited, it must be cited relative to some benchmark spot rate curve. This is necessary because it indicates the credit and sector risks that are being considered when the Z-spread was calculated. While Z-spreads are typically calculated using Treasury securities as the benchmark interest rates, this need not be the case. Vendors of analytical systems commonly allow the user to select a benchmark spot rate curve. Moreover, in non-U.S. markets, Treasury securities are typically not the benchmark. The key point is that an investor should always ask what benchmark was used to compute the Z-spread.

4.2.2 *Option-Adjusted Spread*

The Z-spread seeks to measure the spread over a spot rate curve, thus overcoming the first problem of the nominal spread that we cited earlier. Now let's look at the second shortcoming—failure to take future interest rate volatility into account which could change the cash flows for bonds with embedded options.

4.2.2.1 Valuation Models　What investors seek to do is to buy undervalued securities (securities whose value is greater than their price). Before they can do this though, they need to know what the security is worth (i.e., a fair price to pay). A valuation model is designed to provide precisely this. If a model determines the fair price of a share of common stock is $36 and the market price is currently $24, then the stock is considered to be undervalued. If a bond is selling for less than its fair value, then it too is considered undervalued.

A valuation model need not stop here, however. Market participants find it more convenient to think about yield spread than about price differences. A valuation model can take this difference between the fair price and the market price and convert it into a yield spread measure. Instead of asking, "How much is this security undervalued?", the model can ask, "How much return will I earn in exchange for taking on these risks?"

The option-adjusted spread (OAS) was developed as a way of doing just this: taking the dollar difference between the fair price and market price and converting it into a yield spread measure. Thus, the OAS is used to reconcile the fair price (or value) to the market price by finding a return (spread) that will equate the two (using a trial and error procedure). This is somewhat similar to what we did earlier when calculating yield to maturity, yield to call, etc., only in this case, we are calculating a spread (measured in basis points) rather than a percentage rate of return as we did then.

The OAS is model dependent. That is, the OAS computed depends on the valuation model used. In particular, OAS models differ considerably in how they forecast interest rate changes, leading to variations in the level of OAS. What are two of these key modeling differences?

- Interest rate volatility is a critical assumption. Specifically, when the issuer/
  borrower has the option (e.g., callable bonds and mortgage pass-through
  securities), the higher the interest rate volatility assumed, the lower the OAS.
  In the case of a putable bond, the higher the interest rate volatility assumed, the
  higher the OAS. In comparing OAS of dealer firms, it is important to check on
  the volatility assumption made.

- The OAS is a spread, but what is it a "spread" over? The OAS is a spread over the
  Treasury spot rate curve or the issuer's benchmark used in the analysis. In the
  model, the spot rate curve is actually the result of a series of assumptions that
  allow for changes in interest rates. Again, different models yield different results.

Why is the spread referred to as "option adjusted"? Because the security's embedded
option can change the cash flows; the value of the security should take this change of
cash flow into account. Note that the Z-spread doesn't do this—it ignores the fact that
interest rate changes can affect the cash flows. In essence, it assumes that interest rate
volatility is zero. This is why the Z-spread is also referred to as the zero-volatility OAS.

4.2.2.2 Option Cost

The implied cost of the option embedded in any security can
be obtained by calculating the difference between the OAS at the assumed interest
rate or yield volatility and the Z-spread. That is, since the Z-spread is just the sum of
the OAS and option cost, i.e.,

Z-spread = OAS + Option cost

it follows that:

Option cost = Z-spread − OAS

The reason that the option cost is measured in this way is as follows. In an environment in which interest rates are assumed not to change, the investor would earn the
Z-spread. When future interest rates are uncertain, the spread is different because of
the embedded option(s); the OAS reflects the spread after adjusting for this option.
Therefore, the option cost is the difference between the spread that would be earned
in a static interest rate environment (the Z-spread, or equivalently, the zero-volatility
OAS) and the spread after adjusting for the option (the OAS).

For callable bonds and most mortgage-backed and asset-backed securities, the
option cost is positive. This is because the issuer's ability to alter the cash flows will
result in an OAS that is less than the Z-spread. In the case of a putable bond, the OAS
is greater than the Z-spread so that the option cost is negative. This occurs because
of the investor's ability to alter the cash flows.

In general, when the option cost is positive, this means that the investor has sold
an option to the issuer or borrower. This is true for callable bonds and most mortgage-
backed and asset-backed securities. A negative value for the option cost means that
the investor has purchased an option from the issuer or borrower. A putable bond is
an example of this negative option cost. There are certain securities in the mortgage-
backed securities market that also have an option cost that is negative.

4.2.2.3 Highlighting the Pitfalls of the Nominal Spread

We can use the concepts
presented in this reading to highlight the pitfalls of the nominal spread. First, we can
recast the relationship between the option cost, Z-spread, and OAS as follows:

Z-spread = OAS + Option cost

Next, recall that the nominal spread and the Z-spread may not diverge significantly.
Suppose that the nominal spread is approximately equal to the Z-spread. Then, we can
substitute nominal spread for Z-spread in the previous relationship giving:

Nominal spread ≈ OAS + Option cost

This relationship tells us that a high nominal spread could be hiding a high option cost. The option cost represents the portion of the spread that the investor has given to the issuer or borrower. Thus, while the nominal spread for a security that can be called or prepaid might be, say 200 basis points, the option cost may be 190 and the OAS only 10 basis points. But, an investor is only compensated for the OAS. An investor that relies on the nominal spread may not be adequately compensated for taking on the option risk associated with a security with an embedded option.

4.2.3 *Summary of Spread Measures*

We have just described three spread measures:

- nominal spread;
- zero-volatility spread; and
- option-adjusted spread.

To understand different spread measures we ask two questions:

1. What is the benchmark for computing the spread? That is, what is the spread measured relative to?

2. What is the spread measuring?

The table below provides a summary showing for each of the three spread measures the benchmark and the risks for which the spread is compensating.

Spread Measure	Benchmark	Reflects Compensation for
Nominal	Treasury yield curve	Credit risk, option risk, liquidity risk
Zero-volatility	Treasury spot rate curve	Credit risk, option risk, liquidity risk
Option-adjusted	Treasury spot rate curve	Credit risk, liquidity risk

5   FORWARD RATES

We have seen how a default-free theoretical spot rate curve can be extrapolated from the Treasury yield curve. Additional information useful to market participants can be extrapolated from the default-free theoretical spot rate curve: **forward rates**. Under certain assumptions described later, these rates can be viewed as the market's consensus of future interest rates.

Examples of forward rates that can be calculated from the default-free theoretical spot rate curve are the:

- 6-month forward rate six months from now;
- 6-month forward rate three years from now;
- 1-year forward rate one year from now;
- 3-year forward rate two years from now;
- 5-year forward rates three years from now.

Since the forward rates are implicitly extrapolated from the default-free theoretical spot rate curve, these rates are sometimes referred to as implied forward rates. We begin by showing how to compute the 6-month forward rates. Then we explain how to compute any forward rate.

While we continue to use the Treasury yield curve in our illustrations, as noted earlier, a LIBOR spot rate curve can also be constructed using the bootstrapping methodology and forward rates for LIBOR can be obtained in the same manner as described below.

5.1 Deriving 6-Month Forward Rates

To illustrate the process of extrapolating 6-month forward rates, we will use the yield curve and corresponding spot rate curve from Exhibit 4. We will use a very simple arbitrage principle as we did earlier in this reading to derive the spot rates. Specifically, if two investments have the same cash flows and have the same risk, they should have the same value.

Consider an investor who has a 1-year investment horizon and is faced with the following two alternatives:

- buy a 1-year Treasury bill, or
- buy a 6-month Treasury bill and, when it matures in six months, buy another 6-month Treasury bill.

The investor will be indifferent toward the two alternatives if they produce the same return over the 1-year investment horizon. The investor knows the spot rate on the 6-month Treasury bill and the 1-year Treasury bill. However, he does not know what yield will be on a 6-month Treasury bill purchased six months from now. That is, he does not know the 6-month forward rate six months from now. Given the spot rates for the 6-month Treasury bill and the 1-year Treasury bill, the forward rate on a 6-month Treasury bill is the rate that equalizes the dollar return between the two alternatives.

To see how that rate can be determined, suppose that an investor purchased a 6-month Treasury bill for X. At the end of six months, the value of this investment would be:

$$X(1 + z_1)$$

where z_1 is one-half the bond-equivalent yield (BEY) of the theoretical 6-month spot rate.

Let f represent one-half the forward rate (expressed as a BEY) on a 6-month Treasury bill available six months from now. If the investor were to rollover his investment by purchasing that bill at that time, then the future dollars available at the end of one year from the X investment would be:

$$X(1 + z_1)(1 + f)$$

Now consider the alternative of investing in a 1-year Treasury bill. If we let z_2 represent one-half the BEY of the theoretical 1-year spot rate, then the future dollars available at the end of one year from the X investment would be:

$$X(1 + z_2)^2$$

The reason that the squared term appears is that the amount invested is being compounded for two periods. (Recall that each period is six months.)

The two choices are depicted in Exhibit 11. Now we are prepared to analyze the investor's choices and what this says about forward rates. The investor will be indifferent toward the two alternatives confronting him if he makes the same dollar investment (X) and receives the same future dollars from both alternatives at the end of one year. That is, the investor will be indifferent if:

$$X(1 + z_1)(1 + f) = X(1 + z_2)^2$$

Solving for f, we get:

$$f = \frac{(1+z_2)^2}{(1+z_1)} - 1$$

Doubling f gives the BEY for the 6-month forward rate six months from now.

Exhibit 11	Graphical Depiction of the Six-Month Forward Rate Six Months from Now

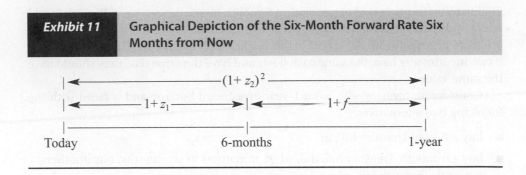

We can illustrate the use of this formula with the theoretical spot rates shown in Exhibit 4. From that exhibit, we know that:

6-month bill spot rate = 0.030, therefore z_1 = 0.0150

1-year bill spot rate = 0.033, therefore z_2 = 0.0165

Substituting into the formula, we have:

$$f = \frac{(1.0165)^2}{(1.0150)} - 1 = 0.0180 = 1.8\%$$

Therefore, the 6-month forward rate six months from now is 3.6% (1.8% × 2) BEY.

Let's confirm our results. If $X invested in the 6-month Treasury bill at 1.5% and the proceeds then reinvested for six months at the 6-month forward rate of 1.8%, the total proceeds from this alternative would be:

$$X(1.0150)(1.018) = 1.03327X$$

Investment of $X in the 1-year Treasury bill at one-half the 1-year rate, 1.0165%, would produce the following proceeds at the end of one year:

$$X(1.0165)^2 = 1.03327X$$

Both alternatives have the same payoff if the 6-month Treasury bill yield six months from now is 1.8% (3.6% on a BEY). This means that, if an investor is guaranteed a 1.8% yield (3.6% BEY) on a 6-month Treasury bill six months from now, he will be indifferent toward the two alternatives.

The same line of reasoning can be used to obtain the 6-month forward rate beginning at any time period in the future. For example, the following can be determined:

■ the 6-month forward rate three years from now;

■ the 6-month forward rate five years from now.

The notation that we use to indicate 6-month forward rates is $_1f_m$ where the subscript 1 indicates a 1-period (6-month) rate and the subscript m indicates the period beginning m periods from now. When m is equal to zero, this means the current rate. Thus, the first 6-month forward rate is simply the current 6-month spot rate. That is, $_1f_0 = z_1$.

The general formula for determining a 6-month forward rate is:

$$_1f_m = \frac{(1+z_{m+1})^{m+1}}{(1+z_m)^m} - 1$$

For example, suppose that the 6-month forward rate four years (eight 6-month periods) from now is sought. In terms of our notation, m is 8 and we seek $_1f_8$. The formula is then:

$$_1f_8 = \frac{(1 + z_9)^9}{(1 + z_8)^8} - 1$$

From Exhibit 4, since the 4-year spot rate is 5.065% and the 4.5-year spot rate is 5.1701%, z_8 is 2.5325% and z_9 is 2.58505%. Then,

$$_1f_8 = \frac{(1.0258505)^9}{(1.025325)^8} - 1 = 3.0064\%$$

Doubling this rate gives a 6-month forward rate four years from now of 6.01%.

Exhibit 12 shows all of the 6-month forward rates for the Treasury yield curve shown in Exhibit 4. The forward rates reported in Exhibit 12 are the annualized rates on a bond-equivalent basis. In Exhibit 13, the short-term forward rates are plotted along with the Treasury par yield curve and theoretical spot rate curve. The graph of the short-term forward rates is called the short-term forward-rate curve. Notice that the short-term forward rate curve lies above the other two curves. This will always be the case if the par yield curve is upward sloping. If the par yield curve is downward sloping, the short-term forward rate curve will be the lowest curve. Notice the unusual shape for the short-term forward rate curve. There is a mathematical reason for this shape. In practice, analysts will use statistical techniques to create a smooth short-term forward rate curve.

Exhibit 12	Six-Month Forward Rates (Annualized Rates on a Bond-Equivalent Basis)

Notation	Forward Rate
$_1f_0$	3.00
$_1f_1$	3.60
$_1f_2$	3.92
$_1f_3$	5.15
$_1f_4$	6.54
$_1f_5$	6.33
$_1f_6$	6.23
$_1f_7$	5.79
$_1f_8$	6.01
$_1f_9$	6.24
$_1f_{10}$	6.48
$_1f_{11}$	6.72
$_1f_{12}$	6.97
$_1f_{13}$	6.36
$_1f_{14}$	6.49
$_1f_{15}$	6.62
$_1f_{16}$	6.76
$_1f_{17}$	8.10
$_1f_{18}$	8.40
$_1f_{19}$	8.71

Exhibit 13	Graph of Short-Term Forward Rate Curve

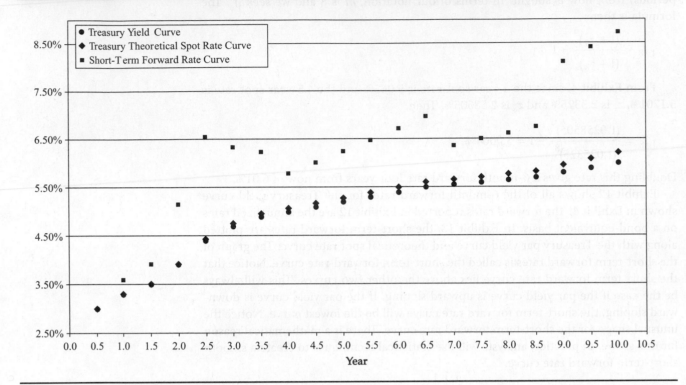

Practice Question 9

Show how the 6-month forward rate 6.5 years (13 periods from now) reported in Exhibit 12 is computed.

5.2 Relationship between Spot Rates and Short-Term Forward Rates

Suppose an investor invests $\$X$ in a 3-year zero-coupon Treasury security. The total proceeds three years (six periods) from now would be:

$$X(1 + z_6)^6$$

The investor could instead buy a 6-month Treasury bill and reinvest the proceeds every six months for three years. The future dollars or dollar return will depend on the 6-month forward rates. Suppose that the investor can actually reinvest the proceeds maturing every six months at the calculated 6-month forward rates shown in Exhibit 12. At the end of three years, an investment of $\$X$ would generate the following proceeds:

$$X(1+z_1)(1+{}_1f_1)(1+{}_1f_2)(1+{}_1f_3)(1+{}_1f_4)(1+{}_1f_5)$$

Since the two investments must generate the same proceeds at the end of three years, the two previous equations can be equated:

$$X(1+z_6)^6 = X(1+z_1)(1+{}_1f_1)(1+{}_1f_2)(1+{}_1f_3)(1+{}_1f_4)(1+{}_1f_5)$$

Solving for the 3-year (6-period) spot rate, we have:

$$z_6 = \left[(1+z_1)(1+{}_1f_1)(1+{}_1f_2)(1+{}_1f_3)(1+{}_1f_4)(1+{}_1f_5)\right]^{1/6} - 1$$

This equation tells us that the 3-year spot rate depends on the current 6-month spot rate and the five 6-month forward rates. In fact, the right-hand side of this equation is a geometric average of the current 6-month spot rate and the five 6-month forward rates.

Let's use the values in Exhibits 4 and 12 to confirm this result. Since the 6-month spot rate in Exhibit 4 is 3%, z_1 is 1.5% and therefore[11]

$$z_6 = \left[(1.015)(1.018)(1.0196)(1.0257)(1.0327)(1.03165)\right]^{1/6} - 1$$
$$= 0.023761 = 2.3761\%$$

Doubling this rate gives 4.7522%. This agrees with the spot rate shown in Exhibit 4.

In general, the relationship between a T-period spot rate, the current 6-month spot rate, and the 6-month forward rates is as follows:

$$z_T = \left[(1+z_1)(1+{_1f_1})(1+{_1f_2})\cdots(1+{_1f_{T-1}})\right]^{1/T} - 1$$

Therefore, discounting at the forward rates will give the same present value as discounting at spot rates.

5.3 Valuation Using Forward Rates

Since a spot rate is simply a package of short-term forward rates, it will not make any difference whether we discount cash flows using spot rates or forward rates. That is, suppose that the cash flow in period T is $1. Then the present value of the cash flow can be found using the spot rate for period T as follows:

$$\text{PV of \$1 in } T \text{ periods} = \frac{1}{\left(1 + z_T\right)^T}$$

Alternatively, since we know that

$$z_T = \left[(1+z_1)(1+{_1f_1})(1+{_1f_2})\cdots(1+{_1f_{T-1}})\right]^{1/T} - 1$$

then, adding 1 to both sides of the equation,

$$(1+z_T) = \left[(1+z_1)(1+{_1f_1})(1+{_1f_2})\cdots(1+{_1f_{T-1}})\right]^{1/T}$$

Raising both sides of the equation to the T-th power we get:

$$(1+z_T)^T = (1+z_1)(1+{_1f_1})(1+{_1f_2})\cdots(1+{_1f_{T-1}})$$

Substituting the right-hand side of the above equation into the present value formula we get:

$$\text{PV of \$1 in } T \text{ periods} = \frac{1}{(1+z_1)(1+{_1f_1})(1+{_1f_2})\cdots(1+{_1f_{T-1}})}$$

In practice, the present value of $1 in T periods is called the forward discount factor for period T.

For example, consider the forward rates shown in Exhibit 12. The forward discount rate for period 4 is found as follows:

$$z_1 = 3\%/2 = 1.5\% \qquad {_1f_1} = 3.6\%/2 = 1.8\%$$
$$_1f_2 = 3.92\%/2 = 1.958\% \qquad {_1f_3} = 5.15\%/2 = 2.577\%$$

---

[11] Actually, the semiannual forward rates are based on annual rates calculated to more decimal places. For example, $f_{1,3}$ is 5.15% in Exhibit 12 but based on the more precise value, the semi-annual rate is 2.577%.

$$\text{Forward discount factors of \$1 in 4 periods} = \frac{\$1}{(1.015)(1.018)(1.01958)(1.02577)}$$

$$= 0.925369$$

To see that this is the same present value that would be obtained using the spot rates, note from Exhibit 4 that the 2-year spot rate is 3.9164%. Using that spot rate, we find:

$$z_4 = 3.9164\%/2 = 1.9582\%$$

$$\text{PV of \$1 in 4 periods} = \frac{\$1}{(1.019582)^4} = 0.925361$$

The answer is the same as the forward discount factor (the slight difference is due to rounding).

Exhibit 14 shows the computation of the forward discount factor for each period based on the forward rates in Exhibit 12. Let's show how both the forward rates and the spot rates can be used to value a 2-year 6% coupon Treasury bond. The present value for each cash flow is found as follows using spot rates:

$$\frac{\text{Cash flow for period } t}{(1 + z_t)^t}$$

The following table uses the spot rates in Exhibit 4 to value this bond:

Spot Rate Period	Semiannual BEY (%)	Spot Rate (%)	PV of $1	Cash Flow	PV of Cash Flow
1	3.0000	1.50000	0.9852217	3	2.955665
2	3.3000	1.65000	0.9677991	3	2.903397
3	3.5053	1.75266	0.9492109	3	2.847633
4	3.9164	1.95818	0.9253619	103	95.312278
				Total	104.018973

Exhibit 14	Calculation of the Forward Discount Factor for Each Period

Periods	Years	Notation	Forward Rate[a]	0.5 × Forward Rate[b]	1 + Forward Rate	Forward Discount Factor
1	0.5	$_1f_0$	3.00%	1.5000%	1.01500	0.985222
2	1.0	$_1f_1$	3.60%	1.8002%	1.01800	0.967799
3	1.5	$_1f_2$	3.92%	1.9583%	1.01958	0.949211
4	2.0	$_1f_3$	5.15%	2.5773%	1.02577	0.925362
5	2.5	$_1f_4$	6.54%	3.2679%	1.03268	0.896079
6	3.0	$_1f_5$	6.33%	3.1656%	1.03166	0.868582
7	3.5	$_1f_6$	6.23%	3.1139%	1.03114	0.842352
8	4.0	$_1f_7$	5.79%	2.8930%	1.02893	0.818668
9	4.5	$_1f_8$	6.01%	3.0063%	1.03006	0.794775
10	5.0	$_1f_9$	6.24%	3.1221%	1.03122	0.770712
11	5.5	$_1f_{10}$	6.48%	3.2407%	1.03241	0.746520

Exhibit 14	Continued					
Periods	**Years**	**Notation**	**Forward Rate**[a]	**0.5 × Forward Rate**[b]	**1 + Forward Rate**	**Forward Discount Factor**
12	6.0	$_1f_{11}$	6.72%	3.3622%	1.03362	0.722237
13	6.5	$_1f_{12}$	6.97%	3.4870%	1.03487	0.697901
14	7.0	$_1f_{13}$	6.36%	3.1810%	1.03181	0.676385
15	7.5	$_1f_{14}$	6.49%	3.2450%	1.03245	0.655126
16	8.0	$_1f_{15}$	6.62%	3.3106%	1.03310	0.634132
17	8.5	$_1f_{16}$	6.76%	3.3778%	1.03378	0.613412
18	9.0	$_1f_{17}$	8.10%	4.0504%	1.04050	0.589534
19	9.5	$_1f_{18}$	8.40%	4.2009%	1.04201	0.565767
20	10.0	$_1f_{19}$	8.72%	4.3576%	1.04357	0.542142

[a]The rates in this column are rounded to two decimal places.
[b]The rates in this column used the forward rates in the previous column carried to four decimal places.

Based on the spot rates, the value of this bond is $104.0190.

Using forward rates and the forward discount factors, the present value of the cash flow in period t is found as follows:

Cash flow in period t × Discount factor for period t

The following table uses the forward rates and the forward discount factors in Exhibit 14 to value this bond:

Period	Semiannual Forward Rate (%)	Forward Discount Factor	Cash Flow	PV of Cash Flow
1	1.5000	0.985222	3	2.955665
2	1.8002	0.967799	3	2.903397
3	1.9583	0.949211	3	2.847633
4	2.5773	0.925362	103	95.312278
			Total	104.018973

The present value of this bond using forward rates is $104.0190.

So, it does not matter whether one discounts cash flows by spot rates or forward rates, the value is the same.

Practice Question 10

Compute the value of a 10% coupon 3-year bond using the forward rates in Exhibit 12.

5.4 Computing Any Forward Rate

Using spot rates, we can compute any forward rate. Using the same arbitrage arguments as used above to derive the 6-month forward rates, any forward rate can be obtained.

There are two elements to the forward rate. The first is when in the future the rate begins. The second is the length of time for the rate. For example, the 2-year forward rate 3 years from now means a rate three years from now for a length of two years. The notation used for a forward rate, f, will have two subscripts—one before f and one after f as shown below:

$$_t f_m$$

The subscript before f is t and is the length of time that the rate applies. The subscript after f is m and is when the forward rate begins. That is,

$$\underset{\text{the length of time of the forward rate}}{} f \underset{\text{when the forward rate begins}}{}$$

Remember our time periods are still 6-month periods. Given the above notation, here is what the following mean:

Notation	Interpretation for the Forward Rate
$_1f_{12}$	6-month (1-period) forward rate beginning 6 years (12 periods) from now
$_2f_8$	1-year (2-period) forward rate beginning 4 years (8 periods) from now
$_6f_4$	3-year (6-period) forward rate beginning 2 years (4 periods) from now
$_8f_{10}$	4-year (8-period) forward rate beginning 5 years (10 periods) from now

To see how the formula for the forward rate is derived, consider the following two alternatives for an investor who wants to invest for $m + t$ periods:

- buy a zero-coupon Treasury bond that matures in $m + t$ periods, or
- buy a zero-coupon Treasury bond that matures in m periods and invest the proceeds at the maturity date in a zero-coupon Treasury bond that matures in t periods.

The investor will be indifferent between the two alternatives if they produce the same return over the $m + t$ investment horizon.

For $100 invested in the first alternative, the proceeds for this investment at the horizon date assuming that the semiannual rate is z_{m+t} is

$$\$100(1+z_{m+t})^{m+t}$$

For the second alternative, the proceeds for this investment at the end of m periods assuming that the semiannual rate is z_m is

$$\$100(1+z_m)^m$$

When the proceeds are received in m periods, they are reinvested at the forward rate, $_t f_m$, producing a value for the investment at the end of $m + t$ periods of

$$\$100(1+z_m)^m(1+{}_t f_m)^t$$

For the investor to be indifferent to the two alternatives, the following relationship must hold:

$$\$100(1+z_{m+t})^{m+t} = \$100(1+z_m)^m(1+{}_t f_m)^t$$

Solving for $_t f_m$ we get:

$$_t f_m = \left[\frac{(1+z_{m+t})^{m+t}}{(1+z_m)^m}\right]^{1/t} - 1$$

Notice that if t is equal to 1, the formula reduces to the 1-period (6-month) forward rate.

To illustrate, for the spot rates shown in Exhibit 4, suppose that an investor wants to know the 2-year forward rate three years from now. In terms of the notation, t is equal to 4 and m is equal to 6. Substituting for t and m into the equation for the forward rate we have:

$$_4 f_6 = \left[\frac{(1+z_{10})^{10}}{(1+z_6)^6} \right]^{1/4} - 1$$

This means that the following two spot rates are needed: z_6 (the 3-year spot rate) and z_{10} (the 5-year spot rate). From Exhibit 4 we know

z_6 (the 3-year spot rate) = 4.752%/2 = 0.02376

z_{10} (the 5-year spot rate) = 5.2772%/2 = 0.026386

then

$$_4 f_6 = \left[\frac{(1.026386)^{10}}{(1.02376)^6} \right]^{1/4} - 1 = 0.030338$$

Therefore, $_4f_6$ is equal to 3.0338% and doubling this rate gives 6.0675% the forward rate on a bond-equivalent basis.

We can verify this result. Investing $100 for 10 periods at the spot rate of 2.6386% will produce the following value:

$$\$100(1.026386)^{10} = \$129.7499$$

By investing $100 for 6 periods at 2.376% and reinvesting the proceeds for 4 periods at the forward rate of 3.030338% gives the same value

$$\$100(1.02376)^6 (1.030338)^4 = \$129.75012$$

Practice Question 11

A. Given the spot rates in Exhibit 4, compute the 6-year forward rate 4 years from now.

B. Demonstrate that the forward rate computed in part A is correct.

SOLUTIONS FOR PRACTICE QUESTIONS

1. The cash flow for this bond is 30 payments of $3 plus a maturity value of $100 thirty 6-month periods from now. Below is the present value of the cash flow when discounted at one-half the yields of 7.2%, 7.6%, and 7.8%. The short-cut formula given in the reading on understanding yield spreads was used so the information is provided for the present value of the coupon payments and the present value of the maturity value.

Annual Rate (BEY)	7.2%	7.6%	7.8%
Semiannual Rate	3.6%	3.8%	3.9%
Present value of			
Coupon payments	54.49	53.16	52.51
Maturity value	34.61	32.66	31.74
Total present value	89.10	85.82	84.25

Since the semiannual discount rate of 3.9% equates the present value of the cash flows to the price of $84.25, 3.9% is the semiannual yield to maturity. Doubling this yield gives a yield to maturity of 7.8% on a bond equivalent basis.

2. **A.** The total future dollars from an investment of $89.32 if the yield is 7% is:

$$\$89.32 \times (1.035)^{40} = \$353.64$$

Decomposing the total future dollars we see that:

Total future dollars	=	$353.64
Return of principal	=	$ 89.32
Total dollar return	=	$264.32

Without reinvestment income, the dollar return is:

Coupon interest	=	$120.00
Capital gain	=	$ 10.68
Dollar return	=	$130.68

The dollar return shortfall is therefore $133.64 ($264.32 − $130.68). This shortfall is made up if the coupon payments can be reinvested at a yield of 7% (the yield on the bond at the time of purchase). For this bond, the reinvestment income is 51% of the total dollar return needed to produce a yield of 7% ($133.64/$264.32).

    B. There are no coupon payments to reinvest because the coupon rate is 0%. Therefore, no portion of the dollar return of a zero-coupon bond comes from reinvestment income.

3. **A.** The bond-equivalent yield is

$$2\left[(1.048)^{0.5} - 1\right] = 4.74\%$$

    B. The annual yield is

$$\left[(1.024)^2 - 1\right] = 4.86\%$$

4. **A.** The cash flows for this bond up to the first call date are 1) 10 coupon payments of $4.50 and 2) $104.50 ten 6-month periods from now. The table below shows the present values of the coupon payments and maturity value for the three interest rates in the question:

Annual Interest Rate (%)	Semiannual Interest Rate (%)	Present Value of 10 Payments of $4.5	Present Value of $104.5 10 Periods from Now	Present Value of Cash Flows
4.4	2.2	40.0019	84.0635	124.0654
4.6	2.3	39.7944	83.2453	123.0397
4.8	2.4	39.5886	82.4360	122.0246

Since a semiannual rate of 2.3% produces a present value for the cash flows of $123.0397 and the price is $123.04, 2.3% is the semiannual yield to call. Doubling this yield gives a 4.6% yield to call on a bond-equivalent basis.

    B. The cash flows for this bond up to the first par call date are 1) 16 coupon payments of $4.50 and 2) $100 sixteen 6-month periods from now. The table below shows the present values of the coupon payments and maturity value for the three interest rates in the question:

Annual Interest Rate (%)	Semiannual Interest Rate (%)	Present Value of 16 Payments of $4.5	Present Value of $100 16 Periods from Now	Present Value of Cash Flows
5.41	2.705	57.8211	65.2431	123.0642
5.62	2.810	57.3548	64.1851	121.5399
5.75	2.875	57.0689	63.5393	120.6082

For the three semiannual interest rates used, the one that makes the present value of the cash flows to the first par call date closest to the price of $123.04 is 2.705%. Doubling this yield gives a 5.41% yield to first par call date on a bond-equivalent basis.

5. The discount margin is the margin that when added to LIBOR will make the present value of the cash flows (assuming LIBOR is unchanged over the life of the floater) equal to the price. When the price is 99.8269, it can be seen from Exhibit 3 that a margin of 84 basis points makes the present value of the cash flows equal to that price. Thus, if the floater's price is 99.8269, the discount margin is 84 basis points.

6. **A.** The yield on a discount basis, d, is:

$$(1 - 0.9825)\left(\frac{360}{115}\right) = 0.0548 = 5.48\%$$

B. The price of this Treasury bill, p, per $1 dollar of maturity value is:

$$1 - 0.059(162/360) = 0.97345$$

7. From Exhibit 4, the coupon rate for the on-the-run issue is 4.4%. Thus, the semiannual coupon payment per $100 of par value is $2.20 (4.4%/2 times $100). The present value of the cash flow is:

$$\frac{2.2}{(1+z_1)^1} + \frac{2.2}{(1+z_2)^2} + \frac{2.2}{(1+z_3)^3} + \frac{2.2}{(1+z_4)^4} + \frac{102.2}{(1+z_5)^5}$$

where z_5 is one half of the 2.5-year theoretical spot rate.

Given the other four spot rates, we can write

$$\frac{2.2}{(1.0150)^1} + \frac{2.2}{(1.0165)^2} + \frac{2.2}{(1.017527)^3} + \frac{2.2}{(1.019582)^4} + \frac{102.2}{(1+z_5)^5} = 100$$

Since the price of the 2.5-year coupon Treasury security is par, the present value must equal par. Therefore,

$$\frac{2.2}{(1.0150)^1} + \frac{2.2}{(1.0165)^2} + \frac{2.2}{(1.017527)^3} + \frac{2.2}{(1.019582)^4} + \frac{102.2}{(1+z_5)^5} = 100$$

Solving the above equation:

$$2.167488 + 2.129158 + 2.088261 + 2.0355795 + \frac{102.20}{(1+z_5)^5} = 100$$

$$8.420702 + \frac{102.20}{(1+z_5)^5} = 100$$

$$\frac{102.20}{(1+z_5)^5} = 91.5793$$

$$(1+z_5)^5 = \frac{102.20}{91.5793}$$

$$z_5 = 0.022188 = 2.2188\%$$

Doubling the semiannual yield gives 4.4376% for the 2.5-year spot rate on a bond-equivalent basis. This rate agrees with the rate in Exhibit 4.

8. From Exhibit 5 it can be seen that if 125 basis points is added to each spot rate, the present value of the cash flow is 105.7165, the assumed price for the non-Treasury issue. Therefore, the Z-spread is 125 basis points.

9. $_1f_{13}$ is found as follows:

$$_1f_{13} = \frac{(1+z_{14})^{14}}{(1+z_{13})^{13}} - 1$$

From Exhibit 4, the annual spot rates for z_{13} and z_{14} are reported. They are 5.6108% and 5.6643%, respectively. Therefore,

$$z_{13} = 0.056108/2 = 0.028054$$
$$z_{14} = 0.056643/2 = 0.028322$$

Substituting we get

$$_1f_{13} = \frac{(1.028322)^{14}}{(1.028054)^{13}} - 1 = 0.0318 = 3.18\%$$

Doubling this rate gives the annualized rate for $_1f_{13}$ on a bond-equivalent basis of 6.36% reported in Exhibit 12.

10. The value is $114.8195 as shown below:

Period	Semiannual Forward Rate (%)	Forward Discount Factor	Cash Flow	PV of Cash Flow
1	1.500	0.985222	$5	$4.926108
2	1.800	0.967799	5	4.838996
3	1.958	0.949211	5	4.746055
4	2.577	0.925362	5	4.626810
5	3.268	0.896079	5	4.480396
6	3.166	0.868582	105	91.201111
		Total		$114.819476

11. A. The forward rate sought is $_{12}f_8$. The formula for this forward rate is therefore:

$$_{12}f_8 = \left[\frac{(1+z_{20})^{20}}{(1+z_8)^8} \right]^{1/12} - 1$$

The spot rates needed are z_8 (the 4-year spot rate) and z_{20} (the 10-year spot rate). From Exhibit 4 we know

$$z_8 \text{ (the 4-year spot rate)} = 5.065\%/2 = 0.025325$$

$$z_{20} \text{ (the 10-year spot rate)} = 6.2169\%/2 = 0.031085$$

then

$$_{12}f_8 = \left[\frac{(1.031085)^{20}}{(1.025325)^8} \right]^{1/12} - 1 = 0.034943$$

Therefore, $_{12}f_8$ is equal to 3.4943% and doubling this rate gives 6.9885% the forward rate on a bond-equivalent basis.

B. We can verify this result. Investing $100 for 20 periods at the spot rate of 3.1085% will produce the following value:

$$\$100(1.031085)^{20} = \$184.4545$$

By investing $100 for 8 periods at 2.5325% and reinvesting the proceeds for 12 periods at the forward rate of 3.4942% gives the same value

$$\$100(1.025325)^8(1.034942)^{12} = \$184.4545$$

SUMMARY

- The sources of return from holding a bond to maturity are the coupon interest payments, any capital gain or loss, and reinvestment income.
- Reinvestment income is the interest income generated by reinvesting coupon interest payments and any principal payments from the time of receipt to the bond's maturity.
- The current yield relates the annual dollar coupon interest to the market price and fails to recognize any capital gain or loss and reinvestment income.
- The yield to maturity is the interest rate that will make the present value of the cash flows from a bond equal to the price plus accrued interest.
- The market convention to annualize a semiannual yield is to double it, and the resulting annual yield is referred to as a bond-equivalent yield.
- When market participants refer to a yield or return measure as computed on a bond-equivalent basis, it means that a semiannual yield or return is doubled.
- The yield to maturity takes into account all three sources of return but assumes that the coupon payments and any principal repayments can be reinvested at an interest rate equal to the yield to maturity.
- The yield to maturity will only be realized if the interim cash flows can be reinvested at the yield to maturity and the bond is held to maturity.
- Reinvestment risk is the risk an investor faces that future reinvestment rates will be less than the yield to maturity at the time a bond is purchased.
- Interest rate risk is the risk that if a bond is not held to maturity, an investor may have to sell it for less than the purchase price.

- The longer the maturity and the higher the coupon rate, the more a bond's return is dependent on reinvestment income to realize the yield to maturity at the time of purchase.

- The yield to call is the interest rate that will make the present value of the expected cash flows to the assumed call date equal to the price plus accrued interest.

- Yield measures for callable bonds include yield to first call, yield to next call, yield to first par call, and yield to refunding.

- The yield to call considers all three sources of potential return but assumes that all cash flows can be reinvested at the yield to call until the assumed call date, the investor will hold the bond to the assumed call date, and the issuer will call the bond on the assumed call date.

- For a putable bond a yield to put is computed assuming that the issue will be put on the first put date.

- The yield to worst is the lowest yield from among all possible yield to calls, yield to puts, and the yield to maturity.

- For mortgage-backed and asset-backed securities, the cash flow yield based on some prepayment rate is the interest rate that equates the present value of the projected principal and interest payments to the price plus accrued interest.

- The cash flow yield assumes that all cash flows (principal and interest payments) can be reinvested at the calculated yield and that the assumed prepayment rate will be realized over the security's life.

- For amortizing securities, reinvestment risk is greater than for standard coupon nonamortizing securities because payments are typically made monthly and include principal as well as interest payments.

- For floating-rate securities, instead of a yield measure, margin measures (i.e., spread above the reference rate) are computed.

- Two margin measures commonly used are spread for life and discount margin.

- The discount margin assumes that the reference rate will not change over the life of the security and that there is no cap or floor restriction on the coupon rate.

- The theoretical spot rate is the interest rate that should be used to discount a default-free cash flow.

- Because there are a limited number of on-the-run Treasury securities traded in the market, interpolation is required to obtain the yield for interim maturities; hence, the yield for most maturities used to construct the Treasury yield curve are interpolated yields rather than observed yields.

- Default-free spot rates can be derived from the Treasury yield curve by a method called bootstrapping.

- The basic principle underlying the bootstrapping method is that the value of a Treasury coupon security is equal to the value of the package of zero-coupon Treasury securities that duplicates the coupon bond's cash flows.

- The nominal spread is the difference between the yield for a non-Treasury bond and a comparable-maturity Treasury coupon security.

- The nominal spread fails to consider the term structure of the spot rates and the fact that, for bonds with embedded options, future interest rate volatility may alter its cash flows.

- The zero-volatility spread or Z-spread is a measure of the spread that the investor will realize over the entire Treasury spot rate curve if the bond is held to maturity, thereby recognizing the term structure of interest rates.

- Unlike the nominal spread, the Z-spread is not a spread off one point on the Treasury yield curve but is a spread over the entire spot rate curve.

- For bullet bonds, unless the yield curve is very steep, the nominal spread will not differ significantly from the Z-spread; for securities where principal is paid over time rather than just at maturity there can be a significant difference, particularly in a steep yield curve environment.

- The option-adjusted spread (OAS) converts the cheapness or richness of a bond into a spread over the future possible spot rate curves.

- An OAS is said to be option adjusted because it allows for future interest rate volatility to affect the cash flows.

- The OAS is a product of a valuation model and, when comparing the OAS of dealer firms, it is critical to check on the volatility assumption (and other assumptions) employed in the valuation model.

- The cost of the embedded option is measured as the difference between the Z-spread and the OAS.

- Investors should not rely on the nominal spread for bonds with embedded options since it hides how the spread is split between the OAS and the option cost.

- OAS is used as a relative value measure to assist in the selection of bonds with embedded options.

- Using arbitrage arguments, forward rates can be extrapolated from the Treasury yield curve or the Treasury spot rate curve.

- The spot rate for a given period is related to the forward rates; specifically, the spot rate is a geometric average of the current 6-month spot rate and the subsequent 6-month forward rates.

PRACTICE PROBLEMS FOR READING 57

1. What are the sources of return any yield measure should incorporate?

2. **A.** Suppose a 10-year 9% coupon bond is selling for $112 with a par value of $100. What is the current yield for the bond?

   B. What is the limitation of the current yield measure?

3. Determine whether the yield to maturity of a 6.5% 20-year bond that pays interest semiannually and is selling for $90.68 is 7.2%, 7.4%, or 7.8%.

4. The following yields and prices were reported in the financial press. Are any of them incorrect assuming that the reported price and coupon rate are correct? If so, explain why. (No calculations are needed to answer this question.)

Bond	Price	Coupon Rate (%)	Current Yield (%)	Yield to Maturity (%)
A	100	6.0	5.0	6.0
B	110	7.0	6.4	6.1
C	114	7.5	7.1	7.7
D	95	4.7	5.2	5.9
E	75	5.6	5.1	4.1

5. Comment on the following statement: "The yield to maturity measure is a useless measure because it doubles a semiannual yield (calling the annual yield a bond-equivalent yield) rather than computing an effective annual yield. This is the major shortcoming of the yield-to-maturity measure."

6. **A.** Suppose that an investor invests $108.32 in a 5-year certificate of deposit that pays 7% annually (on a bond-equivalent basis) or 3.5% semiannually and the interest payments are semiannual. What are the total future dollars of this investment at the end of 5 years (i.e., ten 6-month periods)?

   B. How much total interest is generated from the investment in this certificate of deposit?

   C. Suppose an investor can purchase any 5-year investment for $108.32 that offers a 7% yield on a bond-equivalent basis and pays interest semi-annually, with automatic reinvestment at a rate equal to the yield. What is the total future dollars and the total dollar return from this investment?

   D. Suppose an investor can purchase a 5-year 9% coupon bond that pays interest semiannually and the price of this bond is $108.32. The yield to maturity for this bond is 7% on a bond-equivalent basis. What is the total future dollars and the total dollar return that will be generated from this bond if it is to yield 7%? Assume the reinvestment rate is equal to the yield.

   E. Complete the following for the bond in part D:

Coupon interest	=
Capital gain/loss	=
Reinvestment income	= _____
Total dollar return	=

    F. What percentage of the total dollar return is dependent on reinvestment income?

    G. How is the reinvestment income in part E realized?

7. **A.** Which of the following three bonds has the greatest dependence on reinvestment income to generate the computed yield? Assume that each bond is offering the same yield to maturity. (No calculations are needed to answer this question.)

Bond	Maturity	Coupon Rate (%)
X	25 years	0
Y	20 years	7
Z	20 years	8

    B. Which of the three bonds in part A has the least dependence on reinvestment income to generate the computed yield? Assume that each bond is offering the same yield to maturity. (No calculations are needed to answer this question.)

8. What is the reinvestment risk and interest rate risk associated with a yield to maturity measure?

9. **A.** If the yield to maturity on an annual-pay bond is 5.6%, what is the bond-equivalent yield?

    B. If the yield of a U.S. bond issue quoted on a bond-equivalent basis is 5.6%, what is the yield to maturity on an annual-pay basis?

10. Suppose that a 10% 15-year bond has the following call structure:

- not callable for the next 5 years;
- first callable in 5 years at $105;
- first par call date is in 10 years;
- the price of the bond is $127.5880.

    A. Is the yield to maturity for this bond 7.0%, 7.4%, or 7.8%?

    B. Is the yield to first call for this bond 4.55%, 4.65%, or 4.85%?

    C. Is the yield to first par call for this bond 6.25%, 6.55%, or 6.75%?

11. Suppose a 5% coupon 6-year bond is selling for $105.2877 and is putable in four years at par value. The yield to maturity for this bond is 4%. Determine whether the yield to put is 3.38%, 3.44%, or 3.57%.

12. Suppose that an amortizing security pays interest monthly. Based on the projected principal payments and interest, suppose that the monthly interest rate that makes the present value of the cash flows equal to the price of the security is 0.41%. What is the cash flow yield on a bond-equivalent basis?

13. Two portfolio managers are discussing the investment characteristics of amortizing securities. Manager A believes that the advantage of these securities relative to nonamortizing securities is that since the periodic cash flows include principal payments as well as coupon payments, the manager can generate greater reinvestment income. In addition, the payments are typically monthly so even greater reinvestment income can be generated. Manager B believes that the need to reinvest monthly and the need to invest larger amounts than just coupon interest payments make amortizing securities less attractive. Who do you agree with and why?

14. An investor is considering the purchase of a 5-year floating-rate note that pays interest semiannually. The coupon formula is equal to 6-month LIBOR plus 30 basis points. The current value for 6-month LIBOR is 5% (annual rate). The price of this note is 99.1360. Is the discount margin 40 basis points, 50 basis points, or 55 basis points?

15. How does the discount margin handle any cap on a floater and the fact that the reference rate may change over time?

16. A Treasury bill with 64 days from settlement to maturity is selling for $0.995 per $1 of maturity value. The bill's yield on a discount basis is *closest* to:

    A. 2.81%.

    B. 2.85%.

    C. 2.90%.

17. A. A Treasury bill with 105 days from settlement to maturity is selling for $0.989 per $1 of maturity value. What is the yield on a discount basis?

    B. A Treasury bill with 275 days from settlement to maturity is quoted as having a yield on a discount basis of 3.68%. What is the price of this Treasury bill?

    C. What are the problems with using the yield on a discount basis as measure of a Treasury bill's yield?

18. Explain how a Treasury yield curve is constructed even though there are only a limited number of on-the-run Treasury issues available in the market.

19. Suppose that the annual yield to maturity for the 6-month and 1-year Treasury bill is 4.6% and 5.0%, respectively. These yields represent the 6-month and 1-year spot rates. Also assume the following Treasury yield curve (i.e., the price for each issue is $100) has been estimated for 6-month periods out to a maturity of 3 years:

Years to Maturity	Annual Yield to Maturity (BEY)
1.5	5.4%
2.0	5.8%
2.5	6.4%
3.0	7.0%

Compute the 1.5-year, 2-year, 2.5-year, and 3-year spot rates.

20. Given the spot rates computed in the previous question and the 6-month and 1-year spot rates, compute the arbitrage-free value of a 3-year Treasury security with a coupon rate of 8%.

21. What are the two limitations of the nominal spread as a measure of relative value of two bonds?

22. Suppose that the Treasury spot rate curve is as follows:

Period	Years to Maturity	Spot Rate
1	0.5	5.0%
2	1.0	5.4
3	1.5	5.8
4	2.0	6.4

Period	Years to Maturity	Spot Rate
5	2.5	7.0
6	3.0	7.2
7	3.5	7.4
8	4.0	7.8

Suppose that the market price of a 4-year 6% coupon non-Treasury issue is $91.4083. Determine whether the zero-volatility spread (Z-spread) relative to the Treasury spot rate curve for this issue is 80 basis points, 90 basis points, or 100 basis points.

23. The Prestige Investment Management Company sent a report to its pension client. In the report, Prestige indicated that the yield curve is currently flat (i.e., the yield to maturity for each maturity is the same) and then discussed the nominal spread for the corporate bonds held in the client's portfolio. A trustee of the pension fund was concerned that Prestige focused on the nominal spread rather than the zero-volatility spread or option-adjusted spread for these bond issues. Joan Thomas is Prestige's employee who is the contact person for this account. She received a phone call from the trustee regarding his concern. How should she respond regarding the use of nominal spread rather than zero-volatility spread and option-adjusted spread as a spread measure for corporate bonds?

24. John Tinker is a junior portfolio manager assigned to work for Laura Sykes, the manager of the corporate bond portfolio of a public pension fund. Ms. Sykes asked Mr. Tinker to construct a portfolio profile that she could use in her presentation to the trustees. One of the measures Ms. Sykes insisted that Mr. Tinker include was the option-adjusted spread of each issue. In preparing the portfolio profile, Mr. Tinker encountered the following situations that he did not understand. Provide Mr. Tinker with an explanation.

    A. Mr. Tinker checked with several dealer firms to determine the option-adjusted spread for each issue. For several of the issues, there were substantially different option-adjusted spreads reported. For example, for one callable issue one dealer reported an OAS of 100 basis points, one dealer reported 170 basis points, and a third dealer 200 basis points. Mr. Tinker could not understand how the dealers could have substantially different OAS values when in fact the yield to maturity and nominal spread values for each of the issues did not differ from dealer to dealer.

    B. The dealers that Mr. Tinker checked with furnished him with the nominal spread and the Z-spread for each issue in addition to the OAS. For all the bond issues where there were no embedded options, each dealer reported that the Z-spread was equal to the OAS. Mr. Tinker could not understand why.

    C. One dealer firm reported an option cost for each issue. There were positive, negative, and zero values reported. Mr. Tinker observed that for all the bond issues that were putable, the option cost was negative. For all the option-free bond issues, the reported value was zero.

25. Max Dumas is considering the purchase of a callable corporate bond. He has available to him two analytical systems to value the bond. In one system, System A, the vendor uses the on-the-run Treasury issues to construct the theoretical spot rate that is used to construct a model to compute the OAS. The other analytical system, System B, uses the on-the-run issue for the particular issuer in constructing a model to compute the OAS.

A. Suppose that using System A, Mr. Dumas finds that the OAS for the callable corporate he is considering is 50 basis points. How should he interpret this OAS value?

B. Suppose that using System B, Mr. Dumas finds that the OAS computed is 15 basis points. How should he interpret this OAS value?

C. Suppose that a dealer firm shows Mr. Dumas another callable corporate bond of the same credit quality and duration with an OAS of 40 basis points. Should Mr. Dumas view that this bond is more attractive or less attractive than the issue he is considering for acquisition?

26. Assume the following Treasury spot rates:

Period	Years to Maturity	Spot Rate
1	0.5	5.0%
2	1.0	5.4
3	1.5	5.8
4	2.0	6.4
5	2.5	7.0
6	3.0	7.2
7	3.5	7.4
8	4.0	7.8

Compute:

A. the 6-month forward rate six months from now.

B. the 6-month forward rate one year from now.

C. the 6-month forward rate three years from now.

D. the 2-year forward rate one year from now.

E. the 1-year forward rate two years from now.

27. For the previous question, demonstrate that the 6-month forward rate six months from now is the rate that will produce at the end of one year the same future dollars as investing either 1) at the current 1-year spot rate of 5.4% or 2) at the 6-month spot rate of 5.0% and reinvesting at the 6-month forward rate six months from now.

28. Two sales people of analytical systems are making a presentation to you about the merits of their respective systems. One sales person states that in valuing bonds the system first constructs the theoretical spot rates and then discounts cash flows using these rates. The other sales person interjects that his firm takes a different approach. Rather than using spot rates, forward rates are used to value the cash flows and he believes this is a better approach to valuing bonds compared to using spot rates. How would you respond to the second sales person's comment about his firm's approach?

29. An investor is considering the purchase of three option-free bonds:

Bond	Coupon Rate (%)
1	7.5
2	8.0
3	8.5

All three bonds have the same time remaining to maturity and the same 8.0 percent yield to maturity. If the investor plans to hold the bonds to maturity, the bond with the total dollar return that is *most* dependent on reinvestment income is Bond:

A. 1.

B. 2.

C. 3.

30. With respect to callable bonds, the zero-volatility spread will *most likely* be:

A. less than the option-adjusted spread.

B. greater than the option-adjusted spread.

C. equal to the option-adjusted spread, but substantially less than the nominal spread.

31. With respect to bond yield spreads, is the term structure of spot rates considered when determining the:

	nominal yield spread?	zero-volatility yield spread?
A.	No	No
B.	No	Yes
C.	Yes	No

32. If the Treasury par yield curve is upward sloping, will the short-term forward-rate curve always lie above the Treasury:

	par yield curve?	theoretical spot curve?
A.	No	Yes
B.	Yes	No
C.	Yes	Yes

33. An analyst made the following statement: "Regarding bonds with options, the Z-spread can be computed as approximately the option-adjusted spread (OAS) plus the option cost. Therefore, the Z-spread will sometimes be greater for bonds with options than for bonds without options, and sometimes less." Is the analyst's statement correct with respect to:

	Z-spread calculation?	Z-spread for bonds with options?
A.	No	Yes
B.	Yes	No
C.	Yes	Yes

34. Given the following spot rate curve, the implied forward rate for a six-month loan beginning eighteen months from now is *closest* to:

Maturity	Spot Rate (%)
Six months	6.00
Twelve months	7.00
Eighteen months	8.00
Twenty-four months	9.00
Thirty months	10.00
Thirty-six months	11.00

A. 7.00%.

B. 8.50%.

C. 12.03%.

35. A $1,000 par value, semiannual coupon bond with exactly two years to maturity and a coupon rate of 10 percent is selling for $976.45. Given the current U.S. Treasury spot rates given below and ignoring accrued interest and transactions costs, the zero-volatility spread (static spread) for this bond is *closest* to:

Maturity	Spot Rate (%)
Six months	6.00
Twelve months	7.50
Eighteen months	9.00
Twenty-four months	10.00

A. 100 basis points.

B. 150 basis points.

C. 200 basis points.

36. Consider the following statements about callable bonds:

Statement 1   "Given a callable bond's price and relative to a given spot rate curve, more than one zero-volatility spread (Z-spread) might exist depending on the outcomes of the specific model used to generate the zero-volatility spread."

Statement 2   "Given a callable bond's price and relative to a given spot rate curve, more than one option-adjusted spread (OAS) might exist depending on the outcomes of the specific model used to generate the option-adjusted spread."

Are the statements *most likely* correct or incorrect?

A. Both statements are correct.

B. Statement 1 is incorrect, but Statement 2 is correct.

C. Statement 1 is correct, but Statement 2 is incorrect.

37. The Z-spread for a callable bond is 120 basis points (bp). The reported option-adjusted spread for the bond is 70 bps. The option cost is *closest* to:

A. 50 bps.

B. 70 bps.

C. 190 bps.

38. A coupon-bearing bond purchased when issued at par value was held until maturity during which time interest rates rose. The ex-post realized return of the bond investment *most likely* was:

A. above the YTM at the time of issue.

B. below the YTM at the time of issue.

C. equal to the YTM at the time of issue because the bond was held until maturity.

SOLUTIONS FOR READING 57

1. The three sources are 1) coupon interest, 2) any capital gain (or loss, a reduction in return), and 3) reinvestment income.

2. **A.** The current yield for the bond is

    Annual coupon payment $= 0.09 \times \$100 = \$9$

    Current yield $= \dfrac{\$9}{\$112} = 0.0804 = 8.04\%$

    B. The current yield measure only considers coupon interest and ignores any capital gain or loss (a capital loss of $12 for the bond in our example), and reinvestment income.

3. The present value of the cash flows of a 6.5% 20-year semiannual-pay bond using the three discount rates is shown below:

Discount Rate (Annual BEY)	Semiannual Rate (Half Annual Rate)	Present Value of Cash Flows
7.2%	3.6%	92.64
7.4	3.7	90.68
7.8	3.9	86.94

Since 3.7% equates the present value of the cash flows to the price of 90.68, 3.7% is the semiannual yield to maturity. Doubling that rate gives a 7.4% yield to maturity on a bond-equivalent basis.

4. This question requires no calculations. (Note that the maturity of each bond is intentionally omitted.) The question tests for an understanding of the relationship between coupon rate, current yield, and yield to maturity for a bond trading at par, a discount, and a premium.

    - Bond A's current yield is incorrect. The current yield should be equal to the coupon rate.

    - Bond B is fine. That is, it has the expected relationship between coupon rate, current yield, and yield to maturity for a bond trading at a premium.

    - Bond C's yield to maturity is incorrect. Since the bond is a premium bond, the yield to maturity should be less than the coupon rate.

    - Bond D is fine. That is, it has the expected relationship between coupon rate, current yield, and yield to maturity for a bond trading at a discount.

    - Bond E is incorrect. Both the current yield and the yield to maturity should be greater than the coupon rate since the bond is trading at a discount.

5. The statement is misleading in that while it is true that the yield to maturity computed on a bond-equivalent basis is flawed, it is not the reason why the yield to maturity is limited. The major reason is that it assumes that the bond is held to maturity and the coupon payments are assumed to be reinvested at the computed yield to maturity.

6. **A.** The total future dollars are found as follows:

    $\$108.32(1.035)^{10} = \$152.80$

    B. Since the total future dollars are $152.80 and the investment is $108.32, the total interest from the CD is $44.48.

    C. The answer is the same as for parts A and B. The total future dollars are $152.80. The total dollar return is the same as the total interest, $44.48.

D. The answer is the same as for part C:

Total future dollars	=	$152.80
Total dollar return	=	$44.48

E.

Coupon interest	=	$45.00
Capital gain/loss	=	−$8.32
Reinvestment income	=	$7.80
Total dollar return	=	$44.48

F. The percentage of the total dollar return that must be generated from reinvestment income is 17.5% ($7.80/$44.48).

G. The $7.80 reinvestment income must be generated by reinvesting the semiannual coupon payments from the time of receipt to the maturity date at the semiannual yield to maturity, 3.5% in this example. The reinvestment income earned on a given coupon payment of $4.50 if it is invested from the time of receipt in period t to the maturity date (10 periods in our example) at a 3.5% semiannual rate is:

$$\$4.50(1.035)^{10-t} - \$4.50$$

The reinvestment income for each coupon payment is shown below:

Period	Periods Reinvested	Coupon Payment	Reinvestment Income at 3.5%
1	9	$4.5	$1.63
2	8	4.5	1.43
3	7	4.5	1.23
4	6	4.5	1.03
5	5	4.5	0.84
6	4	4.5	0.66
7	3	4.5	0.49
8	2	4.5	0.32
9	1	4.5	0.16
10	0	4.5	0.00
		Total	7.79

The reinvestment income totals $7.79 which differs from $7.80 due to rounding.

7. A. Bond X has no dependence on reinvestment income since it is a zero-coupon bond. So it is either Bond Y or Bond Z. The two bonds have the same maturity. Since they are both selling at the same yield, Bond Z, the one with the higher coupon rate, is more dependent on reinvestment income.

B. As explained in Part A, since Bond X is a zero-coupon bond, it has the least dependence (in fact, no dependence) on reinvestment income.

8. The reinvestment risk is that to realize the computed yield, it is necessary to reinvest the interim cash flows (i.e., coupon payments in the case of a nonamortizing security and principal plus coupon payments in the case of an amortizing security) at the computed yield. The interest rate risk comes into play because it is assumed the security will be held to the maturity date. If it is not, the yield no longer applies because there is the risk of having to sell the security below its purchase price.

9. A. The bond-equivalent yield is

$$2\left[(1.056)^{0.5} - 1\right] = 0.0552 = 5.52\%$$

B. The annual yield is

$$\left[(1.028)^2 - 1\right] = 0.0568 = 5.68\%$$

10. A. The cash flows for this bond to the maturity date are 1) 30 coupon payments of $5 and 2) $100 at the maturity date. The table below shows the present values of the coupon payments and maturity value for the three interest rates in the question:

Annual Interest Rate (%)	Semiannual Interest Rate (%)	Present Value of 30 Payments of $5	Present Value of $100 30 Periods from Now	Present Value of Cash Flows
7.0	3.5	91.9602	35.6278	127.5880
7.4	3.7	89.6986	33.6231	123.3217
7.8	3.9	87.5197	31.7346	119.2543

Since a semiannual interest rate of 3.5% produces a present value equal to the price of the bond ($127.5880), the yield to maturity is 7% on a bond-equivalent basis.

B. The cash flows for this bond up to the first call date are 1) 10 coupon payments of $5 and 2) $105 ten 6-month periods from now. The table below shows the present values of the coupon payments and maturity value for the three interest rates in the question:

Annual Interest Rate (%)	Semiannual Interest Rate (%)	Present Value of 10 Payments of $5	Present Value of $105 10 Periods from Now	Present Value of Cash Flows
4.55	2.275	44.2735	83.8483	128.1218
4.65	2.325	44.1587	83.4395	127.5982
4.85	2.425	43.9304	82.6284	126.5588

Since of the three interest rates in the question, a semiannual interest rate of 2.325% makes the present value of the cash flows closest to the price of $127.5880, the yield to the first call date is 4.65% on a bond-equivalent basis.

C. The cash flows for this bond up to the first par call date are 1) 20 coupon payments of $5 and 2) $100 twenty 6-month periods from now. The table below shows the present values of the coupon payments and maturity value for the three interest rates in the question:

Annual Interest Rate (%)	Semiannual Interest Rate (%)	Present Value of 20 Payments of $5	Present Value of $100 20 Periods from Now	Present Value of Cash Flows
6.25	3.125	73.5349	54.0407	127.5756
6.55	3.275	72.5308	52.4923	125.0231
6.75	3.375	71.8725	51.4860	123.3585

Since of the three interest rates in the question, a semiannual interest rate of 3.125% makes the present value of the cash flows closest to the price of $127.5880, the yield to the first par call date is 6.25% on a bond-equivalent basis.

11. The cash flows to the put date are 1) 8 coupon payments of $2.50 and 2) $100 (the put price) eight 6-month periods from now. The table below shows the present values of the coupon payments and maturity value for the three interest rates in the question:

Annual Interest Rate (%)	Semiannual Interest Rate (%)	Present Value of 8 Payments of $2.5	Present Value of $100 8 Periods from Now	Present Value of Cash Flows
3.38	1.690	18.5609	87.4529	106.0136
3.44	1.720	18.5367	87.2467	105.7834
3.57	1.785	18.4846	86.8020	105.2866

Since of the three interest rates in the question, a semiannual interest rate of 1.785% makes the present value of the cash flows closest to the price of $105.2877, the yield to the put date is 3.57% on a bond-equivalent basis.

12. First, the semiannual effective yield is computed from the monthly yield by compounding it for six months as follows:

$$\text{Effective semiannual yield} = (1.0041)^6 - 1 = 0.024854 = 2.4854\%$$

Next, the effective semiannual yield is doubled to get the annual cash flow yield on a bond-equivalent basis. Thus, the cash flow yield on a bond-equivalent basis is 4.97% (2 times 2.4854%).

13. You should agree with Manager B. The cash flow yield, as with any other yield measure such as the yield to maturity or any yield to call date, requires that the investor be able to reinvest any interim cash flows in order to realize the computed yield. A cash flow yield is even more dependent on reinvestment income because the interim cash flows are monthly coupon and principal, rather than simply semiannual coupon for a standard coupon bond. Consequently, the reinvestment risk is greater with an amortizing security.

14. The table below shows the present value using the three discount margins:

5-year floater
current LIBOR   5.00%
quoted margin   30 basis points

Period	LIBOR (Annual Rate) (%)	Coupon Rate (%)	Cash Flow ($)	40 5.400%	50 5.500%	55 5.550%
1	5.00	5.300	2.65	2.5803	2.5791	2.5784
2	5.00	5.300	2.65	2.5125	2.5100	2.5088
3	5.00	5.300	2.65	2.4464	2.4429	2.4411
4	5.00	5.300	2.65	2.3821	2.3775	2.3752
5	5.00	5.300	2.65	2.3195	2.3139	2.3110
6	5.00	5.300	2.65	2.2585	2.2519	2.2486
7	5.00	5.300	2.65	2.1991	2.1917	2.1879
8	5.00	5.300	2.65	2.1413	2.1330	2.1289
9	5.00	5.300	2.65	2.0850	2.0759	2.0714
10	5.00	5.300	102.65	78.6420	78.2601	78.0700
			Total	99.5669	99.1360	98.9214

Present Value ($) at Assumed Margin of

When a margin of 50 basis points is used, the present value of the cash flows is equal to the price ($99.1360).

15. The discount margin ignores both and hence is a limitation of this measure. The cap is not considered because the reference rate is assumed to be unchanged at the current value for the reference rate. The only way in which the cap is considered is in the special case where the current value for the reference rate is capped and in this case it assumes that the reference rate will not fall below the cap for the life of the floater.

16. A is correct.

The yield on a discount basis $= d = (1 - p) \times (360/N_{SM})$

Where: $p =$ settlement price per $1 of maturity value

$N_{SM} =$ number of days between settlement and maturity

$d = (1 - 0.995) \times (360/64) = 2.81\%$

17. **A.** The yield on a discount basis, d, is:

$(1 - 0.989)\left(\dfrac{360}{105}\right) = 0.0377 = 3.77\%$

B. The price of this Treasury bill, p, per $1 dollar of maturity value is:

$1 - 0.0368(275/360) = 0.971889$

C. The yield on a discount basis has two major shortcomings. First, it relates the interest return to the maturity or face value rather than the amount invested. Second, it is based on a 360-day year rather than 365-day year as used for Treasury coupon securities.

18. Beyond the 1-year maturity, there are only a few on-the-run Treasury issues available: 2 year, 5 year, and 10 year. For the 30-year maturity, market participants estimate the yield based on the last 30-year Treasury bond that was issued by the U.S. Department of the Treasury. The yield for interim maturities is calculated using an interpolation methodology. The simplest is linear interpolation; however, more elaborate statistical methods can be used.

19. We will use the same notation as in the reading. One-half the annualized spot rate for a 6-month period will be denoted by z_t. We know that the 6-month Treasury bill yield is 4.6% and the 1-year Treasury yield is 5.0%, so

$z_1 = 4.6\%/2 = 2.3\%$ and $z_2 = 5.0\%/2 = 2.5\%$

Now we use the bootstrapping methodology. The 1.5-year Treasury yield from the Treasury yield curve is selling to yield 5.4%. Since the price of the issue is its par value, the coupon rate is 5.4%. So, the cash flow for this issue is:

0.5 year $0.054 \times \$100 \times 0.5 = \$2.70$

1.0 year $0.054 \times \$100 \times 0.5 = \$2.70$

1.5 years $0.054 \times \$100 \times 0.5 + \$100 = \$102.70$

The present value of the cash flows is then:

$\dfrac{2.7}{(1 + z_1)^1} + \dfrac{2.7}{(1 + z_2)^2} + \dfrac{102.7}{(1 + z_3)^3}$

Substituting the first two spot rates we have:

$\dfrac{2.7}{(1.023)^1} + \dfrac{2.7}{(1.025)^2} + \dfrac{102.7}{(1 + z_3)^3}$

The goal is to find z_3. Since the value of this cash flow must be equal to the price of the 1.5-year issue which is par value, we can set the previous equation equal to 100:

$$\frac{2.7}{(1.023)^1} + \frac{2.7}{(1.025)^2} + \frac{102.7}{(1 + z_3)^3} = 100$$

We then solve for z_3 as follows:

$$2.639296 + 2.569899 + \frac{102.7}{(1 + z_3)^3} = 100$$

$$\frac{102.7}{(1 + z_3)^3} = 94.7908$$

$$z_3 = 0.027073 = 2.7073\%$$

Doubling this yield we obtain the bond-equivalent yield of 5.4146%.

The equation for obtaining the 2-year, 2.5-year, and 3-year spot rates are given below.

For the 2-year spot rate, the coupon rate from the Treasury yield curve is 5.8%. So, the present value of the cash flow is:

$$\frac{2.9}{(1 + z_1)^1} + \frac{2.9}{(1 + z_2)^2} + \frac{2.9}{(1 + z_3)^3} + \frac{102.9}{(1 + z_4)^4}$$

Substituting: $z_1 = 2.3\%$, $z_2 = 2.5\%$, and $z_3 = 2.7073\%$ and setting the present value equal to the price of the 2-year issue (100), we obtain:

$$\frac{2.9}{(1.023)^1} + \frac{2.9}{(1.025)^2} + \frac{2.9}{(1.027073)^3} + \frac{102.9}{(1 + z_4)^4} = 100$$

Solving the above equation we would find that z_4 is 2.9148%. Therefore, the 2-year spot rate on a bond-equivalent basis is 5.8297%.

For the 2.5-year spot rate, we use the 2.5-year issue from the par yield curve. The yield is 6.4% and therefore the coupon rate is 6.4%. The present value of the cash flow for this issue is then:

$$\frac{3.2}{(1 + z_1)^1} + \frac{3.2}{(1 + z_2)^2} + \frac{3.2}{(1 + z_3)^3} + \frac{3.2}{(1 + z_4)^4} + \frac{103.2}{(1 + z_5)^5}$$

Substituting: $z_1 = 2.3\%$, $z_2 = 2.5\%$, $z_3 = 2.7073\%$, and $z_4 = 2.9148\%$ and setting the present value equal to the price of the 2.5-year issue (100), we obtain:

$$\frac{3.2}{(1.023)^1} + \frac{3.2}{(1.025)^2} + \frac{3.2}{(1.027073)^3} + \frac{3.2}{(1.029148)^4} + \frac{103.2}{(1 + z_5)^5} = 100$$

Solving the above equation we would find that z_5 is 3.2333%. Therefore, the 2.5-year spot rate on a bond-equivalent basis is 6.4665%.

For the 3-year spot rate, we use the 3-year issue from the par yield curve. The yield is 7.0% and therefore the coupon rate is 7.0%. The present value of the cash flow for this issue is then:

$$\frac{3.5}{(1 + z_1)^1} + \frac{3.5}{(1 + z_2)^2} + \frac{3.5}{(1 + z_3)^3} + \frac{3.5}{(1 + z_4)^4} + \frac{3.5}{(1 + z_5)^5} + \frac{103.5}{(1 + z_6)^6}$$

Substituting: $z_1 = 2.3\%$, $z_2 = 2.5\%$, $z_3 = 2.7073\%$, and $z_4 = 2.9148\%$, and $z_5 = 3.2333\%$ and setting the present value equal to the price of the 3-year issue (100), we obtain:

$$\frac{3.5}{(1.023)^1} + \frac{3.5}{(1.025)^2} + \frac{3.5}{(1.027073)^3} + \frac{3.5}{(1.029148)^4}$$

$$+\frac{3.5}{(1.032333)^5} + \frac{103.5}{(1 + z_6)^6} = 100$$

Solving the above equation we would find that z_6 is 3.5586%. Therefore, the 3-year spot rate on a bond-equivalent basis is 7.1173%.

To summarize the findings for the spot rates:

Period	Year	Annualized Spot Rate (BEY)	z_t
1	0.5	4.6000%	2.3000%
2	1.0	5.0000	2.5000
3	1.5	5.4146	2.7073
4	2.0	5.8297	2.9148
5	2.5	6.4665	3.2333
6	3.0	7.1173	3.5586

20. To obtain the arbitrage-free value of an 8% coupon 3-year Treasury bond, the cash flows for the bond are discounted at the spot rates in the previous question as shown below:

Period	Annual Spot Rate (%)	Semiannual Spot Rate (%)	Cash Flow	PV of CF
1	4.6000	2.3000	$4.0	$3.9101
2	5.0000	2.5000	4.0	3.8073
3	5.4146	2.7073	4.0	3.6919
4	5.8297	2.9148	4.0	3.5657
5	6.4665	3.2333	4.0	3.4116
6	7.1173	3.5586	104.0	84.3171
			Total	$102.7037

The arbitrage-free value of this bond is $102.7037.

21. The nominal spread fails to take into consideration 1) the shape of the yield curve (and therefore spot rates) and 2) any option embedded in a bond.

22. The Z-spread relative to the Treasury spot rate curve is the spread that when added to all the Treasury spot rates will produce a present value for the cash flows equal to the market price. The present value using each of the three spreads in the question—80, 90, and 100 basis points—is shown below:

Period	Years to Maturity	Spot Rate (BEY) (%)	Semiannual Spot Rate (%)	Cash Flow	PV at Assumed Spread (bps)		
					80	90	100
1	0.5	5.0	2.50	$3	$2.9155	$2.9140	$2.9126
2	1.0	5.4	2.70	3	2.8223	2.8196	2.8168
3	1.5	5.8	2.90	3	2.7216	2.7176	2.7137
4	2.0	6.4	3.20	3	2.6042	2.5992	2.5942
5	2.5	7.0	3.50	3	2.4777	2.4717	2.4658
6	3.0	7.2	3.60	3	2.3709	2.3641	2.3573
7	3.5	7.4	3.70	3	2.2645	2.2569	2.2493
8	4.0	7.8	3.90	103	73.5466	73.2652	72.9849
				Total	91.7233	91.4083	91.0947

The last three columns in the table show the assumed spread. One-half of the spread is added to the column showing the semiannual spot rate. Then the cash flow is discounted using the semiannual spot rate plus one-half the assumed spread.

As can be seen, when a 90 basis point spread is used, the present value of the cash flow is equal to the price of the non-Treasury issue, $91.4083. Therefore, the Z-spread is 90 basis points.

23. When the yield curve is flat, all the cash flows are discounted at the same rate. Therefore, if Treasury securities are the benchmark, the nominal spread will be equal to the Z-spread. So, in the case of the corporate bond issues where there is no embedded option, using either measure is acceptable. In contrast, for corporate bonds issues in the portfolio with embedded options, the option-adjusted spread is more appropriate than either the nominal spread or the Z-spread regardless of the shape of the yield curve. Consequently, Joan Thomas would have to agree that the option-adjusted spread should be used for the corporate issues with embedded options.

24. **A.** There are several assumptions that are made in valuing bonds with embedded options. One important assumption is interest rate volatility. Because these assumptions differ from dealer to dealer, the OAS values may differ substantially.

B. The relationship between the OAS, Z-spread, and option cost is as follows:

Option cost = Z-spread − OAS

If a bond has no embedded option, then there is no option cost. That is, the option cost is zero. Substituting zero into the above equation, we have

Z-spread = OAS

That is, the Z-spread is equal to the OAS. This is the reason why Mr. Tinker observed that for the issues with no embedded options the OAS is the same as the Z-spread.

C. A negative value for the option cost means that the investor has purchased an option from the issuer. A putable bond is an example of where the investor purchases an option. This explains why Mr. Tinker finds that a negative value for the option cost was reported for the putable bond issues. When there is no embedded option, the option cost is zero and that is why Mr. Tinker finds this value for issues with this characteristic. A positive value for the option cost means that the investor has sold an option to the issuer. This occurs for callable bond issues, as Mr. Tinker observes.

25. **A.** Because the Treasury securities are the benchmark, the OAS reflects a spread to compensate for credit risk and liquidity risk. (Remember that option risk has already been removed.)

B. Since the benchmark is the issuer's on-the-run yield curve, the spread already reflects credit risk. So, basically the OAS reflects compensation for liquidity risk. (Remember that option risk has already been removed.)

C. The answer depends on the benchmark interest rates used by the dealer firm. If the benchmark interest rates are Treasury rates, then the OAS is better for the issue that Mr. Dumas is considering. If the benchmark is the issuer's on-the-run yield curve, then the issue that the dealer is offering to Mr. Dumas is more attractive. However, the qualifier is that the answer also depends on the interest rate volatility assumed by the dealer and the interest rate volatility assumed by Mr. Dumas when analyzing the issue using System A and System B. Without knowing the assumed interest rate volatilities, no statement can be made about the relative value of these two issues.

26. We will use these notations in the reading:

   f = the forward rate
   t = the subscript before f and will indicate the length of time that the rate applies
   m = the subscript after f and will indicate when the forward rate begins

All periods are equal to six months.

The forward rate is then found as follows:

$$_t f_m = \left[\frac{\left(1 + z_{m+t}\right)^{m+t}}{\left(1 + z_m\right)^m} \right]^{1/t} - 1$$

A. For the 6-month forward rate six months from now, $t = 1$ and $m = 1$. Therefore,

$$_1 f_1 = \left[\frac{\left(1 + z_{1+1}\right)^{1+1}}{\left(1 + z_1\right)^1} \right]^{1/1} - 1$$

or

$$_1 f_1 = \left[\frac{\left(1 + z_2\right)^2}{\left(1 + z_1\right)^1} \right]^1 - 1$$

Since

$$z_1 = 5.0\%/2 = 2.5\% \text{ and } z_2 = 5.4\%/2 = 2.7\%$$

then

$$_1 f_1 = \left[\frac{\left(1.027\right)^2}{\left(1.025\right)^1} \right]^1 - 1 = 0.029004 = 2.9004\%$$

Then the annualized 6-month forward rate six months from now on a bond-equivalent basis is 5.8008%.

B. For the 6-month forward rate one year from now, $t = 1$ and $m = 2$. Therefore,

$$_1f_2 = \left[\frac{\left(1 + z_{2+1}\right)^{2+1}}{\left(1 + z_2\right)^2} \right]^{1/1} - 1$$

or

$$_1f_2 = \left[\frac{\left(1 + z_3\right)^3}{\left(1 + z_2\right)^2} \right]^1 - 1$$

Since

$$z_2 = 5.4\%/2 = 2.7\% \text{ and } z_3 = 5.8\%/2 = 2.9\%$$

then

$$_1f_2 = \left[\frac{\left(1.029\right)^3}{\left(1.027\right)^2} \right]^1 - 1 = 0.033012 = 3.3012\%$$

Then the annualized 6-month forward rate one year from now on a bond-equivalent basis is 6.6023%.

C. For the 6-month forward rate three years from now, $t = 1$ and $m = 6$. Therefore,

$$_1f_6 = \left[\frac{\left(1 + z_{6+1}\right)^{6+1}}{\left(1 + z_6\right)^6} \right]^{1/1} - 1$$

or

$$_1f_6 = \left[\frac{\left(1 + z_7\right)^7}{\left(1 + z_6\right)^6} \right]^{1/1} - 1$$

Since

$$z_6 = 7.2\%/2 = 3.6\% \text{ and } z_7 = 7.4\%/2 = 3.7\%$$

then

$$_1f_6 = \left[\frac{\left(1.037\right)^7}{\left(1.036\right)^6} \right]^{1/1} - 1 = 0.04302 = 4.302\%$$

Then the annualized 6-month forward rate three years from now on a bond-equivalent basis is 8.6041%.

D. For the 2-year forward rate one year from now, $t = 4$ and $m = 2$. Therefore,

$$_4f_2 = \left[\frac{\left(1 + z_{4+2}\right)^{4+2}}{\left(1 + z_2\right)^2} \right]^{1/4} - 1$$

or

$$_4f_2 = \left[\frac{\left(1 + z_6\right)^6}{\left(1 + z_2\right)^2} \right]^{1/4} - 1$$

Since

$$z_2 = 5.4\%/2 = 2.7\% \text{ and } z_6 = 7.2\%/2 = 3.6\%$$

then

$$_4f_2 = \left[\frac{(1.036)^6}{(1.027)^2}\right]^{1/4} - 1 = 0.04053 = 4.053\%$$

Then the annualized 2-year forward rate one year from now on a bond-equivalent basis is 8.1059%.

E. For the 1-year forward rate two years from now, $t = 2$ and $m = 4$. Therefore,

$$_2f_4 = \left[\frac{\left(1 + z_{2+4}\right)^{2+4}}{\left(1 + z_4\right)^4}\right]^{1/2} - 1$$

or

$$_2f_4 = \left[\frac{\left(1 + z_6\right)^6}{\left(1 + z_4\right)^4}\right]^{1/2} - 1$$

Since

$$z_4 = 6.4\%/2 = 3.2\% \text{ and } z_6 = 7.2\%/2 = 3.6\%$$

then

$$_2f_4 = \left[\frac{(1.036)^6}{(1.032)^4}\right]^{1/2} - 1 = 0.04405 = 4.405\%$$

Then the annualized 1-year forward rate two years from now on a bond-equivalent basis is 8.810%.

27. The 6-month forward rate six months from now as found in the previous question is 5.8008%. The two alternatives are:

Alternative 1   Invest $X at the 1-year spot rate of 5.4% for one year

Alternative 2   Invest $X today at the 6-month spot rate of 5.0% and reinvest at the end of six months the proceeds at the 6-month forward rate of 5.8008%

For Alternative 1, the amount at the end of one year will be:

$$\$X(1 + 0.054/2)^2 = 1.054729(\$X)$$

For Alternative 2, the amount at the end of one year will be:

$$\$X(1 + 0.05/2)(1 + 0.058008/2) = 1.054729 \ (\$X)$$

Thus, the two alternatives produce the same future value if the 6-month forward rate six months from now is 5.8008%.

28. Discounting at spot rates and forward rates will produce the same value for a bond. This is because spot rates are nothing more than packages of short-term forward rates. So, the second sales person's comment is wrong about the superiority of forward rates for valuation compared to spot rates.

29. C is correct. All else equal, the bond with the highest coupon will require the highest portion of the total dollar return to come from reinvestment income.

This is particularly true when the bond is selling at a premium, that is, more reinvestment income is required to offset the capital loss on the bond. Bond 3, with a coupon rate of 8.5 percent, is the bond that is *most* dependent on reinvestment income.

30. B is correct. The zero-volatility spread is equal to the option-adjusted spread plus the option cost. Because the option cost for a callable bond is positive, the zero-volatility spread must be greater than the option-adjusted spread.

31. B is correct. One of the drawbacks of the nominal yield spread measure is that the term structure of spot rates is ignored. The zero-volatility yield spread takes the term structure into account by using the entire yield curve to determine the spread over the life of the issue; the nominal yield spread uses only one point on the curve.

32. C is correct. Forward rates are always greater than par or spot rates if the par yield curve is upward sloping. Conversely, forward rates are always less than par or spot rates if the par yield curve is downward sloping.

33. C is correct. For bonds with options, the Z-spread is approximately equal to the OAS plus the cost of the option. However, for some options such as putable bonds the option cost is negative; therefore, the analyst's statement is correct in both respects.

34. C is correct. Solve $((1.045)^4 / (1.04)^3 - 1) \times 2 = 0.1203$ or 12.03%.

35. B is correct. You must use trial-and-error to find the zero-volatility spread. Start with answer A. Add 100 bps to each spot rate. Then divide by two to adjust for semiannual compounding. Find the present values of each cash flow using these discount rates. Add the present values. If they add to the price of the bond, which in this case is $976.45, you've found the static spread. If not, choose a different spread and iteratively repeat the process until the sum of the present values you calculate equals the price of the bond.

    For this problem, solve $5 / (1 + (0.060 + 0.015) / 2) + 5 / (1 + (0.075 + 0.015) / 2)^2 + 5 / (1 + (0.090 + 0.015) / 2)^3 + 105 / (1 + (0.100 + 0.015) / 2)^4 = 97.645$.

36. B is correct. OAS is model dependent, the Z-spread is not.

37. A is correct. The cost of the option is equal to the Z-spread – OAS = 120 bp – 70 bp = 50 bps.

38. A is correct. Interest rates rose and therefore the coupon interest was reinvested at higher rates. Because the bond was held until maturity, the realized yield was higher than the YTM at initial issue. If the bond had not been held until maturity, more information would be needed to answer the question.

Introduction to the Measurement of Interest Rate Risk

by Frank J. Fabozzi, CFA

LEARNING OUTCOMES

Mastery	The candidate should be able to:
☐	**a** distinguish between the full valuation approach (the scenario analysis approach) and the duration/convexity approach for measuring interest rate risk, and explain the advantage of using the full valuation approach;
☐	**b** describe the price volatility characteristics for option-free, callable, prepayable, and putable bonds when interest rates change;
☐	**c** describe positive convexity and negative convexity, and their relation to bond price and yield;
☐	**d** calculate and interpret the effective duration of a bond, given information about how the bond's price will increase and decrease for given changes in interest rates;
☐	**e** calculate the approximate percentage price change for a bond, given the bond's effective duration and a specified change in yield;
☐	**f** distinguish among the alternative definitions of duration and explain why effective duration is the most appropriate measure of interest rate risk for bonds with embedded options;
☐	**g** calculate the duration of a portfolio, given the duration of the bonds comprising the portfolio, and explain the limitations of portfolio duration;
☐	**h** describe the convexity measure of a bond and estimate a bond's percentage price change, given the bond's duration and convexity and a specified change in interest rates;
☐	**i** distinguish between modified convexity and effective convexity;
☐	**j** calculate the price value of a basis point (PVBP), and explain its relationship to duration;
☐	**k** describe the impact of yield volatility on the interest rate risk of a bond.

Fixed Income Analysis for the Chartered Financial Analyst® Program, Second Edition, by Frank J. Fabozzi, CFA. Copyright © 2004 by CFA Institute.

1 INTRODUCTION

In the reading on risks associated with investing in bonds, we discussed the interest rate risk associated with investing in bonds. We know that the value of a bond moves in the opposite direction to a change in interest rates. If interest rates increase, the price of a bond will decrease. For a short bond position, a loss is generated if interest rates fall. However, a manager wants to know more than simply when a position generates a loss. To control interest rate risk, a manager must be able to quantify that result.

What is the key to measuring the interest rate risk? It is the accuracy in estimating the value of the position after an adverse interest rate change. A valuation model determines the value of a position after an adverse interest rate move. Consequently, if a reliable valuation model is not used, there is no way to properly measure interest rate risk exposure.

There are two approaches to measuring interest rate risk—the full valuation approach and the duration/convexity approach.

2 THE FULL VALUATION APPROACH

The most obvious way to measure the interest rate risk exposure of a bond position or a portfolio is to re-value it when interest rates change. The analysis is performed for different scenarios with respect to interest rate changes. For example, a manager may want to measure the interest rate exposure to a 50 basis point, 100 basis point, and 200 basis point instantaneous change in interest rates. This approach requires the re-valuation of a bond or bond portfolio for a given interest rate change scenario and is referred to as the full valuation approach. It is sometimes referred to as **scenario analysis** because it involves assessing the exposure to interest rate change scenarios.

To illustrate this approach, suppose that a manager has a $10 million par value position in a 9% coupon 20-year bond. The bond is option-free. The current price is 134.6722 for a yield (i.e., yield to maturity) of 6%. The market value of the position is $13,467,220 (134.6722% × $10 million). Since the manager owns the bond, she is concerned with a rise in yield since this will decrease the market value of the position. To assess the exposure to a rise in market yields, the manager decides to look at how the value of the bond will change if yields change instantaneously for the following three scenarios: 1) 50 basis point increase, 2) 100 basis point increase, and 3) 200 basis point increase. This means that the manager wants to assess what will happen to the bond position if the yield on the bond increases from 6% to 1) 6.5%, 2) 7%, and 3) 8%. Because this is an option-free bond, valuation is straightforward. In the examples that follow, we will use one yield to discount each of the cash flows. In other words, to simplify the calculations, we will assume a flat yield curve (even though that assumption doesn't fit the examples perfectly). The price of this bond per $100 par value and the market value of the $10 million par position is shown in Exhibit 1. Also shown is the new market value and the percentage change in market value.

Exhibit 1	Illustration of Full Valuation Approach to Assess the Interest Rate Risk of a Bond Position for Three Scenarios

Current bond position: 9% coupon 20-year bond (option-free)
Price: 134.6722
Yield to maturity: 6%
Par value owned: $10 million
Market value of position: $13,467,220.00

	Exhibit 1	Continued				

Scenario	Yield Change (bps)	New Yield (%)	New Price ($)	New Market Value ($)	Percentage Change in Market Value (%)
1	50	6.5	127.7606	12,776,050	−5.13
2	100	7.0	121.3551	12,135,510	−9.89
3	200	8.0	109.8964	10,989,640	−18.40

In the case of a portfolio, each bond is valued for a given scenario and then the total value of the portfolio is computed for a given scenario. For example, suppose that a manager has a portfolio with the following two option-free bonds: 1) 6% coupon 5-year bond and 2) 9% coupon 20-year bond. For the shorter term bond, $5 million of par value is owned and the price is 104.3760 for a yield of 5%. For the longer term bond, $10 million of par value is owned and the price is 134.6722 for a yield of 6%. Suppose that the manager wants to assess the interest rate risk of this portfolio for a 50, 100, and 200 basis point increase in interest rates assuming both the 5-year yield and 20-year yield change by the same number of basis points. Exhibit 2 shows the interest rate risk exposure. Panel A of the exhibit shows the market value of the 5-year bond for the three scenarios. Panel B does the same for the 20-year bond. Panel C shows the total market value of the two-bond portfolio and the percentage change in the market value for the three scenarios.

In the illustration in Exhibit 2, it is assumed that both the 5-year and the 20-year yields changed by the same number of basis points. The full valuation approach can also handle scenarios where the yield curve does not change in a parallel fashion. Exhibit 3 illustrates this for our portfolio that includes the 5-year and 20-year bonds. The scenario analyzed is a yield curve shift combined with shifts in the level of yields. In the illustration in Exhibit 3, the following yield changes for the 5-year and 20-year yields are assumed:

Scenario	Change in 5-Year Rate (bps)	Change in 20-Year Rate (bps)
1	50	10
2	100	50
3	200	100

The last panel in Exhibit 3 shows how the market value of the portfolio changes for each scenario.

Exhibit 2	Illustration of Full Valuation Approach to Assess the Interest Rate Risk of a Two Bond Portfolio (Option-Free) for Three Scenarios Assuming a Parallel Shift in the Yield Curve

Panel A

Bond 1: 6% coupon 5-year bond
Initial price: 104.3760
Yield: 5%
Par value: $5,000,000
Initial market value: $5,218,800

(continued)

Exhibit 2	Continued

Scenario	Yield Change (bps)	New Yield (%)	New Price	New Market Value ($)
1	50	5.5	102.1600	5,108,000
2	100	6.0	100.0000	5,000,000
3	200	7.0	95.8417	4,792,085

Panel B

Bond 2: 9% coupon 20-year bond
Initial price: 134.6722
Yield: 6%
Par value: $10,000,000
Initial market value: $13,467,220

Scenario	Yield Change (bps)	New Yield (%)	New Price	New Market Value ($)
1	50	6.5	127.7605	12,776,050
2	100	7.0	121.3551	12,135,510
3	200	8.0	109.8964	10,989,640

Panel C

Initial Portfolio Market value: $18,686,020.00

Scenario	Yield Change (bps)	Market Value Of Bond 1 ($)	Market Value Of Bond 2 ($)	Portfolio ($)	Percentage Change in Market Value (%)
1	50	5,108,000	12,776,050	17,884,020	−4.29
2	100	5,000,000	12,135,510	17,135,510	−8.30
3	200	4,792,085	10,989,640	15,781,725	−15.54

The full valuation approach seems straightforward. If one has a good valuation model, assessing how the value of a portfolio or individual bond will change for different scenarios for parallel and nonparallel yield curve shifts measures the interest rate risk of a portfolio.

A common question that often arises when using the full valuation approach is which scenarios should be evaluated to assess interest rate risk exposure. For some regulated entities, there are specified scenarios established by regulators. For example, it is common for regulators of depository institutions to require entities to determine the impact on the value of their bond portfolio for a 100, 200, and 300 basis point instantaneous change in interest rates (up and down). (Regulators tend to refer to this as "simulating" interest rate scenarios rather than scenario analysis.) Risk managers and highly leveraged investors such as hedge funds tend to look at extreme scenarios to assess exposure to interest rate changes. This practice is referred to as **stress testing**.

Exhibit 3	Illustration of Full Valuation Approach to Assess the Interest Rate Risk of a Two Bond Portfolio (Option-Free) for Three Scenarios Assuming a Nonparallel Shift in the Yield Curve

Panel A

Bond 1: 6% coupon 5-year bond
Initial price: 104.3760
Yield: 5%
Par value: $5,000,000
Initial market value: $5,218,800

Scenario	Yield Change (bps)	New Yield (%)	New Price	New Market Value ($)
1	50	5.5	102.1600	5,108,000
2	100	6.0	100.0000	5,000,000
3	200	7.0	95.8417	4,792,085

Panel B

Bond 2: 9% coupon 20-year bond
Initial price: 134.6722
Yield: 6%
Par value: $10,000,000
Initial market value: $13,467,220

Scenario	Yield Change (bps)	New Yield (%)	New Price	New Market Value ($)
1	10	6.1	133.2472	13,324,720
2	50	6.5	127.7605	12,776,050
3	100	7.0	121.3551	12,135,510

Panel C

Initial Portfolio Market value: $18,686,020.00

Scenario	Market Value of			Percentage Change in Market Value (%)
	Bond 1 ($)	Bond 2 ($)	Portfolio ($)	
1	5,108,000	13,324,720	18,432,720	−1.36
2	5,000,000	12,776,050	17,776,050	−4.87
3	4,792,085	12,135,510	16,927,595	−9.41

Of course, in assessing how changes in the yield curve can affect the exposure of a portfolio, there are an infinite number of scenarios that can be evaluated. The state-of-the-art technology involves using a complex statistical procedure[1] to determine a likely set of yield curve shift scenarios from historical data.

It seems like the reading should end right here. We can use the full valuation approach to assess the exposure of a bond or portfolio to interest rate changes to evaluate any scenario, assuming—and this must be repeated continuously—*that the*

---

1 The procedure used is principal component analysis.

manager has a good valuation model to estimate what the price of the bonds will be in each interest rate scenario. However, we are not stopping here. In fact, the balance of this reading is considerably longer than this section. Why? The reason is that the full valuation process can be very time consuming. This is particularly true if the portfolio has a large number of bonds, even if a minority of those bonds are complex (i.e., have embedded options). While the full valuation approach is the recommended method, managers want one simple measure that they can use to get an idea of how bond prices will change if rates change in a parallel fashion, rather than having to revalue an entire portfolio. In the reading on the risks associated with investing in bonds, such a measure was introduced—duration. We will discuss this measure as well as a supplementary measure (convexity) in Sections 4 and 5, respectively. To build a foundation to understand the limitations of these measures, we describe the basic price volatility characteristics of bonds in Section 3. The fact that there are limitations of using one or two measures to describe the interest rate exposure of a position or portfolio should not be surprising. These measures provide a starting point for assessing interest rate risk.

3   PRICE VOLATILITY CHARACTERISTICS OF BONDS

In the reading on the risks associated with investing in bonds, we described the characteristics of a bond that affect its price volatility: 1) maturity, 2) coupon rate, and 3) presence of embedded options. We also explained how the level of yields affects price volatility. In this section, we will take a closer look at the price volatility of bonds.

3.1 Price Volatility Characteristics of Option-Free Bonds

Let's begin by focusing on option-free bonds (i.e., bonds that do not have embedded options). A fundamental characteristic of an option-free bond is that the price of the bond changes in the opposite direction to a change in the bond's yield. Exhibit 4 illustrates this property for four hypothetical bonds assuming a par value of $100.

Exhibit 4	Price/Yield Relationship for Four Hypothetical Option-Free Bonds			
	Price ($)			
Yield (%)	**6%/5 Year**	**6%/20 Year**	**9%/5 Year**	**9%/20 Year**
4.00	108.9826	127.3555	122.4565	168.3887
5.00	104.3760	112.5514	117.5041	150.2056
5.50	102.1600	106.0195	115.1201	142.1367
5.90	100.4276	101.1651	113.2556	136.1193
5.99	100.0427	100.1157	112.8412	134.8159
6.00	100.0000	100.0000	112.7953	134.6722
6.01	99.9574	99.8845	112.7494	134.5287
6.10	99.5746	98.8535	112.3373	133.2472
6.50	97.8944	94.4479	110.5280	127.7605
7.00	95.8417	89.3225	108.3166	121.3551
8.00	91.8891	80.2072	104.0554	109.8964

Exhibit 5	Price/Yield Relationship for a Hypothetical Option-Free Bond

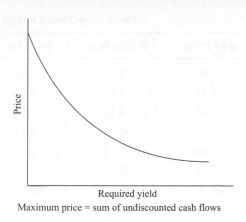

Maximum price = sum of undiscounted cash flows

When the price/yield relationship for any option-free bond is graphed, it exhibits the shape shown in Exhibit 5. Notice that as the yield increases, the price of an option-free bond declines. However, this relationship is not linear (i.e., not a straight line relationship). The shape of the price/yield relationship for any option-free bond is referred to as convex. This price/yield relationship reflects an instantaneous change in the required yield.

The price sensitivity of a bond to changes in the yield can be measured in terms of the dollar price change or the percentage price change. Exhibit 6 uses the four hypothetical bonds in Exhibit 4 to show the percentage change in each bond's price for various changes in yield, assuming that the initial yield for all four bonds is 6%. An examination of Exhibit 6 reveals the following properties concerning the price volatility of an option-free bond:

Property 1:	Although the price moves in the opposite direction from the change in yield, the percentage price change is not the same for all bonds.
Property 2:	For small changes in the yield, the percentage price change for a given bond is roughly the same, whether the yield increases or decreases.
Property 3:	For large changes in yield, the percentage price change is not the same for an increase in yield as it is for a decrease in yield.
Property 4:	For a given large change in yield, the percentage price increase is greater than the percentage price decrease.

While the properties are expressed in terms of percentage price change, they also hold for dollar price changes.

Exhibit 6	Instantaneous Percentage Price Change for Four Hypothetical Bonds (Initial Yield for All Four Bonds Is 6%)

	Percentage Price Change			
New Yield (%)	6%/5 Year	6%/20 Year	9%/5 Year	9%/20 Year
4.00	8.98	27.36	8.57	25.04
5.00	4.38	12.55	4.17	11.53

(continued)

| Exhibit 6 | Continued |

| | Percentage Price Change | | | |
New Yield (%)	6%/5 Year	6%/20 Year	9%/5 Year	9%/20 Year
5.50	2.16	6.02	2.06	5.54
5.90	0.43	1.17	0.41	1.07
5.99	0.04	0.12	0.04	0.11
6.01	−0.04	−0.12	−0.04	−0.11
6.10	−0.43	−1.15	−0.41	−1.06
6.50	−2.11	−5.55	−2.01	−5.13
7.00	−4.16	−10.68	−3.97	−9.89
8.00	−8.11	−19.79	−7.75	−18.40

An explanation for these last two properties of bond price volatility lies in the convex shape of the price/yield relationship. Exhibit 7 illustrates this. The following notation is used in the exhibit

Y = initial yield
Y_1 = lower yield
Y_2 = higher yield
P = initial price
P_1 = price at lower yield Y_1
P_2 = price at higher yield Y_2

What was done in the exhibit was to change the initial yield (Y) up and down by the same number of basis points. That is, in Exhibit 7, the yield is decreased from Y to Y_1 and increased from Y to Y_2 such that the change is the same:

$$Y - Y_1 = Y_2 - Y$$

Also, the change in yield is a large number of basis points.

The vertical distance from the horizontal axis (the yield) to the intercept on the graph shows the price. The change in the initial price (P) when the yield declines from Y to Y_1 is equal to the difference between the new price (P_1) and the initial price (P). That is,

Change in price when yield decreases = $P_1 - P$

The change in the initial price (P) when the yield increases from Y to Y_2 is equal to the difference between the new price (P_2) and the initial price (P). That is,

Change in price when yield increases = $P_2 - P$

Exhibit 7	Graphical Illustration of Properties 3 and 4 for an Option-Free Bond

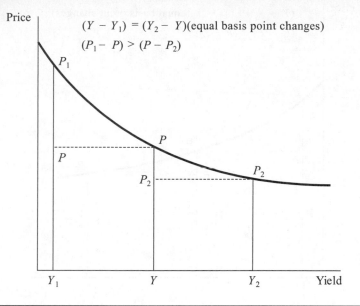

As can be seen in the exhibit, the change in price when yield decreases is not equal to the change in price when yield increases by the same number of basis points. That is,

$$P_1 - P \neq P_2 - P$$

This is what Property 3 states.

A comparison of the price change shows that the change in price when yield decreases is greater than the change in price when yield increases. That is,

$$P_1 - P > P_2 - P$$

This is Property 4.

The implication of Property 4 is that if an investor owns a bond, the capital gain that will be realized if the yield decreases is greater than the capital loss that will be realized if the yield increases by the same number of basis points. For an investor who is short a bond (i.e., sold a bond not owned), the reverse is true: the potential capital loss is greater than the potential capital gain if the yield changes by a given number of basis points.

The convexity of the price/yield relationship impacts Property 4. Exhibit 8 shows a less convex price/yield relationship than Exhibit 7. That is, the price/yield relationship in Exhibit 8 is less bowed than the price/yield relationship in Exhibit 7. Because of the difference in the convexities, look at what happens when the yield increases and decreases by the same number of basis points and the yield change is a large number of basis points. We use the same notation in Exhibits 8 and 9 as in Exhibit 7. Notice that while the price gain when the yield decreases is greater than the price decline when the yield increases, the gain is not much greater than the loss. In contrast, Exhibit 9 has much greater convexity than the bonds in Exhibits 7 and 8, and the price gain is significantly greater than the loss for the bonds depicted in Exhibits 7 and 8.

Exhibit 8	Impact of Convexity on Property 4: Less Convex Bond

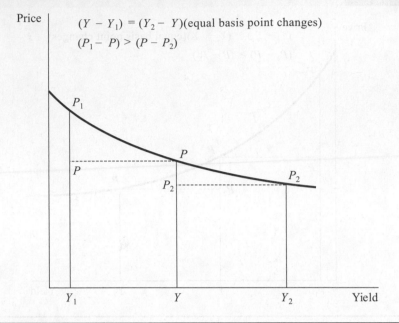

$(Y - Y_1) = (Y_2 - Y)$(equal basis point changes)
$(P_1 - P) > (P - P_2)$

Exhibit 9	Impact of Convexity on Property 4: Highly Convex Bond

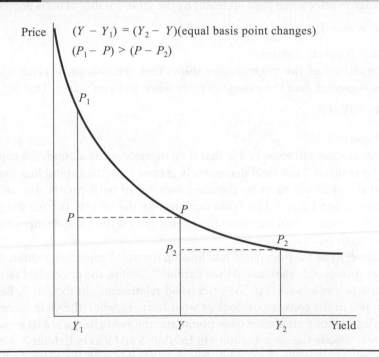

$(Y - Y_1) = (Y_2 - Y)$(equal basis point changes)
$(P_1 - P) > (P - P_2)$

3.2 Price Volatility of Bonds with Embedded Options

Now let's turn to the price volatility of bonds with embedded options. As explained in previous readings, the price of a bond with an embedded option is comprised of two components. The first is the value of the same bond if it had no embedded option (that is, the price if the bond is option free). The second component is the value of the embedded option. In other words, the value of a bond with embedded options is equal to the value of an option-free bond plus or minus the value of embedded options.

The two most common types of embedded options are call (or prepay) options and put options. As interest rates in the market decline, the issuer may call or prepay the debt obligation prior to the scheduled principal payment date. The other type of option is a put option. This option gives the investor the right to require the issuer to purchase the bond at a specified price. Below we will examine the price/yield relationship for bonds with both types of embedded options (calls and puts) and implications for price volatility.

Exhibit 10	Price/Yield Relationship for a Callable Bond and an Option-Free Bond

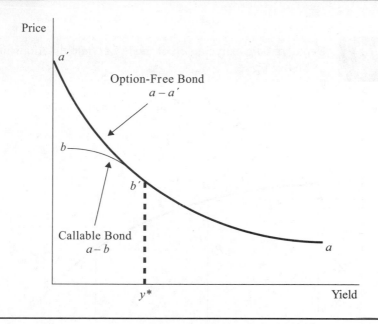

3.2.1 *Bonds with Call and Prepay Options*

In the discussion below, we will refer to a bond that may be called or is prepayable as a callable bond. Exhibit 10 shows the price/yield relationship for an option-free bond and a callable bond. The convex curve given by $a–a'$ is the price/yield relationship for an option-free bond. The unusual shaped curve denoted by $a–b$ in the exhibit is the price/yield relationship for the callable bond.

The reason for the price/yield relationship for a callable bond is as follows. When the prevailing market yield for comparable bonds is higher than the coupon rate on the callable bond, it is unlikely that the issuer will call the issue. For example, if the coupon rate on a bond is 7% and the prevailing market yield on comparable bonds is 12%, it is highly unlikely that the issuer will call a 7% coupon bond so that it can issue a 12% coupon bond. Since the bond is unlikely to be called, the callable bond will have a similar price/yield relationship to an otherwise comparable option-free bond. Consequently, the callable bond will be valued as if it is an option-free bond. However, since there is still some value to the call option,[2] the bond won't trade exactly like an option-free bond.

---

2 This is because there is still some chance that interest rates will decline in the future and the issue will be called.

As yields in the market decline, the concern is that the issuer will call the bond. The issuer won't necessarily exercise the call option as soon as the market yield drops below the coupon rate. Yet, the value of the embedded call option increases as yields approach the coupon rate from higher yield levels. For example, if the coupon rate on a bond is 7% and the market yield declines to 7.5%, the issuer will most likely not call the issue. However, market yields are now at a level at which the investor is concerned that the issue may eventually be called if market yields decline further. Cast in terms of the value of the embedded call option, that option becomes more valuable to the issuer and therefore it reduces the price relative to an otherwise comparable option-free bond.[3] In Exhibit 10, the value of the embedded call option at a given yield can be measured by the difference between the price of an option-free bond (the price shown on the curve a–a') and the price on the curve a–b. Notice that at low yield levels (below y^* on the horizontal axis), the value of the embedded call option is high.

Exhibit 11	Negative Convexity Region of the Price/Yield Relationship for a Callable Bond

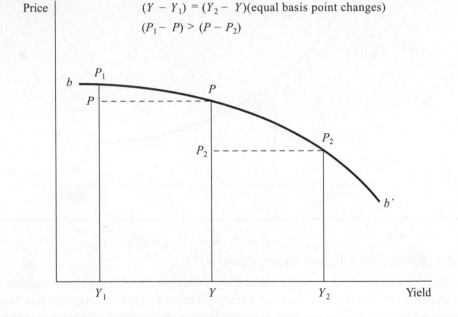

$$(Y - Y_1) = (Y_2 - Y)(\text{equal basis point changes})$$
$$(P_1 - P) > (P - P_2)$$

---

3 For readers who are already familiar with option theory, this characteristic can be restated as follows: When the coupon rate for the issue is below the market yield, the embedded call option is said to be "out-of-the-money." When the coupon rate for the issue is above the market yield, the embedded call option is said to be "in-the-money."

Using the information in Exhibit 10, let's compare the price volatility of a callable bond to that of an option-free bond. Exhibit 11 focuses on the portion of the price/yield relationship for the callable bond where the two curves in Exhibit 10 depart (segment $b'-b$ in Exhibit 10). We know from our earlier discussion that for a large change in yield, the price of an option-free bond increases by more than it decreases (Property 4). Is that what happens for a callable bond in the region of the price/yield relationship shown in Exhibit 11? No, it is not. In fact, as can be seen in the exhibit, the opposite is true! That is, for a given large change in yield, the price appreciation is less than the price decline.

This very important characteristic of a callable bond—that its price appreciation is less than its price decline when rates change by a large number of basis points—is referred to as negative convexity.[4] But notice from Exhibit 10 that callable bonds don't exhibit this characteristic at every yield level. When yields are high (relative to the issue's coupon rate), the bond exhibits the same price/yield relationship as an option-free bond; therefore at high yield levels it also has the characteristic that the gain is greater than the loss. Because market participants have referred to the shape of the price/yield relationship shown in Exhibit 11 as negative convexity, market participants refer to the relationship for an option-free bond as positive convexity. Consequently, a callable bond exhibits negative convexity at low yield levels and positive convexity at high yield levels. This is depicted in Exhibit 12.

Exhibit 12	**Negative and Positive Convexity Exhibited by a Callable Bond**

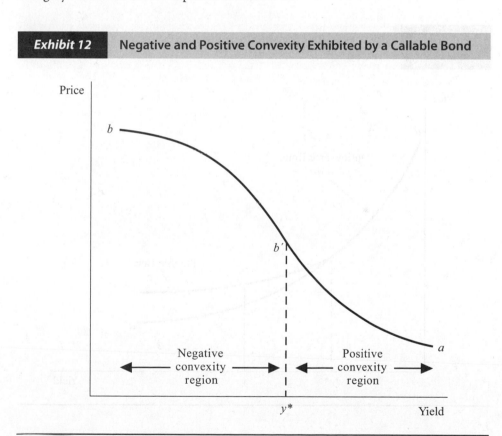

As can be seen from the exhibits, when a bond exhibits negative convexity, the bond compresses in price as rates decline. That is, at a certain yield level there is very little price appreciation when rates decline. When a bond enters this region, the bond is said to exhibit "price compression."

---

4 Mathematicians refer to this shape as being "concave."

3.2.2 *Bonds with Embedded Put Options*

Putable bonds may be redeemed by the bondholder on the dates and at the put price specified in the indenture. Typically, the put price is par value. The advantage to the investor is that if yields rise such that the bond's value falls below the put price, the investor will exercise the put option. If the put price is par value, this means that if market yields rise above the coupon rate, the bond's value will fall below par and the investor will then exercise the put option.

The value of a putable bond is equal to the value of an option-free bond plus the value of the put option. Thus, the difference between the value of a putable bond and the value of an otherwise comparable option-free bond is the value of the embedded put option. This can be seen in Exhibit 13, which shows the price/yield relationship for a putable bond is the curve a–c and for an option-free bond is the curve a–a'.

At low yield levels (low relative to the issue's coupon rate), the price of the putable bond is basically the same as the price of the option-free bond because the value of the put option is small. As rates rise, the price of the putable bond declines, but the price decline is less than that for an option-free bond. The divergence in the price of the putable bond and an otherwise comparable option-free bond at a given yield level (y) is the value of the put option (P_1–P). When yields rise to a level where the bond's price would fall below the put price, the price at these levels is the put price.

Exhibit 13	Price/Yield Relationship for a Putable Bond and an Option-Free Bond

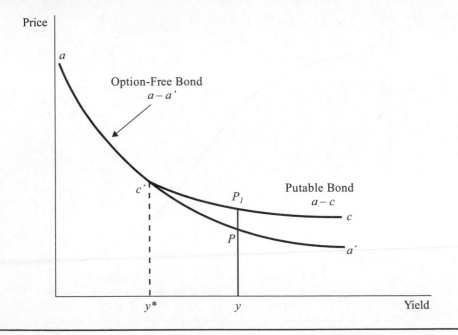

4   DURATION

With the background about the price volatility characteristics of a bond, we can now turn to an alternate approach to full valuation: the duration/convexity approach. As explained in the reading on risks associated with investing in bonds, *duration is a measure of the approximate price sensitivity of a bond to interest rate changes. More specifically, it is the approximate percentage change in price for a 100 basis point change in rates.* We will see in this section that duration is the first (linear) approximation of the percentage price change. To improve the approximation provided by duration, an adjustment for "convexity" can be made. Hence, using duration combined with convexity to estimate the percentage price change of a bond caused by changes in interest rates is called the duration/convexity approach.

4.1 Calculating Duration

In the reading on risks associated with investing in bonds, we explained that the duration of a bond is estimated as follows:

$$\frac{\text{Price if yields decline} - \text{Price if yields rise}}{2(\text{Initial price})(\text{Change in yield in decimal})}$$

If we let

Δy = change in yield in decimal
V_0 = initial price
V_- = price if yields decline by Δy
V_+ = price if yields increase by Δy

then duration can be expressed as

$$\text{Duration} = \frac{V_- - V_+}{2(V_0)(\Delta y)} \tag{1}$$

For example, consider a 9% coupon 20-year option-free bond selling at 134.6722 to yield 6% (see Exhibit 4). Let's change (i.e., shock) the yield down and up by 20 basis points and determine what the new prices will be for the numerator. If the yield is decreased by 20 basis points from 6.0% to 5.8%, the price would increase to 137.5888. If the yield increases by 20 basis points, the price would decrease to 131.8439. Thus,

$\Delta y = 0.002$
$V_0 = 134.6722$
$V_- = 137.5888$
$V_+ = 131.8439$

Then,

$$\text{Duration} = \frac{137.5888 - 131.8439}{2 \times (134.6722) \times (0.002)} = 10.66$$

As explained in the reading on risks associated with investing in bonds, duration is interpreted as the approximate percentage change in price for a 100 basis point change in rates. Consequently, a duration of 10.66 means that the approximate change in price for this bond is 10.66% for a 100 basis point change in rates.

A common question asked about this interpretation of duration is the consistency between the yield change that is used to compute duration using Equation 1 and the interpretation of duration. For example, recall that in computing the duration of the 9% coupon 20-year bond, we used a 20 basis point yield change to obtain the two prices to use in the numerator of Equation 1. Yet, we interpret the duration computed as the approximate percentage price change for a 100 basis point change in yield. The reason is that regardless of the yield change used to estimate duration in Equation 1, the interpretation is the same. If we used a 25 basis point change in yield to compute the prices used in the numerator of Equation 1, the resulting duration is interpreted as the approximate percentage price change for a 100 basis point change in yield. Later we will use different changes in yield to illustrate the sensitivity of the computed duration.

Practice Question 1

  A. Compute the duration of the 9% coupon 20-year option-free bond by changing the yield down and up by 10 basis points. (The relevant values can be found in Exhibit 4.)

  B. Suppose a 6% coupon 20-year option-free bond is selling at par value and therefore offering a yield of 6%. Compute the duration by changing the yield down and up by 10 basis points. (The relevant values can be found in Exhibit 4.)

4.2 Approximating the Percentage Price Change Using Duration

In the reading on risks associated with investing in bonds, we explained how to approximate the percentage price change for a given change in yield and a given duration. Here we will express the process using the following formula:

$$\text{Approximate percentage price change} = -\text{Duration} \times \Delta y_* \times 100 \qquad (2)$$

where Δy^* is the yield change (in decimal) for which the estimated percentage price change is sought.[5] The reason for the negative sign on the right-hand side of Equation 2 is due to the inverse relationship between price change and yield change (e.g., as yields increase, bond prices decrease). The following two examples illustrate how to use duration to estimate a bond's price change.

Example #1: Small change in basis point yield. For example, consider the 9% 20-year bond trading at 134.6722 whose duration we just showed is 10.66. The approximate percentage price change for a 10 basis point increase in yield (i.e., $\Delta y^* = +0.001$) is:

$$\text{Approximate percentage price change} = -10.66 \times (+0.001) \times 100 = -1.066\%$$

How good is this approximation? The actual percentage price change is −1.06% (as shown in Exhibit 6 when yield increases to 6.10%). Duration, in this case, did an excellent job in estimating the percentage price change.

We would come to the same conclusion if we used duration to estimate the percentage price change if the yield declined by 10 basis points (i.e., $\Delta y = -0.001$). In this case, the approximate percentage price change would be +1.066% (i.e., the direction of the estimated price change is the reverse but the magnitude of the change is the same). Exhibit 6 shows that the actual percentage price change is +1.07%.

In terms of estimating the new price, let's see how duration performed. The initial price is 134.6722. For a 10 basis point increase in yield, duration estimates that the price will decline by 1.066%. Thus, the price will decline to 133.2366 (found by multiplying 134.6722 by one minus 0.01066). The actual price from Exhibit 4 if the yield increases by 10 basis points is 133.2472. Thus, the price estimated using duration is close to the actual price.

For a 10 basis point decrease in yield, the actual price from Exhibit 4 is 136.1193, and the estimated price using duration is 136.1078 (a price increase of 1.066%). Consequently, the new price estimated by duration is close to the actual price for a 10 basis point change in yield.

---

[5] The difference between Δy in the duration formula given by Equation 1 and Δy^* in Equation 2 to get the approximate percentage change is as follows. In the duration formula, the Δy is used to estimate duration and, as explained later, for reasonably small changes in yield the resulting value for duration will be the same. We refer to this change as the "rate shock." Given the duration, the next step is to estimate the percentage price change for any change in yield. The Δy^* in Equation 2 is the specific change in yield for which the approximate percentage price change is sought.

Example #2: Large change in basis point yield. Let's look at how well duration does in estimating the percentage price change if the yield increases by 200 basis points instead of 10 basis points. In this case, Δy is equal to +0.02. Substituting into Equation 2, we have

Approximate percentage price change $=-10.66\times(+0.02)\times100=-21.32\%$

How good is this estimate? From Exhibit 6, we see that the actual percentage price change when the yield increases by 200 basis points to 8% is −18.40%. Thus, the estimate is not as accurate as when we used duration to approximate the percentage price change for a change in yield of only 10 basis points. If we use duration to approximate the percentage price change when the yield decreases by 200 basis points, the approximate percentage price change in this scenario is +21.32%. The actual percentage price change as shown in Exhibit 6 is +25.04%.

Let's look at the use of duration in terms of estimating the new price. Since the initial price is 134.6722 and a 200 basis point increase in yield will decrease the price by 21.32%, the estimated new price using duration is 105.9601 (found by multiplying 134.6722 by one minus 0.2132). From Exhibit 4, the actual price if the yield is 8% is 109.8964. Consequently, the estimate is not as accurate as the estimate for a 10 basis point change in yield. The estimated new price using duration for a 200 basis point decrease in yield is 163.3843 compared to the actual price (from Exhibit 4) of 168.3887. Once again, the estimation of the price using duration is not as accurate as for a 10 basis point change. *Notice that whether the yield is increased or decreased by 200 basis points, duration underestimates what the new price will be. We will see why shortly.*

Summary. Let's summarize what we found in our application of duration to approximate the percentage price change:

Yield Change (bps)	Initial Price	New Price		Percent Price Change		Comment
		Based on Duration	Actual	Based on Duration	Actual	
+10	134.6722	133.2366	133.2472	−1.066	−1.06	Estimated price close to new price
−10	134.6722	136.1078	136.1193	+1.066	+1.07	Estimated price close to new price
+200	134.6722	105.9601	109.8964	−21.320	−18.40	Underestimates new price
−200	134.6722	163.3843	168.3887	+21.320	+25.04	Underestimates new price

Should any of this be a surprise to you? No, not after reading Section 3 of this reading and evaluating Equation 2 in terms of the properties for the price/yield relationship discussed in that section. Look again at Equation 2. Notice that whether the change in yield is an increase or a decrease, the approximate percentage price change will be the same except that the sign is reversed. This violates Property 3 and Property 4 with respect to the price volatility of option-free bonds when yields change. Recall that Property 3 states that the percentage price change will not be the same for a large increase and decrease in yield by the same number of basis points. Property 4 states the percentage price increase is greater than the percentage price decrease. These are two reasons why the estimate is inaccurate for a 200 basis point yield change.

Why did the duration estimate of the price change do a good job for a small change in yield of 10 basis points? Recall from Property 2 that the percentage price change will be approximately the same whether there is an increase or decrease in yield by a small number of basis points. We can also explain these results in terms of the graph of the price/yield relationship.

Practice Question 2

Using the duration for the 6% coupon 20-year bond found in part B of Practice Question 1, answer the following questions.

A. What is the approximate percentage price change if interest rates increase by 10 basis points?

B. Comment on the approximation compared to the actual price change as given in Exhibit 6.

C. What is the approximate percentage price change if interest rates decrease by 10 basis points?

D. Comment on the approximation compared to the actual price change as given in Exhibit 6.

E. What is the approximate percentage price change if interest rates increase by 200 basis points?

F. Comment on the approximation compared to the actual price change as given in Exhibit 6.

G. What is the approximate percentage price change if interest rates decrease by 200 basis points?

H. Comment on the approximation compared to the actual price change as given in Exhibit 6.

4.3 Graphical Depiction of Using Duration to Estimate Price Changes

In Section 3, we used the graph of the price/yield relationship to demonstrate the price volatility properties of bonds. We can also use graphs to illustrate what we observed in our examples about how duration estimates the percentage price change, as well as some other noteworthy points.

The shape of the price/yield relationship for an option-free bond is convex. Exhibit 14 shows this relationship. In the exhibit, a tangent line is drawn to the price/yield relationship at yield y^*. (For those unfamiliar with the concept of a tangent line, it is a straight line that just touches a curve at one point within a relevant (local) range. In Exhibit 14, the tangent line touches the curve at the point where the yield is equal to y^* and the price is equal to p^*.) The tangent line is used to *estimate* the new price if the yield changes. If we draw a vertical line from any yield (on the horizontal axis), as in Exhibit 14, the distance between the horizontal axis and the tangent line represents the price approximated by using duration starting with the initial yield y^*.

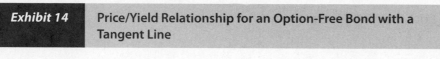

Exhibit 14	Price/Yield Relationship for an Option-Free Bond with a Tangent Line

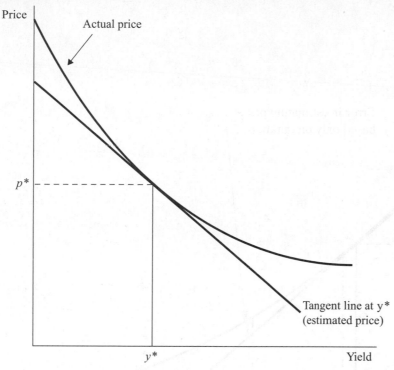

Now how is the tangent line related to duration? Given an initial price and a specific yield change, the tangent line tells us the approximate new price of a bond. The approximate percentage price change can then be computed for this change in yield. But this is precisely what duration (using Equation 2) gives us: the approximate percentage price change for a given change in yield. Thus, using the tangent line, one obtains the same approximate percentage price change as using Equation 2.

This helps us understand why duration did an effective job of estimating the percentage price change, or equivalently the new price, when the yield changes by a small number of basis points. Look at Exhibit 15. Notice that for a small change in yield, the tangent line does not depart much from the price/yield relationship. Hence, when the yield changes up or down by 10 basis points, the tangent line does a good job of estimating the new price, as we found in our earlier numerical illustration.

Exhibit 15	Estimating the New Price Using a Tangent Line

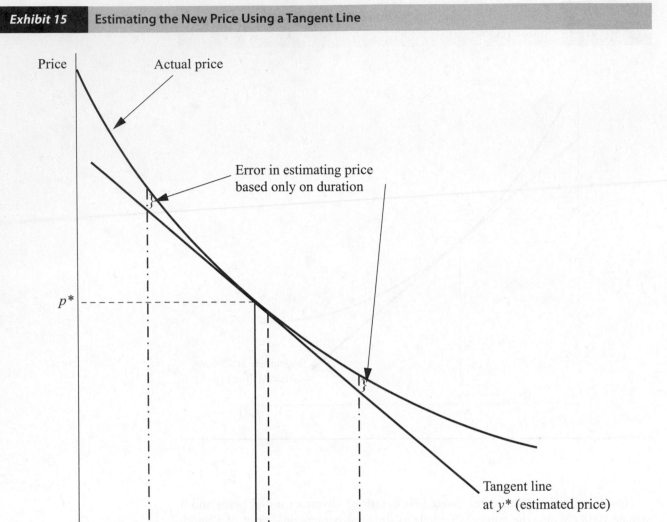

Exhibit 15 shows what happens to the estimate using the tangent line when the yield changes by a large number of basis points. Notice that the error in the estimate gets larger the further one moves from the initial yield. The estimate is less accurate the more convex the bond as illustrated in Exhibit 16.

| **Exhibit 16** | Estimating the New Price for a Large Yield Change for Bonds with Different Convexities |

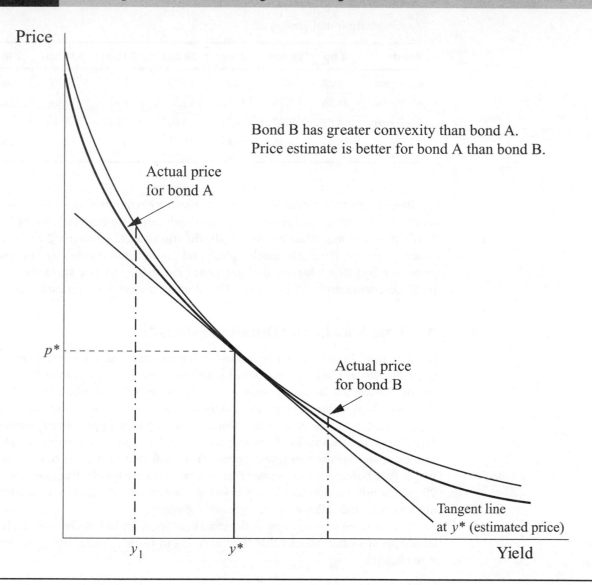

Bond B has greater convexity than bond A.
Price estimate is better for bond A than bond B.

Actual price
for bond A

Actual price
for bond B

Tangent line
at y^* (estimated price)

Also note that, regardless of the magnitude of the yield change, the tangent line always underestimates what the new price will be for an option-free bond because the tangent line is below the price/yield relationship. This explains why we found in our illustration that when using duration, we underestimated what the actual price will be.

The results reported in Exhibit 17 are for option-free bonds. When we deal with more complicated securities, small rate shocks that do not reflect the types of rate changes that may occur in the market do not permit the determination of how prices can change. This is because expected cash flows may change when dealing with bonds with embedded options. In comparison, if large rate shocks are used, we encounter the asymmetry caused by convexity. Moreover, large rate shocks may cause dramatic changes in the expected cash flows for bonds with embedded options that may be far different from how the expected cash flows will change for smaller rate shocks.

| Exhibit 17 | Duration Estimates for Different Rate Shocks |

Assumption: Initial yield is 6%.

Bond	1 bp	10 bps	20 bps	50 bps	100 bps	150 bps	200 bps
6% 5 year	4.27	4.27	4.27	4.27	4.27	4.27	4.27
6% 20 year	11.56	11.56	11.56	11.57	11.61	11.69	11.79
9% 5 year	4.07	4.07	4.07	4.07	4.07	4.08	4.08
9% 20 year	10.66	10.66	10.66	10.67	10.71	10.77	10.86

There is another potential problem with using small rate shocks for complicated securities. The prices that are inserted into the duration formula as given by Equation 1 are derived from a valuation model. The duration measure depends crucially on the valuation model. If the rate shock is small and the valuation model used to obtain the prices for Equation 1 is poor, dividing poor price estimates by a small shock in rates (in the denominator) will have a significant effect on the duration estimate.

4.4 Rate Shocks and Duration Estimate

In calculating duration using Equation 1, it is necessary to shock interest rates (yields) up and down by the same number of basis points to obtain the values for V_- and V_+. In our illustration, 20 basis points was arbitrarily selected. But how large should the shock be? That is, how many basis points should be used to shock the rate?

In Exhibit 17, the duration estimates for our four hypothetical bonds using Equation 1 for rate shocks of 1 basis point to 200 basis points are reported. The duration estimates for the two 5-year bonds are not affected by the size of the shock. The two 5-year bonds are less convex than the two 20-year bonds. But even for the two 20-year bonds, for the size of the shocks reported in Exhibit 17, the duration estimates are not materially affected by the greater convexity.

What is done in practice by dealers and vendors of analytical systems? Each system developer uses rate shocks that they have found to be realistic based on historical rate changes.

4.5 Modified Duration versus Effective Duration

One form of duration that is cited by practitioners is **modified duration**. Modified duration is the approximate percentage change in a bond's price for a 100 basis point change in yield *assuming that the bond's expected cash flows do not change when the yield changes*. What this means is that in calculating the values of V_- and V_+ in Equation 1, the same cash flows used to calculate V_0 are used. Therefore, the change in the bond's price when the yield is changed is due solely to discounting cash flows at the new yield level.

The assumption that the cash flows will not change when the yield is changed makes sense for option-free bonds such as noncallable Treasury securities. This is because the payments made by the U.S. Department of the Treasury to holders of its obligations do not change when interest rates change. However, the same cannot be said for bonds with embedded options (i.e., callable and putable bonds and mortgage-backed securities). For these securities, a change in yield may significantly alter the expected cash flows.

In Section 3, we showed the price/yield relationship for callable and prepayable bonds. Failure to recognize how changes in yield can alter the expected cash flows will produce two values used in the numerator of Equation 1 that are not good estimates of how the price will actually change. The duration is then not a good number to use to estimate how the price will change.

Some valuation models for bonds with embedded options take into account how changes in yield will affect the expected cash flows. Thus, when V_- and V_+ are the values produced from these valuation models, the resulting duration takes into account both the discounting at different interest rates and how the expected cash flows may change. When duration is calculated in this manner, it is referred to as effective duration or option-adjusted duration. (Lehman Brothers refers to this measure in some of its publications as adjusted duration.) Exhibit 18 summarizes the distinction between modified duration and effective duration.

Exhibit 18	Modified Duration versus Effective Duration

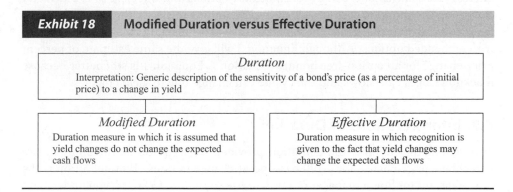

Duration
Interpretation: Generic description of the sensitivity of a bond's price (as a percentage of initial price) to a change in yield

Modified Duration
Duration measure in which it is assumed that yield changes do not change the expected cash flows

Effective Duration
Duration measure in which recognition is given to the fact that yield changes may change the expected cash flows

The difference between modified duration and effective duration for bonds with embedded options can be quite dramatic. For example, a callable bond could have a modified duration of 5 but an effective duration of only 3. For certain collateralized mortgage obligations, the modified duration could be 7 and the effective duration 20! Thus, using modified duration as a measure of the price sensitivity for a security with embedded options to changes in yield would be misleading. Effective duration is the more appropriate measure for any bond with an embedded option.

4.6 Macaulay Duration and Modified Duration

It is worth comparing the relationship between modified duration to another duration measure, **Macaulay duration**. Modified duration can be written as[6]:

$$\frac{1}{(1+\text{Yield}/k)}\left[\frac{1\times\text{PVCF}_1 +2\times\text{PVCF}_2 +\ldots+n\times\text{PVCF}_n}{k\times\text{Price}}\right] \quad (3)$$

where

k = number of periods, or payments, per year (e.g., k = 2 for semiannual-pay bonds and k = 12 for monthly-pay bonds)

n = number of periods until maturity (i.e., number of years to maturity times k)

Yield = yield to maturity of the bond

PVCF_t = present value of the cash flow in period t discounted at the yield to maturity where t = 1, 2, . . ., n

We know that duration tells us the approximate percentage price change for a bond if the yield changes.

---

6 More specifically, this is the formula for the modified duration of a bond on a coupon anniversary date.

The expression in the brackets of the modified duration formula given by Equation 3 is a measure formulated in 1938 by Frederick Macaulay.[7] This measure is popularly referred to as Macaulay duration. Thus, modified duration is commonly expressed as:

$$\text{Modified duration} = \frac{\text{Macaulay duration}}{(1 + \text{Yield}/k)}$$

The general formulation for duration as given by Equation 1 provides a shortcut procedure for determining a bond's modified duration. Because it is easier to calculate the modified duration using the short-cut procedure, most vendors of analytical software will use Equation 1 rather than Equation 3 to reduce computation time.

However, *modified duration is a flawed measure of a bond's price sensitivity to interest rate changes for a bond with embedded options and therefore so is Macaulay duration.* The duration formula given by Equation 3 misleads the user because it masks the fact that changes in the expected cash flows must be recognized for bonds with embedded options. Although Equation 3 will give the same estimate of percent price change for an option-free bond as Equation 1, Equation 1 is still better because it acknowledges cash flows and thus value can change due to yield changes.

4.7 Interpretations of Duration

Throughout this volume, the definition provided for duration is: the approximate percentage price change for a 100 basis point change in rates. That definition is the most relevant for how a manager or investor uses duration. In fact, if you understand this definition, you can easily calculate the change in a bond's value.

For example, suppose we want to know the approximate percentage change in price for a 50 basis point change in yield for our hypothetical 9% coupon 20-year bond selling for 134.6722. Since the duration is 10.66, a 100 basis point change in yield would change the price by about 10.66%. For a 50 basis point change in yield, the price will change by approximately 5.33% (= 10.66%/2). So, if the yield increases by 50 basis points, the price will decrease by about 5.33% from 134.6722 to 127.4942.

Now let's look at some other duration definitions or interpretations that appear in publications and are cited by managers in discussions with their clients.

4.7.1 *Duration Is the "First Derivative"*

Sometimes a market participant will refer to duration as the "first derivative of the price/yield function" or simply the "first derivative." Wow! Sounds impressive. First, "derivative" here has nothing to do with "derivative instruments" (i.e., futures, swaps, options, etc.). A derivative as used in this context is obtained by differentiating a mathematical function using calculus. There are first derivatives, second derivatives, and so on. When market participants say that duration is the first derivative, here is what they mean. The first derivative calculates the slope of a line—in this case, the slope of the tangent line in Exhibit 14. If it were possible to write a mathematical equation for a bond in closed form, the first derivative would be the result of differentiating that equation the first time. Even if you don't know how to do the process of differentiation to get the first derivative, it sounds like you are really smart since it suggests you understand calculus! While it is a correct interpretation of duration, it is an interpretation that in no way helps us understand what the interest rate risk is of a bond. That is, it is an operationally meaningless interpretation.

Why is it an operationally meaningless interpretation? Go back to the $10 million bond position with a duration of 6. Suppose a client is concerned with the exposure

---

7 Frederick Macaulay, *Some Theoretical Problems Suggested by the Movement of Interest Rates, Bond Yields, and Stock Prices in the U.S. Since 1856* (New York: National Bureau of Economic Research, 1938).

of the bond to changes in interest rates. Now, tell that client the duration is 6 and that it is the first derivative of the price function for that bond. What have you told the client? Not much. In contrast, tell that client that the duration is 6 and that duration is the approximate price sensitivity of a bond to a 100 basis point change in rates and you have told the client more relevant information with respect to the bond's interest rate risk.

4.7.2 *Duration Is Some Measure of Time*

When the concept of duration was originally introduced by Macaulay in 1938, he used it as a gauge of the time that the bond was outstanding. More specifically, Macaulay defined duration as the weighted average of the time to each coupon and principal payment of a bond. Subsequently, duration has too often been thought of in temporal terms, i.e., years. This is most unfortunate for two reasons.

First, in terms of dimensions, there is nothing wrong with expressing duration in terms of years because that is the proper dimension of this value. But the proper interpretation is that duration is the price volatility of a zero-coupon bond with that number of years to maturity. So, when a manager says a bond has a duration of 4 years, it is not useful to think of this measure in terms of time, but that the bond has the price sensitivity to rate changes of a 4-year zero-coupon bond.

Second, thinking of duration in terms of years makes it difficult for managers and their clients to understand the duration of some complex securities. Here are a few examples. For a mortgage-backed security that is an interest-only security (i.e., receives coupons but not principal repayment) discussed at Level II, the duration is negative. What does a negative number, say, −4 mean? In terms of our interpretation as a percentage price change, it means that when rates change by 100 basis points, the price of the bond changes by about 4%, but the change is in the same direction as the change in rates.

As a second example, consider an inverse floater created in the collateralized mortgage obligation (CMO) market. The underlying collateral for such a security might be loans with 25 years to final maturity. However, an inverse floater can have a duration that easily exceeds 25. This does not make sense to a manager or client who uses a measure of time as a definition for duration.

As a final example, consider derivative instruments, such as an option that expires in one year. Suppose that it is reported that its duration is 60. What does that mean? To someone who interprets duration in terms of time, does that mean 60 years, 60 days, 60 seconds? It doesn't mean any of these. It simply means that the option tends to have the price sensitivity to rate changes of a 60-year zero-coupon bond.

4.7.3 *Forget First Derivatives and Temporal Definitions*

The bottom line is that one should not care if it is technically correct to think of duration in terms of years (volatility of a zero-coupon bond) or in terms of first derivatives. There are even some who interpret duration in terms of the "half-life" of a security.[8] Subject to the limitations that we will describe as we proceed in this book, duration is the measure of a security's price sensitivity to changes in yield. We will fine tune this definition as we move along.

Users of this interest rate risk measure are interested in what it tells them about the price sensitivity of a bond (or a portfolio) to changes in interest rates. Duration provides the investor with a feel for the dollar price exposure or the percentage price exposure to potential interest rate changes. Try the following definitions on a client who has a portfolio with a duration of 4 and see which one the client finds most useful for understanding the interest rate risk of the portfolio when rates change:

---

8 "Half-life" is the time required for an element to be reduced to half its initial value.

Definition 1:   The duration of 4 for your portfolio indicates that the portfolio's value will change by approximately 4% if rates change by 100 basis points.

Definition 2:   The duration of 4 for your portfolio is the first derivative of the price function for the bonds in the portfolio.

Definition 3:   The duration of 4 for your portfolio is the weighted average number of years to receive the present value of the portfolio's cash flows.

Definition 1 is clearly preferable. It would be ridiculous to expect clients to understand the last two definitions better than the first.

Moreover, interpreting duration in terms of a measure of price sensitivity to interest rate changes allows a manager to make comparisons between bonds regarding their interest rate risk under certain assumptions.

4.8 Portfolio Duration

A portfolio's duration can be obtained by calculating the weighted average of the duration of the bonds in the portfolio. The weight is the proportion of the portfolio that a security comprises. Mathematically, a portfolio's duration can be calculated as follows:

$$w_1 D_1 + w_2 D_2 + w_3 D_3 + \ldots + w_K D_K$$

where

w_i = market value of bond i/market value of the portfolio
D_i = duration of bond i
K = number of bonds in the portfolio

To illustrate this calculation, consider the following 3-bond portfolio in which all three bonds are option free:

Bond	Price ($)	Yield (%)	Par Amount Owned	Market Value	Duration
10% 5 year	100.0000	10	$4 million	$4,000,000	3.861
8% 15 year	84.6275	10	5 million	4,231,375	8.047
14% 30 year	137.8586	10	1 million	1,378,586	9.168

In this illustration, it is assumed that the next coupon payment for each bond is exactly six months from now (i.e., there is no accrued interest). The market value for the portfolio is $9,609,961. Since each bond is option free, modified duration can be used. The market price per $100 par value of each bond, its yield, and its duration are given below:

In this illustration, K is equal to 3 and:

w_1 = $4,000,000/$9,609,961 = 0.416 D_1 = 3.861
w_2 = $4,231,375/$9,609,961 = 0.440 D_2 = 8.047
w_3 = $1,378,586/$9,609,961 = 0.144 D_3 = 9.168

The portfolio's duration is:

$$0.416(3.861) + 0.440(8.047) + 0.144(9.168) = 6.47$$

A portfolio duration of 6.47 means that for a 100 basis point change in the yield for each of the three bonds, the market value of the portfolio will change by approximately 6.47%. But keep in mind, the yield for each of the three bonds must change by 100 basis points for the duration measure to be useful. (In other words, there must be a parallel shift in the yield curve.) This is a *critical assumption* and its importance cannot be overemphasized.

An alternative procedure for calculating the duration of a portfolio is to calculate the dollar price change for a given number of basis points for each security in the portfolio and then add up all the price changes. Dividing the total of the price changes by the initial market value of the portfolio produces a percentage price change that can be adjusted to obtain the portfolio's duration.

For example, consider the 3-bond portfolio shown above. Suppose that we calculate the dollar price change for each bond in the portfolio based on its respective duration for a 50 basis point change in yield. We would then have:

Bond	Market Value	Duration	Change in Value for 50 bps Yield Change
10% 5 year	$4,000,000	3.861	$77,220
8% 15 year	4,231,375	8.047	170,249
14% 30 year	1,378,586	9.168	63,194
		Total	$310,663

Thus, a 50 basis point change in all rates changes the market value of the 3-bond portfolio by $310,663. Since the market value of the portfolio is $9,609,961, a 50 basis point change produced a change in value of 3.23% ($310,663 divided by $9,609,961). Since duration is the approximate percentage change for a 100 basis point change in rates, this means that the portfolio duration is 6.46 (found by doubling 3.23). This is essentially the same value for the portfolio's duration as found earlier.

CONVEXITY ADJUSTMENT

5

The duration measure indicates that regardless of whether interest rates increase or decrease, the approximate percentage price change is the same. However, as we noted earlier, this is not consistent with Property 3 of a bond's price volatility. Specifically, while for small changes in yield the percentage price change will be the same for an increase or decrease in yield, for large changes in yield this is not true. This suggests that duration is only a good approximation of the percentage price change for small changes in yield.

We demonstrated this property earlier using a 9% 20-year bond selling to yield 6% with a duration of 10.66. For a 10 basis point change in yield, the estimate was accurate for both an increase or decrease in yield. However, for a 200 basis point change in yield, the approximate percentage price change was off *considerably*.

The reason for this result is that duration is in fact a first (linear) approximation for a small change in yield.[9] The approximation can be improved by using a second approximation. This approximation is referred to as the "convexity adjustment." It is used to approximate the change in price that is not explained by duration.

The formula for the convexity adjustment to the percentage price change is

Convexity adjustment to the percentage price change =

$$C \times (\Delta y*)^2 \times 100 \tag{4}$$

where $\Delta y* =$ the change in yield for which the percentage price change is sought and

$$C = \frac{V_+ + V_- - 2V_0}{2V_0(\Delta y)^2} \qquad (5)$$

The notation is the same as used in Equation 1 for duration.[10]

For example, for our hypothetical 9% 20-year bond selling to yield 6%, we know from Section 4.1 that for a 20 basis point change in yield ($\Delta y = 0.002$):

$$V_0 = 134.6722, V_- = 137.5888, \text{ and } V_+ = 131.8439$$

Substituting these values into the formula for C:

$$C = \frac{131.8439 + 137.5888 - 2(134.6722)}{2(134.6722)(0.002)^2} = 81.95$$

Suppose that a convexity adjustment is sought for the approximate percentage price change for our hypothetical 9% 20-year bond for a change in yield of 200 basis points. That is, in Equation 4, $\Delta y*$ is 0.02. Then the convexity adjustment is

$$81.95 \times (0.02)^2 \times 100 = 3.28\%$$

If the yield decreases from 6% to 4%, the convexity adjustment to the percentage price change based on duration would also be 3.28%.

The approximate percentage price change based on duration and the convexity adjustment is found by adding the two estimates. So, for example, if yields change from 6% to 8%, the estimated percentage price change would be:

Estimated change using duration	=	−21.32%
Convexity adjustment	=	+3.28%
Total estimated percentage price change	=	−18.04%

The actual percentage price change is −18.40%.

For a decrease of 200 basis points, from 6% to 4%, the approximate percentage price change would be as follows:

Estimated change using duration	=	+21.32%
Convexity adjustment	=	+3.28%
Total estimated percentage price change	=	+24.60%

The actual percentage price change is +25.04%. Thus, duration *combined* with the convexity adjustment does a better job of estimating the sensitivity of a bond's price change to large changes in yield (i.e., better than using duration alone).

5.1 Positive and Negative Convexity Adjustment

Notice that when the convexity adjustment is positive, we have the situation described earlier that the gain is greater than the loss for a given large change in rates. That is, the bond exhibits positive convexity. We can see this in the example above. However, if the convexity adjustment is negative, we have the situation where the loss will be greater than the gain. For example, suppose that a callable bond has an effective duration of 4 and a convexity adjustment for a 200 basis point change of −1.2%.

The bond then exhibits the negative convexity property illustrated in Exhibit 11. The approximate percentage price change after adjusting for convexity is:

---

10 See Footnote 5 for the difference between Δy in the formula for C and $\Delta y*$ in Equation 4.

Estimated change using duration	=	−8.0%
Convexity adjustment	=	−1.2%
Total estimated percentage price change	=	−9.2%

For a decrease of 200 basis points, the approximate percentage price change would be as follows:

Estimated change using duration	=	+8.0%
Convexity adjustment	=	−1.2%
Total estimated percentage price change	=	+6.8%

Notice that the loss is greater than the gain—a property called negative convexity that we discussed in Section 3 and illustrated in Exhibit 11.

Practice Question 3

A. What is the value for C in Equation 4 for a 6% 20-year option-free bond selling at par to yield 6% using an interest rate shock of 10 basis points (i.e., $\Delta y_* = 0.001$)? (The relevant values can be found in Exhibit 4.)

B. Using the convexity adjustment for the 6% coupon 20-year option-free bond selling at 100 to yield 6% found in part A, complete the following:

i. For a 10 basis point increase in interest rates (i.e., $\Delta y_* = 0.001$):

Estimated change using duration	=	_____ %
Convexity adjustment	=	_____ %
Total estimated percentage price change	=	_____ %
Actual percentage price change[a]	=	_____ %

ii. For a 10 basis point decrease in interest rates (i.e., $\Delta y_* = -0.001$):

Estimated change using duration	=	_____ %
Convexity adjustment	=	_____ %
Total estimated percentage price change	=	_____ %
Actual percentage price change[a]	=	_____ %

iii. For a 200 basis point increase in interest rates (i.e., $\Delta y_* = 0.02$):

Estimated change using duration	=	_____ %
Convexity adjustment	=	_____ %
Total estimated percentage price change	=	_____ %
Actual percentage price change[a]	=	_____ %

iv. For a 200 basis point decrease in interest rates (i.e., $\Delta y_* = -0.02$):

Estimated change using duration	=	_____ %
Convexity adjustment	=	_____ %
Total estimated percentage price change	=	_____ %
Actual percentage price change[a]	=	_____ %

---
[a] See Exhibit 6.

5.2 Modified and Effective Convexity Adjustment

The prices used in computing C in Equation 4 to calculate the convexity adjustment can be obtained by assuming that, when the yield changes, the expected cash flows either do not change or they do change. In the former case, the resulting convexity is referred to as modified convexity adjustment. (Actually, in the industry, convexity adjustment is not qualified by the adjective "modified.") In contrast, effective convexity adjustment assumes that the cash flows change when yields change. This is the same distinction made for duration.

As with duration, there is little difference between a modified convexity adjustment and an effective convexity adjustment for option-free bonds. However, for bonds with embedded options, there can be quite a difference between the calculated modified convexity adjustment and an effective convexity adjustment. In fact, for all option-free bonds, either convexity adjustment will have a positive value. For bonds with embedded options, the calculated effective convexity adjustment can be negative when the calculated modified convexity adjustment is positive.

6   PRICE VALUE OF A BASIS POINT

Some managers use another measure of the price volatility of a bond to quantify interest rate risk—the price value of a basis point (PVBP). This measure, also called the dollar value of an 01 (DV01), is the absolute value of the change in the price of a bond for a 1 basis point change in yield. That is,

PVBP = |Initial price − Price if yield is changed by 1 basis point|

Does it make a difference if the yield is increased or decreased by 1 basis point? It does not because of Property 2—the change will be about the same for a small change in basis points.

To illustrate the computation, let's use the values in Exhibit 4. If the initial yield is 6%, we can compute the PVBP by using the prices for either the yield at 5.99% or 6.01%. The PVBP for both for each bond is shown below:

Coupon	6.0%	6.0%	9.0%	9.0%
Maturity	5	20	5	20
Initial price	$100.0000	$100.0000	$112.7953	$134.6722
Price at 5.99%	100.0427	100.1157	112.8412	134.8159
PVBP at 5.99%	$0.0427	$0.1157	$0.0459	$0.1437
Price at 6.01%	99.9574	99.8845	112.7494	134.5287
PVBP at 6.01%	$0.0426	$0.1155	$0.0459	$0.1435

The PVBP is related to duration. In fact, PVBP is simply a special case of dollar duration described in the reading on risks associated with investing in bonds. We know that the duration of a bond is the approximate percentage price change for a 100 basis point change in interest rates. We also know how to compute the approximate percentage price change for any number of basis points given a bond's duration using Equation 2. Given the initial price and the approximate percentage price change for 1 basis point, we can compute the change in price for a 1 basis point change in rates.

For example, consider the 9% 20-year bond. The duration for this bond is 10.66. Using Equation 2, the approximate percentage price change for a 1 basis point increase in interest rates (i.e., $\Delta y = 0.0001$), ignoring the negative sign in Equation 2, is:

$$10.66 \times (0.0001) \times 100 = 0.1066\%$$

Given the initial price of 134.6722, the dollar price change estimated using duration is

$$0.1066\% \times 134.6722 = \$0.1435$$

This is the same price change as shown above for a PVBP for this bond. Below is 1) the PVBP based on a 1 basis point increase for each bond and 2) the estimated price change using duration for a 1 basis point increase for each bond:

Coupon	6.0%	6.0%	9.0%	9.0%
Maturity	5	20	5	20
PVBP for 1 bp increase	$0.0426	$0.1155	$0.0459	$0.1435
Duration of bond	4.2700	11.5600	4.0700	10.6600
Duration estimate	$0.0427	$0.1156	$0.0459	$0.1436

THE IMPORTANCE OF YIELD VOLATILITY

7

What we have not considered thus far is the volatility of interest rates. For example, as we explained in the reading on risks associated with investing in bonds, all other factors equal, the higher the coupon rate, the lower the price volatility of a bond to changes in interest rates. In addition, the higher the level of yields, the lower the price volatility of a bond to changes in interest rates. This is illustrated in Exhibit 19 which shows the price/yield relationship for an option-free bond. When the yield level is high (Y_H, for example, in the exhibit), a change in interest rates does not produce a large change in the initial price. For example, as yields change from Y_H to Y_H'', the price changes a *small* amount from P_H to P_H''. However, when the yield level is low and changes (Y_L to Y_L', for example, in the exhibit), a change in interest rates of the same number of basis points as Y_H to Y_H'' produces a *large* change in the initial price (P_L to P_L').

This can also be cast in terms of duration properties: the higher the coupon, the lower the duration; the higher the yield level, the lower the duration. Given these two properties, a 10-year non-investment grade bond has a lower duration than a current coupon 10-year Treasury note since the former has a higher coupon rate and trades at a higher yield level. Does this mean that a 10-year non-investment grade bond has less interest rate risk than a current coupon 10-year Treasury note? Consider also that a 10-year Swiss government bond has a lower coupon rate than a current coupon 10-year U.S. Treasury note and trades at a lower yield level. Therefore, a 10-year Swiss government bond will have a higher duration than a current coupon 10-year Treasury note. Does this mean that a 10-year Swiss government bond has greater interest rate risk than a current coupon 10-year U.S. Treasury note? The missing link is the relative volatility of rates, which we shall refer to as yield volatility or interest rate volatility.

| Exhibit 19 | The Effect of Yield Level on Price Volatility—Option-Free Bond |

$$(Y_H{}' - Y_H) = (Y_H - Y_H{}'') = (Y_L{}' - Y_L) = (Y_L - Y_L{}'')$$
$$(P_H - P_H{}') < (P_L - P_L{}') \text{ and}$$
$$(P_H - P_H{}'') < (P_L - P_L{}'')$$

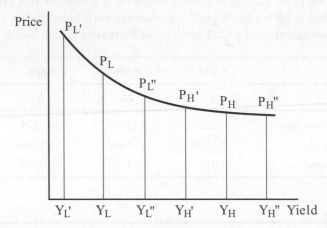

The greater the expected yield volatility, the greater the interest rate risk for a given duration and current value of a position. In the case of non-investment grade bonds, while their durations are less than current coupon Treasuries of the same maturity, the yield volatility of non-investment grade bonds is greater than that of current coupon Treasuries. For the 10-year Swiss government bond, while the duration is greater than for a current coupon 10-year U.S. Treasury note, the yield volatility of 10-year Swiss bonds is considerably less than that of 10-year U.S. Treasury notes.

Consequently, to measure the exposure of a portfolio or position to interest rate changes, it is necessary to measure yield volatility. This requires an understanding of the fundamental principles of probability distributions. The measure of yield volatility is the standard deviation of yield changes. As we will see, depending on the underlying assumptions, there could be a wide range for the yield volatility estimates.

A framework that ties together the price sensitivity of a bond position to interest rate changes and yield volatility is the value-at-risk (VaR) framework. Risk in this framework is defined as the maximum estimated loss in market value of a given position that is expected to occur with a specified probability.

SOLUTIONS FOR PRACTICE QUESTIONS

1. **A.** From Exhibit 4 we know that

    $$V_-(\text{price at } 5.9\% \text{ yield}) = 136.1193$$
    $$V_+(\text{price at } 6.1\% \text{ yield}) = 133.2472$$

    and

    $$\Delta y = 0.001$$
    $$V_0 = 134.6722$$
    $$\text{Duration} = \frac{136.1193 - 133.2472}{2(134.6722)(0.001)} = 10.66$$

Note that this is the same value computed for duration when a 20 basis point rate shock was used. Duration is therefore the same for this bond regardless of whether the yield change used is 20 basis points or 10 basis points.

B. From Exhibit 4 we know that

$$V_-(\text{price } 5.9\% \text{ yield}) = 101.1651$$
$$V_+(\text{price } 6.1\% \text{ yield}) = 98.8535$$

and

$$\Delta y = 0.001$$
$$V_0 = 100$$
$$\text{Duration} = \frac{101.1651 - 98.8535}{2(100)(0.001)} = 11.56$$

2. A. The duration for this bond is 11.56. The approximate percentage price change for a 10 basis point increase in interest rates is

$$= -11.56 \times 0.0010 \times 100 = -1.156\%$$

B. The actual percentage price change from Exhibit 6 is −1.15%. Therefore the estimate is good.

C. The approximate percentage price change for a 10 basis point decrease in interest rates is

$$= -11.56 \times (-0.0010) \times 100 = 1.156\%$$

D. The actual percentage price change from Exhibit 6 is 1.17%. Therefore the estimate is good.

E. The approximate percentage price change for a 200 basis point increase in interest rates is

$$= -11.56 \times 0.02 \times 100 = -23.12\%$$

F. The actual percentage price change from Exhibit 6 is −19.79%. Therefore duration provides a poor estimate and underestimates the new price.

G. The approximate percentage price change for a 200 basis point decrease in interest rates is

$$= -11.56 \times (-0.02) \times 100 = 23.12\%$$

H. The actual percentage price change from Exhibit 6 is 27.36%. Therefore duration provides a poor estimate and underestimates the new price.

3. A. For a rate shock of 10 basis points ($\Delta y = 0.001$)

$$C = \frac{98.8535 + 101.1651 - 2(100)}{2(100)(0.001)^2} = 93.00$$

B. **i.** For a 10 basis point increase in interest rates ($\Delta y^* = 0.001$)

Estimated change using duration	−1.16%
Convexity adjustment	0.0093%
Total estimated percentage price change	−1.15%
Actual percentage price change	−1.15%

ii. For a 10 basis point decrease in interest rates ($\Delta y^* = -0.001$)

Estimated change using duration	1.16%
Convexity adjustment	0.0093%
Total estimated percentage price change	1.17%
Actual percentage price change	1.17%

iii. For a 200 basis point increase in interest rates ($\Delta y^* = 0.02$)

Estimated change using duration	−23.12%
Convexity adjustment	3.72%
Total estimated percentage price change	−19.40%
Actual percentage price change	−19.79%

iv. For a 200 basis point decrease in interest rates ($\Delta y^* = -0.02$)

Estimated change using duration	23.12%
Convexity adjustment	3.72%
Total estimated percentage price change	26.84%
Actual percentage price change	27.36%

SUMMARY

- To control interest rate risk, a manager must be able to quantify what will occur from an adverse change in interest rates.

- A valuation model is used to determine the value of a position after an interest rate movement and therefore, if a reliable valuation model is not used, there is no way to measure interest rate risk exposure.

- There are two approaches to measure interest rate risk: full valuation approach and duration/convexity approach.

- The full valuation approach involves revaluing a bond position (every position in the case of a portfolio) for a scenario of interest rate changes.

- The advantage of the full valuation approach is its accuracy with respect to interest rate exposure for a given interest rate change scenario—accurate relative to the valuation model used—but its disadvantage for a large portfolio is having to revalue each bond for each scenario.

- The characteristics of a bond that affect its price volatility are 1) maturity, 2) coupon rate, and 3) presence of any embedded options.

- The shape of the price/yield relationship for an option-free bond is convex.

- The price sensitivity of a bond to changes in the required yield can be measured in terms of the dollar price change or percentage price change.

- One property of an option-free bond is that although its price moves in the opposite direction of a change in yield, the percentage price change is not the same for all bonds.

- A second property of an option-free bond is that for small changes in the required yield, the percentage price change for a given bond is roughly the same whether the yield increases or decreases.

- A third property of an option-free bond is that for a large change in yield, the percentage price change for an increase in yield is not the same for a decrease in yield.

- A fourth property of an option-free bond is that for a large change in yield, the price of an option-free bond increases more than it decreases.

- "Negative convexity" means that for a large change in interest rates, the amount of the price appreciation is less than the amount of the price depreciation.

- Option-free bonds exhibit positive convexity.

- "Positive convexity" means that for a large change in interest rates, the amount of the price appreciation is greater than the amount of the price depreciation.

- A callable bond exhibits positive convexity at high yield levels and negative convexity at low yield levels where "high" and "low" yield levels are relative to the issue's coupon rate.

- At low yield levels (low relative to the issue's coupon rate), the price of a putable bond is basically the same as the price of an option-free bond because the value of the put option is small; as rates rise, the price of a putable bond declines, but the price decline is less than that for an option-free bond.

- Duration is a first approximation of a bond's price or a portfolio's value to interest rate changes.

- To improve the estimate provided by duration, a convexity adjustment can be used.

- Using duration combined with a convexity adjustment to estimate the percentage price change of a bond to changes in interest rates is called the duration/convexity approach to interest rate risk measurement.

- Duration does a good job of estimating the percentage price change for a small change in interest rates but the estimation becomes poorer the larger the change in interest rates.

- In calculating duration, it is necessary to shock interest rates (yields) up and down by the same number of basis points to obtain the values when rates change.

- In calculating duration for option-free bonds, the size of the interest rate shock is unimportant for reasonable changes in yield.

- For bonds with embedded options, the problem with using a small shock to estimate duration is that divergences between actual and estimated price changes are magnified by dividing by a small change in rate in the denominator of the duration formula; in addition, small rate shocks that do not reflect the types of rate changes that may occur in the market do not permit the determination of how prices can change because expected cash flows may change.

- For bonds with embedded options, if large rate shocks are used the asymmetry caused by convexity is encountered; in addition, large rate shocks may cause dramatic changes in the expected cash flows for bonds with embedded options that may be far different from how the expected cash flows will change for smaller rate shocks.

- Modified duration is the approximate percentage change in a bond's price for a 100 basis point change in yield assuming that the bond's expected cash flows do not change when the yield changes.

- In calculating the values to be used in the numerator of the duration formula, for modified duration the cash flows are not assumed to change and therefore, the change in the bond's price when the yield is changed is due solely to discounting at the new yield levels.

- Effective duration is the approximate percentage change in a bond's price for a 100 basis point change in yield assuming that the bond's expected cash flows do change when the yield changes.

- Modified duration is appropriate for option-free bonds; effective duration should be used for bonds with embedded options.

- The difference between modified duration and effective duration for bonds with an embedded option can be quite dramatic.

- Macaulay duration is mathematically related to modified duration and is therefore a flawed measure of the duration of a bond with an embedded option.

- Interpretations of duration in temporal terms (i.e., some measure of time) or calculus terms (i.e., first derivative of the price/yield relationship) are operationally meaningless and should be avoided.

- The duration for a portfolio is equal to the market-value weighted duration of each bond in the portfolio.

- In applying portfolio duration to estimate the sensitivity of a portfolio to changes in interest rates, it is assumed that the yield for all bonds in the portfolio change by the same amount.

- The duration measure indicates that regardless of whether interest rates increase or decrease, the approximate percentage price change is the same; however, this is not a property of a bond's price volatility for large changes in yield.

- A convexity adjustment can be used to improve the estimate of the percentage price change obtained using duration, particularly for a large change in yield.

- The convexity adjustment is the amount that should be added to the duration estimate for the percentage price change in order to obtain a better estimate for the percentage price change.

- The same distinction made between modified duration and effective duration applies to modified convexity adjustment and effective convexity adjustment.

- For a bond with an embedded option that exhibits negative convexity at some yield level, the convexity adjustment will be negative.

- The price value of a basis point (or dollar value of an 01) is the change in the price of a bond for a 1 basis point change in yield.

- The price value of a basis point is the same as the estimated dollar price change using duration for a 1 basis point change in yield.

- Yield volatility must be recognized in estimating the interest rate risk of a bond and a portfolio.

- Value-at-risk is a measure that ties together the duration of a bond and yield volatility.

PRACTICE PROBLEMS FOR READING 58

1. Explain why you agree or disagree with the following statement:

   The disadvantage of the full valuation approach to measuring interest rate risk is that it requires a revaluation of each bond in the portfolio for each interest rate scenario. Consequently, you need a valuation model. In contrast, for the duration/convexity approach there is no need for a valuation model because the duration and convexity adjustment can be obtained without a valuation model.

2. Explain why you agree or disagree with the following statement:

   The problem with both the full valuation approach and the duration/convexity approach is that they fail to take into account how the change in the yield curve can affect a portfolio's value.

3. Explain why you agree or disagree with the following statement:

   If two bonds have the same duration, then the percentage change in price of the two bonds will be the same for a given change in interest rates.

4. James Smith and Donald Robertson are assistant portfolio managers for Micro Management Partners. In a review of the interest rate risk of a portfolio, Smith and Robertson discussed the riskiness of two Treasury securities. Following is the information about these two Treasuries:

Bond	Price	Modified Duration
A	90	4
B	50	6

   Smith noted that Treasury bond B has more price volatility because of its higher modified duration. Robertson disagreed noting that Treasury bond A has more price volatility despite its lower modified duration. Which manager is correct?

5. At its quarterly meeting, the trustees of the National Baggage Handlers Pension Fund reviewed the status of its bond portfolio. The portfolio is managed by William Renfro of Wiser and Wiser Management Company. The portfolio consists of 20% Treasury bonds, 10% corporate bonds that are noncallable for the life of the bonds, 30% callable corporate bonds, and 40% mortgage-backed securities. The report provided by Wiser and Wiser includes the following information for each bond in the portfolio: 1) modified duration and 2) effective duration. The portfolio's modified duration and effective duration were reported to be 5 and 3, respectively. Renfro attended the board meeting to answer any questions that the trustees might have. Nancy Weston, one of the trustees for the fund, prepared the following list of questions:

   A. What does the duration of a bond mean and how should the board interpret the portfolio duration?

   B. Why is the modified duration and effective duration for each Treasury bond and noncallable corporate bond the same?

Practice Problems and Solutions: 1–17 taken from *Fixed Income Analysis for the Chartered Financial Analyst® Program*, Second Edition, by Frank J. Fabozzi, CFA. Copyright © 2004 by CFA Institute. All other problems and solutions copyright © CFA Institute.

    C. What is the appropriate duration measure, effective duration or modified duration?

    D. How were the effective duration measures obtained?

    E. What are the limitations in using duration?

The minutes of the board meeting indicated the following response by Mr. Renfro to each of these questions:

    A. Duration is a measure of the approximate weighted average life of a bond or a bond portfolio. For example, a portfolio duration of 5 means that the fund will realize the return of the amount invested (in present value terms) in about 5 years.

    B. Because the Treasury bonds in the portfolio are noncallable, modified duration is the same as effective duration. The same is true for the corporate bonds that are noncallable for life.

    C. The appropriate measure is the effective duration since it takes into account the option embedded in the bonds held in the portfolio.

    D. We obtained the effective duration from various sources—dealers firms and commercial vendors. There is a standard formula that all of these sources use to obtain the effective duration. Sometimes, a source may provide an effective duration that is not logical and we override the value by using the modified duration. For example, for some of the collateralized mortgage obligations, one vendor reported an effective duration of 40. This value was obviously wrong since the underlying collateral is 30-year loans; therefore, the duration cannot exceed 30. Moreover, for some of the CMOs, the duration is negative and this is obviously wrong. Again, in such instances we use the modified duration.

    E. Duration is only a good measure for small changes in yield and assumes that the yield curve will shift in a parallel fashion. However, if these assumptions are satisfied, two portfolios with the same duration will perform in exactly the same way.

You are employed by Pension Consultants, a consultant to the labor union. You have been given the minutes of the meeting of the board of trustees with the responses of Mr. Renfro to the questions of Ms. Weston. Prepare a report indicating whether you agree or disagree with Mr. Renfro's responses.

6. Lewis Marlo, an assistant portfolio manager, was reviewing a potential buy list of corporate bonds. The list provided information on the effective duration and effective convexity adjustment assuming a 200 basis point change in interest rates for each corporate bond on the list. The senior portfolio manager, Jane Zorick, noticed that Mr. Marlo crossed out each bond with a negative convexity adjustment. When Ms. Zorick asked Mr. Marlo why, he responded that a negative value meant that the particular corporate bond was unattractive. How do you think Ms. Zorick should respond?

7. A client is reviewing information about the portfolio. For one of the issues in the portfolio the client sees the following:

Issue	Maturity	Duration
X	10 years	13

The client has questioned you as to whether or not the reported duration of 13 is correct. The client's concern is that he has heard that duration is some measure of time for a bond and as such cannot exceed the maturity of the security. Yet, the duration of Issue X exceeds its maturity. What explanation do you give to the client?

8. Suppose that you are given the following information about two callable bonds of the same issuer that can be called immediately:

	Estimated Percentage Change in Price If Interest Rates Change by	
	−50 Basis Points (%)	+50 Basis Points (%)
Bond ABC	+2	−5
Bond XYZ	+11	−8

You are told that both bonds have about the same maturity and the coupon rate of one bond is 7% and the other 13%. Suppose that the yield curve for this issuer is flat at 8%. Based on this information, which bond is the lower coupon bond and which is the higher coupon bond? Explain why.

9. **A.** Why is modified duration an inappropriate measure for a high-coupon callable bond?

   B. What would be a better measure than modified duration?

10. Suppose that a 7% coupon corporate bond is immediately callable. Also suppose that if this issuer issued new bonds the coupon rate would be 12%. Why would the modified duration be a good approximation of the effective duration for this bond?

Questions 11–15 are based on the following price information for four bonds and assuming that all four bonds are trading to yield 5%.

	Coupon	5.0%	5.0%	8.0%	8.0%
Yield (%)	Maturity	4	25	4	25
3.00		107.4859	134.9997	118.7148	187.4992
4.00		103.6627	115.7118	114.6510	162.8472
4.50		101.8118	107.4586	112.6826	152.2102
4.75		100.9011	103.6355	111.7138	147.2621
4.90		100.3593	101.4324	111.1374	144.4042
5.00		100.0000	100.0000	110.7552	142.5435
5.10		99.6423	98.5959	110.3746	140.7175
5.25		99.1085	96.5416	109.8066	138.0421
5.50		98.2264	93.2507	108.8679	133.7465
6.00		96.4902	87.1351	107.0197	125.7298
7.00		93.1260	76.5444	103.4370	111.7278

Percentage price change based on an initial yield of 5%:

	Coupon	5.0%	5.0%	8.0%	8.0%
Yield (%)	Maturity	4 (%)	25 (%)	4 (%)	25 (%)
3.00		7.49	35.00	7.19	31.54
4.00		3.66	15.71	3.52	14.24

(continued)

	Coupon	5.0%	5.0%	8.0%	8.0%
Yield (%)	Maturity	4 (%)	25 (%)	4 (%)	25 (%)
4.50		1.81	7.46	1.74	6.78
4.75		0.90	3.64	0.87	3.31
4.90		0.36	1.43	0.35	1.31
5.00		0.00	0.00	0.00	0.00
5.10		−0.36	−1.40	−0.34	−1.28
5.25		−0.89	−3.46	−0.86	−3.16
5.50		−1.77	−6.75	−1.70	−6.17
6.00		−3.51	−12.86	−3.37	−11.80
7.00		−6.87	−23.46	−6.61	−21.62

11. Assuming all four bonds are selling to yield 5%, compute the following for each bond:

    A. Duration based on a 25 basis point rate shock ($\Delta y = 0.0025$).

    B. Duration based on a 50 basis point rate shock ($\Delta y = 0.0050$).

12. Assuming all four bonds are selling to yield 5%, compute the value for C in the convexity equation for each bond using a 25 basis point rate shock ($\Delta y = 0.0025$).

13. A. Using the duration computed in question 11A, compute the approximate percentage price change using duration for the two 8% coupon bonds assuming that the yield changes by 10 basis points ($\Delta y_* = 0.0010$).

    B. How does the estimated percentage price change compare to the actual percentage price change?

14. A. Using the duration computed in question 11A, compute the approximate percentage price change using duration for the two 8% coupon bonds assuming that the yield changes by 200 basis points ($\Delta y_* = 0.02$).

    B. How does the estimated percentage price change compare to the actual percentage price change?

15. A. Using the value for C computed in question 12, compute the convexity adjustment for the two 25-year bonds assuming that the yield changes by 200 basis points ($\Delta y_* = 0.02$).

    B. Compute the estimated percentage price change using duration (as computed in question 11A) and convexity adjustment if yield changes by 200 basis points.

    C. How does the estimated percentage price change using duration and convexity adjustment compare to the actual percentage price change for a 200 basis point change in yield?

16. A. Given the information below for a 6.2% 18-year bond compute the price value of a basis point:

    Price = 114.1338

    Yield = 5%

    Price if yield is 5.01% = 114.0051

    B. If the duration of the 6.2% 18-year bond is 11.28, what is the estimated price change for a 1 basis point change in yield.

17. Why is information about a bond's duration and convexity adjustment insufficient to quantify interest rate risk exposure?

18. A bond that exhibits negative convexity at low yield levels (relative to the bond's coupon rate) and positive convexity at high yield levels (relative to the bond's coupon rate) is *most likely* a(n):

    A. putable bond.

    B. callable bond.

    C. option-free bond selling at a discount.

19. An analyst accurately calculates that the price of an option-free bond with a 9 percent coupon would experience a 12 percent change if market yields increase 100 basis points. If market yields decrease 100 basis points, the bond's price would *most likely*:

    A. increase by 12%.

    B. increase by less than 12%.

    C. increase by more than 12%.

20. At yield levels that are close to the bond's coupon rate, is the price of an option-free bond higher than the price of an otherwise identical:

	callable bond?	putable bond?
A.	No	No
B.	No	Yes
C.	Yes	No

21. The duration of an option-free bond priced at $900 is 8.5. If yields decrease by 150 basis points, the *most* accurate statement about the actual price of the bond after the decrease in yields is that the actual price will be:

    A. equal to $1,014.75.

    B. greater than $1,014.75.

    C. less than $1,014.75 because the lower level of yields increases the bond's interest rate risk.

22. An investor holds two bonds in her portfolio as follows:

Bond	Market Value ($)	Duration
3-year, 6% coupon	300,521	2.67
10-year, 5% coupon	567,000	6.41

The portfolio's duration is *closest* to:

    A. 4.54.

    B. 5.11.

    C. 5.45.

23. Western Investments holds a fixed-income portfolio comprised of four bonds whose market values and durations are given in the following table.

	Bond A	Bond B	Bond C	Bond D
Market value	$200,000	$300,000	$250,000	$550,000
Duration	4	6	7	8

The portfolio's duration is *closest* to:

A. 6.06.

B. 6.25.

C. 6.73.

24. Consider the following statements about non-callable bonds.

   Statement 1   "For non-callable bonds, duration provides only a linear approximation of a bond's price changes as interest rates change."

   Statement 2   "Incorporating convexity into the analysis of a non-callable bond's price changes as interest rates change always results in higher bond price estimates than derived by using only the bond's duration. This is true whether interest rates increase or decrease."

   Are the statements *most likely* correct or incorrect?

   A. Both statements are correct.

   B. Statement 1 is incorrect, but Statement 2 is correct.

   C. Statement 1 is correct, but Statement 2 is incorrect.

25. The modified duration for a bond is 17.45. The market price of the bond is $1,105. The price value of a basis point for the bond is *closest* to:

   A. $1.93.

   B. $64.81.

   C. $192.82.

26. Consider the following statements about bond price volatility.

   Statement 1   "If interest rates increase dramatically, callable bonds can exhibit negative convexity."

   Statement 2   "The higher the level of interest rates, the lower the price volatility of a bond to changes in interest rates."

   Are the statements most likely correct or incorrect?

   A. Both statements are incorrect.

   B. Statement 1 is incorrect, but Statement 2 is correct.

   C. Statement 1 is correct, but Statement 2 is incorrect.

27. From the time of issuance until the bond matures, which of the following bonds is *most likely* to exhibit negative convexity?

   A. A putable bond.

   B. A callable bond.

   C. An option-free bond selling at a discount.

28. A bond with a par value of $1,000 has a duration of 6.2. If the yield on the bond is expected to change from 8.80 percent to 8.95 percent, the estimated new price for the bond following the expected change in yield is *best* described as being:

   A. 0.93% lower than the bond's current price.

   B. 1.70% lower than the bond's current price.

   C. 10.57% lower than the bond's current price.

SOLUTIONS FOR READING 58

1. While it is true that a disadvantage of the full valuation approach is that it requires revaluing the bonds in the portfolio, it is not true that the duration/convexity approach does not require a valuation model. A valuation model is required in order to obtain the prices when rates are shocked that are used in the duration and convexity adjustment formulas.

2. The duration/convexity approach does not take into consideration how the yield curve can shift. However, this is not correct for the full valuation approach since yield curve scenarios are part of the full valuation method.

3. The statement is not correct. While two bonds may have the same duration, they can have different convexities. In addition, the two bonds may have different prices and coupons thus leading to different percentage price changes for the two bonds.

4. The problem here is in the definition of price volatility. It can be measured in terms of dollar price change or percentage price change. Smith is correct that there is greater price volatility for bond B because of its higher modified duration—that is, a higher percentage price change. Robertson is correct that bond A has greater price volatility but in terms of dollar price change. Specifically, for a 100 basis point change in rates, bond A will change by $3.60 (4% times 90); for bond B the dollar price change will be $3 (6% times 50) for a 100 basis point rate change.

5. **A.** Mr. Renfro's definition is a temporal definition and it is best not to use such an interpretation. Duration is related to the percentage price change of a bond when interest rates change.

   B. Mr. Renfro's response is correct.

   C. Mr. Renfro's response is correct.

   D. The computation of effective duration requires a valuation model to determine what the new prices will be when interest rates change. These models are based on assumptions. When duration is taken from different sources, there is no consistency of assumptions. While it is true that there is a formula for computing duration once the new prices for the bond are determined from a valuation model when rates are shocked, there is no simple valuation formula for bonds with embedded options.

   Mr. Renfro incorrectly overrode duration measures. It is possible—and it does occur in practice—to have a duration for a bond that is greater than the maturity of the bond. A negative duration does occur for some securities as well. For example, certain mortgage-backed securities have a negative duration. A negative duration of −3, for example, would mean that if interest rates increased by 100 basis points, the price of the bond will increase by approximately 3%. That is, the price of the bond moves in the same direction as the change in rates. In fact, for the types of bonds that have a duration longer than maturity and a negative duration, modified duration is not what the manager would want to use.

   E. The first part of the statement is correct. However, the second part is not true. Two portfolios can have the same duration but perform differently when rates change because they have different convexities. Also, the portfolios may have different yield and coupon characteristics.

6. A negative convexity adjustment simply means that a bond's price appreciation will be less than its price decline for a large change in interest rates (200 basis

points in the question). Whether or not a bond with negative convexity is attractive depends on its price and expectations about future interest rate changes.

7. If one interprets duration as some measure of time, it is difficult to understand why a bond will have a duration greater than its maturity. Duration is the approximate percentage price change of a bond for a 100 basis point change in interest rates. It is possible to have a security with a maturity of 10 years and a duration of 13.

8. Bond ABC exhibits negative convexity—for a 100 basis point change in rates, the gain is less than the loss; Bond XYZ exhibits positive convexity. A high coupon bond will exhibit negative convexity. A low coupon bond will exhibit positive convexity. Therefore, bond ABC is probably the high coupon bond while bond XYZ is probably the low coupon bond.

9. **A.** Modified duration is an inappropriate duration measure for a high coupon callable bond because it fails to recognize that as interest rates change, the expected cash flows will change.

   B. A better measure for a high-coupon callable bond is effective or option-adjusted duration.

10. Because the issue's coupon rate is substantially below the prevailing rate at which the issue can be refunded (500 basis points below), this issue is not likely to be called. Basically, if rates are shocked up and down, the expected cash flows are not likely to change because the coupon rate is so far below the market rate. Thus, modified duration—which assumes that the expected cash flow will not change when rates are changed—will be a good approximation for effective duration.

11. **A.** For a 25 basis point rate shock, the duration formula is:

$$\text{Duration} = \frac{V_- - V_+}{2V_0(0.0025)}$$

		5%, 4 Year	5%, 25 Year	8%, 4 Year	8%, 25 Year
Initial value	V_0	100.0000	100.0000	110.7552	142.5435
Value at 4.75%	V_-	100.9011	103.6355	111.7138	147.2621
Value at 5.25%	V_+	99.1085	96.5416	109.8066	138.0421
Duration		3.59	14.19	3.44	12.94

B. For a 50 basis point rate shock, the duration formula is:

$$\text{Duration} = \frac{V_- - V_+}{2V_0(0.0050)}$$

		5%, 4 Year	5%, 25 Year	8%, 4 Year	8%, 25 Year
Initial value	V_0	100.0000	100.0000	110.7552	142.5435
Value at 4.50%	V_-	101.8118	107.4586	112.6826	152.2102
Value at 5.50%	V_+	98.2264	93.2507	108.8679	133.7465
Duration		3.59	14.21	3.44	12.95

12. For a 25 basis point rate shock, the value for C is:

$$C = \frac{V_+ + V_- - 2V_0}{2V_0(0.0025)}$$

		5%, 4 Year	5%, 25 Year	8%, 4 Year	8%, 25 Year
Initial value	V_0	100.0000	100.0000	110.7552	142.5435
Value at 4.75%	V_-	100.9011	103.6355	111.7138	147.2621
Value at 5.25%	V_+	99.1085	96.5416	109.8066	138.0421
C		7.68	141.68	7.23	121.89

13. A. For a 10 basis point change:

> Duration for 8% 4-year bond = 3.44
>
> Duration for 8% 25-year bond = 12.94
>
> $\Delta y_* $ = 0.0010

For the 8% 4-year bond: approximate percentage price change for 10 basis point change in yield ($\Delta y_* = 0.0010$):

> 10 basis point increase:
>
> Approximate percentage price change = $-3.44 \times (0.0010) \times 100$
>
> = -0.34%

> 10 basis point decrease:
>
> Approximate percentage price change = $-3.44 \times (-0.0010) \times 100$
>
> = $+0.34\%$

For the 8% 25-year bond: approximate percentage price change for 10 basis point change in yield (0.0010):

> 10 basis point increase:
>
> Approximate percentage price change = $-12.94 \times (0.0010) \times 100$
>
> = -1.29%

> 10 basis point decrease:
>
> Approximate percentage price change = $-12.94 \times (-0.0010) \times 100$
>
> = $+1.29\%$

B. For the 4-year bond, the estimated percentage price change using duration is excellent for a 10 basis point change, as shown below:

	Duration Estimate (%)	Actual Change (%)
10 bp increase	−0.34	−0.34
10 bp decrease	+0.34	+0.35

For the 25-year bond, the estimated percentage price change using duration is excellent for a 10 basis point change, as shown below:

	Duration Estimate (%)	Actual Change (%)
10 bp increase	−1.29	−1.28
10 bp decrease	+1.29	+1.31

14. **A.** For a 200 basis point change:

Duration for 8% 4-year bond　= 3.44
Duration for 8% 25-year bond = 12.94
Δy_*　　　　　　　　　= 0.02

For the 8% 4-year bond: approximate percentage price change for 200 basis point change in yield ($\Delta y_* = 0.02$):

200 basis point increase:

Approximate percentage price change	$= -3.44 \times (0.02) \times 100$
	$= -6.89\%$

200 basis point decrease:

Approximate percentage price change	$= -3.44 \times (-0.02) \times 100$
	$= +6.89\%$

For the 8% 25-year bond: approximate percentage price change for 200 basis point shock:

200 basis point increase:

Approximate percentage price change	$= -12.94 \times (0.02) \times 100$
	$= -25.88\%$

200 basis point decrease:

Approximate percentage price change	$= -12.94 \times (-0.02) \times 100$
	$= +25.88\%$

B. For the 4-year bond, the estimated percentage price change using duration is very good despite a 200 basis point change, as shown below:

	Duration Estimate (%)	Actual Change (%)
200 bp increase	−6.88	−6.61
200 bp decrease	+6.88	+7.19

For the 25-year bond, the estimated percentage price change using duration is poor for a 200 basis point change, as shown on the next page:

	Duration Estimate (%)	Actual Change (%)
200 bp increase	−25.88	−21.62
200 bp decrease	+25.88	+31.54

15. **A.** The convexity adjustment for the two 25-year bonds is:

For the 5% 25-year bond:

$C = 141.68$

$\Delta y_* = 0.02$

convexity adjustment to percentage price change = $141.68 \times (0.02)^2 \times 100 = 5.67\%$

For the 8% 25-year bond:

$C = 121.89$

convexity adjustment to percentage price change = $121.89 \times (0.02)^2 \times 100 = 4.88\%$

B. Estimated price change using duration and convexity adjustment.

For the 5% 25 year bond:

Duration = 14.19

$\Delta y_* = 0.02$

Approximate percentage price change based on duration = $-14.19 \times 0.02 \times 100 = -28.38\%$

Convexity adjustment = 5.67%

Therefore,

Yield change (Δy_*)	+200 bps
Estimated change using duration	−28.38%
Convexity adjustment	5.67%
Total estimated percentage price change	−22.71%
Yield change (Δy_*)	−200 bps
Estimated change using duration	28.38%
Convexity adjustment	5.67%
Total estimated percentage price change	34.05%

For the 8% 25-year bond:

Duration = 12.94

$\Delta y_* = 0.02$

Approximate percentage price change based on duration = $-12.94 \times 0.02 \times 100 = -25.88\%$

Convexity adjustment = 4.88%

Yield change (Δy_*)	+200 bps
Estimated change using duration	−25.88%
Convexity adjustment	4.88%
Total estimated percentage price change	−21.00%
Yield change (Δy_*)	−200 bps
Estimated change using duration	25.88%
Convexity adjustment	4.88%
Total estimated percentage price change	30.76%

C. For a large change in rates of 200 basis points, duration with the convexity adjustment does a pretty good job of estimating the actual percentage price change, as shown below:

	Duration/Convexity Estimate (%)	Actual Change (%)
For 5% 25-year bond		
200 bp increase	−22.71	−23.46
200 bp decrease	+34.05	+35.00

(continued)

	Duration/Convexity Estimate (%)	Actual Change (%)
For 8% 25-year bond		
200 bp increase	−21.00	−21.62
200 bp decrease	+30.76	+31.54

16. **A.** The price value of a basis point is:

   $114.1338 - $114.0051 = $0.1287

   B. Using Equation 2, the approximate percentage price change for a 1 basis point increase in interest rates (i.e., $\Delta y = 0.0001$), ignoring the negative sign in Equation 2, is:

   $11.28 \times (0.0001) \times 100 = 0.1128\%$

   Given the initial price of 114.1338, the dollar price change estimated using duration is:

   $0.1128\% \times 114.1338 = $0.1287

17. Duration even after adjusting for convexity indicates what the exposure of a bond or bond portfolio will be if interest rates change. However, to capture fully the interest rate exposure, it is necessary to know how volatile interest rates are. For example, in comparing duration of government bonds in different countries, the duration only indicates the sensitivity of the price to changes in interest rates by a given number of basis points. It does not consider the volatility of rates. In a country with little volatility in rates but where the government bonds have a high duration, just looking at duration misleads the investor as to the interest rate risk exposure.

18. B is correct. The likelihood of call is much greater at yield levels that are low (relative to the coupon rate) than at high yield levels. This results in negative convexity at low yield levels.

19. C is correct. An option-free bond will exhibit positive convexity; therefore, price gains will be greater than price losses for any given large change in yields. If an increase in yields produces a loss of 12%, a decrease in yields will produce a gain of more than 12%.

20. C is correct. When yield levels are relatively low, the price of a comparable callable bond will be lower than the price of the option-free bond because the likelihood of a call is substantial. The putable bond will trade at a higher price because of the put option.

21. B is correct. The price adjustment for duration can be calculated as follows:

   $8.5 \times (0.015) \times 100 = 12.75\%$

   $\$900(1.1275) = \$1,014.75$

   This adjusts the price for duration only. Because the bond is option-free and the change in yield is large, using duration alone underestimates the actual price of the bond because of the effect of convexity. Once an adjustment is made for convexity, the price would be greater than $1,014.75.

22. B is correct. The portfolio duration is the weighted-average of the individual bonds in the portfolio and is calculated as follows:

   Total portfolio value = ($300,521 + 567,000) = $867,521.

   The weighted average = $(300,521/867,521) \times 2.67 + (567,000/867,521) \times 6.41 = 5.11$.

23. C is correct. Portfolio duration is the weighted average of the component durations where the weights are the market values of each component divided by the total market value of the portfolio. In this case: $(200 / 1,300) \times 4 + (300 / 1,300) \times 6 + (250 / 1,300) \times 7 + (550 / 1,300) \times 8 = 6.73$.

24. A is correct. Duration is a linear approximation. It is the tangent line to the actual bond pricing curve for a given starting point (interest rate). The actual pricing curve for an option-free bond is convex. Because of convexity, as you move away from the tangency (the starting point), actual prices (i.e., those on the actual pricing curve) will always be above the tangent line.

25. A is correct. Solve $17.45 \times 0.0001 \times \$1,105 = \$1.93$.

26. B is correct. Callable bonds can exhibit negative convexity at *low* interest rates. Bond prices are less responsive to changes in interest rates at high levels of interest rates than they are at low levels of interest rates.

27. B is correct. The likelihood of call is much greater at low yield levels (relative to the coupon rate) than at high yield levels. The price appreciation of a callable (prepayable) bond is less than the bond's price decline when yields change by a large number of basis points. The other two bonds do not have negative convexity.

28. A is correct. The formula is:

$$\% \text{ change in price} = (-\text{Duration})(\text{Change in yield})(100)$$
$$= -6.2(.0015)(100) = -0.93\%.$$

READING

59

Fundamentals of Credit Analysis

by Christopher L. Gootkind, CFA

LEARNING OUTCOMES

Mastery	The candidate should be able to:
☐	**a** describe credit risk and credit-related risks affecting corporate bonds;
☐	**b** describe seniority rankings of corporate debt and explain the potential violation of the priority of claims in a bankruptcy proceeding;
☐	**c** distinguish between corporate issuer credit ratings and issue credit ratings and describe the rating agency practice of "notching";
☐	**d** explain risks in relying on ratings from credit rating agencies;
☐	**e** explain the components of traditional credit analysis;
☐	**f** calculate and interpret financial ratios used in credit analysis;
☐	**g** evaluate the credit quality of a corporate bond issuer and a bond of that issuer, given key financial ratios of the issuer and the industry;
☐	**h** describe factors that influence the level and volatility of yield spreads;
☐	**i** calculate the return impact of spread changes;
☐	**j** explain special considerations when evaluating the credit of high yield, sovereign, and municipal debt issuers and issues.

INTRODUCTION

1

With bonds outstanding worth many trillions of U.S. dollars, the debt markets play a critical role in the global economy. Companies and governments raise capital in the debt market to fund current operations; buy equipment; build factories, roads, bridges, airports, and hospitals; acquire assets, and so on. By channeling savings into productive investments, the debt markets facilitate economic growth. Credit analysis has a crucial function in the debt capital markets—efficiently allocating capital by properly assessing credit risk, pricing it accordingly, and repricing it as risks change. How do fixed-income investors determine the riskiness of that debt, and how do they decide what they need to earn as compensation for that risk?

The author would like to thank several of his Fixed Income Research colleagues at Loomis, Sayles & Company for their assistance with this reading: Paul Batterton, Diana Leader-Cramer, Diana Monteith, Shannon O'Mara, CFA, and Laura Sarlo, CFA.

This reading will cover the basic principles of credit analysis, which may be broadly defined as the process by which credit risk is evaluated. Readers will be introduced to such concepts as the definition of credit risk, credit ratings, components of traditional credit analysis, measures of cash flow, key financial metrics and ratios, bond issuer creditworthiness comparisons within a given industry as well as across industries, the pricing of credit risk in the bond market, and the effects of changes in prices on holding period return.

The reading focuses primarily on analysis of corporate debt; however, credit analysis of sovereign and sub-sovereign (municipal) government bonds will also be addressed. Structured finance, a segment of the debt markets that includes securities backed by pools of assets, such as residential and commercial mortgages as well as other consumer loans, will not be covered here.

The key components of credit risk—default probability and loss severity—are introduced in the next section along with such credit-related risks as spread risk, credit migration risk, and liquidity risk. Section 3 discusses the relationship between credit risk and the capital structure of the firm. Credit ratings and the role of credit rating agencies are addressed in Section 4. Section 5 focuses on the process of analyzing the credit risk of corporations, whereas Section 6 examines the impact of credit spreads on risk and return. Special considerations applicable to the analysis of (i) high-yield (low-quality) corporate bonds and (ii) government bonds are presented in Section 7. Section 8 gives a brief summary, and a set of review questions concludes the reading.

2   CREDIT RISK

Credit risk is the risk of loss resulting from the borrower (issuer of debt) failing to make full and timely payments of interest and/or principal. Credit risk has two components. The first is known as **default risk**, or **default probability**, which is the probability that a borrower defaults—that is, fails to meet its obligation to make full and timely payments of principal and interest, according to the terms of the debt security. The second component is **loss severity** (also known as "loss given default") in the event of default—that is, the portion of a bond's value (including unpaid interest) an investor loses. A default can lead to losses of various magnitudes. In most instances, in the event of default, bondholders will recover some value, so there will not be a total loss on the investment. Thus, credit risk is reflected in the distribution of potential losses that may arise if the investor is not paid in full and on time. Although it is sometimes important to consider the entire distribution of potential losses and their respective probabilities,[1] it is often convenient to summarize the risk with a single default probability and loss severity and to focus on the **expected loss**:

Expected loss = Default probability × Loss severity given default

The loss severity, and hence the expected loss, can be expressed as either a monetary amount (e.g., €450,000) or as a percentage of the principal amount (e.g., 45 percent). The latter form is generally more useful for analysis because it is independent of the amount of investment. Loss severity is often expressed as (1 − Recovery rate), where the recovery rate is the percentage of the principal amount recovered in the event of default.

---

1 As an example, careful attention to the full distribution of potential losses is important in analyzing credit risk in structured finance products because the various tranches usually share unequally in the credit losses on the underlying loans or securities. A particular tranche typically bears none of the losses up to some level of underlying losses, then it bears all of the underlying losses until the tranche is wiped out. Losses on a "thin" tranche are very likely to be either 0 percent or 100 percent, with relatively small probabilities on intermediate loss severities. This situation is not well described by a single "average" loss severity.

Because default risk (default probability) is quite low for most good quality debt issuers, bond investors tend to focus primarily on assessing this likelihood and devote less effort to assessing the potential loss severity arising from default. However, as an issuer's default risk rises, investors will focus more on what the recovery rate might be in the event of default. This issue will be discussed in more detail later. Other important forms of credit-related risk include the following:

Spread risk. Corporate bonds and other "credit-risky" debt instruments typically trade at a yield premium, or spread, to bonds that have been considered "default-risk free," such as U.S. Treasury bonds or German government bonds. Yield spreads, expressed in basis points, widen based on two primary factors: (1) a decline in an issuer's creditworthiness, sometimes referred to as **credit migration** or **downgrade risk**, and (2) an increase in **market liquidity risk**. These two risks are separate but frequently related.

Credit migration (or downgrade) risk. This is the risk that a bond issuer's creditworthiness deteriorates, or migrates lower, leading investors to believe the risk of default is higher and thus causing the yield spreads on the issuer's bonds to widen and the price of its bonds to fall. The term "downgrade" refers to action by the major bond rating agencies, whose role will be covered in more detail in Section 4.

Market liquidity risk. This is the risk that the price at which investors can actually transact—buying or selling—may differ from the price indicated in the market. To compensate investors for the risk that there may not be sufficient market liquidity for them to buy or sell bonds in the quantity they desire, the spread or yield premium on corporate bonds includes a market liquidity component, in addition to a credit risk component. Unlike stocks, which trade on exchanges, most markets bonds trade primarily over the counter, through broker–dealers trading for their own accounts. Their ability and willingness to make markets, as reflected in the bid–ask spread, is an important determinant of market liquidity risk. The two main issuer-specific factors that affect market liquidity risk are (1) the size of the issuer (that is, the amount of publicly traded debt an issuer has outstanding) and (2) the credit quality of the issuer. In general, the less debt an issuer has outstanding, the less frequently its debt trades, and thus the higher the market liquidity risk. And the lower the quality of the issuer, the higher the market liquidity risk.

During times of financial stress or crisis, such as in late 2008, market liquidity can decline sharply, causing yield spreads on corporate bonds, and other credit-risky debt, to widen and their prices to drop. Some research has been done on trying to quantify market liquidity risk,[2] and more is likely to be done in the aftermath of the financial crisis.

Example 1

Defining Credit Risk

1. Which of the following *best* defines credit risk?
   A. The probability of default times the severity of loss given default
   B. The loss of principal and interest payments in the event of bankruptcy
   C. The risk of not receiving full interest and principal payments on a timely basis

---

2 For example, see Francis A. Longstaff, Sanjay Mithal, and Eric Neis, "Corporate Yield Spreads: Default Risk or Liquidity? New Evidence from the Credit Default Swap Market," NBER Working Paper No. 10418 (April 2004).

2. Which of the following is the *best* measure of credit risk?

    A. The expected loss

    B. The severity of loss

    C. The probability of default

3. Which of the following is NOT credit or credit-related risk?

    A. Default risk

    B. Interest rate risk

    C. Downgrade or credit migration risk

Solution to 1:

C is correct. Credit risk is the risk that the borrower will not make full and timely payments.

Solution to 2:

A is correct. The expected loss captures both of the key components of credit risk: (the product of) the likelihood of default and the loss severity in the event of default. Neither component alone fully reflects the risk.

Solution to 3:

B is correct. Bond price changes due to general interest rate movements are not considered credit risk.

3   CAPITAL STRUCTURE, SENIORITY RANKING, AND RECOVERY RATES

The various debt obligations of a given borrower will not necessarily all have the same **seniority ranking**, or priority of payment. In this section, we will introduce the topic of an issuer's capital structure and discuss the various types of debt claims that may arise from that structure, as well as their ranking and how those rankings can influence recovery rates in the event of default.

3.1 Capital Structure

The composition and distribution across operating units of a company's debt and equity—including bank debt, bonds of all seniority rankings, preferred stock, and common equity—is referred to as its **capital structure**. Some companies and industries have straightforward capital structures, with all the debt equally ranked and issued by one main operating entity. Other companies and industries, due to their frequent acquisitions and divestitures (e.g., media companies or conglomerates) or high levels of regulation (e.g., banks and utilities), tend to have more complicated capital structures. Companies in these industries often have many different subsidiaries, or operating companies, that have their own debt outstanding and parent holding companies that also issue debt, with different levels or rankings of seniority. Similarly, the cross-border operations of multi-national corporations tend to increase the complexity of their capital structures.

3.2 Seniority Ranking

Just as borrowers can issue debt with many different maturity dates and coupons, they can also have many different rankings in terms of seniority. The ranking refers to the priority of payment, with the most senior or highest-ranking debt having the first claim on the cash flows and assets of the issuer. This level of seniority can affect the value of an investor's claim in the event of default and restructuring. Broadly, there is **secured debt** and **unsecured debt**. Unsecured bonds are often referred to as debentures. Secured debt means the debtholder has a direct claim—a pledge from the issuer—on certain assets and their associated cash flows. Unsecured bondholders have only a general claim on an issuer's assets and cash flow. In the event of default, unsecured debtholders' claims rank below (i.e., get paid after) those of secured creditors[3] under what's known as the **priority of claims**.

Exhibit 1	Seniority Ranking

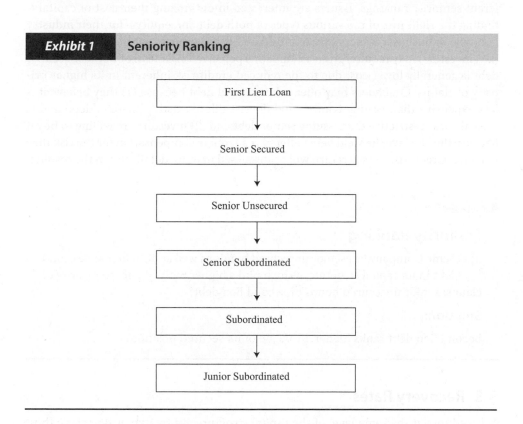

Within each category of debt, there are finer gradations of types and rankings. Within secured debt, there is first mortgage or first lien debt, which is the highest-ranked debt in terms of priority of repayment. **First mortgage debt** refers to the pledge of a specific property (e.g., a power plant for a utility or a specific casino for a gaming company). **First lien debt** refers to a pledge of certain assets that could include buildings but might also include property and equipment, licenses, patents, brands, and so on. There can also be **second lien**, or even third lien, secured debt, which, as the name implies, has a secured interest in the pledged assets but ranks below first lien debt in both collateral protection and priority of payment.

---

3 The term "creditors" is used throughout this reading to mean holders of debt instruments, such as bonds and bank loans. Unless specifically stated, it does not include such obligations as trade credit, tax liens, or employment-related obligations.

Within unsecured debt, there can also be finer gradations and seniority rankings. The highest-ranked unsecured debt is senior unsecured debt. It is the most common type of all corporate bonds outstanding. Other, lower-ranked debt includes **subordinated debt** and junior subordinated debt. Among the various creditor classes, these obligations have among the lowest priority of claims and frequently have little or no recovery in the event of default. That is, their loss severity can be as high as 100 percent. (See Exhibit 1 for seniority ranking.) For regulatory and capital purposes, banks in Europe and the United States have issued debt and debt-like securities that rank even lower than subordinated debt[4] and are intended to provide a capital cushion in times of financial distress. Many of them did not work as intended during the financial crisis that began in 2008, and most were phased out, potentially to be replaced by more effective instruments that automatically convert to equity in certain circumstances.

There are many reasons why companies issue—and investors buy—debt with different seniority rankings. Issuers are interested in optimizing their cost of capital—finding the right mix of the various types of both debt and equity—for their industry and type of business. Issuers may offer secured debt because that is what the market (i.e., investors) may require, given a company's perceived riskiness, or because secured debt is generally lower cost due to the reduced credit risk inherent in its higher priority of claims. Or, issuers may offer subordinated debt because (1) they believe it is less expensive than issuing equity[5] (and doesn't dilute existing shareholders) and is typically less restrictive than issuing senior debt and (2) investors are willing to buy it because they believe the yield being offered is adequate compensation for the risk they perceive. Credit risk versus return will be discussed in more detail later in the reading.

Example 2

Seniority Ranking

The Acme Company has senior unsecured bonds as well as both first and second lien debt in its capital structure. Which ranks higher with respect to priority of claims: senior unsecured bonds or second lien debt?

Solution:

Second lien debt ranks higher, by virtue of its secured position.

3.3 Recovery Rates

All creditors at the same level of the capital structure are treated as one class; thus, a senior unsecured bondholder whose debt is due in 30 years has the same pro rata claim in bankruptcy as one whose debt matures in six months. This provision is referred to as bonds ranking **pari passu** ("on an equal footing") in right of payment.

Defaulted debt will often continue to be traded by investors and broker–dealers based on their assessment that either in liquidation of the bankrupt company's assets or in some form of reorganization, the bonds will have some recovery value. In the case of reorganization, or restructuring (whether through formal bankruptcy or on a voluntary basis), new debt, equity, cash, or some combination thereof could be issued in exchange for the original defaulted debt.

---

4 These have various names such as hybrids, trust preferred, and upper and lower Tier 2 securities. In some cases, the non-payment or deferral of interest does not constitute an event of default, and in other cases, they might convert into perpetual securities—that is, securities with no maturity date.

5 Debtholders require a lower return than equity holders because they have prior claims to an issuer's cash flow and assets. That is, the cost of debt is lower than the cost of equity. In most countries, this cost differential is even greater due to the tax deductibility of interest payments.

As discussed, recovery rates vary by seniority of ranking in a company's capital structure, under the priority of claims treatment in bankruptcy. Over many decades, there have been enough defaults to generate statistically meaningful historical data on recovery rates by seniority ranking. Exhibit 2 provides recovery rates by seniority ranking for North American non-financial companies.[6] For example, as shown in Exhibit 2, investors on average recovered 51.6 percent of the value of senior unsecured debt that defaulted in 2009 but only 28.0 percent of the value of senior subordinated issues that defaulted that year.

Exhibit 2	Average Corporate Debt Recovery Rates Measured by Ultimate Recoveries					
	Emergence Year*			**Default Year**		
Seniority ranking	2010	2009	1987–2010	2010	2009	1987–2010
Senior secured	64.4%	59.0%	63.5%	56.3%	65.6%	63.5%
Senior unsecured	51.0%	48.3%	49.2%	26.5%	51.6%	49.2%
Senior subordinated	20.5%	26.2%	29.4%	21.7%	28.0%	29.4%
Subordinated	53.4%	34.3%	29.3%	0.0%	58.3%	29.3%
Junior subordinated	NA	0.5%	18.4%	NA	0.0%	18.4%

Notes: Emergence year is typically the year the defaulted company emerges from bankruptcy. Default year data refer to the recovery rate of debt that defaulted in that year (i.e., 2009 and 2010) or range of years (i.e., 1987–2010). Data are for North American nonfinancial companies. NA indicates not available. *Source:* Based on data from Moody's Investors Service, Inc.'s Ultimate Recovery Database.

There are a few things worth noting:

1. **Recovery rates can vary widely by industry**. Companies that go bankrupt in industries that are in secular decline (e.g., newspaper publishing) will most likely have lower recovery rates than those that go bankrupt in industries merely suffering from a cyclical economic downturn.

2. **Recovery rates can also vary depending on when they occur in a credit cycle**.[7] As shown in Exhibit 3, at or near the bottom of a credit cycle—which is almost always closely linked with an economic cycle—recoveries will tend to be lower than at other times in the credit cycle. This is because there will be many companies closer to, or already in, bankruptcy, causing valuations to be depressed.

---

6 The recovery rates shown for default years 2009 and 2010 should be viewed as preliminary because some of the numbers are based on the relatively small number of defaults for which final recovery had been determined at the time of the Moody's study. For example, the 2010 senior unsecured recovery rate reflects only two bonds.

7 Credit cycles describe the changing availability—and pricing—of credit. When the economy is strong or improving, the willingness of lenders to extend credit, and on favorable terms, is high. Conversely, when the economy is weak or weakening, lenders pull back, or "tighten" credit, by making it less available and more expensive. This frequently contributes to asset values, such as real estate, declining, causing further economic weakness and higher defaults. Central banks frequently survey banks to assess how "tight" or "loose" their lending standards are. This information, as well as the level and direction of corporate bond default rates, helps provide a good sense of where one is in the credit cycle.

Exhibit 3	Global Recovery Rates by Seniority Ranking, 1990–2010

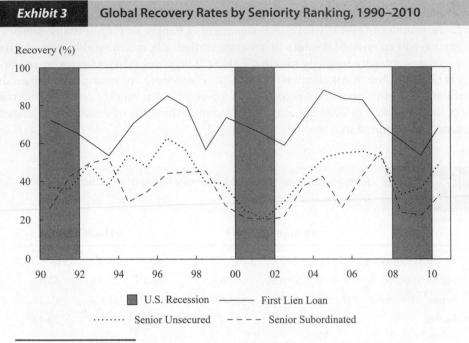

Source: Based on data from Moody's Investors Service, Inc.'s Ultimate Recovery Database.

3. **These recovery rates are averages**. In fact, there can be large variability, both across industries, as noted above, as well as across companies within a given industry. Factors might include composition and proportion of debt across an issuer's capital structure. An abundance of secured debt will lead to smaller recovery rates on lower-ranked debt.

Understanding recovery rates is important because they are a key component of credit analysis and risk. Recall that the best measure of credit risk is expected loss—that is, probability of default times loss severity given default. And loss severity equals (1 – Recovery rate). Having an idea how much one can lose in the event of default is a critical factor in valuing credit, particularly lower-quality credit, as the default risk rises.

Priority of claims: Not always absolute. The priority of claims in bankruptcy—the idea that the highest-ranked creditors get paid out first, followed by the next level, and on down, like a waterfall—is well established and is often described as "absolute." In principle, in the event of bankruptcy or liquidation:

- Creditors with a secured claim have the right to the value of that specific property before any other claim. If the value of the pledged property is less than the amount of the claim, then the difference becomes a senior unsecured claim.

- Unsecured creditors have a right to be paid in full before holders of equity interests (common and preferred shareholders) receive value on their interests.

- Senior creditors take priority over junior (i.e., subordinated) creditors. A creditor is senior unless expressly subordinated.

In practice, however, more junior creditors and even shareholders may receive some consideration without more senior creditors being paid in full. Why might this be the case? In bankruptcy, there are different classes of claimants, and all classes that are impaired (that is, receive less than full claim) get to vote to confirm the plan of reorganization. This vote is subject to the absolute priority of claims. Either by consent of the various parties or by the judge's order, however, absolute priority may not be strictly enforced in the final plan. There may be disputes over the value of various assets in the bankruptcy estate (e.g., what is a plant, or a patent portfolio, worth?) or the present value or timing of payouts. For example, what is the value of the new debt I'm receiving for my old debt of a reorganized company before it emerges from bankruptcy?

Resolution of these disputes takes time, and cases can drag on for months and years. In the meantime, during bankruptcy, substantial expenses are being incurred for legal and accounting fees, and the value of the company may be declining as key employees leave, customers go elsewhere, and so on. Thus, to avoid the time, expense, and uncertainty over disputed issues, such as the value of property in the estate, the legality of certain claims, and so forth, the various claimants have a strong incentive to negotiate and compromise. This frequently leads to more junior creditors and other claimants (e.g., even shareholders) receiving more consideration than they are legally entitled to.

It's worth noting that in the United States, the bias is toward reorganization and recovery of companies in bankruptcy, whereas in other jurisdictions, such as the United Kingdom, the bias is toward liquidation of companies in bankruptcy and maximizing value to the banks and other senior creditors. It's also worth noting that bankruptcy and bankruptcy laws are very complex and can vary greatly by country, so it is difficult to generalize about how creditors will fare. As shown in the earlier chart, there is huge variability in recovery rates for defaulted debt. Every case is different.

Example 3

Priority of Claims

1. Under which circumstance is a subordinated bondholder *most likely* to recover some value in a bankruptcy without a senior creditor getting paid in full? When:

   A. absolute priority rules are enforced.

   B. the various classes of claimants agree to it.

   C. the company is liquidated rather than reorganized.

2. In the event of bankruptcy, claims at the same level of the capital structure are:

   A. on an equal footing, regardless of size, maturity, or time outstanding.

   B. paid in the order of maturity from shortest to longest, regardless of size or time outstanding.

   C. paid on a first-in, first-out (FIFO) basis so that the longest-standing claims are satisfied first, regardless of size or maturity.

Solution to 1:

B is correct. All impaired classes get to vote on the reorganization plan. Negotiation and compromise are often preferable to incurring huge legal and accounting fees in a protracted bankruptcy process that would otherwise reduce the value of the estate for all claimants. This process may allow junior creditors (e.g., subordinated bondholders) to recover some value even though more senior creditors do not get paid in full.

Solution to 2:

A is correct. All claims at the same level of the capital structure are pari passu (on an equal footing).

4 RATINGS AGENCIES, CREDIT RATINGS, AND THEIR ROLE IN THE DEBT MARKETS

The major credit ratings agencies—Moody's Investors Service ("Moody's"), Standard & Poor's ("S&P"), and to a somewhat lesser extent, Fitch Ratings ("Fitch")—play a central, if somewhat controversial, role in the credit markets. For the vast majority of outstanding bonds, at least two of the agencies provide ratings: a symbol-based measure of the potential risk of default of a particular bond or issuer of debt. In the public and quasi-public bond markets,[8] issuers won't offer, and investors won't buy, bonds that do not carry ratings from Moody's and/or S&P (and Fitch). This practice applies for all types of bonds—government or sovereign, government related,[9] supra-national,[10] corporate, municipal, and mortgage- and asset-backed debt. How did the ratings agencies attain such a dominant position in the credit markets? What are credit ratings, and what do they mean? How does the market use credit ratings? What are the risks of relying solely or excessively on credit ratings?

The history of the major ratings agencies goes back more than 100 years. John Moody began publishing credit analysis and opinions on U.S. railroads in 1909. S&P published its first ratings in 1916. They have grown in size and prominence since then. Many bond investors like the fact that there are independent analysts who meet with the issuer and often have access to material, non-public information, such as financial projections that investors cannot receive, to aid in the analysis. What has also proven very attractive to investors is that credit ratings provide direct and easy comparability of the relative credit riskiness of all bond issuers, within and across industries and bond types, although there is some debate about ratings comparability across the types of bonds.[11]

Several factors have led to the near universal use of credit ratings in the bond markets and the dominant role of the major credit rating agencies. These factors include the following:

- Independent assessment of credit risk
- Ease of comparison across bond issuers, issues, and market segments
- Regulatory and statutory reliance and usage[12]
- Issuer payment for ratings[13]
- Huge growth of debt markets
- Development and expansion of bond portfolio management and the accompanying bond indices.

---

8 That is, underwritten by investment banks, as opposed to privately placed on a "best efforts" basis.

9 These are government agencies or instrumentalities that may have implicit or explicit guarantees from the government. Examples include Ginnie Mae in the United States and *Pfandbriefe* in Germany.

10 Supranationals are international financial institutions, such as the International Bank for Reconstruction and Development ("World Bank"), the Asian Development Bank, and the European Investment Bank, that are established by treaty and owned by several member governments.

11 Investigations conducted after the late 2008/early 2009 financial crisis suggested that, for a given rating category, municipal bonds have experienced a lower historical incidence of default than corporate debt.

12 It is common for regulations to make reference to ratings issued by recognized credit ratings agencies. In light of the role played by the agencies in the sub-prime mortgage crisis, however, some jurisdictions (e.g., the United States) are moving to remove such references. Nonetheless, the so-called Basel III global framework for bank supervision developed beginning in 2009 retains such references.

13 The "issuer pay" model allows the distribution of ratings to a broad universe of investors and undoubtedly facilitated widespread reliance on ratings. It is controversial, however, because some believe it creates a conflict of interest among the rating agency, the investor, and the issuer. Studies suggest, however, that ratings are not biased upward and alternate payment models, such as "investor pays," have their own shortcomings, including the "free rider" problem inherent in a business where information is widely available and freely shared. So, despite its potential problems, and some calls for a new payment model, the "issuer pay" model remains entrenched in the market.

However, in the aftermath of the financial crisis of 2008–2009, when the rating agencies were blamed for at least contributing to the crisis with their overly optimistic ratings on securities backed by subprime mortgages, there were attempts to reduce the role and dominant positions of the major credit rating agencies. New rules, regulations, and legislation were passed to require the agencies to be more transparent, reduce conflicts of interest, and stimulate more competition. Challenging the hegemony of Moody's, S&P, and Fitch, additional credit rating agencies have emerged, while existing ones that have a strong presence in their home markets but are not so well known globally, such as Dominion Bond Rating Service (DBRS) in Canada and Mikuni & Co. in Japan, have tried to raise their profiles. The market dominance of the biggest credit rating agencies, however, remains largely intact.

4.1 Credit Ratings

The three major global credit rating agencies—Moody's, S&P, and Fitch—use similar, symbol-based ratings that are basically an assessment of a bond issue's risk of default. Exhibit 4 shows their long-term ratings ranked from highest to lowest.[14]

Exhibit 4	Long-Term Ratings Matrix: Investment Grade vs. Non-Investment Grade			
		Moody's	**S&P**	**Fitch**
Investment Grade	High-Quality Grade	Aaa	AAA	AAA
		Aa1	AA+	AA+
		Aa2	AA	AA
		Aa3	AA–	AA–
	Upper-Medium Grade	A1	A+	A+
		A2	A	A
		A3	A–	A–
	Low-Medium Grade	Baa1	BBB+	BBB+
		Baa2	BBB	BBB
		Baa3	BBB–	BBB–

(continued)

---

14 The rating agencies also provide ratings on short-term debt instruments, such as bank deposits and commercial paper. However, they use different scales: From the highest to lowest rating, Moody's uses P-1, P-2, P-3; S&P uses A-1+, A-1, A-2, A-3; Fitch uses F-1, F-2, F-3. Below that is not prime. Short-term ratings are typically used by money market funds, with the vast majority of the instruments they own rated in the highest (or in the case of S&P, the highest or second-highest) category. These top ratings basically map to a single-A or higher long-term rating.

		Moody's	S&P	Fitch
		Ba1	BB+	BB+
		Ba2	BB	BB
		Ba3	BB–	BB–
		B1	B+	B+
Non-Investment Grade "Junk" or "High Yield"	Low Grade or Speculative Grade	B2	B	B
		B3	B–	B–
		Caa1	CCC+	CCC+
		Caa2	CCC	CCC
		Caa3	CCC–	CCC–
		Ca	CC	CC
		C	C	C
	Default	C	D	D

Exhibit 4 — Continued

Bonds rated triple-A (Aaa or AAA) are said to be "of the highest quality, with minimal credit risk"[15] and thus have extremely low probabilities of default. Double-A (Aa or AA) rated bonds are referred to as "high-quality grade" and are also regarded as having very low default risk. Bonds rated single-A are referred to as "upper-medium grade." Baa (Moody's) or BBB (S&P and Fitch) are called "low-medium grade." Bonds rated Baa3/BBB– or higher are called "investment grade." Bonds rated Ba1 or lower by Moody's and BB– or lower by S&P and Fitch, respectively, have speculative credit characteristics and increasingly higher default risk. As a group, these bonds are referred to in a variety of ways: "low grade," "speculative grade," "non-investment grade," "below investment grade," "high yield," and, in an attempt to reflect the extreme level of risk, some observers refer to these bonds as "junk bonds." The D rating is reserved for securities that are already in default in S&P's and Fitch's scales. For Moody's, bonds rated C are likely, but not necessarily, in default. Generally, issuers of bonds rated investment grade are more consistently able to access the debt markets and can borrow at lower interest rates than those rated below investment grade.

In addition, rating agencies will typically provide outlooks on their respective ratings—positive, stable, or negative—and may provide other indicators on the potential direction of their ratings under certain circumstances, such as "On Review for a Downgrade" or "On CreditWatch for an Upgrade."[16] It should also be noted that, in support of the ratings they publish, the rating agencies also provide extensive written commentary and financial analysis on the obligors they rate, as well as summary industry statistics.

4.2 Issuer vs. Issue Ratings

Rating agencies will typically provide both issuer and issue ratings, particularly as they relate to corporate debt. Terminology used to distinguish between issuer and issue ratings includes corporate family rating (CFR) and corporate credit rating (CCR) or

---

15 Moody's Investors Service, "Ratings Symbols and Definitions" (July 2011).
16 Additional detail on their respective ratings definitions, methodologies, and criteria can be found on each of the major rating agency's websites: www.moodys.com, www.standardandpoors.com, and www.fitch.com.

issuer credit rating and issue credit rating. An issuer credit rating is meant to address an obligor's overall creditworthiness—its ability and willingness to make timely payments of interest and principal on its debt. The issuer credit rating usually applies to its senior unsecured debt.

Issue ratings refer to specific financial obligations of an issuer and take into consideration such factors as ranking in the capital structure (e.g., secured or subordinated). Although **cross-default provisions**, whereby events of default such as non-payment of interest[17] on one bond trigger default on all outstanding debt,[18] implies the same default probability for all issues, specific issues may be assigned different credit ratings—higher or lower—due to a ratings adjustment methodology known as **notching**.

Notching. For the rating agencies, likelihood of default is the primary factor in assigning their ratings. However, there are secondary factors as well. These factors include the priority of payment in the event of a default (e.g., secured versus senior unsecured versus subordinated) as well as potential loss severity in the event of default. Another rating factor is so-called **structural subordination**, which can arise when a corporation with a holding company structure has debt at both its parent holding company and operating subsidiaries. Debt at the operating subsidiaries will get serviced by the cash flow and assets of the subsidiaries before funds can be passed ("upstreamed") to the holding company to service debt at that level.

Recognizing these different payment priorities, and thus the potential for higher (or lower) loss severity in the event of default, the rating agencies have adopted a notching process whereby their credit ratings on issues can be moved up or down from the issuer rating (senior unsecured). As a general rule, the higher the senior unsecured rating, the smaller the notching adjustment will be. The reason behind this is that the higher the rating, the lower the perceived risk of default, so the need to "notch" the rating to capture the potential difference in loss severity is greatly reduced. For lower-rated credits, however, the risk of default is greater and thus the potential difference in loss from a lower (or higher) priority ranking is a bigger consideration in assessing an issue's credit riskiness. Thus, the rating agencies will typically apply larger rating adjustments. For example, S&P applies the following notching guidelines:

> As default risk increases, the concern over what can be recovered takes on greater relevance and, therefore, greater rating significance. Accordingly, the LGD [Loss Given Default] aspect of ratings is given more weight as one moves down the rating spectrum. For example, subordinated debt can be rated up to two notches below a noninvestment grade corporate credit rating, but one notch at most if the corporate credit rating is investment grade. (In the same vein, issues of companies with an 'AAA' rating need not be notched at all.)[19]

Exhibit 5 is an example of S&P's notching criteria, as applied to United Rentals, Inc. (URI). URI is a U.S.-based equipment rental company whose corporate credit—and senior unsecured—rating is single-B. Note how the company's subordinated debt is rated two notches lower, at CCC+.

---

17 This issue will be covered in greater detail in the section on covenants.
18 Nearly all bonds have a cross-default provision. Rare exceptions to this cross-default provision include the deeply subordinated, debt-like securities referenced earlier in this reading.
19 Standard & Poor's, "Rating Each Issue," in *Corporate Ratings Criteria 2008* (New York: Standard and Poor's, 2008): 89.

Exhibit 5	URI's S&P Ratings Detail, 27 May 2011
Corporate credit rating	B/Stable/–
Preferred stock (1 issue)	CCC
Senior unsecured (2 issues)	B
Subordinated (4 issues)	CCC+

Source: Based on data from Standard & Poor's Financial Services, LLC.

4.3 Risks in Relying on Agency Ratings

The dominant position of the rating agencies in the global debt markets, and the near-universal use of their credit ratings on debt securities, suggests that investors believe they do a good job assessing credit risk. In fact, with a few exceptions (e.g., too high ratings on U.S. subprime mortgage-backed securities issued in the mid-2000s, which turned out to be much riskier than expected), their ratings have proved quite accurate as a relative measure of default risk. For example, Exhibit 6 shows historical S&P one-year global corporate default rates by rating category from 1991 to 2010.[20]

Exhibit 6	Global Corporate Annual Default Rates by Rating Category (%)						
	AAA	**AA**	**A**	**BBB**	**BB**	**B**	**CCC/C**
1991	0.00	0.00	0.00	0.55	1.68	13.84	33.87
1992	0.00	0.00	0.00	0.00	0.00	6.99	30.19
1993	0.00	0.00	0.00	0.00	0.70	2.62	13.33
1994	0.00	0.00	0.14	0.00	0.27	3.08	16.67
1995	0.00	0.00	0.00	0.17	0.98	4.59	28.00
1996	0.00	0.00	0.00	0.00	0.67	2.91	4.17
1997	0.00	0.00	0.00	0.25	0.19	3.49	12.00
1998	0.00	0.00	0.00	0.41	0.97	4.61	42.86
1999	0.00	0.17	0.18	0.19	0.95	7.28	32.35
2000	0.00	0.00	0.26	0.37	1.25	7.73	34.12
2001	0.00	0.00	0.35	0.33	3.13	11.24	44.55
2002	0.00	0.00	0.00	1.01	2.81	8.11	44.12
2003	0.00	0.00	0.00	0.23	0.56	4.01	32.93
2004	0.00	0.00	0.08	0.00	0.53	1.56	15.33
2005	0.00	0.00	0.00	0.07	0.20	1.73	8.94
2006	0.00	0.00	0.00	0.00	0.30	0.81	12.38
2007	0.00	0.00	0.00	0.00	0.19	0.25	15.09
2008	0.00	0.38	0.38	0.48	0.78	3.98	26.26
2009	0.00	0.00	0.22	0.54	0.72	10.38	48.68
2010	0.00	0.00	0.00	0.00	0.55	0.80	22.27

(continued)

---

20 S&P uses a static pool methodology here. It measures the percentage of issues that defaulted in a given calendar year based on how they were rated at the beginning of the year.

Exhibit 6	Continued						
	AAA	AA	A	BBB	BB	B	CCC/C
Mean	0.00	0.03	0.08	0.23	0.87	5.00	25.91
Max	0.00	0.38	0.38	1.01	3.13	13.84	48.68
Min	0.00	0.00	0.00	0.00	0.00	0.25	4.17

Source: Based on data from Standard & Poor's Financial Services, LLC.

As Exhibit 6 shows, the highest-rated bonds have extremely low default rates. With very few exceptions, the lower the rating, the higher the annual rate of default, with bonds rated CCC and lower experiencing the highest default rates by far. There are limitations and risks, however, to relying on credit rating agency ratings, including the following:

1. **Credit ratings can be very dynamic**. That is, over a long time period (e.g., many years), credit ratings can migrate—move up or down—significantly from the time of bond issuance. Using Standard & Poor's data, Exhibit 7 shows the average three-year migration (or "transition") by rating from 1981 to 2010. Note that the higher the credit rating, the greater the ratings stability. Even for AAA rated credits, however, only about 70 percent (70 percent in the United States and 68 percent globally) of the time did ratings remain in that rating category over a three-year period. (Of course, AAA rated credits can have their ratings move in only one direction—down.) A very small fraction of AAA rated credits became non-investment grade or defaulted within three years. For single-B rated credits, only about 40 percent (40 percent in the United States and 39 percent globally) of the time did ratings remain in that rating category over three-year periods. This observation about the dynamism of credit ratings isn't meant to be a criticism of the rating agencies. It is meant to demonstrate that creditworthiness can and does change—up or down—and that bond investors should not assume an issuer's credit rating will remain the same from time of purchase through the entire holding period.

Exhibit 7	Average Three-Year Corporate Transition Rates, 1981–2010 (%)								
From/To	AAA	AA	A	BBB	BB	B	CCC/C	D	NR*
United States									
AAA	69.75	16.60	2.47	0.38	0.21	0.13	0.13	0.17	10.15
AA	1.32	65.46	17.75	2.52	0.47	0.42	0.04	0.20	11.82
A	0.11	4.34	67.32	12.05	1.79	0.69	0.14	0.42	13.16
BBB	0.04	0.47	8.61	62.21	8.03	2.47	0.35	1.22	16.60
BB	0.02	0.10	0.78	10.95	43.95	13.59	1.40	5.60	23.61
B	0.01	0.06	0.42	1.08	10.06	40.27	4.94	15.79	27.37
CCC/C	0.00	0.00	0.38	0.98	1.97	12.19	13.47	43.98	27.02

(continued)

Exhibit 7	Continued								
From/To	AAA	AA	A	BBB	BB	B	CCC/C	D	NR*
Global									
AAA	68.09	18.85	2.46	0.34	0.14	0.08	0.11	0.14	9.78
AA	1.30	65.78	18.59	2.24	0.37	0.26	0.03	0.15	11.29
A	0.08	4.53	67.31	11.84	1.42	0.57	0.12	0.34	13.80
BBB	0.03	0.41	8.90	61.42	7.44	2.12	0.36	1.20	18.12
BB	0.01	0.07	0.67	11.31	43.97	12.06	1.37	5.17	25.37
B	0.01	0.05	0.34	1.08	10.90	38.93	4.61	15.25	28.84
CCC/C	0.00	0.00	0.29	0.91	2.05	16.04	12.39	40.47	27.85

*NR means not rated—that is, certain corporate issuers were no longer rated by S&P. This could occur for a variety of reasons, including issuers paying off their debt and no longer needing ratings.

Source: Based on data from Standard & Poor's Financial Services, LLC.

2. **Rating agencies are not infallible**. The mis-rating of billions of dollars of subprime-backed mortgage securities is one example. Other examples include the mis-ratings of U.S. companies Enron and WorldCom and European issuer Parmalat. Like many investors, the rating agencies did not see the accounting fraud being committed in those companies.

3. **Other types of so-called idiosyncratic or event risk are difficult to capture in ratings**. Examples of this include litigation risk, such as that which can affect tobacco companies, or environmental and business risks faced by chemical companies and utility power plants. This would also include such unpredictable events as the earthquake and tsunami that hit Japan in March 2011 and its credit impact on debt issuer Tokyo Electric Power Company (TEPCO). Leveraged transactions, such as debt-financed acquisitions and large stock buybacks, are often difficult to anticipate and thus to capture in credit ratings.

4. **Ratings tend to lag market pricing of credit**. Bond prices and credit spreads frequently move more quickly because of changes in perceived creditworthiness than rating agencies change their ratings (or even outlooks) up or down. Bond prices and relative valuations can move every day, whereas bond ratings, appropriately, don't change that often. Even over long time periods, however, credit ratings can badly lag changes in bond prices. Exhibit 8 shows the price and Moody's rating of a bond from U.S. automaker Ford Motor Company before, during, and after the financial crisis in 2008. Note how the bond's price moved down sharply well before Moody's downgraded its credit rating— multiple times—and also how the bond's price began to recover—and kept recovering—well before Moody's upgraded its credit rating on Ford debt.

Exhibit 8	Ford Motor Company Senior Unsecured Debt: Price vs. Moody's Rating Since 2005

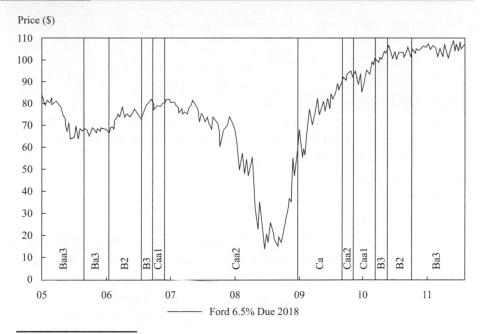

Sources: Data based on Bloomberg Finance L.P. and Moody's Investors Service.

Moreover, particularly for certain speculative-grade credits, two bonds with similar ratings may trade at very different valuations. This is partly a result of the fact that credit ratings primarily try to assess the risk of default, whereas for low-quality credits, the market begins focusing more on expected loss (default probability times loss severity). So, bonds from two separate issuers with comparable (high) risk of default but different recovery rates may have similar ratings but trade at significantly different dollar prices.[21]

Thus, bond investors who wait for rating agencies to change their ratings before making buy and sell decisions in their portfolios may be at risk of underperforming other investors who make portfolio decisions in advance of—or not solely based on—rating agency changes.

As described, there are risks in relying on credit rating agency ratings when investing in bonds. Thus, while the credit rating agencies will almost certainly continue to play a significant role in the bond markets, it's important for investors to perform their own credit analyses and draw their own conclusions regarding the credit risk of a given debt issue or issuer.

---

21 See Christopher L. Gootkind, "Improving Credit Risk Analysis," in *Fixed-Income Management for the 21st Century* (Charlottesville, VA: Association for Investment Management and Research, 2002).

Example 4

Credit Ratings

1. Using the S&P ratings scale, investment grade bonds carry which of the following ratings?

    A. AAA to EEE

    B. BBB– to CCC

    C. AAA to BBB–

2. Using both Moody's and S&P ratings, which of the following pairs of ratings is considered high yield, also known as "below investment grade," "speculative grade," or "junk"?

    A. Baa1/BBB–

    B. B3/CCC+

    C. Baa3/BB+

3. What is the difference between an issuer rating and an issue rating?

    A. The issuer rating applies to all of an issuer's bonds, whereas the issue rating considers a bond's seniority ranking.

    B. The issuer rating is an assessment of an issuer's overall creditworthiness, whereas the issue rating is always higher than the issuer rating.

    C. The issuer rating is an assessment of an issuer's overall creditworthiness, typically reflected as the senior unsecured rating, whereas the issue rating considers a bond's seniority ranking (e.g., secured or subordinated).

4. Based on the practice of notching by the rating agencies, a subordinated bond from a company with an issuer rating of BB would likely carry what rating?

    A. B+

    B. BB

    C. BBB–

5. The fixed-income portfolio manager you work with asked you why a bond from an issuer you cover didn't rise in price when it was upgraded by Fitch from B+ to BB. Which of the following is the *most likely* explanation?

    A. Bond prices never react to rating changes.

    B. The bond doesn't trade often so the price hasn't adjusted to the rating change yet.

    C. The market was expecting the rating change, and so it was already "priced in" to the bond.

6. Amalgamated Corp. and Widget Corp. each have bonds outstanding with similar coupons and maturity dates. Both bonds are rated B2, B–, and B by Moody's, S&P, and Fitch, respectively. The bonds, however, trade at very different prices—the Amalgamated bond trades at €89, whereas the Widget bond trades at €62. What is the *most likely* explanation of the price (and yield) difference?

    A. Widget's credit ratings are lagging the market's assessment of the company's credit deterioration.

B. The bonds have similar risks of default (as reflected in the ratings), but the market believes the Amalgamated bond has a higher expected loss in the event of default.

C. The bonds have similar risks of default (as reflected in the ratings), but the market believes the Widget bond has a higher expected recovery rate in the event of default.

Solution to 1:

C is correct.

Solution to 2:

B is correct. Note that issuers with ratings such as Baa3/BB+ (answer C) are called "crossovers" because one rating is investment grade (the Moody's rating of Baa3) and the other is high yield (the S&P rating of BB+).

Solution to 3:

C is correct.

Solution to 4:

A is correct. The subordinated bond would have its rating notched lower than the company's BB rating, probably by two notches, reflecting the higher weight given to loss severity for below-investment-grade credits.

Solution to 5:

C is correct. The market was anticipating the rating upgrade and had already priced it in. Bond prices often do react to rating changes, particularly multi-notch ones. Even if bonds don't trade, their prices adjust based on dealer quotations given to bond pricing services.

Solution to 6:

A is correct. Widget's credit ratings are probably lagging behind the market's assessment of its deteriorating creditworthiness. Answers B and C both state the situation backwards. If the market believed that the Amalgamated bond had a higher expected loss given default, then that bond would be trading at a lower, not a higher, price. Similarly, if the market believed that the Widget bond had a higher expected recovery rate in the event of default, then that bond would be trading at a higher, not a lower, price.

TRADITIONAL CREDIT ANALYSIS: CORPORATE DEBT SECURITIES

5

The goal of credit analysis is to assess an issuer's ability to satisfy its debt obligations, including bonds and other indebtedness, such as bank loans. These debt obligations are contracts, the terms of which specify the interest rate to be paid, the frequency and timing of payments, the maturity date, and the covenants that describe the permissible and required actions of the borrower. Because corporate bonds are contracts, enforceable by law, credit analysts generally assume an issuer's willingness to pay and concentrate instead on assessing its ability to pay. Thus, the main focus in credit analysis is to understand a company's ability to generate cash flow over the term of its debt obligations. In so doing, analysts must assess both the credit quality of the company and the fundamentals of the industry in which the company operates.

Traditional credit analysis considers the sources, predictability, and sustainability of cash generated by a company to service its debt obligations. This section will focus on corporate credit analysis; in particular, it will emphasize non-financial companies. Financial institutions have very different business models and funding profiles from industrial and utility companies.

5.1 Credit Analysis vs. Equity Analysis: Similarities and Differences

The above description of credit analysis suggests credit and equity analyses should be very similar; in many ways, they are. There are motivational differences, however, between equity and fixed-income investors that are an important aspect of credit analysis. Strictly speaking, management works for the shareholders of a company. Its primary objective is to maximize the value of the company for its owners. In contrast, management's legal duty to its creditors—including bondholders—is to meet the terms of the governing contracts. Growth in the value of a corporation from rising profits and cash flow accrues to the shareholders, while the best outcome for bondholders is to receive full, timely payment of interest and repayment of principal when due. Conversely, shareholders are more exposed to the decline in value as a company's future earnings power and cash flow decline because bondholders have a priority claim on cash flow and assets. Should a company's earnings power and cash flow decline to the extent that it can no longer make its debt payments, however, then bondholders are at risk of loss as well.

In summary, in exchange for a priority claim on cash flow and assets, bondholders do not share in the growth in value of a company (except to the extent that its creditworthiness improves) but have downside risk in the event of default. In contrast, shareholders have theoretically unlimited upside opportunity, but in the event of default, their investment is typically wiped out before the bondholders suffer a loss. This is very similar to the type of payoff patterns seen in financial options. In fact, in recent years, a great deal of credit modeling has been predicated on a sophisticated application of financial option theory and mathematics. Although it is beyond the scope of this present introduction to the subject, it is an expanding area of interest to both institutional investors and rating agencies.

Thus, although the analysis is similar in many respects for both equity and credit, equity analysts are interested in the strategies and investments that will increase a company's value and grow earnings per share. They then compare that earnings power and growth potential with that of other companies in a given industry. Credit analysts will look more at the downside risk by measuring and assessing the sustainability of a company's cash flow relative to its debt levels and interest expense. Importantly for credit analysts, the balance sheet will show the composition of an issuer's debt—the overall amount, how much is coming due and when, and the distribution by seniority ranking. In general, equity analysts will focus more on income and cash flow statements, whereas credit analysts tend to focus more on the balance sheet and cash flow statements.

5.2 The Four Cs of Credit Analysis: A Useful Framework

Traditionally, it has been convenient to consider what is often called the "four Cs of credit analysis"[22]:

---

22 There is no unique list of Cs. In addition to those listed here, one may see "capital" and/or "conditions" on a particular author's list of four (or five) Cs. Conditions typically refers to overall economic conditions. Capital refers to the company's accumulated capital and its specific capital assets and is essentially subsumed within the categories of capacity and collateral. Keep in mind that the list of Cs is a convenient way to summarize the important aspects of the analysis, not a checklist to be applied mechanically.

- Capacity
- Collateral
- Covenants
- Character

Capacity refers to the ability of the borrower to make its debt payments on time; this is the focus of this section. **Collateral** refers to the quality and value of the assets supporting the issuer's indebtedness. **Covenants** are the terms and conditions of lending agreements that the issuer must comply with. **Character** refers to the quality of management. Each of these will now be covered in greater detail.

5.2.1 *Capacity*

Capacity is the ability of a borrower to service its debt. To determine that, credit analysis, in a process similar to equity analysis, starts with industry analysis and then turns to examination of the specific issuer (company analysis).

Industry structure. A useful framework for analyzing industry structure was developed by business school professor and consultant Michael Porter.[23] The framework looks at the five major forces of competition in an industry:

1. **Power of suppliers.** An industry that relies on just a few suppliers has greater credit risk than an industry that has multiple suppliers. Industries and companies with just a few suppliers have limited negotiating power to keep them from raising prices to their customers, whereas industries that have many suppliers can play them off against each other to keep prices in check.

2. **Power of buyers/customers.** Industries that rely heavily on just a few main customers have greater risk because the negotiating power lies with the buyers. For example, a toolmaker that sells 50 percent of its products to one large global retailer has limited negotiating power with its principal customer.

3. **Barriers to entry.** Industries with high entry barriers tend to have lower risk than industries with low entry barriers because competition may not be as fierce and pricing power is strong or at least sufficient. High entry barriers can take many forms, including high capital investment, such as in aerospace; large, established distribution systems, such as in auto dealerships; patent protection, such as in technology or pharmaceutical industries; or a high degree of regulation, such as in utilities.

4. **Substitution risk.** Industries (and companies) that offer products and services that provide great value to their customers, and for which there are not good or cost-competitive substitutes, typically have strong pricing power, generate substantial cash flows, and represent less credit risk than other industries or companies. Certain (patent-protected) drugs are an example, as are large jet airplanes. Over time, however, disruptive technologies and inventions can increase substitution risk. For example, years ago, airplanes began displacing many trains and steamships. Newspapers were considered to have a nearly unassailable market position until television and then the internet became substitutes for how people received news and information. Over time, recorded music has shifted from records to tapes, to compact discs, to mp3s and other forms of digital media.

5. **Level of competition.** Industries with heavy competition—characterized by a large number of participants, none of whom has significant market share—tend to have less cash flow predictability and, therefore, represent higher credit risk

---

[23] Michael E. Porter, *Competitive Strategy: Techniques for Analyzing Industries and Competitors* (New York; The Free Press, 1980).

than industries with less competition. Regulation can play an important role in competition as well. For example, regulated utilities typically have a monopoly position in a given market, which results in relatively stable and predictable cash flows. (They often carry higher debt levels, however, as a result of that monopoly position and the more stable cash flows.)

It is also important to consider how companies in an industry generate revenues and earn profits. Is it an industry with high fixed costs and capital investment or one with modest fixed costs? These structures generate revenues and earn profits in very different ways. Two of the best examples of industries with high fixed costs, also referred to as "having high operating leverage," are airlines and hotels. Many of their costs are fixed—running a hotel, flying a plane—so they cannot easily cut costs. If an insufficient number of people stay at a company's hotel, or fly in its planes, then the company will have trouble covering its fixed costs and will be at risk of losing lots of money. With high occupancy, however, revenues are strong, fixed costs get more than covered, and the company can earn substantial profits.

Industry fundamentals. After understanding an industry's structure, the next step is to assess its fundamentals, including its sensitivity to macroeconomic factors, its growth prospects, its profitability, and its business need—or lack thereof—for strong credit quality. Judgments about these can be made by looking at the following:

- *Cyclical or non-cyclical.* This is a crucial assessment because industries that are cyclical—that is, have greater sensitivity to broader economic performance—have more volatile revenues, margins, and cash flows and thus are inherently riskier than non-cyclical industries. Consumer product and health care companies are typically considered non-cyclical, whereas auto and steel companies can be very cyclical. Companies in cyclical industries should carry lower levels of debt relative to their ability to generate cash flow over an economic cycle than companies in less-cyclical or non-cyclical industries.

- *Growth prospects.* Although growth is typically a greater focus for equity analysts than for credit analysts, bond investors have an interest in growth as well. Industries that have little or no growth tend to consolidate via mergers and acquisitions. Depending upon how these are financed (e.g., using stock or debt) and the economic benefits (or lack thereof) of the merger, they may or may not be favorable to corporate bond investors. Weaker competitors in slow-growth industries may begin to struggle financially, adversely affecting their creditworthiness.

- *Published industry statistics.* Analysts can get a strong sense of an industry's fundamentals and performance by researching statistics that are published by and available from a number of different sources, including the rating agencies, investment banks, industry publications, and frequently, government agencies.

Company fundamentals. Following analysis of an industry's structure and fundamentals, the next step is to assess the fundamentals of the company: the corporate borrower. Analysts should examine the following:

- Competitive position
- Track record/operating history
- Management's strategy and execution
- Ratios and ratio analysis

Competitive position. Based on their knowledge of the industry structure and fundamentals, analysts assess a company's competitive position within the industry. What is its market share? How has it changed over time: Is it increasing, decreasing, holding steady? Is it well above (or below) its peers? How does it compare with respect to cost structure? How might it change its competitive position? What sort of financing might that require?

Track record/Operating history. How has the company performed over time? It's useful to go back several years and analyze the company's financial performance, perhaps during times of both economic growth and contraction. What are the trends in revenues, profit margins, and cash flow? Capital expenditures represent what percent of revenues? What are the trends on the balance sheet—use of debt versus equity? Was this track record developed under the current management team? If not, when did the current management team take over?

Management's strategy and execution. What is management's strategy for the company: to compete and to grow? Does it make sense, and is it plausible? How risky is it, and how differentiated is it from its industry peers? Is it venturing into unrelated businesses? Does the analyst have confidence in management's ability to execute? What is management's track record, both at this company and at previous ones? Credit analysts also want to know and understand how management's strategy will affect its balance sheet. Does management plan to manage the balance sheet prudently, in a manner that doesn't adversely affect bondholders? Analysts can learn about management's strategy from reading comments, discussion, and analysis that are included with financial statements filed with appropriate regulators, listening to conference calls about earnings or other big announcements (e.g., acquisitions), going to company websites to find earnings releases and copies of slides of presentations at various industry conferences, visiting and speaking with the company, and so on.

Example 5

Industry and Company Analysis

1. Given a hotel company, a chemical company, and a consumer products company, which is *most likely* to be able to support a high debt load over an economic cycle?

   A. The hotel company, because people need a place to stay when they travel.

   B. The chemical company, because chemicals are a key input to many products.

   C. The consumer products company, because consumer products are typically resistant to recessions.

2. Why do heavily regulated monopoly companies, such as utilities, carry high debt loads?

   A. Regulators require them to carry high debt loads.

   B. They generate strong and stable cash flows, enabling them to support high levels of debt.

   C. They are not very profitable and need to borrow heavily to maintain their plant and equipment.

3. XYZ Corp. manufactures a commodity product in a highly competitive industry in which no company has significant market share and where there are low barriers to entry. Which of the following *best* describes XYZ's ability to take on substantial debt?

   A. Its ability is very limited because companies in industries with those characteristics generally cannot support high debt loads.

B. Its ability is strong because companies in industries with those characteristics generally have high margins and cash flows that can support significant debt.

C. We don't have enough information to answer the question.

Solution to 1:

C is correct. Consumer products companies are considered non-cyclical, whereas hotel and chemical companies are more cyclical and thus more vulnerable to economic downturns.

Solution to 2:

B is correct. Because such monopolies' financial returns are generally dictated by the regulators, they generate consistent cash flows and are, therefore, able to support high debt levels. In addition, significant barriers to entry arising from high capital investment requirements and the regulatory process can contribute to debt capacity.

Solution to 3:

A is correct. Companies in industries with those characteristics typically have low margins and limited cash flow and thus cannot support high debt levels.

Ratios and ratio analysis. To provide context and metrics to the analysis and understanding of a company's fundamentals—based on the industry in which it operates, its competitive position, its strategy and execution—a number of financial ratios derived from the company's principal financial statements are examined: the income statement, balance sheet, and cash flow statement. Credit analysts calculate a number of ratios to assess the financial health of a company, identify trends over time, and compare companies across an industry to get a sense of relative creditworthiness. Note that typical values of these ratios vary widely from one industry to another because of different industry characteristics previously identified: competitive structure, economic cyclicality, regulation, and so on.

We will categorize the key credit analysis ratios into three different groups:

■ Profitability and cash flow

■ Leverage

■ Coverage

Profitability and cash flow measures. It is from profitability and cash flow generation that companies can service their debt. Credit analysts typically look at operating profit margins and operating income to get a sense of a company's underlying profitability and see how it varies over time. Operating income is defined as operating revenues minus operating expenses and is commonly referred to as "earnings before interest and taxes" (EBIT). Credit analysts focus on EBIT because it is useful to determine a company's performance prior to costs arising from its capital structure (i.e., how much debt it carries versus equity). And "before taxes" is used because interest expense is paid before income taxes are calculated.

There are several measures of cash flow used in credit analysis; some are more conservative than others because they make certain adjustments for cash that gets used in managing and maintaining the business or in making payments to shareholders.

■ **Earnings before interest, taxes, depreciation, and amortization (EBITDA).** EBITDA is a commonly used measure of cash flow that takes operating income and adds back depreciation and amortization expense because those are non-cash items. This is a somewhat crude measure of cash flow because it excludes certain cash-related expenses of running a business, such as capital expenditures and changes in (non-cash) working capital. Thus, despite its popularity as a cash flow metric, analysts look at other measures in addition to EBITDA.

- **Funds from operations (FFO).** Standard & Poor's defines funds from operations as net income from continuing operations plus depreciation, amortization, deferred income taxes, and other non-cash items.[24]

- **Free cash flow before dividends.**[25] This measures excess cash flow generated by the company (excluding non-recurring items) before payments to shareholders or that could be used to pay down debt or pay dividends. It includes net income plus depreciation and amortization minus capital expenditures minus increase (plus decrease) in non-cash working capital, and excludes non-recurring items. Companies that have negative free cash flow before payments to shareholders will be consuming cash they have or will need to rely on additional financing—from banks, bond investors, or equity investors. This obviously represents higher credit risk.

- **Free cash flow after dividends.** This measure just takes the preceding calculation and subtracts dividend payments. If this number is positive, it represents cash that could be used to pay down debt or build up cash on the balance sheet. Either outcome is a form of deleveraging, which is favorable from a credit risk standpoint. Some credit analysts will calculate net debt by subtracting balance sheet cash from total debt, although they shouldn't assume the cash will be used to pay down debt. Actual debt paid down from free cash flow is a stronger form of deleveraging. Some analysts will also deduct stock buybacks to get the "truest" form of free cash flow that can be used to de-lever on either a gross or net debt basis; however, others view stock buybacks as more discretionary and as having less certain timing than dividends, and thus treat those two forms of shareholder payments differently when calculating free cash flow.

Leverage ratios. There are a few measures of leverage used by credit analysts. The most common are the debt/capital, debt/EBITDA, and FFO/debt ratios. Note that many analysts adjust a company's reported debt levels for debt-like liabilities, such as underfunded pensions and other retiree benefits, as well as operating leases. When adjusting for leases, analysts will typically add back the imputed interest or rent expense to various cash flow measures.

- **Debt/capital**. Capital is calculated as total debt plus shareholders equity. This ratio shows the percent of a company's capital base that is financed with debt. A lower percentage of debt indicates lower credit risk. This traditional ratio is generally used for investment-grade corporate issuers. Where goodwill or other intangible assets are significant (and subject to obsolescence, depletion, or other forms of devaluation), it is often informative to also compute the debt to capital ratio after assuming a write-down of the after-tax value of such assets.

- **Debt/EBITDA.** This ratio is a common leverage measure. Analysts use it on a "snapshot" basis, as well as to look at trends over time and at projections and to compare companies in a given industry. Rating agencies often use it as a trigger for rating actions, and banks reference it in loan covenants. A higher ratio

---

[24] The funds from operations differs only slightly from the better known cash flow from operations in that it excludes working capital changes. The idea behind using FFO in credit analysis is to take out the near-term swings and seasonality in working capital that can potentially distort the amount of operating cash flow a business is generating. Over time, the working capital swings are expected to even out. Analysts tend to look at both FFO and cash flow from operations, particularly for businesses with large working capital swings (e.g., very cyclical manufacturing companies).

[25] In other parts of the CFA curriculum, this is referred to as free cash flow to the firm (FCFF). These can be regarded as interchangeable.

indicates more leverage and thus higher credit risk. Note that this ratio can be very volatile for companies with high cash flow variability, such as those in cyclical industries and with high operating leverage (fixed costs).

▪ **FFO/debt.** Credit rating agencies like using this leverage ratio. They publish key median and average ratios, such as this one, by rating category so analysts can get a sense of why an issuer is assigned a certain credit rating, as well as where that rating may migrate based on changes to such key ratios as this one.

Coverage ratios. Coverage ratios measure an issuer's ability to meet—to "cover"—its interest payments. The two most common are the EBITDA/interest expense and EBIT/interest expense ratios.

▪ **EBITDA/interest expense.** This measurement of interest coverage is a bit more liberal than the one that uses EBIT because it does not subtract out the impact of (non-cash) depreciation and amortization expense. A higher ratio indicates better credit quality.

▪ **EBIT/interest expense.** Because EBIT does not include depreciation and amortization, it is considered a more conservative measure of interest coverage. This ratio is now used less frequently than EBITDA/interest expense.

Exhibit 9 is a good example of the key average credit ratios by rating category for industrial companies over a three-year period, as published by Standard & Poor's.

Exhibit 9	**Industrial Comparative Ratio Analysis**							
Credit Rating	EBITDA Margin (%)	Return on Capital (%)	EBIT Interest Coverage (x)	EBITDA Interest Coverage (x)	FFO/Debt (%)	Free Operations Cash Flow/ Debt (%)	Debt/ EBITDA (x)	Debt/Debt plus Equity (%)
AAA								
U.S.	29.6	36.8	60.2	68.0	251.1	197.0	0.4	15.7
EMEA	NA	NA	NA	NA	NA	NA	NA	NA
AA								
U.S.	24.6	24.5	16.8	20.5	69.9	52.3	1.2	36.0
EMEA	25.2	21.7	14.4	17.6	163.9	82.5	0.9	23.7
A								
U.S.	24.2	21.0	22.0	29.0	96.7	65.9	1.5	36.0
EMEA	21.5	17.1	9.0	12.3	92.8	60.1	1.6	34.5
BBB								
U.S.	21.8	16.1	8.8	12.2	54.0	32.8	2.7	46.3
EMEA	19.7	13.1	5.3	7.9	52.1	23.7	2.6	44.9
BB								
U.S.	23.4	11.8	4.1	6.2	35.7	13.6	3.3	54.9
EMEA	20.3	11.0	5.3	7.2	31.8	9.7	3.3	51.0
B								
U.S.	19.4	8.0	1.6	2.9	17.5	5.1	6.6	84.0
EMEA	20.5	6.8	1.7	3.4	19.1	2.2	7.0	78.4

Notes: Data are as of 24 August 2011. EMEA is Europe, Middle East, and Africa.
Source: Based on data from Standard & Poor's Financial Services, LLC.

Comments on issuer liquidity. An issuer's access to liquidity is also an important consideration in credit analysis. Companies with strong liquidity represent lower credit risk than those with weak liquidity, other factors being equal. The financial crisis of 2008–2009 showed companies and investors that access to liquidity via the debt and equity markets should not be taken for granted, particularly for those that do not have strong balance sheets or steady operating cash flow.

When assessing an issuer's liquidity, credit analysts tend to look at the following:

- **Cash on the balance sheet.** Cash holdings provide the greatest assurance of having sufficient liquidity to make promised payments.

- **Net working capital.** The big U.S. automakers used to have enormous negative working capital, despite having high levels of cash on the balance sheet. This proved disastrous when the financial crisis hit in 2008 and the economy contracted sharply. Auto sales—and thus revenues—fell, the auto companies cut production, and working capital consumed billions of dollars in cash as accounts payable came due when the companies most needed liquidity.

- **Operating cash flow.** Analysts will project this figure out a few years and consider the risk that it may be lower than expected.

- **Committed bank lines.** Committed but untapped lines of credit provide contingent liquidity in the event that the company is unable to tap other, potentially cheaper, financing in the public debt markets.

- **Debt coming due and committed capital expenditures in the next one to two years.** Analysts will compare the sources of liquidity with the amount of debt coming due as well as with committed capital expenditures to ensure that companies can repay their debt and still invest in the business if the capital markets are somehow not available.

As will be discussed in more detail in the section on special considerations for high-yield credits, issuer liquidity is a bigger consideration for high-yield companies than for investment grade companies.

Example 6

Watson Pharmaceuticals, Inc. is a U.S.-based specialty health care company. As a credit analyst, you have been asked to assess its creditworthiness—on its own, relative to another competitor and its overall industry, and compared with a similarly rated company in a different industry. Using the financial statements provided in Exhibits 10 through 13 for the three years ending 31 December 2008, 2009, and 2010, address the following:

1. Calculate Watson Pharmaceuticals' operating profit margin, EBITDA, and free cash flow. (Note: The company did not pay dividends in 2008–2010.)

2. Determine Watson's leverage ratios: debt/EBITDA, debt/capital, free cash flow/debt.

3. Calculate Watson's interest coverage using both EBIT and EBITDA.

4. Using the statistics provided on the pharmaceutical industry and on competitor Johnson & Johnson, compare the credit ratios of Watson and Johnson & Johnson and explain the relative creditworthiness and ratings of the two companies.

5. Contrast the credit ratios of Watson with Luxembourg-based ArcelorMittal, one of the world's largest global steelmakers. Comment on the volatility of the credit ratios of the two companies. Which company looks to be more cyclical? What industry factors might explain some of the differences? In comparing the creditworthiness of these two companies, what other factors might be considered to offset greater volatility of credit ratios?

Exhibit 10	A: Watson Pharmaceuticals' Financial Statements		

Consolidated Statements of Operations (dollars in millions except per share amounts)	Years Ended December 31		
	2008	**2009**	**2010**
Net revenues	**2,535.5**	**2,793.0**	**3,566.9**
Operating expenses:			
Cost of sales (excludes amortization)	1,502.8	1,596.8	1,998.5
Research and development	170.1	197.3	296.1
Selling and marketing	232.9	263.1	320.0
General and administrative	190.5	257.1	436.1
Amortization	80.7	92.6	180.0
Loss on asset sales and impairments	0.3	2.2	30.8
Total operating expenses	**2,177.3**	**2,409.1**	**3,261.5**
Operating income	**358.2**	**383.9**	**305.4**
Other (expense) income:			
Interest income	9.0	5.0	1.6
Interest expense	(28.2)	(34.2)	(84.1)
Other income	19.3	7.9	27.7
Total other (expense) income, net	0.1	(21.3)	(54.8)
Income before income taxes and noncontrolling interest	**358.3**	**362.6**	**250.6**
Provision for income taxes	119.9	140.6	67.3
Net income	**238.4**	**222.0**	**183.3**
Loss attributable to noncontrolling interest	—	—	1.1
Net income attributable to common shareholders	**238.4**	**222.0**	**184.4**

Source: Based on data from Watson Pharmaceuticals' Company Annual Report (2010).

Exhibit 10B	Watson Pharmaceuticals' Financial Statements		

Consolidated Balance Sheets (dollars in millions)	Years Ended December 31		
	2008	**2009**	**2010**
ASSETS			
Current assets:			
Cash and cash equivalents	507.6	201.4	282.8

Exhibit 10B   Continued

Consolidated Balance Sheets	Years Ended December 31		
(dollars in millions)	2008	2009	2010
Marketable securities	13.2	13.6	11.1
Accounts receivable	305.0	517.4	560.9
Inventories, net	473.1	692.3	631.0
Prepaid expenses and other current assets	48.5	213.9	134.2
Deferred tax assets	111.0	130.9	179.4
Total current assets	**1,458.4**	**1,769.5**	**1,799.4**
Property and equipment, net	658.5	694.2	642.3
Investments and other assets	80.6	114.5	84.5
Deferred tax assets	52.3	110.8	141.0
Product rights and other intangibles, net	560.0	1,713.5	1,632.0
Goodwill	868.1	1,501.0	1,528.1
Total assets	**3,677.9**	**5,903.5**	**5,827.3**

LIABILITIES AND EQUITY

Current liabilities:

	2008	2009	2010
Accounts payable and accrued expenses	381.3	614.3	741.1
Income taxes payable	15.5	78.4	39.9
Short-term debt and current portion of long-term debt	53.2	307.6	—
Deferred tax liabilities	15.9	31.3	20.8
Deferred revenue	16.1	16.3	18.9
Total current liabilities	**482.0**	**1,047.9**	**820.7**
Long-term debt	824.7	1,150.2	1,016.1
Deferred revenue	30.1	31.9	18.2
Other long-term liabilities	4.9	118.7	183.1
Other taxes payable	53.3	76.0	65.1
Deferred tax liabilities	174.3	455.7	441.5
Total liabilities	**1,569.3**	**2,880.4**	**2,544.7**

Equity:

	2008	2009	2010
Preferred stock	—	—	—
Common stock	0.4	0.4	0.4
Additional paid-in capital	995.9	1,686.9	1,771.8
Retained earnings	1,418.1	1,640.1	1,824.5
Accumulated other comprehensive (loss) income	(3.2)	1.9	(2.5)

(continued)

Exhibit 10B	**Continued**		
Consolidated Balance Sheets	\ \ \ **Years Ended December 31**		
(dollars in millions)	2008	2009	2010
Treasury stock, at cost (9.7 and 9.6 shares held, respectively)	(302.6)	(306.2)	(312.5)
Total stockholders' equity	**2,108.6**	**3,023.1**	**3,281.7**
Noncontrolling interest	—	—	0.9
Total equity	**2,108.6**	**3,023.1**	**3,282.6**
Total liabilities and equity	**3,677.9**	**5,903.5**	**5,827.3**

Source: Based on data from Watson Pharmaceuticals' Company Annual Report (2010).

Exhibit 10C	**Watson Pharmaceuticals' Financial Statements**		
Consolidated Statements of Cash Flow	\ \ \ **Years Ended December 31**		
(dollars in millions)	2008	2009	2010
Cash flows from operating activities:			
Net income	238.4	222.0	183.3
Reconciliation to net cash provided by operating activities:			
Depreciation	90.0	96.4	101.9
Amortization	80.7	92.6	180.0
Provision for inventory reserve	45.7	51.0	50.0
Share-based compensation	18.5	19.1	23.5
Deferred income tax (benefit) provision	3.5	(19.0)	(118.3)
(Gain) loss on sale of securities	(9.6)	1.1	(27.3)
Loss on asset sales and impairment	0.3	2.6	29.8
Increase in allowance for doubtful accounts	1.2	3.4	9.5
Accretion of preferred stock and contingent payment consideration	—	2.2	38.4
Other, net	(13.9)	(7.6)	11.3
Changes in working capital	(38.2)	(87.0)	88.9
Net cash provided by operating activities	416.6	376.8	571.0
Cash flows from investing activities:			
Additions to property and equipment	(63.5)	(55.4)	(56.6)
Additions to product rights and other intangibles	(37.0)	(16.5)	(10.9)
Additions to marketable securities	(8.2)	(8.0)	(5.5)
Additions to long-term investments	—	—	(43.7)
Proceeds from sale of property and equipment	—	3.0	2.7

Exhibit 10C	Continued

Consolidated Statements of Cash Flow	Years Ended December 31		
(dollars in millions)	2008	2009	2010
Proceeds from sale of marketable securities	6.7	9.0	9.5
Proceeds from sale of investments	8.2	—	95.4
Acquisition of business, net of cash acquired	—	(968.2)	(67.5)
Other investing activities, net	0.4	—	2.5
Net cash used in investing activities	(93.4)	(1,036.1)	(74.1)
Cash flows from financing activities:			
Proceeds from issuance of long-term debt	—	1,109.9	—
Principal payments on debt	(95.6)	(786.6)	(459.7)
Proceeds from borrowings on short-term debt	67.9	—	—
Proceeds from stock plans	8.4	33.4	54.7
Repurchase of common stock	(0.9)	(3.6)	(6.3)
Net cash provided by (used in) financing activities	(20.2)	353.1	(411.3)
Effect of currency exchange rate changes	—	—	(4.2)
Net increase (decrease) in cash and cash equivalents	303.0	(306.2)	81.4
Cash and cash equivalents at beginning of period	204.6	507.6	201.4
Cash and cash equivalents at end of period	507.6	201.4	282.8

Source: Based on data from Watson Pharmaceuticals' Company Annual Report (2010).

Exhibit 11	Johnson & Johnson's Credit Ratios

	2008	2009	2010
Operating margin	25.1%	25.2%	26.8%
Debt/EBITDA	0.6x	0.8x	0.9x
EBITDA/Interest	43.3x	40.7x	42.8x
FCF/Debt	58.1%	61.1%	48.9%
Debt/Capital	21.8%	22.3%	22.9%

Source: Company Filings, Loomis, Sayles & Company.

Exhibit 12	Pharmaceuticals: U.S. Industry Credit Ratios (average of past three fiscal years as of 27 June 2011)

	Corp. Credit Rating (1)	Return on Capital (%)	EBIT Interest Coverage (x)	EBITDA Interest Coverage (x)	FFO/ Debt (%)	Free Operating Cash Flow/ Debt (%)	Debt/ EBITDA (x)	Debt/ Debt plus Equity (%)
Abbott Laboratories	AA/Stable/ A-1+	23.7	12.4	15.7	65.4	48.4	1.3	36.3
Allergan, Inc.	A+/Stable/ A-1	17.0	12.8	16.9	51.2	37.3	1.4	30.5
Axcan Intermediate Holdings Inc.	BB−/ Stable/−	14.0	2.2	3.1	20.2	18.6	2.7	55.2
Bristol-Myers Squibb	A+/Stable/ A-1	31.7	14.3	15.0	105.3	82.8	0.7	23.0
Catalent	B+/Stable/−	2.5	0.5	1.8	4.0	2.0	8.9	82.5
Eli Lilly and Company	AA/Stable/ A-1+	39.6	18.6	22.7	116.6	101.9	0.7	33.1
Johnson & Johnson	AAA/Stable/ A-1+	31.8	30.9	36.4	209.6	175.7	0.4	14.0
King Pharmaceuticals, Inc.	BB/Stable/−	16.0	10.9	14.9	68.3	58.2	1.2	26.3
Merck & Co., Inc.	AA−/ Positive/A-1+	28.2	22.3	20.2	150.8	114.1	0.6	12.1
Mylan Inc.	BB/Stable/−	7.5	2.0	3.1	11.7	4.4	5.6	63.5
Pfizer Inc.	AA/Stable/ A-1+	22.5	21.4	25.9	141.9	179.6	0.4	12.2
Valeant Pharmaceuticals International	BB−/ Stable/−	15.1	3.3	4.9	22.0	21.1	2.9	67.0
Watson Pharmaceuticals, Inc.	BBB−/ Stable/ −	11.5	9.5	14.2	39.4	29.4	2.0	33.6
Median		17.0	12.4	15.0	65.4	48.4	1.3	33.1

Source: Standard and Poor's Financial Services LLC (S&P). (1) As of June 27, 2010.

Exhibit 13	ArcelorMittal Credit Ratios		
	2008	**2009**	**2010**
Operating margin	10.2%	−2.4%	4.6%
Debt/EBITDA	2.0x	8.0x	3.3x
EBITDA/Interest	7.4x	1.1x	3.6x

Exhibit 13	Continued		
	2008	**2009**	**2010**
FCF/Debt	20.0%	13.0%	−2.1%
Debt/Capital	36.5%	27.5%	28.2%

Source: Company Filings, Loomis, Sayles & Company.

Solutions:

1. Operating profit margin (%) = Operating income/Revenue

    2008: 358.2/2535.5 = 0.141 or 14.1 percent

    2009: 383.9/2793.0 = 0.137 or 13.7 percent

    2010: 305.4/3566.9 = 0.086 or 8.6 percent

   EBITDA = Operating income + Depreciation + Amortization

    2008: 358.2 + 90.0 + 80.7 = 528.9

    2009: 383.9 + 96.4 + 92.6 = 572.9

    2010: 305.4 + 101.9 + 180.0 = 587.3

   FCF = Cash flow from operations − Capital expenditures − Dividends

    2008: 416.6 − (63.5 + 37.0 − 0.0) − 0 = 316.1

    2009: 376.8 − (55.4 + 16.5 − 3.0) − 0 = 307.9

    2010: 571.0 − (56.6 + 10.9 − 2.7) − 0 = 506.2

   where

   Capital expenditures = Additions to property and equipment + Additions to product rights and intangibles − Proceeds of sale of property and equipment

   Note that "Additions to product rights and intangibles" is included in capital expenditures here because such activities are likely to be both material and recurring for a health care/drug company. For other types of businesses, the analyst might elect to exclude this item from capital expenditures when calculating FCF.

2. Debt/EBITDA

    Total debt = Short-term debt and Current portion of long-term debt + Long-term debt

    2008: Debt: 53.2 + 824.7 = 877.9

     Debt/EBITDA: 877.9/528.9 = 1.7x

    2009: Debt: 307.6 + 1150.2 = 1457.8

     Debt/EBITDA: 1457.8/572.9 = 2.5x

    2010: Debt: 0 + 1016.1 = 1016.1

     Debt/EBITDA: 1016.1/587.3 = 1.7x

    Debt/Capital (%)

     Capital = Debt + Equity

     2008: Capital: 877.9 + 2108.6 = 2986.5

      Debt/Capital: 877.9/2986.5 = 29.4 percent

     2009: Capital: 1457.8 + 3023.1 = 4480.9

      Debt/Capital: 1457.8/4480.9 = 32.5 percent

2010: Capital: 1016.1 + 3282.6 = 4298.7

    Debt/Capital: 1016.1/4298.7 = 23.6 percent

FCF/Debt (%)

    2008: 316.1/877.9 = 36.0 percent

    2009: 307.9/1457.8 = 21.1 percent

    2010: 506.2/1016.1 = 49.8 percent

3. EBIT/Interest expense

    2008: 358.2/28.2 = 12.7x

    2009: 383.9/34.2 = 11.2x

    2010: 305.4/84.1 = 3.6x

  EBITDA/Interest expense

    2008: 528.9/28.2 = 18.8x

    2009: 572.9/34.2 = 16.8x

    2010: 587.3/84.1 = 7.0x

4. Based just on these credit ratios, Johnson & Johnson (J&J) has a higher operating margin, better leverage ratios, a much better Debt/EBITDA, a better FCF/debt over the three years (though slightly lower in 2010), a lower debt/capital (although pretty close in 2010), and a much better interest coverage as measured by EBITDA/interest. Collectively, those ratios suggest J&J is a stronger credit than Watson.

Watson Pharmaceuticals' Credit Ratios	2008	2009	2010
Operating margin	14.1%	13.7%	8.6%
Debt/EBITDA	1.7x	2.5x	1.7x
EBITDA/Interest	18.8x	16.8x	7.0x
FCF/Debt	36.0%	21.1%	49.8%
Debt/Capital	29.4%	32.5%	23.6%

Johnson & Johnson's Credit Ratios	2008	2009	2010
Operating margin	25.1%	25.2%	26.8%
Debt/EBITDA	0.6x	0.8x	0.9x
EBITDA/Interest	43.3x	40.7x	42.8x
FCF/Debt	58.1%	61.1%	48.9%
Debt/Capital	21.8%	22.3%	22.9%

5. By the five credit ratios shown in the tables, Watson has a higher and less volatile operating margin than ArcelorMittal, lower leverage (except debt/capital in 2009), and higher interest coverage. Based on the volatility of its cash flow and operating margin, Arcelor appears to be a much more cyclical credit. Coupled with its higher debt levels, one would expect Arcelor to have a lower credit rating. To mitigate the impact of its more volatile credit ratios, Arcelor might have very high levels of liquidity. Its size and global diversity may also be a "plus." In addition, it could have favorable supplier and customer contracts, and/or its profitability might be improving as, for example, competitors that are sub-scale and/or employing aggressively low pricing strategies are forced to retrench or exit the industry.

Watson Pharmaceuticals' Credit Ratios	2008	2009	2010
Operating margin	14.1%	13.7%	8.6%
Debt/EBITDA	1.7x	2.5x	1.7x
EBITDA/Interest	18.8x	16.8x	7.0x
FCF/Debt	36.0%	21.1%	49.8%
Debt/Capital	29.4%	32.5%	23.6%

ArcelorMittal's Credit Ratios	2008	2009	2010
Operating margin	10.2%	−2.4%	4.6%
Debt/EBITDA	2.0x	8.0x	3.3x
EBITDA/Interest	7.4x	1.1x	3.6x
FCF/Debt	20.0%	13.0%	−2.1%
Debt/Capital	36.5%	27.5%	28.2%

5.2.2 *Collateral*

Collateral, or asset value, analysis is typically emphasized more with weaker credit quality companies. As discussed earlier, credit analysts focus primarily on probability of default, which is mostly about an issuer's ability to generate sufficient cash flow to support its debt payments, as well as its ability to refinance maturing debt. Only when the default probability rises to a sufficient level do analysts typically consider asset or collateral value in the context of loss severity in the event of default.

Analysts do think about the value and quality of a company's assets; however, these are difficult to observe directly. Factors to consider include the nature and amount of intangible assets on the balance sheet. Some assets, such as patents, are clearly valuable and can be sold if necessary to cover liabilities. Goodwill, on the other hand, is not considered a high-quality asset. In fact, sustained weak financial performance most likely implies that a company's goodwill will be written down, reinforcing its poor quality. Another factor to consider is the amount of depreciation an issuer takes relative to its capital expenditures: Low capital expenditures relative to depreciation expense could imply that management is insufficiently investing in its business, which will lead to lower-quality assets, potentially reduced future operating cash flow, and higher loss severity in the event of default.

A market-based signal that credit analysts use to impute the quality of a publicly traded company's assets, and its ability to support its debt, is equity market capitalization. For instance, a company whose stock trades below book value may have lower-quality assets than is suggested by the amount reported on the balance sheet.

As economies become more service- and knowledge-based and those types of companies issue debt, it's important to understand that these issuers rely more on human and intellectual capital than on "hard assets." In generating profits and cash flow, these companies are not as asset intensive. One example would be software companies. Another example would be investment management firms. Human- and intellectual-capital-based companies may generate a lot of cash flow, but their collateral value is questionable, unless there are patents and other forms of intellectual property and "intangible capital" that may not appear directly on the balance sheet but could be valuable in the event of financial distress or default.

Regardless of the nature of the business, the key point of collateral analysis is to assess the value of the assets relative to the issuer's level—and seniority ranking—of debt.

5.2.3 Covenants

Covenants are meant to protect creditors while also giving management sufficient flexibility to operate its business on behalf of and for the benefit of the shareholders. They are integral to credit agreements, whether they are bonds or bank loans, and they spell out what the issuer's management is (1) obligated to do and (2) limited in doing. The former are called "affirmative covenants," whereas the latter are called "negative" or "restrictive covenants." Obligations would include such duties as making interest and principal payments and filing audited financial statements on a timely basis. Covenants might also require a company to redeem debt in the event of the company being acquired[26] or to keep the ratio of debt to EBITDA below some pre-scribed amount. The limitations might include a cap on the amount of cash that can be paid out to shareholders relative to earnings, or perhaps on the amount of additional secured debt that can be issued. Covenant violations can be an event of default unless they are cured in a short time or a waiver is granted.

For corporate bonds, covenants are described in the bond **prospectus**, the document that is part of a new bond issue. The prospectus describes the terms of the bond issue, as well as supporting financial statements, to help investors perform their analyses and make investment decisions as to whether or not to submit orders to buy the new bonds. Actually, the **bond indenture** is the governing legal credit agreement and is typically incorporated by reference in the prospectus.

Covenants are an important but underappreciated part of credit analysis. Strong covenants protect bond investors from the possibility of management taking actions that would hurt an issuer's creditworthiness. For example, without appropriate covenants management might pay large dividends, undertake stock buybacks well in excess of free cash flow, sell the company in a leveraged buyout,[27] or take on a lot of secured debt that structurally subordinates unsecured bondholders. All of these actions would enrich shareholders at the expense of bondholders. Recall that management works for the shareholders and that bonds are contracts, with management's only real obligation to creditors being to uphold the terms of the contract. Weak covenants pose additional risks to bond investors.

The bond-buying investor base is very large and diverse, particularly for investment-grade debt. It includes insurance companies, investment management firms, pension funds, mutual funds, hedge funds, sovereign wealth funds, and so on. Although there are some very large investment firms, the buyer base is fragmented and does not—and legally cannot—act as a syndicate. Thus, bondholders are generally not able to negotiate strong covenants on most new bond issues. Therefore, covenants provide limited protection to investment-grade bondholders and often only somewhat stronger protection to high-yield investors. Covenants on new bond issues tend to be stronger during weak economic or market conditions because investors seek more protection during such times. There are a few organized institutional investor groups focused on strengthening covenants: the Credit Roundtable[28] in the United States and the European Model Covenant Initiative in the United Kingdom.

---

26 This is often referred to as a "change of control" covenant.
27 A leveraged buyout (LBO) is an acquisition of a company by private investors using high levels of debt and relatively little equity.
28 See www.creditroundtable.org.

Covenant language is often very technical and written in "legalese," so it can be helpful to have an in-house person with a legal background to review and interpret the specific covenant terms and wording. One might also use a third-party service specializing in covenant analysis, such as Covenant Review.[29]

We will go into more detail on specific covenants in the section on special considerations for high-yield bonds.

5.2.4 *Character*

The character of a corporate borrower can also be difficult to observe. The analysis of character as a factor in credit analysis dates to when loans were made to companies owned by individuals. Most corporate bond issuers are now publicly owned by shareholders or privately owned by pools of capital, such as private equity firms. Management often has little ownership in a corporation, so analysis and assessment of character is different than it would be for owner-managed firms. Credit analysts can make judgments about management's character in the following ways:

- An assessment of the soundness of management's strategy.

- Management's track record in executing past strategies, particularly if they led to bankruptcy or restructuring. A company run by executives whose prior positions/ventures resulted in significant distress might still be able to borrow in the debt markets, but it would likely have to borrow on a secured basis and/ or pay a higher rate of interest.

- Use of aggressive accounting policies and/or tax strategies. Examples might include using a significant amount of off-balance-sheet financing, capitalizing versus immediately expensing items, timing revenue recognition, and/ or frequently changing auditors. These are potential warning flags to other behaviors or actions that may adversely impact an issuer's creditworthiness.

- Any history of fraud or malfeasance—a major warning flag to credit analysts.

- Previous poor treatment of bondholders—for example, management actions that resulted in major credit rating downgrades. These actions might include a debt-financed acquisition, a large special dividend to shareholders, or a major debt-financed stock buyback program.

Example 7

The Four Cs

1. Which of the following would not be a bond covenant?

   A. The issuer must file financial statements with the bond trustee on a timely basis.

   B. The company can buy back as much stock as it likes.

   C. If the company offers security to any creditors, it must offer security to this bond issue.

2. Why should credit analysts be concerned if a company's stock trades below book value?

   A. It means the company is probably going bankrupt.

   B. It means the company will probably incur lots of debt to buy back its undervalued stock.

---

[29] See www.covenantreview.com.

    C. It's a signal that the company's asset value on its balance sheet may be impaired and have to be written down, suggesting less collateral protection for creditors.

3. If management is of questionable character, how can investors incorporate this assessment into their credit analysis and investment decisions?

    A. They can choose not to invest based on the increased credit risk.

    B. They can insist on getting collateral (security) and/or demand a higher return.

    C. They can choose not to invest or insist on additional security and/or higher return.

Solution to 1:

B is correct. Covenants describe what the borrower is (1) obligated to do or (2) limited in doing. It's the absence of covenants that would permit a company to buy back as much stock as it likes. A requirement that the company offer security to this bond issue if it offers security to other creditors (answer C) is referred to as a "negative pledge."

Solution to 2:

C is correct.

Solution to 3:

C is correct. Investors can always say no if they are not comfortable with the credit risk presented by a bond or issuer. They may also decide to lend to a borrower with questionable character only on a secured basis and/or demand a higher return for the perceived higher risk.

6   CREDIT RISK VS. RETURN: YIELDS AND SPREADS[30]

As in other types of investing, taking more risk in credit offers higher potential return, but with more volatility and less certainty of earning that return. Using credit ratings as a proxy for risk, Exhibit 14 shows the composite yield to maturity[31] for bonds of all maturities within each rating category in the U.S. and European bond markets according to Barclays Capital, one of the largest providers of fixed-income market indices.

| Exhibit 14 | Corporate Yields by Rating Category as of 30 June 2011 |

Barclays Capital Indices	Investment Grade				Non-Investment Grade				
	AAA (%)	AA (%)	A (%)	BBB (%)	BB (%)	B (%)	CCC (%)	CC (%)	D (%)
U.S.	3.09	3.10	3.64	4.35	6.50	7.93	10.27	14.11	22.73
Pan European	3.33	3.58	4.14	4.98	6.90	8.67	17.12	13.81	54.80

Source: Based on data from Barclays Capital.

---

30 The material in this section applies to all bonds subject to credit risk. For simplicity, in what follows all such bonds are sometimes referred to as "corporate" bonds.

31 High-yield bonds are often quoted on a "yield to call" (YTC) or "yield to worst" (YTW) basis because so many of them are callable before maturity, whereas most investment-grade bonds are non-callable, or at least callable at such punitive premiums that issuers are not likely to exercise that option.

Note that the lower the credit quality, the higher the quoted yield. The realized yield, or return, will almost always be different because of changes in interest rates and the various forms of credit risk discussed earlier. For example, in the aggregate credit losses will "eat up" some of the yield premium offered by lower-quality bonds versus higher-quality credits. Trailing 12-month returns by credit rating category, and the volatility (standard deviation) of those returns, are shown in Exhibit 15.

Exhibit 15	U.S. Trailing 12-Month Returns by Rating Category, 31 December 1996–30 June 2011

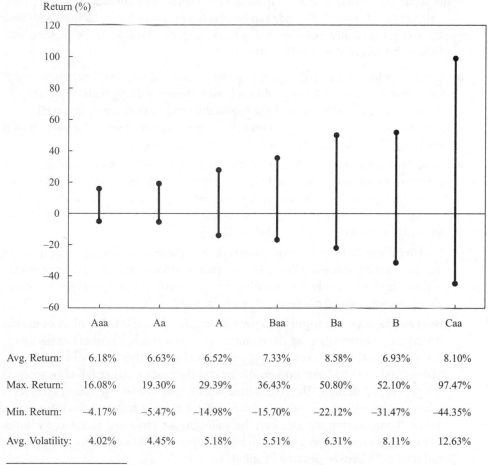

Return (%)

	Aaa	Aa	A	Baa	Ba	B	Caa
Avg. Return:	6.18%	6.63%	6.52%	7.33%	8.58%	6.93%	8.10%
Max. Return:	16.08%	19.30%	29.39%	36.43%	50.80%	52.10%	97.47%
Min. Return:	−4.17%	−5.47%	−14.98%	−15.70%	−22.12%	−31.47%	−44.35%
Avg. Volatility:	4.02%	4.45%	5.18%	5.51%	6.31%	8.11%	12.63%

Source: Based on data from Barclays Capital and Loomis, Sayles & Company.

As shown in the exhibit, the higher the credit risk, the greater the return potential and the higher the volatility of that return. This pattern is consistent with other types of investing that involves risk and return (although average returns on single-B rated bonds appear anomalous in this example).

For extremely liquid bonds that are deemed to have virtually no default risk (e.g., German government bonds, or *Bunds*), the yield is a function of real interest rates plus an expected inflation rate and a maturity premium. Of course, those factors are present in corporate bonds as well. In addition, the yield on corporate bonds will include a liquidity premium and a credit spread intended to compensate investors for these additional risks as well as for the expected level of credit losses. Thus, the yield on a corporate bond can be decomposed as

Yield on corporate bond = Real risk-free interest rate + Expected inflation rate + Maturity premium + Liquidity premium + Credit spread

Changes in any of these components will alter the yield, price, and return on the bond.

Investors in corporate bonds focus primarily on the yield spread relative to a comparable, default-free bond, which is composed of the liquidity premium and the credit spread:

Yield spread = Liquidity premium + Credit spread

The market's willingness to bear risk will affect each of these components. In general, however, it is not possible to directly observe the market's assessment of the components separately—analysts can only observe the total yield spread.

Spreads on all corporate bonds can be affected by a number of factors, with lower-quality issuers typically experiencing greater spread volatility. These factors, which are frequently linked, include the following:

- **Credit cycle.** As the credit cycle improves, credit spreads will narrow. Conversely, a deteriorating credit cycle will cause credit spreads to widen. Spreads are tightest at or near the top of the credit cycle, when financial markets believe risk is low, whereas they are widest at or near the bottom of the credit cycle, when financial markets believe risk is high.

- **Broader economic conditions.** Not surprisingly, weakening economic conditions will push investors to desire a greater risk premium and drive overall credit spreads wider. Conversely, a strengthening economy will cause credit spreads to narrow because investors anticipate credit metrics will improve due to rising corporate cash flow, thus reducing the risk of default.

- **Financial market performance overall, including equities.** In weak financial markets, credit spreads will widen, whereas in strong markets, credit spreads will narrow. In a steady, low-volatility environment, credit spreads will typically also narrow, as investors tend to "reach for yield."

- **Broker–dealers' willingness to provide sufficient capital for market making.** Bonds trade primarily over the counter, so investors need broker–dealers to commit capital for market-making purposes. During the financial crisis in 2008–2009, several large broker–dealer counterparties either failed or were taken over by another. This, combined with financial and regulatory stresses faced by virtually all the other broker–dealers, greatly reduced the total capital available for making markets and the willingness to buy/sell credit-risky bonds. Future regulatory reform may well lead to persistent or even permanent reductions in broker-provided capital.

- **General market supply and demand.** In periods of heavy new issue supply, credit spreads will widen if there is insufficient demand. In periods of high demand for bonds, spreads will move tighter.

Each of the first four factors played a role during the financial crisis of 2008–2009, causing spreads to widen dramatically, as shown in Exhibit 16, before narrowing sharply as governments intervened and markets stabilized. This is shown in two panels—one for investment grade, another for high yield—because of the much greater spread volatility in high-yield bonds, particularly CCC rated credits. This spread volatility is reflected in the different spread ranges on the y-axes. OAS is option-adjusted spread, which incorporates the value of the embedded call option in certain corporate bonds that issuers have the right to exercise before maturity.[32]

---

[32] The details of valuing bonds with embedded options and the calculation of OAS are covered in Level II of the CFA curriculum.

Exhibit 16	U.S. Investment-Grade and High-Yield Corporate Spreads

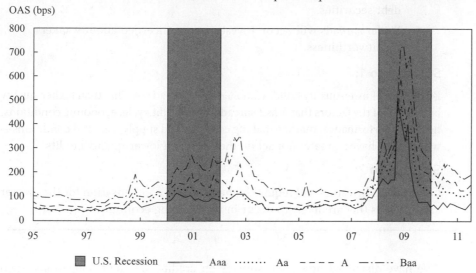

A. Investment-Grade Corporate Spreads

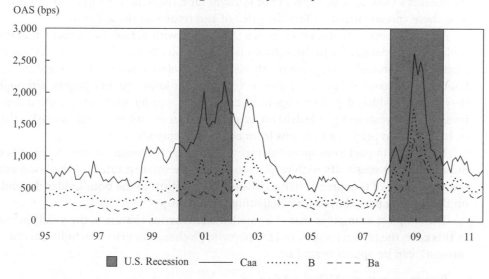

B. High-Yield Corporate Spreads

Sources: Based on data from Barclays Capital and Loomis Sayles & Company.

Example 8

Yield Spreads

1. Which bonds are likely to exhibit the greatest spread volatility?

    A. Bonds from issuers rated AA

    B. Bonds from issuers rated BB

    C. Bonds from issuers rated A

2. If investors become increasingly worried about the economy—say, as shown by declining stock prices—what is the *most likely* impact on credit spreads?

> **A.** There will be no change to credit spreads. They aren't affected by equity markets.
>
> **B.** Narrower spreads will occur. Investors will move out of equities into debt securities.
>
> **C.** Wider spreads will occur. Investors are concerned about weaker creditworthiness.
>
> ### Solution to 1:
>
> B is correct. Lower-quality bonds exhibit greater spread volatility than higher-quality bonds. All of the factors that affect spreads—the credit cycle, economic conditions, financial performance, market-making capacity, and supply/demand conditions—will tend to have a greater impact on the pricing of lower-quality credits.
>
> ### Solution to 2:
>
> C is correct. Investors will require higher yields as compensation for the greater credit losses that are likely to occur in a weakening economy.

We have discussed how yield spreads on credit-risky debt obligations, such as corporate bonds, can fluctuate based on a number of factors, including changes in the market's view of issuer-specific or idiosyncratic risk. The next question to ask is how these spread changes affect the price of and return on these bonds.

Although bond investors do concern themselves with default risks, recall that the probability of default for higher-quality bonds is typically very low: For investment-grade bonds, annual defaults are nearly always well below 1 percent (recall Exhibit 6). On the other hand, default rates can be very high for lower-quality issuers, although they can vary widely depending upon the credit cycle, among other things. What most investors in investment-grade debt focus on more than default risk is spread risk—that is, the effect on prices and returns from changes in spreads.

The return impact from spread changes is driven by two main factors: the modified duration (price sensitivity with respect to changes in interest rates) of the bond and the magnitude of the spread change. The effect on return to the bondholder depends on the holding period used for calculating the return.

The simplest example is that of a small, instantaneous change in the yield spread. In this case, the return impact, i.e., the percentage change in price (including accrued interest), can be approximated by

$$\text{Return impact} \approx -\text{MDur} \times \Delta\text{Spread}$$

where MDur is the modified duration. The negative sign in this equation reflects the fact that because bond prices and yields move in opposite directions, narrower spreads have a positive impact on bond prices and thus returns, whereas wider spreads have a negative impact on bond returns. Note that if the spread change is expressed in basis points, then the return impact will also be in basis points, whereas if the spread change is expressed as a decimal, the return impact will also be expressed as a decimal. Either way, the result is easily re-expressed as a percent.

For larger spread changes (and thus larger yield changes), the impact of convexity needs to be incorporated into the approximation:

$$\text{Return impact} \approx -(\text{MDur} \times \Delta\text{Spread}) + \tfrac{1}{2}\text{Cvx} \times (\Delta\text{Spread})^2$$

In this case, one must be careful to ensure that convexity (denoted by Cvx) is appropriately scaled to be consistent with the way the spread change is expressed. In general, for bonds without embedded options, one can scale convexity so that it has the same order of magnitude as the duration squared and then express the spread change as a decimal. For example, for a bond with duration of 5.0 and reported convexity of 0.235, one would re-scale convexity to 23.5 before applying the formula. For a 1 percent (i.e., 100 bps) increase in spread, the result would be

$$\text{Return impact} = (-5.0 \times 0.01) + \tfrac{1}{2} \times 23.5 \times (0.01)^2 = -0.04765 \text{ or } -4.765 \text{ percent}$$

The return impact of instantaneous spread changes is illustrated in Exhibit 17 using two bonds from British Telecom, the U.K. telecommunications company. The bonds, denominated in British pounds, are priced to provide a certain spread over British government bonds (gilts) of a similar maturity. From the starting spread, in increments of 25 bps and for both wider and narrower spreads, the new price and actual return for each spread change are calculated. In addition, the exhibit shows the approximate returns with and without the convexity term. As can be seen, the approximation using only duration is reasonably accurate for small spread changes but for larger changes, the convexity term generally provides a meaningful improvement.

Exhibit 17	Impact of Duration on Price for a Given Change in Spread

Issuer: British Telecom, 8.625%, maturing on 26 March 2020

Price: £129.475	Modified Duration: 6.084	Spread to Gilt Curve: 248 b.p.
Accrued interest: 6.3	Convexity: 47.4	YTM: 4.31

					Scenarios				
Spread Δ (b.p.)	−100	−75	−50	−25	0	25	50	75	100
Spread (b.p.)	148	173	198	223	248	273	298	323	348
New Price (£)	137.90	135.73	133.60	131.52	129.48	127.47	125.51	123.59	121.71
New Price + Accrued (£)	144.20	142.03	139.90	137.82	135.78	133.77	131.81	129.89	128.01
Price Δ (£)	8.43	6.26	4.13	2.05	0.00	−2.01	−3.96	−5.88	−7.77
Return (%)									
Actual	6.21%	4.61%	3.04%	1.51%	0.00%	−1.48%	−2.92%	−4.33%	−5.72%
Approx: Dur only	6.08%	4.56%	3.04%	1.52%	0.00%	−1.52%	−3.04%	−4.56%	−6.08%
Approx: Dur & Cvx	6.32%	4.70%	3.10%	1.54%	0.00%	−1.51%	−2.98%	−4.43%	−5.85%

Issuer: British Telecom, 6.375%, maturing on 23 June 2037

Price: £110.093	Modified Duration: 13.064	Spread to Gilt Curve: 247 b.p.
Accrued interest: 3.117	Convexity: 253.5	YTM: 5.62

					Scenarios				
Spread Δ (b.p.)	−100	−75	−50	−25	0	25	50	75	100
Spread (b.p.)	147	172	197	222	247	272	297	322	347
New Price (£)	125.99	121.72	117.65	113.78	110.09	106.58	103.23	100.04	97.00
New Price + Accrued (£)	129.11	124.84	120.77	116.90	113.21	109.70	106.35	103.16	100.11
Price Δ (£)	15.90	11.63	7.56	3.69	0.00	−3.51	−6.86	−10.05	−13.10
Return (%)									
Actual	14.04%	10.27%	6.68%	3.26%	0.00%	−3.10%	−6.06%	−8.88%	−11.57%
Approx: Dur only	13.06%	9.80%	6.53%	3.27%	0.00%	−3.27%	−6.53%	−9.80%	−13.06%
Approx: Dur & Cvx	14.33%	10.51%	6.85%	3.35%	0.00%	−3.19%	−6.22%	−9.09%	−11.80%

Source: Based on data from Bloomberg Finance, L.P. (settle date is 19 December 2011).

Note that the price change for a given spread change is higher for the longer-duration bond—in this case, the 2037 maturity British Telecom bond—than for the shorter-duration bond. Longer-duration corporate bonds are referred to as having "higher spread sensitivity"; that is, their prices, and thus returns, are more volatile with respect to changes in spread. It is essentially the same concept as duration for any bond: The longer the duration of a bond, the greater the price volatility for a given change in interest rates/yields.

In addition, investors want to be compensated for the fact that the further one is from a bond's maturity (i.e., the longer the bond), the greater the uncertainty about an issuer's future creditworthiness. Based on credit analysis, an investor might be confident that an issuer's risk of default is relatively low in the near term; however, looking many years into the future, the investor's uncertainty grows because of factors that are increasingly difficult, if not impossible, to forecast (e.g., poor management strategy or execution, technological obsolescence, natural or man-made disasters, corporate leveraging events). This increase in credit risk over time can be seen in Exhibit 18. Note that in this Standard & Poor's study,[33] one-year default rates for the 2010 issuance pool are 0 percent for all rating categories of B+ or higher. The three-year default rates for bonds issued in 2008 are materially higher, and the observed defaults include bonds originally rated up to BBB– (i.e., low investment grade). The 10-year default rates for bonds issued in 2001 are appreciably higher than the 3-year default rates, and the defaults include bonds initially rated as high as A+ (i.e., solid investment grade). In addition to the risk of default rising over time, the data also show quite conclusively that the lower the credit rating, the higher the risk of default. Finally, note the very high risk of default for bonds rated CCC or lower over all time horizons. This is consistent with Exhibit 7 earlier in the reading, which showed significant three-year ratings variability ("migration"), with much of the migration to lower credit ratings (i.e., higher risk of default).

Exhibit 18	Default Rate by Rating Category (%) (Non-financials)		
Credit Rating	1 Year (2010 pool)	3 Year (2008 pool)	10 Year (2001 pool)
AAA	0.00	0.00	0.00
AA+	0.00	0.00	0.00
AA	0.00	0.00	0.00
AA–	0.00	0.00	0.00
A+	0.00	0.00	1.76
A	0.00	0.00	1.70
A–	0.00	0.00	0.87
BBB+	0.00	0.00	5.03
BBB	0.00	0.00	4.55
BBB–	0.00	1.04	12.80
BB+	0.00	2.12	15.38
BB	0.00	3.53	19.91
BB–	0.00	6.14	26.84
B+	0.00	12.73	33.69
B	0.76	22.08	39.02

33 From S&P, "2010 Annual Global Corporate Default Study and Ratings Transitions," Standard & Poor's report (30 March 2011). Detailed descriptions of the underlying methodology are available in Appendix I of the report.

Exhibit 18	Continued		

Credit Rating	1 Year (2010 pool)	3 Year (2008 pool)	10 Year (2001 pool)
B–	2.07	25.23	55.83
CCC/C	21.99	56.63	65.31

Source: Based on data from S&P, "2010 Annual Global Corporate Default Study and Ratings Transitions," Standard & Poor's report (30 March 2011).

It is also worth noting that bid–ask spreads (in yield terms) translate into higher transaction costs for longer-duration bonds; investors want to be compensated for that as well. For these reasons, spread curves (often called **credit curves**), like yield curves, are typically upward sloping. That is, longer-maturity bonds of a given issuer typically trade at wider spreads than shorter-maturity bonds to their respective comparable-maturity government bonds.[34] Exhibit 19, using the U.S. telecommunications company AT&T as an example, shows the upward-sloping credit curve by plotting the yields of its bonds versus their maturity. (As a large and frequent issuer, AT&T has many bonds outstanding across the yield curve.)

Exhibit 19	AT&T Credit Curve vs. U.S. Treasury Curve

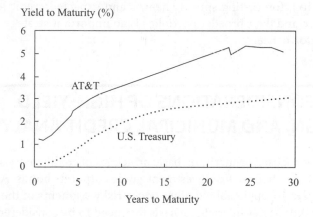

Source: Based on data from Bloomberg Finance, L.P., as of 5 October 2011.

---

34 There are some exceptions to this—bonds that trade at a high premium price over par due to having coupons that are well above the bond's yield to maturity and bonds that trade at distressed levels due to credit concerns. Many investors are averse to paying high premium prices for bonds that have credit risk because of the greater potential price decline—towards a recovery price in the event of default—from a credit-adverse event. Thus, high-coupon intermediate-maturity bonds can trade at similar or wider spreads to longer-maturity bonds. For distressed credits, the high risk of default causes all bonds for a given issuer to migrate toward the same expected recovery price. In this case, the shorter-maturity and shorter-duration bonds will have a higher quoted yield to maturity, and wider spread, than the longer-maturity and longer-duration bonds. This follows from the return impact formulas. The shorter the duration, the higher the yield (including spread) must go to bring the price down to a given expected recovery price.

Example 9

Return Impact

Calculate the return impact on a 10-year corporate bond with a 4.75 percent coupon priced at 100, with an instantaneous 50 bps widening in spread due to the issuer's announcement that it was adding substantial debt to finance an acquisition, resulting in a two-notch downgrade by the rating agencies. The bond has a modified duration of 7.9 and its convexity is 74.9.

Solution:

The impact from the 50 bps spread widening is:

$$
\begin{aligned}
\text{Return impact} \quad &\approx -(\text{MDur} \times \Delta\text{Spread}) + \tfrac{1}{2}\,\text{Cvx} \times (\Delta\text{Spread})^2 \\
&= -(0.0050 \times 7.9) + (0.5 \times 74.9) \times (0.0050)^2 \\
&= -0.0386, \text{ or } -3.86 \text{ percent}
\end{aligned}
$$

Because yields and bond prices move in opposite directions, the wider spread caused the bond price to fall. Using a bond-pricing calculator, the exact return is −3.85 percent, so this approximation was very accurate.

In summary, spread changes can have a significant impact on the performance of credit-risky bonds over a given holding period, and the higher the modified duration of the bond(s), the greater the price impact from changes in spread. Wider spreads hurt bond performance, whereas narrower spreads help bond performance. For bond investors who actively manage their portfolios (i.e., don't just buy bonds and hold them to maturity), forecasting spread changes and expected credit losses on both individual bonds and their broader portfolios is an important strategy for enhancing investment performance.

7   SPECIAL CONSIDERATIONS OF HIGH-YIELD, SOVEREIGN, AND MUNICIPAL CREDIT ANALYSIS

Thus far, we have focused primarily on basic principles of credit analysis and investing with emphasis on higher-quality, investment-grade corporate bonds. Although many of these principles are applicable to other credit-risky segments of the bond market, there are some differences in credit analysis that need to be considered. This section focuses on special considerations in evaluating the credit of debt issuers from the following three market segments: high-yield corporate bonds, sovereign bonds, and municipal bonds.

7.1 High Yield

Recall that high-yield, or non-investment-grade, corporate bonds are those rated below Baa3/BBB− by the major rating agencies. These bonds are sometimes referred to as "junk bonds" because of the higher risk inherent in their weak balance sheets and/or poor or less-proven business prospects.

There are many reasons companies are rated below investment grade, including

■ Highly leveraged capital structure

■ Weak or limited operating history

■ Limited or negative free cash flow

- Highly cyclical business
- Poor management
- Risky financial policies
- Lack of scale and/or competitive advantages
- Large off-balance-sheet liabilities
- Declining industry (e.g., newspaper publishing)

Companies with weak balance sheets and/or business profiles have lower margin for error and greater risk of default relative to higher-quality investment-grade names. And the higher risk of default means more attention must be paid to recovery analysis (or loss severity, in the event of default). Consequently, high-yield analysis typically is more in-depth than investment-grade analysis and thus has special considerations. This includes the following:

- Greater focus on issuer liquidity and cash flow
- Detailed financial projections
- Detailed understanding and analysis of the debt structure
- Understanding of an issuer's corporate structure
- Covenants
- Equity-like approach to high yield analysis

Liquidity. Liquidity—that is, having cash and/or the ability to generate or raise cash—is important to all issuers. It is absolutely critical for high-yield companies. Investment-grade companies typically have substantial cash on their balance sheets, generate a lot of cash from operations relative to their debt (or else they wouldn't be investment grade!), and/or are presumed to have alternate sources of liquidity, such as bank lines and commercial paper.[35] For these reasons, investment-grade companies can more easily roll over (refinance) maturing debt. On the other hand, high-yield companies may not have those options available. For example, there is no high-yield commercial paper market, and bank credit facilities often carry tighter restrictions for high-yield companies. Both bad company-specific news and difficult financial market conditions can lead to high-yield companies being unable to access the debt markets. And although the vast majority of investment-grade corporate debt issuers have publicly traded equity and can thus use that equity as a financing option, many high-yield companies are privately held and thus don't have access to public equity markets.

Thus, issuer liquidity is a key focus in high-yield analysis. Sources of liquidity, from strongest to weakest, are the following:

1. Cash on the balance sheet
2. Working capital
3. Operating cash flow
4. Bank credit facilities
5. Equity issuance
6. Asset sales

Cash on the balance sheet is easy to see and self-evident as a source for repaying debt.[36] As mentioned earlier in this reading, working capital can be a large source

---

35 Commercial paper (CP) is short-term funding—fewer than 270 days—used by many large, investment-grade corporations on a daily basis. In practice, issuance of CP requires solid, long-term, investment-grade ratings, mostly A rated or better, with a much smaller market for BBB rated companies.

36 Note that some cash may be "trapped" in other countries for certain tax, business, or regulatory reasons, and may not be easily accessible, or repatriation—bringing the money back to the home country—could trigger cash tax payments.

or use of liquidity, depending on its amount, its use in a company's cash-conversion cycle, and its role in a company's operations. Operating cash flow is a ready source of liquidity as sales turn to receivables, which turn to cash over a fairly short time period. Bank lines, or credit facilities, can be an important source of liquidity, though there may be some covenants relating to the use of the bank lines which are crucial to know and will be covered a little later. Equity issuance may not be a reliable source of liquidity because an issuer is private or because of poor market conditions if a company does have publicly traded equity. Asset sales are the least reliable source of liquidity because both the potential value and the actual time of closing can be highly uncertain.

The amount of these liquidity sources should be compared with the amount and timing of upcoming debt maturities. A large amount of debt coming due in the next 6–12 months alongside low sources of liquidity will be a warning flag for bond investors and could push an issuer into default because investors may choose not to buy new bonds intended to pay off the existing debt. Insufficient liquidity—that is, running out of cash or no longer having access to external financing to refinance or pay off existing debt—is the principal reason issuers default. Although liquidity is important for industrial companies, it is an absolute necessity for financial firms, as seen in the case of Lehman Brothers and other troubled firms during the financial crisis of 2008. Financial institutions are highly levered and often highly dependent on funding longer-term assets with short-term term liabilities.

Financial Projections. Because high-yield companies have less room for error, it's important to forecast, or project, future earnings and cash flow out several years, perhaps including several scenarios, to assess whether the issuer's credit profile is stable, improving, or declining and thus whether it needs other sources of liquidity or is at risk of default. Ongoing capital expenditures and working capital changes should be incorporated as well. Special emphasis should be given to realistic "stress" scenarios that could expose a borrower's vulnerabilities.

Debt Structure. High-yield companies tend to have many layers of debt in their capital structures, with varying levels of seniority and, therefore, different potential recovery rates in the event of default. (Recall the historical table of default recovery rates based on seniority in Exhibit 2.) A high-yield issuer will often have at least some of the following types of obligations in its debt structure:

- (Secured) Bank debt[37]
- Second lien debt
- Senior unsecured debt
- Subordinated debt, which may include convertible bonds[38]
- Preferred stock[39]

The lower the ranking in the debt structure, the lower the credit rating and the lower the expected recovery in the event of default. In exchange for these associated higher risks, investors will normally demand higher yields.

As discussed in Section 5, the standard leverage calculation used by credit analysts is debt/EBITDA and is quoted as a multiple (e.g., "5.2x levered"). For an issuer with several layers of debt with different expected recovery rates, high-yield analysts should calculate leverage at each level of the debt structure.

---

37 Because of the higher risk of default, in most instances bank debt will be secured for high-yield issuers.
38 Convertible bonds are debt instruments that give holders the option to convert to a fixed number of shares of common stock. They can be at any level of the capital structure but are frequently issued as senior subordinated debt.
39 Preferred stock has elements of both debt and equity. It typically receives a fixed payment like a bond does and has higher priority of claims than common stock. As a type of equity, however, it is subordinated to all forms of debt.

Example 10

Debt Structure and Leverage

Freescale Semiconductor specializes in semiconductors that are used in autos, communication equipment, and industrial machinery. This high-yield-rated company's debt structure is complicated because of the many levels of seniority that resulted from the company's 2006 leveraged buyout by a consortium of private equity firms. Exhibit 20 is a simplified depiction of the company's debt structure, as well as some key credit-related statistics.

Exhibit 20	Freescale Semiconductor Debt and Leverage Structure as of Year-End 2010

Financial Information ($ millions)

Cash	$ 1,050
Total debt	$ 7,611
Net debt	$ 6,561
Interest expense	$ 590
EBITDA	$ 990

Debt Structure ($ millions)

Secured debt (bank loan and bonds)	$ 4,899
Senior unsecured bonds	$ 1,948
Subordinated bonds	$ 764
TOTAL DEBT	$ 7,611

Source: Company Filings, Loomis Sayles & Company.

Using the information provided, address the following:

1. Calculate the total financial leverage through each level of debt, including total gross leverage.

2. Calculate the net leverage through the total debt structure.

3. Why might Freescale have so much secured debt relative to unsecured debt (both senior and subordinated)? (Note: This question draws on concepts from earlier sections.)

Solutions to 1 and 2:

	Gross Leverage (Debt/EBITDA)	Net Leverage (Debt – Cash)/ EBITDA
Secured debt leverage		
(Total secured debt/EBITDA)		
4899/990	4.9x	
Senior unsecured leverage		
(Secured debt + Senior unsecured debt)/EBITDA		
(4899 + 1948)/990	6.9x	

(continued)

	Gross Leverage (Debt/EBITDA)	Net Leverage (Debt – Cash)/ EBITDA
Total leverage (includes subordinated) (Total debt/EBITDA) 7611/990	7.7x	
Net leverage (leverage net of cash through entire debt structure) (Total debt – Cash)/EBITDA		6.6x

Solution to 3:

Freescale might have that much secured debt because (1) it was less expensive than issuing more unsecured debt on which investors would have demanded a higher yield and/or (2) given the riskiness of the business (semiconductors that are sold into cyclical industries, such as autos), the operating leverage of the business model, and the riskiness of the balance sheet (lots of debt from a leveraged buyout), investors would only lend the company money on a secured basis.

High-yield companies that have a lot of secured debt (typically bank debt) relative to unsecured debt are said to have a "top-heavy" capital structure. With this structure, there is less capacity to take on more bank debt in the event of financial stress. Along with the often more stringent covenants associated with bank debt and its generally shorter maturity compared with other forms of debt, this means that these issuers are more susceptible to default, as well as to lower recovery for the various less secured creditors.

Corporate Structure. Many debt-issuing corporations, including high-yield companies, utilize a holding company structure with a parent and several operating subsidiaries. Knowing where an issuer's debt resides (parent versus subsidiaries) and how cash can move from subsidiary to parent ("upstream") and vice versa ("downstream") should be key components of the analysis of high-yield issuers.

In a holding company structure, the parent owns stock in its subsidiaries. Typically, the parent doesn't generate much of its own earnings or cash flow but instead receives funds from its subsidiaries in the form of dividends from their earnings. And the subsidiaries' dividends are generally paid out of earnings after they satisfy of all their other obligations, such as debt payments. To the extent that their earnings and cash flow are weak, subsidiaries may be limited in their ability to pay dividends to the parent. Moreover, subsidiaries that carry a lot of their own debt may have restrictions or limitations on how much cash they can provide to the parent via dividends or another form, such as an intercompany loan. These restrictions and limitations on cash moving between parent and subsidiaries can have a major impact on their respective abilities to meet their debt obligations. The parent's reliance on cash flow from its subsidiaries means the parent's debt is structurally subordinated to the subsidiaries' debt and thus will usually have a lower recovery rating in default.

For companies with very complex holding companies, there may also be one or more intermediate holding companies, each carrying their own debt, and in some cases, they may not own 100 percent of the subsidiaries' stock. This structure is sometimes seen in high-yield companies that have been put together through many mergers and acquisitions or that were part of a leveraged buyout.[40]

Exhibit 21 returns to United Rentals, Inc. (URI), a high-yield company highlighted earlier as an example of the credit rating agency notching process. URI has a capital structure consisting of a parent company that has debt—in this case, convertible senior notes—as well as subsidiaries with outstanding debt. And in the case of URI's United Rentals North America subsidiary, it has several layers of debt by seniority.

Exhibit 21	URI's Capital Structure

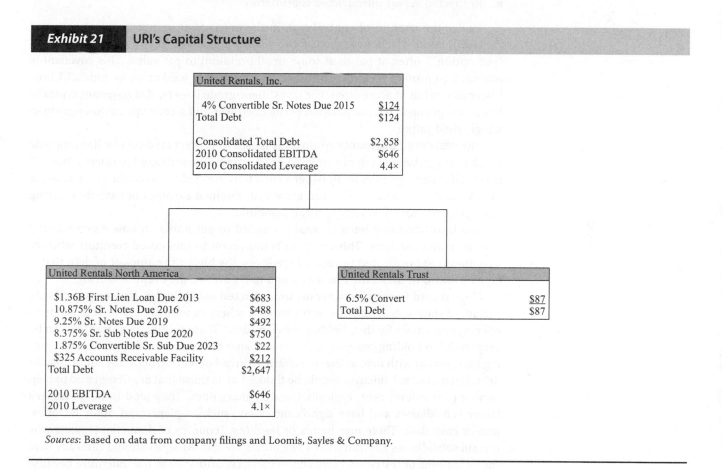

Sources: Based on data from company filings and Loomis, Sayles & Company.

Thus, high-yield investors should analyze and understand an issuer's corporate structure, including the distribution of debt between the parent and its subsidiaries. Leverage ratios should be calculated at each of the debt-issuing entities, as well as on a consolidated basis.

Also important is that although the debt of an operating subsidiary may be "closer to" and better secured by particular assets of the subsidiary, the credit quality of a parent company might still be superior. The parent company could, while being less directly secured by any particular assets, still benefit from the diversity and availability of all the cash flows in the consolidated system. In short, credit quality is not simply an automatic analysis of debt provisions and liens.

---

40 For holding companies with complex corporate structures, such as multiple subsidiaries with their own capital structures, a default in one subsidiary may not trigger a cross-default. Astute analysts will look for that in indentures and other legal documentation.

Covenant Analysis. As discussed earlier, analysis of covenants is very important for all bonds. It is especially important for high-yield credits because of their reduced margin of safety. Key covenants for high-yield issuers may include the following:

- Change of control put
- Restricted payments
- Limitations on liens and additional indebtedness
- Restricted versus unrestricted subsidiaries

Under the **change of control put**, in the event of an acquisition (a "change of control"), bondholders have the right to require the issuer to buy back their debt (a "put option"), often at par or at some small premium to par value. This covenant is intended to protect creditors from being exposed to a weaker, more indebted borrower as a result of acquisition. For investment-grade issuers, this covenant typically has a two-pronged test: acquisition of the borrower and a consequent downgrade to a high-yield rating.

The **restricted payments** covenant is meant to protect creditors by limiting how much cash can be paid out to shareholders over time. The restricted payments "basket" is typically sized relative to an issuer's cash flow and debt outstanding—or is being raised—and is an amount that can grow with retained earnings or cash flow, giving management more flexibility to make pay-outs.

The **limitations on liens** covenant is meant to put limits on how much secured debt an issuer can have. This covenant is important to unsecured creditors who are structurally subordinated to secured creditors; the higher the amount of debt that is layered ahead of them, the less they stand to recover in the event of default.

With regard to **restricted versus unrestricted subsidiaries**, issuers may classify certain of their subsidiaries as restricted and others as unrestricted as it pertains to offering guarantees for their holding company debt. These subsidiary guarantees can be very useful to holding company creditors because they put their debt on equal standing (pari passu) with debt at the subsidiaries instead of with structurally subordinated debt. Restricted subsidiaries should be thought of as those that are designated to help service parent-level debt, typically through guarantees. They tend to be an issuer's larger subsidiaries and have significant assets, such as plants and other facilities, and/or cash flow. There may be tax or legal (e.g., country of domicile) reasons why certain subsidiaries are restricted while others are not. Analysts should carefully read the definitions of restricted versus unrestricted subsidiaries in the indenture because sometimes the language is so loosely written that the company can reclassify subsidiaries from one type to another with a simple vote by a board of directors or trustees.

For high-yield investors, it is also important to know what covenants are in an issuer's bank credit agreements. These agreements are typically filed with the securities commission in the country where the loan document was drafted. Bank covenants can be more restrictive than bond covenants and may include so-called **maintenance covenants**, such as leverage tests, whereby the ratio of, say, debt/EBITDA may not exceed "x" times. In the event a covenant is breached, the bank is likely to block further loans under the agreement until the covenant is cured. If not cured, the bank may accelerate full payment of the facility, triggering a default.

Equity-like approach to high-yield analysis. High-yield bonds are sometimes thought of as a "hybrid" between higher-quality bonds, such as investment-grade corporate debt, and equity securities. Their more volatile price and spread movements are less influenced by interest rate changes than are higher-quality bonds, and they show greater correlation with movements in equity markets. Indeed, as shown in Exhibit 22, historical returns on high-yield bonds and the standard deviation of those returns fall somewhere between investment-grade bonds and equities.

Exhibit 22	U.S. Trailing 12-Month Returns by Asset Class, 31 December 1988–30 June 2011

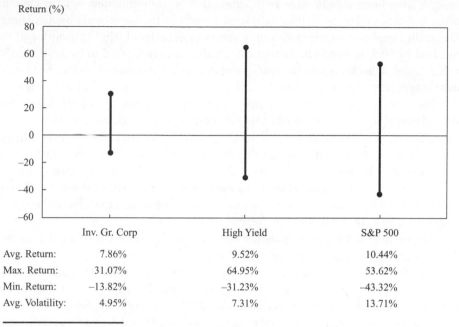

Return (%)

	Inv. Gr. Corp	High Yield	S&P 500
Avg. Return:	7.86%	9.52%	10.44%
Max. Return:	31.07%	64.95%	53.62%
Min. Return:	−13.82%	−31.23%	−43.32%
Avg. Volatility:	4.95%	7.31%	13.71%

Sources: Based on data from Barclays, Haver Analytics, and Loomis, Sayles & Company.

Consequently, an equity market-like approach to analyzing a high-yield issuer can be useful. One approach is to calculate an issuer's enterprise value. Enterprise value (EV) is usually calculated by adding equity market capitalization and total debt and then subtracting excess cash.[41,42] Enterprise value is a measure of what a business is worth (before any takeover premium) because an acquirer of the company would have to either pay off or assume the debt and it would receive the acquired company's cash.

Bond investors like using EV because it shows the amount of equity "cushion" beneath the debt. It can also give a sense of (1) how much more leverage management might attempt to put on a company in an effort to increase equity returns or (2) how likely—and how expensive—a credit-damaging leveraged buyout might be. Similar to how stock investors look at equity multiples, bond investors may calculate and compare EV/EBITDA and debt/EBITDA across several issuers as part of their analysis. Narrow differences between the EV/EBITDA and debt/EBITDA ratios for a given issuer indicate a small equity cushion and, therefore, potentially higher risk for bond investors.

7.2 Sovereign Debt

Governments around the world issue debt to help finance their general operations, including current expenses such as wages for government employees, and investments in long-term assets such as infrastructure and education. Government bonds in developed countries (such as the United States) have traditionally been viewed as the default risk-free rate off of which all other credits are priced. Fiscal challenges in

---

41 Excess cash takes total cash and subtracts any negative working capital.
42 Unlike the vast majority of investment-grade companies, many high-yield issuers do not have publicly traded equity. For those issuers, one can use comparable public company equity data to estimate EV.

developed countries exacerbated by the 2008 crisis, however, have called into question the notion of a "risk-free rate," even for some of the highest-quality government borrowers. As their capital markets have developed, an increasing number of sovereigns have been able to issue both external debt (denominated in hard currency, often the U.S. dollar) as well as local debt (issued in the sovereign's own currency). Generally, weaker sovereigns can only access international (that is, non-local) debt markets by issuing bonds in foreign currencies that are viewed to be safer stores of value. Local—also known as internal—debt is somewhat easier to service because the debt is typically denominated in the country's own currency, subject to its own laws, and the central bank can print additional money to service the government's local debt. Twenty years ago, many emerging market countries[43] could only issue external debt. Today, many are able to issue local debt and have successfully built domestic yield curves of local bonds across the maturity spectrum. All sovereigns are best able to service both external and local debt if they run "twin surpluses"—that is, a government budget surplus as well as a current account surplus. Running a current account surplus means the country is a net exporter of capital to the world and is not dependent on external financing.

Despite ongoing financial globalization and the development of local bond markets, sovereign defaults continue. Defaults are often precipitated by such events as war, political upheaval, major currency devaluation, a sharp deterioration in trade, or dramatic price declines in a country's key commodity exports. But default risks for some developed countries escalated after 2009 as government revenues dropped precipitously following the financial crisis, expenditures surged, and financial markets focused on the long-term sustainability of public finances, given aging populations and rising social security needs. Some of the weaker and more highly indebted members of the eurozone became unable to access the debt markets at economical rates and had to seek loans from the International Monetary Fund (IMF) and the European Union. These weaker governments had previously been able to borrow at much lower rates because of their membership in the European Union and adoption of the euro. Intra-eurozone yield spreads widened and countries were shut out of markets, however, as the global financial crisis exacted a high toll on their public finances and, in some cases, their banking systems, which became contingent liabilities for the sovereigns. In Ireland, the government guaranteed most bank liabilities, causing the country's debt burden to increase dramatically.

Like corporate analysis, sovereign credit analysis is based on a combination of qualitative and quantitative factors. Ultimately, the two key issues for sovereign analysis are 1) a government's ability to pay and 2) its willingness to pay. Willingness to pay is important because, due to the principle of sovereign immunity, investors are generally unable to force a sovereign to pay its debts.

To illustrate the most important considerations in sovereign credit analysis, we present a basic framework for evaluating sovereign credit and assigning sovereign debt ratings.[44] The framework highlights the specific characteristics analysts should expect in a top-quality sovereign credit. Some of these are self-explanatory (e.g., absence of corruption). For others, a brief rationale and/or range of values is included to clarify interpretation. Most, but not all, of these items are included in rating agency Standard & Poor's methodology.

---

43 There is no commonly accepted definition of emerging market countries. The World Bank considers GDP/Capita to be a useful measure, with below-average GDP/Capita likely indicating an emerging market. Other factors include the degree of openness and maturity of the economy, as well as a country's political stability.

44 This outline was developed from the detailed exposition of Standard & Poor's methodology given in "Sovereign Government Rating Methodology and Assumptions," June 2011.

Political and economic profile

- *Institutional effectiveness and political risks*
  - *Effectiveness, stability, and predictability of policy making and institutions*
    - Successful management of past political, economic, and/or financial crises
    - Ability and willingness to implement reforms to address fiscal challenges
    - Predictable policy framework
    - Absence of challenges to political institutions
    - Checks and balances in the system
    - Absence of corruption
    - Unbiased law enforcement and respect for rule of law and property rights
    - Independent/unfettered media and sources of economic data
  - *Perceived commitment to honor debts*
- *Economic structure and growth prospects*
  - Income per capita: More prosperous countries generally have a broader and deeper tax base with which to support debt.
  - Trend growth prospects: Trend GDP growth is primarily a reflection of productivity. Above-average trend growth indicates greater ability to service debt from future revenue and, therefore, greater creditworthiness.
  - Sources and stability of growth: Stable, broad-based growth and absence of excessive private sector credit expansion indicate stronger sovereign credit.
  - Size of the public sector relative to private sector: A smaller, leaner public sector is more likely to be able to enact necessary changes because it should be less beholden to special interest groups, including public employee unions.
  - Growth and age distribution of population: A relatively young and growing population contributes to trend GDP growth and an expanding tax base and mitigates the burden of social services, health care, and pensions, which are disproportionately costly for aging populations.

Flexibility and performance profile

- *External liquidity and international investment position*
  - Status of currency: Sovereigns that control a reserve currency or a very actively traded currency are able to use their own currency in many international transactions and are less vulnerable to adverse shifts in global investor portfolios.
  - External liquidity: Countries with a substantial supply of foreign exchange (foreign exchange reserves plus current account receipts) relative to projected external funding needs (current account payments plus debt maturities) are less vulnerable to interruption of external liquidity.
  - External debt: Countries with low external debt relative to current account receipts are better able to service their foreign currency debt. This is similar to that of a coverage ratio for a corporation.
- *Fiscal performance, flexibility, and debt burden*
  - Trend change in general government debt as a percent of GDP: Stable or declining debt as a percent of GDP indicates a strong credit; a rising ratio is ultimately unsustainable and is, therefore, a sign of diminishing creditworthiness.

- Perceived willingness and ability to increase revenue or cut expenditure to ensure debt service.

- General government interest expense as a percent of revenue: Less than 5 percent is good; greater than 15 percent is poor.

- Net general government debt as a percent of GDP: Less than 30 percent is good; more than 100 percent is poor.

- Contingent liabilities arising from financial sector, public enterprises, and guarantees: Less than 30 percent of GDP is good; more than 80 percent is very poor.

▪ *Monetary flexibility*

- *Ability to use monetary policy to address domestic economic objectives* (e.g., growth)

  ▪ Exchange rate regime: A freely floating currency allows maximum effectiveness for monetary policy. A fixed-rate regime limits effectiveness and flexibility. A hard peg, such as a currency board or monetary union, affords no independent monetary policy.

- *Credibility of monetary policy*

  ▪ Operationally independent central bank: An independent central bank is less likely to "debase the currency" by excessive money creation (e.g., in order to fund government deficits).

  ▪ Clear central bank mandate/objectives

  ▪ Track record of low and stable inflation

  ▪ Central government's ability to issue substantial long-term, fixed-rate debt in local currency: This is a sign of market confidence in the currency as a store of value.

- *Effectiveness of monetary policy transmission via domestic capital markets*

  ▪ Well-developed banking system

  ▪ Active money market and corporate bond market

  ▪ Greater reliance on market-based policy tools (e.g., open market operations) and limited reliance on blunt, administrative policy tools (e.g., reserve requirements)

In light of a sovereign government's various powers—taxation, regulation, monetary policy, and ultimately, the sovereign's ability to "print money" to repay debt—within its own economy, it is virtually always at least as good a credit in its local currency as it is in foreign currency. Thus, credit rating agencies often distinguish between local and foreign currency bonds, with local currency ratings as much as two notches higher. Of course, if a sovereign were to rely heavily on printing money to repay debt, it would fuel high inflation or hyperinflation and increase default risk on local debt as well.[45]

---

45 According to Reinhart and Rogoff in their book *This Time Is Different*, between 1800 and 2009 there have been more than 250 defaults on external sovereign debt and at least 68 defaults on internal debt. Reinhart and Rogoff use a broader definition of default that includes very high levels of inflation (more than 20 percent).

Example 11

Sovereign Debt

Exhibit 23 shows several key sovereign statistics for Portugal.

Exhibit 23	Key Sovereign Statistics for Portugal					
€ (billions), except where noted	2005	2006	2007	2008	2009	2010
Nominal GDP	153.7	160.3	169.3	171.2	168.6	172.6
Population (millions)	10.6	10.6	10.6	10.6	10.6	10.6
Unemployment (%)	8.6	8.6	8.9	8.5	10.6	12.0
Exports as share GDP (%)	20.3	22.2	22.6	22.6	18.8	21.3
Current account as share GDP (%)	−10.3	−10.7	−10.1	−12.6	−10.9	−10.0
Government revenues	61.3	64.8	69.7	70.7	67.0	71.8
Government expenditures	70.4	71.4	75.1	77.1	84.1	88.7
Budget balance (surplus/deficit)	−9.0	−6.5	−5.4	−6.4	−17.1	−16.9
Government interest payments	3.8	4.2	5.1	5.3	4.9	5.2
Primary balance (surplus/deficit)	−5.3	−2.2	−0.4	−1.1	−12.2	−11.7
Government debt	96.5	102.4	115.6	123.1	139.9	161.3
Interest rate on new debt (%)	3.4	3.9	4.4	4.5	4.2	5.4

Sources: Based on data from Haver Analytics, Eurostat, and Instituto Nacional de Estatistica (Portugal).

1. Calculate the government debt/GDP ratio for Portugal over the years 2005–2010.
2. Calculate GDP/Capita for the same period.
3. Based on those calculations, as well as other data from Exhibit 23, what can you say about Portugal's credit trend?

Solutions to 1 and 2:

	2005	2006	2007	2008	2009	2010
Gross government debt/GDP	63%	64%	68%	72%	83%	93%
GDP/Capita	14,500	15,123	15,972	16,151	15,906	16,283

Solution to 3:

The credit trend is deteriorating. Government debt/GDP is rising rapidly. The government is running a budget deficit, and the country is running a sizable current account deficit, which means it must attract funding from outside the country. Interest payments are generally rising, as is the interest rate on new debt.

7.3 Municipal Debt

While sovereigns are the largest issuers of government debt, non-sovereign—sometimes called sub-sovereign—government entities issue bonds as well. This would include state, provincial, and local governments (e.g., cities, towns, and counties, often referred to as municipalities) as well as the various agencies and authorities they create. For example, the City of Tokyo (Tokyo Metropolitan Government) has debt outstanding, as does the Lombardy region in Italy, the City of Buenos Aires in Argentina, and the State of California in the United States.

When people talk about municipal debt securities, however, they are usually referring to the U.S. municipal bond market because of its size. This market is approximately $3.7 trillion in size, roughly 10 percent of the total U.S. bond market,[46] and is composed of both tax-exempt[47] and, to a lesser extent, taxable bonds issued by state and local governments and their agencies. Municipal borrowers may also issue bonds on behalf of private entities, such as non-profit colleges or hospitals. Historically, for any given rating category, these bonds have much lower default rates than corporate bonds with the same ratings. For example, according to Moody's Investors Service, the 10-year average cumulative default rate from 1970 through 2009 was 0.09 percent for municipal bonds, compared with an 11.06 percent 10-year average cumulative default rate for all corporate debt.[48] The majority of municipal bonds are either general obligation bonds or revenue bonds.

General obligation (GO) bonds are unsecured bonds issued with the full faith and credit of the issuing government, typically a city, county, or state. These bonds are supported by the taxing authority of the issuer. The credit analysis of GO bonds has some similarities to sovereign debt analysis (e.g., the ability to levy and collect taxes and fees to help service debt). Almost without exception, however, municipalities must balance their operating budgets (i.e., exclusive of long-term capital projects) annually and they have no ability to use monetary policy the way many sovereigns can. The economic analysis focuses on employment, per capita income (and changes in it over time), per capita debt (and changes in it over time), the tax base (depth, breadth, diversification, stability, etc.), demographics, and net population growth, as well as an analysis of whether the state or municipality has the infrastructure and location to attract and support new jobs. Analysis should look at the volatility and variability of revenues during times of both economic strength and weakness. An overreliance on one or two types of tax revenue—particularly a volatile one, such as capital gains taxes or sales taxes—can signal increased credit risk. Pensions and other post-retirement obligations may not show up directly on the state or municipality's balance sheet, and many of these entities have underfunded pensions that need to be addressed. Adding the unfunded pension and post-retirement obligations to the debt reveals a more realistic picture of the issuer's debt and longer-term obligations. The relative ease or difficulty in managing the annual budgeting process and the government's ability to operate consistently within its budget are also important credit analysis considerations.

Disclosure by state and local governments varies widely, with some of the smaller issuers providing limited financial information. Reporting requirements are inconsistent, so the financial reports may not be available for six months or more after the closing of a reporting period.

---

46 Securities Industry and Financial Markets Association (SIFMA), "Outstanding U.S. Bond Market Data," (Q3 2011).
47 Tax exempt refers to the fact that interest received on these bonds is not subject to U.S. federal income taxes and, in many cases, is exempt for in-state residents from state and local taxes as well.
48 Moody's Investors Service, "U.S. Municipal Bond Defaults and Recoveries, 1970–2009," Moody's Special Comment (February 2010).

Exhibit 24 compares several key debt statistics from two of the largest states in the United States: California and Texas. California has one of the lowest credit ratings of any of the states, whereas Texas has one of the highest. Note the higher debt burden (and ranking) across several measures: Total debt, Debt/Capita, Debt/Personal income, and debt as a percent of state GDP. What is not shown here is that California also has a higher tax burden and greater difficulty balancing its budget on an annual basis than Texas.

Exhibit 24	Municipal Debt Comparison: California vs. Texas	
	California	**Texas**
Ratings:		
Moody's Investors Service	A1	Aaa
Standard & Poor's	A–	AA+
Fitch	A–	AAA
Unemployment rate (%)	12.40	8.20
Personal income per capita ($)	43,641	37,774
Debt burden, net ($/rank):		
Total (millions)	94,715 (1)	15,433 (9)
Per capita	2,542 (8)	612 (39)
As a percent of 2009 personal income	6.00 (9)	1.60 (40)
As a percent of 2010 GDP	4.73 (8)	1.05 (41)

Sources: Based on data from the U.S. Bureau of Labor Statistics (as of 2010), the U.S. Census Bureau (as of 2008), and Moody's Investors Service (as of 2010).

Revenue bonds are issued for specific project financing (e.g., financing for a new sewer system, a toll road, bridge, hospital, a sports arena, etc.). Revenue bonds have a higher degree of risk than GO bonds because they are dependent on a single source of revenue. The analysis of these bonds is a combination of an analysis of the project and the finances around the particular project. The project analysis focuses on the need and projected utilization of the project, as well as on the economic base supporting the project. The financial analysis has some similarities to the analysis of a corporate bond in that it is focused on operating results, cash flow, liquidity, capital structure, and the ability to service and repay the debt. A key credit metric for revenue-backed municipal bonds is the debt service coverage ratio (DSCR), which measures how much revenue is available to cover debt payments (principal and interest) after operating expenses. Many revenue bonds have a minimum DSCR covenant; the higher the DSCR, the stronger the creditworthiness.

CONCLUSION AND SUMMARY

8

In this reading, we introduced readers to the basic principles of credit analysis. We described the importance of the credit markets and the various types of credit risk. We discussed the role and importance of credit ratings and the methodology associated with assigning ratings, as well as the risks of relying on credit ratings. The reading covered the key components of credit analysis and the financial ratios used to help measure creditworthiness.

We also discussed risk versus return when investing in credit and how spread changes affect holding period returns. In addition, we addressed the special considerations to take into account when doing credit analysis of high-yield companies, sovereign borrowers, and municipal bonds.

- Credit risk is the risk of loss resulting from the borrower failing to make full and timely payments of interest and/or principal.

- The key components of credit risk are risk of default and loss severity in the event of default. The product of the two is expected loss. Investors in higher-quality bonds tend not to focus on loss severity because default risk for those securities is low.

- Loss severity equals (1 – Recovery rate).

- Other forms of credit-related risk include downgrade risk (also called credit migration risk) and market liquidity risk. Either of these can cause yield spreads—yield premiums—to rise and bond prices to fall.

- Downgrade risk refers to a decline in an issuer's creditworthiness. Downgrades will cause its bonds to trade at wider yields and thus lower prices.

- Market liquidity risk refers to a widening of the bid–ask spread on an issuer's bonds. Lower-quality bonds tend to have greater market liquidity risk than higher-quality bonds, and during times of market or financial stress, market liquidity risk rises.

- The composition of an issuer's debt and equity is referred to as its "capital structure." Debt ranks ahead of all forms of equity with respect to priority of payment, and within the debt component of the capital structure, there can be varying levels of seniority.

- With respect to priority of claims, secured debt ranks ahead of unsecured debt, and within unsecured debt, senior debt ranks ahead of subordinated debt. In the typical case, all of an issuer's bonds have the same probability of default due to cross-default provisions in most indentures. Higher priority of claim means higher recovery rate—lower loss severity—in the event of default.

- For issuers with more complex corporate structures—for example, a parent holding company that has operating subsidiaries—debt at the holding company is structurally subordinated to the subsidiary debt, although the possibility of more diverse assets and earnings streams from other sources could still result in the parent having higher effective credit quality than a particular subsidiary.

- Recovery rates can vary greatly by issuer and industry. They are influenced by the composition of an issuer's capital structure, where in the economic and credit cycle the default occurred, and what the market's view of the future prospects are for the issuer and its industry.

- The priority of claims in bankruptcy is not always absolute. It can be influenced by several factors, including some leeway accorded to bankruptcy judges, government involvement, or a desire on the part of the more senior creditors to settle with the more junior creditors and allow the issuer to emerge from bankruptcy as a going concern, rather than risking smaller and delayed recovery in the event of a liquidation of the borrower.

- Credit rating agencies, such as Moody's, Standard & Poor's, and Fitch, play a central role in the credit markets. Nearly every bond issued in the broad debt markets carries credit ratings, which are opinions about a bond issue's creditworthiness. Credit ratings enable investors to compare the credit risk of debt issues and issuers within a given industry, across industries, and across geographic markets.

■ Bonds rated Aaa to Baa3 by Moody's and AAA to BBB– by Standard & Poor's (S&P) and/or Fitch (higher to lower) are referred to as "investment grade." Bonds rated lower than that—Ba1 or lower by Moody's and BB+ or lower by S&P and/ or Fitch—are referred to as "below investment grade" or "speculative grade." Below-investment-grade bonds are also called "high-yield" or "junk" bonds.

■ The rating agencies rate both issuers and issues. Issuer ratings are meant to address an issuer's overall creditworthiness—its risk of default. Ratings for issues incorporate such factors as their rankings in the capital structure.

■ The rating agencies will notch issue ratings up or down to account for such factors as capital structure ranking for secured or subordinated bonds, reflecting different recovery rates in the event of default. Ratings may also be notched due to structural subordination.

■ There are risks in relying too much on credit agency ratings. Because creditworthiness is dynamic, initial/current ratings do not necessarily reflect the evolution of credit quality over an investor's holding period. Importantly, bond ratings do not always capture price risk because valuations often adjust before ratings change and the notching process may not adequately reflect the price decline of a bond that is lower ranked in the capital structure. Similarly, because ratings primarily reflect the probability of default but not necessarily the severity of loss given default, bonds with the same rating may have significantly different expected losses (default probability times loss severity). And like analysts, credit rating agencies may have difficulty forecasting certain credit-negative outcomes, such as adverse litigation, leveraging corporate transactions, and such low likelihood/high severity events as earthquakes and hurricanes.

■ The role of corporate credit analysis is to assess the company's ability to make timely payments of interest and repay principal at maturity. Analysts focus on an issuer's ability to generate cash flow by doing an assessment of the company as well as the industry in which it operates.

■ Credit analysis is similar to equity analysis. It is important to understand, however, that bonds are contracts and that management's duty to bondholders and other creditors is limited to the terms of the contract. In contrast, management's duty to shareholders is to act in their best interest by trying to maximize the value of the company—perhaps even at the expense of bondholders at times.

■ Credit analysts tend to focus more on the downside risk given the asymmetry of risk/return, whereas equity analysts focus more on upside opportunity from earnings growth, and so on.

■ The "4 Cs" of credit analysis—capacity, collateral, covenants, and character— provide a useful framework for evaluating credit risk.

■ Credit analysis focuses on an issuer's ability to generate cash flow. The analysis starts with an industry assessment—structure and fundamentals—and continues with an analysis of an issuer's competitive position, management strategy, and track record. Key credit ratios focus on debt leverage and interest coverage and use such measures as EBITDA, free cash flow, funds from operations, balance sheet debt, and adjustments, such as leases, pensions, and other retiree benefits.

■ Credit ratios are used to calculate an issuer's creditworthiness, as well as to compare its credit quality with peer companies.

- An issuer's ability to access liquidity is also an important consideration in credit analysis.

- The higher the credit risk, the greater the offered/required yield and potential return demanded by investors. Over time, bonds with more credit risk offer higher returns but with greater volatility of return than bonds with lower credit risk.

- The yield on a credit-risky bond comprises the yield on a default risk–free bond with a comparable maturity plus a yield premium, or "spread," that comprises a credit spread and a liquidity premium. That spread is intended to compensate investors for credit risk—risk of default and loss severity in the event of default—and the credit-related risks that can cause spreads to widen and prices to decline—downgrade or credit migration risk, as well as market liquidity risk.

   Yield spread = Liquidity premium + Credit spread.

- In times of financial market stress, the liquidity premium can increase sharply, causing spreads to widen on all credit-risky bonds, with lower-quality issuers most affected. In times of credit improvement or stability, however, credit spreads can narrow sharply as well, providing attractive investment returns.

- Credit curves—the plot of yield spreads for a given bond issuer across the yield curve—are typically upward sloping, with the exception of high premium-priced bonds and distressed bonds, where credit curves can be inverted because of the fear of default, when all creditors at a given ranking in the capital structure will receive the same recovery rate without regard to debt maturity.

- The impact of spread changes on holding period returns for credit-risky bonds are a product of two primary factors: the basis point spread change and the sensitivity of price to yield as reflected by (end-of-period) modified duration and convexity. Spread narrowing enhances holding period returns, whereas spread widening has a negative impact on holding period returns. Longer-duration bonds have greater price and return sensitivity to changes in spread than shorter-duration bonds.

   $$\text{Return impact} \approx -(\text{MDur} \times \Delta\text{Spread}) + \tfrac{1}{2}\text{Cvx} \times (\Delta\text{Spread})^2$$

- For high-yield bonds, with their greater risk of default, more emphasis should be placed on an issuer's sources of liquidity, as well as on its debt structure and corporate structure. Credit risk can vary greatly across an issuer's debt structure depending on the seniority ranking. Many high-yield companies often have complex capital structures, resulting in different levels of credit risk depending on where the debt resides.

- Covenant analysis is especially important for high-yield bonds. Key covenants include payment restrictions, limitation on liens, change of control, coverage maintenance tests (often limited to bank loans), and any guarantees from restricted subsidiaries. Covenant language can be very technical and legalistic, so it may help to seek legal or expert assistance.

- An equity-like approach to high-yield analysis can be helpful. Calculating and comparing enterprise value with EBITDA and debt/EBITDA can show a level of equity "cushion" or support beneath an issuer's debt.

- Sovereign credit analysis includes assessing both an issuer's ability and willingness to pay its debt obligations. Willingness to pay is important because, due to sovereign immunity, a sovereign government cannot be forced to pay its debts.

- In assessing sovereign credit risk, a helpful framework is to focus on five broad areas: (1) institutional effectiveness and political risks, (2) economic structure and growth prospects, (3) external liquidity and international investment position, (4) fiscal performance, flexibility, and debt burden, and (5) monetary flexibility.

- Among the characteristics of a high-quality sovereign credit are the absence of corruption and/or challenges to political framework; governmental checks and balances; respect for rule of law and property rights; commitment to honor debts; high per capita income with stable, broad-based growth prospects; control of a reserve or actively traded currency; currency flexibility; low external debt and external financing needs relative to external receipts; stable or declining ratio of debt to GDP; low debt service as a percent of revenue; low ratio of net debt to GDP; operationally independent central bank; track record of low and stable inflation; and a well-developed banking system and active money market.

- In the United States, there are two basic kinds of municipal debt: general obligation bonds and revenue-backed bonds.

- General obligation (GO) bonds are backed by the taxing authority of the issuing municipality (e.g., state or city). The credit analysis of GO bonds has some similarities to sovereign analysis—debt burden per capita versus income per capita, tax burden, demographics, and economic diversity. Underfunded and "off-balance-sheet" liabilities, such as pensions for public employees and retirees, are debt-like in nature.

- Revenue-backed bonds support specific projects, such as toll roads, bridges, airports, and other infrastructure. The creditworthiness comes from the revenues generated by usage fees and tolls levied.

PRACTICE PROBLEMS FOR READING 59

1. The risk that a bond's creditworthiness declines is *best* described by:
   A. credit migration risk.
   B. market liquidity risk.
   C. spread widening risk.

2. Stedsmart Ltd and Fignermo Ltd are alike with respect to financial and operating characteristics, except that Stedsmart Ltd has less publicly traded debt outstanding than Fignermo Ltd. Therefore, Stedsmart Ltd is *most likely* to have:
   A. no market liquidity risk.
   B. lower market liquidity risk.
   C. higher market liquidity risk.

3. In the event of default, debentures' claims will *most likely* rank:
   A. above that of secured debt holders.
   B. below that of secured debt holders.
   C. the same as that of secured debt holders.

4. In the event of default, the recovery rate of which of the following bonds would *most likely* be the highest?
   A. First mortgage debt
   B. Senior unsecured debt
   C. Junior subordinate debt

5. During bankruptcy proceedings of a firm, the priority of claims was not strictly adhered to. Which of the following is the *least likely* explanation for this outcome?
   A. Senior creditors compromised.
   B. The value of secured assets was less than the amount of the claims.
   C. The judge's order resulted in actual claims not adhering to strict priority of claims.

6. Although rating agencies assess the creditworthiness of debt issuers and issues, the *least likely* reason that a fixed income analyst should conduct an independent analysis of credit risk is because rating agencies:
   A. may at times mis-rate issues.
   B. often lag the market in pricing credit risk.
   C. cannot foresee future debt-financed acquisitions.

7. Jaco Meyer, a credit analyst, is analyzing the human capital of a company. Such an analysis will *most likely* give Meyer insight into the:
   A. quality of the company's management.
   B. strength of the company's balance sheet.
   C. power of the company's customers.

8. If goodwill makes up a large percentage of a company's total assets, this *most likely* indicates that:
   A. the company has low free cash flow before dividends.
   B. there is a low likelihood that the market price of the company's common stock is below book value.
   C. a large percentage of the company's assets are of low quality.

9. In order to analyze the **collateral** of a company a credit analyst should assess the:

    A. cash flows of the company.

    B. soundness of management's strategy.

    C. value of the company's assets in relation to the level of debt.

10. In order to determine the **capacity** of a company, it would be *most* appropriate to analyze the:

    A. company's strategy.

    B. growth prospects of the industry.

    C. aggressiveness of the company's accounting policies.

11. A credit analyst is evaluating the credit worthiness of three companies: a construction company, a travel and tourism company, and a beverage company. Both the construction and travel and tourism companies are cyclical, whereas the beverage company is non-cyclical. The construction company has the highest debt level of the three companies. The highest credit risk is *most likely* exhibited by the:

    A. construction company.

    B. beverage company.

    C. travel and tourism company.

12. Based on the information provided in Exhibit 1, the EBITDA interest coverage ratio of Adidas AG is *closest* to:

    A. 7.91x.

    B. 10.12x.

    C. 12.99x.

Exhibit 1	Adidas AG Excerpt from Consolidated Income Statement Year ending 31 December 2010 (€ in millions)
Gross profit	5,730
Royalty and commission income	100
Other operating income	110
Other operating expenses	5,046
Operating profit	894
Interest income	25
Interest expense	113
Income before taxes	806
Income taxes	238
Net income	568

Additional information:
Depreciation and amortization: €249 million

Source: Adidas AG Annual Financial Statements, December 2010

13. The following information is from the annual report of Adidas AG for December 2010:

    - Depreciation and amortization: €249 million

    - Total assets: €10,618 million

    - Total debt: €1,613 million

    - Shareholders' equity: €4,616 million

The debt/capital ratio of Adidas AG is *closest* to:

A. 15.19%.

B. 25.90%.

C. 34.94%.

14. Funds from operations (FFO) of Pay Handle Ltd increased in 2011. In 2011 the total debt of the company remained unchanged, while additional common shares were issued. Pay Handle Ltd's ability to service its debt in 2011, as compared to 2010, *most likely*:

A. improved.

B. worsened.

C. remained the same.

15. Based on the information in Exhibit 2, Grupa Zywiec SA's credit risk is *most likely*:

A. lower than the industry.

B. higher than the industry.

C. the same as the industry.

Exhibit 2	European Food, Beverage, and Tobacco Industry and Grupa Zywiec SA Selected Financial Ratios for 2010				

	Total debt/Total capital (%)	FFO/Total debt (%)	Return on capital (%)	Total debt/ EBITDA (x)	EBITDA interest coverage (x)
Grupa Zywiec SA	47.1	77.5	19.6	1.2	17.7
Industry Median	42.4	23.6	6.55	2.85	6.45

16. Based on the information in Exhibit 3, the credit rating of Davide Campari-Milano S.p.A. is *most likely*:

A. lower than Associated British Foods plc.

B. higher than Associated British Foods plc.

C. the same as Associated British Foods plc.

Exhibit 3	European Food, Beverage, and Tobacco Industry; Associated British Foods plc; and Davide Campari-Milano S.p.A Selected Financial Ratios, 2010				

Company	Total debt/ total capital (%)	FFO/ total debt (%)	Return on capital (%)	Total debt/ EBITDA (x)	EBITDA interest coverage (x)
Associated British Foods plc	0.2	84.3	0.1	1.0	13.9
Davide Campari-Milano S.p.A.	42.9	22.9	8.2	3.2	3.2
European Food, Beverage, and Tobacco Median	42.4	23.6	6.55	2.85	6.45

17. Holding all other factors constant, the *most likely* effect of low demand and heavy new issue supply on bond yield spreads is that yield spreads will:

    A. widen.

    B. tighten.

    C. not be affected.

18. A credit analyst is assessing a two-year, 13.5% coupon bond with a 1.77 duration. Because of a recent slump in operating revenue, the bond's yield to maturity has increased from 7.20% to 7.50%. The impact of the change in yield to maturity on the return of the bond is *closest* to:

    A. 0.53%.

    B. −0.53%.

    C. −0.60%.

SOLUTIONS FOR READING 59

1. A is correct. Credit migration risk or downgrade risk refers to the risk that a bond issuer's creditworthiness may deteriorate or migrate lower. The result is that investors view the risk of default to be higher, causing the spread on the issuer's bonds to widen.

2. C is correct. Market liquidity risk refers to the risk that the price at which investors transact may be different from the price indicated in the market. Market liquidity risk is increased by (1) less debt outstanding and/or (2) a lower issue credit rating. Because Stedsmart Ltd is comparable to Fignermo Ltd except for less publicly traded debt outstanding, it should have higher market liquidity risk.

3. B is correct. Secured debt holders have a direct claim on certain assets and their associated cash flows whereas unsecured debt holders only have a general claim on the issuer's assets and cash flow.

4. A is correct. First mortgage debt is the highest ranked debt in terms of priority of claims and is considered secured debt. First mortgage debt will also have the expected highest recovery rate. First mortgage debt refers to the pledge of specific property. Neither senior unsecured nor junior subordinate debt has any claims on specific assets.

5. B is correct. Whether or not secured assets are sufficient for the claims, this would not influence priority of claims. The difference between pledge assets and the claim becomes senior unsecured debt and still adheres to the guidelines of priority of claims.

6. C is correct. Neither an analyst nor ratings agencies can anticipate unexpected events.

7. B is correct. An analysis of the human capital of a company is the purpose of assessing the strength of its balance sheets or, stated differently, the value and quality of assets supporting the issuer's indebtedness (i.e., collateral).

8. C is correct. Goodwill is viewed as a lower quality asset compared with tangible assets that can be sold and more easily converted into cash.

9. C is correct. The value of assets in relation to the level of debt is important to assess the collateral of the company; that is, the quality and value of the assets that support the debt levels of the company.

10. B is correct. The growth prospects of the industry provide the analyst insight regarding the capacity of the company.

11. A is correct. The construction company is both highly leveraged which increases credit risk and in a highly cyclical industry which results in more volatile earnings. The beverage company is in a non-cyclical industry with less volatile earnings.

12. B is correct. The interest expense is €113 million and EBITDA = Operating profit + Depreciation and amortization = €894 + 249 million = €1,143 million. EBITDA interest coverage = EBITDA/Interest expense = 1,143/113 = 10.12 times.

13. B is correct. Total debt is €1,613 million with Total capital = Total debt + Shareholders' equity = €1,613 + 4,616 = €6,229 million. The Debt/Capital ratio = 1,613/6,229 = 25.90%.

14. A is correct. If the debt of the company remained unchanged but FFO increased, more cash is available to service debt compared to the previous

year. Additionally, the debt/capital ratio has improved. It would imply that the ability of Pay Handle Ltd to service their debt has improved.

15. A is correct. Based on four of the five credit ratios, Grupa Zywiec SA's credit quality is superior to that of the industry.

16. A is correct. Davide Campari-Milano S.p.A. has more financial leverage and less interest coverage than Associated British Foods plc, which implies greater credit risk.

17. A is correct. Low demand implies wider yield spreads, while heavy supply will widen spreads even further.

18. B is correct. Return impact $\approx -(\Delta \text{Spread} \times \text{Duration}_{End})$

Higher credit risk implies widening of the spread by 30 basis points and a lower return.

Return impact = $-(30 \text{ basis points} \times 1.77 \text{ years}) = -53.1 \text{ basis points} = -0.531\%$

Glossary

A priori probability   A probability based on logical analysis rather than on observation or personal judgment.

Abnormal profit   Equal to accounting profit less the implicit opportunity costs not included in total accounting costs; the difference between total revenue (TR) and total cost (TC).

Abnormal return   The amount by which a security's actual return differs from its expected return, given the security's risk and the market's return.

Absolute dispersion   The amount of variability present without comparison to any reference point or benchmark.

Absolute frequency   The number of observations in a given interval (for grouped data).

Accelerated book build   An offering of securities by an investment bank acting as principal that is accomplished in only one or two days.

Accelerated methods   Depreciation methods that allocate a relatively large proportion of the cost of an asset to the early years of the asset's useful life.

Account   With the accounting systems, a formal record of increases and decreases in a specific asset, liability, component of owners' equity, revenue, or expense.

Accounting (or explicit) costs   Payments to non-owner parties for services or resources they supply to the firm.

Accounting loss   When accounting profit is negative.

Accounting profit   (income before taxes or pretax income) Income as reported on the income statement, in accordance with prevailing accounting standards, before the provisions for income tax expense.

Accounts payable   Amounts that a business owes to its vendors for goods and services that were purchased from them but which have not yet been paid.

Accounts receivable (commercial receivables or trade receivables)   Amounts customers owe the company for products that have been sold as well as amounts that may be due from suppliers (such as for returns of merchandise).

Accounts receivable turnover   Ratio of sales on credit to the average balance in accounts receivable.

Accrued expenses (accrued liabilities)   Liabilities related to expenses that have been incurred but not yet paid as of the end of an accounting period—an example of an accrued expense is rent that has been incurred but not yet paid, resulting in a liability "rent payable."

Accrued interest   Interest earned but not yet paid.

Accrued revenue   Revenue that has been earned but not yet billed to customers as of the end of an accounting period.

Accumulated depreciation   An offset to property, plant, and equipment (PPE) reflecting the amount of the cost of PPE that has been allocated to current and previous accounting periods.

Acid-test ratio   A stringent measure of liquidity that indicates a company's ability to satisfy current liabilities with its most liquid assets, calculated as (cash + short-term marketable investments + receivables) divided by current liabilities.

Acquisition method   A method of accounting for a business combination where the acquirer is required to measure each identifiable asset and liability at fair value. This method was the result of a joint project of the IASB and FASB aiming at convergence in standards for the accounting of business combinations.

Action lag   Delay from policy decisions to implementation.

Active investment   An approach to investing in which the investor seeks to outperform a given benchmark.

Active return   The return on a portfolio minus the return on the portfolio's benchmark.

Active strategy   In reference to short-term cash management, an investment strategy characterized by monitoring and attempting to capitalize on market conditions to optimize the risk and return relationship of short-term investments.

Activity ratio   (or participation ratio) The ratio of the labor force to total population of working age.

Activity ratios   (asset utilization or operating efficiency ratios) Ratios that measure how efficiently a company performs day-to-day tasks, such as the collection of receivables and management of inventory.

Add-on interest   A procedure for determining the interest on a bond or loan in which the interest is added onto the face value of a contract.

Addition rule for probabilities   A principle stating that the probability that A or B occurs (both occur) equals the probability that A occurs, plus the probability that B occurs, minus the probability that both A and B occur.

Aggregate demand   The quantity of goods and services that households, businesses, government, and foreign customers want to buy at any given level of prices.

Aggregate demand curve   Inverse relationship between the price level and real output.

Aggregate income   The value of all the payments earned by the suppliers of factors used in the production of goods and services.

Aggregate output   The value of all the goods and services produced in a specified period of time.

Aggregate supply   The quantity of goods and services producers are willing to supply at any given level of price.

Aggregate supply curve   The level of domestic output that companies will produce at each price level.

Aging schedule   A breakdown of accounts into categories of days outstanding.

All-or-nothing (AON) orders   An order that includes the instruction to trade only if the trade fills the entire quantity (size) specified.

Allocationally efficient   Said of a market, a financial system, or an economy that promotes the allocation of resources to their highest value uses.

Allowance for bad debts   An offset to accounts receivable for the amount of accounts receivable that are estimated to be uncollectible.

Alternative investment markets Market for investments other than traditional securities investments (i.e., traditional common and preferred shares and traditional fixed income instruments). The term usually encompasses direct and indirect investment in real estate (including timberland and farmland) and commodities (including precious metals); hedge funds, private equity, and other investments requiring specialized due diligence.

Alternative trading systems (**electronic communications networks** or **multilateral trading facilities**) Trading venues that function like exchanges but that do not exercise regulatory authority over their subscribers except with respect to the conduct of the subscribers' trading in their trading systems.

American depository receipt A U.S. dollar-denominated security that trades like a common share on U.S. exchanges.

American depository share The underlying shares on which American depository receipts are based. They trade in the issuing company's domestic market.

American option An option that can be exercised at any time until its expiration date.

American-style contracts An option that can be exercised at any time until its expiration date.

Amortisation The process of allocating the cost of intangible long-term assets having a finite useful life to accounting periods; the allocation of the amount of a bond premium or discount to the periods remaining until bond maturity.

Amortised cost The historical cost (initially recognised cost) of an asset, adjusted for amortisation and impairment.

Amortization The process of allocating the cost of intangible longterm assets having a finite useful life to accounting periods; the allocation of the amount of a bond premium or discount to the periods remaining until bond maturity.

Annual percentage rate The cost of borrowing expressed as a yearly rate.

Annuity A finite set of level sequential cash flows.

Annuity due An annuity having a first cash flow that is paid immediately.

Anticipation stock Excess inventory that is held in anticipation of increased demand, often because of seasonal patterns of demand.

Antidilutive With reference to a transaction or a security, one that would increase earnings per share (EPS) or result in EPS higher than the company's basic EPS—antidilutive securities are not included in the calculation of diluted EPS.

Arbitrage 1) The simultaneous purchase of an undervalued asset or portfolio and sale of an overvalued but equivalent asset or portfolio, in order to obtain a riskless profit on the price differential. Taking advantage of a market inefficiency in a risk-free manner. 2) The condition in a financial market in which equivalent assets or combinations of assets sell for two different prices, creating an opportunity to profit at no risk with no commitment of money. In a well-functioning financial market, few arbitrage opportunities are possible. 3) A risk-free operation that earns an expected positive net profit but requires no net investment of money.

Arbitrageurs Traders who engage in arbitrage (see *arbitrage*).

Arithmetic mean The sum of the observations divided by the number of observations.

Arms index A flow of funds indicator applied to a broad stock market index to measure the relative extent to which money is moving into or out of rising and declining stocks.

Asian call option A European-style option with a value at maturity equal to the difference between the stock price at maturity and the average stock price during the life of the option, or $0, whichever is greater.

Ask (offer) The price at which a dealer or trader is willing to sell an asset, typically qualified by a maximum quantity (ask size).

Ask size The maximum quantity of an asset that pertains to a specific ask price from a trader. For example, if the ask for a share issue is $30 for a size of 1,000 shares, the trader is offering to sell at $30 up to 1,000 shares.

Asset allocation The process of determining how investment funds should be distributed among asset classes.

Asset beta The unlevered beta; reflects the business risk of the assets; the asset's systematic risk.

Asset class A group of assets that have similar characteristics, attributes, and risk/return relationships.

Asset utilization ratios Ratios that measure how efficiently a company performs day-to-day tasks, such as the collection of receivables and management of inventory.

Asset-based loan A loan that is secured with company assets.

Asset-based valuation models Valuation based on estimates of the market value of a company's assets.

Assets Resources controlled by an enterprise as a result of past events and from which future economic benefits to the enterprise are expected to flow.

Assignment of accounts receivable The use of accounts receivable as collateral for a loan.

At-the-money An option in which the underlying value equals the exercise price.

Automated Clearing House (ACH) An electronic payment network available to businesses, individuals, and financial institutions in the United States, U.S. Territories, and Canada.

Automatic stabilizer A countercyclical factor that automatically comes into play as an economy slows and unemployment rises.

Available-for-sale Debt and equity securities not classified as either held-to-maturity or held-for-trading securities. The investor is willing to sell but not actively planning to sell. In general, available-for-sale securities are reported at fair value on the balance sheet.

Available-for-sale securities Debt and equity securities not classified as either held-to-maturity or held-for-trading securities. The investor is willing to sell but not actively planning to sell. In general, available-for-sale securities are reported at fair value on the balance sheet.

Average fixed cost Total fixed cost divided by quantity.

Average product Measures the productivity of inputs on average and is calculated by dividing total product by the total number of units for a given input that is used to generate that output.

Average revenue Quantity sold divided into total revenue.

Average total cost Total costs divided by quantity.

Average variable cost Total variable cost divided by quantity.

Back simulation Another term for the historical method of estimating VAR. This term is somewhat misleading in that the method involves not a *simulation* of the past but rather what *actually happened* in the past, sometimes adjusted to reflect the fact that a different portfolio may have existed in the past than is planned for the future.

Balance of trade deficit When the domestic economy is spending more on foreign goods and services than foreign economies are spending on domestic goods and services.

Balance sheet (statement of financial position or statement of financial condition) The financial statement that presents an entity's current financial position by disclosing resources the entity controls (its assets) and the claims on those resources (its liabilities and equity claims), as of a particular point in time (the date of the balance sheet).

Balance sheet ratios Financial ratios involving balance sheet items only.

Balanced With respect to a government budget, one in which spending and revenues (taxes) are equal.

Bank discount basis A quoting convention that annualizes, on a 360-day year, the discount as a percentage of face value.

Bar chart A price chart with four bits of data for each time interval—the high, low, opening, and closing prices. A vertical line connects the high and low. A cross-hatch left indicates the opening price and a cross-hatch right indicates the close.

Barter economy An economy where economic agents as house-holds, corporations, and governments "pay" for goods and services with another good or service.

Base rates The reference rate on which a bank bases lending rates to all other customers.

Basic EPS Net earnings available to common shareholders (i.e., net income minus preferred dividends) divided by the weighted average number of common shares outstanding

Basket of listed depository receipts An exchange-traded fund (ETF) that represents a portfolio of depository receipts.

Behavioral finance A field of finance that examines the psychological variables that affect and often distort the investment decision making of investors, analysts, and portfolio managers.

Behind the market Said of prices specified in orders that are worse than the best current price; e.g., for a limit buy order, a limit price below the best bid.

Bernoulli random variable A random variable having the outcomes 0 and 1.

Bernoulli trial An experiment that can produce one of two outcomes.

Best bid The highest bid in the market.

Best efforts offering An offering of a security using an investment bank in which the investment bank, as agent for the issuer, promises to use its best efforts to sell the offering but does not guarantee that a specific amount will be sold.

Best offer The lowest offer (ask price) in the market.

Beta A measure of systematic risk that is based on the covariance of an asset's or portfolio's return with the return of the overall market.

Bid The price at which a dealer or trader is willing to buy an asset, typically qualified by a maximum quantity.

Bid size The maximum quantity of an asset that pertains to a specific bid price from a trader.

Binomial model A model for pricing options in which the underlying price can move to only one of two possible new prices.

Binomial random variable The number of successes in n Bernoulli trials for which the probability of success is constant for all trials and the trials are independent.

Binomial tree The graphical representation of a model of asset price dynamics in which, at each period, the asset moves up with probability p or down with probability $(1 - p)$.

Block brokers A broker (agent) that provides brokerage services for large-size trades.

Blue chip Widely held large market capitalization companies that are considered financially sound and are leaders in their respective industry or local stock market.

Bollinger Bands A price-based technical analysis indicator consisting of a moving average plus a higher line representing the moving average plus a set number of standard deviations from average price (for the same number of periods as used to calculate the moving average) and a lower line that is a moving average minus the same number of standard deviations.

Bond equivalent yield A calculation of yield that is annualized using the ratio of 365 to the number of days to maturity. Bond equivalent yield allows for the restatement and comparison of securities with different compounding periods.

Bond indenture The governing legal credit agreement, typically incorporated by reference in the prospectus.

Bond market vigilantes Bond market participants who might reduce their demand for long-term bonds, thus pushing up their yields.

Bond option An option in which the underlying is a bond; primarily traded in over-the-counter markets.

Bond yield plus risk premium approach An estimate of the cost of common equity that is produced by summing the before-tax cost of debt and a risk premium that captures the additional yield on a company's stock relative to its bonds. The additional yield is often estimated using historical spreads between bond yields and stock yields.

Bond-equivalent basis A basis for stating an annual yield that annualizes a semiannual yield by doubling it.

Bond-equivalent yield The yield to maturity on a basis that ignores compounding.

Bonus issue of shares A type of dividend in which a company distributes additional shares of its common stock to shareholders instead of cash.

Book building Investment bankers' process of compiling a "book" or list of indications of interest to buy part of an offering.

Book value (or carrying value) The net amount shown for an asset or liability on the balance sheet; book value may also refer to the company's excess of total assets over total liabilities.

Boom An expansionary phase characterized by economic growth "testing the limits" of the economy.

Bottom-up analysis With reference to investment selection processes, an approach that involves selection from all securities within a specified investment universe, i.e., without prior narrowing of the universe on the basis of macroeconomic or overall market considerations.

Break point In the context of the weighted average cost of capital (WACC), a break point is the amount of capital at which the cost of one or more of the sources of capital changes, leading to a change in the WACC.

Breakeven point The number of units produced and sold at which the company's net income is zero (revenues = total costs); in the case of perfect competition, the quantity where price, average revenue, and marginal revenue equal average total cost.

Broad money Encompasses narrow money plus the entire range of liquid assets that can be used to make purchases.

Broker 1) An agent who executes orders to buy or sell securities on behalf of a client in exchange for a commission. 2) *See* Futures commission merchants.

Brokered market A market in which brokers arrange trades among their clients.

Broker–dealer A financial intermediary (often a company) that may function as a principal (dealer) or as an agent (broker) depending on the type of trade.

Budget constraint A constraint on spending or investment imposed by wealth or income.

Budget surplus/deficit The difference between government revenue and expenditure for a stated fixed period of time.

Business risk The risk associated with operating earnings. Operating earnings are uncertain because total revenues and many of the expenditures contributed to produce those revenues are uncertain.

Buy-side firm An investment management company or other investor that uses the services of brokers or dealers (i.e., the client of the sell side firms).

Buyback A transaction in which a company buys back its own shares. Unlike stock dividends and stock splits, share repurchases use corporate cash.

Buyout fund A fund that buys all the shares of a public company so that, in effect, the company becomes private.

CBOE Volatility Index A measure of near-term market volatility as conveyed by S&P 500 stock index option prices.

CD equivalent yield A yield on a basis comparable to the quoted yield on an interest-bearing money market instrument that pays interest on a 360-day basis; the annualized holding period yield, assuming a 360-day year.

Call An option that gives the holder the right to buy an underlying asset from another party at a fixed price over a specific period of time.

Call market A market in which trades occur only at a particular time and place (i.e., when the market is called).

Call money rate The interest rate that buyers pay for their margin loan.

Call option An option that gives the holder the right to buy an underlying asset from another party at a fixed price over a specific period of time.

Callable common shares Shares that give the issuing company the option (or right), but not the obligation, to buy back the shares from investors at a call price that is specified when the shares are originally issued.

Candlestick chart A price chart with four bits of data for each time interval. A candle indicates the opening and closing price for the interval. The body of the candle is shaded if the opening price was higher than the closing price, and the body is clear if the opening price was lower than the closing price. Vertical lines known as wicks or shadows extend from the top and bottom of the candle to indicate the high and the low prices for the interval.

Cannibalization Cannibalization occurs when an investment takes customers and sales away from another part of the company.

Cap 1) A contract on an interest rate, whereby at periodic payment dates, the writer of the cap pays the difference between the market interest rate and a specified cap rate if, and only if, this difference is positive. This is equivalent to a stream of call options on the interest rate. 2) A combination of interest rate call options designed to hedge a borrower against rate increases on a floating-rate loan.

Capacity The ability of the borrower to make its debt payments on time.

Capital allocation line (CAL) A graph line that describes the combinations of expected return and standard deviation of return available to an investor from combining the optimal portfolio of risky assets with the risk-free asset.

Capital asset pricing model (also CAPM) An equation describing the expected return on any asset (or portfolio) as a linear function of its beta relative to the market portfolio.

Capital budgeting The allocation of funds to relatively long-range projects or investments.

Capital consumption allowance A measure of the wear and tear (depreciation) of the capital stock that occurs in the production of goods and services.

Capital deepening investment Increases the stock of capital relative to labor.

Capital expenditure Expenditure on physical capital (fixed assets).

Capital market expectations An investor's expectations concerning the risk and return prospects of asset classes.

Capital market line (CML) The line with an intercept point equal to the risk-free rate that is tangent to the efficient frontier of risky assets; represents the efficient frontier when a risk-free asset is available for investment.

Capital markets Financial markets that trade securities of longer duration, such as bonds and equities.

Capital rationing A capital rationing environment assumes that the company has a fixed amount of funds to invest.

Capital stock The accumulated amount of buildings, machinery, and equipment used to produce goods and services.

Capital structure The mix of debt and equity that a company uses to finance its business; a company's specific mixture of long-term financing.

Caplet Each component call option in a cap.

Captive finance subsidiary A wholly-owned subsidiary of a company that is established to provide financing of the sales of the parent company.

Carrying amount The amount at which an asset or liability is valued according to accounting principles.

Carrying value The net amount shown for an asset or liability on the balance sheet; book value may also refer to the company's excess of total assets over total liabilities.

Cartel Participants in collusive agreements that are made openly and formally.

Cash In accounting contexts, cash on hand (e.g., petty cash and cash not yet deposited to the bank) and demand deposits held in banks and similar accounts that can be used in payment of obligations.

Cash conversion cycle (net operating cycle) A financial metric that measures the length of time required for a company to convert cash invested in its operations to cash received as a result of its operations; equal to days of inventory on hand + days of sales outstanding − number of days of payables.

Cash equivalents Very liquid short-term investments, usually maturing in 90 days or less.

Cash flow additivity principle The principle that dollar amounts indexed at the same point in time are additive.

Cash flow from operating activities The net amount of cash provided from operating activities.

Cash flow from operations The net amount of cash provided from operating activities.

Cash price The price for immediate purchase of the underlying asset.

Cash settlement A procedure used in certain derivative transactions that specifies that the long and short parties engage in the equivalent cash value of a delivery transaction.

Central banks The dominant bank in a country, usually with official or semi-official governmental status.

Change in polarity principle A tenet of technical analysis that once a support level is breached, it becomes a resistance level. The same holds true for resistance levels; once breached, they become support levels.

Change of control put A covenant giving bondholders the right to require the issuer to buy back their debt, often at par or at some small premium to par value, in the event that the borrower is acquired.

Character The quality of a debt issuer's management.

Chart of accounts A list of accounts used in an entity's accounting system.

Cheapest-to-deliver bond A bond in which the amount received for delivering the bond is largest compared with the amount paid in the market for the bond.

Classified balance sheet A balance sheet organized so as to group together the various assets and liabilities into subcategories (e.g., current and noncurrent).

Clawback A requirement that the GP return any funds distributed as incentive fees until the LPs have received back their initial investment and a percentage of the total profit.

Clearing instructions Instructions that indicate how to arrange the final settlement ("clearing") of a trade.

Clearinghouse An entity associated with a futures market that acts as middleman between the contracting parties and guarantees to each party the performance of the other.

Closed-end fund A mutual fund in which no new investment money is accepted. New investors invest by buying existing shares, and investors in the fund liquidate by selling their shares to other investors.

Coefficient of variation (CV) The ratio of a set of observations' standard deviation to the observations' mean value.

Coincident economic indicators Turning points that are usually close to those of the overall economy; they are believed to have value for identifying the economy's present state.

Collateral The quality and value of the assets supporting an issuer's indebtedness.

Combination A listing in which the order of the listed items does not matter.

Commercial paper Unsecured short-term corporate debt that is characterized by a single payment at maturity.

Commercial receivables (Trade receivables or accounts receivable) Amounts customers owe the company for products that have been sold as well as amounts that may be due from suppliers (such as for returns of merchandise).

Committed capital The amount that the limited partners have agreed to provide to the private equity fund.

Committed lines of credit A bank commitment to extend credit up to a pre-specified amount; the commitment is considered a short-term liability and is usually in effect for 364 days (one day short of a full year).

Commodity swap A swap in which the underlying is a commodity such as oil, gold, or an agricultural product.

Common shares A type of security that represent an ownership interest in a company.

Common stock See *common shares*.

Common-size analysis The restatement of financial statement items using a common denominator or reference item that allows one to identify trends and major differences; an example is an income statement in which all items are expressed as a percent of revenue.

Company analysis Analysis of an individual company.

Comparable company A company that has similar business risk; usually in the same industry and preferably with a single line of business.

Competitive strategy A company's plans for responding to the threats and opportunities presented by the external environment.

Complements Said of goods which tend to be used together; technically, two goods whose cross-price elasticity of demand is negative.

Complete markets Informally, markets in which the variety of distinct securities traded is so broad that any desired payoff in a future state-of-the-world is achievable.

Complete preferences The assumption that a consumer is able to make a comparison between any two possible bundles of goods.

Completed contract A method of revenue recognition in which the company does not recognize any revenue until the contract is completed; used particularly in long-term construction contracts.

Component cost of capital The rate of return required by suppliers of capital for an individual source of a company's funding, such as debt or equity.

Compounding The process of accumulating interest on interest.

Comprehensive income The change in equity of a business enterprise during a period from nonowner sources; includes all changes in equity during a period except those resulting from investments by owners and distributions to owners; comprehensive income equals net income plus other comprehensive income.

Conditional expected value The expected value of a stated event given that another event has occurred.

Conditional probability The probability of an event given (conditioned on) another event.

Conditional variances The variance of one variable, given the outcome of another.

Consistent With reference to estimators, describes an estimator for which the probability of estimates close to the value of the population parameter increases as sample size increases.

Conspicuous consumption Consumption of high status goods, such as a luxury automobile or a very expensive piece of jewelry.

Constant maturity treasury (or CMT) A hypothetical U.S. Treasury note with a constant maturity. A CMT exists for various years in the range of 2 to 10.

Constant returns to scale The characteristic of constant per-unit costs in the presence of increased production.

Constant-cost industry When firms in the industry experience no change in resource costs and output prices over the long run.

Constituent securities With respect to an index, the individual securities within an index.

Consumer choice theory The theory relating consumer demand curves to consumer preferences.

Consumer surplus The difference between the value that a consumer places on units purchased and the amount of money that was required to pay for them.

Consumption basket A specific combination of the goods and services that a consumer wants to consume.

Consumption bundle A specific combination of the goods and services that a consumer wants to consume.

Continuation patterns A type of pattern used in technical analysis to predict the resumption of a market trend that was in place prior to the formation of a pattern.

Continuous random variable A random variable for which the range of possible outcomes is the real line (all real numbers between $-\infty$ and $+\infty$ or some subset of the real line).

Continuous time Time thought of as advancing in extremely small increments.

Continuous trading market A market in which trades can be arranged and executed any time the market is open.

Continuously compounded return The natural logarithm of 1 plus the holding period return, or equivalently, the natural logarithm of the ending price over the beginning price.

Contra account An account that offsets another account.

Contraction The period of a business cycle after the peak and before the trough; often called a *recession* or, if exceptionally severe, called a *depression*.

Contractionary Tending to cause the real economy to contract.

Contractionary fiscal policy A fiscal policy that has the objective to make the real economy contract.

Contribution margin The amount available for fixed costs and profit after paying variable costs; revenue minus variable costs.

Conventional cash flow A conventional cash flow pattern is one with an initial outflow followed by a series of inflows.

Convergence The tendency for differences in output per capita across countries to diminish over time; in technical analysis, a term that describes the case when an indicator moves in the same manner as the security being analyzed.

Conversion factor An adjustment used to facilitate delivery on bond futures contracts in which any of a number of bonds with different characteristics are eligible for delivery.

Convertible preference shares A type of equity security that entitles shareholders to convert their shares into a specified number of common shares.

Core inflation The inflation rate calculated based on a price index of goods and services except food and energy.

Correlation A number between –1 and +1 that measures the comovement (linear association) between two random variables.

Correlation coefficient A number between –1 and +1 that measures the consistency or tendency for two investments to act in a similar way. It is used to determine the effect on portfolio risk when two assets are combined.

Cost averaging The periodic investment of a fixed amount of money.

Cost of capital The rate of return that suppliers of capital require as compensation for their contribution of capital.

Cost of debt The cost of debt financing to a company, such as when it issues a bond or takes out a bank loan.

Cost of goods sold For a given period, equal to beginning inventory minus ending inventory plus the cost of goods acquired or produced during the period.

Cost of preferred stock The cost to a company of issuing preferred stock; the dividend yield that a company must commit to pay preferred stockholders.

Cost recovery method A method of revenue recognition in which the seller does not report any profit until the cash amounts paid by the buyer—including principal and interest on any financing from the seller—are greater than all the seller's costs for the merchandise sold.

Cost structure The mix of a company's variable costs and fixed costs.

Cost-push Type of inflation in which rising costs, usually wages, compel businesses to raise prices generally.

Counterparty risk The risk that the other party to a contract will fail to honor the terms of the contract.

Cournot assumption Assumption in which each firm determines its profit-maximizing production level assuming that the other firms' output will not change.

Covariance A measure of the co-movement (linear association) between two random variables.

Covariance matrix A matrix or square array whose entries are covariances; also known as a variance–covariance matrix.

Covenants The terms and conditions of lending agreements that the issuer must comply with.

Covered call An option strategy involving the holding of an asset and sale of a call on the asset.

Credit With respect to double-entry accounting, a credit records increases in liability, owners' equity, and revenue accounts or decreases in asset accounts; with respect to borrowing, the willingness and ability of the borrower to make promised payments on the borrowing.

Credit analysis The evaluation of credit risk; the evaluation of the creditworthiness of a borrower or counterparty.

Credit curve A curve showing the relationship between time to maturity and yield spread for an issuer with comparable bonds of various maturities outstanding, usually upward sloping.

Credit migration risk (or downgrade risk) The risk that a bond issuer's creditworthiness deteriorates, or migrates lower, leading investors to believe the risk of default is higher.

Credit risk (or default risk) The risk of loss caused by a counterparty's or debtor's failure to make a promised payment.

Credit scoring model A statistical model used to classify borrowers according to creditworthiness.

Credit-worthiness The perceived ability of the borrower to pay what is owed on the borrowing in a timely manner; it represents the ability of a company to withstand adverse impacts on its cash flows.

Cross-default provisions Provisions whereby events of default such as non-payment of interest on one bond trigger default on all outstanding debt; implies the same default probability for all issues.

Cross-price elasticity of demand The percent change in quantity demanded for a given small change in the price of another good; the responsiveness of the demand for Product A that is associated with the change in price of Product B.

Cross-sectional analysis Analysis that involves comparisons across individuals in a group over a given time period or at a given point in time.

Cross-sectional data Observations over individual units at a point in time, as opposed to time-series data.

Crossing networks Trading systems that match buyers and sellers who are willing to trade at prices obtained from other markets.

Crowding out The thesis that government borrowing may divert private sector investment from taking place.

Cumulative distribution function A function giving the probability that a random variable is less than or equal to a specified value.

Cumulative preference shares Preference shares for which any dividends that are not paid accrue and must be paid in full before dividends on common shares can be paid.

Cumulative relative frequency For data grouped into intervals, the fraction of total observations that are less than the value of the upper limit of a stated interval.

Cumulative voting Voting that allows shareholders to direct their total voting rights to specific candidates, as opposed to having to allocate their voting rights evenly among all candidates.

Currencies Monies issued by national monetary authorities.

Currency option An option that allows the holder to buy (if a call) or sell (if a put) an underlying currency at a fixed exercise rate, expressed as an exchange rate.

Currency swap   A swap in which each party makes interest payments to the other in different currencies.

Current assets   (or liquid assets) Assets that are expected to be consumed or converted into cash in the near future, typically one year or less.

Current cost   With reference to assets, the amount of cash or cash equivalents that would have to be paid to buy the same or an equivalent asset today; with reference to liabilities, the undiscounted amount of cash or cash equivalents that would be required to settle the obligation today.

Current government spending   With respect to government expenditures, spending on goods and services that are provided on a regular, recurring basis including health, education, and defense.

Current liabilities   Short-term obligations, such as accounts payable, wages payable, or accrued liabilities, that are expected to be settled in the near future, typically one year or less.

Current ratio   A liquidity ratio calculated as current assets divided by current liabilities.

Cyclical   See *Cyclical companies.*

Cyclical companies   Companies with sales and profits that regularly expand and contract with the business cycle or state of economy.

Daily settlement   See *Marking to market.*

Dark pools   Alternative trading systems that do not display the orders that their clients send to them.

Data mining   (or data snooping) The practice of determining a model by extensive searching through a dataset for statistically significant patterns.

Data snooping   See *Data mining.*

Date of book closure   The date that a shareholder listed on the corporation's books will be deemed to have ownership of the shares for purposes of receiving an upcoming dividend; two business days after the ex-dividend date.

Date of record   The date that a shareholder listed on the corporation's books will be deemed to have ownership of the shares for purposes of receiving an upcoming dividend; two business days after the ex-dividend date.

Day order   An order that is good for the day on which it is submitted. If it has not been filled by the close of business, the order expires unfilled.

Day trader   A trader holding a position open somewhat longer than a scalper but closing all positions at the end of the day.

Days in receivables   Estimate of the average number of days it takes to collect on credit accounts.

Days of inventory on hand (DOH)   An activity ratio equal to the number of days in the period divided by inventory turnover over the period.

Day's sales outstanding   Estimate of the average number of days it takes to collect on credit accounts.

Dead cross   A technical analysis term that describes a situation where a short-term moving average crosses from above a longer-term moving average to below it; this movement is considered bearish.

Dealers   A financial intermediary that acts as a principal in trades.

Dealing securities   Securities held by banks or other financial intermediaries for trading purposes.

Debit   With respect to double-entry accounting, a debit records increases of asset and expense accounts or decreases in liability and owners' equity accounts.

Debt incurrence test   A financial covenant made in conjunction with existing debt that restricts a company's ability to incur additional debt at the same seniority based on one or more financial tests or conditions.

Debt-rating approach   A method for estimating a company's before-tax cost of debt based upon the yield on comparably rated bonds for maturities that closely match that of the company's existing debt.

Debt-to-assets ratio   A solvency ratio calculated as total debt divided by total assets.

Debt-to-capital ratio   A solvency ratio calculated as total debt divided by total debt plus total shareholders' equity.

Debt-to-equity ratio   A solvency ratio calculated as total debt divided by total shareholders' equity.

Declaration date   The day that the corporation issues a statement declaring a specific dividend.

Decreasing returns to scale   Increase in cost per unit resulting from increased production.

Decreasing-cost industry   An industry in which per-unit costs and output prices are lower when industry output is increased in the long run.

Deductible temporary differences   Temporary differences that result in a reduction of or deduction from taxable income in a future period when the balance sheet item is recovered or settled.

Deep-in-the-money   Options that are far in-the-money.

Deep-out-of-the-money   Options that are far out-of-the-money.

Default risk   (or default probability): The probability that a borrower defaults or fails to meet its obligation to make full and timely payments of principal and interest, according to the terms of the debt security.

Default risk premium   An extra return that compensates investors for the possibility that the borrower will fail to make a promised payment at the contracted time and in the contracted amount.

Defensive companies   Companies with sales and profits that have little sensitivity to the business cycle or state of the economy.

Defensive interval ratio   A liquidity ratio that estimates the number of days that an entity could meet cash needs from liquid assets; calculated as (cash + short-term marketable investments + receivables) divided by daily cash expenditures.

Deferred income   A liability account for money that has been collected for goods or services that have not yet been delivered; payment received in advance of providing a good or service.

Deferred revenue   A liability account for money that has been collected for goods or services that have not yet been delivered; payment received in advance of providing a good or service.

Deferred tax assets   A balance sheet asset that arises when an excess amount is paid for income taxes relative to accounting profit. The taxable income is higher than accounting profit and income tax payable exceeds tax expense. The company expects to recover the difference during the course of future operations when tax expense exceeds income tax payable.

Deferred tax liabilities   A balance sheet liability that arises when a deficit amount is paid for income taxes relative to accounting profit. The taxable income is less than the accounting profit and income tax payable is less than tax expense. The company expects to eliminate the liability over the course of future operations when income tax payable exceeds tax expense.

Defined benefit pension plans   Plan in which the company promises to pay a certain annual amount (defined benefit) to the employee after retirement. The company bears the investment risk of the plan assets.

Defined contribution pension plans   Individual accounts to which an employee and typically the employer makes contributions, generally on a tax-advantaged basis. The amounts of contributions are defined at the outset, but the future value of the benefit is unknown. The employee bears the investment risk of the plan assets.

Deflation   Negative inflation.

Degree of confidence   The probability that a confidence interval includes the unknown population parameter.

Degree of financial leverage   (DFL) The ratio of the percentage change in net income to the percentage change in operating income; the sensitivity of the cash flows available to owners when operating income changes.

Degree of operating leverage   (DOL) The ratio of the percentage change in operating income to the percentage change in units sold; the sensitivity of operating income to changes in units sold.

Degree of total leverage   The ratio of the percentage change in net income to the percentage change in units sold; the sensitivity of the cash flows to owners to changes in the number of units produced and sold.

Degrees of freedom (df)   The number of independent observations used.

Delivery   A process used in a deliverable forward contract in which the long pays the agreed-upon price to the short, which in turn delivers the underlying asset to the long.

Delivery option   The feature of a futures contract giving the short the right to make decisions about what, when, and where to deliver.

Delta   The relationship between the option price and the underlying price, which reflects the sensitivity of the price of the option to changes in the price of the underlying.

Demand shock   A typically unexpected disturbance to demand, such as an unexpected interruption in trade or transportation.

Demand-pull   Type of inflation in which increasing demand raises prices generally, which then are reflected in a business's costs as workers demand wage hikes to catch up with the rising cost of living.

Dependent   With reference to events, the property that the probability of one event occurring depends on (is related to) the occurrence of another event.

Depository bank   A bank that raises funds from depositors and other investors and lends it to borrowers.

Depository institutions   Commercial banks, savings and loan banks, credit unions, and similar institutions that raise funds from depositors and other investors and lend it to borrowers.

Depository receipt   A security that trades like an ordinary share on a local exchange and represents an economic interest in a foreign company.

Depreciation   The process of systematically allocating the cost of long-lived (tangible) assets to the periods during which the assets are expected to provide economic benefits.

Depression   See *contraction*.

Derivative   A financial instrument whose value depends on the value of some underlying asset or factor (e.g., a stock price, an interest rate, or exchange rate).

Derivative pricing rule   A pricing rule used by crossing networks in which a price is taken (derived) from the price that is current in the asset's primary market.

Derivatives dealers   Commercial and investment banks that make markets in derivatives.

Descriptive statistics   The study of how data can be summarized effectively.

Development capital   Minority equity investments in more mature companies that are looking for capital to expand or restructure operations, enter new markets, or finance major acquisitions.

Diffuse prior   The assumption of equal prior probabilities.

Diffusion index   Reflects the proportion of the index's components that are moving in a pattern consistent with the overall index.

Diluted EPS   The EPS that would result if all dilutive securities were converted into common shares.

Diluted shares   The number of shares that would be outstanding if all potentially dilutive claims on common shares (e.g., convertible debt, convertible preferred stock, and employee stock options) were exercised.

Diminishing balance method   An accelerated depreciation method, i.e., one that allocates a relatively large proportion of the cost of an asset to the early years of the asset's useful life.

Diminishing marginal productivity   Describes a state in which each additional unit of input produces less output than previously.

Direct debit program   An arrangement whereby a customer authorizes a debit to a demand account; typically used by companies to collect routine payments for services.

Direct format   (direct method) With reference to the cash flow statement, a format for the presentation of the statement in which cash flow from operating activities is shown as operating cash receipts less operating cash disbursements.

Direct method   See *direct format*.

Direct taxes   Taxes levied directly on income, wealth, and corporate profits.

Direct write-off method   An approach to recognizing credit losses on customer receivables in which the company waits until such time as a customer has defaulted and only then recognizes the loss.

Disbursement float   The amount of time between check issuance and a check's clearing back against the company's account.

Discount   To reduce the value of a future payment in allowance for how far away it is in time; to calculate the present value of some future amount. Also, the amount by which an instrument is priced below its face value.

Discount interest   A procedure for determining the interest on a loan or bond in which the interest is deducted from the face value in advance.

Discount rate   With reference to U.S. banking, the rate for member banks borrowing directly from the U.S. Federal Reserve System.

Discounted cash flow models   Valuation models that estimate the intrinsic value of a security as the present value of the future benefits expected to be received from the security.

Discouraged worker   A person who has stopped looking for a job or has given up seeking employment.

Discrete random variable   A random variable that can take on at most a countable number of possible values.

Discriminatory pricing rule   A pricing rule used in continuous markets in which the limit price of the order or quote that first arrived determines the trade price.

Diseconomies of scale   Increase in cost per unit resulting from increased production.

Dispersion   The variability around the central tendency.

Display size The size of an order displayed to public view.

Distressed investing Investing in securities of companies in financial difficulties. Private equity funds typically buy the debt of mature companies in financial difficulties.

Divergence In technical analysis, a term that describes the case when an indicator moves differently from the security being analyzed.

Diversification ratio The ratio of the standard deviation of an equally weighted portfolio to the standard deviation of a randomly selected security.

Dividend A distribution paid to shareholders based on the number of shares owned.

Dividend discount model (DDM) A present value model that estimates the intrinsic value of an equity share based on the present value of its expected future dividends.

Dividend discount model based approach An approach for estimating a country's equity risk premium. The market rate of return is estimated as the sum of the dividend yield and the growth rate in dividends for a market index. Subtracting the risk-free rate of return from the estimated market return produces an estimate for the equity risk premium.

Dividend payout ratio The ratio of cash dividends paid to earnings for a period.

Dividend yield Annual dividends per share divided by share price.

Divisor A number (denominator) used to determine the value of a price return index. It is initially chosen at the inception of an index and subsequently adjusted by the index provider, as necessary, to avoid changes in the index value that are unrelated to changes in the prices of its constituent securities.

Double bottoms In technical analysis, a reversal pattern that is formed when the price reaches a low, rebounds, and then sells off back to the first low level; used to predict a change from a downtrend to an uptrend.

Double coincidence of wants A prerequisite to barter trades, in particular that both economic agents in the transaction want what the other is selling.

Double declining balance depreciation An accelerated depreciation method that involves depreciating the asset at double the straight-line rate. This rate is multiplied by the book value of the asset at the beginning of the period (a declining balance) to calculate depreciation expense.

Double top In technical analysis, a reversal pattern that is formed when an uptrend reverses twice at roughly the same high price level; used to predict a change from an uptrend to a downtrend.

Double-entry accounting The accounting system of recording transactions in which every recorded transaction affects at least two accounts so as to keep the basic accounting equation (assets = liabilities + owners' equity) in balance.

Down transition probability The probability that an asset's value moves down in a model of asset price dynamics.

Drag on liquidity When receipts lag, creating pressure from the decreased available funds.

Drawdown A reduction in net asset value (NAV).

DuPont analysis An approach to decomposing return on investment, e.g., return on equity, as the product of other financial ratios.

Duration A measure of an option-free bond's average maturity. Specifically, the weighted average maturity of all future cash flows paid by a security, in which the weights are the present value of these cash flows as a fraction of the bond's price. A measure of a bond's price sensitivity to interest rate movements.

Dutch Book theorem A result in probability theory stating that inconsistent probabilities create profit opportunities.

Earnings per share The amount of income earned during a period per share of common stock.

Earnings surprise The portion of a company's earnings that is unanticipated by investors and, according to the efficient market hypothesis, merits a price adjustment.

Economic costs All the remuneration needed to keep a productive resource in its current employment or to acquire the resource for productive use; the sum of total accounting costs and implicit opportunity costs.

Economic indicator A variable that provides information on the state of the overall economy.

Economic loss The amount by which accounting profit is less than normal profit.

Economic order quantity–reorder point (EOQ–ROP) An approach to managing inventory based on expected demand and the predictability of demand; the ordering point for new inventory is determined based on the costs of ordering and carrying inventory, such that the total cost associated with inventory is minimized.

Economic profit (abnormal or supernormal profit) Equal to accounting profit less the implicit opportunity costs not included in total accounting costs; the difference between total revenue (TR) and total cost (TC).

Economic rent The surplus value that results when a particular resource or good is fixed in supply and market price is higher than what is required to bring the resource or good onto the market and sustain its use.

Economic stabilization Reduction of the magnitude of economic fluctuations.

Economies of scale Reduction in cost per unit resulting from increased production.

Effective annual rate The amount by which a unit of currency will grow in a year with interest on interest included.

Effective annual yield (EAY) An annualized return that accounts for the effect of interest on interest; EAY is computed by compounding 1 plus the holding period yield forward to one year, then subtracting 1.

Efficient market A market in which asset prices reflect new information quickly and rationally.

Elasticity The percentage change in one variable for a percentage change in another variable; a measure of how sensitive one variable is to a change in the value of another variable.

Elasticity of supply A measure of the sensitivity of quantity supplied to a change in price.

Electronic communications networks See *Alternative trading systems*.

Electronic funds transfer (EFT) The use of computer networks to conduct financial transactions electronically.

Elliott wave theory A technical analysis theory that claims that the market follows regular, repeated waves or cycles.

Empirical probability The probability of an event estimated as a relative frequency of occurrence.

Employed The number of people with a job.

Enterprise value A measure of a company's total market value from which the value of cash and short-term investments have been subtracted.

Equal weighting An index weighting method in which an equal weight is assigned to each constituent security at inception.

Equity   Assets less liabilities; the residual interest in the assets after subtracting the liabilities.

Equity forward   A contract calling for the purchase of an individual stock, a stock portfolio, or a stock index at a later date at an agreed-upon price.

Equity options   Options on individual stocks; also known as stock options.

Equity risk premium   The expected return on equities minus the risk-free rate; the premium that investors demand for investing in equities.

Equity swap   A swap transaction in which at least one cash flow is tied to the return to an equity portfolio position, often an equity index.

Estimate   The particular value calculated from sample observations using an estimator.

Estimation   With reference to statistical inference, the subdivision dealing with estimating the value of a population parameter.

Estimator   An estimation formula; the formula used to compute the sample mean and other sample statistics are examples of estimators.

Eurodollar   A dollar deposited outside the United States.

European option   An option that can only be exercised on its expiration date.

European-style contracts   An option that can only be exercised on its expiration date.

European-style option (or European option)   An option that can only be exercised on its expiration date.

Event   Any outcome or specified set of outcomes of a random variable.

Ex-date   The first date that a share trades without (i.e. "ex") the dividend.

Ex-dividend date   The first date that a share trades without (i.e. "ex") the dividend.

Excess kurtosis   Degree of peakedness (fatness of tails) in excess of the peakedness of the normal distribution.

Exchange for physicals (EFP)   A permissible delivery procedure used by futures market participants, in which the long and short arrange a delivery procedure other than the normal procedures stipulated by the futures exchange.

Exchanges   Places where traders can meet to arrange their trades.

Execution instructions   Instructions that indicate how to fill an order.

Exercise   The process of using an option to buy or sell the underlying.

Exercise price   The fixed price at which an option holder can buy or sell the underlying.

Exercise rate   The fixed rate at which the holder of an interest rate option can buy or sell the underlying.

Exercise value   The value obtained if an option is exercised based on current conditions.

Exercising the option   The process of using an option to buy or sell the underlying.

Exhaustive   Covering or containing all possible outcomes.

Expansion   The period of a business cycle after its lowest point and before its highest point.

Expansionary   Tending to cause the real economy to grow.

Expansionary fiscal policy   Fiscal policy aimed at achieving real economic growth.

Expected inflation   The level of inflation that economic agents expect in the future.

Expected loss   Default probability times loss severity given default.

Expected value   The probability-weighted average of the possible outcomes of a random variable.

Expenses   Outflows of economic resources or increases in liabilities that result in decreases in equity (other than decreases because of distributions to owners); reductions in net assets associated with the creation of revenues.

Experience curve   A curve that shows the direct cost per unit of good or service produced or delivered as a typically declining function of cumulative output.

Externality   An effect of a market transaction that is borne by parties other than those who transacted.

Extra dividend   A dividend paid by a company that does not pay dividends on a regular schedule, or a dividend that supplements regular cash dividends with an extra payment.

FIFO method   The first in, first out, method of accounting for inventory, which matches sales against the costs of items of inventory in the order in which they were placed in inventory.

FX swap   The combination of a spot and a forward FX transaction.

Face value   The amount of cash payable by a company to the bondholders when the bonds mature; the promised payment at maturity separate from any coupon payment.

Factor   A common or underlying element with which several variables are correlated.

Fair value   The amount at which an asset could be exchanged, or a liability settled, between knowledgeable, willing parties in an arm's-length transaction; the price that would be received to sell an asset or paid to transfer a liability in an orderly transaction between market participants.

Fed funds rate   The U.S. interbank lending rate on overnight borrowings of reserves.

Federal funds rate   The U.S. interbank lending rate on overnight borrowings of reserves.

Fiat money   Money that is not convertible into any other commodity.

Fibonacci sequence   A sequence of numbers starting with 0 and 1, and then each subsequent number in the sequence is the sum of the two preceding numbers. In Elliott Wave Theory, it is believed that market waves follow patterns that are the ratios of the numbers in the Fibonacci sequence.

Fiduciary call   A combination of a European call and a risk-free bond that matures on the option expiration day and has a face value equal to the exercise price of the call.

Fill or kill   See *Immediate or cancel order.*

Financial flexibility   The ability to react and adapt to financial adversities and opportunities.

Financial leverage   The extent to which a company can effect, through the use of debt, a proportional change in the return on common equity that is greater than a given proportional change in operating income; also, short for the financial leverage ratio.

Financial leverage ratio   A measure of financial leverage calculated as average total assets divided by average total equity.

Financial risk   The risk that environmental, social, or governance risk factors will result in significant costs or other losses to a company and its shareholders; the risk arising from a company's obligation to meet required payments under its financing agreements.

Financing activities   Activities related to obtaining or repaying capital to be used in the business (e.g., equity and long-term debt).

First lien debt Debt secured by a pledge of certain assets that could include buildings, but may also include property and equipment, licenses, patents, brands, etc.

First mortgage debt Debt secured by a pledge of a specific property.

First-degree price discrimination Where a monopolist is able to charge each customer the highest price the customer is willing to pay.

Fiscal multiplier The ratio of a change in national income to a change in government spending.

Fiscal policy The use of taxes and government spending to affect the level of aggregate expenditures.

Fisher effect The thesis that the real rate of interest in an economy is stable over time so that changes in nominal interest rates are the result of changes in expected inflation.

Fisher index The geometric mean of the Laspeyres index.

Fixed charge coverage A solvency ratio measuring the number of times interest and lease payments are covered by operating income, calculated as (EBIT + lease payments) divided by (interest payments + lease payments).

Fixed costs Costs that remain at the same level regardless of a company's level of production and sales.

Fixed price tender offer Offer made by a company to repurchase a specific number of shares at a fixed price that is typically at a premium to the current market price.

Fixed rate perpetual preferred stock Nonconvertible, non-callable preferred stock that has a fixed dividend rate and no maturity date.

Flags A technical analysis continuation pattern formed by parallel trendlines, typically over a short period.

Float In the context of customer receipts, the amount of money that is in transit between payments made by customers and the funds that are usable by the company.

Float factor An estimate of the average number of days it takes deposited checks to clear; average daily float divided by average daily deposit.

Float-adjusted market-capitalization weighting An index weighting method in which the weight assigned to each constituent security is determined by adjusting its market capitalization for its market float.

Floor A series of put options on an interest rate, with each option expiring at the date on which the floating loan rate will be reset, and with each option having the same exercise rate. A floor in general can have an underlying other than the interest rate.

Floor traders Market makers that buy and sell by quoting a bid and an ask price. They are the primary providers of liquidity to the market.

Floorlet Each component put option in a floor.

Flotation cost Fees charged to companies by investment bankers and other costs associated with raising new capital.

Foreign currency reserves Holding by the central bank of non-domestic currency deposits and non-domestic bonds.

Foreign exchange gains (or losses) Gains (or losses) that occur when the exchange rate changes between the investor's currency and the currency that foreign securities are denominated in.

Forward contract An agreement between two parties in which one party, the buyer, agrees to buy from the other party, the seller, an underlying asset at a later date for a price established at the start of the contract.

Forward rate The fixed price or rate at which the transaction scheduled to occur at the expiration of a forward contract will take place. This price is agreed on at the initiation date of the contract.

Forward rate agreement (FRA) A forward contract calling for one party to make a fixed interest payment and the other to make an interest payment at a rate to be determined at the contract expiration.

Fractile A value at or below which a stated fraction of the data lies.

Fractional reserve banking Banking in which reserves constitute a fraction of deposits.

Free cash flow The actual cash that would be available to the company's investors after making all investments necessary to maintain the company as an ongoing enterprise (also referred to as free cash flow to the firm); the internally generated funds that can be distributed to the company's investors (e.g., shareholders and bondholders) without impairing the value of the company.

Free cash flow to equity (FCFE) The cash flow available to a company's common shareholders after all operating expenses, interest, and principal payments have been made, and necessary investments in working and fixed capital have been made.

Free cash flow to the firm (FCFF) The cash flow available to the company's suppliers of capital after all operating expenses have been paid and necessary investments in working capital and fixed capital have been made.

Free float The number of shares that are readily and freely tradable in the secondary market.

Free-cash-flow-to-equity models Valuation models based on discounting expected future free cash flow to equity.

Frequency distribution A tabular display of data summarized into a relatively small number of intervals.

Frequency polygon A graph of a frequency distribution obtained by drawing straight lines joining successive points representing the class frequencies.

Full price The price of a security with accrued interest.

Fundamental analysis The examination of publicly available information and the formulation of forecasts to estimate the intrinsic value of assets.

Fundamental value (also **intrinsic value**) The underlying or true value of an asset based on an analysis of its qualitative and quantitative characteristics.

Fundamental weighting An index weighting method in which the weight assigned to each constituent security is based on its underlying company's size. It attempts to address the disadvantages of market-capitalization weighting by using measures that are independent of the constituent security's price.

Funds of funds Funds that hold a portfolio of hedge funds.

Future value (FV) The amount to which a payment or series of payments will grow by a stated future date.

Futures commission merchants (FCMs) Individuals or companies that execute futures transactions for other parties off the exchange.

Futures contract A variation of a forward contract that has essentially the same basic definition but with some additional features, such as a clearinghouse guarantee against credit losses, a daily settlement of gains and losses, and an organized electronic or floor trading facility.

GDP deflator A gauge of prices and inflation that measures the aggregate changes in prices across the overall economy.

Gains Asset inflows not directly related to the ordinary activities of the business.

Game theory The set of tools decision makers use to incorporate responses by rival decision makers into their strategies.

Gamma A numerical measure of how sensitive an option's delta is to a change in the underlying.

General partner The partner that runs the business and theoretically bears unlimited liability.

Geometric mean A measure of central tendency computed by taking the nth root of the product of n non-negative values.

Giffen good A good that is consumed more as the price of the good rises.

Gilts Bonds issued by the U.K. government.

Giro system An electronic payment system used widely in Europe and Japan.

Global depository receipt A depository receipt that is issued outside of the company's home country and outside of the United States.

Global minimum-variance portfolio The portfolio on the minimum-variance frontier with the smallest variance of return.

Global registered share A common share that is traded on different stock exchanges around the world in different currencies.

Gold standard With respect to a currency, if a currency is on the gold standard a given amount can be converted into a prespecified amount of gold.

Golden cross A technical analysis term that describes a situation where a short-term moving average crosses from below a longer-term moving average to above it; this movement is considered bullish.

Good-on-close (market on close) An execution instruction specifying that an order can only be filled at the close of trading.

Good-on-open An execution instruction specifying that an order can only be filled at the opening of trading.

Good-till-cancelled order An order specifying that it is valid until the entity placing the order has cancelled it (or, commonly, until some specified amount of time such as 60 days has elapsed, whichever comes sooner).

Goodwill An intangible asset that represents the excess of the purchase price of an acquired company over the value of the net assets acquired.

Greenmail The purchase of the accumulated shares of a hostile investor by a company that is targeted for takeover by that investor, usually at a substantial premium over market price.

Gross domestic product The market value of all final goods and services produced within the economy in a given period of time (output definition) or, equivalently, the aggregate income earned by all households, all companies, and the government within the economy in a given period of time (income definition).

Gross margin Sales minus the cost of sales (i.e., the cost of goods sold for a manufacturing company).

Gross profit Sales minus the cost of sales (i.e., the cost of goods sold for a manufacturing company).

Gross profit margin The ratio of gross profit to revenues.

Grouping by function With reference to the presentation of expenses in an income statement, the grouping together of expenses serving the same function, e.g. all items that are costs of goods sold.

Grouping by nature With reference to the presentation of expenses in an income statement, the grouping together of expenses by similar nature, e.g., all depreciation expenses.

Growth cyclical A term sometimes used to describe companies that are growing rapidly on a long-term basis but that still experience above-average fluctuation in their revenues and profits over the course of a business cycle.

Harmonic mean A type of weighted mean computed by averaging the reciprocals of the observations, then taking the reciprocal of that average.

Head and shoulders pattern In technical analysis, a reversal pattern that is formed in three parts: a left shoulder, head, and right shoulder; used to predict a change from an uptrend to a downtrend.

Headline inflation The inflation rate calculated based on the price index that includes all goods and services in an economy.

Hedge funds Private investment vehicles that typically use leverage, derivatives, and long and short investment strategies.

Held for trading (trading securities) Debt or equity financial assets bought with the intention to sell them in the near term, usually less than three months; securities that a company intends to trade.

Held-to-maturity Debt (fixed-income) securities that a company intends to hold to maturity; these are presented at their original cost, updated for any amortization of discounts or premiums.

Herding Clustered trading that may or may not be based on information.

Hidden order An order that is exposed not to the public but only to the brokers or exchanges that receive it.

High water marks The highest value, net of fees, which a fund has reached. It reflects the highest cumulative return used to calculate an incentive fee.

Histogram A bar chart of data that have been grouped into a frequency distribution.

Historical cost In reference to assets, the amount paid to purchase an asset, including any costs of acquisition and/or preparation; with reference to liabilities, the amount of proceeds received in exchange in issuing the liability.

Historical equity risk premium approach An estimate of a country's equity risk premium that is based upon the historical averages of the risk-free rate and the rate of return on the market portfolio.

Historical simulation Another term for the historical method of estimating VAR. This term is somewhat misleading in that the method involves not a *simulation* of the past but rather what *actually happened* in the past, sometimes adjusted to reflect the fact that a different portfolio may have existed in the past than is planned for the future.

Holder-of-record date The date that a shareholder listed on the corporation's books will be deemed to have ownership of the shares for purposes of receiving an upcoming dividend; two business days after the ex-dividend date.

Holding period return The return that an investor earns during a specified holding period; a synonym for total return.

Holding period return (HPR) The return that an investor earns during a specified holding period; a synonym for total return.

Holding period yield (HPY) The return that an investor earns during a specified holding period; holding period return with reference to a fixed-income instrument.

Homogeneity of expectations The assumption that all investors have the same economic expectations and thus have the same expectations of prices, cash flows, and other investment characteristics.

Horizontal analysis   Common-size analysis that involves comparing a specific financial statement with that statement in prior or future time periods; also, cross-sectional analysis of one company with another.

Horizontal demand schedule   Implies that at a given price, the response in the quantity demanded is infinite.

Household   A person or a group of people living in the same residence, taken as a basic unit in economic analysis.

Hurdle rate   The rate of return that must be met for a project to be accepted.

Hypothesis   With reference to statistical inference, a statement about one or more populations.

Hypothesis testing   With reference to statistical inference, the subdivision dealing with the testing of hypotheses about one or more populations.

IRR rule   An investment decision rule that accepts projects or investments for which the IRR is greater than the opportunity cost of capital.

Iceberg order   An order in which the display size is less than the order's full size.

If-converted method   A method for accounting for the effect of convertible securities on earnings per share (EPS) that specifies what EPS would have been if the convertible securities had been converted at the beginning of the period, taking account of the effects of conversion on net income and the weighted average number of shares outstanding.

Immediate or cancel order   (fill or kill) An order that is valid only upon receipt by the broker or exchange. If such an order cannot be filled in part or in whole upon receipt, it cancels immediately.

Impact lag   The lag associated with the result of actions affecting the economy with delay.

Imperfect competition   A market structure in which an individual firm has enough share of the market (or can control a certain segment of the market) such that it is able to exert some influence over price.

Implicit price deflator for GDP   A gauge of prices and inflation that measures the aggregate changes in prices across the overall economy.

In-the-money   Options that, if exercised, would result in the value received being worth more than the payment required to exercise.

Incentive fee (or performance fee)   Funds distributed by the general partner to the limited partner(s) based on realized profits.

Income   Increases in economic benefits in the form of inflows or enhancements of assets, or decreases of liabilities that result in an increase in equity (other than increases resulting from contributions by owners).

Income constraint   The constraint on a consumer to spend, in total, no more than his income.

Income elasticity of demand   A measure of the responsiveness of demand to changes in income, defined as the percentage change in quantity demanded divided by the percentage change in income.

Income statement   (statement of operations or profit and loss statement) A financial statement that provides information about a company's profitability over a stated period of time.

Income tax paid   The actual amount paid for income taxes in the period; not a provision, but the actual cash outflow.

Income tax payable   The income tax owed by the company on the basis of taxable income.

Income trust   A type of equity ownership vehicle established as a trust issuing ownership shares known as units.

Increasing marginal returns   Where the marginal product of a resource increases as additional units of that input are employed.

Increasing returns to scale   Reduction in cost per unit resulting from increased production.

Increasing-cost industry   An industry in which per-unit costs and output prices are higher when industry output is increased in the long run.

Incremental cash flow   The cash flow that is realized because of a decision; the changes or increments to cash flows resulting from a decision or action.

Independent   With reference to events, the property that the occurrence of one event does not affect the probability of another event occurring.

Independent and identically distributed (IID)   With respect to random variables, the property of random variables that are independent of each other but follow the identical probability distribution.

Independent projects   Independent projects are projects whose cash flows are independent of each other.

Index of Leading Economic Indicators   A composite of economic variables used by analysts to predict future economic conditions.

Indexing   An investment strategy in which an investor constructs a portfolio to mirror the performance of a specified index.

Indifference curve   A curve representing all the combinations of two goods or attributes such that the consumer is entirely indifferent among them.

Indifference curve map   A group or family of indifference curves, representing a consumer's entire utility function.

Indirect format   (indirect method) With reference to cash flow statements, a format for the presentation of the statement which, in the operating cash flow section, begins with net income then shows additions and subtractions to arrive at operating cash flow.

Indirect format   With reference to cash flow statements, a format for the presentation of the statement which, in the operating cash flow section, begins with net income then shows additions and subtractions to arrive at operating cash flow.

Indirect method   See *indirect format*.

Indirect taxes   Taxes such as taxes on spending, as opposed to direct taxes.

Industry   A group of companies offering similar products and/or services.

Industry analysis   The analysis of a specific branch of manufacturing, service, or trade.

Inelastic   Insensitive to price changes.

Inelastic supply   Said of supply that is insensitive to the price of goods sold.

Inflation   The percentage increase in the general price level from one period to the next; a sustained rise in the overall level of prices in an economy.

Inflation Reports   A type of economic publication put out by many central banks.

Inflation premium   An extra return that compensates investors for expected inflation.

Inflation rate   The percentage change in a price index—that is, the speed of overall price level movements.

Inflation uncertainty   The degree to which economic agents view future rates of inflation as difficult to forecast.

Information cascade The transmission of information from those participants who act first and whose decisions influence the decisions of others.

Information-motivated traders Traders that trade to profit from information that they believe allows them to predict future prices.

Informationally efficient A market in which asset prices reflect new information quickly and rationally.

Informationally efficient market A market in which asset prices reflect new information quickly and rationally.

Initial margin The amount that must be deposited in a clearinghouse account when entering into a futures contract.

Initial margin requirement The margin requirement on the first day of a transaction as well as on any day in which additional margin funds must be deposited.

Initial public offering (IPO) The first issuance of common shares to the public by a formerly private corporation.

Installment method With respect to revenue recognition, a method that specifies that the portion of the total profit of the sale that is recognized in each period is determined by the percentage of the total sales price for which the seller has received cash.

Installment sales With respect to revenue recognition, a method that specifies that the portion of the total profit of the sale that is recognized in each period is determined by the percentage of the total sales price for which the seller has received cash.

Intangible assets Assets lacking physical substance, such as patents and trademarks.

Interest Payment for lending funds.

Interest coverage A solvency ratio calculated as EBIT divided by interest payments.

Interest rate A rate of return that reflects the relationship between differently dated cash flows; a discount rate.

Interest rate call An option in which the holder has the right to make a known interest payment and receive an unknown interest payment.

Interest rate cap A series of call options on an interest rate, with each option expiring at the date on which the floating loan rate will be reset, and with each option having the same exercise rate. A cap in general can have an underlying other than an interest rate.

Interest rate collar A combination of a long cap and a short floor, or a short cap and a long floor. A collar in general can have an underlying other than an interest rate.

Interest rate floor A series of put options on an interest rate, with each option expiring at the date on which the floating loan rate will be reset, and with each option having the same exercise rate. A floor in general can have an underlying other than the interest rate.

Interest rate forward See *Forward rate agreement.*

Interest rate option An option in which the underlying is an interest rate.

Interest rate put An option in which the holder has the right to make an unknown interest payment and receive a known interest payment.

Interest rate swap A swap in which the underlying is an interest rate. Can be viewed as a currency swap in which both currencies are the same and can be created as a combination of currency swaps.

Intergenerational data mining A form of data mining that applies information developed by previous researchers using a dataset to guide current research using the same or a related dataset.

Intermarket analysis A field within technical analysis that combines analysis of major categories of securities—namely, equities, bonds, currencies, and commodities—to identify market trends and possible inflections in a trend.

Internal rate of return (IRR) The discount rate that makes net present value equal 0; the discount rate that makes the present value of an investment's costs (outflows) equal to the present value of the investment's benefits (inflows).

Interquartile range The difference between the third and first quartiles of a dataset.

Interval With reference to grouped data, a set of values within which an observation falls.

Interval scale A measurement scale that not only ranks data but also gives assurance that the differences between scale values are equal.

Intrinsic value See *Fundamental value.*

Inventory The unsold units of product on hand.

Inventory blanket lien The use of inventory as collateral for a loan. Though the lender has claim to some or all of the company's inventory, the company may still sell or use the inventory in the ordinary course of business.

Inventory investment Net change in business inventory.

Inventory turnover An activity ratio calculated as cost of goods sold divided by average inventory.

Investing activities Activities which are associated with the acquisition and disposal of property, plant, and equipment; intangible assets; other long-term assets; and both long-term and short-term investments in the equity and debt (bonds and loans) issued by other companies.

Investment banks Financial intermediaries that provide advice to their mostly corporate clients and help them arrange transactions such as initial and seasoned securities offerings.

Investment opportunity schedule A graphical depiction of a company's investment opportunities ordered from highest to lowest expected return. A company's optimal capital budget is found where the investment opportunity schedule intersects with the company's marginal cost of capital.

Investment policy statement (IPS) A written planning document that describes a client's investment objectives and risk tolerance over a relevant time horizon, along with constraints that apply to the client's portfolio.

Investment property Property used to earn rental income or capital appreciation (or both).

January effect (also turn-of-the-year effect) Calendar anomaly that stock market returns in January are significantly higher compared to the rest of the months of the year, with most of the abnormal returns reported during the first five trading days in January.

Joint probability The probability of the joint occurrence of stated events.

Joint probability function A function giving the probability of joint occurrences of values of stated random variables.

Just-in-time (JIT) method Method of managing inventory that minimizes in-process inventory stocks.

Keynesians Economists who believe that fiscal policy can have powerful effects on aggregate demand, output, and employment when there is substantial spare capacity in an economy.

Kondratieff wave A 54-year long economic cycle postulated by Nikolai Kondratieff.

Kurtosis The statistical measure that indicates the peakedness of a distribution.

LIFO layer liquidation   (LIFO liquidation) With respect to the application of the LIFO inventory method, the liquidation of old, relatively low-priced inventory; happens when the volume of sales rises above the volume of recent purchases so that some sales are made from relatively old, low-priced inventory.

LIFO method   The last in, first out, method of accounting for inventory, which matches sales against the costs of items of inventory in the reverse order the items were placed in inventory (i.e., inventory produced or acquired last are assumed to be sold first).

Labor force   The portion of the working age population (over the age of 16) that is employed or is available for work but not working (unemployed).

Labor productivity   The quantity of goods and services (real GDP) that a worker can produce in one hour of work.

Laddering strategy   A form of active strategy which entails scheduling maturities on a systematic basis within the investment portfolio such that investments are spread out equally over the term of the ladder.

Lagging economic indicators   Turning points that take place later than those of the overall economy; they are believed to have value in identifying the economy's past condition.

Laspeyres index   A price index created by holding the composition of the consumption basket constant.

Law of diminishing returns   The smallest output that a firm can produce such that its long run average costs are minimized.

Law of one price   The condition in a financial market in which two equivalent financial instruments or combinations of financial instruments can sell for only one price. Equivalent to the principle that no arbitrage opportunities are possible.

Lead underwriter   The lead investment bank in a syndicate of investment banks and broker–dealers involved in a securities underwriting.

Leading economic indicators   Turning points that usually precede those of the overall economy; they are believed to have value for predicting the economy's future state, usually near-term.

Legal tender   Something that must be accepted when offered in exchange for goods and services.

Lender of last resort   An entity willing to lend money when no other entity is ready to do so.

Leptokurtic   Describes a distribution that is more peaked than a normal distribution.

Level of significance   The probability of a Type I error in testing a hypothesis.

Leverage   In the context of corporate finance, leverage refers to the use of fixed costs within a company's cost structure. Fixed costs that are operating costs (such as depreciation or rent) create operating leverage. Fixed costs that are financial costs (such as interest expense) create financial leverage.

Leveraged buyout   (LBO) A transaction whereby the target company management team converts the target to a privately held company by using heavy borrowing to finance the purchase of the target company's outstanding shares.

Liabilities   Present obligations of an enterprise arising from past events, the settlement of which is expected to result in an outflow of resources embodying economic benefits; creditors' claims on the resources of a company.

Life-cycle stage   The stage of the life cycle: embryonic, growth, shakeout, mature, declining.

Likelihood   The probability of an observation, given a particular set of conditions.

Limit down   A limit move in the futures market in which the price at which a transaction would be made is at or below the lower limit.

Limit move   A condition in the futures markets in which the price at which a transaction would be made is at or beyond the price limits.

Limit order   Instructions to a broker or exchange to obtain the best price immediately available when filling an order, but in no event accept a price higher than a specified (limit) price when buying or accept a price lower than a specified (limit) price when selling.

Limit order book   The book or list of limit orders to buy and sell that pertains to a security.

Limit up   A limit move in the futures market in which the price at which a transaction would be made is at or above the upper limit.

Limitations on liens   Meant to put limits on how much secured debt an issuer can have.

Limited partners   Partners with limited liability. Limited partnerships in hedge and private equity funds are typically restricted to investors who are expected to understand and to be able to assume the risks associated with the investments

Line chart   In technical analysis, a plot of price data, typically closing prices, with a line connecting the points.

Linear interpolation   The estimation of an unknown value on the basis of two known values that bracket it, using a straight line between the two known values.

Linear scale   (or arithmetic scale) A scale in which equal distances correspond to equal absolute amounts.

Liquid market   Said of a market in which traders can buy or sell with low total transaction costs when they want to trade.

Liquidating dividend   A dividend that is a return of capital rather than a distribution from earnings or retained earnings.

Liquidation   To sell the assets of a company, division, or subsidiary piecemeal, typically because of bankruptcy; the form of bankruptcy that allows for the orderly satisfaction of creditors' claims after which the company ceases to exist.

Liquidity   The ability to purchase or sell an asset quickly and easily at a price close to fair market value. The ability to meet short-term obligations using assets that are the most readily converted into cash.

Liquidity premium   An extra return that compensates investors for the risk of loss relative to an investment's fair value if the investment needs to be converted to cash quickly.

Liquidity ratios   Financial ratios measuring the company's ability to meet its short-term obligations.

Liquidity risk   The risk that a financial instrument cannot be purchased or sold without a significant concession in price due to the size of the market.

Liquidity trap   A condition in which the demand for money becomes infinitely elastic (horizontal demand curve) so that injections of money into the economy will not lower interest rates or affect real activity.

Load fund   A mutual fund in which, in addition to the annual fee, a percentage fee is charged to invest in the fund and/or for redemptions from the fund.

Locals   Market makers that buy and sell by quoting a bid and an ask price. They are the primary providers of liquidity to the market.

Lockbox system   A payment system in which customer payments are mailed to a post office box and the banking institution retrieves and deposits these payments several times a day, enabling the company to have use of the fund sooner than in a centralized system in which customer payments are sent to the company.

Locked limit   A condition in the futures markets in which a transaction cannot take place because the price would be beyond the limits.

Lockup period   The minimum period before investors are allowed to make withdrawals or redeem shares from a fund.

Logarithmic scale   A scale in which equal distances represent equal proportional changes in the underlying quantity.

London Interbank Offered Rate (LIBOR)   The Eurodollar rate at which London banks lend dollars to other London banks; considered to be the best representative rate on a dollar borrowed by a private, high-quality borrower.

Long   The buyer of a derivative contract. Also refers to the position of owning a derivative.

Long position   A position in an asset or contract in which one owns the asset or has an exercisable right under the contract.

Long-lived assets   (or long-term assets) Assets that are expected to provide economic benefits over a future period of time, typically greater than one year.

Long-run average total cost curve   The curve describing average total costs when no costs are considered fixed.

Long-run industry supply curve   A curve describing the relationship between quantity supplied and output prices when no costs are considered fixed.

Long-term contract   A contract that spans a number of accounting periods.

Long-term equity anticipatory securities   (also LEAPS) Options originally created with expirations of several years.

Longitudinal data   Observations on characteristic(s) of the same observational unit through time.

Look-ahead bias   A bias caused by using information that was unavailable on the test date.

Loss severity   Portion of a bond's value (including unpaid interest) an investor loses in the event of default.

Losses   Asset outflows not directly related to the ordinary activities of the business.

Lower bound   The lowest possible value of an option.

M²   A measure of what a portfolio would have returned if it had taken on the same total risk as the market index.

Macaulay duration   The duration without dividing by 1 plus the bond's yield to maturity. The term, named for one of the economists who first derived it, is used to distinguish the calculation from modified duration. (See also *modified duration*.)

Maintenance covenants   Covenants in bank loan agreements that require the borrower to satisfy certain financial ratio tests while the loan is outstanding.

Maintenance margin   The minimum amount that is required by a futures clearinghouse to maintain a margin account and to protect against default. Participants whose margin balances drop below the required maintenance margin must replenish their accounts.

Maintenance margin requirement   The margin requirement on any day other than the first day of a transaction.

Management buy-ins   Leveraged buyout in which the current management team is being replaced and the acquiring team will be involved in managing the company.

Management buyout   (MBO) An event in which a group of investors consisting primarily of the company's existing management purchase all of its outstanding shares and take the company private.

Management fee   (or base fee) A fee based on assets under management or committed capital, as applicable.

Manufacturing resource planning (MRP)   The incorporation of production planning into inventory management. A MRP analysis provides both a materials acquisition schedule and a production schedule.

Margin call   A notice to deposit additional cash or securities in a margin account.

Margin loan   Money borrowed from a broker to purchase securities.

Marginal cost   The cost of producing an additional unit of a good.

Marginal probability   The probability of an event *not* conditioned on another event.

Marginal product   Measures the productivity of each unit of input and is calculated by taking the difference in total product from adding another unit of input (assuming other resource quantities are held constant).

Marginal propensity to consume   The proportion of an additional unit of disposable income that is consumed or spent; the change in consumption for a small change in income.

Marginal propensity to save   The proportion of an additional unit of disposable income that is saved (not spent).

Marginal rate of substitution   The rate at which one is willing to give up one good to obtain more of another.

Marginal revenue   The change in total revenue divided by the change in quantity sold; simply, the additional revenue from selling one more unit.

Marginal revenue product   The amount of additional revenue received from employing an additional unit of an input.

Marginal value curve   A curve describing the highest price consumers are willing to pay for each additional unit of a good.

Mark-to-market   The revaluation of a financial asset or liability to its current market value or fair value.

Market   A means of bringing buyers and sellers together to exchange goods and services.

Market anomaly   Change in the price or return of a security that cannot directly be linked to current relevant information known in the market or to the release of new information into the market.

Market bid–ask spread   The difference between the best bid and the best offer.

Market float   The number of shares that are available to the investing public.

Market liquidity risk   The risk that the price at which investors can actually transact—buying or selling—may differ from the price indicated in the market.

Market model   A regression equation that specifies a linear relationship between the return on a security (or portfolio) and the return on a broad market index.

Market multiple models   Valuation models based on share price multiples or enterprise value multiples.

Market order   Instructions to a broker or exchange to obtain the best price immediately available when filling an order.

Market structure   The competitive environment (perfect competition, monopolistic competition, oligopoly, and monopoly).

Market value   The price at which an asset or security can currently be bought or sold in an open market.

Market-capitalization weighting   (or value weighting) An index weighting method in which the weight assigned to each constituent security is determined by dividing its market capitalization by the total market capitalization (sum of the market capitalization) of all securities in the index.

Market-on-close An execution instruction specifying that an order can only be filled at the close of trading.

Marketable limit order A buy limit order in which the limit price is placed above the best offer, or a sell limit order in which the limit price is placed below the best bid. Such orders generally will partially or completely fill right away.

Marking to market A procedure used primarily in futures markets in which the parties to a contract settle the amount owed daily. Also known as the *daily settlement*.

Markowitz efficient frontier The graph of the set of portfolios offering the maximum expected return for their level of risk (standard deviation of return).

Matching principle The accounting principle that expenses should be recognized when the associated revenue is recognized.

Matching strategy An active investment strategy that includes intentional matching of the timing of cash outflows with investment maturities.

Matrix pricing In the fixed income markets, to price a security on the basis of valuation-relevant characteristics (e.g. debt-rating approach).

Maturity premium An extra return that compensates investors for the increased sensitivity of the market value of debt to a change in market interest rates as maturity is extended.

Maturity value The amount of cash payable by a company to the bondholders when the bonds mature; the promised payment at maturity separate from any coupon payment.

Mean absolute deviation With reference to a sample, the mean of the absolute values of deviations from the sample mean.

Mean excess return The average rate of return in excess of the risk-free rate.

Mean–variance analysis An approach to portfolio analysis using expected means, variances, and covariances of asset returns.

Measure of central tendency A quantitative measure that specifies where data are centered.

Measure of location A quantitative measure that describes the location or distribution of data; includes not only measures of central tendency but also other measures such as percentiles.

Measure of value A standard for measuring value; a function of money.

Measurement scales A scheme of measuring differences. The four types of measurement scales are nominal, ordinal, interval, and ratio.

Median The value of the middle item of a set of items that has been sorted into ascending or descending order; the 50th percentile.

Medium of exchange Any asset that can be used to purchase goods and services or to repay debts; a function of money.

Menu costs A cost of inflation in which businesses constantly have to incur the costs of changing the advertised prices of their goods and services.

Mesokurtic Describes a distribution with kurtosis identical to that of the normal distribution.

Mezzanine financing Debt or preferred shares with a relationship to common equity due to a feature such as attached warrants or conversion options and that is subordinate to both senior and high yield debt. It is referred to as mezzanine because of its location on the balance sheet.

Minimum efficient scale The smallest output that a firm can produce such that its long run average cost is minimized.

Minimum-variance portfolio The portfolio with the minimum variance for each given level of expected return.

Minsky moment Named for Hyman Minksy: A point in a business cycle when, after individuals become overextended in borrowing to finance speculative investments, people start realizing that something is likely to go wrong and a panic ensues leading to asset sell-offs.

Mismatching strategy An active investment strategy whereby the timing of cash outflows is not matched with investment maturities.

Modal interval With reference to grouped data, the most frequently occurring interval.

Mode The most frequently occurring value in a set of observations.

Model risk The use of an inaccurate pricing model for a particular investment, or the improper use of the right model.

Modern portfolio theory (MPT) The analysis of rational portfolio choices based on the efficient use of risk.

Modified duration A measure of a bond's price sensitivity to interest rate movements. Equal to the Macaulay duration of a bond divided by one plus its yield to maturity.

Momentum oscillators A graphical representation of market sentiment that is constructed from price data and calculated so that it oscillates either between a high and a low or around some number.

Monetarists Economists who believe that the rate of growth of the money supply is the primary determinant of the rate of inflation.

Monetary policy Actions taken by a nation's central bank to affect aggregate output and prices through changes in bank reserves, reserve requirements, or its target interest rate.

Monetary transmission mechanism The process whereby a central bank's interest rate gets transmitted through the economy and ultimately affects the rate of increase of prices.

Money A generally accepted medium of exchange and unit of account.

Money creation The process by which changes in bank reserves translate into changes in the money supply.

Money market The market for short-term debt instruments (oneyear maturity or less).

Money market The market for short-term debt instruments (one-year maturity or less).

Money market yield A yield on a basis comparable to the quoted yield on an interest-bearing money market instrument that pays interest on a 360-day basis; the annualized holding period yield, assuming a 360-day year.

Money multiplier Describes how a change in reserves is expected to affect the money supply; in its simplest form, 1 divided by the reserve requirement.

Money neutrality The thesis that an increase in the money supply leads in the long-run to an increase in the price level, while leaving real variables like output and employment unaffected.

Money-weighted rate of return The internal rate of return on a portfolio, taking account of all cash flows.

Moneyness The relationship between the price of the underlying and an option's exercise price.

Monopolist Said of an entity that is the only seller in its market.

Monopolistic competition Highly competitive form of imperfect competition; the competitive characteristic is a notably large number of firms, while the monopoly aspect is the result of product differentiation.

Monopoly In pure monopoly markets, there are no substitutes for the given product or service. There is a single seller, which exercises considerable power over pricing and output decisions.

Monte Carlo simulation   An approach to estimating a probability distribution of outcomes to examine what might happen if particular risks are faced. This method is widely used in the sciences as well as in business to study a variety of problems.

Moving average   The average of the closing price of a security over a specified number of periods. With each new period, the average is recalculated.

Moving-average convergence/divergence oscillator   (MACD) A momentum oscillator that is constructed based on the difference between short-term and long-term moving averages of a security's price.

Multi-factor model   A model that explains a variable in terms of the values of a set of factors.

Multi-market indices   Comprised of indices from different countries, designed to represent multiple security markets.

Multi-step format   With respect to the format of the income statement, a format that presents a subtotal for gross profit (revenue minus cost of goods sold).

Multilateral trading facilities   See *Alternative trading systems*.

Multiplication rule for probabilities   The rule that the joint probability of events *A* and *B* equals the probability of *A* given *B* times the probability of *B*.

Multiplier models   Valuation models based on share price multiples or enterprise value multiples.

Multivariate distribution   A probability distribution that specifies the probabilities for a group of related random variables.

Multivariate normal distribution   A probability distribution for a group of random variables that is completely defined by the means and variances of the variables plus all the correlations between pairs of the variables.

Mutual fund   A professionally managed investment pool in which investors in the fund typically each have a pro-rata claim on the income and value of the fund.

Mutually exclusive projects   Mutually exclusive projects compete directly with each other. For example, if Projects A and B are mutually exclusive, you can choose A or B, but you cannot choose both.

***n* Factorial**   For a positive integer *n*, the product of the first *n* positive integers; 0 factorial equals 1 by definition. *n* factorial is written as *n*!.

NDFs   See *Nondeliverable forwards*.

NPV rule   An investment decision rule that states that an investment should be undertaken if its NPV is positive but not undertaken if its NPV is negative.

Narrow money   The notes and coins in circulation in an economy, plus other very highly liquid deposits.

Nash equilibrium   When two or more participants in a non-coop-erative game have no incentive to deviate from their respective equilibrium strategies given their opponent's strategies.

National income   The income received by all factors of production used in the generation of final output. National income equals gross domestic product (or, in some countries, gross national product) minus the capital consumption allowance and a statistical discrepancy.

Natural rate of unemployment   Effective unemployment rate, below which pressure emerges in labor markets.

Neo-Keynesians   A group of dynamic general equilibrium models that assume slow-to-adjust prices and wages.

Net book value   The remaining (undepreciated) balance of an asset's purchase cost. For liabilities, the face value of a bond minus any unamortized discount, or plus any unamortized premium.

Net income   The difference between revenue and expenses; what remains after subtracting all expenses (including depreciation, interest, and taxes) from revenue.

Net operating cycle   An estimate of the average time that elapses between paying suppliers for materials and collecting cash from the subsequent sale of goods produced.

Net present value   (NPV) The present value of an investment's cash inflows (benefits) minus the present value of its cash outflows (costs).

Net profit margin   (**profit margin** or **return on sales**)An indicator of profitability, calculated as net income divided by revenue; indicates how much of each dollar of revenues is left after all costs and expenses.

Net realizable value   Estimated selling price in the ordinary course of business less the estimated costs necessary to make the sale.

Net revenue   Revenue after adjustments (e.g., for estimated returns or for amounts unlikely to be collected).

Net tax rate   The tax rate net of transfer payments.

Netting   When parties agree to exchange only the net amount owed from one party to the other.

Neutral rate of interest   The rate of interest that neither spurs on nor slows down the underlying economy.

New Keynesians   A group of dynamic general equilibrium models that assume slow-to-adjust prices and wages.

New classical macroeconomics   An approach to macroeconomics that seeks the macroeconomic conclusions of individuals maximizing utility on the basis of rational expectations and companies maximizing profits.

New-issue DRP   Dividend reinvestment plan in which the company meets the need for additional shares by issuing them instead of purchasing them.

No-load fund   A mutual fund in which there is no fee for investing in the fund or for redeeming fund shares, although there is an annual fee based on a percentage of the fund's net asset value.

Node   Each value on a binomial tree from which successive moves or outcomes branch.

Nominal GDP   The value of goods and services measured at current prices.

Nominal rate   A rate of interest based on the security's face value.

Nominal risk-free interest rate   The sum of the real risk-free interest rate and the inflation premium.

Nominal scale   A measurement scale that categorizes data but does not rank them.

Non-accelerating inflation rate of unemployment   Effective unemployment rate, below which pressure emerges in labor markets.

Non-cumulative preference shares   Preference shares for which dividends that are not paid in the current or subsequent periods are forfeited permanently (instead of being accrued and paid at a later date).

Non-current assets   Assets that are expected to benefit the company over an extended period of time (usually more than one year).

Non-current liability   An obligation that broadly represents a probable sacrifice of economic benefits in periods generally greater than one year in the future.

Non-cyclical   A company whose performance is largely independent of the business cycle.

Non-participating preference shares   Preference shares that do not entitle shareholders to share in the profits of the company. Instead, shareholders are only entitled to receive a fixed dividend payment and the par value of the shares in the event of liquidation.

Non-renewable resources   Finite resources that are depleted once they are consumed, such as oil and coal.

Non-satiation   The assumption that the consumer could never have so much of a preferred good that she would refuse any more, even if it were free; sometimes referred to as the "more is better" assumption.

Nonconventional cash flow   In a nonconventional cash flow pattern, the initial outflow is not followed by inflows only, but the cash flows can flip from positive (inflows) to negative (outflows) again (or even change signs several times).

Noncurrent assets   Assets that are expected to benefit the company over an extended period of time (usually more than one year).

Nondeliverable forwards   Cash-settled forward contracts, used predominately with respect to foreign exchange forwards.

Nonparametric test   A test that is not concerned with a parameter, or that makes minimal assumptions about the population from which a sample comes.

Nonsystematic risk   Unique risk that is local or limited to a particular asset or industry that need not affect assets outside of that asset class.

Normal distribution   A continuous, symmetric probability distribution that is completely described by its mean and its variance.

Normal profit   The level of accounting profit needed to just cover the implicit opportunity costs ignored in accounting costs.

Notching   Ratings adjustment methodology where specific issues from the same borrower may be assigned different credit ratings.

Notes payable   Amounts owed by a business to creditors as a result of borrowings that are evidenced by (short-term) loan agreements.

Notice period   The length of time (typically 30 to 90 days) in advance that investors may be required to notify a fund of their intent to redeem.

Number of days of inventory   An activity ratio equal to the number of days in a period divided by the inventory ratio for the period; an indication of the number of days a company ties up funds in inventory.

Number of days of payables   An activity ratio equal to the number of days in a period divided by the payables turnover ratio for the period; an estimate of the average number of days it takes a company to pay its suppliers.

Number of days of receivables   Estimate of the average number of days it takes to collect on credit accounts.

Objective probabilities   Probabilities that generally do not vary from person to person; includes a priori and objective probabilities.

Offer   The price at which a dealer or trader is willing to sell an asset, typically qualified by a maximum quantity (ask size).

Official interest rate   (or official policy rate, policy rate) An interest rate that a central bank sets and announces publicly; normally the rate at which it is willing to lend money to the commercial banks.

Official policy rate   An interest rate that a central bank sets and announces publicly; normally the rate at which it is willing to lend money to the commercial banks.

Offsetting   A transaction in exchange-listed derivative markets in which a party re-enters the market to close out a position.

Oligopoly   Market structure with a relatively small number of firms supplying the market.

One-sided hypothesis test   A test in which the null hypothesis is rejected only if the evidence indicates that the population parameter is greater than (smaller than) θ_0. The alternative hypothesis also has one side.

One-tailed hypothesis test   A test in which the null hypothesis is rejected only if the evidence indicates that the population parameter is greater than (smaller than) θ_0. The alternative hypothesis also has one side.

Open market operations   Activities that involve the purchase and sale of government bonds from and to commercial banks and/or designated market makers.

Open-end fund   A mutual fund that accepts new investment money and issues additional shares at a value equal to the net asset value of the fund at the time of investment.

Open-market DRP   Dividend reinvestment plan in which the company purchases shares in the open market to acquire the additional shares credited to plan participants.

Operating activities   Activities that are part of the day-to-day business functioning of an entity, such as selling inventory and providing services.

Operating breakeven   The number of units produced and sold at which the company's operating profit is zero (revenues = operating costs).

Operating cash flow   The net amount of cash provided from operating activities.

Operating cycle   A measure of the time needed to convert raw materials into cash from a sale; it consists of the number of days of inventory and the number of days of receivables.

Operating efficiency ratios   Ratios that measure how efficiently a company performs day-to-day tasks, such as the collection of receivables and management of inventory.

Operating leverage   The use of fixed costs in operations.

Operating profit   (operating income) A company's profits on its usual business activities before deducting taxes.

Operating profit margin   (operating margin) A profitability ratio calculated as operating income (i.e., income before interest and taxes) divided by revenue.

Operating risk   The risk attributed to the operating cost structure, in particular the use of fixed costs in operations; the risk arising from the mix of fixed and variable costs; the risk that a company's operations may be severely affected by environmental, social, and governance risk factors.

Operational independence   A bank's ability to execute monetary policy and set interest rates in the way it thought would best meet the inflation target.

Operationally efficient   Said of a market, a financial system, or an economy that has relatively low transaction costs.

Opportunity cost   The value that investors forgo by choosing a particular course of action; the value of something in its best alternative use.

Option   (option contract) A financial instrument that gives one party the right, but not the obligation, to buy or sell an underlying asset from or to another party at a fixed price over a specific period of time. Also referred to as contingent claims.

Option contract   See *option*.

Option premium   The amount of money a buyer pays and seller receives to engage in an option transaction.

Option price   The amount of money a buyer pays and seller receives to engage in an option transaction.

Order   A specification of what instrument to trade, how much to trade, and whether to buy or sell.

Order precedence hierarchy   With respect to the execution of orders to trade, a set of rules that determines which orders execute before other orders.

Order-driven markets   A market (generally an auction market) that uses rules to arrange trades based on the orders that traders submit; in their pure form, such markets do not make use of dealers.

Ordinal scale   A measurement scale that sorts data into categories that are ordered (ranked) with respect to some characteristic.

Ordinary annuity   An annuity with a first cash flow that is paid one period from the present.

Ordinary shares   (common stock or common shares) Equity shares that are subordinate to all other types of equity (e.g., preferred equity).

Other comprehensive income   Items of comprehensive income that are not reported on the income statement; comprehensive income minus net income.

Other receivables   Amounts owed to the company from parties other than customers.

Out-of-sample test   A test of a strategy or model using a sample outside the time period on which the strategy or model was developed.

Out-of-the-money   Options that, if exercised, would require the payment of more money than the value received and therefore would not be currently exercised.

Outcome   A possible value of a random variable.

Overbought   A market condition in which market sentiment is thought to be unsustainably bullish.

Oversold   A market condition in which market sentiment is thought to be unsustainably bearish.

Owner-of-record date   The date that a shareholder listed on the corporation's books will be deemed to have ownership of the shares for purposes of receiving an upcoming dividend; two business days after the ex-dividend date.

Owners' equity   (shareholders' equity) The excess of assets over liabilities; the residual interest of shareholders in the assets of an entity after deducting the entity's liabilities.

Paasche index   An index formula using the current composition of a basket of products.

Paired comparisons test   A statistical test for differences based on paired observations drawn from samples that are dependent on each other.

Paired observations   Observations that are dependent on each other.

Pairs arbitrage trade   A trade in two closely related stocks involving the short sale of one and the purchase of the other.

Panel data   Observations through time on a single characteristic of multiple observational units.

Parameter   A descriptive measure computed from or used to describe a population of data, conventionally represented by Greek letters.

Parametric test   Any test (or procedure) concerned with parameters or whose validity depends on assumptions concerning the population generating the sample.

Pari passu   On an equal footing.

Participating preference shares   Preference shares that entitle shareholders to receive the standard preferred dividend plus the opportunity to receive an additional dividend if the company's profits exceed a pre-specified level.

Passive investment   A buy and hold approach in which an investor does not make portfolio changes based on short-term expectations of changing market or security performance.

Passive strategy   In reference to short-term cash management, it is an investment strategy characterized by simple decision rules for making daily investments.

Payable date   The day that the company actually mails out (or electronically transfers) a dividend payment.

Payment date   The day that the company actually mails out (or electronically transfers) a dividend payment.

Payments system   The system for the transfer of money.

Payoff   The value of an option at expiration.

Payout   Cash dividends and the value of shares repurchased in any given year.

Payout policy   A company's set of principles guiding payouts.

Peak   The highest point of a business cycle.

Peer group   A group of companies engaged in similar business activities whose economics and valuation are influenced by closely related factors.

Pennants   A technical analysis continuation pattern formed by trendlines that converge to form a triangle, typically over a short period.

Per capita real GDP   Real GDP divided by the size of the population, often used as a measure of the average standard of living in a country.

Per unit contribution margin   The amount that each unit sold contributes to covering fixed costs—that is, the difference between the price per unit and the variable cost per unit.

Percentage-of-completion   A method of revenue recognition in which, in each accounting period, the company estimates what percentage of the contract is complete and then reports that percentage of the total contract revenue in its income statement.

Percentiles   Quantiles that divide a distribution into 100 equal parts.

Perfect competition   (also price taker) A market structure in which the individual firm has virtually no impact on market price, because it is assumed to be a very small seller among a very large number of firms selling essentially identical products.

Performance appraisal   The evaluation of risk-adjusted performance; the evaluation of investment skill.

Performance evaluation   The measurement and assessment of the outcomes of investment management decisions.

Performance measurement   The calculation of returns in a logical and consistent manner.

Period costs   Costs (e.g., executives' salaries) that cannot be directly matched with the timing of revenues and which are thus expensed immediately.

Permanent differences   Differences between tax and financial reporting of revenue (expenses) that will not be reversed at some future date. These result in a difference between the company's effective tax rate and statutory tax rate and do not result in a deferred tax item.

Permutation   An ordered listing.

Perpetuity   A perpetual annuity, or a set of never-ending level sequential cash flows, with the first cash flow occurring one period from now.

Personal consumption expenditures   All domestic personal consumption; the basis for a price index for such consumption called the PCE price index.

Personal disposable income   Equal to personal income less personal taxes.

Personal income   A broad measure of household income that includes all income received by households, whether earned or unearned; measures the ability of consumers to make purchases.

Plain vanilla swap An interest rate swap in which one party pays a fixed rate and the other pays a floating rate, with both sets of payments in the same currency.

Planning horizon A time period in which all factors of production are variable, including technology, physical capital, and plant size.

Platykurtic Describes a distribution that is less peaked than the normal distribution.

Point and figure chart A technical analysis chart that is constructed with columns of X's alternating with columns of O's such that the horizontal axis represents only the number of changes in price without reference to time or volume.

Point estimate A single numerical estimate of an unknown quantity, such as a population parameter.

Point of sale (POS) Systems that capture transaction data at the physical location in which the sale is made.

Policy rate An interest rate that a central bank sets and announces publicly; normally the rate at which it is willing to lend money to the commercial banks.

Population All members of a specified group.

Population mean The arithmetic mean value of a population; the arithmetic mean of all the observations or values in the population.

Population standard deviation A measure of dispersion relating to a population in the same unit of measurement as the observations, calculated as the positive square root of the population variance.

Population variance A measure of dispersion relating to a population, calculated as the mean of the squared deviations around the population mean.

Portfolio company In private equity, the company that is being invested in.

Portfolio demand for money The demand to hold speculative money balances based on the potential opportunities or risks that are inherent in other financial instruments.

Portfolio planning The process of creating a plan for building a portfolio that is expected to satisfy a client's investment objectives.

Position The quantity of an asset that an entity owns or owes.

Position trader A trader who typically holds positions open overnight.

Posterior probability An updated probability that reflects or comes after new information.

Potential GDP The level of real GDP that can be produced at full employment; measures the productive capacity of the economy.

Power of a test The probability of correctly rejecting the null—that is, rejecting the null hypothesis when it is false.

Precautionary money balances Money held to provide a buffer against unforeseen events that might require money.

Precautionary stocks A level of inventory beyond anticipated needs that provides a cushion in the event that it takes longer to replenish inventory than expected or in the case of greater than expected demand.

Preference shares (or preferred stock) A type of equity interest which ranks above common shares with respect to the payment of dividends and the distribution of the company's net assets upon liquidation. They have characteristics of both debt and equity securities.

Preferred stock See *Preference shares*.

Premium The amount of money a buyer pays and seller receives to engage in an option transaction.

Prepaid expense A normal operating expense that has been paid in advance of when it is due.

Present value (PV) The present discounted value of future cash flows: For assets, the present discounted value of the future net cash inflows that the asset is expected to generate; for liabilities, the present discounted value of the future net cash outflows that are expected to be required to settle the liabilities.

Present value models (or discounted cash flow models) Valuation models that estimate the intrinsic value of a security as the present value of the future benefits expected to be received from the security.

Pretax margin A profitability ratio calculated as earnings before taxes divided by revenue.

Price The market price as established by the interactions of the market demand and supply factors.

Price discovery A feature of futures markets in which futures prices provide valuable information about the price of the underlying asset.

Price elasticity of demand Measures the percentage change in the quantity demanded, given a percentage change in the price of a given product.

Price index Represents the average prices of a basket of goods and services.

Price limits Limits imposed by a futures exchange on the price change that can occur from one day to the next.

Price multiple A ratio that compares the share price with some sort of monetary flow or value to allow evaluation of the relative worth of a company's stock.

Price priority The principle that the highest priced buy orders and the lowest priced sell orders execute first.

Price relative A ratio of an ending price over a beginning price; it is equal to 1 plus the holding period return on the asset.

Price return Measures *only* the price appreciation or percentage change in price of the securities in an index or portfolio.

Price return index (or price index) An index that reflects *only* the price appreciation or percentage change in price of the constituent securities.

Price stability In economics, refers to an inflation rate that is low on average and not subject to wide fluctuation.

Price takers Producers that must accept whatever price the market dictates.

Price to book value A valuation ratio calculated as price per share divided by book value per share.

Price to cash flow A valuation ratio calculated as price per share divided by cash flow per share.

Price to earnings ratio (P/E ratio) The ratio of share price to earnings per share.

Price to sales A valuation ratio calculated as price per share divided by sales per share.

Price weighting An index weighting method in which the weight assigned to each constituent security is determined by dividing its price by the sum of all the prices of the constituent securities.

Price-to-earnings ratio (also P/E) The ratio of share price to earnings per share.

Priced risk Risk for which investors demand compensation for bearing (e.g. equity risk, company-specific factors, macroeconomic factors).

Primary capital markets (primary markets) The market where securities are first sold and the issuers receive the proceeds.

Primary market The market where securities are first sold and the issuers receive the proceeds.

Prime brokers Brokers that provide services including custody, administration, lending, short borrowing, and trading.

Principal The amount of funds originally invested in a project or instrument; the face value to be paid at maturity.

Principal business activity The business activity from which a company derives a majority of its revenues and/or earnings.

Principal value The amount of cash payable by a company to the bondholders when the bonds mature; the promised payment at maturity separate from any coupon payment.

Prior probabilities Probabilities reflecting beliefs prior to the arrival of new information.

Priority of claims Priority of payment, with the most senior or highest ranking debt having the first claim on the cash flows and assets of the issuer.

Private equity securities Securities that are not listed on public exchanges and have no active secondary market. They are issued primarily to institutional investors via non-public offerings, such as private placements.

Private investment in public equity An investment in the equity of a publicly traded firm that is made at a discount to the market value of the firm's shares.

Private placement When corporations sell securities directly to a small group of qualified investors, usually with the assistance of an investment bank.

Probability A number between 0 and 1 describing the chance that a stated event will occur.

Probability density function A function with non-negative values such that probability can be described by areas under the curve graphing the function.

Probability distribution A distribution that specifies the probabilities of a random variable's possible outcomes.

Probability function A function that specifies the probability that the random variable takes on a specific value.

Producer price index Reflects the price changes experienced by domestic producers in a country.

Production function Provides the quantitative link between the level of output that the economy can produce and the inputs used in the production process.

Production opportunity frontier Curve describing the maximum number of units of one good a company can produce, for any given number of the other good that it chooses to manufacture.

Productivity The amount of output produced by workers in a given period of time–for example, output per hour worked; measures the efficiency of labor.

Profit The return that owners of a company receive for the use of their capital and the assumption of financial risk when making their investments.

Profit and loss (P&L) statement A financial statement that provides information about a company's profitability over a stated period of time.

Profit margin An indicator of profitability, calculated as net income divided by revenue; indicates how much of each dollar of revenues is left after all costs and expenses.

Profitability ratios Ratios that measure a company's ability to generate profitable sales from its resources (assets).

Project sequencing To defer the decision to invest in a future project until the outcome of some or all of a current project is known. Projects are sequenced through time, so that investing in a project creates the option to invest in future projects.

Promissory note A written promise to pay a certain amount of money on demand.

Property, plant, and equipment Tangible assets that are expected to be used for more than one period in either the production or supply of goods or services, or for administrative purposes.

Prospectus The document that describes the terms of a new bond issue and helps investors perform their analysis on the issue.

Protective put An option strategy in which a long position in an asset is combined with a long position in a put.

Pseudo-random numbers Numbers produced by random number generators.

Pull on liquidity When disbursements are paid too quickly or trade credit availability is limited, requiring companies to expend funds before they receive funds from sales that could cover the liability.

Pure discount instruments Instruments that pay interest as the difference between the amount borrowed and the amount paid back.

Pure-play method A method for estimating the beta for a company or project; it requires using a comparable company's beta and adjusting it for financial leverage differences.

Put An option that gives the holder the right to sell an underlying asset to another party at a fixed price over a specific period of time.

Put/call ratio A technical analysis indicator that evaluates market sentiment based upon the volume of put options traded divided by the volume of call options traded for a particular financial instrument.

Putable common shares Common shares that give investors the option (or right) to sell their shares (i.e., "put" them) back to the issuing company at a price that is specified when the shares are originally issued.

Put–call parity An equation expressing the equivalence (parity) of a portfolio of a call and a bond with a portfolio of a put and the underlying, which leads to the relationship between put and call prices.

Quantile (or fractile) A value at or below which a stated fraction of the data lies.

Quantitative easing An expansionary monetary policy based on aggressive open market purchase operations.

Quantity The amount of a product that consumers are willing and able to buy at each price level.

Quantity demanded The amount of a product that consumers are willing and able to buy at each price level.

Quantity equation of exchange An expression that over a given period, the amount of money used to purchase all goods and services in an economy, $M \times V$, is equal to monetary value of this output, $P \times Y$.

Quantity theory of money Asserts that total spending (in money terms) is proportional to the quantity of money.

Quartiles Quantiles that divide a distribution into four equal parts.

Quasi-fixed cost A cost that stays the same over a range of production but can change to another constant level when production moves outside of that range.

Quick assets Assets that can be most readily converted to cash (e.g., cash, short-term marketable investments, receivables).

Quick ratio A stringent measure of liquidity that indicates a company's ability to satisfy current liabilities with its most liquid assets, calculated as (cash + short-term marketable investments + receivables) divided by current liabilities.

Quintiles Quantiles that divide a distribution into five equal parts.

Quote-driven market A market in which dealers acting as principals facilitate trading.

Quoted interest rate (also stated annual interest rate) A quoted interest rate that does not account for compounding within the year.

Random number An observation drawn from a uniform distribution.

Random number generator An algorithm that produces uniformly distributed random numbers between 0 and 1.

Random variable A quantity whose future outcomes are uncertain.

Range The difference between the maximum and minimum values in a dataset.

Ratio scales A measurement scale that has all the characteristics of interval measurement scales as well as a true zero point as the origin.

Real GDP The value of goods and services produced, measured at base year prices.

Real income Income adjusted for the effect of inflation on the purchasing power of money.

Real interest rate Nominal interest rate minus the expected rate of inflation.

Real risk-free interest rate The single-period interest rate for a completely risk-free security if no inflation were expected.

Realizable (settlement) value With reference to assets, the amount of cash or cash equivalents that could currently be obtained by selling the asset in an orderly disposal; with reference to liabilities, the undiscounted amount of cash or cash equivalents expected to be paid to satisfy the liabilities in the normal course of business.

Rebalancing Adjusting the weights of the constituent securities in an index.

Rebalancing policy The set of rules that guide the process of restoring a portfolio's asset class weights to those specified in the strategic asset allocation.

Recession A period during which real GDP decreases (i.e., negative growth) for at least two successive quarters, or a period of significant decline in total output, income, employment, and sales usually lasting from six months to a year.

Recognition lag The lag in government response to an economic problem resulting from the delay in confirming a change in the state of the economy.

Record date The date that a shareholder listed on the corporation's books will be deemed to have ownership of the shares for purposes of receiving an upcoming dividend; two business days after the ex-dividend date.

Redemptions Withdrawals of funds by investors.

Refinancing rate A type of central bank policy rate.

Regulatory risk The risk associated with the uncertainty of how derivative transactions will be regulated or with changes in regulations.

Relative dispersion The amount of dispersion relative to a reference value or benchmark.

Relative frequency With reference to an interval of grouped data, the number of observations in the interval divided by the total number of observations in the sample.

Relative price The price of a specific good or service in comparison with those of other goods and services.

Relative strength analysis A comparison of the performance of one asset with the performance of another asset or a benchmark based on changes in the ratio of the securities' respective prices over time.

Relative strength index A technical analysis momentum oscillator that compares a security's gains with its losses over a set period.

Renewable resources Resources that can be replenished, such as a forest.

Rent Payment for the use of property.

Reorganization Agreements made by a company in bankruptcy under which a company's capital structure is altered and/or alternative arrangements are made for debt repayment; U.S. Chapter 11 bankruptcy. The company emerges from bankruptcy as a going concern.

Repo rates Short-term collateralized lending rates.

Repurchase agreement The sale of securities together with an agreement for the seller to buy back the securities at a later date at a higher price; often called a repo. Typically a short-term agreement; if long term, called a term repo.

Reserve requirement The requirement for banks to hold reserves in proportion to the size of deposits.

Residual claim The owners' remaining claim on the company's assets after the liabilities are deducted.

Resistance In technical analysis, a price range in which selling activity is sufficient to stop the rise in the price of a security.

Restricted payments A bond covenant meant to protect creditors by limiting how much cash can be paid out to shareholders over time.

Retail method An inventory accounting method in which the sales value of an item is reduced by the gross margin to calculate the item's cost.

Retracement In technical analysis, a reversal in the movement of a security's price such that it is counter to the prevailing longerterm price trend.

Return on assets (ROA) A profitability ratio calculated as net income divided by average total assets; indicates a company's net profit generated per dollar invested in total assets.

Return on equity (ROE) A profitability ratio calculated as net income divided by average shareholders' equity.

Return on sales An indicator of profitability, calculated as net income divided by revenue; indicates how much of each dollar of revenues is left after all costs and expenses.

Return on total capital A profitability ratio calculated as EBIT divided by the sum of short- and long-term debt and equity.

Return-generating model A model that can provide an estimate of the expected return of a security given certain parameters and estimates of the values of the independent variables in the model.

Revaluation model The process of valuing long-lived assets at fair value, rather than at cost less accumulated depreciation. Any resulting profit or loss is either reported on the income statement and/or through equity under revaluation surplus.

Revenue The amount charged for the delivery of goods or services in the ordinary activities of a business over a stated period; the inflows of economic resources to a company over a stated period.

Reversal patterns A type of pattern used in technical analysis to predict the end of a trend and a change in direction of the security's price.

Reverse stock split A reduction in the number of shares outstanding with a corresponding increase in share price, but no change to the company's underlying fundamentals.

Revolving credit agreements The strongest form of short-term bank borrowing facilities; they are in effect for multiple years (e.g., 3–5 years) and may have optional medium-term loan features.

Rho The sensitivity of the option price to the risk-free rate.

Ricardian equivalence An economic theory that implies that it makes no difference whether a government finances a deficit by increasing taxes or issuing debt.

Risk averse The assumption that an investor will choose the least risky alternative.

Risk aversion   The degree of an investor's inability and unwillingness to take risk.

Risk budgeting   The establishment of objectives for individuals, groups, or divisions of an organization that takes into account the allocation of an acceptable level of risk.

Risk management   The process of identifying the level of risk an entity wants, measuring the level of risk the entity currently has, taking actions that bring the actual level of risk to the desired level of risk, and monitoring the new actual level of risk so that it continues to be aligned with the desired level of risk.

Risk premium   An extra return expected by investors for bearing some specified risk.

Risk tolerance   The amount of risk an investor is willing and able to bear to achieve an investment goal.

Robust   The quality of being relatively unaffected by a violation of assumptions.

Rule of 72   The principle that the approximate number of years necessary for an investment to double is 72 divided by the stated interest rate.

Safety stock   A level of inventory beyond anticipated needs that provides a cushion in the event that it takes longer to replenish inventory than expected or in the case of greater than expected demand.

Safety-first rules   Rules for portfolio selection that focus on the risk that portfolio value will fall below some minimum acceptable level over some time horizon.

Sales   Generally, a synonym for revenue; "sales" is generally understood to refer to the sale of goods, whereas "revenue" is understood to include the sale of goods or services.

Sales returns and allowances   An offset to revenue reflecting any cash refunds, credits on account, and discounts from sales prices given to customers who purchased defective or unsatisfactory items.

Sales risk   Uncertainty with respect to the quantity of goods and services that a company is able to sell and the price it is able to achieve; the risk related to the uncertainty of revenues.

Salvage value   (or residual value) The amount the company estimates that it can sell the asset for at the end of its useful life.

Sample   A subset of a population.

Sample excess kurtosis   A sample measure of the degree of a distribution's peakedness in excess of the normal distribution's peakedness.

Sample kurtosis   A sample measure of the degree of a distribution's peakedness.

Sample mean   The sum of the sample observations, divided by the sample size.

Sample selection bias   Bias introduced by systematically excluding some members of the population according to a particular attribute—for example, the bias introduced when data availability leads to certain observations being excluded from the analysis.

Sample skewness   A sample measure of degree of asymmetry of a distribution.

Sample standard deviation   The positive square root of the sample variance.

Sample statistic   A quantity computed from or used to describe a sample.

Sample variance   A sample measure of the degree of dispersion of a distribution, calculated by dividing the sum of the squared deviations from the sample mean by the sample size minus 1.

Sampling   The process of obtaining a sample.

Sampling distribution   The distribution of all distinct possible values that a statistic can assume when computed from samples of the same size randomly drawn from the same population.

Sampling error   The difference between the observed value of a statistic and the quantity it is intended to estimate.

Sampling plan   The set of rules used to select a sample.

Say's law   Named for French economist J.B. Say: All that is produced will be sold because supply creates its own demand.

Scalper   A trader who offers to buy or sell futures contracts, holding the position for only a brief period of time. Scalpers attempt to profit by buying at the bid price and selling at the higher ask price.

Scenario analysis   Analysis that shows the changes in key financial quantities that result from given (economic) events, such as the loss of customers, the loss of a supply source, or a catastrophic event; a risk management technique involving examination of the performance of a portfolio under specified situations. Closely related to stress testing.

Scrip dividend schemes   Dividend reinvestment plan in which the company meets the need for additional shares by issuing them instead of purchasing them.

Seasoned offering   An offering in which an issuer sells additional units of a previously issued security.

Seats   Memberships in a derivatives exchange.

Second lien   A secured interest in the pledged assets that ranks below first lien debt in both collateral protection and priority of payment.

Second-degree price discrimination   When the monopolist charges different per-unit prices using the quantity purchased as an indicator of how highly the customer values the product.

Secondary market   The market where securities are traded among investors.

Secondary precedence rules   Rules that determine how to rank orders placed at the same time.

Sector   A group of related industries.

Sector indices   Indices that represent and track different economic sectors—such as consumer goods, energy, finance, health care, and technology—on either a national, regional, or global basis.

Secured debt   Debt in which the debtholder has a direct claim—a pledge from the issuer—on certain assets and their associated cash flows.

Security characteristic line   A plot of the excess return of a security on the excess return of the market.

Security market index   A portfolio of securities representing a given security market, market segment, or asset class.

Security market line   (also SML) The graph of the capital asset pricing model.

Security selection   The process of selecting individual securities; typically, security selection has the objective of generating superior risk-adjusted returns relative to a portfolio's benchmark.

Self-investment limits   With respect to investment limitations applying to pension plans, restrictions on the percentage of assets that can be invested in securities issued by the pension plan sponsor.

Sell-side firm   A broker or dealer that sells securities to and provides independent investment research and recommendations to investment management companies.

Semi-strong-form efficient market   A market in which security prices reflect all publicly known and available information.

Semideviation The positive square root of semivariance (sometimes called semistandard deviation).

Semilogarithmic Describes a scale constructed so that equal intervals on the vertical scale represent equal rates of change, and equal intervals on the horizontal scale represent equal amounts of change.

Semivariance The average squared deviation below the mean.

Seniority ranking Priority of payment of various debt obligations.

Sensitivity analysis Analysis that shows the range of possible outcomes as specific assumptions are changed.

Separately managed account (SMA) An investment portfolio managed exclusively for the benefit of an individual or institution.

Settlement date The date on which the parties to a swap make payments.

Settlement period The time between settlement dates.

Settlement price The official price, designated by the clearinghouse, from which daily gains and losses will be determined and marked to market.

Share repurchase A transaction in which a company buys back its own shares. Unlike stock dividends and stock splits, share repurchases use corporate cash.

Shareholder wealth maximization To maximize the market value of shareholders' equity.

Shareholder-of-record date The date that a shareholder listed on the corporation's books will be deemed to have ownership of the shares for purposes of receiving an upcoming dividend; two business days after the ex-dividend date.

Shareholders' equity Assets less liabilities; the residual interest in the assets after subtracting the liabilities.

Sharpe ratio The average return in excess of the risk-free rate divided by the standard deviation of return; a measure of the average excess return earned per unit of standard deviation of return.

Shelf registration A registration of an offering well in advance of the offering; the issuer may not sell all shares registered in a single transaction.

Short The seller of a derivative contract. Also refers to the position of being short a derivative.

Short position A position in an asset or contract in which one has sold an asset one does not own, or in which a right under a contract can be exercised against oneself.

Short selling A transaction in which borrowed securities are sold with the intention to repurchase them at a lower price at a later date and return them to the lender.

Short-run average total cost curve The curve describing average total costs when some costs are considered fixed.

Short-run supply curve The section of the marginal cost curve that lies above the minimum point on the average variable cost curve.

Shortfall risk The risk that portfolio value will fall below some minimum acceptable level over some time horizon.

Shutdown point The point at which average revenue is less than average variable cost.

Simple interest The interest earned each period on the original investment; interest calculated on the principal only.

Simple random sample A subset of a larger population created in such a way that each element of the population has an equal probability of being selected to the subset.

Simple random sampling The procedure of drawing a sample to satisfy the definition of a simple random sample.

Simulation Computer-generated sensitivity or scenario analysis that is based on probability models for the factors that drive outcomes.

Simulation trial A complete pass through the steps of a simulation.

Single-step format With respect to the format of the income statement, a format that does not subtotal for gross profit (revenue minus cost of goods sold).

Skewed Not symmetrical.

Skewness A quantitative measure of skew (lack of symmetry); a synonym of skew.

Solvency With respect to financial statement analysis, the ability of a company to fulfill its long-term obligations.

Solvency ratios Ratios that measure a company's ability to meet its long-term obligations.

Sovereign yield spread An estimate of the country spread (country equity premium) for a developing nation that is based on a comparison of bonds yields in country being analyzed and a developed country. The sovereign yield spread is the difference between a government bond yield in the country being analyzed, denominated in the currency of the developed country, and the Treasury bond yield on a similar maturity bond in the developed country.

Spearman rank correlation coefficient A measure of correlation applied to ranked data.

Special dividend A dividend paid by a company that does not pay dividends on a regular schedule, or a dividend that supplements regular cash dividends with an extra payment.

Special purpose entity (special purpose vehicle or variable interest entity) A non-operating entity created to carry out a specified purpose, such as leasing assets or securitizing receivables; can be a corporation, partnership, trust, limited liability, or partnership formed to facilitate a specific type of business activity.

Special purpose vehicle See *Special purpose entity*.

Specific identification method An inventory accounting method that identifies which specific inventory items were sold and which remained in inventory to be carried over to later periods.

Speculative demand for money (or portfolio demand for money) The demand to hold speculative money balances based on the potential opportunities or risks that are inherent in other financial instruments.

Speculative money balances Monies held in anticipation that other assets will decline in value.

Speculative value The difference between the market price of the option and its intrinsic value, determined by the uncertainty of the underlying over the remaining life of the option.

Sponsored A type of depository receipt in which the foreign company whose shares are held by the depository has a direct involvement in the issuance of the receipts.

Spot markets Markets that trade assets for immediate delivery.

Spot price The price for immediate purchase of the underlying asset.

Spread risk Bond price risk arising from changes in the yield spread on credit-risky bonds; reflects changes in the market's assessment and/or pricing of credit migration (or downgrade) risk and market liquidity risk.

Stackelberg model A prominent model of strategic decision-making in which firms are assumed to make their decisions sequentially.

Stagflation When a high inflation rate is combined with a high level of unemployment and a slowdown of the economy.

Standard cost With respect to inventory accounting, the planned or target unit cost of inventory items or services.

Standard deviation The positive square root of the variance; a measure of dispersion in the same units as the original data.

Standard normal distribution The normal density with mean (μ) equal to 0 and standard deviation (σ) equal to 1.

Standardizing A transformation that involves subtracting the mean and dividing the result by the standard deviation.

Standing limit orders A limit order at a price below market and which therefore is waiting to trade.

Stated annual interest rate (also quoted interest rate) A quoted interest rate that does not account for compounding within the year.

Statement of cash flows (cash flow statement) A financial statement that reconciles beginning-of-period and end-of-period balance sheet values of cash; provides information about an entity's cash inflows and cash outflows as they pertain to operating, investing, and financing activities.

Statement of changes in equity (statement of owners' equity) A financial statement that reconciles the beginning-of-period and end-of-period balance sheet values of shareholders' equity; provides information about all factors affecting shareholders' equity.

Statement of financial condition The financial statement that presents an entity's current financial position by disclosing resources the entity controls (its assets) and the claims on those resources (its liabilities and equity claims), as of a particular point in time (the date of the balance sheet).

Statement of financial position The financial statement that presents an entity's current financial position by disclosing resources the entity controls (its assets) and the claims on those resources (its liabilities and equity claims), as of a particular point in time (the date of the balance sheet).

Statement of operations A financial statement that provides information about a company's profitability over a stated period of time.

Statement of owners' equity (Statement of changes in shareholders' equity) A financial statement that reconciles the beginning of-period and end-of-period balance sheet values of shareholders' equity; provides information about all factors affecting shareholders' equity.

Statement of retained earnings A financial statement that reconciles beginning-of-period and end-of-period balance sheet values of retained income; shows the linkage between the balance sheet and income statement.

Statistic A quantity computed from or used to describe a sample of data.

Statistical inference Making forecasts, estimates, or judgments about a larger group from a smaller group actually observed; using a sample statistic to infer the value of an unknown population parameter.

Statistically significant A result indicating that the null hypothesis can be rejected; with reference to an estimated regression coefficient, frequently understood to mean a result indicating that the corresponding population regression coefficient is different from 0.

Statutory voting A common method of voting where each share represents one vote.

Stock dividend A type of dividend in which a company distributes additional shares of its common stock to shareholders instead of cash.

Stock-out losses Profits lost from not having sufficient inventory on hand to satisfy demand.

Stop order (or stop-loss order) An order in which a trader has specified a stop price condition.

Stop-loss order See *Stop order*.

Store of value The quality of tending to preserve value.

Store of wealth Goods that depend on the fact that they do not perish physically over time, and on the belief that others would always value the good.

Straight-line method A depreciation method that allocates evenly the cost of a long-lived asset less its estimated residual value over the estimated useful life of the asset.

Strategic analysis Analysis of the competitive environment with an emphasis on the implications of the environment for corporate strategy.

Strategic asset allocation The set of exposures to IPS-permissible asset classes that is expected to achieve the client's long-term objectives given the client's investment constraints.

Strategic groups Groups sharing distinct business models or catering to specific market segments in an industry.

Stress testing A set of techniques for estimating losses in extremely unfavorable combinations of events or scenarios.

Strike The fixed price at which an option holder can buy or sell the underlying.

Strike price The fixed price at which an option holder can buy or sell the underlying.

Strike rate The fixed rate at which the holder of an interest rate option can buy or sell the underlying.

Striking price The fixed price at which an option holder can buy or sell the underlying.

Strong-form efficient market A market in which security prices reflect all public and private information.

Structural (or cyclically adjusted) budget deficit The deficit that would exist if the economy was at full employment (or full potential output).

Structural subordination Arises in a holding company structure when the debt of operating subsidiaries is serviced by the cash flow and assets of the subsidiaries before funds can be passed to the holding company to service debt at the parent level.

Structured note A variation of a floating-rate note that has some type of unusual characteristic such as a leverage factor or in which the rate moves opposite to interest rates.

Subjective probability A probability drawing on personal or subjective judgment.

Subordinated debt A class of unsecured debt that ranks below a firm's senior unsecured obligations.

Substitutes Said of two goods or services such that if the price of one increases the demand for the other tends to increase, holding all other things equal (e.g., butter and margarine).

Sunk cost A cost that has already been incurred.

Supernormal profit Equal to accounting profit less the implicit opportunity costs not included in total accounting costs; the difference between total revenue (TR) and total cost (TC).

Supply shock A typically unexpected disturbance to supply.

Support In technical analysis, a price range in which buying activity is sufficient to stop the decline in the price of a security.

Survey approach An estimate of the equity risk premium that is based upon estimates provided by a panel of finance experts.

Survivorship bias The bias resulting from a test design that fails to account for companies that have gone bankrupt, merged, or are otherwise no longer reported in a database.

Sustainable growth rate The rate of dividend (and earnings) growth that can be sustained over time for a given level of return on equity, keeping the capital structure constant and without issuing additional common stock.

Sustainable rate of economic growth The rate of increase in the economy's productive capacity or potential GDP.

Swap An agreement between two parties to exchange a series of future cash flows.

Swap contract An agreement between two parties to exchange a series of future cash flows.

Swap spread The difference between the fixed rate on an interest rate swap and the rate on a Treasury note with equivalent maturity; it reflects the general level of credit risk in the market.

Swaption An option to enter into a swap.

Synthetic call The combination of puts, the underlying, and riskfree bonds that replicates a call option.

Synthetic put The combination of calls, the underlying, and riskfree bonds that replicates a put option.

Systematic risk Risk that affects the entire market or economy; it cannot be avoided and is inherent in the overall market. Systematic risk is also known as non diversifiable or market risk.

Systematic sampling A procedure of selecting every kth member until reaching a sample of the desired size. The sample that results from this procedure should be approximately random.

t-Test A hypothesis test using a statistic (t-statistic) that follows a t-distribution.

TRIN A flow of funds indicator applied to a broad stock market index to measure the relative extent to which money is moving into or out of rising and declining stocks.

Tactical asset allocation The decision to deliberately deviate from the strategic asset allocation in an attempt to add value based on forecasts of the near-term relative performance of asset classes.

Target balance A minimum level of cash to be held available— estimated in advance and adjusted for known funds transfers, seasonality, or other factors.

Target capital structure A company's chosen proportions of debt and equity.

Target independent A bank's ability to determine the definition of inflation that they target, the rate of inflation that they target, and the horizon over which the target is to be achieved.

Target semideviation The positive square root of target semivariance.

Target semivariance The average squared deviation below a target value.

Tax base The amount at which an asset or liability is valued for tax purposes.

Tax expense An aggregate of an entity's income tax payable (or recoverable in the case of a tax benefit) and any changes in deferred tax assets and liabilities. It is essentially the income tax payable or recoverable if these had been determined based on accounting profit rather than taxable income.

Tax loss carry forward A taxable loss in the current period that may be used to reduce future taxable income.

Taxable income The portion of an entity's income that is subject to income taxes under the tax laws of its jurisdiction.

Taxable temporary differences Temporary differences that result in a taxable amount in a future period when determining the taxable profit as the balance sheet item is recovered or settled.

Technical analysis A form of security analysis that uses price and volume data, which is often displayed graphically, in decision making.

Technology The process a company uses to transform inputs into outputs.

Tenor The original time to maturity on a swap.

Terminal stock value (or terminal value) The expected value of a share at the end of the investment horizon—in effect, the expected selling price.

Terminal value The expected value of a share at the end of the investment horizon—in effect, the expected selling price.

Termination date The date of the final payment on a swap; also, the swap's expiration date.

Theory of the consumer The branch of microeconomics that deals with consumption—the demand for goods and services—by utility-maximizing individuals.

Theory of the firm The branch of microeconomics that deals with the supply of goods and services by profit-maximizing firms.

Theta The rate at which an option's time value decays.

Third-degree price discrimination When the monopolist segregates customers into groups based on demographic or other characteristics and offers different pricing to each group.

Time to expiration The time remaining in the life of a derivative, typically expressed in years.

Time value The difference between the market price of the option and its intrinsic value, determined by the uncertainty of the underlying over the remaining life of the option.

Time value of money The principles governing equivalence relationships between cash flows with different dates.

Time-period bias The possibility that when we use a time-series sample, our statistical conclusion may be sensitive to the starting and ending dates of the sample.

Time-series data Observations of a variable over time.

Time-weighted rate of return The compound rate of growth of one unit of currency invested in a portfolio during a stated measurement period; a measure of investment performance that is not sensitive to the timing and amount of withdrawals or additions to the portfolio.

Top-down analysis With reference to investment selection processes, an approach that starts with macro selection (i.e., identifying attractive geographic segments and/or industry segments) and then addresses selection of the most attractive investments within those segments.

Total comprehensive income The change in equity during a period resulting from transaction and other events, other than those changes resulting from transactions with owners in their capacity as owners.

Total costs The summation of all costs, where costs are classified according to fixed or variable.

Total factor productivity A scale factor that reflects the portion of growth that is not accounted for by explicit factor inputs (e.g. capital and labor).

Total fixed cost The summation of all expenses that do not change when production varies.

Total probability rule A rule explaining the unconditional probability of an event in terms of probabilities of the event conditional on mutually exclusive and exhaustive scenarios.

Total probability rule for expected value A rule explaining the expected value of a random variable in terms of expected values of the random variable conditional on mutually exclusive and exhaustive scenarios.

Total product The aggregate sum of production for the firm during a time period.

Total return Measures the price appreciation, or percentage change in price of the securities in an index or portfolio, plus any income received over the period.

Total return index An index that reflects the price appreciation or percentage change in price of the constituent securities plus any income received since inception.

Total return swap A swap in which one party agrees to pay the total return on a security. Often used as a credit derivative, in which the underlying is a bond.

Total revenue Price times the quantity of units sold.

Total variable cost The summation of all variable expenses.

Tracking error The standard deviation of the differences between a portfolio's returns and its benchmark's returns; a synonym of active risk.

Tracking risk (tracking error) The standard deviation of the differences between a portfolio's returns and its benchmark's returns; a synonym of active risk.

Trade credit A spontaneous form of credit in which a purchaser of the goods or service is financing its purchase by delaying the date on which payment is made.

Trade payables Amounts that a business owes to its vendors for goods and services that were purchased from them but which have not yet been paid.

Trade receivables (commercial receivables or accounts receivable) Amounts customers owe the company for products that have been sold as well as amounts that may be due from suppliers (such as for returns of merchandise).

Trading securities (held-for-trading securities) Securities held by a company with the intent to trade them.

Traditional investment markets Markets for traditional investments, which include all publicly traded debts and equities and shares in pooled investment vehicles that hold publicly traded debts and/or equities.

Transactions money balances Money balances that are held to finance transactions.

Transactions motive In the context of inventory management, the need for inventory as part of the routine production–sales cycle.

Transfer payments Welfare payments made through the social security system that exist to provide a basic minimum level of income for low-income households.

Transitive preferences The assumption that when comparing any three distinct bundles, A, B, and C, if A is preferred to B and simultaneously B is preferred to C, then it must be true that A is preferred to C.

Treasury Inflation-Protected Securities A bond issued by the United States Treasury Department that is designed to protect the investor from inflation by adjusting the principal of the bond for changes in inflation.

Treasury shares Shares that were issued and subsequently repurchased by the company.

Treasury stock Shares that were issued and subsequently repurchased by the company.

Treasury stock method A method for accounting for the effect of options (and warrants) on earnings per share (EPS) that specifies what EPS would have been if the options and warrants had been exercised and the company had used the proceeds to repurchase common stock.

Tree diagram A diagram with branches emanating from nodes representing either mutually exclusive chance events or mutually exclusive decisions.

Trend A long-term pattern of movement in a particular direction.

Treynor ratio A measure of risk-adjusted performance that relates a portfolio's excess returns to the portfolio's beta.

Triangle patterns In technical analysis, a continuation chart pattern that forms as the range between high and low prices narrows, visually forming a triangle.

Trimmed mean A mean computed after excluding a stated small percentage of the lowest and highest observations.

Triple bottoms In technical analysis, a reversal pattern that is formed when the price forms three troughs at roughly the same price level; used to predict a change from a downtrend to an uptrend.

Triple tops In technical analysis, a reversal pattern that is formed when the price forms three peaks at roughly the same price level; used to predict a change from an uptrend to a downtrend.

Trough The lowest point of a business cycle.

Trust receipt arrangement The use of inventory as collateral for a loan. The inventory is segregated and held in trust, and the proceeds of any sale must be remitted to the lender immediately.

Turn-of-the-year effect Calendar anomaly that stock market returns in January are significantly higher compared to the rest of the months of the year, with most of the abnormal returns reported during the first five trading days in January.

Two-fund separation theorem The theory that all investors regardless of taste, risk preferences, and initial wealth will hold a combination of two portfolios or funds: a risk-free asset and an optimal portfolio of risky assets.

Two-sided hypothesis test A test in which the null hypothesis is rejected in favor of the alternative hypothesis if the evidence indicates that the population parameter is either smaller or larger than a hypothesized value.

Two-tailed hypothesis test A test in which the null hypothesis is rejected in favor of the alternative hypothesis if the evidence indicates that the population parameter is either smaller or larger than a hypothesized value.

Two-week repo rate The interest rate on a two-week repurchase agreement; may be used as a policy rate by a central bank.

Type I error The error of rejecting a true null hypothesis.

Type II error The error of not rejecting a false null hypothesis.

Unanticipated (unexpected) inflation The component of inflation that is a surprise.

Unbilled revenue (accrued revenue) Revenue that has been earned but not yet billed to customers as of the end of an accounting period.

Unclassified balance sheet A balance sheet that does not show subtotals for current assets and current liabilities.

Unconditional probability The probability of an event *not* conditioned on another event.

Underemployed A person who has a job but has the qualifications to work a significantly higher-paying job.

Underlying An asset that trades in a market in which buyers and sellers meet, decide on a price, and the seller then delivers the asset to the buyer and receives payment. The underlying is the asset or other derivative on which a particular derivative is based. The market for the underlying is also referred to as the spot market.

Underwritten offering An offering in which the (lead) investment bank guarantees the sale of the issue at an offering price that it negotiates with the issuer.

Unearned fees Unearned fees are recognized when a company receives cash payment for fees prior to earning them.

Unearned revenue (**deferred revenue** or **deferred income**) A liability account for money that has been collected for goods or services that have not yet been delivered; payment received in advance of providing a good or service.

Unemployed People who are actively seeking employment but are currently without a job.

Unemployment rate The ratio of unemployed to the labor force.

Unexpected inflation The component of inflation that is a surprise.

Unit labor cost The average labor cost to produce one unit of output.

Unit normal distribution The normal density with mean (μ) equal to 0 and standard deviation (σ) equal to 1.

Units-of-production method A depreciation method that allocates the cost of a long-lived asset based on actual usage during the period.

Univariate distribution A distribution that specifies the probabilities for a single random variable.

Unlimited funds An unlimited funds environment assumes that the company can raise the funds it wants for all profitable projects simply by paying the required rate of return.

Unsecured debt Debt which gives the debtholder only a general claim on an issuer's assets and cash flow.

Unsponsored A type of depository receipt in which the foreign company whose shares are held by the depository has no involvement in the issuance of the receipts.

Up transition probability The probability that an asset's value moves up.

Utility function A mathematical representation of the satisfaction derived from a consumption basket.

Utils A unit of utility.

Validity instructions Instructions which indicate when the order may be filled.

Valuation The process of determining the value of an asset or service.

Valuation allowance A reserve created against deferred tax assets, based on the likelihood of realizing the deferred tax assets in future accounting periods.

Valuation ratios Ratios that measure the quantity of an asset or flow (e.g., earnings) in relation to the price associated with a specified claim (e.g., a share or ownership of the enterprise).

Value at risk (VAR) A money measure of the minimum value of losses expected during a specified time period at a given level of probability.

Variable costs Costs that fluctuate with the level of production and sales.

Variance The expected value (the probability-weighted average) of squared deviations from a random variable's expected value.

Variation margin Additional margin that must be deposited in an amount sufficient to bring the balance up to the initial margin requirement.

Veblen good A good that increases in desirability with price.

Vega The relationship between option price and volatility.

Venture capital Investments that provide "seed" or start-up capital, early-stage financing, or mezzanine financing to companies that are in the early stages of development and require additional capital for expansion.

Venture capital fund A fund for private equity investors that provides financing for development-stage companies.

Vertical analysis Common-size analysis using only one reporting period or one base financial statement; for example, an income statement in which all items are stated as percentages of sales.

Vertical demand schedule Implies that some fixed quantity is demanded, regardless of price.

Volatility As used in option pricing, the standard deviation of the continuously compounded returns on the underlying asset.

Voluntarily unemployed A person voluntarily outside the labor force, such as a jobless worker refusing an available vacancy.

Vote by proxy A mechanism that allows a designated party—such as another shareholder, a shareholder representative, or management—to vote on the shareholder's behalf.

Warehouse receipt arrangement The use of inventory as collateral for a loan; similar to a trust receipt arrangement except there is a third party (i.e., a warehouse company) that supervises the inventory.

Weak-form efficient market hypothesis The belief that security prices fully reflect all past market data, which refers to all historical price and volume trading information.

Wealth effect An increase (decrease) in household wealth increases (decreases) consumer spending out of a given level of current income.

Weighted average cost method An inventory accounting method that averages the total cost of available inventory items over the total units available for sale.

Weighted average cost of capital A weighted average of the aftertax required rates of return on a company's common stock, preferred stock, and long-term debt, where the weights are the fraction of each source of financing in the company's target capital structure.

Weighted mean An average in which each observation is weighted by an index of its relative importance.

Weighted-average cost of capital A weighted average of the aftertax required rates of return on a company's common stock, preferred stock, and long-term debt, where the weights are the fraction of each source of financing in the company's target capital structure.

Wholesale price index Reflects the price changes experienced by domestic producers in a country.

Winsorized mean A mean computed after assigning a stated percent of the lowest values equal to one specified low value, and a stated percent of the highest values equal to one specified high value.

Working capital The difference between current assets and current liabilities.

Working capital management The management of a company's short-term assets (such as inventory) and short-term liabilities (such as money owed to suppliers).

Yield The actual return on a debt security if it is held to maturity.

Yield spread The difference between the yield on a bond and the yield on a default-free security, usually a government note, of the same maturity. The yield spread is primarily determined by the market's perception of the credit risk on the bond.

Yield to maturity The annual return that an investor earns on a bond if the investor purchases the bond today and holds it until maturity.

Zero-cost collar A transaction in which a position in the underlying is protected by buying a put and selling a call with the premium from the sale of the call offsetting the premium from the purchase of the put. It can also be used to protect a floating-rate borrower against interest rate increases with the premium on a long cap offsetting the premium on a short floor.

Index